For B.C.—

Now you will know
from whence I have plagiarized
all of my best lines!

With all my thanks and
respect,

Barbara
8-85

THE PORTABLE

DOROTHY PARKER

THE PORTABLE

DOROTHY PARKER

REVISED AND ENLARGED EDITION

With a new Introduction by Brendan Gill

The Viking Press : New York

PUBLISHERS' NOTE

The original *Portable Dorothy Parker* appeared in 1944 as the fourth volume in a new series which had been launched with a wartime anthology of American prose and verse designed by Alexander Woollcott for servicemen overseas. Of the first ten Portables (they now number more than seventy-five), seven have been dropped or replaced by new editions; only *Shakespeare, The World Bible,* and *Dorothy Parker* have remained continuously in print and selling steadily through time and change. Whether this juxtaposition was fortuitous or not, it seems time to give Mrs. Parker a new look, a broader coverage, with an introductory appraisal by a critic of a succeeding generation, who can judge her more nearly *sub specie aeternitatis.*

Though the volume has been completely reset, the text of the original Portable as chosen by her in 1943 is retained intact. It contained only stories and poems, and was drawn almost entirely from her two collected volumes: *Here Lies* (the stories; 1936) and *Not So Deep as a Well* (the poems; 1939). These in turn had been made up, with a few additions and subtractions, from her two earlier books of stories and three of verse. For the Portable she added three or four subsequent stories and one poem, and again eliminated some, especially poems, no longer to her taste.

She went on writing fitfully for the magazines until her death in 1967, but there were no more published volumes; only four stories, and no poems, were available for this revised edition of the Portable. A selection of her book reviews, however, as *The New Yorker*'s famous "Constant Reader," was issued in 1970, and this has been included complete, along with some of her later reviews from *Esquire.* Other examples of her literary journalism, not even considered for the original Portable, are her debutante play reviews from

Vanity Fair ("juvenilia" if you like) and as substitute for Benchley in *The New Yorker*. These, with a few miscellaneous pieces, are included to give the full range on which her vogue was based and to suggest the kind of personal approach, so much her innovation, that marked the period and influenced the scene. Part of the original introduction by Somerset Maugham, writing as a friendly contemporary, is reprinted as an afterword for its historic interest.

The additional contents were selected by editors of The Viking Press, with the help and general approval of Mrs. Parker's friend and executrix, Miss Lillian Hellman. Brendan Gill, who has written the new introduction, is free of any responsibility for the plan or for the choices. In 1972 the Parker estate, including her literary rights, passed under her will to the National Association for the Advancement of Colored People. To its executives, the publishers express thanks for permission to publish this expanded Portable.

Contents

Publishers' Note
Introduction by Brendan Gill

INTRODUCTION
by Brendan Gill

I

There are writers who die to the world long before they are dead, and if this is sometimes by choice, more often it is a fate imposed on them by others and not easily dealt with. A writer enjoys a vogue,. and, the vogue having passed, either he consents to endure the obscurity into which he has been thrust or he struggles against it in vain, with a bitterness that tends to increase as his powers diminish. No matter how well or badly he behaves, the result is the same. If the work is of a certain quality, it survives the passing of the vogue, but the maker of the work no longer effectually exists. Even though he goes on writing, he dwells in the limbo of the half-forgotten, and his obituary notices are read with a flippant, unthinking incredulity: who would have guessed that the tattered old teller of tales had had it in him to hang on so fiercely? What on earth had he been waiting for? Hoping for? Dreading?

A protracted life-in-death is all the more striking in the case of writers who make a reputation in youth and then live on into age. It is most striking of all in the case of young writers whose theme is the pleasingness of death, and for whom it amounts in the world's eyes to a betrayal of their theme when they are observed to cling far more tenaciously to life than their happier contemporaries have managed to do. Dorothy Parker's career was of this nature. She enjoyed an early vogue, which passed, leaving her work to be judged on its merits, and because the subject of so large a portion of her verses was the seductiveness of a neat, brisk doing away with herself, many people were astonished to read of her death, in 1967, from natural causes, as an old lady of seventy-three. Under the circumstances, it seemed to them a tardy end, and by an irony that had been one of Mrs. Parker's chief stocks in trade she would have been the first to agree with them. She had indeed taken an un-

xiii

conscionably long time to leave a world of which she had always claimed to hold a low opinion. Her husbands, her lovers, and most of her friends had preceded her; for a person who boasted of wooing death, she had proved the worst of teases—an elderly flirt of the sort that she herself at thirty would have savaged in a paragraph.

There had been, of course, more at stake for her than a reluctance to keep old promises made in poems. The gap between her life and her work had grown very wide. The fact was that as she put on years she seemed unable to make a favorite of either life or death; she refused to take sides. It was as if she had hung on not fiercely or grimly but because she lacked the tiny tremor of will required to give up. She had had fame, and for long periods in Hollywood a very large income. The world would have said that she had every opportunity to fulfill her talent, and now she lived alone, with a raspy little concierge of a dog, in a hotel room in Manhattan and waited for nothing and hoped for nothing and got through the day, often enough with a bottle. She had been tiresome when she drank in youth, and with age she could scarcely be expected to improve; the occasions for drink were not merry ones. There were, besides, no suitable companions left to raise hell with— no incomparably joyous Benchleys to babble nonsense to, no Hemingways to hero-worship. Even if there had been, she would surely have found ways to alienate them. Early in life she had developed a strong bent for cutting ties with friends; to the born wisecracker, uttering the one funny word too many is the last appetite that fails.

Mrs. Parker had been a writer whose robust and acid lucidities had been much feared and admired, and it was sad that she should be making such a messy finish; she was never so muddled as not to see that and to make her apologies for it. By the standards of her prime, what she was engaged in committing—what, plainly, she was helpless not to commit— was an inexcusable social and aesthetic blunder: she was becoming the guest who is aware that he has outstayed his welcome and who yet makes no attempt to pack his things and go.

II

Readers coming to Mrs. Parker for the first time may find it as hard to understand the high place she held in the literary world of forty or fifty years ago as to understand the critical disregard into which she subsequently fell. The first precaution for such readers is to bear in mind the fact that the so-called world that gave her her reputation was really only a province, and, like all provinces, it considered itself much bigger and more important than it was. Its arbiters did well to praise Mrs. Parker, but she was a better writer than they took her for, and the difference between who she was and who they supposed she was held considerable risks for her. Not the least of these risks was the likelihood that when her champions came to be swept away into the dustbin, she, too, would be swept away. The small literary set that centered on New York in the twenties and thirties and that hailed Mrs. Parker as one of its leading lights was made up largely of second- and third-raters. Mrs. Parker perceived this in her middle years and passed judgment on her old colleagues with the acerbity of one who has been over-praised by people unfit to offer either praise or blame. She *was* one of their leading lights; to be that, she might have said, it would have sufficed to be a glowworm. She pointed out that the major American writers of the period had not been members of any set; they had lived and worked far from the coterie of self-promoters who gathered under the heading of the Algonquin Round Table. Hemingway, Faulkner, Lardner, Fitzgerald, Dos Passos, Cather, Crane, and O'Neill were not to be found cracking jokes and singing each other's praises or waspishly stinging each other into tantrums on West 44th Street. Some of Mrs. Parker's companions at the Algonquin were exceptionally attractive people (Robert Benchley, Robert E. Sherwood, Marc Connelly) and some of them were exceptionally unattractive (Alexander Woollcott, George S. Kaufman, Edna Ferber), but, companionship aside, by any reasonable historic measure what a trifling harvest was to be gained from them! If a number of Mrs. Parker's short stories and poems will last and if some of

Benchley's humorous pieces will also last, still, it is hard to think of works by other members of that well-touted little clique that are likely to survive the century.

Mrs. Parker's reputation suffered from the literary company she kept; it suffered also from the fact that the milieu that was her natural subject matter—the narrow sector of American society that could be summed up as Eastern, urban, intellectual, and middle class—underwent a sudden and overwhelming change during the Depression. The people Mrs. Parker had kept under close scrutiny and about whom she had written with authority seemed so remote from the realities of the post-Depression period as to be stamped, for a time, with a kind of retroactive invalidity. In the forties and fifties they simply did not matter any more, and the reading public was tempted to conclude, mistakenly, that they ought never to have mattered. Little by little over the years, the period and the people who gave it its character have recovered importance. By now we find it worth while to make an effort to apprehend them fairly, according to the tone and temper of their day, and in order to do so we turn with relish to Mrs. Parker.

No doubt it will strike young readers as odd, but the twenties in which Mrs. Parker began work were considered an era of extreme and perhaps dangerous permissiveness, especially in regard to the social experiments being carried out by women. Drinking, smoking, sniffing cocaine, bobbing one's hair, dancing the Charleston, necking, getting "caught"—it was hard to imagine that things could go much farther before civilization itself broke down. The young women who set the pace were called sophisticated, though few of them were; their shocking motto was "Anything goes," and they meant it. New York was their noisy Sodom, and Mrs. Parker's verse gave glimpses of the license to be met with there and its heavy cost in terms of one's emotions. These verses, which became something of a national rage, were thought to be strong stuff: brusque, bitter, and unwomanly in their presumed cynicism. They gave the average reader an impression of going recklessly far in asserting a woman's equal rights inside a sexual relationship, including the right of infidelity. The verses do not seem brusque, bitter, and unwomanly today; moreover, the verses that at the time of their first publication appealed to readers as the real thing, full of a pain of loss splendidly borne, are the ones likeliest now to set our teeth on edge, as being tainted with a glib gallantry every bit as false as the revolting cuddly high spirits of Mrs. Parker's literary mortal enemy, A. A. Milne. Mrs. Parker was quoted incessantly by her admirers; the quotations were almost always from poems that current readers would regard as among her cleverest but least heartfelt:

> And let her loves, when she is dead,
>   Write this above her bones:
> "No more she lives to give us bread
>   Who asked her only stones."

*

> By the time you swear you're his,
>   Shivering and sighing,
> And he swears his passion is
>   Infinite, undying—
> Lady, make a note of this:
>   One of you is lying.

*

> Princes, never I'd give offense.
>   Won't you think of me tenderly?
> Here's my strength and my weakness, gents—
>   I loved them until they loved me.

*

> Razors pain you;
> Rivers are damp;
> Acids stain you;
> And drugs cause cramp.
> Guns aren't lawful;
> Nooses give;
> Gas smells awful;
> You might as well live.

The most popular woman poet of the twentieth century, prior to Mrs. Parker, was Edna St. Vincent Millay, who was often thought to have served as a literary model for her. It was not altogether so; for one thing, Miss Millay was a much more skillful prosodist than Mrs. Parker, with a mastery of many forms of verse that Mrs. Parker never attempted, and, for another, Miss Millay enjoyed a far wider range of expressible feelings, which she spent a lifetime of hard intellectual effort exploring. She struggled to achieve greatness, and if the effort failed, it produced a number of sufficiently remarkable volumes of poems. Mrs. Parker worked less hard and less steadily, and she flinched from thorough self-examination: the depths were there, and she would glance into them from time to time, but she was not prepared to descend into them and walk their bounds. Her true literary mentor was that forbidding male spinster, A. E. Housman, who with the help of high intelligence, classical learning, and an exquisite ear, contrived to turn a reiterated whining into superior poetry. One reads Housman today not for the sense but for the sound, wishing often that it were not necessary to understand his long-drawn-out adolescent howl and could listen, instead, to the matchless positioning of his syllables—"For this of old the trader/Unpearled the Indian seas." Housman pretended to look into the depths, but they were other people's depths and not his. Such lines as his audacious mock-Roman "Life, to be sure, is nothing much to lose" often moved Mrs. Parker to strike just the wrong note of lofty, sentimental not-caring; her verses are also marred on occasions by "lads" if not "chaps," and she shares Housman's tendency to shower congratulations upon anyone who takes his life when young. (Like Mrs. Parker, Housman was to live into his seventies and die of natural causes. He believed in suicide, but with this proviso—that it was for others.) Mrs. Parker wrote what was essentially light verse; it was not Housman's perennial ruefulness that she ought to have imitated, but the witty aplomb of her contemporary, Ogden Nash. Along with, in her sunnier moods, Miss Millay, Nash broke up the old forms and fashioned new ones that accommodated to perfection the spoken language of the period. Nevertheless, Mrs. Parker was someone to be taken seriously. Edmund Wilson wrote at the time that he had been "sometimes accused of overrating the more popular irony of Mrs. Dorothy Parker. It is true that Mrs. Parker's epigrams have the accent of the Hotel Algonquin rather than that of the coffee houses of the eighteenth century. But I believe that, if we admire, as it is fashionable to do, the light verse of Prior and Gay, we should admire Mrs. Parker also. She writes well: her wit is the wit of her particular time and place, but it is often as cleanly economic at the same time that it is flatly brutal as the wit of the age of Pope; and, within its small scope, it is a criticism of life. It has its roots in contemporary reality, and that is what I am pleading for in poetry."

Wilson expressed that opinion of Mrs. Parker nearly fifty years ago; it continues to be a sound one, and the poems that we admire today are those that most ably sum up her particular time and place. It is a world that has grown very distant from ours, but because she was true to its nature it remains, with certain attendant risks, visitable. In 1944, in the course of reviewing the first edition of this book, Wilson wrote in *The New Yorker* that, while he found Mrs. Parker's poems a little dated, her prose seemed to him as sharp and funny as in the years when it was first coming out. Again, a sensible judgment, worth quoting after almost thirty years. If it is easier to visit the world of the twenties and thirties through Mrs. Parker's short stories and soliloquies than through her verse, it is also more rewarding; to a startling degree, they have a substance, a solidity, that the poems do little to prepare us for. Not the least hint of the Round Table is detectable in the stories—no sassy showing off, no making a leg at the reader. The author keeps her distance, and sometimes it is a distance great enough to remind one of Flaubert. She has written her tales with grave care and given them a surface as hard and smooth as stone, and there is no need for her to flutter about in the foreground and call attention to her cleverness. We perceive from one sentence to the next that we are in the hands of a skilled and confident guide and that each story can be marched through from beginning to end without our stumbling into uncertain or gratuitous asides. One has only to sample the superlatively self-assured opening sentences of two or three of the stories:

> He was a very good-looking young man indeed, shaped to be annoyed.

> If the Bains had striven for years, they could have been no more successful in making their living-room into a small but admirably complete museum of objects suggesting strain, discomfort, or the tomb.

> The woman with the pink velvet poppies twined round the assisted gold of her hair . . .

The force of that "assisted," slipped so unobtrusively into the text, is like a hammer-blow. The opening paragraph of her late story, "The Lovely Leave," displays the Parker style at its simplest and best; not a word amiss:

> Her husband had telephoned her by long distance to tell her about the leave. She had not expected the call, and she had no words arranged. She threw away whole seconds explaining her surprise at hearing him, and reporting that it was raining hard in New York, and asking was it terribly hot where he was. He had stopped her to say, look, he didn't have time to talk long; and he had told her quickly that his squadron was to be moved to another field the next week and on the way he would have twenty-four hours' leave. It was difficult for her to hear. Behind his voice came a jagged chorus of young male voices, all crying the syllable "Hey!"

At the time she was writing them, Mrs. Parker's soliloquies caused a great stir among her readers and especially among her fellow writers. These soliloquies were like star turns by an acrobat working up at the top of the tent without a net, and part of the pleasure they gave lay in the reader's wondering how she could possibly bring off a feat so difficult. Like most feats of this order, they were made to look easy by the person performing them—what did they consist of, after all, but an unidentified woman nattering away to herself as a succession of thoughts tumbled helter-skelter across her consciousness?—but it soon turned out that, simple as the principle of the feats was, mastery of it was next to impossible; Mrs. Parker had few imitators. One of the more celebrated of her soliloquies was "The Telephone Call," which began:

> Please, God, let him telephone me now. Dear God, let him call me now. I won't ask anything else of You, truly I won't. It isn't very much to ask. It would be so little to You, God, such a little, little thing. Only let him telephone now. Please, God. Please, please, please.

Another was called "The Little Hours" and began:

> Now what's this? What's the object of all this darkness all over me? They haven't gone and buried me alive while my back was turned, have they? Ah, now would you think they'd do a thing like that! Oh, no, I know what it is. I'm awake. That's it. I've waked up in the middle of the night. Well, isn't that nice. Isn't that simply ideal.

In Wilson's review of the first edition of the Portable, he drew a contrast between the twenties and the forties that was notably unfavorable to the latter:

> The thing that I have particularly felt is the difference between the general tone, the psychological and literary atmosphere, of the period—the twenties and the earlier thirties—when most of these pieces of Mrs. Parker's were written, and the atmosphere of the present time. It was suddenly brought home to me how much freer people were—in their emotion, in their ideas, and in expressing themselves. In the twenties they could love, they could travel, they could stay up late at night, as extravagantly as they pleased; they could think or say or write whatever seemed to them amusing or interesting. There was a good deal of irresponsibility, and a lot of money and energy wasted, and the artistic activities of the time suffered from the general vices, but it was a much more favorable climate for writing than the period we are in now.

The passage was written during the Second World War, under circumstances grimmer than any we have known since in this country. For the young writers of the seventies the situation is not unlike the one that Wilson remembered the young writers of the twenties having enjoyed and—certainly in his own case and in that of Mrs. Parker—gained intellectual stimulus from. Writers today are free to love and travel and stay up late (a curious privilege for Wilson to have noted: neither in the forties nor at any other period in his long life did he feel obliged to go to bed early), and they are free to think or say or write whatever seems to them amusing or interesting. In the light of continued warfare abroad and continued social injustice at home, they cannot be as carefree in their emotions as Wilson hints that he and his contemporaries were—there are dark thoughts that no amount of love and travel will expunge—but money and energy are in ample supply, and the squandering of them is not always as irresponsible as it looks. We are indeed in possession of a favorable climate for writing, and this may be one of the reasons that many of us are more powerfully drawn to the twenties than the usual processes of nostalgia would account for. A very deep and wide gulf separates us from those years, but we do not feel in the least estranged from them, as we do from the forties and fifties—sharper than ever to us are the lineaments of the writers we admire as we look back upon them over half a century. It is not surprising that we choose for good companions Fitzgerald, Lardner, Hemingway, and the other boys in the back room, nor is it surprising that there should pop up among them, glass in hand, hat askew, her well-bred voice full of soft apologies, the droll, tiny figure of Mrs. Parker.

III

The essential facts of her life, long as it was, are quickly told; and this is a mercy, since few careers, after a brilliant start, can be seen to have so continuously and sadly extinguished themselves. She was born Dorothy Rothschild, in 1893, at her family's summer place in West End, New Jersey. Her mother, who died in Dorothy's infancy, was Scottish; her father, a well-to-do garment manufacturer, had no connection with the banking Rothschilds. She grew up in New York, intensely disliking her strict father and even stricter stepmother; she attended a Catholic convent school in Manhattan and Miss Dana's School in Morristown, New Jersey; and in 1916, having sold some verses to Frank Crowninshield, the editor of *Vogue*, she was given an editorial position on that magazine. Her task was to write captions for fashion photographs and drawings, and her salary was ten dollars a week. She became one of Crowninshield's innumerable platonic protégées, and within a year he offered her a far better position on another magazine of which he was the editor—the charming and elegant *Vanity Fair*. She was to become its drama critic, and since she appears to have manifested no previous interest in the theater, Crowninshield must have been following one of his celebrated canny whims. At about the same time, she married a good-looking young man from Hartford named Edwin Pond Parker II. They were divorced some years later, but she continued to use his name, which she preferred to her own. She felt a constant resentment at being Jewish; life might have pleased her better if it had been her mother who had been Jewish and her father Scottish, and she had been born a Marston.

On *Vanity Fair* she met Benchley and Sherwood, two other congenital unemployables whom Crowninshield had perceived literary virtues in, and her career as the wittiest member of the Algonquin Round Table was launched. She made wisecracks—often quite admirable wisecracks—as easily as most people say, "Is it hot enough for you?" or, "Please pass the bread." Having left *Vanity Fair*, she became one of the handful of writers who helped form the character of *The New Yorker*, founded by Harold Ross in 1925. Her short stories in the magazine, at first scarcely more than scraps of lacerating dialogue, led to the development of what was afterward assumed by critics to be a recognizable genre—*The New Yorker* short story—though none of the writers of these stories, including Mrs. Parker, O'Hara, Fuchs, Cheever, and Salinger, would agree that the genre existed. (Mrs. Parker's work was to appear in the magazine at irregular intervals from 1926 until 1955.) She went abroad and met the Gerald Murphys and the

Hemingways and the Fitzgeralds. She worked hard at her writing, and when her book of poems, *Enough Rope*, was published, it became a best seller. In the thirties she married an actor-writer named Alan Campbell, who was eleven years younger than she and bisexual; he had in common with her an ancestry half-Jewish and half-Scottish. Though it was probably the case that no man could have remained married to her for long, Campbell was not only a devoted husband but also a capable manager of their professional and domestic affairs, and the marriage lasted longer than any of her friends had predicted. They went to Hollywood as a writing team, at a salary of something over five thousand dollars a week. They also bought a farm in Bucks County, Pennsylvania. To her delight, at the age of forty-two she became pregnant; she lost the baby in the third month. Back in Hollywood, she became an ever more ardent left-wing political activist, to the jeopardy of Campbell's and her screenwriting career. They worked on many movies, rarely to her satisfaction. During the Second World War Campbell, though well past draft age, volunteered for the Army and served overseas. They were divorced in 1947 and remarried in 1950; they separated two years later and then settled down to a marriage of sorts in 1956. Campbell died in 1963 in Hollywood, and Mrs. Parker—again, as nearly always, Mrs. Parker—returned to New York. Her last original writing of importance was a play, *The Ladies of the Corridor*, in which she collaborated with Arnaud d'Usseau. In his review of it in *The New Yorker*, Wolcott Gibbs described the play as an account of life in a residential hotel in the East Sixties "that is the last resort of those [women] who have lost their husbands, whose children have grown up and moved away, and who have nothing to do with their remaining years except go to the movies, attend to their little dogs, and discuss one another's affairs with intense and delighted malignance." Gibbs found a good deal to admire in the play. "Some familiarity with the past performances of both authors," he wrote, "leads me to conclude that Mrs. Parker, who is in the habit these days of irritably deprecating her reputation as a wit, is responsible not only for the precise and deadly wit that frequently punctuates the script but also for the acute understanding of human loneliness, cruelty, stupidity, and occasional glowing, unpredictable fortitude that gives the characters their intermittent flashes of absolute fidelity to life." Mrs. Parker had worked hard on the play; she hoped it would enjoy a big success and provide her, no matter how belatedly, with a fresh start in life. The majority of the reviews of the play proved unfavorable, and it closed after forty-five performances. Mrs. Parker said of it afterward, "It was the only thing I ever did that I was proud of."

IV

Mrs. Parker was given to making reckless remarks, and it may be that she made that particular reckless remark on other occasions in her life. It was not true, or was true only for as long as she needed it to be. Certainly she had been proud of many poems and many stories; certainly she had been proud when she was asked to assemble them for a Viking Portable. She was less proud of the screenwriting she had done, and rightly so, for in nearly every case it had been pawed over by others and disimproved in the traditional Hollywood fashion. She wrote a large number of book reviews, mostly for *The New Yorker* and *Esquire*, and although, at the time, she may have thought of them as fugitive journeyman pieces, she fussed over them with as much care as if they were fiction. She did not have, like Wilson, a natural gift for literary journalism—where he cast the widest possible net and hauled up, to the world's astonishment, an unprecedented variety of fascinating sea monsters, Mrs. Parker dealt with books and writers on a small scale, sometimes with a facetiousness bred of unease. Evidently she feared that the praise she bestowed in her reviews would give readers less pleasure than the malicious one-line dismissals for which she was famous ("Tonstant Weader fwowed up").

Astonishingly, in the light of her harum-scarum ways, a large body of work had been accumulated. The book reviews and play reviews and other journalism aside, there stood the volumes in their not unimpressive number, and glancing along the row one saw that, whether by chance or design, the titles amounted to a capsule autobiography. *Enough Rope, Sunset Gun, Laments for the Living, Death and Taxes, After Such Pleasures; Not So Deep as a Well, Here Lies*—with a single exception, the titles all speak directly or indirectly of death, and the exception is concerned with man's loss of something profoundly good: the contentment after making love that is more than satiety. Why cannot we as cocks and lions jocund be? Why cannot we turn away even at the moment of highest joy from the distress of our continuously prefigured death? Under whatever disguise, this was Mrs. Parker's theme, and she never feared to sound its heartbreaking note throughout fifty years of writing. She was one of the wittiest people in the world and one of the saddest; if even now we go on laughing at something she happened to say very late at night in some long-since-vanished bar, we do so at our peril. Man is the animal that knows he dies, and the death's head grinning in the mirror back of all those lighted bottles is our own. There is nothing good in life, Mrs. Parker said, that will not be taken away. One of the things she admired most in Hemingway was how he had struggled to face this problem both in his life and in his writing. He had been so sure in youth that he would not choose his father's way out of life, by suicide, and Mrs. Parker had been so sure in youth that she could find no other means of dealing with the pain of being; and so Hemingway had killed himself and she had lived on, and toward the end there were only ghosts in the corners of the hotel room, silently reproaching her for having had the cowardice to live. It was no use asking them when she had ever claimed to be brave. If, as she said, she had always been the greatest little hoper in the world, she had known that hope was a form of folly and had nothing to do with either courage or wisdom.

> Hope it was that tutored me,
>   And Love that taught me more;
> And now I learn at Sorrow's knee
>   The self-same lore.

People ought to be one of two things, young or old. No; what's the use of fooling? People ought to be one of two things, young or dead.

But she had been young, and it had not been satisfactory. It was precisely then, in the years, say, from sixteen to twenty-three, that she was confirmed in her bleak view of how things are. We know little about her during those years, except that she had left the school she disliked and the family she disliked and was making her own difficult way in the world. Delicate and bold and virginal in her teens, she must have been determined even then to be found worthy of heartrending misadventures. There are hints of them in the early poems—hints that, given a choice between happiness and unhappiness, she would be prompted by some devil in her to choose unhappiness. She had the imagination of disaster, as so many people do who have lost a mother in infancy, and she cultivated this form of imagination and made it flourish. Her knack for causing things to end badly amounted, in her friends' eyes, to genius, and one cannot help thinking with sympathy of the miserable days and nights through which she drove a succession of distracted lovers. Edna St. Vincent Millay's confident, "We were very young, we were very merry,/We went back and forth all night on the ferry" would not have served the purposes of little Dottie Rothschild, standing tiptoe on the brink of doom: "Lips that taste of tears, they say,/Are the best for kissing." The lines are from the first poem in her first book, and we are not surprised to see that the poem is entitled "Threnody." She began her career as a poet with a song of lamentation and she ended it with what she called a war song, in which she urged her soldier-husband to be unfaithful to her. The span of her work is narrow and what it embraces is often slight, but the author of it is perhaps luckier than she supposed herself to be: as a writer, she had not counted on surviving, and the continued interest in her work in schools and colleges, where she is being read by the great-grandchildren of her contemporaries, would startle and delight her. There were circumstances under which, with an effort, she could refrain from making wisecracks; though it is risky to assume that an occasion for paying homage to her would be among them, we do well to take that chance. Mrs. Parker had, after all, when she chose to display them, perfect manners. She would be eager to conceal from us, for our sakes, how much readier she was to accept abuse than praise. Greatly daring, we salute her. For here she is.

PART ONE

The Original Portable

as Arranged by

Dorothy Parker in 1944

The Lovely Leave

Her husband had telephoned her by long distance to tell her about the leave. She had not expected the call, and she had no words arranged. She threw away whole seconds explaining her surprise at hearing him, and reporting that it was raining hard in New York, and asking was it terribly hot where he was. He had stopped her to say, look, he didn't have time to talk long; and he had told her quickly that his squadron was to be moved to another field the next week and on the way he would have twenty-four hours' leave. It was difficult for her to hear. Behind his voice came a jagged chorus of young male voices, all crying the syllable "Hey!"

"Ah, don't hang up yet," she said. "Please. Let's talk another minute, just another——"

"Honey, I've got to go," he said. "The boys all want a crack at the telephone. See you a week from today, around five. 'By."

Then there had been a click as his receiver went back into place. Slowly she cradled her telephone, looking at it as if all frustrations and bewilderments and separations were its fault. Over it she had heard his voice, coming from far away. All the months, she had tried not to think of the great blank distance between them; and now that far voice made her know she had thought of nothing else. And his speech had been brisk and busy. And from back of him had come gay, wild young voices, voices he heard every day and she did not, voices of those who shared his new life. And he had heeded them and not her, when she begged for another minute. She took her hand off the telephone and held it away from her with the fingers spread stiffly apart, as if it had touched something horrid.

Then she told herself to stop her nonsense. If you looked for things to make you feel hurt and wretched and unnecessary, you were certain to find them, more easily each time, so easily, soon, that you did not even realize you had gone out searching.

3

Women alone often developed into experts at the practice. She must never join their dismal league.

What was she dreary about, anyway? If he had only a little while to talk, then he had only a little while to talk, that was all. Certainly he had had time to tell her he was coming, to say that they would be together soon. And there she was, sitting scowling at the telephone, the kind, faithful telephone that had brought her the lovely news. She would see him in a week. Only a week. She began to feel, along her back and through her middle, little quivers of excitement, like tiny springs uncoiling into spirals.

There must be no waste to this leave. She thought of the preposterous shyness that had fallen upon her when he had come home before. It was the first time she had seen him in uniform. There he stood, in their little apartment, a dashing stranger in strange, dashing garments. Until he had gone into the army, they had never spent a night apart in all their marriage; and when she saw him, she dropped her eyes and twisted her handkerchief and could bring nothing but monosyllables from her throat. There must be no such squandering of minutes this time. There must be no such gangling diffidence to lop even an instant from their twenty-four hours of perfect union. Oh, Lord, only twenty-four hours. . . .

No. That was exactly the wrong thing to do; that was directly the wrong way to think. That was the way she had spoiled it before. Almost as soon as the shyness had left her and she felt she knew him again, she had begun counting. She was so filled with the desperate consciousness of the hours sliding away—only twelve more, only five, oh, dear God, only one left—that she had no room for gaiety and ease. She had spent the golden time in grudging its going.

She had been so woebegone of carriage, so sad and slow of word as the last hour went, that he, nervous under the pall, had spoken sharply and there had been a quarrel. When he had had to leave for his train, there were no clinging farewells, no tender words to keep. He had gone to the door and opened it and stood with it against his shoulder while he shook out his flight cap and put it on, adjusting it with great care, one inch over the eye, one inch above the ear. She stood in the middle of the living-room, cool and silent, looking at him.

When his cap was precisely as it should be, he looked at her.

"Well," he said. He cleared his throat. "Guess I'd better get going."

"I'm sure you had," she said.

He studied his watch intently. "I'll just make it," he said.

"I'm sure you will," she said.

She turned, not with an actual shrug, only with the effect of one, and went to the window and looked out, as if casually remarking the weather. She heard the door close loudly and then the grind of the elevator.

When she knew he was gone, she was cool and still no longer. She ran about the little flat, striking her breast and sobbing.

Then she had two months to ponder what had happened, to see how she had wrought the ugly small ruin. She cried in the nights.

She need not brood over it any more. She had her lesson; she could forget how she had learned it. This new leave would be the one to remember, the one he and she would have, to keep forever. She was to have a second chance, another twenty-four hours with him. After all, that is no short while, you know; that is, if you do not think of it as a thin little row of hours dropping off like beads from a broken string. Think of it as a whole long day and a whole long night, shining and sweet, and you will be all but awed by your fortune. For how many people are there who have the memory of a whole long day and a whole long night, shining and sweet, to carry with them in their hearts until they die?

To keep something, you must take care of it. More, you must understand just what sort of care it requires. You must know the rules and abide by them. She could do that. She had been doing it all the months, in the writing of her letters to him. There had been rules to be learned in that matter, and the first of them was the hardest: never say to him what you want him to say to you. Never tell him how sadly you miss him, how it grows no better, how each day without him is sharper than the day before. Set down for him the gay happenings about you, bright little anecdotes, not invented, necessarily, but attractively embellished. Do not bedevil him with the pinings of your faithful heart because he is your husband, your man, your love. For you are writing to none of these. You are writing to a soldier.

She knew those rules. She would have said that she would rather die, and she would have meant something very near the words, than send a letter of complaint or sadness or cold anger to her husband, a soldier far away, strained and weary from his work, giving all he had for the mighty cause. If in her letters she could be all he wanted her to be, how much easier to be it when they were together. Letters were difficult; every word had to be considered and chosen. When they were together again, when they could see and hear and touch each other, there would be no stiltedness. They would talk and laugh together. They would have tenderness and excitement. It would be as if they had never been separated. Perhaps they never had been. Perhaps a strange new life and strange empty miles and strange gay voices had no existence for two who were really one.

She had thought it out. She had learned the laws of what not to do. Now she could give herself up to the ecstasy of waiting his coming.

It was a fine week. She counted the time again, but now it was sweet to see it go. Two days after tomorrow, day after tomorrow, tomorrow. She lay awake in the dark, but it was a thrilling wakefulness. She went tall and straight by day, in pride in her warrior. On the street, she looked with amused pity at women who walked with men in civilian suits.

She bought a new dress; black—he liked black dresses—simple—he liked plain dresses—and so expensive that she would not think of its price. She charged it, and realized that for months to come she would tear up the bill without removing it from its envelope. All right—this was no time to think of months to come.

The day of the leave was a Saturday. She flushed with gratitude to the army for this coincidence, for after one o'clock, Saturday was her own. She went from her office without stopping for lunch, and bought perfume and toilet water and bath oil. She had a bit of each remaining in bottles on her dressing table and in her bathroom, but it made her feel desired and secure to have rich new stores of them. She bought a nightgown, a delightful thing of soft chiffon patterned with little bouquets, with innocent puffs of sleeves and a Romney neck and a blue sash. It could never withstand laundering, a French cleaner must care for it—all right. She hurried home with it, to fold it in a satin sachet.

Then she went out again and bought the materials for cocktails and whiskies-and-sodas, shuddering at their cost. She went a dozen blocks to buy the kind of salted biscuits he liked with drinks. On the way back she passed a florist's shop in the window of which were displayed potted fuchsia. She made no attempt to resist them. They were too charming, with their delicate parchment-colored inverted cups and their graceful magenta bells. She bought six pots of them. Suppose she did without lunches the next week—all right.

When she was done with the little living-room, it looked gracious and gay. She ranged the pots of fuchsia along the window sill, she drew out a table and set it with glasses and bottles, she plumped the pillows and laid bright-covered magazines about invitingly. It was a place where someone entering eagerly would find delighted welcome.

Before she changed her dress, she telephoned downstairs to the man who tended both the switchboard and the elevator.

"Oh," she said, when he eventually answered. "Oh, I just want to say, when my husband, Lieutenant McVicker, comes, please send him right up."

There was no necessity for the call. The wearied attendant would have brought up anyone to any flat without the additional stress of a telephoned announcement. But she wanted to say the words. She wanted to say "my husband" and she wanted to say "lieutenant."

She sang, when she went into the bedroom to dress. She had a sweet, uncertain little voice that made the lusty song ludicrous.

> *"Off we go, into the wild blue yonder,*
>   *Climbing high into the sun, sun, sun, sun.*
> *Here they come; zooming to meet our thunder—*
>   *At 'em boys, give 'er the gun!"*

She kept singing, in a preoccupied way, while she gave close attention to her lips and her eyelashes. Then she was silent and held her breath as she drew on the new dress. It was good to her. There was a reason for the cost of those perfectly plain black dresses. She stood looking at herself in the mirror with deep interest, as if she watched a chic unknown, the details of whose costume she sought to memorize.

As she stood there, the bell rang. It rang three times, loud and quick. He had come.

She gasped, and her hands fluttered over the dressing table. She seized the perfume atomizer and sprayed scent violently all about her head and shoulders, some of it reaching them. She had already perfumed herself, but she wanted another minute, another moment, anything. For it had taken her again—the outrageous shyness. She could not bring herself to go to the door and open it. She stood, shaking, and squirted perfume.

The bell rang three times loud and quick again, and then an endless peal.

"Oh, *wait*, can't you?" she cried. She threw down the atomizer, looked wildly around the room as if for a hiding-place, then sternly made herself tall and sought to control the shaking of her body. The shrill noise of the bell seemed to fill the flat and crowd the air out of it.

She started for the door. Before she reached it, she stopped, held her hands over her face, and prayed, "Oh, please let it be all right," she whispered. "Please keep me from doing wrong things. Please let it be lovely."

Then she opened the door. The noise of the bell stopped. There he stood in the brightly lighted little hall. All the long sad nights, and all the strong and sensible vows. And now he had come. And there she stood.

"Well, for heaven's sake!" she said. "I had no idea there was anybody out here. Why, you were just as quiet as a little mouse."

"Well! Don't you ever open the door?" he said.

"Can't a woman have time to put on her shoes?" she said.

He came in and closed the doors behind him. "Ah, darling," he said. He put his arms around her. She slid her cheek along his lips, touched her forehead to his shoulder, and broke away from him.

"Well!" she said. "Nice to see you, Lieutenant. How's the war?"

"How are you?" he said. "You look wonderful."

"Me?" she said. "Look at you."

He was well worth looking at. His fine clothes complemented his fine body. The precision of his appointments was absolute, yet he seemed to have no consciousness of it. He stood straight, and he moved with grace and assurance. His face was browned. It was thin, so thin that the bones showed under the cheeks and down the jaws; but there was no look of strain in it. It was smooth and serene and confident. He was the American officer, and there was no finer sight than he.

"Well!" she said. She made herself raise her eyes to his and found suddenly that it was no longer difficult. "Well, we can't just stand here saying 'well' at each other. Come on in and sit down. We've got a long time ahead of us—oh, Steve, isn't it wonderful! Hey. Didn't you bring a bag?"

"Why, you see," he said, and stopped. He slung his cap over onto the table among the bottles and glasses. "I left the bag at the station. I'm afraid I've got sort of rotten news, darling."

She kept her hands from flying to her breast.

"You—you're going overseas right away?" she said.

"Oh, Lord, no," he said. "Oh, no, no, no. I said this was rotten news. No. They've changed the orders, baby. They've taken back all leaves. We're to go right on to the new field. I've got to get a train at six-ten."

She sat down on the sofa. She wanted to cry; not silently with slow crystal tears, but with wide mouth and smeared face. She wanted to throw herself stomach-down on the floor, and kick and scream, and go limp if anyone tried to lift her.

"I think that's awful," she said. "I think that's just filthy."

"I know," he said. "But there's nothing to do about it. This is the army, Mrs. Jones."

"Couldn't you have said something?" she said. "Couldn't you have told them you've had only one leave in six months? Couldn't you have said all the chance your wife had to see you again was just this poor little twenty-four hours? Couldn't you have explained what it meant to her? Couldn't you?"

"Come on, now, Mimi," he said. "There's a war on."

"I'm sorry," she said. "I was sorry as soon as I'd said it. I was sorry while I was saying it. But—oh, it's so hard!"

"It's not easy for anybody," he said. "You don't know how the boys were looking forward to their leaves."

"Oh, I don't give a damn about the boys!" she said.

"That's the spirit that'll win for our side," he said. He sat down in the biggest chair, stretched his legs and crossed his ankles.

"You don't care about anything but those pilots," she said.

"Look, Mimi," he said. "We haven't got time to do this. We haven't got time to get into a fight and say a lot of things we don't mean. Everything's all—all speeded up, now. There's no time left for this."

"Oh, I know," she said. "Oh, Steve, don't I know!"

She went over and sat on the arm of his chair and buried her face in his shoulder.

"This is more like it," he said. "I've kept thinking about this." She nodded against his blouse.

"If you knew what it was to sit in a decent chair again," he said.

She sat up. "Oh," she said. "It's the chair. I'm so glad you like it."

"They've got the worst chairs you ever saw, in the pilots' room," he said. "A lot of busted-down old rockers—honestly, rockers—that big-hearted patriots contributed, to get them out of the attic. If they haven't better furniture at the new field. I'm going to do something about it, even if I have to buy the stuff myself."

"I certainly would, if I were you," she said. "I'd go without food and clothing and laundry, so the boys would be happy sitting down. I wouldn't even save out enough for air mail stamps, to write to my wife once in a while."

She rose and moved about the room.

"Mimi, what's the matter with you?" he said. "Are you—are you jealous of the pilots?"

She counted as far as eight, to herself. Then she turned and smiled at him.

"Why—I guess I am—" she said. "I guess that's just what I must be. Not only of the pilots. Of the whole air corps. Of the whole Army of the United States."

"You're wonderful," he said.

"You see," she said with care, "you have a whole new life—I have half an old one. Your life is so far away from mine, I don't see how they're ever going to come back together."

"That's nonsense," he said.

"No, please wait," she said. "I get strained and—and frightened, I guess, and I say things I could cut my throat for saying. But you know what I really feel about you. I'm so proud of you I can't find words for it. I know you're doing the most important thing in the world, maybe the only important thing in the world. Only—oh, Steve, I wish to heaven you didn't love doing it so much!"

"Listen," he said.

"No," she said. "You mustn't interrupt a lady. It's unbecoming an officer, like carrying packages in the street. I'm just trying to tell you a little about how I feel. I can't get used to being so completely left out. You don't wonder what I do, you don't want to find out what's in my head—why, you never even ask me how I am!"

"I do so!" he said. "I asked you how you were the minute I came in."

"That was white of you," she said.

"Oh, for heaven's sake!" he said. "I didn't have to ask you. I could see how you look. You look wonderful. I told you that."

She smiled at him. "Yes, you did, didn't you?" she said.
"And you sounded as if you meant it. Do you really like my
dress?"

"Oh, yes," he said. "I always liked that dress on you."

It was as if she turned to wood. "This dress," she said,
enunciating with insulting distinctness, "is brandnew. I have
never had it on before in my life. In case you are interested, I
bought it especially for this occasion."

"I'm sorry, honey," he said. "Oh, sure, now I see it's not the
other one at all. I think it's great. I like you in black."

"At moments like this," she said, "I almost wish I were in it
for another reason."

"Stop it," he said. "Sit down and tell me about yourself.
What have you been doing?"

"Oh, nothing," she said.

"How's the office?" he said.

"Dull," she said. "Dull as mud."

"Who have you seen?" he said.

"Oh, nobody," she said.

"Well, what do you *do?*" he said.

"In the evenings?" she said. "Oh, I sit here and knit and
read detective stories that it turns out I've read before."

"I think that's all wrong of you," he said. "I think it's
asinine to sit here alone, moping. That doesn't do any good to
anybody. Why don't you go out more?"

"I hate to go out with just women," she said.

"Well, why do you have to?" he said. "Ralph's in town, isn't
he? And John and Bill and Gerald. Why don't you go out with
them? You're silly not to."

"It hadn't occurred to me," she said, "that it was silly to
keep faithful to one's husband."

"Isn't that taking rather a jump?" he said. "It's possible to
go to dinner with a man and stay this side adultery. And don't
use words like 'one's.' You're awful when you're elegant."

"I know," she said. "I never have any luck when I try. No.
You're the one that's awful, Steve. You really are. I'm trying to
show you a glimpse of my heart, to tell you how it feels when
you're gone, how I don't want to be with anyone if I can't be

with you. And all you say is, I'm not doing any good to anybody. That'll be nice to think of when you go. You don't know what it's like for me here alone. You just don't know."

"Yes, I do," he said. "I know, Mimi." He reached for a cigarette on the little table beside him, and the bright magazine by the cigarette-box caught his eye. "Hey, is this this week's? I haven't seen it yet." He glanced through the early pages.

"Go ahead and read if you want to," she said. "Don't let me disturb you."

"I'm not reading," he said. He put down the magazine. "You see, I don't know what to say, when you start talking about showing me glimpses of your heart, and all that. I know. I know you must be having a rotten time. But aren't you feeling fairly sorry for yourself?"

"If *I'm* not," she said, "who would be?"

"What do you want anyone to be sorry for you for?" he said. "You'd be all right if you'd stop sitting around alone. I'd like to think of you having a good time while I'm away."

She went over to him and kissed him on the forehead.

"Lieutenant," she said, "you are a far nobler character than I am. Either that," she said, "or there is something else back of this."

"Oh, shut up," he said. He pulled her down to him and held her there. She seemed to melt against him, and stayed there, still.

Then she felt him take his left arm from around her and felt his head raised from its place against hers. She looked up at him. He was craning over her shoulder, endeavoring to see his wrist watch.

"Oh, now, really!" she said. She put her hands against his chest and pushed herself vigorously away from him.

"It goes so quickly," he said softly, with his eyes on his watch. "We've—we've only a little while, darling."

She melted again. "Oh, Steve," she whispered. "Oh, dearest."

"I do want to take a bath," he said. "Get up, will you, baby?"

She got right up. "You're going to take a bath?" she said.

"Yes," he said. "You don't mind, do you?"

"Oh, not in the least," she said. "I'm sure you'll enjoy it. It's one of the pleasantest ways of killing time, I always think."

"You know how you feel after a long ride on a train," he said.

"Oh, surely," she said.

He rose and went into the bedroom. "I'll hurry up," he called back to her.

"Why?" she said.

Then she had a moment to consider herself. She went into the bedroom after him, sweet with renewed resolve. He had hung his blouse and necktie neatly over a chair and he was unbuttoning his shirt. As she came in, he took it off. She looked at the beautiful brown triangle of his back. She would do anything for him, anything in the world.

"I—I'll go run your bath water," she said. She went into the bathroom, turned on the faucets of the tub, and set the towels and mat ready. When she came back into the bedroom he was just entering it from the living-room, naked. In his hand he carried the bright magazine he had glanced at before. She stopped short.

"Oh," she said. "You're planning to read in the tub?"

"If you knew how I'd been looking forward to this!" he said. "Boy, a hot bath in a tub! We haven't got anything but showers, and when you take a shower, there's a hundred boys waiting, yelling at you to hurry up and get out."

"I suppose they can't bear being parted from you," she said.

He smiled at her. "See you in a couple of minutes," he said, and went on into the bathroom and closed the door. She heard the slow slip and slide of water as he laid himself in the tub.

She stood just as she was. The room was lively with the perfume she had sprayed, too present, too insistent. Her eyes went to the bureau drawer where lay, wrapped in soft fragrance, the nightgown with the little bouquets and the Romney neck. She went over to the bathroom door, drew back her right foot, and kicked the base of the door so savagely that the whole frame shook.

"What, dear?" he called. "Want something?"

"Oh, nothing," she said. "Nothing whatever. I've got everything any woman could possibly want, haven't I?"

"What?" he called. "I can't hear you, honey."

"Nothing," she screamed.

She went into the living-room. She stood, breathing heavily, her finger nails scarring her palms, as she looked at the fuchsia blossoms, with their dirty parchment-colored cups, their vulgar magenta bells.

Her breath was quiet and her hands relaxed when he came into the living-room again. He had on his trousers and shirt, and his necktie was admirably knotted. He carried his belt. She turned to him. There were things she had meant to say, but she could do nothing but smile at him, when she saw him. Her heart turned liquid in her breast.

His brow was puckered. "Look, darling," he said. "Have you got any brass polish?"

"Why, no," she said. "We haven't even got any brass."

"Well, have you any nail polish—the colorless kind? A lot of the boys use that."

"I'm sure it must look adorable on them," she said. "No, I haven't anything but rose-colored polish. Would that be of any use to you, heaven forbid?"

"No," he said, and he seemed worried. "Red wouldn't be any good at all. Hell, I don't suppose you've got a Blitz Cloth, have you? Or a Shine-O?"

"If I had the faintest idea what you were talking about," she said, "I might be better company for you."

He held the belt out toward her. "I want to shine my buckle," he said.

"Oh . . . my . . . dear . . . sweet . . . gentle . . . Lord," she said. "We've got about ten minutes left, and you want to shine your belt buckle."

"I don't like to report to a new C.O. with a dull belt buckle," he said.

"It was bright enough for you to report to your wife in, wasn't it?" she said.

"Oh, stop that," he said. "You just won't understand, that's all."

"It isn't that I won't understand," she said. "It's that I can't remember. I haven't been with a Boy Scout for so long."

He looked at her. "You're being great, aren't you?" he said. He looked around the room. "There must be a cloth around somewhere—oh, this will do." He caught up a pretty little cocktail napkin from the table of untouched bottles and glasses, sat down with his belt laid over his knees, and rubbed at the buckle.

She watched him for a moment, then rushed over to him and grasped his arm.

"Please," she said. "Please, I didn't mean it, Steve."

"Please let me do this, will you?" he said. He wrenched his arm from her hand and went on with his polishing.

"You tell me I won't understand!" she cried. "You won't understand anything about anybody else. Except those crazy pilots."

"They're all right!" he said. "They're fine kids. They're going to make great fighters." He went on rubbing at his buckle.

"Oh, I know it!" she said. "You know I know it. I don't mean it when I say things against them. How would I dare to mean it? They're risking their lives and their sight and their sanity, they're giving everything for——"

"Don't do that kind of talk, will you?" he said. He rubbed the buckle.

"I'm not doing any kind of talk!" she said. "I'm trying to tell you something. Just because you've got on that pretty suit, you think you should never hear anything serious, never anything sad or wretched or disagreeable. You make me sick, that's what you do! I know, I know—I'm not trying to take anything away from you, I realize what you're doing, I told you what I think of it. Don't, for heaven's sake, think I'm mean enough to grudge you any happiness and excitement you can get out of it. I know it's hard for you. But it's never lonely, that's all I mean.

You have companionships no—no wife can ever give you. I suppose it's the sense of hurry, maybe, the consciousness of living on borrowed time, the—the knowledge of what you're all going into together that makes the comradeship of men in war so firm, so fast. But won't you please try to understand how I feel? Won't you understand that it comes out of bewilderment and disruption and—and being frightened, I guess? Won't you understand what makes me do what I do, when I hate myself while I'm doing it? Won't you please understand? Darling, won't you please?"

He laid down the little napkin. "I can't go through this kind of thing, Mimi," he said. "Neither can you." He looked at his watch. "Hey, it's time for me to go."

She stood tall and stiff. "I'm sure it is," she said.

"I'd better put on my blouse," he said.

"You might as well," she said.

He rose, wove his belt through the loops of his trousers, and went into the bedroom. She went over to the window and stood looking out, as if casually remarking the weather.

She heard him come back into the room, but she did not turn around. She heard his steps stop, knew he was standing there.

"Mimi," he said.

She turned toward him, her shoulders back, her chin high, cool, regal. Then she saw his eyes. They were no longer bright and gay and confident. Their blue was misty and they looked troubled; they looked at her as if they pleaded with her.

"Look, Mimi," he said, "do you think I want to do this? Do you think I want to be away from you? Do you think that this is what I thought I'd be doing now? In the years—well, in the years when we ought to be together."

He stopped. Then he spoke again, but with difficulty. "I can't talk about it. I can't even think about it—because if I did I couldn't do my job. But just because I don't talk about it doesn't mean I want to be doing what I'm doing. I want to be with you, Mimi. That's where I belong. You know that, darling. Don't you?"

He held his arms open to her. She ran to them. This time,

she did not slide her cheek along his lips.

When he had gone, she stood a moment by the fuchsia plants, touching delicately, tenderly, the enchanting parchment-colored caps, the exquisite magenta bells.

The telephone rang. She answered it, to hear a friend of hers inquiring about Steve, asking how he looked and how he was, urging that he come to the telephone and say hello to her.

"He's gone," she said. "All their leaves were canceled. He wasn't here an hour."

The friend cried sympathy. It was a shame, it was simply awful, it was absolutely terrible.

"No, don't say that," she said. "I know it wasn't very much time. But oh, it was lovely!"

Arrangement in Black and White

The woman with the pink velvet poppies twined round the assisted gold of her hair traversed the crowded room at an interesting gait combining a skip with a sidle, and clutched the lean arm of her host.

"Now I got you!" she said. "Now you can't get away!"

"Why, hello," said her host. "Well. How are you?"

"Oh, I'm finely," she said. "Just simply finely. Listen. I want you to do me the most terrible favor. Will you? Will you please? Pretty please?"

"What is it?" said her host.

"Listen," she said. "I want to meet Walter Williams. Honestly, I'm just simply crazy about that man. Oh, when he sings! When he sings those spirituals! Well, I said to Burton, 'It's a good thing for you Walter Williams is colored,' I said, 'or you'd have lots of reason to be jealous.' I'd really love to meet him. I'd like to tell him I've heard him sing. Will you be an angel and introduce me to him?"

"Why, certainly," said her host. "I thought you'd met him. The party's for him. Where is he, anyway?"

"He's over there by the bookcase," she said. "Let's wait till those people get through talking to him. Well, I think you're simply marvelous, giving this perfectly marvelous party for him, and having him meet all these white people, and all. Isn't he terribly grateful?"

"I hope not," said her host.

"I think it's really terribly nice," she said. "I do. I don't see why on earth it isn't perfectly all right to meet colored people. I haven't any feeling at all about it—not one single bit. Burton—oh, he's just the other way. Well, you know, he comes from Virginia, and you know how they are."

"Did he come tonight?" said her host.

"No, he couldn't," she said. "I'm a regular grass widow tonight. I told him when I left, 'There's no telling what I'll do,'

I said. He was just so tired out, he couldn't move. Isn't it a shame?"

"Ah," said her host.

"Wait till I tell him I met Walter Williams!" she said. "He'll just about die. Oh, we have more arguments about colored people. I talk to him like I don't know what, I get so excited. 'Oh, don't be so silly,' I say. But I must say for Burton, he's heaps broader-minded than lots of these Southerners. He's really awfully fond of colored people. Well, he says himself, he wouldn't have white servants. And you know, he had this old colored nurse, this regular old nigger mammy, and he just simply loves her. Why, every time he goes home, he goes out in the kitchen to see her. He does, really, to this day. All he says is, he says he hasn't got a word to say against colored people as long as they keep their place. He's always doing things for them—giving them clothes and I don't know what all. The only thing he says, he says he wouldn't sit down at the table with one for a million dollars. 'Oh,' I say to him, 'you make me sick, talking like that.' I'm just terrible to him. Aren't I terrible?"

"Oh, no, no, no," said her host. "No, no."

"I am," she said. "I know I am. Poor Burton! Now, me, I don't feel that way at all. I haven't the slightest feeling about colored people. Why, I'm just crazy about some of them. They're just like children—just as easygoing, and always singing and laughing and everything. Aren't they the happiest things you ever saw in your life? Honestly, it makes me laugh just to hear them. Oh, I like them. I really do. Well, now, listen, I have this colored laundress, I've had her for years, and I'm devoted to her. She's a real character. And I want to tell you, I think of her as my friend. That's the way I think of her. As I say to Burton, 'Well, for heaven's sakes, we're all human beings!' Aren't we?"

"Yes," said her host. "Yes, indeed."

"Now this Walter Williams," she said. "I think a man like that's a real artist. I do. I think he deserves an awful lot of credit. Goodness, I'm so crazy about music or anything, I don't care *what* color he is. I honestly think if a person's an artist, nobody ought to have any feeling at all about meeting them.

That's absolutely what I say to Burton. Don't you think I'm right?"

"Yes," said her host. "Oh, yes."

"That's the way I feel," she said. "I just can't understand people being narrow-minded. Why, I absolutely think it's a privilege to meet a man like Walter Williams. Yes, I do. I haven't any feeling at all. Well, my goodness, the good Lord made him, just the same as He did any of us. Didn't He?"

"Surely," said her host. "Yes, indeed."

"That's what I say," she said. "Oh, I get so furious when people are narrow-minded about colored people. It's just all I can do not to say something. Of course, I do admit when you get a bad colored man, they're simply terrible. But as I say to Burton, there are some bad white people, too, in this world. Aren't there?"

"I guess there are," said her host.

"Why, I'd really be glad to have a man like Walter Williams come to my house and sing for us, some time," she said. "Of course, I couldn't ask him on account of Burton, but I wouldn't have any feeling about it at all. Oh, can't he sing! Isn't it marvelous, the way they all have music in them? It just seems to be right *in* them. Come on, let's us go on over and talk to him. Listen, what shall I do when I'm introduced? Ought I to shake hands? Or what?"

"Why, do whatever you want," said her host.

"I guess maybe I'd better," she said. "I wouldn't for the world have him think I had any feeling. I think I'd better shake hands, just the way I would with anybody else. That's just exactly what I'll do."

They reached the tall young Negro, standing by the bookcase. The host performed introductions; the Negro bowed.

"How do you do?" he said.

The woman with the pink velvet poppies extended her hand at the length of her arm and held it so for all the world to see, until the Negro took it, shook it, and gave it back to her.

"Oh, how do you do, Mr. Williams," she said. "Well, how do you do. I've just been saying, I've enjoyed your singing so awfully much. I've been to your concerts, and we have you on the phonograph and everything. Oh, I just enjoy it!"

She spoke with great distinctness, moving her lips meticulously, as if in parlance with the deaf.

"I'm so glad," he said.

"I'm just simply crazy about that 'Water Boy' thing you sing," she said. "Honestly, I can't get it out of my head. I have my husband nearly crazy, the way I go around humming it all the time. Oh, he looks just as black as the ace of—Well. Tell me, where on earth do you ever get all those songs of yours? How do you ever get hold of them?"

"Why," he said, "there are so many different——"

"I should think you'd love singing them," she said. "It must be more fun. All those darling old spirituals—oh, I just love them! Well, what are you doing, now? Are you still keeping up your singing? Why don't you have another concert, some time?"

"I'm having one the sixteenth of this month," he said.

"Well, I'll be there," she said. "I'll be there, if I possibly can. You can count on me. Goodness, here comes a whole raft of people to talk to you. You're just a regular guest of honor! Oh, who's that girl in white? I've seen her some place."

"That's Katherine Burke," said her host.

"Good Heavens," she said, "is that Katherine Burke? Why, she looks entirely different off the stage. I thought she was much better-looking. I had no idea she was so terribly dark. Why, she looks almost like—Oh, I think she's a wonderful actress! Don't you think she's a wonderful actress, Mr. Williams? Oh, I think she's marvelous. Don't you?"

"Yes, I do," he said.

"Oh, I do, too," she said. "Just wonderful. Well, goodness, we must give someone else a chance to talk to the guest of honor. Now, don't forget, Mr. Williams, I'm going to be at that concert if I possibly can. I'll be there applauding like everything. And if I can't come, I'm going to tell everybody I know to go, anyway. Don't you forget!"

"I won't," he said. "Thank you so much."

The host took her arm and piloted her into the next room.

"Oh, my dear," she said. "I nearly died! Honestly, I give you my word, I nearly passed away. Did you hear that terrible break I made? I was just going to say Katherine Burke looked almost like a nigger. I just caught myself in time. Oh, do you think he noticed?"

"I don't believe so," said her host.

"Well, thank goodness," she said, "because I wouldn't have embarrassed him for anything. Why, he's awfully nice. Just as nice as he can be. Nice manners, and everything. You know, so many colored people, you give them an inch, and they walk all over you. But he doesn't try any of that. Well, he's got more sense, I suppose. He's really nice. Don't you think so?"

"Yes," said her host.

"I liked him," she said. "I haven't any feeling at all because he's a colored man. I felt just as natural as I would with anybody. Talked to him just as naturally, and everything. But honestly, I could hardly keep a straight face. I kept thinking of Burton. Oh, wait till I tell Burton I called him 'Mister'!"

The Sexes

The young man with the scenic cravat glanced nervously down the sofa at the girl in the fringed dress. She was examining her handkerchief; it might have been the first one of its kind she had seen, so deep was her interest in its material, form, and possibilities. The young man cleared his throat, without necessity or success, producing a small, syncopated noise.

"Want a cigarette?" he said.

"No, thank you," she said. "Thank you ever so much just the same."

"Sorry I've only got these kind," he said. "You got any of your own?"

"I really don't know," she said. "I probably have, thank you."

"Because if you haven't," he said, "it wouldn't take me a minute to go up to the corner and get you some."

"Oh, thank you, but I wouldn't have you go to all that trouble for anything," she said. "It's awfully sweet of you to think of it. Thank you ever so much."

"Will you for God's sakes stop thanking me?" he said.

"Really," she said, "I didn't know I was saying anything out of the way. I'm awfully sorry if I hurt your feelings. I know what it feels like to get your feelings hurt. I'm sure I didn't realize it was an insult to say 'thank you' to a person. I'm not exactly in the habit of having people swear at me because I say 'thank you' to them."

"I did not swear at you!" he said.

"Oh, you didn't?" she said. "I see."

"My God," he said, "all I said, I simply asked you if I couldn't go out and get you some cigarettes. Is there anything in that to get up in the air about?"

"Who's up in the air?" she said. "I'm sure I didn't know it was a criminal offense to say I wouldn't dream of giving you all

24

that trouble. I'm afraid I must be awfully stupid, or something."

"Do you want me to go out and get you some cigarettes; or don't you?" he said.

"Goodness," she said, "if you want to go so much, please don't feel you have to stay here. I wouldn't have you feel you had to stay for anything."

"Ah, don't be that way, will you?" he said.

"Be what way?" she said. "I'm not being any way."

"What's the matter?" he said.

"Why, nothing," she said. "Why?"

"You've been funny all evening," he said. "Hardly said a word to me, ever since I came in."

"I'm terribly sorry you haven't been having a good time," she said. "For goodness' sakes, don't feel you have to stay here and be bored. I'm sure there are millions of places you could be having a lot more fun. The only thing, I'm a little bit sorry I didn't know before, that's all. When you said you were coming over tonight, I broke a lot of dates to go to the theater and everything. But it doesn't make a bit of difference. I'd much rather have you go and have a good time. It isn't very pleasant to sit here and feel you're boring a person to death."

"I'm not bored!" he said. "I don't want to go any place! Ah, honey, won't you tell me what's the matter? Ah, please."

"I haven't the faintest idea what you're talking about," she said. "There isn't a thing on earth the matter. I don't know what you mean."

"Yes, you do," he said. "There's something the trouble. Is it anything I've done, or anything?"

"Goodness," she said, "I'm sure it isn't any of my business, anything you do. I certainly wouldn't feel I had any right to criticize."

"Will you stop talking like that?" he said. "Will you, please?"

"Talking like what?" she said.

"You know," he said. "That's the way you were talking over the telephone today, too. You were so snotty when I called you up, I was afraid to talk to you."

"I beg your pardon," she said. "What did you say I was?"

"Well, I'm sorry," he said. "I didn't mean to say that. You get me so balled up."

"You see," she said, "I'm really not in the habit of hearing language like that. I've never had a thing like that said to me in my life."

"I told you I was sorry, didn't I?" he said. "Honest, honey, I didn't mean it. I don't know how I came to say a thing like that. Will you excuse me? Please?"

"Oh, certainly," she said. "Goodness, don't feel you have to apologize to me. It doesn't make any difference at all. It just seems a little bit funny to have somebody you were in the habit of thinking was a gentleman come to your home and use language like that to you, that's all. But it doesn't make the slightest bit of difference."

"I guess nothing I say makes any difference to you," he said. "You seem to be sore at me."

"I'm sore at you?" she said. "I can't understand what put that idea in your head. Why should I be sore at you?"

"That's what I'm asking you," he said. "Won't you tell me what I've done? Have I done something to hurt your feelings, honey? The way you were, over the phone, you had me worried all day. I couldn't do a lick of work."

"I certainly wouldn't like to feel," she said, "that I was interfering with your work. I know there are lots of girls that don't think anything of doing things like that, but I think it's terrible. It certainly isn't very nice to sit here and have someone tell you you interfere with his business."

"I didn't say that!" he said. "I didn't say it!"

"Oh, didn't you?" she said. "Well, that was the impression I got. It must be my stupidity."

"I guess maybe I better go," he said. "I can't get right. Everything I say seems to make you sorer and sorer. Would you rather I'd go?"

"Please do just exactly whatever you like," she said. "I'm sure the last thing I want to do is have you stay here when you'd rather be some place else. Why don't you go some place where you won't be bored? Why don't you go up to Florence

Leaming's? I know she'd love to have you."

"I don't want to go up to Florence Leaming's!" he said. "What would I want to go up to Florence Leaming's for? She gives me a pain."

"Oh, really?" she said. "She didn't seem to be giving you so much of a pain at Elsie's party last night, I notice. I notice you couldn't even talk to anybody else, that's how much of a pain she gave you."

"Yeah, and you know why I was talking to her?" he said.

"Why, I suppose you think she's attractive," she said. "I suppose some people do. It's perfectly natural. Some people think she's quite pretty."

"I don't know whether she's pretty or not," he said. "I wouldn't know her if I saw her again. Why I was talking to her was you wouldn't even give me a tumble, last night. I came up and tried to talk to you, and you just said, 'Oh, how do you do'—just like that, 'Oh, how do you do'—and you turned right away and wouldn't look at me."

"I wouldn't look at you?" she said. "Oh, that's awfully funny. Oh, that's marvelous. You don't mind if I laugh, do you?"

"Go ahead and laugh your head off," he said. "But you wouldn't."

"Well, the minute you came in the room," she said, "you started making such a fuss over Florence Leaming, I thought you never wanted to see anybody else. You two seemed to be having such a wonderful time together, goodness knows I wouldn't have butted in for anything."

"My God," he said, "this what's-her-name girl came up and began talking to me before I even saw anybody else, and what could I do? I couldn't sock her in the nose, could I?"

"I certainly didn't see you try," she said.

"You saw me try to talk to you, didn't you?" he said. "And what did you do? 'Oh, how do you do.' Then this what's-her-name came up again, and there I was, stuck. Florence Leaming! I think she's terrible. Know what I think of her? I think she's a damn little fool. That's what I think of her."

"Well, of course," she said, "that's the impression she

always gave me, but I don't know. I've heard people say she's pretty. Honestly I have."

"Why, she can't be pretty in the same room with you," he said.

"She has got an awfully funny nose," she said. "I really feel sorry for a girl with a nose like that."

"She's got a terrible nose," he said. "You've got a beautiful nose. Gee, you've got a pretty nose."

"Oh, I have not," she said. "You're crazy."

"And beautiful eyes," he said, "and beautiful hair and a beautiful mouth. And beautiful hands. Let me have one of the little hands. Ah, look atta little hand! Who's got the prettiest hands in the world? Who's the sweetest girl in the world?"

"I don't know," she said. "Who?"

"You don't know!" he said. "You do so, too, know."

"I do not," she said. "Who? Florence Leaming?"

"Oh, Florence Leaming, my eye!" he said. "Getting sore about Florence Leaming! And me not sleeping all last night and not doing a stroke of work all day because you wouldn't speak to me! A girl like you getting sore about a girl like Florence Leaming!"

"I think you're just perfectly crazy," she said. "I was not sore! What on earth ever made you think I was? You're simply crazy. Ow, my new pearl beads! Wait a second till I take them off. There!"

The Standard of Living

Annabel and Midge came out of the tea room with the arrogant slow gait of the leisured, for their Saturday afternoon stretched ahead of them. They had lunched, as was their wont, on sugar, starches, oils, and butter-fats. Usually they ate sandwiches of spongy new white bread greased with butter and mayonnaise; they ate thick wedges of cake lying wet beneath ice cream and whipped cream and melted chocolate gritty with nuts. As alternates, they ate patties, sweating beads of inferior oil, containing bits of bland meat bogged in pale, stiffening sauce; they ate pastries, limber under rigid icing, filled with an indeterminate yellow sweet stuff, not still solid, not yet liquid, like salve that has been left in the sun. They chose no other sort of food, nor did they consider it. And their skin was like the petals of wood anemones, and their bellies were as flat and their flanks as lean as those of young Indian braves.

Annabel and Midge had been best friends almost from the day that Midge had found a job as stenographer with the firm that employed Annabel. By now, Annabel, two years longer in the stenographic department, had worked up to the wages of eighteen dollars and fifty cents a week; Midge was still at sixteen dollars. Each girl lived at home with her family and paid half her salary to its support.

The girls sat side by side at their desks, they lunched together every noon, together they set out for home at the end of the day's work. Many of their evenings and most of their Sundays were passed in each other's company. Often they were joined by two young men, but there was no steadiness to any such quartet; the two young men would give place, unlamented, to two other young men, and lament would have been inappropriate, really, since the newcomers were scarcely distinguishable from their predecessors. Invariably the girls spent the fine idle hours of their hot-weather Saturday afternoons together. Constant use had not worn ragged the fabric of their friendship.

They looked alike, though the resemblance did not lie in their features. It was in the shape of their bodies, their movements, their style, and their adornments. Annabel and Midge did, and completely, all that young office workers are besought not to do. They painted their lips and their nails, they darkened their lashes and lightened their hair, and scent seemed to shimmer from them. They wore thin, bright dresses, tight over their breasts and high on their legs, and tilted slippers, fancifully strapped. They looked conspicuous and cheap and charming.

Now, as they walked across to Fifth Avenue with their skirts swirled by the hot wind, they received audible admiration. Young men grouped lethargically about newsstands awarded them murmurs, exclamations, even—the ultimate tribute— whistles. Annabel and Midge passed without the condescension of hurrying their pace; they held their heads higher and set their feet with exquisite precision, as if they stepped over the necks of peasants.

Always the girls went to walk on Fifth Avenue on their free afternoons, for it was the ideal ground for their favorite game. The game could be played anywhere, and, indeed, was, but the great shop windows stimulated the two players to their best form.

Annabel had invented the game; or rather she had evolved it from an old one. Basically, it was no more than the ancient sport of what-would-you-do-if-you-had-a-million dollars? But Annabel had drawn a new set of rules for it, had narrowed it, pointed it, made it stricter. Like all games, it was the more absorbing for being more difficult.

Annabel's version went like this: You must suppose that somebody dies and leaves you a million dollars, cool. But there is a condition to the bequest. It is stated in the will that you must spend every nickel of the money on yourself.

There lay the hazard of the game. If, when playing it, you forgot, and listed among your expenditures the rental of a new apartment for your family, for example, you lost your turn to the other player. It was astonishing how many—and some of them among the experts, too—would forfeit all their innings by such slips.

It was essential, of course, that it be played in passionate seriousness. Each purchase must be carefully considered and, if necessary, supported by argument. There was no zest to playing wildly. Once Annabel had introduced the game to Sylvia, another girl who worked in the office. She explained the rules to Sylvia and then offered her the gambit "What would be the first thing you'd do?" Sylvia had not shown the decency of even a second of hesitation. "Well," she said, "the first thing I'd do, I'd go out and hire somebody to shoot Mrs. Gary Cooper, and then . . ." So it is to be seen that she was no fun.

But Annabel and Midge were surely born to be comrades, for Midge played the game like a master from the moment she learned it. It was she who added the touches that made the whole thing cozier. According to Midge's innovations, the eccentric who died and left you the money was not anybody you loved, or, for the matter of that, anybody you even knew. It was somebody who had seen you somewhere and had thought, "That girl ought to have lots of nice things. I'm going to leave her a million dollars when I die." And the death was to be neither untimely nor painful. Your benefactor, full of years and comfortably ready to depart, was to slip softly away during sleep and go right to heaven. These embroideries permitted Annabel and Midge to play their game in the luxury of peaceful consciences.

Midge played with a seriousness that was not only proper but extreme. The single strain on the girls' friendship had followed an announcement once made by Annabel that the first thing she would buy with her million dollars would be a silver-fox coat. It was as if she had struck Midge across the mouth. When Midge recovered her breath, she cried that she couldn't imagine how Annabel could do such a thing—silver-fox coats were common! Annabel defended her taste with the retort that they were not common, either. Midge then said that they were so. She added that everybody had a silver-fox coat. She went on, with perhaps a slight loss of head, to declare that she herself wouldn't be caught dead in silver fox.

For the next few days, though the girls saw each other as constantly, their conversation was careful and infrequent, and they did not once play their game. Then one morning, as soon as Annabel entered the office, she came to Midge and said that she had changed her mind. She would not buy a silver-fox coat with any part of her million dollars. Immediately on receiving the legacy, she would select a coat of mink.

Midge smiled and her eyes shone. "I think," she said, "you're doing absolutely the right thing."

Now, as they walked along Fifth Avenue, they played the game anew. It was one of those days with which September is repeatedly cursed; hot and glaring, with slivers of dust in the wind. People drooped and shambled, but the girls carried themselves tall and walked a straight line, as befitted young heiresses on their afternoon promenade. There was no longer need for them to start the game at its formal opening. Annabel went direct to the heart of it.

"All right," she said. "So you've got this million dollars. So what would be the first thing you'd do?"

"Well, the first thing I'd do," Midge said, "I'd get a mink coat." But she said it mechanically, as if she were giving the memorized answer to an expected question.

"Yes," Annabel said, "I think you ought to. The terribly dark kind of mink." But she, too, spoke as if by rote. It was too hot; fur, no matter how dark and sleek and supple, was horrid to the thoughts.

They stepped along in silence for a while. Then Midge's eye was caught by a shop window. Cool, lovely gleamings were there set off by chaste and elegant darkness.

"No," Midge said, "I take it back. I wouldn't get a mink coat the first thing. Know what I'd do? I'd get a string of pearls. Real pearls."

Annabel's eyes turned to follow Midge's.

"Yes," she said, slowly. "I think that's kind of a good idea. And it would make sense, too. Because you can wear pearls with anything."

Together they went over to the shop window and stood pressed against it. It contained but one object—a double row of great, even pearls clasped by a deep emerald around a little pink velvet throat.

"What do you suppose they cost?" Annabel said.

"Gee, I don't know," Midge said. "Plenty, I guess."

"Like a thousand dollars?" Annabel said.

"Oh, I guess like more," Midge said. "On account of the emerald."

"Well, like ten thousand dollars?" Annabel said.

"Gee, I wouldn't even know," Midge said.

The devil nudged Annabel in the ribs. "Dare you to go in and price them," she said.

"Like fun!" Midge said.

"Dare you," Annabel said.

"Why, a store like this wouldn't even be open this afternoon," Midge said.

"Yes, it is so, too," Annabel said. "People just came out. And there's a doorman on. Dare you."

"Well," Midge said. "But you've got to come too."

They tendered thanks, icily, to the doorman for ushering them into the shop. It was cool and quiet, a broad, gracious room with paneled walls and soft carpet. But the girls wore expressions of bitter disdain, as if they stood in a sty.

A slim, immaculate clerk came to them and bowed. His neat face showed no astonishment at their appearance.

"Good afternoon," he said. He implied that he would never forget it if they would grant him the favor of accepting his soft-spoken greeting.

"Good afternoon," Annabel and Midge said together, and in like freezing accents.

"Is there something—?" the clerk said.

"Oh, we're just looking," Annabel said. It was as if she flung the words down from a dais.

The clerk bowed.

"My friend and myself merely happened to be passing," Midge said, and stopped, seeming to listen to the phrase. "My friend here and myself," she went on, "merely happened to be wondering how much are those pearls you've got in your window."

"Ah, yes," the clerk said. "The double rope. That is two hundred and fifty thousand dollars, Madam."

"I see," Midge said.

The clerk bowed. "An exceptionally beautiful necklace," he said. "Would you care to look at it?"

"No, thank you," Annabel said.

"My friend and myself merely happened to be passing," Midge said.

They turned to go; to go, from their manner, where the tumbrel awaited them. The clerk sprang ahead and opened the door. He bowed as they swept by him.

The girls went on along the Avenue and disdain was still on their faces.

"Honestly!" Annabel said. "Can you imagine a thing like that?"

"Two hundred and fifty thousand dollars!" Midge said. "That's a quarter of a million dollars right there!"

"He's got his nerve!" Annabel said.

They walked on. Slowly the disdain went, slowly and completely as if drained from them, and with it went the regal carriage and tread. Their shoulders dropped and they dragged their feet; they bumped against each other, without notice or apology, and caromed away again. They were silent and their eyes were cloudy.

Suddenly Midge straightened her back, flung her head high, and spoke, clear and strong.

"Listen, Annabel," she said. "Look. Suppose there was this terribly rich person, see? You don't know this person, but this person has seen you somewhere and wants to do something for you. Well, it's a terribly old person, see? And so this person dies, just like going to sleep, and leaves you ten million dollars. Now, what would be the first thing you'd do?"

Mr. Durant

Not for some ten days had Mr. Durant known any such ease of mind. He gave himself up to it, wrapped himself, warm and soft, as in a new and an expensive cloak. God, for Whom Mr. Durant entertained a good-humored affection, was in His heaven, and all was again well with Mr. Durant's world.

Curious how this renewed peace sharpened his enjoyment of the accustomed things about him. He looked back at the rubber works, which he had just left for the day, and nodded approvingly at the solid red pile, at the six neat stories rising impressively into the darkness. You would go far, he thought, before you would find a more up-and-coming outfit, and there welled in him a pleasing, proprietary sense of being a part of it.

He gazed amiably down Center Street, noting how restfully the lights glowed. Even the wet, dented pavement, spotted with thick puddles, fed his pleasure by reflecting the discreet radiance above it. And to complete his comfort, the car for which he was waiting, admirably on time, swung into view far down the track. He thought, with a sort of jovial tenderness, of what it would bear him to; of his dinner—it was fish-chowder night—of his children, of his wife, in the order named. Then he turned his kindly attention to the girl who stood near him, obviously awaiting the Center Street car, too. He was delighted to feel a sharp interest in her. He regarded it as being distinctly creditable to himself that he could take a healthy notice of such matters once more. Twenty years younger—that's what he felt.

Rather shabby, she was, in her rough coat with its shagginess rubbed off here and there. But there was a something in the way her cheaply smart turban was jammed over her eyes, in the way her thin young figure moved under the loose coat. Mr. Durant pointed his tongue, and moved it delicately along his cool, smooth upper lip.

The car approached, clanged to a stop before them. Mr.

Durant stepped gallantly aside to let the girl get in first. He did not help her to enter, but the solicitous way in which he superintended the process gave all the effect of his having actually assisted her.

Her tight little skirt slipped up over her thin, pretty legs as she took the high step. There was a run in one of her flimsy silk stockings. She was doubtless unconscious of it; it was well back toward the seam, extending, probably from her garter, half-way down the calf. Mr. Durant had an odd desire to catch his thumb-nail in the present end of the run, and to draw it on down until the slim line of the dropped stitches reached to the top of her low shoe. An indulgent smile at his whimsy played about his mouth, broadening to a grin of affable evening greeting for the conductor, as he entered the car and paid his fare.

The girl sat down somewhere far up at the front. Mr. Durant found a desirable seat toward the rear, and craned his neck to see her. He could catch a glimpse of a fold of her turban and a bit of her brightly rouged cheek, but only at a cost of holding his head in a strained, and presently painful, position. So, warmed by the assurance that there would always be others, he let her go, and settled himself restfully. He had a ride of twenty minutes or so before him. He allowed his head to fall gently back, to let his eyelids droop, and gave himself to his thoughts. Now that the thing was comfortably over and done with, he could think of it easily, almost laughingly. Last week, now, and even part of the week before, he had had to try with all his strength to force it back every time it wrenched itself into his mind. It had positively affected his sleep. Even though he was shielded by his newly acquired amused attitude, Mr. Durant felt indignation flood within him when he recalled those restless nights.

He had met Rose for the first time about three months before. She had been sent up to his office to take some letters for him. Mr. Durant was assistant manager of the rubber company's credit department; his wife was wont to refer to him as one of the officers of the company, and, though she often spoke thus of him to people in his presence, he never troubled to go more fully into detail about his position. He rated a room, a desk, and a telephone to himself; but not a stenographer. When he wanted to give dictation or to have some letters typewritten, he telephoned around to the various other officers until he found a girl who was not busy with her own work. That was how Rose had come to him.

She was not a pretty girl. Distinctly, no. But there was a rather sweet fragility about her, and an almost desperate timidity that Mr. Durant had once found engaging, but that he now thought of with a prickling irritation. She was twenty, and the glamour of youth was around her. When she bent over her work, her back showing white through her sleazy blouse, her clean hair coiled smoothly on her thin neck, her straight, childish legs crossed at the knee to support her pad, she had an undeniable appeal.

But not pretty—no. Her hair wasn't the kind that went up well, her eyelashes and lips were too pale, she hadn't much knack about choosing and wearing her cheap clothes. Mr. Durant, in reviewing the thing, felt a surprise that she should ever have attracted him. But it was a tolerant surprise, not an impatient one. Already he looked back on himself as being just a big boy in the whole affair.

It did not occur to him to feel even a flicker of astonishment that Rose should have responded so eagerly to him, an immovably married man of forty-nine. He never thought of himself in that way. He used to tell Rose, laughingly, that he was old enough to be her father, but neither of them ever really believed it. He regarded her affection for him as the most natural thing in the world—there she was, coming from a much smaller town, never the sort of girl to have had admirers; naturally, she was dazzled at the attentions of a man who, as Mr. Durant put it, was approaching the prime. He had been charmed with the idea of there having been no other men in her life; but lately, far from feeling flattered at being the first and only one, he had come to regard it as her having taken a sly advantage of him, to put him in that position.

It had all been surprisingly easy. Mr. Durant knew it would be almost from the first time he saw her. That did not lessen its interest in his eyes. Obstacles discouraged him, rather than led him on. Elimination of bother was the main thing.

Rose was not a coquettish girl. She had that curious directness that some very timid people possess. There were her scruples, of course, but Mr. Durant readily reasoned them away. Not that he was a master of technique, either. He had had some experiences, probably a third as many as he habitually thought of himself as having been through, but none that taught him much of the delicate shadings of wooing. But then, Rose's simplicity asked exceedingly little.

She was never one to demand much of him, anyway. She never thought of stirring up any trouble between him and his wife, never besought him to leave his family and go away with her, even for a day. Mr. Durant valued her for that. It did away with a lot of probable fussing.

It was amazing how free they were, how little lying there was to do. They stayed in the office after hours—Mr. Durant found many letters that must be dictated. No one thought anything of that. Rose was busy most of the day, and it was only considerate that Mr. Durant should not break in on her employer's time, only natural that he should want as good a stenographer as she was to attend to his correspondence.

Rose's only relative, a married sister, lived in another town. The girl roomed with an acquaintance named Ruby, also employed at the rubber works, and Ruby, who was much taken up with her own affairs of the emotions, never appeared to think it strange if Rose was late to dinner. or missed the meal entirely. Mr. Durant readily explained to his wife that he was detained by a rush of business. It only increased his importance, to her, and spurred her on to devising especially pleasing dishes, and solicitously keeping them hot for his return. Sometimes, important in their guilt, Rose and he put out the light in the little office and locked the door, to trick the other employees into thinking that they had long ago gone home. But no one ever so much as rattled the doorknob, seeking admission.

It was all so simple that Mr. Durant never thought of it as anything outside the usual order of things. His interest in Rose did not blunt his appreciation of chance attractive legs or provocative glances. It was an entanglement of the most restful, comfortable nature. It even held a sort of homelike quality, for him.

And then everything had to go and get spoiled. "Wouldn't you know?" Mr. Durant asked himself, with deep bitterness.

Ten days before, Rose had come weeping to his office. She had the sense to wait till after hours, for a wonder, but anybody might have walked in and seen her blubbering there; Mr. Durant felt it to be due only to the efficient management of his personal God that no one had. She wept, as he sweepingly put it, all over the place. The color left her cheeks and collected damply in her nose, and rims of vivid pink grew around her pale eyelashes. Even her hair became affected; it came away from the pins, and stray ends of it wandered limply over her neck. Mr. Durant hated to look at her, could not bring himself to touch her.

All his energies were expended in urging her for God's sake to keep quiet; he did not ask her what was the matter. But it came out, between bursts of unpleasant-sounding sobs. She was "in trouble." Neither then nor in the succeeding days did she and Mr. Durant ever use any less delicate phrase to describe her condition. Even in their thoughts, they referred to it that way.

She had suspected it, she said, for some time, but she hadn't wanted to bother him about it until she was absolutely sure. "Didn't want to bother me!" thought Mr. Durant.

Naturally, he was furious. Innocence is a desirable thing, a dainty thing, an appealing thing, in its place; but carried too far, it is merely ridiculous. Mr. Durant wished to God that he had never seen Rose. He explained this desire to her.

But that was no way to get things done. As he had often jovially remarked to his friends, he knew "a thing or two." Cases like this could be what people of the world called "fixed up"—New York society women, he understood, thought virtually nothing of it. This case could be fixed up, too. He got Rose to go home, telling her not to worry, he would see that everything was all right. The main thing was to get her out of sight, with that nose and those eyes.

But knowing a thing or two and putting the knowledge into practice turned out to be vastly different things. Mr. Durant did not know whom to seek for information. He pictured himself inquiring of his intimates if they could tell him of "someone that this girl he had heard about could go to." He could hear his voice uttering the words, could hear the nervous laugh that would accompany them, the terrible flatness of them as they left his lips. To confide in one person would be confiding in at least one too many. It was a progressing town, but still small enough for gossip to travel like a typhoon. Not that he thought for a moment that his wife would believe any such thing, if it reached her; but where would be the sense in troubling her?

Mr. Durant grew pale and jumpy over the thing as the days went by. His wife worried herself into one of her sick spells over his petulant refusals of second helpings. There daily arose in him an increasing anger that he should be drawn into conniving to find a way to break the law of his country—probably the law of every country in the world. Certainly of every decent, Christian place.

It was Ruby, finally, who got them out of it. When Rose confessed to him that she had broken down and told Ruby, his rage leaped higher than any words. Ruby was secretary to the vice-president of the rubber company. It would be pretty, wouldn't it, if she let it out? He had lain wide-eyed beside his wife all that night through. He shuddered at the thought of chance meetings with Ruby in the hall.

But Ruby had made it delightfully simple, when they did meet. There were no reproachful looks, no cold turnings away of the head. She had given him her usual smiling "good-morning," and added a little upward glance, mischievous, understanding, with just that least hint of admiration in it. There was a sense of intimacy, of a shared secret binding them cozily together. A fine girl, that Ruby!

Ruby had managed it all without any fuss. Mr. Durant was not directly concerned in the planning. He heard of it only through Rose, on the infrequent occasions when he had had to see her. Ruby knew, through some indistinct friends of hers, of "a woman." It would be twenty-five dollars. Mr. Durant had gallantly insisted upon giving Rose the money. She had started to sniffle about taking it, but he had finally prevailed. Not that he couldn't have used the twenty-five very nicely himself, just then, with Junior's teeth, and all!

Well, it was all over now. The invaluable Ruby had gone with Rose to "the woman"; had that very afternoon taken her to the station and put her on a train for her sister's. She had even thought of wiring the sister beforehand that Rose had had influenza and must have a rest.

Mr. Durant had urged Rose to look on it as just a little vacation. He promised, moreover, to put in a good word for her whenever she wanted her job back. But Rose had gone pink about the nose again at the thought. She had sobbed her rasping sobs, then had raised her face from her stringy hand-kerchief and said, with an entirely foreign firmness, that she never wanted to see the rubber works or Ruby or Mr. Durant again. He had laughed indulgently, had made himself pat her thin back. In his relief at the outcome of things, he could be generous to the pettish.

He chuckled inaudibly, as he reviewed that last scene. "I suppose she thought she'd make me sore, saying she was never coming back," he told himself. "I suppose I was supposed to get down on my knees and coax her."

It was fine to dwell on the surety that it was all done with. Mr. Durant had somewhere picked up a phrase that seemed ideally suited to the occasion. It was to him an admirably dashing expression. There was something stylish about it; it was the sort of thing you would expect to hear used by men who wore spats and swung canes without self-consciousness. He employed it now, with satisfaction.

"Well, that's that," he said to himself. He was not sure that he didn't say it aloud.

The car slowed, and the girl in the rough coat came down toward the door. She was jolted against Mr. Durant—he would have sworn she did it purposely—uttered a word of laughing apology, gave him what he interpreted as an inviting glance. He half rose to follow her, then sank back again. After all, it was a wet night, and his corner was five blocks farther on. Again there came over him the cozy assurance that there would always be others.

In high humor, he left the car at his street, and walked in the direction of his house. It was a mean night, but the insinuating cold and the black rain only made more graphic his picture of the warm, bright house, the great dish of steaming fish chowder, the well-behaved children and wife that awaited him. He walked rather slowly to make them seem all the better for the wait, humming a little on his way down the neat sidewalk, past the solid, reputably shabby houses.

Two girls ran past him, holding their hands over their heads to protect their hats from the wet. He enjoyed the click of their heels on the pavement, their little bursts of breathless laughter, their arms upraised in a position that brought out all the neat lines of their bodies. He knew who they were—they lived three doors down from him, in the house with the lamp-post in front of it. He had often lingeringly noticed their fresh prettiness. He hurried, so that he might see them run up the steps, their narrow skirts sliding up over their legs. His mind went back to the girl with the run in her stocking, and amusing thoughts filled him as he entered his own house.

His children rushed, clamoring, to meet him, as he unlocked the door. There was something exciting going on, for Junior and Charlotte were usually too careful-mannered to cause people discomfort by rushing and babbling. They were nice, sensible children, good at their lessons, and punctilious about brushing their teeth, speaking the truth, and avoiding playmates who used bad words. Junior would be the very picture of his father, when they got the bands off his teeth, and little Charlotte strongly resembled her mother. Friends often commented on what a nice arrangement it was.

Mr. Durant smiled good-naturedly through their racket, carefully hanging up his coat and hat. There was even pleasure for him in the arrangement of his apparel on the cool, shiny knob of the hatrack. Everytning was pleasant, tonight. Even the children's noise couldn't irritate him.

Eventually he discovered the cause of the commotion. It was a little stray dog that had come to the back door. They were out in the kitchen helping Freda, and Charlotte thought she heard something scratching, and Freda said nonsense, but Charlotte went to the door, anyway, and there was this little dog, trying to get in out of the wet. Mother helped them give it a bath, and Freda fed it, and now it was in the living-room. Oh, Father, couldn't they keep it, please, couldn't they, couldn't they, please, Father, couldn't they? It didn't have any collar on it— so you see it didn't belong to anybody. Mother said all right, if he said so, and Freda liked it fine.

Mr. Durant still smiled his gentle smile. "We'll see," he said.

The children looked disappointed, but not despondent. They would have liked more enthusiasm, but "we'll see," they knew by experience, meant a leaning in the right direction.

Mr. Durant proceeded to the living-room, to inspect the visitor. It was not a beauty. All too obviously, it was the living souvenir of a mother who had never been able to say no. It was a rather stocky little beast with shaggy white hair and occasional, rakishly placed patches of black. There was a suggestion of Sealyham terrier about it, but that was almost blotted out by hosts of reminiscences of other breeds. It looked, on the whole, like a composite photograph of Popular Dogs. But you could tell at a glance that it had a way with it. Scepters have been tossed aside for that.

It lay, now, by the fire, waving its tragically long tail wistfully, its eyes pleading with Mr. Durant to give it a fair trial. The children had told it to lie down there, and so it did not move. That was something it could do toward repaying them.

Mr. Durant warmed to it. He did not dislike dogs, and he somewhat fancied the picture of himself as a soft-hearted fellow who extended shelter to friendless animals. He bent, and held out a hand to it.

"Well, sir," he said, genially. "Come here, good fellow."

The dog ran to him, wriggling ecstatically. It covered his cold hand with joyous, though respectful kisses, then laid its warm, heavy head on his palm. "You are beyond a doubt the greatest man in America," it told him with its eyes.

Mr. Durant enjoyed appreciation and gratitude. He patted the dog graciously.

"Well, sir, how'd you like to board with us?" he said. "I guess you can plan to settle down." Charlotte squeezed Junior's arm wildly. Neither of them, though, thought it best to crowd their good fortune by making any immediate comment on it.

Mrs. Durant entered from the kitchen, flushed with her final attentions to the chowder. There was a worried line between her eyes. Part of the worry was due to the dinner, and part to the disturbing entrance of the little dog into the family life. Anything not previously included in her day's schedule threw Mrs. Durant into a state resembling that of one convalescing from shellshock. Her hands jerked nervously, beginning gestures that they never finished.

Relief smoothed her face when she saw her husband patting the dog. The children, always at ease with her, broke their silence and jumped about her, shrieking that Father said it might stay.

"There, now—didn't I tell you what a dear, good father you had?" she said in the tone parents employ when they have happened to guess right. "That's fine, Father. With that big yard and all, I think we'll make out all right. She really seems to be an awfully good little——"

Mr. Durant's hand stopped sharply in its patting motions, as if the dog's neck had become red-hot to his touch. He rose, and looked at his wife as at a stranger who had suddenly begun to behave wildly.

"She?" he said. He maintained the look and repeated the word. "She?"

Mrs. Durant's hands jerked.

"Well—" she began, as if about to plunge into a recital of extenuating circumstances. "Well—yes," she concluded.

The children and the dog looked nervously at Mr. Durant, feeling something was gone wrong. Charlotte whimpered wordlessly.

"Quiet!" said her father, turning suddenly upon her. "I said it could stay, didn't I? Did you ever know Father to break a promise?"

Charlotte politely murmured, "No, Father," but conviction was not hers. She was a philosophical child, though, and she decided to leave the whole issue to God, occasionally jogging Him up a bit with prayer.

Mr. Durant frowned at his wife, and jerked his head backward. This indicated that he wished to have a few words with her, for adults only, in the privacy of the little room across the hall, known as "Father's den."

He had directed the decoration of his den, had seen that it had been made a truly masculine room. Red paper covered its walls, up to the wooden rack on which were displayed ornamental steins, of domestic manufacture. Empty pipe-racks—Mr. Durant smoked cigars—were nailed against the red paper at frequent intervals. On one wall was an indifferent reproduction of a drawing of a young woman with wings like a vampire bat, and on another, a water-colored photograph of "September Morn," the tints running a bit beyond the edges of the figure as if the artist's emotions had rendered his hand unsteady. Over the table was carefully flung a tanned and fringed hide with the profile of an unknown Indian maiden painted on it, and the rocking-chair held a leather pillow bearing the picture, done by pyrography, of a girl in a fencing costume which set off her distressingly dated figure.

Mr. Durant's books were lined up behind the glass of the bookcase. They were all tall, thick books, brightly bound, and they justified his pride in their showing. They were mostly accounts of favorites of the French court, with a few volumes on odd personal habits of various monarchs, and the adventures of former Russian monks. Mrs. Durant, who never had time to get around to reading, regarded them with awe, and thought of her husband as one of the country's leading bibliophiles. There were books, too, in the living-room, but those she had inherited or been given. She had arranged a few on the living-room table; they looked as if they had been placed there by the Gideons.

Mr. Durant thought of himself as an indefatigable collector and an insatiable reader. But he was always disappointed in his books, after he had sent for them. They were never so good as the advertisements had led him to believe.

Into his den Mr. Durant preceded his wife, and faced her, still frowning. His calm was not shattered, but it was punctured. Something annoying always had to go and come up. Wouldn't you know?

"Now you know perfectly well, Fan, we can't have that dog around," he told her. He used the low voice reserved for underwear and bathroom articles and kindred shady topics. There was all the kindness in his tones that one has for a backward child, but a Gibraltar-like firmness was behind it. "You must be crazy to even think we could for a minute. Why, I wouldn't give a she-dog house-room, not for any amount of money. It's disgusting, that's what it is."

"Well, but, Father—" began Mrs. Durant, her hands again going off into their convulsions.

"Disgusting," he repeated. "You have a female around, and you know what happens. All the males in the neighborhood will be running after her. First thing you know, she'd be having puppies—and the way they look after they've had them, and all! That would be nice for the children to see, wouldn't it? I should think you'd think of the children, Fan. No, sir, there'll be nothing like that around here, not while I know it. Disgusting!"

"But the children," she said. "They'll be just simply——"

"Now you just leave all that to me," he reassured her. "I told them the dog could stay, and I've never broken a promise yet, have I? Here's what I'll do—I'll wait till they're asleep, and then I'll just take this little dog and put it out. Then, in the morning, you can tell them it ran away during the night, see?"

She nodded. Her husband patted her shoulder, in its crapy-smelling black silk. His peace with the world was once more intact, restored by this simple solution of the little difficulty. Again his mind wrapped itself in the knowledge that everything was all fixed, all ready for a nice, fresh start. His arm was still about his wife's shoulder as they went on in to dinner.

The Waltz

Why, *thank you so much. I'd adore to.*

I don't want to dance with him. I don't want to dance with anybody. And even if I did, it wouldn't be him. He'd be well down among the last ten. I've seen the way he dances; it looks like something you do on Saint Walpurgis Night. Just think, not a quarter of an hour ago, here I was sitting, feeling so sorry for the poor girl he was dancing with. And now *I'm* going to be the poor girl. Well, well. Isn't it a small world?

And a peach of a world, too. A true little corker. Its events are so fascinatingly unpredictable, are not they? Here I was, minding my own business, not doing a stitch of harm to any living soul. And then he comes into my life, all smiles and city manners, to sue me for the favor of one memorable mazurka. Why, he scarcely knows my name, let alone what it stands for. It stands for Despair, Bewilderment, Futility, Degradation, and Premeditated Murder, but little does he wot. I don't wot his name, either; I haven't any idea what it is. Jukes, would be my guess from the look in his eyes. How do you do, Mr. Jukes? And how is that dear little brother of yours, with the two heads?

Ah, now why did he have to come around me, with his low requests? Why can't he let me lead my own life? I ask so little—just to be left alone in my quiet corner of the table, to do my evening brooding over all my sorrows. And he must come, with his bows and his scrapes and his may-I-have-this-ones. And I had to go and tell him that I'd adore to dance with him. I cannot understand why I wasn't struck right down dead. Yes, and being struck dead would look like a day in the country, compared to struggling out a dance with this boy. But what could I do? Everyone else at the table had got up to dance, except him and me. There was I, trapped. Trapped like a trap in a trap.

What can you say, when a man asks you to dance with him?

I most certainly will *not* dance with you, I'll see you in hell first. Why, thank you, I'd like to awfully, but I'm having labor pains. Oh, yes, *do* let's dance together—it's so nice to meet a man who isn't a scaredy-cat about catching my beri-beri. No. There was nothing for me to do, but say I'd adore to. Well, we might as well get it over with. All right, Cannonball, let's run out on the field. You won the toss; you can lead.

Why, I think it's more of a waltz, really. Isn't it? We might just listen to the music a second. Shall we? Oh, yes, it's a waltz. Mind? Why, I'm simply thrilled. I'd love to waltz with you.

I'd love to waltz with you. I'd love to waltz with you. I'd love to have my tonsils out, I'd love to be in a midnight fire at sea. Well, it's too late now. We're getting under way. *Oh.* Oh, dear. Oh, dear, dear, dear. Oh, this is even worse than I thought it would be. I suppose that's the one dependable law of life—everything is always worse than you thought it was going to be. Oh, if I had any real grasp of what this dance would be like, I'd have held out for sitting it out. Well, it will probably amount to the same thing in the end. We'll be sitting it out on the floor in a minute, if he keeps this up.

I'm so glad I brought it to his attention that this is a waltz they're playing. Heaven knows what might have happened, if he had thought it was something fast; we'd have blown the sides right out of the building. Why does he always want to be somewhere that he isn't? Why can't we stay in one place just long enough to get acclimated? It's this constant rush, rush, rush, that's the curse of American life. That's the reason that we're all of us so—*Ow!* For God's sake, don't *kick,* you idiot; this is only second down. Oh, my shin. My poor, poor shin, that I've had ever since I was a little girl!

Oh, no, no, no. Goodness, no. It didn't hurt the least little bit. And anyway it was my fault. Really it was. Truly. Well, you're just being sweet, to say that. It really was all my fault.

I wonder what I'd better do—kill him this instant, with my naked hands, or wait and let him drop in his traces. Maybe it's best not to make a scene. I guess I'll just lie low, and watch the pace get him. He can't keep this up indefinitely—he's only flesh and blood. Die he must, and die he shall, for what he did to me.

I don't want to be of the over-sensitive type, but you can't tell me that kick was unpremeditated. Freud says there are no accidents. I've led no cloistered life, I've known dancing partners who have spoiled my slippers and torn my dress; but when it comes to kicking, I am Outraged Womanhood. When you kick me in the shin, *smile*.

Maybe he didn't do it maliciously. Maybe it's just his way of showing his high spirits. I suppose I ought to be glad that one of us is having such a good time. I suppose I ought to think myself lucky if he brings me back alive. Maybe it's captious to demand of a practically strange man that he leave your shins as he found them. After all, the poor boy's doing the best he can. Probably he grew up in the hill country, and never had no larnin'. I bet they had to throw him on his back to get shoes on him.

Yes, it's lovely, isn't it? It's simply lovely. It's the loveliest waltz. Isn't it? Oh, I think it's lovely, too.

Why, I'm getting positively drawn to the Triple Threat here. He's my hero. He has the heart of a lion, and the sinews of a buffalo. Look at him—never a thought of the consequences, never afraid of his face, hurling himself into every scrimmage, eyes shining, cheeks ablaze. And shall it be said that I hung back? No, a thousand times no. What's it to me if I have to spend the next couple of years in a plaster cast? Come on, Butch, right through them! Who wants to live forever?

Oh, Oh, dear. Oh, he's all right, thank goodness. For a while I thought they'd have to carry him off the field. Ah, I couldn't bear to have anything happen to him. I love him. I love him better than anybody in the world. Look at the spirit he gets into a dreary, commonplace waltz; how effete the other dancers seem, beside him. He is youth and vigor and courage, he is strength and gaiety and—*Ow!* Get off my instep, you hulking peasant! What do you think I am, anyway—a gangplank? *Ow!*

No, of course it didn't hurt. Why, it didn't a bit. Honestly. And it was all my fault. You see, that little step of yours—well, it's perfectly lovely, but it's just a tiny bit tricky to follow at first. Oh, did you work it up yourself? You really did? Well, aren't you amazing! Oh, now I think I've got it. Oh, I think it's

*lovely. I was watching you do it when you were dancing before.
It's awfully effective when you look at it.*

It's awfully effective when you look at it. I bet I'm awfully
effective when you look at me. My hair is hanging along my
cheeks, my skirt is swaddling about me, I can feel the cold
damp of my brow. I must look like something out of "The Fall
of the House of Usher." This sort of thing takes a fearful toll of
a woman my age. And he worked up his little step himself, he
with his degenerate cunning. And it was just a tiny bit tricky at
first, but now I think I've got it. Two stumbles, slip, and a
twenty-yard dash; yes. I've got it. I've got several other things,
too, including a split shin and a bitter heart. I hate this
creature I'm chained to. I hated him the moment I saw his
leering, bestial face. And here I've been locked in his noxious
embrace for the thirty-five years this waltz has lasted. Is that
orchestra never going to stop playing? Or must this obscene
travesty of a dance go on until hell burns out?

*Oh, they're going to play another encore. Oh, goody. Oh,
that's lovely. Tired? I should say I'm not tired. I'd like to go on
like this forever.*

I should say I'm not tired. I'm dead, that's all I am. Dead,
and in what a cause! And the music is never going to stop
playing, and we're going on like this, Double-Time Charlie and
I, throughout eternity. I suppose I won't care any more, after
the first hundred thousand years. I suppose nothing will matter
then, not heat nor pain nor broken heart nor cruel, aching
weariness. Well. It can't come too soon for me.

I wonder why I didn't tell him I was tired. I wonder why I
didn't suggest going back to the table. I could have said let's
just listen to the music. Yes, and if he would, that would be the
first bit of attention he has given it all evening. George Jean
Nathan said that the lovely rhythms of the waltz should be
listened to in stillness and not be accompanied by strange
gyrations of the human body. I think that's what he said. I
think it was George Jean Nathan. Anyhow, whatever he said
and whoever he was and whatever he's doing now, he's better
off than I am. That's safe. Anybody who isn't waltzing with this
Mrs. O'Leary's cow I've got here is having a good time.

Still if we were back at the table, I'd probably have to talk to him. Look at him—what could you say to a thing like that! Did you go to the circus this year, what's your favorite kind of ice cream, how do you spell cat? I guess I'm as well off here. As well off as if I were in a cement mixer in full action.

I'm past all feeling now. The only way I can tell when he steps on me is that I can hear the splintering of bones. And all the events of my life are passing before my eyes. There was the time I was in a hurricane in the West Indies, there was the day I got my head cut open in the taxi smash, there was the night the drunken lady threw a bronze ash-tray at her own true love and got me instead, there was that summer that the sailboat kept capsizing. Ah, what an easy, peaceful time was mine, until I fell in with Swifty, here. I didn't know what trouble was, before I got drawn into this *danse macabre*. I think my mind is beginning to wander. It almost seems to me as if the orchestra were stopping. It couldn't be, of course; it could never, never be. And yet in my ears there is a silence like the sound of angel voices. . . .

Oh, they've stopped, the mean things. They're not going to play any more. Oh, darn. Oh, do you think they would? Do you really think so, if you gave them twenty dollars? Oh, that would be lovely. And look, do tell them to play this same thing. I'd simply adore to go on waltzing.

The Wonderful Old Gentleman

If the Bains had striven for years, they could have been no more successful in making their living-room into a small but admirably complete museum of objects suggesting strain, discomfort, or the tomb. Yet they had never even tried for the effect. Some of the articles that the room contained were wedding-presents; some had been put in from time to time as substitutes as their predecessors succumbed to age and wear; a few had been brought along by the Old Gentleman when he had come to make his home with the Bains some five years before.

It was curious how perfectly they all fitted into the general scheme. It was as if they had all been selected by a single enthusiast to whom time was but little object, so long as he could achieve the eventual result of transforming the Bain living-room into a home chamber of horrors, modified a bit for family use.

It was a high-ceilinged room, with heavy, dark old woodwork, that brought long and unavoidable thoughts of silver handles and weaving worms. The paper was the color of stale mustard. Its design, once a dashing affair of a darker tone splashed with twinkling gold, had faded into lines and smears that resolved themselves, before the eyes of the sensitive, into hordes of battered heads and tortured profiles, some eyeless, some with clotted gashes for mouths.

The furniture was dark and cumbersome and subject to painful creakings—sudden, sharp creaks that seemed to be wrung from its brave silence only when it could bear no more. A close, earthy smell came from its dulled tapestry cushions, and try as Mrs. Bain might, furry gray dust accumulated in the crevices.

The center-table was upheld by the perpetually strained arms of three carved figures, insistently female to the waist, then trailing discreetly off into a confusion of scrolls and scales.

Upon it rested a row of blameless books, kept in place at the ends by the straining shoulder-muscles of two bronze-colored plaster elephants, forever pushing at their tedious toil.

On the heavily carved mantel was a gayly colored figure of a curly-headed peasant boy, ingeniously made so that he sat on the shelf and dangled one leg over. He was in the eternal act of removing a thorn from his chubby foot, his round face realistically wrinkled with the cruel pain. Just above him hung a steel-engraving of a chariot-race, the dust flying, the chariots careening wildly, the drivers ferociously lashing their maddened horses, the horses themselves caught by the artist the moment before their hearts burst, and they dropped in their traces.

The opposite wall was devoted to the religious in art; a steel-engraving of the Crucifixion, lavish of ghastly detail; a sepia-print of the martyrdom of Saint Sebastian, the cords cutting deep into the arms writhing from the stake, arrows bristling in the thick, soft-looking body; a water-color copy of a "Mother of Sorrows," the agonized eyes raised to a cold heaven, great, bitter tears forever on the wan cheeks, paler for the grave-like draperies that wrapped the head.

Beneath the windows hung a painting in oil of two lost sheep, huddled hopelessly together in the midst of a wild blizzard. This was one of the Old Gentleman's contributions to the room. Mrs. Bain was wont to observe of it that the frame was worth she didn't know how much.

The wall-space beside the door was reserved for a bit of modern art that had once caught Mr. Bain's eye in a stationer's window—a colored print, showing a railroad-crossing, with a train flying relentlessly toward it, and a low, red automobile trying to dash across the track before the iron terror shattered it into eternity. Nervous visitors who were given chairs facing this scene usually made opportunity to change their seats before they could give their whole minds to the conversation.

The ornaments, placed with careful casualness on the table and the upright piano, included a small gilt lion of Lucerne, a little, chipped, plaster Laocoön, and a savage china kitten eternally about to pounce upon a plump and helpless china mouse. This last had been one of the Old Gentleman's own wedding-gifts. Mrs. Bain explained, in tones low with awe, that it was very old.

The ash-receivers, of Oriental manufacture, were in the form of grotesque heads, tufted with bits of gray human hair, and given bulging, dead, glassy eyes and mouths stretched into great gapes, into which those who had the heart for it might flick their ashes. Thus the smallest details of the room kept loyally to the spirit of the thing, and carried on the effect.

But the three people now sitting in the Bains' living-room were not in the least oppressed by the decorative scheme. Two of them, Mr. and Mrs. Bain, not only had had twenty-eight years of the room to accustom themselves to it, but had been stanch admirers of it from the first. And no surroundings, however morbid, could close in on the aristocratic calm of Mrs. Bain's sister, Mrs. Whittaker.

She graciously patronized the very chair she now sat in, smiled kindly on the glass of cider she held in her hand. The Bains were poor, and Mrs. Whittaker had, as it is ingenuously called, married well, and none of them ever lost sight of these facts.

But Mrs. Whittaker's attitude of kindly tolerance was not confined to her less fortunate relatives. It extended to friends of her youth, working people, the arts, politics, the United States in general, and God, Who had always supplied her with the best of service. She could have given Him an excellent reference at any time.

The three people sat with a comfortable look of spending the evening. There was an air of expectancy about them, a not unpleasant little nervousness, as of those who wait for a curtain to rise. Mrs. Bain had brought in cider in the best tumblers, and had served some of her nut cookies in the plate painted by hand with clusters of cherries—the plate she had used for sandwiches when, several years ago, her card club had met at her house.

She had thought it over a little tonight, before she lifted out the cherry plate, then quickly decided and resolutely heaped it with cookies. After all, it was an occasion—informal, perhaps, but still an occasion. The Old Gentleman was dying upstairs. At five o'clock that afternoon the doctor had said that it would be a surprise to him if the Old Gentleman lasted till the middle of the night—a big surprise, he had augmented.

There was no need for them to gather at the Old Gentleman's bedside. He would not have known any of them. In fact, he had not known them for almost a year, addressing them by wrong names and asking them grave, courteous questions about the health of husbands or wives or children who belonged to other branches of the family. And he was quite unconscious now.

Miss Chester, the nurse who had been with him since "this last stroke," as Mrs. Bain importantly called it, was entirely competent to attend and watch him. She had promised to call them if, in her tactful words, she saw any signs.

So the Old Gentleman's daughters and son-in-law waited in the warm living-room, and sipped their cider, and conversed in low, polite tones.

Mrs. Bain cried a little in pauses in the conversation. She had always cried easily and often. Yet, in spite of her years of practice, she did not do it well. Her eyelids grew pink and sticky, and her nose gave her no little trouble, necessitating almost constant sniffling. She sniffled loudly and conscientiously, and frequently removed her pince-nez to wipe her eyes with a crumpled handkerchief, gray with damp.

Mrs. Whittaker, too, bore a handkerchief, but she appeared to be holding it in waiting. She was dressed, in compliment to the occasion, in her black crepe de Chine, and she had left her lapis-lazuli pin, her olivine bracelet, and her topaz and amethyst rings at home in her bureau drawer, retaining only her lorgnette on its gold chain, in case there should be any reading to be done.

Mrs. Whittaker's dress was always studiously suited to its occasion; thus, her bearing had always that calm that only the correctly attired may enjoy. She was an authority on where to place monograms on linen, how to instruct working folk, and what to say in letters of condolence. The word "lady" figured largely in her conversation. Blood, she often predicted, would tell.

Mrs. Bain wore a rumpled white shirt-waist and the old blue skirt she saved for "around the kitchen." There had been time to change, after she had telephoned the doctor's verdict to her sister, but she had not been quite sure whether it was the thing to do. She had thought that Mrs. Whittaker might expect her to display a little distraught untidiness at a time like this; might even go in for it in a mild way herself.

Now Mrs. Bain looked at her sister's elaborately curled, painstakingly brown coiffure, and nervously patted her own straggling hair, gray at the front, with strands of almost lime-color in the little twist at the back. Her eyelids grew wet and sticky again, and she hung her glasses over one forefinger while she applied the damp handkerchief. After all, she reminded herself and the others, it was her poor father.

Oh, but it was really the best thing, Mrs. Whittaker explained in her gentle, patient voice.

"You wouldn't want to see Father go on like this," she pointed out. Mr. Bain echoed her, as if struck with the idea. Mrs. Bain had nothing to reply to them. No, she wouldn't want to see the Old Gentleman go on like this.

Five years before, Mrs. Whittaker had decided that the Old Gentleman was getting too old to live alone with only old Annie to cook for him and look after him. It was only a question of a little time before it "wouldn't have looked right," his living alone, when he had his children to take care of him. Mrs. Whittaker always stopped things before they got to the stage where they didn't look right. So he had come to live with the Bains.

Some of his furniture had been sold; a few things, such as his silver, his tall clock, and the Persian rug he had bought at the Exposition, Mrs. Whittaker had found room for in her own house; and some he brought with him to the Bains'.

Mrs. Whittaker's house was much larger than her sister's, and she had three servants and no children. But, as she told her friends, she had held back and let Allie and Lewis have the Old Gentleman.

"You see," she explained, dropping her voice to the tones reserved for not very pretty subjects, "Allie and Lewis are— well, they haven't a great deal."

So it was gathered that the Old Gentleman would do big things for the Bains when he came to live with them. Not exactly by paying board—it is a little too much to ask your father to pay for his food and lodging, as if he were a stranger. But, as Mrs. Whittaker suggested, he could do a great deal in the way of buying needed things for the house and keeping everything going.

And the Old Gentleman did contribute to the Bain household. He bought an electric heater and an electric fan, new curtains, storm-windows, and light fixtures, all for his bedroom; and had a nice little bathroom for his personal use made out of the small guest-room adjoining it.

He shopped for days until he found a coffee-cup large enough for his taste; he bought several large ash-trays, and a dozen extra-size bath-towels, that Mrs. Bain marked with his initials. And every Christmas and birthday he gave Mrs. Bain a round, new, shining ten-dollar gold piece. Of course, he presented gold pieces to Mrs. Whittaker, too, on like ap-appropriate occasions. The Old Gentleman prided himself always on his fair-mindedness. He often said that he was not one to show any favoritism.

Mrs. Whittaker was Cordelia-like to her father during his declining years. She came to see him several times a month, bringing him jelly or potted hyacinths. Sometimes she sent her car and chauffeur for him, so that he might take an easy drive through the town, and Mrs. Bain might be afforded a chance to drop her cooking and accompany him. When Mrs. Whittaker was away on trips with her husband, she almost never neglected to send her father picture post-cards of various points of interest.

The Old Gentleman appreciated her affection, and took pride in her. He enjoyed being told that she was like him.

"That Hattie," he used to tell Mrs. Bain, "she's a fine woman—a fine woman."

As soon as she had heard that the Old Gentleman was dying Mrs. Whittaker had come right over, stopping only to change her dress and have her dinner. Her husband was away in the woods with some men, fishing. She explained to the Bains that there was no use in disturbing him—it would have been impossible for him to get back that night. As soon as—well, if anything happened she would telegraph him, and he could return in time for the funeral.

Mrs. Bain was sorry that he was away. She liked her ruddy, jovial, loud-voiced brother-in-law.

"It's too bad that Clint couldn't be here," she said, as she had said several times before. "He's so fond of cider," she added.

"Father," said Mrs. Whittaker, "was always very fond of Clint." Already the Old Gentleman had slipped into the past tense.

"Everybody likes Clint," Mr. Bain stated.

He was included in the "everybody." The last time he had failed in business, Clint had given him the clerical position he had since held over at the brush works. It was pretty generally understood that this had been brought about through Mrs. Whittaker's intervention, but still they were Clint's brush works, and it was Clint who paid him his salary. And forty dollars a week is indubitably forty dollars a week.

"I hope he'll be sure and be here in time for the funeral," said Mrs. Bain. "It will be Wednesday morning, I suppose, Hat?"

Mrs. Whittaker nodded.

"Or perhaps around two o'clock Wednesday afternoon," she amended. "I always think that's a nice time. Father has his frock coat, Allie?"

"Oh, yes," Mrs. Bain said eagerly. "And it's all clean and lovely. He has everything. Hattie, I noticed the other day at Mr. Newton's funeral they had more of a blue necktie on him, so I suppose they're wearing them—Mollie Newton always has everything just so. But I don't know——"

"I think," said Mrs. Whittaker firmly, "that there is nothing lovelier than black for an old gentleman."

"Poor Old Gentleman," said Mr. Bain, shaking his head. "He would have been eighty-five if he just could have lived till next September. Well, I suppose it's all for the best."

He took a small draft of cider and another cooky.

"A wonderful, wonderful life," summarized Mrs. Whittaker. "And a wonderful, wonderful old gentleman."

"Well, I should say so," said Mrs. Bain. "Why, up to the last year he was as interested in everything! It was, 'Allie, how much do you have to give for your eggs now?' and 'Allie, why don't you change your butcher?—this one's robbing you,' and 'Allie, who was that you were talking to on the telephone?' all day long! Everybody used to speak of it."

"And he used to come to the table right up to this stroke," Mr. Bain related, chuckling reminiscently. "My, he used to raise Cain when Allie didn't cut up his meat fast enough to suit him. Always had a temper, *I'll* tell you, the Old Gentleman did. Wouldn't stand for us having anybody in to meals—he didn't like that worth a cent. Eighty-four years old, and sitting right up there at the table with us!"

They vied in telling instances of the Old Gentleman's intelligence and liveliness, as parents cap one another's anecdotes of precocious children.

"It's only the past year that he had to be helped up-and down-stairs," said Mrs. Bain. "Walked up-stairs all by himself, and more than eighty years old!"

Mrs. Whittaker was amused.

"I remember you said that once when Clint was here," she remarked, "and Clint said, 'Well, if you can't walk up-stairs by the time you're eighty, when are you going to learn?' "

Mrs. Bain smiled politely, because her brother-in-law had said it. Otherwise she would have been shocked and wounded.

"Yes, sir," said Mr. Bain. "Wonderful."

"The only thing I could have wished," Mrs. Bain said, after a pause—"I could have wished he'd been a little different about Paul. Somehow I've never felt quite right since Paul went way up to that cold place out West."

Mrs. Whittaker's voice fell into the key used for the subject that has been gone over and over and over again.

"Now, Allie," she said, "you know yourself that was the best thing that could have happened. Father told you that himself, often and often. Paul was young, and he wanted to have all his young friends running in and out of the house, banging doors and making all sorts of racket, and it would have been a terrible nuisance for Father. You must realize that Father was more than eighty years old, Allie."

"Yes, I know," Mrs. Bain said. Her eyes went to the photograph of her son in his lumberjack's shirt, and she sighed.

"And besides," Mrs. Whittaker pointed out triumphantly, "now that Miss Chester's here in Paul's room, there wouldn't have been any room for him. So you see!"

There was rather a long pause. Then Mrs. Bain edged toward the other thing that had been weighing upon her.

"Hattie," she said, "I suppose—I suppose we'd ought to let Matt know?"

"I shouldn't," said Mrs. Whittaker composedly. She always took great pains with her "shall's" and "will's." "I only hope that he doesn't see it in the papers in time to come on for the funeral. If you want to have your brother turn up drunk at the services, Allie, *I* don't."

"But I thought he'd straightened up," said Mr. Bain. "Thought he was all right since he got married."

"Yes, I know, I know, Lewis," Mrs. Whittaker said wearily. "I've heard all about that. All I say is, *I* know what Matt is."

"John Loomis was telling me," reported Mr. Bain, "he was going through Akron, and he stopped off to see Matt. Said they had a nice little place, and he seemed to be getting along fine. Said she seemed like a cracker-jack housekeeper."

Mrs. Whittaker smiled.

"Yes," she said, "John Loomis and Matt were always two of a kind—you couldn't believe a word either of them said. Probably she did seem to be a good housekeeper. I've no doubt she acted the part very well. Matt never made any bones of the fact that she was on the stage once, for almost a year. Excuse me from having that woman come to Father's funeral. If you want to know what *I* think, *I* think that Matt marrying a woman like that had a good deal to do with hastening Father's death."

The Bains sat in awe.

"And after all Father did for Matt, too," added Mrs. Whittaker, her voice shaken.

"Well, I should think so," Mr. Bain was glad to agree. "I remember how the Old Gentleman used to try and help Matt get along. He'd go down, like it was to Mr. Fuller, that time Matt was working at the bank, and he'd explain to him, 'Now, Mr. Fuller,' he'd say, 'I don't know whether you know it, but this son of mine has always been what you might call the black sheep of the family. He's been kind of a drinker,' he'd say, 'and he's got himself into trouble a couple of times, and if you'd just keep an eye on him, so's to see he keeps straight, it'd be a favor to me.'

"Mr. Fuller told me about it himself. Said it was wonderful the way the Old Gentleman came right out and talked just as frankly to him. Said *he'd* never had any idea Matt was that way—wanted to hear all about it."

Mrs. Whittaker nodded sadly.

"Oh, I know," she said. "Time and again Father would do that. And then, as like as not, Matt would get one of his sulky fits, and not turn up at his work."

"And when Matt would be out of work," Mrs. Bain said, "the way Father'd hand him out his car-fare, and I don't know what all! When Matt was a grown man, going on thirty years old, Father would take him down to Newins & Malley's and buy him a whole new outfit—pick out everything himself. He always used to say Matt was the kind that would get cheated out of his eye-teeth if he went into a store alone."

"My, Father hated to see anybody make a fool of themselves about money," Mrs. Whittaker commented. "Remember how he always used to say, 'Any fool can make money, but it takes a wise man to keep it'?"

"I suppose he must be a pretty rich man," Mr. Bain said, abruptly restoring the Old Gentleman to the present.

"Oh—rich!" Mrs. Whittaker's smile was at its kindliest. "But he managed his affairs very well, Father did, right up to the last. Everything is in splendid shape, Clint says."

"He showed you the will, didn't he, Hat?" asked Mrs. Bain, forming bits of her sleeve into little plaits between her thin, hard fingers.

"Yes," said her sister. "Yes, he did. He showed me the will. A little over a year ago, I think it was, wasn't it? You know, just before he started to fail, that time."

She took a small bite of cooky.

"*Awfully* good," she said. She broke into a little bubbly laugh, the laugh she used at teas and wedding receptions and fairly formal dinners. "You know," she went on, as one sharing a good story, "he's gone and left all that old money to me. 'Why, Father!' I said, as soon as I'd read that part. But it seems he'd gotten some sort of idea in his head that Clint and I would be able to take care of it better than anybody else, and you know what Father was, once he made up that mind of his. You can just imagine how *I* felt. I couldn't say a thing."

She laughed again, shaking her head in amused bewilderment.

"Oh, and Allie," she said, "he's left you all the furniture he brought here with him, and all the things he bought since he came. And Lewis is to have his set of Thackeray. And that money he lent Lewis, to try and tide him over in the hardware business that time—that's to be regarded as a gift."

She sat back and looked at them, smiling.

"Lewis paid back most all of that money Father lent him that time," Mrs. Bain said. "There was only about two hundred dollars more, and then he would have had it all paid up."

"That's to be regarded as a gift," insisted Mrs. Whittaker. She leaned over and patted her brother-in-law's arm. "Father always liked you, Lewis," she said softly.

"Poor Old Gentleman," murmured Mr. Bain.

"Did it—did it say anything about Matt?" asked Mrs. Bain.

"Oh, Allie!" Mrs. Whittaker gently reproved her. "When you think of all the money Father spent and spent on Matt, it seems to me he did more than enough—more than enough.

And then when Matt went away off there to live, and married that woman, and never a word about it—Father hearing it all through strangers—well, I don't think any of us realize how it hurt Father. He never said much about it, but I don't think he ever got over it. I'm always so thankful that poor dear Mother didn't live to see how Matt turned out."

"Poor Mother," said Mrs. Bain shakily, and brought the grayish handkerchief into action once more. "I can hear her now, just as plain. 'Now, children,' she used to say, 'do for goodness' sake let's all try and keep your father in a good humor.' If I've heard her say it once, I've heard her say it a hundred times. Remember, Hat?"

"Do I remember!" said Mrs. Whittaker. "And do you remember how they used to play whist, and how furious Father used to get when he lost?"

"Yes," Mrs. Bain cried excitedly, "and how Mother used to have to cheat, so as to be sure and not win from him? She got so she used to be able to do it just as well!"

They laughed softly, filled with memories of the gone days. A pleasant, thoughtful silence fell around them.

Mrs. Bain patted a yawn to extinction, and looked at the clock.

"Ten minutes to eleven," she said. "Goodness, I had no idea it was anywhere near so late. I wish—" She stopped just in time, crimson at what her wish would have been.

"You see, Lew and I have got in the way of going to bed early," she explained. "Father slept so light, we couldn't have people in like we used to before he came here, to play a little bridge or anything, on account of disturbing him. And if we wanted to go to the movies or anywhere, he'd go on so about being left alone that we just kind of gave up going."

"Oh, the Old Gentleman always let you know what he wanted," said Mr. Bain, smiling. "He was a wonder, *I'll* tell you. Nearly eighty-five years old!"

"Think of it," said Mrs. Whittaker.

A door clicked open above them, and feet ran quickly and not lightly down the stairs. Miss Chester burst into the room.

"Oh, Mrs. Bain!" she cried. "Oh, the Old Gentleman! Oh,

he's gone! I noticed him kind of stirring and whimpering a little, and he seemed to be trying to make motions at his warm milk, like as if he wanted some. So I put the cup up to his mouth, and he sort of fell over, and just like that he was gone, and the milk all over him."

Mrs. Bain instantly collapsed into passionate weeping. Her husband put his arm tenderly about her, and murmured a series of "Now-now's."

Mrs. Whittaker rose, set her cider-glass carefully on the table, shook out her handkerchief, and moved toward the door.

"A lovely death," she pronounced. "A wonderful, wonderful life, and now a beautiful, peaceful death. Oh, it's the best thing, Allie; it's the best thing."

"Oh, it is, Mrs. Bain; it's the best thing," Miss Chester said earnestly. "It's really a blessing. That's what it is."

Among them they got Mrs. Bain up the stairs.

Song of the Shirt, 1941

It was one of those extraordinarily bright days that make things look somehow bigger. The Avenue seemed to stretch wider and longer, and the buildings to leap higher into the skies. The window-box blooms were not just a mass and a blur; it was as if they had been enlarged, so that you could see the design of the blossoms and even their separate petals. Indeed you could sharply see all sorts of pleasant things that were usually too small for your notice—the lean figurines on radiator caps, and the nice round gold knobs on flagpoles, the flowers and fruits on ladies' hats and the creamy dew applied to the eyelids beneath them. There should be more of such days.

The exceptional brightness must have had its effect upon unseen objects, too, for Mrs. Martindale, as she paused to look up the Avenue, seemed actually to feel her heart grow bigger than ever within her. The size of Mrs. Martindale's heart was renowned among her friends, and they, as friends will, had gone around babbling about it. And so Mrs. Martindale's name was high on the lists of all those organizations that send out appeals to buy tickets and she was frequently obliged to be photographed seated at a table, listening eagerly to her neighbor, at some function for the good of charity. Her big heart did not, as is so sadly often the case, inhabit a big bosom. Mrs. Martindale's breasts were admirable, delicate yet firm, pointing one to the right, one to the left; angry at each other, as the Russians have it.

Her heart was the warmer, now, for the fine sight of the Avenue. All the flags looked brand-new. The red and the white and the blue were so vivid they fairly vibrated, and the crisp stars seemed to dance on their points. Mrs. Martindale had a flag, too, clipped to the lapel of her jacket. She had had quantities of rubies and diamonds and sapphires just knocking about, set in floral designs on evening bags and vanity boxes and cigarette-cases; she had taken the lot of them to her

jeweller, and he had assembled them into a charming little Old
Glory. There had been enough of them for him to devise a
rippled flag, and that was fortunate, for those flat flags looked
sharp and stiff. There were numbers of emeralds, formerly
figuring as leaves and stems in the floral designs, which were of
course of no use to the present scheme and so were left over, in
an embossed leather case. Some day, perhaps, Mrs. Martindale
would confer with her jeweller about an arrangement to employ
them. But there was no time for such matters now.

There were many men in uniform walking along the Avenue
under the bright banners. The soldiers strode quickly and
surely, each on to a destination. The sailors, two by two,
ambled, paused at a corner and looked down a street, gave it
up and went slower along their unknown way. Mrs. Martindale's heart grew again as she looked at them. She had a
friend who made a practice of stopping uniformed men on the
street and thanking them, individually, for what they were
doing for *her*. Mrs. Martindale felt that this was going unnecessarily far. Still, she did see, a little bit, what her friend
meant.

And surely no soldier or sailor would have objected to being
addressed by Mrs. Martindale. For she was lovely, and no other
woman was lovely like her. She was tall, and her body streamed
like a sonnet. Her face was formed all of triangles, as a cat's is,
and her eyes and her hair were blue-gray. Her hair did not
taper in its growth about her forehead and temples; it sprang
suddenly, in great thick waves, from a straight line across her
brow. Its blue-gray was not premature. Mrs. Martindale
lingered in her fragrant forties. Has not afternoon been ad-
judged the fairest time of the day?

To see her, so delicately done, so finely finished, so softly
sheltered by her very loveliness, you might have laughed to hear
that she was a working-woman. "Go on!" you might have said,
had such been your unfortunate manner of expressing
disbelief. But you would have been worse than coarse; you
would have been wrong. Mrs. Martindale worked, and worked
hard. She worked doubly hard, for she was unskilled at what
she did, and she disliked the doing of it. But for two months

she had worked every afternoon five afternoons of every week, and had shirked no moment. She received no remuneration for her steady services. She gave them because she felt she should do so. She felt that you should do what you could, hard and humbly. She practiced what she felt.

The special office of the war-relief organization where Mrs. Martindale served was known to her and her coworkers as Headquarters; some of them had come to call it H.Q. These last were of the group that kept agitating for the adoption of a uniform—the design had not been thoroughly worked out, but the idea was of something nurselike, only with a fuller skirt and a long blue cape and white gauntlets. Mrs. Martindale was not in agreement with this faction. It had always been hard for her to raise her voice in opposition, but she did, although softly. She said that while of course there was nothing *wrong* about a uniform, certainly nobody could possibly say there was anything *wrong* with the idea, still it seemed—well, it seemed not quite right to make the work an excuse, well, for fancy dress, if they didn't mind her saying so. Naturally, they wore their coifs at Headquarters, and if anybody wanted to take your photograph in your coif, you should go through with it, because it was good for the organization and publicized its work. But please, not whole uniforms, said Mrs. Martindale. Really, *please*, Mrs. Martindale said.

Headquarters was, many said, the stiffest office of all the offices of all the war-relief organizations in the city. It was not a place where you dropped in and knitted. Knitting, once you have caught the hang of it, is agreeable work, a relaxation from what strains life may be putting upon you. When you knit, save when you are at those bits where you must count stitches, there is enough of your mind left over for you to take part in conversations, and for you to be receptive of news and generous with it. But at Headquarters they sewed. They did a particularly difficult and tedious form of sewing. They made those short, shirtlike coats, fastened in back with tapes, that are put on patients in hospitals. Each garment must have two sleeves, and all the edges must be securely bound. The material was harsh to the touch and the smell, and impatient of the needle of the novice. Mrs. Martindale had made three and had another almost half done. She had thought that after the first one the others would be easier and quicker of manufacture. They had not been.

There were sewing machines at Headquarters, but few of the workers understood the running of them. Mrs. Martindale herself was secretly afraid of a machine; there had been a nasty story, never traced to its source, of somebody who put her thumb in the wrong place, and down came the needle, right through nail and all. Besides, there was something—you didn't know quite how to say it—something more of sacrifice, of service, in making things by hand. She kept on at the task that never grew lighter. It was wished that there were more of her caliber.

For many of the workers had given up the whole thing long before their first garment was finished. And many others, pledged to daily attendance, came only now and then. There was but a handful like Mrs. Martindale.

All gave their services, although there were certain doubts about Mrs. Corning, who managed Headquarters. It was she who oversaw the work, who cut out the garments, and explained to the workers what pieces went next to what other pieces. (It did not always come out as intended. One amateur seamstress toiled all the way to the completion of a coat that had one sleeve depending from the middle of the front. It was impossible to keep from laughing; and a sharp tongue suggested that it might be sent in as it was, in case an elephant was brought to bed. Mrs. Martindale was the first to say "Ah, don't! She worked so hard over it.") Mrs. Corning was a cross woman, hated by all. The high standards of Headquarters were important to the feelings of the workers, but it was agreed that there was no need for Mrs. Corning to scold so shrilly when one of them moistened the end of her thread between her lips before thrusting it into her needle.

"Well, really," one of the most spirited among the rebuked had answered her. "If a little clean spit's the worst they're ever going to get on them . . ."

The spirited one had returned no more to Headquarters, and

there were those who felt that she was right. The episode drew new members into the school of thought that insisted Mrs. Corning was paid for what she did.

When Mrs. Martindale paused in the clear light and looked along the Avenue, it was at a moment of earned leisure. She had just left Headquarters. She was not to go back to it for many weeks, nor were any of the other workers. Somewhere the cuckoo had doubtless sung, for summer was coming in. And what with everybody leaving town, it was only sensible to shut Headquarters until autumn. Mrs. Martindale, and with no guilt about it, had looked forward to a holiday from all that sewing.

Well, she was to have none, it turned out. While the workers were gaily bidding farewells and calling out appointments for the autumn, Mrs. Corning had cleared her throat hard to induce quiet and had made a short speech. She stood beside a table piled with cut-out sections of hospital coats not yet sewn together. She was a graceless woman, and though it may be assumed that she meant to be appealing, she sounded only disagreeable. There was, she said, a desperate need, a dreadful need, for hospital garments. More were wanted right away, hundreds and thousands of them; the organization had had a cable that morning, urging and pleading. Headquarters was closing until September—that meant all work would stop. Certainly they had all earned a vacation. And yet, in the face of the terrible need, she could not help asking—she would like to call for volunteers to take coats with them, to work on at home.

There was a little silence, and then a murmur of voices, gaining in volume and in assurance as the owner of each realized that it was not the only one. Most of the workers, it seemed, would have been perfectly willing, but they felt that they absolutely must give their entire time to their children, whom they had scarcely *seen* because of being at Headquarters so constantly. Others said they were just plain too worn out, and that was all there was to it. It must be admitted that for some moments Mrs. Martindale felt with this latter group. Then shame waved over her like a blush, and swiftly, quietly, with the blue-gray head held high, she went to Mrs. Corning.

"Mrs. Corning," she said. "I should like to take twelve, please."

Mrs. Corning was nicer than Mrs. Martindale had ever seen her. She put out her hand and grasped Mrs. Martindale's.

"Thank you," she said, and her shrill voice was gentle.

But then she had to go and be the way she always had been before. She snatched her hand from Mrs. Martindale's and turned to the table, starting to assemble garments.

"And please, Mrs. Martindale," she said, shrilly, "kindly try and remember to keep the seams straight. Wounded people can be made terribly uncomfortable by crooked seams, you know. And if you could manage to get your stitches even, the coat would look much more professional and give our organization a higher standing. And time is terribly important. They're in an awful hurry for these. So if you could just manage to be a little quicker, it would help a lot."

Really, if Mrs. Martindale hadn't offered to take the things, she would have . . .

The twelve coats still in sections, together with the coat that was half finished, made a formidable bundle. Mrs. Martindale had to send down for her chauffeur to come and carry it to her car for her. While she waited for him, several of the workers came up, rather slowly, and volunteered to sew at home. Four was the highest number of garments promised.

Mrs. Martindale did say good-by to Mrs. Corning, but she expressed no pleasure at the hope of seeing her again in the autumn. You do what you can, and you do it because you should. But all you can do is all you can do.

Out on the Avenue, Mrs. Martindale was herself again. She kept her eyes from the great package the chauffeur had placed in the car. After all, she might, and honorably, allow herself a recess. She need not go home and start sewing again immediately. She would send the chauffeur home with the bundle, and walk in the pretty air, and not think of unfinished coats.

But the men in uniform went along the Avenue under the snapping flags, and in the sharp, true light you could see all their faces; their clean bones and their firm skin and their eyes, the confident eyes of the soldiers and the wistful eyes of the sailors. They were so young, all of them, and all of them doing what they could, doing everything they could, doing it hard and humbly, without question and without credit. Mrs. Martindale put her hand to her heart. Some day, maybe, some day some of them might be lying on hospital cots . . .

Mrs. Martindale squared her delicate shoulders and entered her car.

"Home, please," she told her chauffeur. "And I'm in rather a hurry."

At home, Mrs. Martindale had her maid unpack the clumsy bundle and lay the contents in her up-stairs sitting-room. Mrs. Martindale took off her outdoor garments and bound her head, just back of the first great blue-gray wave, in the soft linen coif she had habitually worn at Headquarters. She entered her sitting-room, which had recently been redone in the color of her hair and her eyes; it had taken a deal of mixing and matching, but it was a success. There were touches, splashes rather, of magenta about, for Mrs. Martindale complemented brilliant colors and made them and herself glow sweeter. She looked at the ugly, high pile of unmade coats, and there was a second when her famous heart shrank. But it swelled to its norm again as she felt what she must do. There was no good thinking about those twelve damned new ones. Her job immediately was to get on with the coat she had half made.

She sat down on quilted blue-gray satin and set herself to her task. She was at the most hateful stretch of the garment—the binding of the rounded neck. Everything pulled out of place, and nothing came out even, and a horrid starchy smell rose from the thick material, and the stitches that she struggled to put so prettily appeared all different sizes and all faintly gray. Over and over, she had to rip them out for their imperfection, and load her needle again without moistening the thread between her lips, and see them wild and straggling once more. She felt almost ill from the tussle with the hard, monotonous work.

Her maid came in, mincingly, and told her that Mrs. Wyman wished to speak to her on the telephone; Mrs. Wyman wanted to ask a favor of her. Those were two of the penalties attached to the possession of a heart the size of Mrs. Martindale's—people were constantly telephoning to ask her favors and she was constantly granting them. She put down her sewing, with a sigh that might have been of one thing or of another, and went to the telephone.

Mrs. Wyman, too, had a big heart, but it was not well set. She was a great, hulking, stupidly dressed woman, with flapping cheeks and bee-stung eyes. She spoke with rapid diffidence, inserting apologies before she needed to make them, and so was a bore and invited avoidance.

"Oh, my dear," she said now to Mrs. Martindale, "I'm so sorry to bother you. Please do forgive me. But I do want to ask you to do me the most tremendous favor. Please do excuse me. But I want to ask you, do you possibly happen to know of anybody who could possibly use my little Mrs. Christie?"

"Your Mrs. Christie?" Mrs. Martindale asked. "Now, I don't think—or do I?"

"You know," Mrs. Wyman said. "I wouldn't have bothered you for the world, with all you do and all, but you know my little Mrs. Christie. She has that daughter that had infantile, and she has to support her, and I just don't know *what* she's going to do. I wouldn't have bothered you for the world, only I've been sort of thinking up jobs for her to do for me right along, but next week we're going to the ranch, and I really don't know *what* will become of her. And the crippled daughter and all. They just won't be able to *live!*"

Mrs. Martindale made a soft little moan. "Oh, how awful," she said. "How perfectly awful. Oh, I wish I could—tell me, what can I do?"

"Well, if you could just think of somebody that could use her," Mrs. Wyman said. "I wouldn't have bothered you, honestly I wouldn't, but I just didn't know who to turn to. And Mrs. Christie's really a wonderful little woman—she can do anything. Of course, the thing is, she has to work at home, because she wants to take care of the crippled child—well, you can't blame her, really. But she'll call for things and bring them back. And she's so quick, and so good. Please do forgive me for bothering you, but if you could just think——"

"Oh, there must be somebody!" Mrs. Martindale cried. "I'll think of somebody. I'll rack my brains, truly I will. I'll call you up as soon as I think."

Mrs. Martindale went back to her blue-gray quilted satin. Again she took up the unfinished coat. A shaft of the exceptionally bright sunlight shot past a vase of butterfly orchids and settled upon the waving hair under the gracious coif. But Mrs. Martindale did not turn to meet it. Her blue-gray eyes were bent on the drudgery of her fingers. This coat, and then the twelve others beyond it. The need, the desperate, dreadful need, and the terrible importance of time. She took a stitch and another stitch and another stitch and another stitch; she looked at their wavering line, pulled the thread from her needle, ripped out three of the stitches, rethreaded her needle, and stiched again. And as she stitched, faithful to her promise and to her heart, she racked her brains.

Enough Rope

Threnody

Lilacs blossom just as sweet
Now my heart is shattered.
If I bowled it down the street,
Who's to say it mattered?
If there's one that rode away
What would I be missing?
Lips that taste of tears, they say,
Are the best for kissing.

Eyes that watch the morning star
Seem a little brighter;
Arms held out to darkness are
Usually whiter.
Shall I bar the strolling guest,
Bind my brow with willow,
When, they say, the empty breast
Is the softer pillow?

That a heart falls tinkling down,
Never think it ceases.
Every likely lad in town
Gathers up the pieces.
If there's one gone whistling by
Would I let it grieve me?
Let him wonder if I lie;
Let him half believe me.

The Small Hours

No more my little song comes back;
   And now of nights I lay
My head on down, to watch the black
   And wait the unfailing gray.

Oh, sad are winter nights, and slow;
   And sad's a song that's dumb;
And sad it is to lie and know
   Another dawn will come.

The False Friends

They laid their hands upon my head,
They stroked my cheek and brow;
And time could heal a hurt, they said,
And time could dim a vow.

And they were pitiful and mild
Who whispered to me then,
"The heart that breaks in April, child,
Will mend in May again."

Oh, many a mended heart they knew.
So old they were, and wise.
And little did they have to do
To come to me with lies!

Who flings me silly talk of May
Shall meet a bitter soul;
For June was nearly spent away
Before my heart was whole.

The Trifler

Death's the lover that I'd be taking;
  Wild and fickle and fierce is he.
Small's his care if my heart be breaking—
  Gay young Death would have none of me.

Hear them clack of my haste to greet him!
  No one other my mouth had kissed.
I had dressed me in silk to meet him—
  False young Death would not hold the tryst.

Slow's the blood that was quick and stormy,
  Smooth and cold is the bridal bed;
I must wait till he whistles for me—
  Proud young Death would not turn his head.

I must wait till my breast is wilted,
  I must wait till my back is bowed,
I must rock in the corner, jilted—
  Death went galloping down the road.

Gone's my heart with a trifling rover.
  Fine he was in the game he played—
Kissed, and promised, and threw me over,
  And rode away with a prettier maid.

A Very Short Song

Once, when I was young and true,
  Someone left me sad—
Broke my brittle heart in two;
  And that is very bad.

Love is for unlucky folk,
  Love is but a curse.
Once there was a heart I broke;
  And that, I think, is worse.

A Well-Worn Story

In April, in April,
My one love came along,
And I ran the slope of my high hill
To follow a thread of song.

His eyes were hard as porphyry
With looking on cruel lands;
His voice went slipping over me
Like terrible silver hands.

Together we trod the secret lane
And walked the muttering town.
I wore my heart like a wet, red stain
On the breast of a velvet gown.

In April, in April,
My love went whistling by,
And I stumbled here to my high hill
Along the way of a lie.

Now what should I do in this place
But sit and count the chimes,
And splash cold water on my face
And spoil a page with rhymes?

Convalescent

How shall I wail, that wasn't meant for weeping?
Love has run and left me, oh, what then?
Dream, then, I must, who never can be sleeping;
What if I should meet Love, once again?

What if I met him, walking on the highway?
Let him see how lightly I should care.
He'd travel his way, I would follow my way;
Hum a little song, and pass him there.

What if at night, beneath a sky of ashes,
He should seek my doorstep, pale with need?
There could he lie, and dry would be my lashes;
Let him stop his noise, and let me read.

Oh, but I'm gay, that's better off without him;
Would he'd come and see me, laughing here.
Lord! Don't I know I'd have my arms about him,
Crying to him, "Oh, come in, my dear!"

The Dark Girl's Rhyme

Who was there had seen us
    Wouldn't bid him run?
Heavy lay between us
    All our sires had done.

There he was, a-springing
    Of a pious race,
Setting hags a-swinging
    In a market-place;

Sowing turnips over
    Where the poppies lay;
Looking past the clover,
    Adding up the hay;

Shouting through the Spring song,
    Clumping down the sod;
Toadying, in sing-song,
    To a crabbed god.

There I was, that came of
    Folk of mud and flame—
I that had my name of
    Them without a name.

Up and down a mountain
  Streeled my silly stock;
Passing by a fountain,
  Wringing at a rock;

Devil-gotten sinners,
  Throwing back their heads,
Fiddling for their dinners,
  Kissing for their beds.

Not a one had seen us
  Wouldn't help him flee.
Angry ran between us
  Blood of him and me.

How shall I be mating
  Who have looked above—
Living for a hating,
  Dying of a love?

Epitaph

The first time I died, I walked my ways;
I followed the file of limping days.

I held me tall, with my head flung up,
But I dared not look on the new moon's cup.

I dared not look on the sweet young rain,
And between my ribs was a gleaming pain.

The next time I died, they laid me deep.
They spoke worn words to hallow my sleep.

They tossed me petals, they wreathed me fern,
They weighted me down with a marble urn.

And I lie here warm, and I lie here dry,
And watch the worms slip by, slip by.

Light of Love

Joy stayed with me a night—
Young and free and fair—
And in the morning light
He left me there.

Then Sorrow came to stay,
And lay upon my breast;
He walked with me in the day,
And knew me best.

I'll never be a bride,
Nor yet celibate,
So I'm living now with Pride—
A cold bedmate.

He must not hear nor see,
Nor could he forgive
That Sorrow still visits me
Each day I live.

Wail

Love has gone a-rocketing.
    That is not the worst;
I could do without the thing,
    And not be the first.

Joy has gone the way it came.
    That is nothing new;
I could get along the same—
    Many people do.

Dig for me the narrow bed,
    Now I am bereft.
All my pretty hates are dead,
    And what have I left?

The Satin Dress

Needle, needle, dip and dart,
Thrusting up and down,
Where's the man could ease a heart
Like a satin gown?

See the stitches curve and crawl
Round the cunning seams—
Patterns thin and sweet and small
As a lady's dreams.

Wantons go in bright brocade;
Brides in organdie;
Gingham's for the plighted maid;
Satin's for the free!

Wool's to line a miser's chest;
Crape's to calm the old;
Velvet hides an empty breast
Satin's for the bold!

Lawn is for a bishop's yoke;
Linen's for a nun;
Satin is for wiser folk—
Would the dress were done!

Satin glows in candlelight—
Satin's for the proud!
They will say who watch at night,
"What a fine shroud!"

Somebody's Song

This is what I vow:
He shall have my heart to keep;

Sweetly will we stir and sleep,
    All the years, as now.
Swift the measured sands may run;
Love like this is never done;
He and I are welded one:
    This is what I vow.

This is what I pray:
Keep him by me tenderly;
Keep him sweet in pride of me,
    Ever and a day;
Keep me from the old distress;
Let me, for our happiness,
Be the one to love the less:
    This is what I pray.

This is what I know:
Lovers' oaths are thin as rain;
Love's a harbinger of pain—
    Would it were not so!
Ever is my heart a-thirst,
Ever is my love accurst;
He is neither last nor first:
    This is what I know.

Braggart

The days will rally, wreathing
Their crazy tarantelle;
And you must go on breathing,
But I'll be safe in hell.

Like January weather,
The years will bite and smart,
And pull your bones together
To wrap your chattering heart.

83

The pretty stuff you're made of
Will crack and crease and dry.
The thing you are afraid of
Will look from every eye.

You will go faltering after
The bright, imperious line,
And split your throat on laughter,
And burn your eyes with brine.

You will be frail and musty
With peering, furtive head,
Whilst I am young and lusty
Among the roaring dead.

Epitaph
for a Darling Lady

All her hours were yellow sands,
Blown in foolish whorls and tassels;
Slipping warmly through her hands;
Patted into little castles.

Shiny day on shiny day
Tumbled in a rainbow clutter,
As she flipped them all away,
Sent them spinning down the gutter.

Leave for her a red young rose,
Go your way, and save your pity;
She is happy, for she knows
That her dust is very pretty.

To a Much Too
Unfortunate Lady

He will love you presently
If you be the way you be.
Send your heart a-skittering,
He will stoop, and lift the thing.
Be your dreams as thread, to tease
Into patterns he shall please.
Let him see your passion is
Ever tenderer than his. . . .
Go and bless your star above,
Thus are you, and thus is Love.

He will leave you white with woe,
If you go the way you go.
If your dreams were thread to weave
He will pluck them from his sleeve.
If your heart had come to rest,
He will flick it from his breast.
Tender though the love he bore,
You had loved a little more. . . .
Lady, go and curse your star,
Thus Love is, and thus you are.

Paths

I shall tread, another year,
    Ways I walked with Grief,
Past the dry, ungarnered ear
    And the brittle leaf.

I shall stand, a year apart,
    Wondering, and shy,
Thinking, "Here she broke her heart;
    Here she pled to die."

I shall hear the pheasants call,
   And the raucous geese;
Down these ways, another Fall,
   I shall walk with Peace.

But the pretty path I trod
   Hand-in-hand with Love—
Underfoot, the nascent sod,
   Brave young boughs above.

And the stripes of ribbon grass
   By the curling way—
I shall never dare to pass
   To my dying day.

Hearthside

Half across the world from me
Lie the lands I'll never see—
I, whose longing lives and dies
Where a ship has sailed away;
I, that never close my eyes
But to look upon Cathay.

Things I may not know nor tell
Wait, where older waters swell;
Ways that flowered at Sappho's tread,
Winds that sighed in Homer's strings,
Vibrant with the singing dead,
Golden with the dust of wings.

Under deeper skies than mine,
Quiet valleys dip and shine,
Where their tender grasses heal
Ancient scars of trench and tomb
I shall never walk: nor kneel
Where the bones of poets bloom.

If I seek a lovelier part,
Where I travel goes my heart;
Where I stray my thought must go;
With me wanders my desire.
Best to sit and watch the snow,
Turn the lock, and poke the fire.

Rainy Night

Ghosts of all my lovely sins,
  Who attend too well my pillow,
Gay the wanton rain begins;
  Hide the limp and tearful willow.

Turn aside your eyes and ears,
  Trail away your robes of sorrow,
You shall have my further years—
  You shall walk with me tomorrow.

I am sister to the rain;
  Fey and sudden and unholy,
Petulant at the windowpane,
  Quickly lost, remembered slowly.

I have lived with shades, a shade;
  I am hung with graveyard flowers.
Let me be tonight arrayed
  In the silver of the showers.

Every fragile thing shall rust;
  When another April passes
I may be a furry dust,
  Sifting through the brittle grasses.

All sweet sins shall be forgot;
  Who will live to tell their siring?
Hear me now, nor let me rot
  Wistful still, and still aspiring.

Ghosts of dear temptations, heed;
  I am frail, be you forgiving.
See you not that I have need
  To be living with the living?

Sail, tonight, the Styx's breast;
  Glide among the dim processions
Of the exquisite unblest,
  Spirits of my shared transgressions,

Roam with young Persephone,
  Plucking poppies for your slumber . . .
With the morrow, there shall be
  One more wraith among your number.

The New Love

If it shine or if it rain,
  Little will I care or know.
Days, like drops upon a pane,
  Slip, and join, and go.

At my door's another lad;
  Here's his flower in my hair.
If he see me pale and sad,
  Will he see me fair?

I sit looking at the floor.
  Little will I think or say
If he seek another door;
  Even if he stay.

Anecdote

So silent I when Love was by
  He yawned, and turned away;
But Sorrow clings to my apron-strings,
  I have so much to say.

For a Sad Lady

And let her loves, when she is dead,
   Write this above her bones:
"No more she lives to give us bread
   Who asked her only stones."

Recurrence

We shall have our little day.
Take my hand and travel still
Round and round the little way,
Up and down the little hill.

It is good to love again;
Scan the renovated skies,
Dip and drive the idling pen,
Sweetly tint the paling lies.

Trace the dripping, pierced heart,
Speak the fair, insistent verse,
Vow to God, and slip apart,
Little better, little worse.

Would we need not know before
How shall end this prettiness;
One of us must love the more,
One of us shall love the less.

Thus it is, and so it goes;
We shall have our day, my dear.
Where, unwilling, dies the rose
Buds the new, another year.

Story of Mrs. W——

My garden blossoms pink and white,
  A place of decorous murmuring,
Where I am safe from August night
  And cannot feel the knife of Spring.

And I may walk the pretty place
  Before the curtsying hollyhocks
And laundered daisies, round of face—
  Good little girls, in party frocks.

My trees are amiably arrayed
  In pattern on the dappled sky,
And I may sit in filtered shade
  And watch the tidy years go by.

And I may amble pleasantly
  And hear my neighbors list their bones
And click my tongue in sympathy,
  And count the cracks in paving-stones.

My door is grave in oaken strength,
  The cool of linen calms my bed,
And there at night I stretch my length
  And envy no one but the dead.

The Dramatists

A string of shiny days we had,
  A spotless sky, a yellow sun;
And neither you nor I was sad
  When that was through and done.

But when, one day, a boy comes by
  And pleads me with your happiest vow,
"There was a lad I knew——" I'll sigh;
  "I do not know him now."

And when another girl shall pass
  And speak a little name I said,
Then you will say, "There was a lass—
  I wonder is she dead."

And each of us will sigh, and start
  A-talking of a faded year,
And lay a hand above a heart,
  And dry a pretty tear.

August

When my eyes are weeds,
And my lips are petals, spinning
Down the wind that has beginning
Where the crumpled beeches start
In a fringe of salty reeds;
When my arms are elder-bushes,
And the rangy lilac pushes
Upward, upward through my heart;

Summer, do your worst!
Light your tinsel moon, and call on
Your performing stars to fall on
Headlong through your paper sky;
Nevermore shall I be cursed
By a flushed and amorous slattern,
With her dusty laces' pattern
Trailing, as she straggles by.

The White Lady

I cannot rest, I cannot rest
  In straight and shiny wood,
My woven hands upon my breast—
  The dead are all so good!

The earth is cool across their eyes;
   They lie there quietly.
But I am neither old nor wise;
   They do not welcome me.

Where never I walked alone before,
   I wander in the weeds;
And people scream and bar the door,
   And rattle at their beads.

We cannot rest, we never rest
   Within a narrow bed
Who still must love the living best—
   Who hate the pompous dead!

I Know I Have Been Happiest

I know I have been happiest at your side;
But what is done, is done, and all's to be.
And small the good, to linger dolefully—
Gayly it lived, and gallantly it died.
I will not make you songs of hearts denied,
And you, being man, would have no tears of me,
And should I offer you fidelity,
You'd be, I think, a little terrified.

Yet this the need of woman, this her curse:
To range her little gifts, and give, and give,
Because the throb of giving's sweet to bear.
To you, who never begged me vows or verse,
My gift shall be my absence, while I live;
But after that, my dear, I cannot swear.

Testament

Oh, let it be a night of lyric rain
And singing breezes, when my bell is tolled.
I have so loved the rain that I would hold
Last in my ears its friendly, dim refrain.
I shall lie cool and quiet, who have lain
Fevered, and watched the book of day unfold.
Death will not see me flinch; the heart is bold
That pain has made incapable of pain.

Kinder the busy worms than ever love;
It will be peace to lie there, empty-eyed,
My bed made secret by the leveling showers,
My breast replenishing the weeds above.
And you will say of me, "Then has she died?
Perhaps I should have sent a spray of flowers."

I Shall Come Back

I shall come back without fanfaronade
Of wailing wind and graveyard panoply;
But, trembling, slip from cool Eternity—
A mild and most bewildered little shade.
I shall not make sepulchral midnight raid,
But softly come where I had longed to be
In April twilight's unsung melody,
And I, not you, shall be the one afraid.

Strange, that from lovely dreamings of the dead
I shall come back to you, who hurt me most.
You may not feel my hand upon your head,
I'll be so new and inexpert a ghost.
Perhaps you will not know that I am near—
And that will break my ghostly heart, my dear.

Condolence

They hurried here, as soon as you had died,
Their faces damp with haste and sympathy,
And pressed my hand in theirs, and smoothed my knee,
And clicked their tongues, and watched me, mournful-
    eyed.
Gently they told me of that Other Side—
How, even then, you waited there for me,
And what ecstatic meeting ours would be.
Moved by the lovely tale, they broke, and cried.

And when I smiled, they told me I was brave,
And they rejoiced that I was comforted,
And left, to tell of all the help they gave.
But I had smiled to think how you, the dead,
So curiously preoccupied and grave,
Would laugh, could you have heard the things they said.

The Immortals

If you should sail for Trebizond, or die,
Or cry another name in your first sleep,
Or see me board a train, and fail to sigh,
Appropriately, I'd clutch my breast and weep.
And you, if I should wander through the door,
Or sin, or seek a nunnery, or save
My lips and give my cheek, would tread the floor
And aptly mention poison and the grave.

Therefore the mooning world is gratified,
Quoting how prettily we sigh and swear;
And you and I, correctly side by side,
Shall live as lovers when our bones are bare
And though we lie forever enemies,
Shall rank with Abelard and Héloïse.

A Portrait

Because my love is quick to come and go—
A little here, and then a little there—
What use are any words of mine to swear
My heart is stubborn, and my spirit slow
Of weathering the drip and drive of woe?
What is my oath, when you have but to bare
My little, easy loves; and I can dare
Only to shrug, and answer, "They are so"?

You do not know how heavy a heart it is
That hangs about my neck—a clumsy stone
Cut with a birth, a death, a bridal-day.
Each time I love, I find it still my own,
Who take it, now to that lad, now to this,
Seeking to give the wretched thing away.

Portrait of the Artist

Oh, lead me to a quiet cell
  Where never footfall rankles,
And bar the window passing well,
  And gyve my wrists and ankles.

Oh, wrap my eyes with linen fair,
  With hempen cord go bind me,
And, of your mercy, leave me there,
  Nor tell them where to find me.

Oh, lock the portal as you go,
  And see its bolts be double. . . .
Come back in half an hour or so,
  And I will be in trouble.

Some men, some men
Cannot pass a
Book shop.
(Lady, make your mind up, and wait your life away.)

Some men, some men
Cannot pass a
Crap game.
(He said he'd come at moonrise, and here's another
    day!)

Some men, some men
Cannot pass a
Bar-room.
(Wait about, and hang about, and that's the way it
    goes.)

Some men, some men
Cannot pass a
Woman.
(Heaven never send me another one of those!)

Some men, some men
Cannot pass a
Golf course.
(Read a book, and sew a seam, and slumber if you can.)

Some men, some men
Cannot pass a
Haberdasher's.
(All your life you wait around for some damn man!)

Unfortunate
Coincidence

By the time you swear you're his,
    Shivering and sighing,
And he vows his passion is
    Infinite, undying—
Lady, make a note of this:
    One of you is lying.

Comment

Oh, life is a glorious cycle of song,
A medley of extemporanea;
And love is a thing that can never go wrong;
And I am Marie of Roumania.

Inventory

Four be the things I am wiser to know:
Idleness, sorrow, a friend, and a foe.

Four be the things I'd been better without:
Love, curiosity, freckles, and doubt.

Three be the things I shall never attain:
Envy, content, and sufficient champagne.

Three be the things I shall have till I die:
Laughter and hope and a sock in the eye.

Now at Liberty

Little white love, your way you've taken;
    Now I am left alone, alone.

Little white love, my heart's forsaken.
   (Whom shall I get by telephone?)
Well do I know there's no returning;
   Once you go out, it's done, it's done.
All of my days are gray with yearning.
   (Nevertheless, a girl needs fun.)

Little white love, perplexed and weary,
   Sadly your banner fluttered down.
Sullen the days, and dreary, dreary.
   (Which of the boys is still in town?)
Radiant and sure, you came a-flying;
   Puzzled, you left on lagging feet.
Slow in my breast, my heart is dying.
   (Nevertheless, a girl must eat.)

Little white love, I hailed you gladly;
   Now I must wave you out of sight.
Ah, but you used me badly, badly.
   (Who'd like to take me out tonight?)
All of the blundering words I've spoken,
   Little white love, forgive, forgive.
Once you went out, my heart fell, broken.
   (Nevertheless, a girl must live.)

Plea

Secrets, you said, would hold us two apart;
   You'd have me know of you your least transgression,
And so the intimate places of your heart,
   Kneeling, you bared to me, as in confession.
Softly you told of loves that went before—
   Of clinging arms, of kisses gladly given;
Luxuriously clean of heart once more,
   You rose up, then, and stood before me, shriven.

When this, my day of happiness, is through,
  And love, that bloomed so fair, turns brown and
    brittle,
There is a thing that I shall ask of you—
  I, who have given so much, and asked so little.
Some day, when there's another in my stead,
  Again you'll feel the need of absolution,
And you will go to her, and bow your head,
  And offer her your past, as contribution.

When with your list of loves you overcome her,
For Heaven's sake, keep this one secret from her!

Pattern

Leave me to my lonely pillow.
  Go, and take your silly posies;
Who has vowed to wear the willow
  Looks a fool, tricked out in roses.

Who are you, my lad, to ease me?
  Leave your pretty words unspoken.
Tinkling echoes little please me,
  Now my heart is freshly broken.

Over young are you to guide me,
  And your blood is slow and sleeping.
If you must, then sit beside me. . . .
  Tell me, why have I been weeping?

De Profundis

Oh, is it, then, Utopian
To hope that I may meet a man
Who'll not relate, in accents suave,
The tales of girls he used to have?

Résumé

Razors pain you;
Rivers are damp;
Acids stain you;
And drugs cause cramp.
Guns aren't lawful;
Nooses give;
Gas smells awful;
You might as well live.

They Part

And if, my friend, you'd have it end,
   There's naught to hear or tell.
But need you try to black my eye
   In wishing me farewell.

Though I admit an edged wit
   In woe is warranted,
May I be frank? . . . Such words as "—"
   Are better left unsaid.

There's rosemary for you and me;
   But is it usual, dear,
To hire a man, and fill a van
   By way of *souvenir?*

Ballade
of a Great Weariness

There's little to have but the things I had,
   There's little to bear but the things I bore.
There's nothing to carry and naught to add,
   And glory to Heaven, I paid the score.

There's little to do but I did before,
  There's little to learn but the things I know;
And this is the sum of a lasting lore:
  Scratch a lover, and find a foe.

And couldn't it be I was young and mad
  If ever my heart on my sleeve I wore?
There's many to claw at a heart unclad,
  And little the wonder it ripped and tore.
There's one that'll join in their push and roar,
  With stories to jabber, and stones to throw;
He'll fetch you a lesson that costs you sore—
  Scratch a lover, and find a foe.

So little I'll offer to you, my lad;
  It's little in loving I set my store.
There's many a maid would be flushed and glad,
  And better you'll knock at a kindlier door.
I'll dig at my lettuce, and sweep my floor—
  Forever, forever I'm done with woe—
And happen I'll whistle about my chore,
  "Scratch a lover, and find a foe."

L'ENVOI

Oh, beggar or prince, no more, no more!
  Be off and away with your strut and show.
The sweeter the apple, the blacker the core—
  Scratch a lover, and find a foe!

Renunciation

Chloe's hair, no doubt, was brighter;
  Lydia's mouth more sweetly sad;
Hebe's arms were rather whiter;
  Languorous-lidded Helen had

Eyes more blue than e'er the sky was;
    Lalage's was subtler stuff;
Still, you used to think that I was
    Fair enough.

Now you're casting yearning glances
    At the pale Penelope;
Cutting in on Claudia's dances;
    Taking Iris out to tea.
Iole you find warm-hearted;
    Zoe's cheek is far from rough—
Don't you think it's time we parted? ...
    Fair enough!

The Veteran

When I was young and bold and strong,
Oh, right was right, and wrong was wrong!
My plume on high, my flag unfurled,
I rode away to right the world.
"Come out, you dogs, and fight!" said I,
And wept there was but once to die.

But I am old; and good and bad
Are woven in a crazy plaid.
I sit and say, "The world is so;
And he is wise who lets it go.
A battle lost, a battle won—
The difference is small, my son."

Inertia rides and riddles me;
The which is called Philosophy.

Verse for a Certain Dog

Such glorious faith as fills your limpid eyes,
　Dear little friend of mine, I never knew.
All-innocent are you, and yet all-wise.
　(For Heaven's sake, stop worrying that shoe!)
You look about, and all you see is fair;
　This mighty globe was made for you alone.
Of all the thunderous ages, you're the heir.
　(Get off the pillow with that dirty bone!)

A skeptic world you face with steady gaze;
　High in young pride you hold your noble head,
Gayly you meet the rush of roaring days.
　(*Must* you eat puppy biscuit on the bed?)
Lancelike your courage, gleaming swift and strong,
　Yours the white rapture of a winged soul,
Yours is a spirit like a Mayday song.
　(God help you, if you break the goldfish bowl!)

"Whatever is, is good"—your gracious creed.
　You wear your joy of living like a crown.
Love lights your simplest act, your every deed.
　(Drop it, I tell you—put that kitten down!)
You are God's kindliest gift of all—a friend.
　Your shining loyalty unflecked by doubt,
You ask but leave to follow to the end.
　(Couldn't you wait until I took you out?)

Prophetic Soul

Because your eyes are slant and slow,
　Because your hair is sweet to touch,
My heart is high again; but oh,
　I doubt if this will get me much.

Godspeed

Oh, seek, my love, your newer way;
   I'll not be left in sorrow.
So long as I have yesterday,
   Go take your damned tomorrow!

Song of
Perfect Propriety

Oh, I should like to ride the seas,
   A roaring buccaneer;
A cutlass banging at my knees,
   A dirk behind my ear.
And when my captives' chains would clank
   I'd howl with glee and drink,
And then fling out the quivering plank
   And watch the beggars sink.

I'd like to straddle gory decks,
   And dig in laden sands,
And know the feel of throbbing necks
   Between my knotted hands.
Oh, I should like to strut and curse
   Among my blackguard crew. . . .
But I am writing little verse,
   As little ladies do.

Oh, I should like to dance and laugh
   And pose and preen and sway,
And rip the hearts of men in half,
   And toss the bits away.
I'd like to view the reeling years
   Through unastonished eyes,
And dip my finger-tips in tears,
   And give my smiles for sighs.

I'd stroll beyond the ancient bounds,
   And tap at fastened gates,
And hear the prettiest of sound—
   The clink of shattered fates.
My slaves I'd like to bind with thongs
   That cut and burn and chill. . . .
But I am writing little songs,
   As little ladies will.

Social Note

Lady, lady, should you meet
One whose ways are all discreet,
One who murmurs that his wife
Is the lodestar of his life,
One who keeps assuring you
That he never was untrue,
Never loved another one . . .
   Lady, lady, better run!

One Perfect Rose

A single flow'r he sent me, since we met.
   All tenderly his messenger he chose;
Deep-hearted, pure, with scented dew still wet—
   One perfect rose.

I knew the language of the floweret;
   "My fragile leaves," it said, "his heart enclose."
Love long has taken for his amulet
   One perfect rose.

Why is it no one ever sent me yet
   One perfect limousine, do you suppose?
Ah no, it's always just my luck to get
   One perfect rose.

Ballade at Thirty-Five

This, no song of an ingénue,
  This, no ballad of innocence;
This, the rhyme of a lady who
  Followed ever her natural bents.
  This, a solo of sapience,
This, a chantey of sophistry,
  This, the sum of experiments—
I loved them until they loved me.

Decked in garments of sable hue,
  Daubed with ashes of myriad Lents,
Wearing shower bouquets of rue,
  Walk I ever in penitence.
  Oft I roam, as my heart repents,
Through God's acre of memory,
  Marking stones, in my reverence,
"I loved them until they loved me."

Pictures pass me in long review—
  Marching columns of dead events.
I was tender and, often, true;
  Ever a prey to coincidence.
  Always knew I the consequence;
Always saw what the end would be.
  We're as Nature has made us—hence
I loved them until they loved me.

L'ENVOI

Princes, never I'd give offense,
  Won't you think of me tenderly?
Here's my strength and my weakness, gents—
  I loved them until they loved me.

The Thin Edge

With you, my heart is quiet here,
And all my thoughts are cool as rain.
I sit and let the shifting year
Go by before the windowpane,
And reach my hand to yours, my dear . . .
I wonder what it's like in Spain.

Love Song

My own dear love, he is strong and bold
   And he cares not what comes after.
His words ring sweet as a chime of gold,
   And his eyes are lit with laughter.
He is jubilant as a flag unfurled—
   Oh, a girl, she'd not forget him.
My own dear love, he is all my world—
   And I wish I'd never met him.

My love, he's mad, and my love, he's fleet,
   And a wild young wood-thing bore him!
The ways are fair to his roaming feet,
   And the skies are sunlit for him.
As sharply sweet to my heart he seems
   As the fragrance of acacia.
My own dear love, he is all my dreams—
   And I wish he were in Asia.

My love runs by like a day in June,
   And he makes no friends of sorrows.
He'll tread his galloping rigadoon
   In the pathway of the morrows.
He'll live his days where the sunbeams start,
   Nor could storm or wind uproot him.
My own dear love, he is all my heart—
   And I wish somebody'd shoot him.

Indian Summer

In youth, it was a way I had
To do my best to please,
And change, with every passing lad,
To suit his theorics.

But now I know the things I know,
And do the things I do;
And if you do not like me so,
To hell, my love, with you!

Philosophy

If I should labor through daylight and dark,
Consecrate, valorous, serious, true,
Then on the world I may blazon my mark;
And what if I don't, and what if I do?

For an Unknown Lady

Lady, if you'd slumber sound,
Keep your eyes upon the ground.
If you'd toss and turn at night,
Slip your glances left and right.
Would the mornings find you gay,
Never give your heart away.
Would they find you pale and sad,
Fling it to a whistling lad.
Ah, but when his pleadings burn,
Will you let my words return?
Will you lock your pretty lips,
And deny your finger-tips,
Veil away your tender eyes,

Just because some words were wise?
If he whistles low and clear
When the insistent moon is near
And the secret stars are known—
Will your heart be still your own
Just because some words were true? . . .
Lady, I was told them, too!

The Leal

The friends I made have slipped and strayed,
  And who's the one that cares?
A trifling lot and best forgot—
  And that's my tale, and theirs.

Then if my friendships break and bend,
  There's little need to cry
The while I know that every foe
  Is faithful till I die.

Words of Comfort to Be
Scratched on a Mirror

Helen of Troy had a wandering glance;
Sappho's restriction was only the sky;
Ninon was ever the chatter of France;
But oh, what a good girl am I!

Faute de Mieux

Travel, trouble, music, art,
  A kiss, a frock, a rhyme—
I never said they feed my heart,
  But still they pass my time.

Men

They hail you as their morning star
Because you are the way you are.
If you return the sentiment,
They'll try to make you different;
And once they have you, safe and sound,
They want to change you all around.
Your moods and ways they put a curse on;
They'd make of you another person.
They cannot let you go your gait;
They influence and educate.
They'd alter all that they admired.
They make me sick, they make me tired.

News Item

Men seldom make passes
At girls who wear glasses.

Song of One of the Girls

Here in my heart I am Helen;
  I'm Aspasia and Hero, at least.
I'm Judith, and Jael, and Madame de Staël;
  I'm Salome, moon of the East.

Here in my soul I am Sappho;
  Lady Hamilton am I, as well.
In me Recamier vies with Kitty O'Shea,
  With Dido, and Eve, and poor Nell.

I'm of the glamorous ladies
  At whose beckoning history shook.
But you are a man, and see only my pan,
  So I stay at home with a book.

Lullaby

Sleep, pretty lady, the night is enfolding you;
    Drift, and so lightly, on crystalline streams.
Wrapped in its perfumes, the darkness is holding you;
    Starlight bespangles the way of your dreams.
Chorus the nightingales, wistfully amorous;
    Blessedly quiet, the blare of the day.
All the sweet hours may your visions be glamorous—
    Sleep, pretty lady, as long as you may.

Sleep, pretty lady, the night shall be still for you;
    Silvered and silent, it watches you rest.
Each little breeze, in its eagerness, will for you
    Murmur the melodies ancient and blest.
So in the midnight does happiness capture us;
    Morning is dim with another day's tears.
Give yourself sweetly to images rapturous—
    Sleep, pretty lady, a couple of years.

Sleep, pretty lady, the world awaits day with you;
    Girlish and golden, the slender young moon.
Grant the fond darkness its mystical way with you;
    Morning returns to us ever too soon.
Roses unfold, in their loveliness, all for you;
    Blossom the lilies for hope of your glance.
When you're awake, all the men go and fall for you—
    Sleep, pretty lady, and give me a chance.

Roundel

She's passing fair; but so demure is she,
So quiet is her gown, so smooth her hair,
That few there are who note her and agree
    She's passing fair.

Yet when was ever beauty held more rare
Than simple heart and maiden modesty?
What fostered charms with virtue could compare?

Alas, no lover ever stops to see;
The best that she is offered is the air.
Yet—if the passing mark is minus D
    She's passing fair.

A Certain Lady

Oh, I can smile for you, and tilt my head,
    And drink your rushing words with eager lips,
And paint my mouth for you a fragrant red,
    And trace your brows with tutored finger-tips.
When you rehearse your list of loves to me,
    Oh, I can laugh and marvel, rapturous-eyed.
And you laugh back, nor can you ever see
    The thousand little deaths my heart has died.
And you believe, so well I know my part,
    That I am gay as morning, light as snow,
And all the straining things within my heart
    You'll never know.

Oh, I can laugh and listen, when we meet,
    And you bring tales of fresh adventurings—
Of ladies delicately indiscreet,
    Of lingering hands, and gently whispered things.
And you are pleased with me, and strive anew
    To sing me sagas of your late delights.
Thus do you want me—marveling, gay, and true—
    Nor do you see my staring eyes of nights.
And when, in search of novelty, you stray,
    Oh, I can kiss you blithely as you go. . . .
And what goes on, my love, while you're away,
    You'll never know.

Observation

If I don't drive around the park,
I'm pretty sure to make my mark.
If I'm in bed each night by ten,
I may get back my looks again.
If I abstain from fun and such,
I'll probably amount to much;
But I shall stay the way I am,
Because I do not give a damn.

Symptom Recital

I do not like my state of mind;
I'm bitter, querulous, unkind.
I hate my legs, I hate my hands,
I do not yearn for lovelier lands.
I dread the dawn's recurrent light;
I hate to go to bed at night.
I snoot at simple, earnest folk.
I cannot take the gentlest joke.
I find no peace in paint or type.
My world is but a lot of tripe.
I'm disillusioned, empty-breasted.
For what I think, I'd be arrested.
I am not sick, I am not well.
My quondam dreams are shot to hell.
My soul is crushed, my spirit sore;
I do not like me any more.
I cavil, quarrel, grumble, grouse.
I ponder on the narrow house.
I shudder at the thought of men. . . .
I'm due to fall in love again.

Rondeau Redoublé

[and scarcely worth the trouble, at that]

The same to me are somber days and gay.
   Though joyous dawns the rosy morn, and bright,
Because my dearest love is gone away
   Within my heart is melancholy night.

My heart beats low in loneliness, despite
   That riotous Summer holds the earth in sway.
In cerements my spirit is bedight;
   The same to me are somber days and gay.

Though breezes in the rippling grasses play,
   And waves dash high and far in glorious might,
I thrill no longer to the sparkling day,
   Though joyous dawns the rosy morn, and bright.

Ungraceful seems to me the swallow's flight;
   As well might heaven's blue be sullen gray;
My soul discerns no beauty in their sight
   Because my dearest love is gone away.

Let roses fling afar their crimson spray,
   And virgin daisies splash the fields with white,
Let bloom the poppy hotly as it may,
   Within my heart is melancholy night.

And this, O love, my pitiable plight
   Whenever from my circling arms you stray;
This little world of mine has lost its light. . . .
   I hope to God, my dear, that you can say
            The same to me.

Fighting Words

Say my love is easy had,
　　Say I'm bitten raw with pride,
Say I am too often sad—
　　Still behold me at your side.

Say I'm neither brave nor young,
　　Say I woo and coddle care,
Say the devil touched my tongue—
　　Still you have my heart to wear.

But say my verses do not scan,
　　And I get me another man!

The Choice

He'd have given me rolling lands,
　　Houses of marble, and billowing farms,
Pearls, to trickle between my hands,
　　Smoldering rubies, to circle my arms.
You—you'd only a lilting song,
　　Only a melody, happy and high,
You were sudden and swift and strong—
　　Never a thought for another had I.

He'd have given me laces rare,
　　Dresses that glimmered with frosty sheen,
Shining ribbons to wrap my hair,
　　Horses to draw me, as fine as a queen.
You—you'd only to whistle low,
　　Gayly I followed wherever you led.
I took you, and I let him go—
　　Somebody ought to examine my head!

General Review of the
Sex Situation

Woman wants monogamy;
Man delights in novelty.
Love is woman's moon and sun;
Man has other forms of fun.
Woman lives but in her lord;
Count to ten, and man is bored.
With this the gist and sum of it,
What earthly good can come of it?

Pictures in the Smoke

Oh, gallant was the first love, and glittering and fine;
    The second love was water, in a clear white cup;
The third love was his, and the fourth was mine;
    And after that, I always get them all mixed up.

Inscription for the
Ceiling of a Bedroom

Daily dawns another day;
I must up, to make my way.
Though I dress and drink and eat,
Move my fingers and my feet,
Learn a little, here and there,
Weep and laugh and sweat and swear,
Hear a song, or watch a stage,
Leave some words upon a page,
Claim a foe, or hail a friend—
Bed awaits me at the end.

Though I go in pride and strength,
I'll come back to bed at length.
Though I walk in blinded woe,
Back to bed I'm bound to go.
High my heart, or bowed my head,
All my days but lead to bed.
Up, and out, and on; and then
Ever back to bed again,
Summer, Winter, Spring, and Fall—
I'm a fool to rise at all!

Nocturne

Always I knew that it could not last
  (Gathering clouds, and the snowflakes flying),
Now it is part of the golden past
  (Darkening skies, and the night-wind sighing);
It is but cowardice to pretend.
  Cover with ashes our love's cold crater—
Always I've known that it had to end
  Sooner or later.

Always I knew it would come like this
  (Pattering rain, and the grasses springing),
Sweeter to you is a new love's kiss
  (Flickering sunshine, and young birds singing).
Gone are the raptures that once we knew,
  Now you are finding a new joy greater—
Well, I'll be doing the same thing, too,
  Sooner or later.

Interview

The ladies men admire, I've heard,
Would shudder at a wicked word.
Their candle gives a single light;

They'd rather stay at home at night.
They do not keep awake till three,
Nor read erotic poetry.
They never sanction the impure,
Nor recognize an overture.
They shrink from powders and from paints.
So far, I have had no complaints.

Experience

Some men break your heart in two,
    Some men fawn and flatter,
Some men never look at you;
    And that cleans up the matter.

Neither Bloody
nor Bowed

They say of me, and so they should,
It's doubtful if I come to good.
I see acquaintances and friends
Accumulating dividends,
And making enviable names
In science, art, and parlor games.
But I, despite expert advice,
Keep doing things I think are nice,
And though to good I never come—
Inseparable my nose and thumb!

The Burned Child

Love has had his way with me.
    This my heart is torn and maimed
Since he took his play with me.
    Cruel well the bow-boy aimed,

Shot, and saw the feathered shaft
   Dripping bright and bitter red.
He that shrugged his wings and laughed—
   Better had he left me dead.

Sweet, why do you plead me, then,
   Who have bled so sore of that?
Could I bear it once again? . . .
   Drop a hat, dear, drop a hat!

A Telephone Call

Please, God, let him telephone me now. Dear God, let him call me now. I won't ask anything else of You, truly I won't. It isn't very much to ask. It would be so little to You, God, such a little, little thing. Only let him telephone now. Please, God. Please, please, please.

If I didn't think about it, maybe the telephone might ring. Sometimes it does that. If I could think of something else. If I could think of something else. Maybe if I counted five hundred by fives, it might ring by that time. I'll count slowly. I won't cheat. And if it rings when I get to three hundred, I won't stop; I won't answer it until I get to five hundred. Five, ten, fifteen, twenty, twenty-five, thirty, thirty-five, forty, forty-five, fifty. . . . Oh, please ring. Please.

This is the last time I'll look at the clock. I will not look at it again. It's ten minutes past seven. He said he would telephone at five o'clock. "I'll call you at five, darling." I think that's where he said "darling." I'm almost sure he said it there. I know he called me "darling" twice, and the other time was when he said good-by. "Good-by, darling." He was busy, and he can't say much in the office, but he called me "darling" twice. He couldn't have minded my calling him up. I know you shouldn't keep telephoning them—I know they don't like that. When you do that, they know you are thinking about them and wanting them, and that makes them hate you. But I hadn't talked to him in three days—not in three days. And all I did was ask him how he was; it was just the way anybody might have called him up. He couldn't have minded that. He couldn't have thought I was bothering him. "No, of course you're not," he said. And he said he'd telephone me. He didn't have to say that. I didn't ask him to, truly I didn't. I'm sure I didn't. I don't think he would say he'd telephone me, and then just never do it. Please don't let him do that, God. Please don't.

119

"I'll call you at five, darling." "Good-by, darling." He was busy, and he was in a hurry, and there were people around him, but he called me "darling" twice. That's mine, that's mine. I have that, even if I never see him again. Oh, but that's so little. That isn't enough. Nothing's enough, if I never see him again. Please let me see him again, God. Please, I want him so much. I want him so much. I'll be good, God. I will try to be better, I will, if You will let me see him again. If You let him telephone me. Oh, let him telephone me now.

Ah, don't let my prayer seem too little to You, God. You sit up there, so white and old, with all the angels about You and the stars slipping by. And I come to You with a prayer about a telephone call. Ah, don't laugh, God. You see, You don't know how it feels. You're so safe, there on Your throne, with the blue swirling under You. Nothing can touch You; no one can twist Your heart in his hands. This is suffering, God, this is bad, bad suffering. Won't You help me? For Your Son's sake, help me. You said You would do whatever was asked of You in His name. Oh, God, in the name of Thine only beloved Son, Jesus Christ, our Lord, let him telephone me now.

I must stop this. I mustn't be this way. Look. Suppose a young man says he'll call a girl up, and then something happens, and he doesn't. That isn't so terrible, is it? Why, it's going on all over the world, right this minute. Oh, what do I care what's going on all over the world? Why can't that telephone ring? Why can't it, why can't it? Couldn't you ring? Ah, please, couldn't you? You damned, ugly, shiny thing. It would hurt you to ring, wouldn't it? Oh, that would hurt you. Damn you, I'll pull your filthy roots out of the wall, I'll smash your smug black face in little bits. Damn you to hell.

No, no, no. I must stop. I must think about something else. This is what I'll do. I'll put the clock in the other room. Then I can't look at it. If I do have to look at it, then I'll have to walk into the bedroom, and that will be something to do. Maybe, before I look at it again, he will call me. I'll be so sweet to him, if he calls me. If he says he can't see me tonight, I'll say, "Why, that's all right, dear. Why, of course it's all right." I'll be the way I was when I first met him. Then maybe he'll like me again. I was always sweet, at first. Oh, it's so easy to be sweet to people before you love them.

I think he must still like me a little. He couldn't have called me "darling" twice today, if he didn't still like me a little. It isn't all gone, if he still likes me a little; even if it's only a little, little bit. You see, God, if You would just let him telephone me, I wouldn't have to ask You anything more. I would be sweet to him, I would be gay, I would be just the way I used to be, and then he would love me again. And then I would never have to ask You for anything more. Don't You see, God? So won't You please let him telephone me? Won't You please, please, please?

Are You punishing me, God, because I've been bad? Are You angry with me because I did that? Oh, but, God, there are so many bad people—You could not be hard only to me. And it wasn't very bad; it couldn't have been bad. We didn't hurt anybody, God. Things are only bad when they hurt people. We didn't hurt one single soul; You know that. You know it wasn't bad, don't You, God? So won't You let him telephone me now?

If he doesn't telephone me, I'll know God is angry with me. I'll count five hundred by fives, and if he hasn't called me then, I will know God isn't going to help me, ever again. That will be the sign. Five, ten, fifteen, twenty, twenty-five, thirty, thirty-five, forty, forty-five, fifty, fifty-five. . . . It was bad. I knew it was bad. All right, God, send me to hell. You think You're frightening me with Your hell, don't You? You think Your hell is worse than mine.

I mustn't. I mustn't do this. Suppose he's a little late calling me up—that's nothing to get hysterical about. Maybe he isn't going to call—maybe he's coming straight up here without telephoning. He'll be cross if he sees I have been crying. They don't like you to cry. He doesn't cry. I wish to God I could make him cry. I wish I could make him cry and tread the floor and feel his heart heavy and big and festering in him. I wish I could hurt him like hell.

He doesn't wish that about me. I don't think he even knows how he makes me feel. I wish he could know, without my telling him. They don't like you to tell them they've made you cry.

They don't like you to tell them you're unhappy because of them. If you do, they think you're possessive and exacting. And then they hate you. They hate you whenever you say anything you really think. You always have to keep playing little games. Oh, I thought we didn't have to; I thought this was so big I could say whatever I meant. I guess you can't, ever. I guess there isn't ever anything big enough for that. Oh, if he would just telephone, I wouldn't tell him I had been sad about him. They hate sad people. I would be so sweet and so gay, he couldn't help but like me. If he would only telephone. If he would only telephone.

Maybe that's what he is doing. Maybe he is coming on here without calling me up. Maybe he's on his way now. Something might have happened to him. No, nothing could ever happen to him. I can't picture anything happening to him. I never picture him run over. I never see him lying still and long and dead. I wish he were dead. That's a terrible wish. That's a lovely wish. If he were dead, he would be mine. If he were dead, I would never think of now and the last few weeks. I would remember only the lovely times. It would be all beautiful. I wish he were dead. I wish he were dead, dead, dead.

This is silly. It's silly to go wishing people were dead just because they don't call you up the very minute they said they would. Maybe the clock's fast; I don't know whether it's right. Maybe he's hardly late at all. Anything could have made him a little late. Maybe he had to stay at his office. Maybe he went home, to call me up from there, and somebody came in. He doesn't like to telephone me in front of people. Maybe he's worried, just a little, little bit, about keeping me waiting. He might even hope that I would call him up. I could do that. I could telephone him.

I mustn't. I mustn't, I mustn't. Oh, God, please don't let me telephone him. Please keep me from doing that. I know, God, just as well as You do, that if he were worried about me, he'd telephone no matter where he was or how many people there were around him. Please make me know that, God. I don't ask You to make it easy for me—You can't do that, for all that You could make a world. Only let me know it, God. Don't let me go on hoping. Don't let me say comforting things to myself. Please don't let me hope, dear God. Please don't.

I won't telephone him. I'll never telephone him again as long as I live. He'll rot in hell, before I'll call him up. You don't have to give me strength, God; I have it myself. If he wanted me, he could get me. He knows where I am. He knows I'm waiting here. He's so sure of me, so sure. I wonder why they hate you, as soon as they are sure of you. I should think it would be so sweet to be sure.

It would be so easy to telephone him. Then I'd know. Maybe it wouldn't be a foolish thing to do. Maybe he wouldn't mind. Maybe he'd like it. Maybe he has been trying to get me. Sometimes people try and try to get you on the telephone, and they say the number doesn't answer. I'm not just saying that to help myself; that really happens. You know that really happens, God. Oh, God, keep me away from that telephone. Keep me away. Let me still have just a little bit of pride. I think I'm going to need it, God. I think it will be all I'll have.

Oh, what does pride matter, when I can't stand it if I don't talk to him? Pride like that is such a silly, shabby little thing. The real pride, the big pride, is in having no pride. I'm not saying that just because I want to call him. I am not. That's true, I know that's true. I will be big. I will be beyond little prides.

Please, God, keep me from telephoning him. Please, God.

I don't see what pride has to do with it. This is such a little thing, for me to be bringing in pride, for me to be making such a fuss about. I may have misunderstood him. Maybe he said for me to call him up, at five. "Call me at five, darling." He could have said that, perfectly well. It's so possible that I didn't hear him right. "Call me at five, darling." I'm almost sure that's what he said. God, don't let me talk this way to myself. Make me know, please make me know.

I'll think about something else. I'll just sit quietly. If I could sit still. If I could sit still. Maybe I could read. Oh, all the books are about people who love each other, truly and sweetly. What do they want to write about that for? Don't they know it isn't true? Don't they know it's a lie, it's a God damned lie? What do they have to tell about that for, when they know how it hurts? Damn them, damn them, damn them.

I won't. I'll be quiet. This is nothing to get excited about. Look. Suppose he were someone I didn't know very well. Suppose he were another girl. Then I'd just telephone and say, "Well, for goodness' sake, what happened to you?" That's what I'd do, and I'd never even think about it. Why can't I be casual and natural, just because I love him? I can be. Honestly, I can be. I'll call him up, and be so easy and pleasant. You see if I won't, God. Oh, don't let me call him. Don't, don't, don't.

God, aren't You really going to let him call me? Are You sure, God? Couldn't You please relent? Couldn't You? I don't even ask You to let him telephone me this minute, God: only let him do it in a little while. I'll count five hundred by fives. I'll do it so slowly and so fairly. If he hasn't telephoned then, I'll call him. I will. Oh, please, dear God, dear kind God, my blessed Father in Heaven, let him call before then. Please, God. Please.

Five, ten, fifteen, twenty, twenty-five, thirty, thirty-five. . . .

Here We Are

The young man in the new blue suit finished arranging the glistening luggage in tight corners of the Pullman compartment. The train had leaped at curves and bounced along straightaways, rendering balance a praiseworthy achievement and a sporadic one; and the young man had pushed and hoisted and tucked and shifted the bags with concentrated care.

Nevertheless, eight minutes for the settling of two suitcases and a hat-box is a long time.

He sat down, leaning back against bristled green plush, in the seat opposite the girl in beige. She looked as new as a peeled egg. Her hat, her fur, her frock, her gloves were glossy and stiff with novelty. On the arc of the thin, slippery sole of one beige shoe was gummed a tiny oblong of white paper, printed with the price set and paid for that slipper and its fellow, and the name of the shop that had dispensed them.

She had been staring raptly out of the window, drinking in the big weathered signboards that extolled the phenomena of codfish without bones and screens no rust could corrupt. As the young man sat down, she turned politely from the pane, met his eyes, started a smile and got it about half done, and rested her gaze just above his right shoulder.

"Well!" the young man said.

"Well!" she said.

"Well, here we are," he said.

"Here we are," she said. "Aren't we?"

"I should say we were," he said. "Eeyop. Here we are."

"Well!" she said.

"Well!" he said. "Well. How does it feel to be an old married lady?"

"Oh, it's too soon to ask me that," she said. "At least—I mean. Well, I mean, goodness, we've only been married about three hours, haven't we?"

The young man studied his wrist-watch as if he were just acquiring the knack of reading time.

"We have been married," he said, "exactly two hours and twenty-six minutes."

"My," she said. "It seems like longer."

"No," he said. "It isn't hardly half-past six yet."

"It seems like later," she said. "I guess it's because it starts getting dark so early."

"It does, at that," he said. "The nights are going to be pretty long from now on. I mean. I mean—well, it starts getting dark early."

"I didn't have any idea what time it was," she said. "Everything was so mixed up, I sort of don't know where I am, or what it's all about. Getting back from the church, and then all those people, and then changing all my clothes, and then everybody throwing things, and all. Goodness, I don't see how people do it every day."

"Do what?" he said.

"Get married," she said. "When you think of all the people, all over the world, getting married just as if it was nothing. Chinese people and everybody. Just as if it wasn't anything."

"Well, let's not worry about people all over the world," he said. "Let's don't think about a lot of Chinese. We've got something better to think about. I mean. I mean—well, what do we care about them?"

"I know," she said. "But I just sort of got to thinking of them, all of them, all over everywhere, doing it all the time. At least, I mean—getting married, you know. And it's—well, it's sort of such a big thing to do, it makes you feel queer. You think of them, all of them, all doing it just like it wasn't anything. And how does anybody know what's going to happen next?"

"Let them worry," he said. "We don't have to. We know darn well what's going to happen next. I mean. I mean—well, we know it's going to be great. Well, we know we're going to be happy. Don't we?"

"Oh, of course," she said. "Only you think of all the people, and you have to sort of keep thinking. It makes you feel funny.

An awful lot of people that get married, it doesn't turn out so well. And I guess they all must have thought it was going to be great."

"Come on, now," he said. "This is no way to start a honeymoon, with all this thinking going on. Look at us—all married and everything done. I mean. The wedding all done and all."

"Ah, it was nice, wasn't it?" she said. "Did you really like my veil?"

"You looked great," he said. "Just great."

"Oh, I'm terribly glad," she said. "Ellie and Louise looked lovely, didn't they? I'm terribly glad they did finally decide on pink. They looked perfectly lovely."

"Listen," he said. "I want to tell you something. When I was standing up there in that old church waiting for you to come up, and I saw those two bridesmaids, I thought to myself, I thought, 'Well, I never knew Louise could look like that!' Why, she'd have knocked anybody's eye out."

"Oh, really?" she said. "Funny. Of course, everybody thought her dress and hat were lovely, but a lot of people seemed to think she looked sort of tired. People have been saying that a lot, lately. I tell them I think it's awfully mean of them to go around saying that about her. I tell them they've got to remember that Louise isn't so terribly young any more, and they've got to expect her to look like that. Louise can say she's twenty-three all she wants to, but she's a good deal nearer twenty-seven."

"Well, she was certainly a knock-out at the wedding," he said. "Boy!"

"I'm terribly glad you thought so," she said. "I'm glad someone did. How did you think Ellie looked?"

"Why, I honestly didn't get a look at her," he said.

"Oh, really?" she said. "Well, I certainly think that's too bad. I don't suppose I ought to say it about my own sister, but I never saw anybody look as beautiful as Ellie looked today. And always so sweet and unselfish, too. And you didn't even notice her. But you never pay attention to Ellie, anyway. Don't think I haven't noticed it. It makes me feel just terrible. It makes me feel just awful, that you don't like my own sister."

"I do like her!" he said. "I'm crazy for Ellie. I think she's a great kid."

"Don't think it makes any difference to Ellie!" she said. "Ellie's got enough people crazy about her. It isn't anything to her whether you like her or not. Don't flatter yourself she cares! Only, the only thing is, it makes it awfully hard for me you don't like her, that's the only thing. I keep thinking, when we come back and get in that apartment and everything, it's going to be awfully hard for me that you won't want my own sister to come and see me. It's going to make it awfully hard for me that you won't ever want my family around. I know how you feel about my family. Don't think I haven't seen it. Only, if you don't ever want to see them, that's your loss. Not theirs. Don't flatter yourself!"

"Oh, now, come on!" he said. "What's all this talk about not wanting your family around? Why, you know how I feel about your family. I think your old lady—I think your mother's swell. And Ellie. And your father. What's all this talk?"

"Well, I've seen it," she said. "Don't think I haven't. Lots of people they get married, and they think it's going to be great and everything, and then it all goes to pieces because people don't like people's families, or something like that. Don't tell me! I've seen it happen."

"Honey," he said, "what is all this? What are you getting all angry about? Hey, look, this is our honeymoon. What are you trying to start a fight for? Ah, I guess you're just feeling sort of nervous."

"Me?" she said. "What have I got to be nervous about? I mean. I mean, goodness, I'm not nervous."

"You know, lots of times," he said, "they say that girls get kind of nervous and yippy on account of thinking about—I mean. I mean—well, it's like you said, things are all so sort of mixed up and everything, right now. But afterwards, it'll be all right. I mean. I mean—well, look, honey, you don't look any too comfortable. Don't you want to take your hat off? And let's don't ever fight, ever. Will we?"

"Ah, I'm sorry I was cross," she said. "I guess I did feel a little bit funny. All mixed up, and then thinking of all those people all over everywhere, and then being sort of 'way off here, all alone with you. It's so sort of different. It's sort of such a big thing. You can't blame a person for thinking, can you? Yes, don't let's ever, ever fight. We won't be like a whole lot of them. We won't fight or be nasty or anything. Will we?"

"You bet your life we won't," he said.

"I guess I will take this darned old hat off," she said. "It kind of presses. Just put it up on the rack, will you, dear? Do you like it, sweetheart?"

"Looks good on you," he said.

"No, but I mean," she said, "do you really like it?"

"Well, I'll tell you," he said. "I know this is the new style and everything like that, and it's probably great. I don't know anything about things like that. Only I like the kind of a hat like that blue hat you had. Gee, I liked that hat."

"Oh, really?" she said. "Well, that's nice. That's lovely. The first thing you say to me, as soon as you get me off on a train away from my family and everything, is that you don't like my hat. The first thing you say to your wife is you think she has terrible taste in hats. That's nice, isn't it?"

"Now, honey," he said, "I never said anything like that. I only said——"

"What you don't seem to realize," she said, "is this hat cost twenty-two dollars. Twenty-two dollars. And that horrible old blue thing you think you're so crazy about, that cost three ninety-five."

"I don't give a darn what they cost," he said. "I only said—I said I liked that blue hat. I don't know anything about hats. I'll be crazy about this one as soon as I get used to it. Only it's kind of not like your other hats. I don't know about the new styles. What do I know about women's hats?"

"It's too bad," she said, "you didn't marry somebody that would get the kind of hats you'd like. Hats that cost three ninety-five. Why didn't you marry Louise? You always think she looks so beautiful. You'd love her taste in hats. Why didn't you marry her?"

"Ah, now, honey," he said. "For heaven's sakes!"

"Why didn't you marry her?" she said. "All you've done, ever since we got on this train, is talk about her. Here I've sat and sat, and just listened to you saying how wonderful Louise is. I suppose that's nice, getting me all off here alone with you, and then raving about Louise right in front of my face. Why didn't you ask her to marry you? I'm sure she would have jumped at the chance. There aren't so many people asking her to marry them. It's too bad you didn't marry her. I'm sure you'd have been much happier."

"Listen, baby," he said, "while you're talking about things like that, why didn't you marry Joe Brooks? I suppose he could have given you all the twenty-two-dollar hats you wanted, I suppose!"

"Well, I'm not so sure I'm not sorry I didn't," she said. "There! Joe Brooks wouldn't have waited until he got me all off alone and then sneered at my taste in clothes. Joe Brooks wouldn't ever hurt my feelings. Joe Brooks has always been fond of me. There!"

"Yeah," he said. "He's fond of you. He was so fond of you he didn't even send a wedding present. That's how fond of you he was."

"I happen to know for a fact," she said, "that he was away on business, and as soon as he comes back he's going to give me anything I want, for the apartment."

"Listen," he said. "I don't want anything he gives you in our apartment. Anything he gives you, I'll throw right out the window. That's what I think of your friend Joe Brooks. And how do you know where he is and what he's going to do, anyway? Has he been writing to you?"

"I suppose my friends can correspond with me," she said. "I didn't hear there was any law against that."

"Well, I suppose they can't!" he said. "And what do you think of that? I'm not going to have my wife getting a lot of letters from cheap traveling salesmen!"

"Joe Brooks is not a cheap traveling salesman!" she said. "He is not! He gets a wonderful salary."

"Oh yeah?" he said. "Where did you hear that?"

"He told me so himself," she said.

"Oh, he told you so himself," he said. "I see. He told you so himself."

"You've got a lot of right to talk about Joe Brooks," she said. "You and your friend Louise. All you ever talk about is Louise."

"Oh, for heaven's sakes!" he said. "What do I care about Louise? I just thought she was a friend of yours, that's all. That's why I ever even noticed her."

"Well, you certainly took an awful lot of notice of her today," she said. "On our wedding day! You said yourself when you were standing there in the church you just kept thinking of her. Right up at the altar. Oh, right in the presence of God! And all you thought about was Louise."

"Listen, honey," he said, "I never should have said that. How does anybody know what kind of crazy things come into their heads when they're standing there waiting to get married? I was just telling you that because it was so kind of crazy. I thought it would make you laugh."

"I know," she said. "I've been all sort of mixed up today, too. I told you that. Everything so strange and everything. And me all the time thinking about all those people all over the world, and now us here all alone, and everything. I know you get all mixed up. Only I did think, when you kept talking about how beautiful Louise looked, you did it with malice and forethought."

"I never did anything with malice and forethought!" he said. "I just told you that about Louise because I thought it would make you laugh."

"Well, it didn't," she said.

"No, I know it didn't," he said. "It certainly did not. Ah, baby, and we ought to be laughing, too. Hell, honey lamb, this is our honeymoon. What's the matter?"

"I don't know," she said. "We used to squabble a lot when we were going together and then engaged and everything, but I thought everything would be so different as soon as you were married. And now I feel so sort of strange and everything. I feel so sort of alone."

"Well, you see, sweetheart," he said, "we're not really

married yet. I mean. I mean—well, things will be different afterwards. Oh, hell. I mean, we haven't been married very long."

"No," she said.

"Well, we haven't got much longer to wait now," he said. "I mean—well, we'll be in New York in about twenty minutes. Then we can have dinner, and sort of see what we feel like doing. Or I mean. Is there anything special you want to do tonight?"

"What?" she said.

"What I mean to say," he said, "would you like to go to a show or something?"

"Why, whatever you like," she said. "I sort of didn't think people went to theaters and things on their—I mean, I've got a couple of letters I simply must write. Don't let me forget."

"Oh," he said. "You're going to write letters tonight?"

"Well, you see," she said. "I've been perfectly terrible. What with all the excitement and everything. I never did thank poor old Mrs. Sprague for her berry spoon, and I never did a thing about those book ends the McMasters sent. It's just too awful of me. I've got to write them this very night."

"And when you've finished writing your letters," he said, "maybe I could get you a magazine or a bag of peanuts."

"What?" she said.

"I mean," he said, "I wouldn't want you to be bored."

"As if I could be bored with you!" she said. "Silly! Aren't we married? Bored!"

"What I thought," he said, "I thought when we got in, we could go right up to the Biltmore and anyway leave our bags, and maybe have a little dinner in the room, kind of quiet, and then do whatever we wanted. I mean. I mean—well, let's go right up there from the station."

"Oh, yes, let's," she said. "I'm so glad we're going to the Biltmore. I just love it. The twice I've stayed in New York we've always stayed there, Papa and Mamma and Ellie and I, and I was crazy about it. I always sleep so well there. I go right off to sleep the minute I put my head on the pillow."

"Oh, you do?" he said.

"At least, I mean," she said. "Way up high it's so quiet."

"We might go to some show or other tomorrow night instead of tonight," he said. "Don't you think that would be better?"

"Yes, I think it might," she said.

He rose, balanced a moment, crossed over and sat down beside her.

"Do you really have to write those letters tonight?" he said.

"Well," she said, "I don't suppose they'd get there any quicker than if I wrote them tomorrow."

There was a silence with things going on in it.

"And we won't ever fight any more, will we?" he said.

"Oh, no," she said. "Not ever! I don't know what made me do like that. It all got so sort of funny, sort of like a nightmare, the way I got thinking of all those people getting married all the time; and so many of them, everything spoils on account of fighting and everything. I got all mixed up thinking about them. Oh, I don't want to be like them. But we won't be, will we?"

"Sure we won't," he said.

"We won't go all to pieces," she said. "We won't fight. It'll all be different, now we're married. It'll all be lovely. Reach me down my hat, will you, sweetheart? It's time I was putting it on. Thanks. Ah, I'm so sorry you don't like it '

"I do so like it!" he said.

"You said you didn't," she said. "You said you thought it was perfectly terrible."

"I never said any such thing," he said. "You're crazy."

"All right, I may be crazy," she said. "Thank you very much. But that's what you said. Not that it matters—it's just a little thing. But it makes you feel pretty funny to think you've gone and married somebody that says you have perfectly terrible taste in hats. And then goes and says you're crazy, beside."

"Now, listen here," he said. "Nobody said any such thing. Why, I love that hat. The more I look at it the better I like it. I think it's great."

"That isn't what you said before," she said.

"Honey," he said. "Stop it, will you? What do you want to start all this for? I love the damned hat. I mean, I love your hat.

I love anything you wear. What more do you want me to say?"

"Well, I don't want you to say it like that," she said.

"I said I think it's great," he said. "That's all I said."

"Do you really?" she said. "Do you honestly? Ah, I'm so glad. I'd hate you not to like my hat. It would be—I don't know, it would be sort of such a bad start."

"Well, I'm crazy for it," he said. "Now we've got that settled, for heaven's sakes. Ah, baby. Baby lamb. We're not going to have any bad starts. Look at us—we're on our honeymoon. Pretty soon we'll be regular old married people. I mean. I mean, in a few minutes we'll be getting in to New York, and then we'll be going to the hotel, and then everything will be all right. I mean—well, look at us! Here we are married! Here we are!"

"Yes, here we are," she said. "Aren't we?"

Dusk before Fireworks

He was a very good-looking young man indeed, shaped to be annoyed. His voice was intimate as the rustle of sheets, and he kissed easily. There was no tallying the gifts of Charvet handkerchiefs, *art moderne* ash-trays, monogrammed dressing-gowns, gold key-chains, and cigarette-cases of thin wood, inlaid with views of Parisian comfort stations, that were sent him by ladies too quickly confident, and were paid for with the money of unwitting husbands, which is acceptable any place in the world. Every woman who visited his small, square apartment promptly flamed with the desire to assume charge of its redecoration. During his tenancy, three separate ladies had achieved this ambition. Each had left behind her, for her brief monument, much too much glazed chintz.

The glare of the latest upholstery was dulled, now, in an April dusk. There was a soft blur of mauve and gray over chairs and curtains, instead of the daytime pattern of heroic-sized double poppies and small, sad elephants. (The most recent of the volunteer decorators was a lady who added interest to her ways by collecting all varieties of elephants save those alive or stuffed; her selection of the chintz had been made less for the cause of contemporary design than in the hope of keeping ever present the wistful souvenirs of her hobby and, hence, of herself. Unhappily, the poppies, those flowers for forgetfulness, turned out to be predominant in the pattern.)

The very good-looking young man was stretched in a chair that was legless and short in back. It was a strain to see in that chair any virtue save the speeding one of modernity. Certainly it was a peril to all who dealt with it; they were far from their best within its arms, and they could never have wished to be remembered as they appeared while easing into its depths or struggling out again. All, that is, save the young man. He was a long young man, broad at the shoulders and chest and narrow everywhere else, and his muscles obeyed him at the exact instant of command. He rose and lay, he moved and was still, always in beauty. Several men disliked him, but only one woman really hated him. She was his sister. She was stump-shaped, and she had straight hair.

On the sofa opposite the difficult chair there sat a young woman, slight and softly dressed. There was no more to her frock than some dull, dark silk and a little chiffon, but the recurrent bill for it demanded, in bitter black and white, a sum well on toward the second hundred. Once the very good-looking young man had said that he liked women in quiet and conservative clothes, carefully made. The young woman was of those unfortunates who remember every word. This made living peculiarly trying for her when it was later demonstrated that the young man was also partial to ladies given to garments of slap-dash cut, and color like the sound of big brass instruments.

The young woman was temperately pretty in the eyes of most beholders; but there were a few, mainly hand-to-mouth people. artists and such, who could not look enough at her. Half a year before, she had been sweeter to see. Now there was tension about her mouth and unease along her brow, and her eyes looked wearied and troubled. The gentle dusk became her. The young man who shared it with her could not see these things.

She stretched her arms and laced her fingers high above her head.

"Oh, this is nice," she said. "It's nice being here."

"It's nice and peaceful," he said. "Oh, Lord. Why can't people just be peaceful? That's little enough to ask, isn't it? Why does there have to be so much hell, all the time?"

She dropped her hands to her lap.

"There doesn't have to be at all," she said. She had a quiet voice, and she said her words with every courtesy to each of them, as if she respected language, "There's never any need for hell."

"There's an awful lot of it around, sweet," he said.

"There certainly is," she said. "There's just as much hell as there are hundreds of little shrill, unnecessary people. It's the second-raters that stir up hell; first-rate people wouldn't. You need never have another bit of it in your beautiful life if—if you'll pardon my pointing—you could just manage to steel yourself against that band of spitting hell-cats that is included in your somewhat over-crowded acquaintance, my lamb. Ah, but I mean it, Hobie, dear. I've been wanting to tell you for so long. But it's so rotten hard to say. If I say it, it makes me sound just like one of them—makes me seem inexpensive and jealous. Surely, you know, after all this time, I'm not like that. It's just that I worry so about you. You're so fine, you're so lovely, it nearly kills me to see you just eaten up by a lot of things like Margot Wadsworth and Mrs. Holt and Evie Maynard and those. You're so much better than that. You know that's why I'm saying it. You know I haven't got a stitch of jealousy in me. Jealous! Good heavens, if I were going to be jealous, I'd be it about someone worth while, and not about any silly, stupid, idle, worthless, selfish, hysterical, vulgar, promiscuous, sex-ridden——"

"Darling!" he said.

"Well, I'm sorry," she said. "I guess I'm sorry. I didn't really mean to go into the subject of certain of your friends. Maybe the way they behave isn't their fault," said she, lying in her teeth. "After all, you can't expect them to know what it's about. Poor things, they'll never know how sweet it can be, how lovely it always is when we're alone together. It is, isn't it? Ah, Hobie, isn't it?"

The young man raised his slow lids and looked at her. He smiled with one end of his beautiful curly mouth.

"Uh-huh," he said.

He took his eyes from hers and became busy with an ash-tray and a spent cigarette. But he still smiled.

"Ah, don't," she said. "You promised you'd forget about—about last Wednesday. You said you'd never remember it again. Oh, whatever made me do it! Making scenes. Having tantrums. Rushing out into the night. And then coming crawling back. Me, that wanted to show you how different a woman could be! Oh, please, please don't let's think about it. Only tell me I wasn't as terrible as I know I was."

"Darling," he said, for he was often a young man of simple statements, "you were the worst I ever saw."

"And doesn't that come straight from Sir Hubert!" she said. "Oh, dear. Oh, dear, oh, dear. What can I say? 'Sorry' isn't nearly enough. I'm broken, I'm in little bits. Would you mind doing something about putting me together again?"

She held out her arms to him.

The young man rose, came over to the sofa, and kissed her. He had intended a quick, good-humored kiss, a moment's stop on a projected trip out to his little pantry to mix cocktails. But her arms clasped him so close and so gladly that he dismissed the plan. He lifted her to her feet, and did not leave her.

Presently she moved her head and hid her face above his heart.

"Listen," she said, against cloth. "I want to say it all now, and then never say it any more. I want to tell you that there'll never, never be anything like last Wednesday again. What we have is so much too lovely ever to cheapen. I promise, oh, I promise you, I won't ever be like—like anybody else."

"You couldn't be, Kit," he said.

"Ah, think that always," she said, "and say it sometimes. It's so sweet to hear. Will you, Hobie?"

"For your size," he said, "you talk an awful lot." His fingers slid to her chin and held her face for his greater convenience.

After a while she moved again.

"Guess who I'd rather be, right this minute, than anybody in the whole world," she said.

"Who?" he said.

"Me," she said.

The telephone rang.

The telephone was in the young man's bedroom, standing in frequent silence on the little table by his bed. There was no door to the bed-chamber; a plan which had disadvantages, too. Only a curtained archway sequestered its intimacies from those of the living-room. Another archway, also streaming chintz, gave from the bedroom upon a tiny passage, along which were ranged the bathroom and the pantry. It was only by entering either of these, closing the door behind, and turning the faucets on to the full that any second person in the apartment could avoid hearing what was being said over the telephone. The young man sometimes thought of removing to a flat of more sympathetic design.

"There's that damn telephone," the young man said.

"Isn't it?" the young woman said. "And wouldn't it be?"

"Let's not answer it," he said. "Let's let it ring."

"No, you mustn't," she said. "I must be big and strong. Anyway, maybe it's only somebody that just died and left you twenty million dollars. Maybe it isn't some other woman at all. And if it is, what difference does it make? See how sweet and reasonable I am? Look at me being generous."

"You can afford to be, sweetheart," he said.

"I know I can," she said. "After all, whoever she is, she's way off on an end of a wire, and I'm right here."

She smiled up at him. So it was nearly half a minute before he went away to the telephone.

Still smiling, the young woman stretched her head back, closed her eyes and flung her arms wide. A long sigh raised her breast. Thus she stood, then she went and settled back on the sofa. She essayed whistling softly, but the issuing sounds would not resemble the intended tune and she felt, though interested, vaguely betrayed. Then she looked about the dusk-filled room. Then she pondered her finger nails, bringing each bent hand close to her eyes, and could find no fault. Then she smoothed her skirt along her legs and shook out the chiffon frills at her wrists. Then she spread her little handkerchief on her knee and with exquisite care traced the "Katherine" embroidered in script across one of its corners. Then she gave it all up and did nothing but listen.

"Yes?" the young man was saying. "Hello? Hello. I *told* you this is Mr. Ogden. Well, I *am* holding the wire. I've *been* holding the wire. *You're* the one that went away. Hello? Ah, now listen—Hello? Hey. Oh, what the hell *is* this? Come back, will you? Operator! Hello, *Yes*, this is Mr. Ogden. Who? Oh, hello, Connie. How are you, dear? What? You're what? Oh, that's too bad. What's the matter? Why can't you? Where are you, in Greenwich? Oh, I see. When, now? Why, Connie, the only thing is I've got to go right out. So if you came in to town now, it really wouldn't do much—Well, I couldn't very well do that, dear. I'm keeping these people waiting as it is. I say I'm late now, I was just going out the door when you called. Why, I'd better not say that, Connie, because there's no telling when I'll be able to break away. Look, why don't you wait and come in to town tomorrow some time? What? Can't you tell me now? Oh— Well— Oh, Connie, there's no reason to talk like that. Why, of course I'd do anything in the world I could, but I tell you I can't tonight. No, no, no, no, no, it isn't that at all. No, it's nothing like that, I tell you. These people are friends of my sister's, and it's just one of those things you've got to do. Why don't you be a good girl and go to bed early, and then you'll feel better tomorrow? Hm? Will you do that? What? Of course I do, Connie. I'll try to later on if I can, dear. Well, all right, if you want to, but I don't know what time I'll be home. Of course I do. Of course I do. Yes, *do*, Connie. You be a good girl, won't you? 'By, dear."

The young man returned, through the chintz. He had a rather worn look. It was, of course, becoming to him.

"God," he said, simply.

The young woman on the sofa looked at him as if through clear ice.

"And how *is* dear Mrs. Holt?" she said.

"Great," he said. "Corking. Way up at the top of her form." He dropped wearily into the low chair. "She says she has something she wants to tell me."

"It can't be her age," she said.

He smiled without joy. "She says it's too hard to say over the wire," he said.

"Then it may be her age," she said. "She's afraid it might sound like her telephone number."

"About twice a week," he said, "Connie has something she must tell you right away, that she couldn't possibly say over the telephone. Usually it turns out she's caught the butler drinking again."

"I see," she said.

"Well," he said. "Poor little Connie."

"Poor little Connie," she said. "Oh, my God. That saber-toothed tigress. Poor little Connie."

"Darling, why do we have to waste time talking about Connie Holt?" he said. "Can't we just be peaceful?"

"Not while that she-beast prowls the streets," she said. "Is she coming in to town tonight?"

"Well, she was," he said, "but then she more or less said she wouldn't."

"Oh, she will," she said. "You get right down out of that fool's paradise you're in. She'll shoot out of Greenwich like a bat out of hell, if she thinks there's a chance of seeing you. Ah, Hobie, you don't really want to see that old thing, do you? Do you? Because if you do—Well, I suppose maybe you do. Naturally, if she has something she must tell you right away, you want to see her. Look, Hobie, you know you can see me any time. It isn't a bit important, seeing me tonight. Why don't you call up Mrs. Holt and tell her to take the next train in? She'd get here quicker by train than by motor, wouldn't she? Please go ahead and do it. It's quite all right about me. Really."

"You know," he said, "I knew that was coming. I could tell it by the way you were when I came back from the telephone. Oh, Kit, what makes you want to talk like that? You know damned well the last thing I want to do is see Connie Holt. You know how I want to be with you. Why do you want to work up all this? I watched you just sit there and deliberately talk yourself into it, starting right out of nothing. Now what's the idea of that? Oh, good Lord, what's the matter with women, anyway?"

"Please don't call me 'women,' " she said.

"I'm sorry, darling," he said. "I didn't mean to use bad words." He smiled at her. She felt her heart go liquid, but she did her best to be harder won.

"Doubtless," she said, and her words fell like snow when there is no wind, "I spoke ill-advisedly. If I said, as I must have, something to distress you, I can only beg you to believe that that was my misfortune, and not my intention. It seemed to me as if I were doing only a courteous thing in suggesting that you need feel no obligation about spending the evening with me, when you would naturally wish to be with Mrs. Holt. I simply felt that—Oh, the hell with it! I'm no good at this. Of course I didn't mean it, dearest. If you had said, 'All right,' and had gone and told her to come in, I should have died. I just said it because I wanted to hear you say it was me you wanted to be with. Oh, I need to hear you say that, Hobie. It's—it's what I live on, darling."

"Kit," he said, "you ought to know, without my saying it. You know. It's this feeling you *have* to say things—that's what spoils everything."

"I suppose so," she said. "I suppose I know so. Only—the thing is, I get so mixed up, I just—I just can't go on. I've got to be reassured, dearest. I didn't need to be at first, when everything was gay and sure, but things aren't—well, they aren't the same now. There seem to be so many others that— So I need so terribly to have you tell me that it's me and not anybody else. Oh, I *had* to have you say that, a few minutes ago. Look, Hobie. How do you think it makes me feel to sit here and hear you lie to Connie Holt—to hear you say you have to go out with friends of your sister's? Now why couldn't you say you had a date with me? Are you ashamed of me, Hobie? Is that it?"

"Oh, Kit," he said, "for heaven's sake! I don't know why I did it. I did it before I even thought. I did it—well, sort of instinctively, I guess, because it seemed to be the easiest thing to do. I suppose I'm just weak."

"No!" she said. "You weak? Well! And is there any other news tonight?"

"I know I am," he said. "I know it's weak to do anything in the world to avoid a scene."

"Exactly what," she said, "is Mrs. Holt to you and you to her that she may make a scene if she learns that you have an engagement with another woman?"

"Oh, God!" he said. "I told you I don't give a damn about Connie Holt. She's nothing to me. Now will you for God's sake let it drop?"

"Oh, she's nothing to you," she said. "I see. Naturally, that would be why you called her 'dear' every other word."

"If I did," he said, "I never knew I was saying it. Good Lord, that doesn't mean anything. It's simply a—a form of nervousness, I suppose. I say it when I can't think what to call people. Why, I call telephone operators 'dear.' "

"I'm sure you do!" she said.

They glared. It was the young man who gave first. He went and sat close to her on the sofa, and for a while there were only murmurs. Then he said, "Will you stop? Will you stop it? Will you always be just like this—just sweet and the way you're meant to be and no fighting?"

"I will," she said. "Honest, I mean to. Let's not let anything come between us again ever. Mrs. Holt, indeed! Hell with her."

"Hell with her," he said. There was another silence, during which the young man did several things that he did extraordinarily well.

Suddenly the young woman stiffened her arms and pushed him away from her.

"And how do I know," she said, "that the way you talk to me about Connie Holt isn't just the way you talk to her about me when I'm not here? How do I know that?"

"Oh, my Lord," he said. "Oh, my dear, sweet Lord. Just when everything was all right. Ah, stop it, will you, baby? Let's just be quiet. Like this. See?"

A little later he said, "Look, sweet, how about a cocktail? Mightn't that be an idea? I'll go make them. And would you like the lights lighted?"

"Oh, no," she said. "I like it better in the dusk, like this. It's sweet. Dusk is so personal, somehow. And this way you can't see those lampshades. Hobie, if you knew how I hate your lampshades!"

"Honestly?" he said, with less injury than bewilderment in his voice. He looked at the shades as if he saw them for the first time. They were of vellum, or some substance near it, and upon each was painted a panorama of the right bank of the Seine, with the minute windows of the buildings cut out, under the direction of a superior mind, so that light might come through. "What's the matter with them, Kit?"

"Dearest, if you don't know, I can't ever explain it to you," she said. "Among other things, they're banal, inappropriate, and unbeautiful. They're exactly what Evie Maynard *would* have chosen. She thinks, just because they show views of Paris, that they're pretty darned sophisticated. She is that not uncommon type of woman that thinks any reference to la belle France is an invitation to the waltz. 'Not uncommon.' If that isn't the mildest word-picture that ever was painted of that——"

"Don't you like the way she decorated the apartment?" he said.

"Sweetheart," she said, "I think it's poisonous. You know that."

"Would you like to do it over?" he said.

"I should say not," she said. "Look, Hobie, don't you remember me? I'm the one that doesn't want to decorate your flat. Now do you place me? But if I ever *did*, the first thing I should do would be to paint these walls putty color—no, I guess first I'd tear off all this chintz and fling it to the winds, and then I'd——"

The telephone rang.

The young man threw one stricken glance at the young woman and then sat motionless. The jangles of the bell cut the dusk like little scissors.

"I think," said the young woman, exquisitely, "that your telephone is ringing. Don't let me keep you from answering it. As a matter of fact, I really must go powder my nose."

She sprang up, dashed through the bedroom, and into the bathroom. There was the sound of a closed door, the grind of a firmly turned key, and then immediately the noise of rushing waters.

When she returned, eventually, to the living-room, the young man was pouring pale, cold liquid into small glasses. He gave one to her, and smiled at her over it. It was his wistful smile. It was of his best.

"Hobie," she said, "is there a livery stable anywhere around here where they rent wild horses?"

"What?" he said.

"Because if there is," she said, "I wish you'd call up and ask them to send over a couple of teams. I want to show you they couldn't drag me into asking who that was on the telephone."

"Oh," he said, and tried his cocktail. "Is this dry enough, sweet? Because you like them dry, don't you? Sure it's all right? Really? Ah, wait a second, darling. Let *me* light your cigarette. There. Sure you're all right?"

"I can't stand it," she said. "I just lost all my strength of purpose—maybe the maid will find it on the floor in the morning. Hobart Ogden, who was that on the telephone?"

"Oh, that?" he said. "Well, that was a certain lady who shall be nameless."

"I'm sure she should be," she said. "She doubtless has all the other qualities of a—Well, I didn't quite say it, I'm keeping my head. Ah, dearest, was that Connie Holt again?"

"No, that was the funniest thing," he said. "That was Evie Maynard. Just when we were talking about her."

"Well, well, well," she said. "Isn't it a small world? And what's on her mind, if I may so flatter her? Is *her* butler tight, too?"

"Evie hasn't got a butler," he said. He tried smiling again, but found it better to abandon the idea and concentrate on refilling the young woman's glass. "No, she's just dizzy, the same as usual. She's got a cocktail party at her apartment, and they all want to go out on the town, that's all."

"Luckily," she said, "you had to go out with these friends of your sister's. You were just going out the door when she called."

"I never told her any such thing!" he said. "I said I had a date I'd been looking forward to all week."

"Oh, you didn't mention any names?" she said.

"There's no reason why I should, to Evie Maynard," he said. "It's none of her affair, any more than what she's doing and who she's doing it with is any concern of mine. She's nothing in my life. You know that. I've hardly seen her since she did the apartment. I don't care if I never see her again. I'd *rather* I never saw her again."

"I should think that might be managed, if you've really set your heart on it," she said.

"Well, I do what I can," he said. "She wanted to come in now for a cocktail, she and some of those interior decorator boys she has with her, and I told her absolutely no."

"And you think that will keep her away?" she said. "Oh, no. She'll be here. She and her feathered friends. Let's see—they ought to arrive just about the time that Mrs. Holt has thought it over and come in to town. Well. It's shaping up into a lovely evening, isn't it?"

"Great," he said. "And if I may say so, you're doing everything you can to make it harder, you little sweet." He poured more cocktails. "Oh, Kit, why are you being so nasty? Don't do it, darling. It's not like you. It's so unbecoming to you."

"I know it's horrible," she said. "It's—well, I do it in defense, I suppose, Hobie. If I didn't say nasty things, I'd cry. I'm afraid to cry; it would take me so long to stop. I—oh, I'm so hurt, dear. I don't know what to think. All these women. All these awful women. If they were fine, if they were sweet and gentle and intelligent, I shouldn't mind. Or maybe I should. I don't know. I don't know much of anything, any more. My mind goes round and round. I thought what we had was so different. Well—it wasn't. Sometimes I think it would be better never to see you any more. But then I know I couldn't stand that. I'm too far gone now. I'd do anything to be with you! And so I'm just another of those women to you. And I used to come first, Hobie—oh, I did! I did!"

"You did!" he said. "And you do!"

"And I always will?" she said.

"And you always will," he said, "as long as you'll only be your own self. Please be sweet again, Kit. Like this, darling. Like this, child."

Again they were close, and again there was no sound.

The telephone rang.

They started as if the same arrow had pierced them. Then the young woman moved slowly back.

"You know," she said, musingly, "this is my fault. I did this. It was me. I was the one that said let's meet here, and not at my house. I said it would be quieter, and I had so much I wanted to talk to you about. I said we could be quiet and alone here. Yes. I said that."

"I give you my word," he said, "that damn thing hasn't rung in a week."

"It was lucky for me, wasn't it?" she said, "that I happened to be here the last time it did. I am known as Little Miss Horseshoes. Well. Oh, please do answer it, Hobic. It drives me even crazier to have it ring like this."

"I hope to God," the young man said, "that it's a wrong number." He held her to him, hard. "Darling," he said. Then he went to the telephone.

"Hello," he said into the receiver. "Yes? Oh, hello there. How are you, dear—how are you? Oh, did you? Ah, that's too bad. Why, you see I was out with these friends of my—I was out till quite late. Oh, you did? Oh, that's too bad, dear, you waited up all that time. No, I did *not* say that, Margot, I said I'd come if I possibly could. That's exactly what I said. I did so. Well, then you misunderstood me. Well, you must have. Now, there's no need to be unreasonable about it. Listen, what I said, I said I'd come if it was possible, but I didn't think there was a chance. If you think hard, you'll remember, dear. Well, I'm terribly sorry, but I don't see what you're making so much fuss about. It was just a misunderstanding, that's all. Why don't you calm down and be a good little girl? Won't you? Why, I can't tonight, dear. Because I *can't*. Well, I have a date I've had for a long time. Yes. Oh, no, it isn't anything like that! Oh, now, please, Margot! Margot, please don't! Now don't do that! I tell you I won't be here. All right, come ahead, but I won't be in. Listen, I can't talk to you when you're like this. I'll call you tomorrow, dear. I tell you I won't be *in*, dear! Please be good. Certainly I do. Look. I have to run now. I'll call you, dear. 'By."

The young man came back to the living-room, and sent his somewhat shaken voice ahead of him.

"How about another cocktail, sweet?" he said. "Don't you think we really ought—" Through the thickening dark, he saw the young woman. She stood straight and tense. Her fur scarf was knotted about her shoulders, and she was drawing on her second glove.

"What's this about?" the young man said.

"I'm so sorry," the young woman said, "but I truly must go home."

"Oh, really?" he said. "May I ask why?"

"It's sweet of you," she said, "to be interested enough to want to know. Thank you so much. Well, it just happens, I can't stand any more of this. There is somewhere, I think, some proverb about a worm's eventually turning. It is doubtless from the Arabic. They so often are. Well, good night, Hobie, and thank you so much for those delicious cocktails. They've cheered me up wonderfully."

She held out her hand. He caught it tight in both of his.

"Ah, now listen," he said. "Please don't do this, Kit. Please, don't, darling. Please. This is just the way you were last Wednesday."

"Yes," she said. "And for exactly the same reason. Please give me back my hand. Thank you. Well, good night, Hobie, and good luck, always."

"All right," he said. "If this is what you want to do."

"Want to do!" she said. "It's nothing *I* want. I simply felt it would be rather easier for you if you could be alone, to receive your telephone calls. Surely you cannot blame me for feeling a bit *de trop*."

"My Lord, do you think I want to talk to those fools?" he said. "What can I do? Take the telephone receiver off? Is that what you want me to do?"

"It's a good trick of yours," she said. "I gather that was what you did last Wednesday night, when I kept trying to call you after I'd gone home, when I was in holy agony there."

"I did not!" he said. "They must have been calling the wrong number. I tell you I was alone here all the time you were gone."

"So you said," she said.

"I don't lie to you, Kit," he said.

"That," she said, "is the most outrageous lie you have ever told me. Good night, Hobie."

Only from the young man's eyes and voice could his anger be judged. The beautiful scroll of his mouth never straightened.

He took her hand and bowed over it.

"Good night, Kit," he said.

"Good night," she said. "Well, good night. I'm sorry it must end like this. But if you want other things—well, they're what you want. You can't have both them and me. Good night, Hobie."

"Good night, Kit," he said.

"I'm sorry," she said. "It does seem too bad. Doesn't it?"

"It's what you want," he said.

"I?" she said. "It's what *you* do."

"Oh, Kit, can't you understand?" he said. "You always used to. Don't you know how I am? I just say things and do things that don't mean anything, just for the sake of peace, just for the sake of not having a feud. That's what gets me in trouble. You don't have to do it, I know. You're luckier than I am."

"Luckier?" she said. "Curious word."

"Well, stronger, then," he said. "Finer. Honester. Decenter. All those. Ah, don't do this, Kit. Please. Please take those things off, and come sit down."

"Sit down?" she said. "And wait for the ladies to gather?"

"They're not coming," he said.

"How do you know?" she said. "They've come here before, haven't they? How do you know they won't come tonight?"

"I don't know!" he said. "I don't know what the hell they'll do. I don't know what the hell you'll do, any more. And I thought you were different!"

"I was different," she said, "just so long as you thought I was different."

"Ah, Kit," he said, "Kit. Darling. Come and be the way we were. Come and be sweet and peaceful. Look. Let's have a cocktail, just to each other, and then let's go out to some quiet place for dinner, where we can talk. Will you?"

"Well—" she said. "If you think——"

"I think," he said.

The telephone rang.

"Oh, my *God!*" shrieked the young woman. "Go answer it, you damned—you damned *stallion!*"

She rushed for the door, opened it, and was gone. She was,

after all, different. She neither slammed the door nor left it stark open.

The young man stood, and he shook his remarkable head slowly. Slowly, too, he turned and went into the bedroom.

He spoke into the telephone receiver drearily at first, then he seemed to enjoy both hearing and speaking. He used a woman's name in address. It was not Connie; it was not Evie; it was not Margot. Glowingly he besought the unseen one to meet him; tepidly he agreed to await her coming where he was. He besought her, then, to ring his bell first three times and then twice, for admission. No, no, no, he said, this was not for any reason that might have occurred to her; it was simply that some business friend of his had said something about dropping in, and he wanted to make sure there would be no such intruders. He spoke of his hopes, indeed his assurances, of an evening of sweetness and peace. He said "Good-by," and he said "dear."

The very good-looking young man hung up the receiver, and looked long at the dial of his wrist-watch, now delicately luminous. He seemed to be calculating. So long for a young woman to reach her home, and fling herself upon her couch, so long for tears, so long for exhaustion, so long for remorse, so long for rising tenderness. Thoughtfully he lifted the receiver from its hook and set it on end upon the little table.

Then he went into the living-room, and sped the dark before the tiny beams that sifted through the little open windows in the panoramas of Paris.

You Were Perfectly Fine

The pale young man eased himself carefully into the low chair, and rolled his head to the side, so that the cool chintz comforted his cheek and temple.

"Oh, dear," he said. "Oh, dear, oh, dear, oh, dear. Oh."

The clear-eyed girl, sitting light and erect on the couch, smiled brightly at him.

"Not feeling so well today?" she said.

"Oh, I'm great," he said. "Corking, I am. Know what time I got up? Four o'clock this afternoon, sharp. I kept trying to make it, and every time I took my head off the pillow, it would roll under the bed. This isn't my head I've got on now. I think this is something that used to belong to Walt Whitman. Oh, dear, oh, dear, oh, dear."

"Do you think maybe a drink would make you feel better?" she said.

"The hair of the mastiff that bit me?" he said. "Oh, no, thank you. Please never speak of anything like that again. I'm through. I'm all, all through. Look at that hand; steady as a humming-bird. Tell me, was I very terrible last night?"

"Oh, goodness," she said, "everybody was feeling pretty high. You were all right."

"Yeah," he said. "I must have been dandy. Is everybody sore at me?"

"Good heavens, no," she said. "Everyone thought you were terribly funny. Of course, Jim Pierson was a little stuffy, there, for a minute at dinner. But people sort of held him back in his chair, and got him calmed down. I don't think anybody at the other tables noticed it at all. Hardly anybody."

"He was going to sock me?" he said. "Oh, Lord. What did I do to him?"

"Why, you didn't do a thing," she said. "You were perfectly fine. But you know how silly Jim gets, when he thinks anybody is making too much fuss over Elinor."

"Was I making a pass at Elinor?" he said. "Did I do that?"

"Of course you didn't," she said. "You were only fooling, that's all. She thought you were awfully amusing. She was having a marvelous time. She only got a little tiny bit annoyed just once, when you poured the clam-juice down her back."

"My God," he said. "Clam-juice down that back. And every vertebra a little Cabot. Dear God. What'll I ever do?"

"Oh, she'll be all right," she said. "Just send her some flowers, or something. Don't worry about it. It isn't anything."

"No, I won't worry," he said. "I haven't got a care in the world. I'm sitting pretty. Oh, dear, oh, dear. Did I do any other fascinating tricks at dinner?"

"You were fine," she said. "Don't be so foolish about it. Everybody was crazy about you. The maître d'hôtel was a little worried because you wouldn't stop singing, but he really didn't mind. All he said was, he was afraid they'd close the place again, if there was so much noise. But he didn't care a bit, himself. I think he loved seeing you have such a good time. Oh, you were just singing away, there, for about an hour. It wasn't so terribly loud, at all."

"So I sang," he said. "That must have been a treat. I sang."

"Don't you remember?" she said. "You just sang one song after another. Everybody in the place was listening. They loved it. Only you kept insisting that you wanted to sing some song about some kind of fusiliers or other, and everybody kept shushing you, and you'd keep trying to start it again. You were wonderful. We were all trying to make you stop singing for a minute, and eat something, but you wouldn't hear of it. My, you were funny."

"Didn't I eat any dinner?" he said.

"Oh, not a thing," she said. "Every time the waiter would offer you something, you'd give it right back to him, because you said that he was your long-lost brother, changed in the cradle by a gypsy band, and that anything you had was his. You had him simply roaring at you."

"I bet I did," he said. "I bet I was comical. Society's Pet, I must have been. And what happened then, after my overwhelming success with the waiter?"

"Why, nothing much," she said. "You took a sort of dislike to some old man with white hair, sitting across the room, because you didn't like his necktie and you wanted to tell him about it. But we got you out, before he got really mad."

"Oh, we got out," he said. "Did I walk?"

"Walk! Of course you did," she said. "You were absolutely all right. There was that nasty stretch of ice on the sidewalk, and you did sit down awfully hard, you poor dear. But good heavens, that might have happened to anybody."

"Oh, sure," he said. "Louisa Alcott or anybody. So I fell down on the sidewalk. That would explain what's the matter with my—Yes. I see. And then what, if you don't mind?"

"Ah, now, Peter!" she said. "You can't sit there and say you don't remember what happened after that! I did think that maybe you were just a little tight at dinner—oh, you were perfectly all right, and all that, but I did know you were feeling pretty gay. But you were so serious, from the time you fell down—I never knew you to be that way. Don't you know, how you told me I had never seen your real self before? Oh, Peter, I just couldn't bear it, if you didn't remember that lovely long ride we took together in the taxi! Please, you do remember that, don't you? I think it would simply kill me, if you didn't."

"Oh, yes," he said. "Riding in the taxi. Oh, yes, sure. Pretty long ride, hmm?"

"Round and round and round the park," she said. "Oh, and the trees were shining so in the moonlight. And you said you never knew before that you really had a soul."

"Yes," he said. "I said that. That was me."

"You said such lovely, lovely things," she said. "And I'd never known, all this time, how you had been feeling about me, and I'd never dared to let you see how I felt about you. And then last night—oh, Peter dear, I think that taxi ride was the most important thing that ever happened to us in our lives."

"Yes," he said. "I guess it must have been."

"And we're going to be so happy," she said. "Oh, I just want to tell everybody! But I don't know—I think maybe it would be sweeter to keep it all to ourselves."

"I think it would be," he said.

"Isn't it lovely?" she said.

"Yes," he said. "Great."

"Lovely!" she said.

"Look here," he said, "do you mind if I have a drink? I mean, just medicinally, you know. I'm off the stuff for life, so help me. But I think I feel a collapse coming on."

"Oh, I think it would do you good," she said. "You poor boy, it's a shame you feel so awful. I'll go make you a whisky and soda."

"Honestly," he said, "I don't see how you could ever want to speak to me again, after I made such a fool of myself, last night. I think I'd better go join a monastery in Tibet."

"You crazy idiot!" she said. "As if I could ever let you go away now! Stop talking like that. You were perfectly fine."

She jumped up from the couch, kissed him quickly on the forehead, and ran out of the room.

The pale young man looked after her and shook his head long and slowly, then dropped it in his damp and trembling hands.

"Oh, dear," he said. "Oh, dear, oh, dear, oh, dear."

Mrs. Hofstadter on
Josephine Street

That summer, the Colonel and I leased a bungalow named 947 West Catalpa Boulevard, rumored completely furnished: three forks, but twenty-four nutpicks. Then we went to an employment agency, to hunt for treasure. The lady at the employment agency was built in terraces; she was of a steady pink, presumably all over, and a sky-wide capability. She bit into each of her words and seemed to find it savory, and she finished every sentence to the last crumb. When I am in the presence of such people I am frequently asked, "And what's the matter with Sister today? Has the cat got her tongue?" But they make the Colonel want to tell them what he done to Philadelphia Jack O'Brien.

So the Colonel did the talking for our team. The lady at the employment agency was of the prompt impression that I was something usually kept in the locked wing; she gave me a quick, kind nod, as who should say "Now you just sit there quietly and count those twelve fingers of yours," and then she and the Colonel left me out of the whole project. We wanted, the Colonel said, a man; a man to market, to cook, to serve, to remember about keeping the cigarette-boxes filled, and to clean the little house. We wanted a man, he said, because maids, at least those in our experience, talked a good deal of the time. We were worn haggard with unsolicited autobiographies. We must insist, he said, that our servant be, before all things, still.

"My wife," said the Colonel—the lady and I waited for him to add, "the former Miss Kallikak"—"my wife must never be disturbed."

"*I* see," the lady said. She sighed a little.

"She writes," the Colonel said.

"And pretty soon now," the lady and I inferred, "we must look around for someone to come in a couple of hours a week and teach her to read."

The Colonel went on talking about what we wanted. It was but little. The simplest food, he said. The lady nodded compassionately at him; surely she pictured him standing with extended dish trying to coax me in from eating clay. The quietest life, he said, the earliest hours, the fewest guests—it was a holiday, really, to live with us. We asked only someone to stand between us and the telephone, someone to flick from the doorstep young gentlemen soliciting subscriptions to magazines, someone to keep, at other times and in so far as possible, his face shut.

"Don't you say another word!" the lady said. She smacked that "say" as if it had been delicious with salt and onion. "Not one other word. I've got just the thing!"

Horace Wrenn, she said, was the thing. He was colored, she said, but fine. I was so deeply pondering the selection of "but" that I missed several courses in her repast of words. When next I heard her, a new name had sprung in.

"He's been with Mrs. Hofstadter off and on," she said. She looked triumphant. I looked as if all my life I had heard that anybody who had ever been with Mrs. Hofstadter, either off or on, was beyond question the thing. The Colonel looked much as usual.

"Mrs. Hofstadter on Josephine Street," the lady explained. "That's our loveliest residential district. She has a lovely home there. She's one of our loveliest families. Mrs. Hofstadter—well, wait till you see what *she* says!"

She took from her desk a sheet of notepaper spread with a handwriting like the lesser rivers on maps. It was Mrs. Hofstadter on Josephine Street's letter of recommendation of Horace Wrenn, and it must have been a sort of blending of the Ninety-Eighth Psalm with Senator Vest's tribute to his dog. Whatever it was, it was too good for the likes of us to see. The lady held it tight and slipped her gaze along its lines with clucks and smacks of ecstasy and cries of "Well, look at this, will you—'honest, economical, good carver'—well!" and "My, this *is* a reference for you!"

Then she locked the letter in her desk, and she talked to the Colonel. He is to be had only with difficulty, but she got him, and good. She congratulated him upon the softness of his fortune. She marveled that it was given him to find, and without effort, the blue rose. She envied him the life that would be his when perfection came to house with him. She sighed for the exquisite dishes, the smooth attentions that were to be offered him, ever in silence, by competence and humility, blent and incarnate. He was to have, she told him, just everything, and that without moving a hand or answering a question. There was only one little catch to it, she said; and the Colonel went gray. Horace could not come to us until the day after the next one. Mrs. Hofstadter on Josephine Street's daughter was to be married, and Horace had charge of the breakfast. It was touching to hear the Colonel plead his willingness to wait.

"Well, then I guess that's all," the lady said, briskly. She rose. "If you aren't the luckiest! You just run right along home now, and wait for Horace." Her air added, "And take Soft Susie, the Girl Who Is Like Anybody Else Till the Moon Comes Up, with you. We want no naturals here!"

We went home, sweet in thought of the luxury to come; though the Colonel, who is of a melancholy cast, took to worrying a little because Horace might not go back to New York with us when the summer was over.

Until the arrival of Horace, we did what is known as making out somehow, which is a big phrase for it. It was found to be best, after fair trial, for me to stay out of the kitchen altogether. So the Colonel did the cooking, and tomatoes kept creeping into everything, which gave him delusions of persecution. It was also found better for me to avoid any other room. The last time I made the bed, the Colonel came in and surveyed the result.

"What is this?" he inquired. "Some undergraduate prank?"

Horace arrived in the afternoon, toward the cool of the day. No bell or knocker heralded his coming; simply, he was with us in the living-room. He carried a suitcase of some leathery material, and upon his head he retained a wide white straw hat with drooping brim, rather like something chosen by a duchess for garden-party wear. He was tall and broad, with an enormous cinder-colored face crossed by gold-encircled spectacles.

He spoke to us. As if coated with grease, words slid from his great lips, and his tones were those of one who cozens the sick.

"Here," he said, "is Horace. Horace has come to take care of you."

He set down his suitcase and removed his hat, revealing oiled hair, purple in the sunlight, plaided over with thin, dusty lines; Horace employed a hair-net. He laid his hat upon a table. He advanced and gave to each of us one of his hands. I received the left, the middle finger of which was missing, leaving in its stead a big, square gap.

"I want you to feel," he said, "that I am going to think of this as my home. That is the way I will think of it. I always try to think the right thing. When I told my friends I was coming here, I said to them, I said, 'That is my home from now on.' You are going to meet my friends; yes, you are. I want you to meet my friends. My friends can tell you more about me than I can. Mrs. Hofstadter always says to me, 'Horace,' she says, 'I never heard anything like it,' she says. 'Your friends just can't say enough for you.' I have a great many friends, boy friends and lady friends. Mrs. Hofstadter always tells me, 'Horace,' she says, 'I never seen anybody had so many friends.' Mrs. Hofstadter on Josephine Street. She has a lovely home there; I want you to see her home. When I told her I was coming here, 'Oh, my, Horace,' she said, 'what'm I ever going to do without you?' I have served Mrs. Hofstadter for years, right there on Josephine Street. 'Oh, my, Horace,' she said, 'how'm I going to get along without Horace?' But I had promised to come to you folks, and Horace never goes back on his word. I am a big man, and I always try to do the big thing."

"Well, look," said the Colonel, "suppose I show you where your room is and you can——"

"I want you," Horace said, "to get to know me. And I'm going to get to know you, too; yes, I am. I always try to do the right thing for the folks I serve. I want you to get to know that girl of mine, too. When I tell my friends I have a daughter twelve years of age in September, 'Horace,' they say, 'I can hardly believe it!' You're going to meet that girl of mine; yes, you are. She'll come up here, and she'll talk right up to you; yes, and she'll sit down and play that piano there—play it all day long. I don't say it because I'm her father, but that's the brightest girl *you* ever seen. People say she's Horace all over. Mrs. Hofstadter on Josephine Street, she said to me, 'Horace,' she said, 'I can't hardly tell which is the girl and which is Horace.' Oh, there's nothing of her mother's side about *that* girl! I never could get on with her mother. I try never to say an unkind thing about nobody. I'm a big man, and I always try to do the big thing. But I never could live with her mother more than fifteen minutes at a time."

"Look," the Colonel said, "the kitchen's right in there, and your room is just off it, and you can——"

"Why, do you know," Horace said, "that girl of mine, she's taken for white every day in the week. Yes, sir. I bet you there's a hundred people, right in this town, never dreams that girl of mine's a colored girl. And you're going to meet my sister, too, some of these days pretty soon. My sister's just about the finest hairdresser *you* ever set *your* eyes on. And never touches a colored head, either. She's just about like what I am. I try never to say an unkind thing, I don't hold nothing against the colored race, but Horace just doesn't mix up with them, that's all."

I thought of a man I had known once named Aaron Eisenberg, who changed his name to Erik Colton. Nothing ever became of him.

"Look," the Colonel said, "your room's right off the kitchen, and if you've got a white coat with you you can——"

"Has Horace got a white coat!" Horace said. "Has he got a white coat! Why, when you see Horace in that white coat of his, you're going to say, just like Mrs. Hofstadter on Josephine Street says, 'Horace,' you're going to say, 'I never seen anybody look any nicer.' Yes, *sir*, I've got that white coat. I never forget anything; that's one thing I *don't* do. Now do you know what Horace is going to do for you? Do you *know* what he's going to do? Well, he's going out there in that kitchen, just like it was Mrs. Hofstadter's lovely big kitchen of hers, and he's going to fix you the best dinner *you* ever et in *your* life. I always try to make everybody happy; when people are happy, then I'm happy. That's the way I am. Mrs. Hofstadter said to me, sitting right there in her lovely home on Josephine Street, 'Horace,' she said, 'I don't know who these people are you're going to's,' she said, 'but I can tell you,' Mrs. Hofstadter said, 'they're going to be happy.' I just said, 'Thank you, Mrs. Hofstadter.' That's all I said. I've served her many years. And you're going to see that lovely home of hers, some of these days; yes, you are."

He gathered up his hat and his suitcase, smiled slowly upon us, and went into the kitchen.

The Colonel walked over to the window and stood for a while, looking out of it.

I said, "You know, I think if we play our cards right we can find out who Horace used to work for."

"For whom Horace used to work," the Colonel said, mechanically.

Horace returned. He wore a white coat and an apron that covered him in front to his shoe-leather. My mind went to Pullman dining-cars, and I remembered, with no pleasure, preserved figs and cream.

"Here's Horace," he said. "Now Horace is all ready to try and make you happy. Do you know what Horace is going to do for you, some of these days? Do you *know* what he's going to do? Well, he's just going to make you one of those mint juleps of his, that's what *he's* going to do! Mrs. Hofstadter of Josephine Street always says, 'Horace,' she says, 'when you going to make one of those mint juleps of yours?' Well, I'll tell you what Horace does; he doesn't care how much trouble he takes, when he's making people happy. First he goes to work and he takes some pineapple syrup and he puts it in a glass, and then he puts in just a liddle, lid-dle bit of that juice off them bottles full of red cherries, and then he puts in the gin and the ginger ale, and then he gets him a big, long piece of pineapple and he lays *that* in, and then when he gets the orange in and puts that old red cherry on top—well! That's the way *Horace* does when he fixes a mint julep."

The Colonel is from the old South. He left the room.

Horace came at me with his head lowered and a great

forefinger pointed at the level of my eyes. I was terrified for only a moment. Then I saw it for gigantic archness.

"Wait'll you hear," he said, "wait'll you hear how that telephone is going to ring, soon as my friends find out this is Horace's home. Why I bet you right this minute, Mrs. Hofstadter on Josephine Street's telephone is ringing away, first this one and then that one, 'Where's Horace?' 'How'm I going to reach Horace?' I don't talk about myself, I always try to be just the way I'd want you to be with me, but you're going to say you never seen anybody had so many lady friends. Yes, *sir,* and when you meet them, you're going to say, 'Horace,' you're going to say, 'why, Horace, I'd take any one of them for as white as I am any day in the week.' That's what *you're* going to say. Wait'll you hear the fun there's going to be around this place when that telephone starts, 'How are you, Horace?' 'What are you doing, Horace?' 'When'm I going to see you, Horace?' I'm not going to talk about myself any more than I'd want you to talk about *yourself,* but you wait'll you see all those friends I have. Why, Mrs. Hofstadter on Josephine Street always says, 'Horace,' she says, 'I never——' "

The Colonel came back. "Look, Horace," he said, "would you——"

"Well, now, say, if you want to talk about friends," Horace said, "I just don't mind telling you that out at Mrs. Hofstadter on Josephine Street's daughter's wedding here yesterday, there wasn't a guest there wasn't a friend of Horace's. There they all was, oh, a hundred, a hundred fifty people, all of them talking right up, 'Hello, Horace,' 'Glad to see you, Horace.' Yes, sir, and not a colored face there, either. I just said, 'Thank you.' I always try to say the right thing, and that's what I said. Mrs. Hofstadter, she said to me, 'Horace,' she said——"

"Horace," I said, nor knew, perhaps, that it would stand my only complete speech with him, "may I have a glass of water, please?"

"Can you have a glass of water!" Horace said. "Can you have a glass of water! Well, I'll tell you just what Horace is going to do. He's going out there in that kitchen, and he's going to bring you just the biggest, coldest glass of water *you* ever had in *your* life. There's going to be nothing too good for *you*, now Horace is here. Why, he's going to do for you just like you was Mrs. Hofstadter, out in her lovely home on Josephine Street; yes, he is."

He left, turning his head archly back over his shoulder to bestow his parting smile.

The Colonel said, "I wonder which Mrs. Hofstadter that is."

"I keep getting her mixed up with the one that lives somewhere near Josephine Street," I said.

Horace returned with the water, and spoke to us. Through his preparations for dinner, he spoke to us. Through dinner, which was held at six o'clock, according to the custom obtaining in Mrs. Hofstadter on Josephine Street's lovely home, he spoke to us. We sat there. Once the Colonel asked Horace for something, and so learned his lesson forever. Better go without a service than bring on rich and recommended assurances of the tender perfection of its fulfillment.

I cannot remember the menu. I can bring back, while faintness spirals upward through me, an impression of waxen gray gravy, loose pink gelatine, and butter at blood-heat, specialties finer than which Mrs. Hofstadter on Josephine Street had never et. Over more definite items, memory draws her merciful gray curtain. She does, for that matter, over all the events of Horace's stay with us. I do not know how long that was. There were no days, there were no nights, there was no time. There was only space; space filled with Horace.

The Colonel, for it is a man's world, was away from the bungalow during the day. Horace was there. Horace was always there. I have known no being so present in a house as was Horace. I never knew him to open a door, I never heard his approaching footfall; Horace was out of the room and then, a thousand times more frequently, Horace was in it. I sat at my typewriter, and Horace stood across from it and spoke to me.

And in the evenings, when the Colonel returned, Horace spoke to us. All his conversation was for us, for none of his friends, boy friends or lady friends, ever called him to hold talk; it may be that Mrs. Hofstadter on Josephine Street could not bring herself to share his telephone number. The Colonel and I did not look at each other; after a little while we avoided each other's eyes. Perhaps it was that we did not wish to see each other in our shame. I do not know; I know nothing about those days. I am sure, after confirmation, that we did not think, either of us, "In heaven's name, what manner of worm is this I have married?" We had no thoughts, no spirits, no actions. We ceased to move from room to room, even from chair to chair. We stayed where we were, two vile, dead things, slowly drowned in warmish, sweetish oil. There we were, for eternity, world without end, with Horace.

But an end came. I have never known what brought it on, nor have I wanted to learn. Once your pardon arrives, what's it to you what induced the governor's signature? The Colonel said, afterward, that Horace said it once too often; but that is all I ever knew. All I know is that I came into the living-room one morning, one heavenly morning of sunshine, and heard the Colonel's voice upraised in the kitchen. People who happened to be passing through the town on trains at that time could also have heard the Colonel's voice upraised in the kitchen.

He was giving, it seemed, advice to Horace. "You go," it ran, "and you go now!"

I heard Horace's tones, those of one quieting a problem child, but they were so low I received few words. "—spoken to this way," I distinguished, and "—loveliest people in this town. Why, Mrs. Hofstadter on Josephine Street, she wouldn't never——"

Then the Colonel's voice had everything its way again. He gave a fresh piece of advice. He suggested, as a beginning, that Horace take Mrs. Hofstadter and take her lovely home and take her whole goddam Josephine Street——

The Colonel was free. He was so free that he stood, straight shouldered on the sunlit porch, and sated his eyes on the back of Horace, receding down the path. Mrs. Hofstadter on Josephine Street's words had come true. She had not known who those people were that Horace was going to's, but she had known they were going to be happy. We were alone; tomatoes might start following us around again, but that was the worst that could happen to us.

So it was ten minutes before the telephone rang. Crazed with joy at the return of my tongue, I answered it. I heard a large voice, slithering along the wire like warm cottonseed oil.

"This," it said, "is Horace. Horace is speaking. I am a big man and I always try to do the big thing, and I want to tell you that I am sorry Horace left your home so impetuous; yes, I am: I want you to know that Horace is going to come back to your home again and serve you, just like for so many years he served——"

But somehow the receiver clicked into place and I never had to hear her name again.

Soldiers of the Republic

That Sunday afternoon we sat with the Swedish girl in the big café in Valencia. We had vermouth in thick goblets, each with a cube of honey-combed gray ice in it. The waiter was so proud of that ice he could hardly bear to leave the glasses on the table, and thus part from it forever. He went to his duty—all over the room they were clapping their hands and hissing to draw his attention—but he looked back over his shoulder.

It was dark outside, the quick, new dark that leaps down without dusk on the day; but, because there were no lights in the streets, it seemed as set and as old as midnight. So you wondered that all the babies were still up. There were babies everywhere in the café, babies serious without solemnity and interested in a tolerant way in their surroundings.

At the table next ours, there was a notably small one; maybe six months old. Its father, a little man in a big uniform that dragged his shoulders down, held it carefully on his knee. It was doing nothing whatever, yet he and his thin young wife, whose belly was already big again under her sleazy dress, sat watching it in a sort of ecstasy of admiration, while their coffee cooled in front of them. The baby was in Sunday white; its dress was patched so delicately that you would have thought the fabric whole had not the patches varied in their shades of whiteness. In its hair was a bow of new blue ribbon, tied with absolute balance of loops and ends. The ribbon was of no use; there was not enough hair to require restraint. The bow was sheerly an adornment, a calculated bit of dash.

"Oh, for God's sake, stop that!" I said to myself. "All right, so it's got a piece of blue ribbon on its hair. All right, so its mother went without eating so it could look pretty when its father came home on leave. All right, so it's her business, and none of yours. All right, so what have you got to cry about?"

The big, dim room was crowded and lively. That morning

there had been a bombing from the air, the more horrible for broad daylight. But nobody in the café sat tense and strained, nobody desperately forced forgetfulness. They drank coffee or bottled lemonade, in the pleasant, earned ease of Sunday afternoon, chatting of small, gay matters, all talking at once, all hearing and answering.

There were many soldiers in the room, in what appeared to be the uniforms of twenty different armies until you saw that the variety lay in the differing ways the cloth had worn or faded. Only a few of them had been wounded; here and there you saw one stepping gingerly, leaning on a crutch or two canes, but so far on toward recovery that his face had color. There were many men, too, in civilian clothes—some of them soldiers home on leave, some of them governmental workers, some of them anybody's guess. There were plump, comfortable wives, active with paper fans, and old women as quiet as their grandchildren. There were many pretty girls and some beauties, for whom you did not remark, "There's a charming Spanish type," but said, "What a beautiful girl!" The women's clothes were not new, and their material was too humble ever to have warranted skillful cutting.

"It's funny," I said to the Swedish girl, "how when nobody in a place is best-dressed, you don't notice that everybody isn't."

"Please?" the Swedish girl said.

No one, save an occasional soldier, wore a hat. When we had first come to Valencia, I lived in a state of puzzled pain as to why everybody on the streets laughed at me. It was not because "West End Avenue" was writ across my face as if left there by a customs officer's chalked scrawl. They like Americans in Valencia, where they have seen good ones—the doctors who left their practices and came to help, the calm young nurses, the men of the International Brigade. But when I walked forth, men and women courteously laid their hands across their splitting faces and little children, too innocent for dissembling, doubled with glee and pointed and cried, *"Olé!"* Then, pretty late, I made my discovery, and left my hat off; and there was laughter no longer. It was not one of those comic hats, either; it was just a hat.

The café filled to overflow, and I left our table to speak to a friend across the room. When I came back to the table, six soldiers were sitting there. They were crowded in, and I scraped past them to my chair. They looked tired and dusty and little, the way that the newly dead look little, and the first things you saw about them were the tendons in their necks. I felt like a prize sow.

They were all in conversation with the Swedish girl. She has Spanish, French, German, anything in Scandinavian, Italian, and English. When she has a moment for regret, she sighs that her Dutch is so rusty she can no longer speak it, only read it, and the same is true of her Rumanian.

They had told her, she told us, that they were at the end of forty-eight hours' leave from the trenches, and, for their holiday, they had all pooled their money for cigarettes, and something had gone wrong, and the cigarettes had never come through to them. I had a pack of American cigarettes—in Spain rubies are as nothing to them—and I brought it out, and by nods and smiles and a sort of breast stroke, made it understood that I was offering it to those six men yearning for tobacco. When they saw what I meant, each one of them rose and shook my hand. Darling of me to share my cigarettes with the men on their way back to the trenches. Little Lady Bountiful. The prize sow.

Each one lit his cigarette with a contrivance of yellow rope that stank when afire and was also used, the Swedish girl translated, for igniting grenades. Each one received what he had ordered, a glass of coffee, and each one murmured appreciatively over the tiny cornucopia of coarse sugar that accompanied it. Then they talked.

They talked through the Swedish girl, but they did to us that thing we all do when we speak our own language to one who has no knowledge of it. They looked us square in the face, and spoke slowly, and pronounced their words with elaborate movements of their lips. Then, as their stories came, they poured them at us so vehemently, so emphatically that they were sure we must understand. They were so convinced we would understand that we were ashamed for not understanding.

But the Swedish girl told us. They were all farmers and farmers' sons, from a district so poor that you try not to remember there is that kind of poverty. Their village was next that one where the old men and the sick men and the women and children had gone, on a holiday, to the bullring; and the planes had come over and dropped bombs on the bullring, and the old men and the sick men and the women and the children were more than two hundred.

They had all, the six of them, been in the war for over a year, and most of that time they had been in the trenches. Four of them were married. One had one child, two had three children, one had five. They had not had word from their families since they had left for the front. There had been no communication; two of them had learned to write from men fighting next them in the trench, but they had not dared to write home. They belonged to a union, and union men, of course, are put to death if taken. The village where their families lived had been captured, and if your wife gets a letter from a union man, who knows but they'll shoot her for the connection?

They told about how they had not heard from their families for more than a year. They did not tell it gallantly or whimsically or stoically. They told it as if—Well, look. You have been in the trenches, fighting, for a year. You have heard nothing of your wife and your children. They do not know if you are dead or alive or blinded. You do not know where they are, or if they are. You must talk to somebody. That is the way they told about it.

One of them, some six months before, had heard of his wife and his three children—they had such beautiful eyes, he said— from a brother-in-law in France. They were all alive then, he was told, and had a bowl of beans a day. But his wife had not complained of the food, he heard. What had troubled her was

·that she had no thread to mend the children's ragged clothes. So that troubled him, too.

"She has no thread," he kept telling us. "My wife has no thread to mend with. No thread."

We sat there, and listened to what the Swedish girl told us they were saying. Suddenly one of them looked at the clock, and then there was excitement. They jumped up, as a man, and there were calls for the waiter and rapid talk with him, and each of them shook the hand of each of us. We went through more swimming motions to explain to them that they were to take the rest of the cigarettes—fourteen cigarettes for six soldiers to take to war—and then they shook our hands again. Then all of us said *"Salud!"* as many times as could be for six of them and three of us, and then they filed out of the café, the six of them, tired and dusty and little, as men of a mighty horde are little.

Only the Swedish girl talked, after they had gone. The Swedish girl has been in Spain since the start of the war. She has nursed splintered men, and she has carried stretchers into the trenches and, heavier laden, back to the hospital. She has seen and heard too much to be knocked into silence.

Presently it was time to go, and the Swedish girl raised her hands above her head and clapped them twice together to summon the waiter. He came, but he only shook his head and his hand, and moved away.

The soldiers had paid for our drinks.

Too Bad

"My dear," Mrs. Marshall said to Mrs. Ames, "I never was so surprised in my life. Never in my life. Why, Grace and I were like that—just like *that*."

She held up her right hand, the upstanding first and second fingers rigidly close together, in illustration.

Mrs. Ames shook her head sadly, and offered the cinnamon toast.

"Imagine!" said Mrs. Marshall, refusing it though with a longing eye. "We were going to have dinner with them last Tuesday night, and then I got this letter from Grace from this little place up in Connecticut, saying she was going to be up there she didn't know how long, and she thought, when she came back, she'd probably take just one big room with a kitchenette. Ernest was living down at the club, she said."

"But what did they do about their apartment?" Mrs. Ames's voice was high with anxiety.

"Why, it seems his sister took it, furnished and all—by the way, remind me, I must go and see her," said Mrs. Marshall. "They wanted to move into town, anyway, and they were looking for a place."

"Doesn't she feel terribly about it—his sister?" asked Mrs. Ames.

"Oh—terribly." Mrs. Marshall dismissed the word as inadequate. "My dear, think how everybody that knew them feels. Think how I feel. I don't know when I've had a thing depress me more. If it had been anybody but the Weldons!"

Mrs. Ames nodded.

"That's what I said," she reported.

"That's what everybody says." Mrs. Marshall quickly took away any undeserved credit. "To think of the Weldons separating! Why, I always used to say to Jim, 'Well, there's one happily married couple, anyway,' I used to say, 'so congenial, and with that nice apartment, and all.' And then, right out of a clear sky, they go and separate. I simply can't understand what on earth made them do it. It just seems too awful!"

Again Mrs. Ames nodded, slowly and sadly.

"Yes, it always seems too bad, a thing like that does," she said. "It's too bad."

II

Mrs. Ernest Weldon wandered about the orderly living-room, giving it some of those little feminine touches. She was not especially good as a touch-giver. The idea was pretty, and appealing to her. Before she was married, she had dreamed of herself as moving softly about her new dwelling, deftly moving a vase here or straightening a flower there, and thus transforming it from a house to a home. Even now, after seven years of marriage, she liked to picture herself in the gracious act.

But, though she conscientiously made a try at it every night as soon as the rose-shaded lamps were lit, she was always a bit bewildered as to how one went about performing those tiny miracles that make all the difference in the world to a room. The living-room, it seemed to her, looked good enough as it was—as good as it would ever look, with that mantelpiece and the same old furniture. Delia, one of the most thoroughly feminine of creatures, had subjected it to a long series of emphatic touches earlier in the day, and none of her handiwork had since been disturbed. But the feat of making all the difference in the world, so Mrs. Weldon had always heard, was not a thing to be left to servants. Touch-giving was a wife's job. And Mrs. Weldon was not one to shirk the business she had entered.

With an almost pitiable air of uncertainty, she strayed over to the mantel, lifted a small Japanese vase, and stood with it in her hand, gazing helplessly around the room. The white-enameled bookcase caught her eye, and gratefully she crossed to it and set the vase upon it, carefully rearranging various ornaments to make room. To relieve the congestion, she took up a framed photograph of Mr. Weldon's sister in evening gown and eye-glasses, again looked all about, and then set it timidly on the piano. She smoothed the piano-cover ingratiatingly, straightened the copies of "A Day in Venice," "To a Wild Rose," and Kreisler's "Caprice Viennois," which stood ever upon the rack, walked over to the tea-table and effected a change of places between the cream-jug and the sugar-bowl.

Then she stepped back, and surveyed her innovations. It was amazing how little difference they made to the room.

Sighing, Mrs. Weldon turned her attention to a bowl of daffodils, slightly past their first freshness. There was nothing to be done there; the omniscient Delia had refreshed them with clear water, had clipped their stems, and removed their more passé sisters. Still Mrs. Weldon bent over them pulling them gently about.

She liked to think of herself as one for whom flowers would thrive, who must always have blossoms about her, if she would be truly happy. When her living-room flowers died, she almost never forgot to stop in at the florist's, the next day, and get a fresh bunch. She told people, in little bursts of confidence, that she loved flowers. There was something almost apologetic in her way of uttering her tender avowal, as if she would beg her listeners not to consider her too bizarre in her taste. It seemed rather as though she expected the hearer to fall back, startled, at her words, crying, "Not really! Well, what *are* we coming to?"

She had other little confessions of affection, too, that she made from time to time; always with a little hesitation, as if understandably delicate about baring her heart, she told her love for color, the country, a good time, a really interesting play, nice materials, well-made clothes, and sunshine. But it was her fondness for flowers that she acknowledged oftenest. She seemed to feel that this, even more than her other predilections, set her apart from the general.

Mrs. Weldon gave the elderly daffodils a final pat, now, and once more surveyed the room, to see if any other repairs suggested themselves. Her lips tightened as the little Japanese vase met her gaze; distinctly, it had been better off in the first place. She set it back, the irritation that the sight of the mantel always gave her welling within her.

She had hated the mantelpiece from the moment they had first come to look at the apartment. There were other things that she had always hated about the place, too—the long, narrow hall, the dark dining-room, the inadequate closets. But Ernest had seemed to like the apartment well enough, so she had said nothing, then or since. After all, what was the use of fussing? Probably there would always be drawbacks, wherever they lived. There were enough in the last place they had had.

So they had taken the apartment on a five-year lease—there were four years and three months to go. Mrs. Weldon felt suddenly weary. She lay down on the davenport, and pressed her thin hand against her dull brown hair.

Mr. Weldon came down the street, bent almost double in his battle with the wind from the river. His mind went over its nightly dark thoughts on living near Riverside Drive, five blocks from a subway station—two of those blocks loud with savage gales. He did not much like their apartment, even when he reached it. As soon as he had seen that dining-room, he had realized that they must always breakfast by artificial light—a thing he hated. But Grace had never appeared to notice it, so he had held his peace. It didn't matter much, anyway, he explained to himself. There was pretty sure to be something wrong, everywhere. The dining-room wasn't much worse than that bedroom on the court, in the last place. Grace had never seemed to mind that, either.

Mrs. Weldon opened the door at his ring.

"Well!" she said, cheerily.

They smiled brightly at each other.

"Hel-lo," he said. "Well! You home?"

They kissed, slightly. She watched with polite interest while he hung up his hat and coat, removed the evening papers from his pocket, and handed one to her.

"Bring the papers?" she said, taking it.

She preceded him along the narrow hall to the living-room, where he let himself slowly down into his big chair, with a sound between a sigh and a groan. She sat opposite him, on the davenport. Again they smiled brightly at each other.

"Well, what have you been doing with yourself today?" he inquired.

She had been expecting the question. She had planned before he came in, how she would tell him all the little events of her day—how the woman in the grocer's shop had had an argument with the cashier, and how Delia had tried out a new salad for lunch with but moderate success, and how Alice Marshall had come to tea and it was quite true that Norma Matthews was going to have another baby. She had woven them into a lively little narrative, carefully choosing amusing phrases of description; had felt that she was going to tell it well and with spirit, and that he might laugh at the account of the occurrence in the grocer's. But now, as she considered it, it seemed to her a long, dull story. She had not the energy to begin it. And he was already smoothing out his paper.

"Oh, nothing," she said, with a gay little laugh. "Did you have a nice day?"

"Why—" he began. He had had some idea of telling her how he had finally put through that Detroit thing, and how tickled J. G. had seemed to be about it. But his interest waned, even as he started to speak. Besides, she was engrossed in breaking off a loose thread from the wool fringe of one of the pillows beside her.

"Oh, pretty fair," he said.

"Tired?" she asked.

"Not so much," he answered. "Why—want to do anything tonight?"

"Why, not unless you do," she said, brightly. "Whatever you say."

"Whatever *you say*," he corrected her.

The subject closed. There was a third exchange of smiles, and then he hid most of himself behind his paper.

Mrs. Weldon, too, turned to the newspaper. But it was an off night for news—a long speech of somebody's, a plan for a garbage dump, a proposed dirigible, a four-day-old murder mystery. No one she knew had died or become engaged or married, or had attended any social functions. The fashions depicted on the woman's page were for Miss Fourteen-to-Sixteen. The advertisements ran mostly to bread, and sauces, and men's clothes and sales of kitchen utensils. She put the paper down.

She wondered how Ernest could get so much enjoyment out of a newspaper. He could occupy himself with one for almost an hour, and then pick up another and go all through the same news with unabated interest. She wished that she could. She wished, even more than that, that she could think of something to say. She glanced around the room for inspiration.

"See my pretty daffy-down-dillies?" she said, finding it. To anyone else, she would have referred to them as daffodils.

Mr. Weldon looked in the direction of the flowers.

"M-m-mm," he said in admission, and returned to the news.

She looked at him, and shook her head despondently. He did not see, behind the paper; nor did she see that he was not reading. He was waiting, his hands gripping the printed sheet till their knuckles were blue-white, for her next remark.

It came.

"I love flowers," she said, in one of her little rushes of confidence.

Her husband did not answer. He sighed, his grip relaxed, and he went on reading.

Mrs. Weldon searched the room for another suggestion.

"Ernie," she said, "I'm so comfortable. Wouldn't you like to get up and get my handkerchief off the piano for me?"

He rose instantly. "Why, certainly," he said.

The way to ask people to fetch handkerchiefs, he thought as he went back to his chair, was to ask them to do it, and not try to make them think that you were giving them a treat. Either come right out and ask them, would they or wouldn't they, or else get up and get your handkerchief yourself.

"Thank you ever so much," his wife said with enthusiasm.

Delia appeared in the doorway. "Dinner," she murmured bashfully, as if it were not quite a nice word for a young woman to use, and vanished.

"Dinner," cried Mrs. Weldon gaily, getting up.

"Just a minute," issued indistinctly from behind the newspaper.

Mrs. Weldon waited. Then her lips compressed, and she went over and playfully took the paper from her husband's hands. She smiled carefully at him, and he smiled back at her.

"You go ahead in," he said, rising. "I'll be right with you. I've just got to wash up."

She looked after him, and something like a volcanic eruption took place within her. You'd think that just one night—just one little night—he might go and wash before dinner was announced. Just one night—it didn't seem much to ask. But she said nothing. God knew it was aggravating, but after all, it wasn't worth the trouble of fussing about.

She was waiting, cheerful and bright, courteously refraining from beginning her soup, when he took his place at the table.

"Oh, tomato soup, eh?" he said.

"Yes," she answered. "You like it, don't you?"

"Who—me?" he said. "Oh, yes. Yes, indeed."

She smiled at him.

"Yes, I thought you liked it," she said.

"You like it, too, don't you?" he inquired.

"Oh, yes," she assured him. "Yes, I like it ever so much. I'm awfully fond of tomato soup."

"Yes," he said, "there's nothing much better than tomato soup on a cold night."

She nodded.

"I think it's nice, too," she confided.

They had had tomato soup for dinner probably three times a month during their married life.

The soup was finished, and Delia brought in the meat.

"Well, that looks pretty good," said Mr. Weldon, carving it. "We haven't had steak for a long time."

"Why, yes, we have, too, Ern," his wife said eagerly. "We had it—let me see, what night were the Baileys here?—we had it Wednesday night—no, Thursday night. Don't you remember?"

"Did we?" he said. "Yes, I guess you're right. It seemed longer, somehow."

Mrs. Weldon smiled politely. She could not think of any way to prolong the discussion.

What did married people talk about, anyway, when they were alone together? She had seen married couples—not dubious ones but people she really knew were husbands and wives—at the theater or in trains, talking together as animatedly as if they were just acquaintances. She always watched them, marvelingly, wondering what on earth they found to say.

She could talk well enough to other people. There never seemed to be enough time for her to finish saying all she wanted to to her friends; she recalled how she had run on to Alice Marshall, only that afternoon. Both men and women found her attractive to listen to; not brilliant, not particularly funny, but still amusing and agreeable. She was never at a loss for something to say, never conscious of groping around for a topic. She had a good memory for bits of fresh gossip, or little stories of some celebrity that she had read or heard somewhere, and a knack of telling them entertainingly. Things people said to her stimulated her to quick replies, and more amusing narratives. They weren't especially scintillating people, either; it was just that they talked to her.

That was the trick of it. If nobody said anything to you, how were you to carry on a conversation from there? Inside, she was always bitter and angry at Ernest for not helping her out.

Ernest, too, seemed to be talkative enough when he was with others. People were always coming up and telling her how much they had enjoyed meeting her husband, and what fun he was. They weren't just being polite. There was no reason why they should go out of their way to say it.

Even when she and Ernest had another couple in to dinner or bridge, they both talked and laughed easily, all evening long. But as soon as the guests said goodnight and what an awfully nice evening it had been, and the door had closed behind them, there the Weldons were again, without a word to say to each other. It would have been intimate and amusing to have talked over their guests' clothes and skill at bridge and probable domestic and financial affairs, and she would do it the next day, with great interest, too, to Alice Marshall, or some other one of her friends. But she couldn't do it with Ernest. Just as she started to, she found she simply couldn't make the effort.

So they would put away the card-table and empty the ash-receivers, with many "Oh, I beg your pardon's" and "No, no— I was in your way's," and then Ernest would say, "Well, I guess I'll go along to bed," and she would answer, "All right—I'll be in in a minute," and they would smile cheerfully at each other, and another evening would be over.

She tried to remember what they used to talk about before they were married, when they were engaged. It seemed to her that they never had had much to say to each other. But she hadn't worried about it then; indeed, she had felt the satisfaction of the correct, in their courtship, for she had always heard that true love was inarticulate. Then, besides, there had been always kissing and things, to take up your mind. But it had turned out that true marriage was apparently equally dumb. And you can't depend on kisses and all the rest of it to while away the evenings, after seven years.

You'd think that you would get used to it, in seven years, would realize that that was the way it was, and let it go at that. You don't, though. A thing like that gets on your nerves. It isn't one of those cozy, companionable silences that people occasionally fall into together. It makes you feel as if you must do something about it, as if you weren't performing your duty. You have the feeling a hostess has when her party is going badly, when her guests sit in corners and refuse to mingle. It makes you nervous and self-conscious, and you talk desperately about tomato soup, and say things like "daffy-down-dilly."

Mrs. Weldon cast about in her mind for a subject to offer her husband. There was Alice Marshall's new system of reducing— no, that was pretty dull. There was the case she had read in the morning's paper about the man of eighty-seven who had taken, as his fourth wife, a girl of twenty—he had probably seen that, and as long as he hadn't thought it worth repeating, he wouldn't think it worth hearing. There was the thing the Baileys' little boy had said about Jesus—no, she had told him that the night before.

She looked over at him, desultorily eating his rhubarb pie. She wished he wouldn't put that greasy stuff on his head. Perhaps it was necessary, if his hair really was falling out, but it did seem that he might find some more attractive remedy, if he only had the consideration to look around for one. Anyway, why must his hair fall out? There was something a little disgusting about people with falling hair.

"Like your pie, Ernie?" she asked vivaciously.

"Why, I don't know," he said, thinking it over. "I'm not so crazy about rhubarb, I don't think. Are you?"

"No, I'm not so awfully crazy about it," she answered. "But then, I'm not really crazy about any kind of pie."

"Aren't you really?" he said, politely surprised. "I like pie pretty well—some kinds of pie."

"Do you?" The polite surprise was hers now.

"Why, yes," he said. "I like a nice huckleberry pie or a nice lemon meringue pie, or a—" He lost interest in the thing himself, and his voice died away.

He avoided looking at her left hand, which lay on the edge of the table, palm upward. The long, gray-white ends of her nails protruded beyond the tips of her fingers, and the sight made him uncomfortable. Why in God's name must she wear her finger nails that preposterous length, and file them to those horrible points? If there was anything that he hated, it was a woman with pointed finger nails.

They returned to the living-room, and Mr. Weldon again eased himself down into his chair, reaching for the second paper.

"Quite sure there isn't anything you'd like to do tonight?" he asked solicitously. "Like to go to the movies, or anything?"

"Oh, no," she said. "Unless there's something you want to do."

"No, no," he answered. "I just thought maybe you wanted to."

"Not unless you do," she said.

He began on his paper, and she wandered aimlessly about the room. She had forgotten to get a new book from the library, and it had never in her life occurred to her to reread a book that she had once completed. She thought vaguely of playing solitaire, but she did not care enough about it to go to the trouble of getting out the cards, and setting up the table. There was some sewing that she could do, and she thought that she might presently go into the bedroom and fetch the nightgown that she was making for herself. Yes, she would probably do that, in a little while.

Ernest would read industriously, and, along toward the middle of the paper, he would start yawning aloud. Something happened inside Mrs. Weldon when he did this. She would murmur that she had to speak to Delia, and hurry to the kitchen. She would stay there rather a long time, looking vaguely into jars and inquiring half-heartedly about laundry lists, and, when she returned, he would have gone in to get ready for bed.

In a year, three hundred of their evenings were like this. Seven times three hundred is more than two thousand.

Mrs. Weldon went into the bedroom, and brought back her sewing. She sat down, pinned the pink satin to her knee, and began whipping narrow lace along the top of the half-made garment. It was fussy work. The fine thread knotted and drew, and she could not get the light adjusted so that the shadow of her head did not fall on her work. She grew a little sick, from the strain on her eyes.

Mr. Weldon turned a page, and yawned aloud. "Wah-huh-huh-huh-huh," he went, on a descending scale. He yawned again, and this time climbed the scale.

III

"My dear," Mrs. Ames said to Mrs. Marshall, "don't you really think that there must have been some other woman?"

"Oh, I simply couldn't think it was anything like that," said Mrs. Marshall. "Not Ernest Weldon. So devoted—home every night at half-past six, and such good company, and so jolly, and all. I don't see how there *could* have been."

"Sometimes," observed Mrs. Ames, "those awfully jolly men at home are just the kind."

"Yes, I know," Mrs. Marshall said. "But not Ernest Weldon. Why, I used to say to Jim, 'I never saw such a devoted husband in my life,' I said. Oh, not Ernest Weldon."

"I don't suppose," began Mrs. Ames, and hesitated. "I don't suppose," she went on, intently pressing the bit of sodden lemon in her cup with her teaspoon, "that Grace—that there was ever anyone—or anything like that?"

"Oh, heavens, no," cried Mrs. Marshall. "Grace Weldon just gave her whole life to that man. It was Ernest this and Ernest that every minute. I simply can't understand it. If there was one earthly reason—if they ever fought, or if Ernest drank, or anything like that. But they got along so beautifully together—why, it just seems as if they must have been crazy to go and do a thing like this. Well, I can't begin to tell you how blue it's made me. It seems so awful!"

"Yes," said Mrs. Ames, "it certainly is too bad."

The Last Tea

The young man in the chocolate-brown suit sat down at the table, where the girl with the artificial camellia had been sitting for forty minutes.

"Guess I must be late," he said. "Sorry you been waiting."

"Oh, goodness!" she said. "I just got here myself, just about a second ago. I simply went ahead and ordered because I was dying for a cup of tea. I was late, myself. I haven't been here more than a minute."

"That's good," he said. "Hey, hey, easy on the sugar—one lump is fair enough. And take away those cakes. Terrible! Do I feel terrible!"

"Ah," she said, "you do? Ah. Whadda matter?"

"Oh, I'm ruined," he said. "I'm in terrible shape."

"Ah, the poor boy," she said. "Was it feelin' mizzable? Ah, and it came way up here to meet me! You shouldn't have done that—I'd have understood. Ah, just think of it coming all the way up here when it's so sick!"

"Oh, that's all right," he said. "I might as well be here as any place else. Any place is like any other place, the way I feel today. Oh, I'm all shot."

"Why, that's just awful," she said. "Why, you poor sick thing. Goodness, I hope it isn't influenza. They say there's a lot of it around."

"Influenza!" he said. "I wish that was all I had. Oh, I'm poisoned. I'm through. I'm off the stuff for life. Know what time I got to bed? Twenty minutes past five, A.M., this morning. What a night! What an evening!"

"I thought," she said, "that you were going to stay at the office and work late. You said you'd be working every night this week."

"Yeah, I know," he said. "But it gave me the jumps, thinking about going down there and sitting at that desk. I

182

went up to May's—she was throwing a party. Say, there was somebody there said they knew you."

"Honestly?" she said. "Man or woman?"

"Dame," he said. "Name's Carol McCall. Say, why haven't I been told about her before? That's what I call a girl. What a looker she is!"

"Oh, really?" she said. "That's funny—I never heard of anyone that thought that. I've heard people say she was sort of nice-looking, if she wouldn't make up so much. But I never heard of anyone that thought she was pretty."

"Pretty is right," he said. "What a couple of eyes she's got on her!"

"Really?" she said. "I never noticed them particularly. But I haven't seen her for a long time—sometimes people change, or something."

"She says she used to go to school with you," he said.

"Well, we went to the same school," she said. "I simply happened to go to public school because it happened to be right near us, and Mother hated to have me crossing streets. But she was three or four classes ahead of me. She's ages older than I am."

"She's three or four classes ahead of them all," he said. "Dance! Can she step! 'Burn your clothes, baby,' I kept telling her. I must have been fried pretty."

"I was out dancing myself, last night," she said. "Wally Dillon and I. He's just been pestering me to go out with him. He's the most wonderful dancer. Goodness! I didn't get home until I don't know what time. I must look just simply a wreck. Don't I?"

"You look all right," he said.

"Wally's crazy," she said. "The things he says! For some crazy reason or other, he's got it into his head that I've got beautiful eyes, and, well, he just kept talking about them till I didn't know where to look, I was so embarrassed. I got so red, I thought everybody in the place would be looking at me. I got just as red as a brick. Beautiful eyes! Isn't he crazy?"

"He's all right," he said. "Say, this little McCall girl, she's had all kinds of offers to go into moving pictures. 'Why don't you go ahead and go?' I told her. But she says she doesn't feel like it."

"There was a man up at the lake, two summers ago," she said. "He was a director or something with one of the big moving-picture people—oh, he had all kinds of influence!—and he used to keep insisting and insisting that I ought to be in the movies. Said I ought to be doing sort of Garbo parts. I used to just laugh at him. Imagine!"

"She's had about a million offers," he said. "I told her to go ahead and go. She keeps getting these offers all the time."

"Oh, really?" she said. "Oh, listen, I knew I had something to ask you. Did you call me up last night, by any chance?"

"Me?" he said. "No, I didn't call you."

"While I was out, Mother said this man's voice kept calling up," she said. "I thought maybe it might be you, by some chance. I wonder who it could have been. Oh—I guess I know who it was. Yes, that's who it was!"

"No, I didn't call you," he said. "I couldn't have seen a telephone, last night. What a head I had on me, this morning! I called Carol up, around ten, and she said she was feeling great. Can that girl hold her liquor!"

"It's a funny thing about me," she said. "It just makes me feel sort of sick to see a girl drink. It's just something in me, I guess. I don't mind a man so much, but it makes me feel perfectly terrible to see a girl get intoxicated. It's just the way I am, I suppose."

"Does she carry it!" he said. "And then feels great the next day. There's a girl! Hey, what are you doing there? I don't want any more tea, thanks. I'm not one of these tea boys. And these tea rooms give me the jumps. Look at all those old dames, will you? Enough to give you the jumps."

"Of course, if you'd rather be some place, drinking, with I don't know what kinds of people," she said, "I'm sure I don't see how I can help that. Goodness, there are enough people that are glad enough to take me to tea. I don't know how many people keep calling me up and pestering me to take me to tea. Plenty of people!"

"All right, all right, I'm here, aren't I?" he said. "Keep your hair on."

"I could name them all day," she said.

"All right," he said. "What's there to crab about?"

"Goodness, it isn't any of my business what you do," she said. "But I hate to see you wasting your time with people that aren't nearly good enough for you. That's all."

"No need worrying over me," he said. "I'll be all right. Listen. You don't have to worry."

"It's just I don't like to see you wasting your time," she said, "staying up all night and then feeling terribly the next day. Ah, I was forgetting he was so sick. Ah, I was mean, wasn't I, scolding him when he was so mizzable. Poor boy. How's he feel now?"

"Oh, I'm all right," he said. "I feel fine. You want anything else? How about getting a check? I got to make a telephone call before six."

"Oh, really?" she said. "Calling up Carol?"

"She said she might be in around now," he said.

"Seeing her tonight?" she said.

"She's going to let me know when I call up," he said. "She's probably got about a million dates. Why?"

"I was just wondering," she said. "Goodness, I've got to fly! I'm having dinner with Wally, and he's so crazy, he's probably there now. He's called me up about a hundred times today."

"Wait till I pay the check," he said, "and I'll put you on a bus."

"Oh, don't bother," she said. "It's right at the corner. I've got to fly. I suppose you want to stand and call up your friend from here?"

"It's an idea," he said. "Sure you'll be all right?"

"Oh, sure," she said. Busily she gathered her gloves and purse, and left her chair. He rose, not quite fully, as she stopped beside him.

"When'll I see you again?" she said.

"I'll call you up," he said. "I'm all tied up, down at the office and everything. Tell you what I'll do. I'll give you a ring."

"Honestly, I have more dates!" she said. "It's terrible. I

don't know when I'll have a minute. But you call up, will you?"

"I'll do that," he said. "Take care of yourself."

"You take care of yourself," she said. "Hope you'll feel all right."

"Oh, I'm fine," he said. "Just beginning to come back to life."

"Be sure and let me know how you feel," she said. "Will you? Sure, now? Well, good-by. Oh, have a good time tonight!"

"Thanks," he said. "Hope you have a good time, too."

"Oh, I will," she said. "I expect to. I've got to rush! Oh, I nearly forgot! Thanks ever so much for the tea. It was lovely."

"Be yourself, will you?" he said.

"It was," she said. "Well. Now don't forget to call me up, will you? Sure? Well, good-by."

"Solong," he said.

She walked on down the little lane between the blue-painted tables.

Big Blonde

Hazel Morse was a large, fair woman of the type that incites some men when they use the word "blonde" to click their tongues and wag their heads roguishly. She prided herself upon her small feet and suffered for her vanity, boxing them in snub-toed, high-heeled slippers of the shortest bearable size. The curious things about her were her hands, strange terminations to the flabby white arms splattered with pale tan spots—long, quivering hands with deep and convex nails. She should not have disfigured them with little jewels.

She was not a woman given to recollections. At her middle thirties, her old days were a blurred and flickering sequence, an imperfect film, dealing with the actions of strangers.

In her twenties, after the deferred death of a hazy widowed mother, she had been employed as a model in a wholesale dress establishment—it was still the day of the big woman, and she was then prettily colored and erect and high-breasted. Her job was not onerous, and she met numbers of men and spent numbers of evenings with them, laughing at their jokes and telling them she loved their neckties. Men liked her, and she took it for granted that the liking of many men was a desirable thing. Popularity seemed to her to be worth all the work that had to be put into its achievement. Men liked you because you were fun, and when they liked you they took you out, and there you were. So, and successfully, she was fun. She was a good sport. Men liked a good sport.

No other form of diversion, simpler or more complicated, drew her attention. She never pondered if she might not be better occupied doing something else. Her ideas, or, better, her acceptances, ran right along with those of the other substantially built blondes in whom she found her friends.

When she had been working in the dress establishment some years she met Herbie Morse. He was thin, quick, attractive, with shifting lines about his shiny, brown eyes and a habit of fiercely biting at the skin around his finger nails. He drank largely; she found that entertaining. Her habitual greeting to him was an allusion to his state of the previous night.

"Oh, what a peach you had," she used to say, through her easy laugh. "I thought I'd die, the way you kept asking the waiter to dance with you."

She liked him immediately upon their meeting. She was enormously amused at his fast, slurred sentences, his interpolations of apt phrases from vaudeville acts and comic strips; she thrilled at the feel of his lean arm tucked firm beneath the sleeve of her coat; she wanted to touch the wet, flat surface of his hair. He was as promptly drawn to her. They were married six weeks after they had met.

She was delighted at the idea of being a bride; coquetted with it, played upon it. Other offers of marriage she had had, and not a few of them, but it happened that they were all from stout, serious men who had visited the dress establishment as buyers; men from Des Moines and Houston and Chicago and, in her phrase, even funnier places. There was always something immensely comic to her in the thought of living elsewhere than New York. She could not regard as serious proposals that she share a western residence.

She wanted to be married. She was nearing thirty now, and she did not take the years well. She spread and softened, and her darkening hair turned her to inexpert dabblings with peroxide. There were times when she had little flashes of fear about her job. And she had had a couple of thousand evenings of being a good sport among her male acquaintances. She had come to be more conscientious than spontaneous about it.

Herbie earned enough, and they took a little apartment far uptown. There was a Mission-furnished dining-room with a hanging central light globed in liver-colored glass; in the living-room were an "over-stuffed suite," a Boston fern, and a reproduction of the Henner "Magdalene" with the red hair and the blue draperies; the bedroom was in gray enamel and old rose, with Herbie's photograph on Hazel's dressing-table and Hazel's likeness on Herbie's chest of drawers.

She cooked—and she was a good cook—and marketed and chatted with the delivery boys and the colored laundress. She loved the flat, she loved her life, she loved Herbie. In the first months of their marriage, she gave him all the passion she was ever to know.

She had not realized how tired she was. It was a delight, a new game, a holiday, to give up being a good sport. If her head ached or her arches throbbed, she complained piteously, babyishly. If her mood was quiet, she did not talk. If tears came to her eyes, she let them fall.

She fell readily into the habit of tears during the first year of her marriage. Even in her good sport days, she had been known to weep lavishly and disinterestedly on occasion. Her behavior at the theater was a standing joke. She could weep at anything in a play—tiny garments, love both unrequited and mutual, seduction, purity, faithful servitors, wedlock, the triangle.

"There goes Haze," her friends would say, watching her. "She's off again."

Wedded and relaxed, she poured her tears freely. To her who had laughed so much, crying was delicious. All sorrows became her sorrows; she was Tenderness. She would cry long and softly over newspaper accounts of kidnaped babies, deserted wives, unemployed men, strayed cats, heroic dogs. Even when the paper was no longer before her, her mind revolved upon these things and the drops slipped rhythmically over her plump cheeks.

"Honestly," she would say to Herbie, "all the sadness there is in the world when you stop to think about it!"

"Yeah," Herbie would say.

She missed nobody. The old crowd, the people who had brought her and Herbie together, dropped from their lives, lingeringly at first. When she thought of this at all, it was only to consider it fitting. This was marriage. This was peace.

But the thing was that Herbie was not amused.

For a time, he had enjoyed being alone with her. He found the voluntary isolation novel and sweet. Then it palled with a ferocious suddenness. It was as if one night, sitting with her in the steam-heated living-room, he would ask no more; and the next night he was through and done with the whole thing.

He became annoyed by her misty melancholies. At first, when he came home to find her softly tired and moody, he kissed her neck and patted her shoulder and begged her to tell her Herbie what was wrong. She loved that. But time slid by, and he found that there was never anything really, personally, the matter.

"Ah, for God's sake," he would say. "Crabbing again. All right, sit here and crab your head off. I'm going out."

And he would slam out of the flat and come back late and drunk.

She was completely bewildered by what happened to their marriage. First they were lovers; and then, it seemed without transition, they were enemies. She never understood it.

There were longer and longer intervals between his leaving his office and his arrival at the apartment. She went through agonies of picturing him run over and bleeding, dead and covered with a sheet. Then she lost her fears for his safety and grew sullen and wounded. When a person wanted to be with a person, he came as soon as possible. She desperately wanted him to want to be with her; her own hours only marked the time till he would come. It was often nearly nine o'clock before he came home to dinner. Always he had had many drinks, and their effect would die in him, leaving him loud and querulous and bristling for affronts.

He was too nervous, he said, to sit and do nothing for an evening. He boasted, probably not in all truth, that he had never read a book in his life.

"What am I expected to do—sit around this dump on my tail all night?" he would ask, rhetorically. And again he would slam out.

She did not know what to do. She could not manage him. She could not meet him.

She fought him furiously. A terrific domesticity had come upon her, and she would bite and scratch to guard it. She wanted what she called "a nice home." She wanted a sober, tender husband, prompt at dinner, punctual at work. She wanted sweet, comforting evenings. The idea of intimacy with other men was terrible to her; the thought that Herbie might be seeking entertainment in other women set her frantic.

It seemed to her that almost everything she read—novels from the drug-store lending library, magazine stories, women's pages in the papers—dealt with wives who lost their husbands' love. She could bear those, at that, better than accounts of neat, companionable marriage and living happily ever after.

She was frightened. Several times when Herbie came home in the evening, he found her determinedly dressed—she had had to alter those of her clothes that were not new, to make them fasten—and rouged.

"Let's go wild tonight, what do you say?" she would hail him. "A person's got lots of time to hang around and do nothing when they're dead."

So they would go out, to chop houses and the less expensive cabarets. But it turned out badly. She could no longer find amusement in watching Herbie drink. She could not laugh at his whimsicalities, she was so tensely counting his indulgences. And she was unable to keep back her remonstrances—"Ah, come on, Herb, you've had enough, haven't you? You'll feel something terrible in the morning."

He would be immediately enraged. All right, crab; crab, crab, crab, crab, that was all she ever did. What a lousy sport *she* was! There would be scenes, and one or the other of them would rise and stalk out in fury.

She could not recall the definite day that she started drinking, herself. There was nothing separate about her days. Like drops upon a window-pane, they ran together and trickled away. She had been married six months; then a year; then three years.

She had never needed to drink, formerly. She could sit for most of a night at a table where the others were imbibing earnestly and never droop in looks or spirits, nor be bored by the doings of those about her. If she took a cocktail, it was so unusual as to cause twenty minutes or so of jocular comment. But now anguish was in her. Frequently, after a quarrel, Herbie would stay out for the night, and she could not learn from him where the time had been spent. Her heart felt tight and sore in her breast, and her mind turned like an electric fan.

She hated the taste of liquor. Gin, plain or in mixtures, made her promptly sick. After experiment, she found that Scotch whisky was best for her. She took it without water, because that was the quickest way to its effect.

Herbie pressed it on her. He was glad to see her drink. They both felt it might restore her high spirits, and their good times together might again be possible.

" 'Atta girl," he would approve her. "Let's see you get boiled, baby."

But it brought them no nearer. When she drank with him, there would be a little while of gaiety and then, strangely without beginning, they would be in a wild quarrel. They would wake in the morning not sure what it had all been about, foggy as to what had been said and done, but each deeply injured and bitterly resentful. There would be days of vengeful silence.

There had been a time when they had made up their quarrels, usually in bed. There would be kisses and little names and assurances of fresh starts. . . . "Oh, it's going to be great now, Herb. We'll have swell times. I was a crab. I guess I must have been tired. But everything's going to be swell. You'll see."

Now there were no gentle reconciliations. They resumed friendly relations only in the brief magnanimity caused by liquor, before more liquor drew them into new battles. The scenes became more violent. There were shouted invectives and pushes, and sometimes sharp slaps. Once she had a black eye. Herbie was horrified next day at sight of it. He did not go to work; he followed her about, suggesting remedies and heaping dark blame on himself. But after they had had a few drinks— "to pull themselves together"—she made so many wistful references to her bruise that he shouted at her and rushed out and was gone for two days.

Each time he left the place in a rage, he threatened never to come back. She did not believe him, nor did she consider separation. Somewhere in her head or her heart was the lazy, nebulous hope that things would change and she and Herbie settle suddenly into soothing married life. Here were her home, her furniture, her husband, her station. She summoned no alternatives.

She could no longer bustle and potter. She had no more vicarious tears; the hot drops she shed were for herself. She walked ceaselessly about the rooms, her thoughts running mechanically round and round Herbie. In those days began the hatred of being alone that she was never to overcome. You could be by yourself when things were all right, but when you were blue you got the howling horrors.

She commenced drinking alone, little, short drinks all through the day. It was only with Herbie that alcohol made her nervous and quick in offense. Alone, it blurred sharp things for her. She lived in a haze of it. Her life took on a dream-like quality. Nothing was astonishing.

A Mrs. Martin moved into the flat across the hall. She was a great blonde woman of forty, a promise in looks of what Mrs. Morse was to be. They made acquaintance, quickly became inseparable. Mrs. Morse spent her days in the opposite apartment. They drank together, to brace themselves after the drinks of the nights before.

She never confided her troubles about Herbie to Mrs. Martin. The subject was too bewildering to her to find comfort in talk. She let it be assumed that her husband's business kept him much away. It was not regarded as important; husbands, as such, played but shadowy parts in Mrs. Martin's circle.

Mrs. Martin had no visible spouse; you were left to decide for yourself whether he was or was not dead. She had an admirer, Joe, who came to see her almost nightly. Often he brought several friends with him—"The Boys," they were called. The Boys were big, red, good-humored men, perhaps forty-five, perhaps fifty. Mrs. Morse was glad of invitations to join the parties—Herbie was scarcely ever at home at night now. If he did come home, she did not visit Mrs. Martin. An evening alone with Herbie meant inevitably a quarrel, yet she would stay with him. There was always her thin and wordless idea that, maybe, this night, things would begin to be all right.

The Boys brought plenty of liquor along with them whenever

they came to Mrs. Martin's. Drinking with them, Mrs. Morse became lively and good-natured and audacious. She was quickly popular. When she had drunk enough to cloud her most recent battle with Herbie, she was excited by their approbation. Crab, was she? Rotten sport, was she? Well, there were some that thought different.

Ed was one of The Boys. He lived in Utica—had "his own business" there, was the awed report—but he came to New York almost every week. He was married. He showed Mrs. Morse the then current photographs of Junior and Sister, and she praised them abundantly and sincerely. Soon it was accepted by the others that Ed was her particular friend.

He staked her when they all played poker; sat next her and occasionally rubbed his knee against hers during the game. She was rather lucky. Frequently she went home with a twenty-dollar bill or a ten-dollar bill or a handful of crumpled dollars. She was glad of them. Herbie was getting, in her words, something awful about money. To ask him for it brought an instant row.

"What the hell do you do with it?" he would say. "Shoot it all on Scotch?"

"I try to run this house half-way decent," she would retort. "Never thought of that, did you? Oh, no, his lordship couldn't be bothered with that."

Again, she could not find a definite day, to fix the beginning of Ed's proprietorship. It became his custom to kiss her on the mouth when he came in, as well as for farewell, and he gave her little quick kisses of approval all through the evening. She liked this rather more than she disliked it. She never thought of his kisses when she was not with him.

He would run his hand lingeringly over her back and shoulders.

"Some dizzy blonde, eh?" he would say. "Some doll."

One afternoon she came home from Mrs. Martin's to find Herbie in the bedroom. He had been away for several nights, evidently on a prolonged drinking bout. His face was gray, his hands jerked as if they were on wires. On the bed were two old suitcases, packed high. Only her photograph remained on his bureau, and the wide doors of his closet disclosed nothing but coat-hangers.

"I'm blowing," he said. "I'm through with the whole works. I got a job in Detroit."

She sat down on the edge of the bed. She had drunk much the night before, and the four Scotches she had had with Mrs. Martin had only increased her fogginess.

"Good job?" she said.

"Oh, yeah," he said. "Looks all right."

He closed a suitcase with difficulty, swearing at it in whispers.

"There's some dough in the bank," he said. "The bank book's in your top drawer. You can have the furniture and stuff."

He looked at her, and his forehead twitched.

"God damn it, I'm through, I'm telling you," he cried. "I'm through."

"All right, all right," she said. "I heard you, didn't I?"

She saw him as if he were at one end of a cannon and she at the other. Her head was beginning to ache bumpingly, and her voice had a dreary, tiresome tone. She could not have raised it.

"Like a drink before you go?" she asked.

Again he looked at her, and a corner of his mouth jerked up.

"Cockeyed again for a change, aren't you?" he said. "That's nice. Sure, get a couple of shots, will you?"

She went to the pantry, mixed him a stiff highball, poured herself a couple of inches of whisky and drank it. Then she gave herself another portion and brought the glasses into the bedroom. He had strapped both suitcases and had put on his hat and overcoat.

He took his highball.

"Well," he said, and he gave a sudden, uncertain laugh. "Here's mud in your eye."

"Mud in your eye," she said.

They drank. He put down his glass and took up the heavy suitcases.

"Got to get a train around six," he said.

She followed him down the hall. There was a song, a song

that Mrs. Martin played doggedly on the phonograph, running loudly through her mind. She had never liked the thing.

> *"Night and daytime,*
> *Always playtime.*
> *Ain't we got fun?"*

At the door he put down the bags and faced her.

"Well," he said. "Well, take care of yourself. You'll be all right, will you?"

"Oh, sure," she said.

He opened the door, then came back to her, holding out his hand.

" 'By, Haze," he said. "Good luck to you."

She took his hand and shook it.

"Pardon my wet glove," she said.

When the door had closed behind him, she went back to the pantry.

She was flushed and lively when she went in to Mrs. Martin's that evening. The Boys were there, Ed among them. He was glad to be in town, frisky and loud and full of jokes. But she spoke quietly to him for a minute.

"Herbie blew today," she said. "Going to live out west."

"That so?" he said. He looked at her and played with the fountain pen clipped to his waistcoat pocket.

"Think he's gone for good, do you?" he asked.

"Yeah," she said. "I know he is. I know. Yeah."

"You going to live on across the hall just the same?" he said. "Know what you're going to do?"

"Gee, I don't know," she said. "I don't give much of a damn."

"Oh, come on, that's no way to talk," he told her. "What you need—you need a little snifter. How about it?"

"Yeah," she said. "Just straight."

She won forty-three dollars at poker. When the game broke up, Ed took her back to her apartment.

"Got a little kiss for me?" he asked.

He wrapped her in his big arms and kissed her violently. She was entirely passive. He held her away and looked at her.

"Little tight, honey?" he asked, anxiously. "Not going to be sick, are you?"

"Me?" she said. "I'm swell."

II

When Ed left in the morning, he took her photograph with him. He said he wanted her picture to look at, up in Utica. "You can have that one on the bureau," she said.

She put Herbie's picture in a drawer, out of her sight. When she could look at it, she meant to tear it up. She was fairly successful in keeping her mind from racing around him. Whisky slowed it for her. She was almost peaceful, in her mist.

She accepted her relationship with Ed without question or enthusiasm. When he was away, she seldom thought definitely of him. He was good to her; he gave her frequent presents and a regular allowance. She was even able to save. She did not plan ahead of any day, but her wants were few, and you might as well put money in the bank as have it lying around.

When the lease of her apartment neared its end, it was Ed who suggested moving. His friendship with Mrs. Martin and Joe had become strained over a dispute at poker; a feud was impending.

"Let's get the hell out of here," Ed said. "What I want you to have is a place near the Grand Central. Make it easier for me."

So she took a little flat in the Forties. A colored maid came in every day to clean and to make coffee for her—she was "through with that housekeeping stuff," she said, and Ed, twenty years married to a passionately domestic woman, admired this romantic uselessness and felt doubly a man of the world in abetting it.

The coffee was all she had until she went out to dinner, but alcohol kept her fat. Prohibition she regarded only as a basis for jokes. You could always get all you wanted. She was never noticeably drunk and seldom nearly sober. It required a larger daily allowance to keep her misty-minded. Too little, and she was achingly melancholy.

Ed brought her to Jimmy's. He was proud, with the pride of

the transient who would be mistaken for a native, in his knowledge of small, recent restaurants occupying the lower floors of shabby brownstone houses; places where, upon mentioning the name of an habitué friend, might be obtained strange whisky and fresh gin in many of their ramifications. Jimmy's place was the favorite of his acquaintances.

There, through Ed, Mrs. Morse met many men and women, formed quick friendships. The men often took her out when Ed was in Utica. He was proud of her popularity.

She fell into the habit of going to Jimmy's alone when she had no engagement. She was certain to meet some people she knew, and join them. It was a club for her friends, both men and women.

The women at Jimmy's looked remarkably alike, and this was curious, for, through feuds, removals, and opportunities of more profitable contacts, the personnel of the group changed constantly. Yet always the newcomers resembled those whom they replaced. They were all big women and stout, broad of shoulder and abundantly breasted, with faces thickly clothed in soft, high-colored flesh. They laughed loud and often, showing opaque and lusterless teeth like squares of crockery. There was about them the health of the big, yet a slight, unwholesome suggestion of stubborn preservation. They might have been thirty-six or forty-five or anywhere between.

They composed their titles of their own first names with their husbands' surnames—Mrs. Florence Miller, Mrs. Vera Riley, Mrs. Lilian Block. This gave at the same time the solidity of marriage and the glamour of freedom. Yet only one or two were actually divorced. Most of them never referred to their dimmed spouses; some, a shorter time separated, described them in terms of great biological interest. Several were mothers, each of an only child—a boy at school somewhere, or a girl being cared for by a grandmother. Often, well on toward morning, there would be displays of kodak portraits and of tears.

They were comfortable women, cordial and friendly and irrepressibly matronly. Theirs was the quality of ease. Become fatalistic, especially about money matters, they unworried. Whenever their funds dropped alarmingly, a new donor appeared; this had always happened. The aim of each was to have one man, permanently, to pay all her bills, in return for which she would have immediately given up other admirers and probably would have become exceedingly fond of him; for the affections of all of them were, by now, unexacting, tranquil, and easily arranged. This end, however, grew increasingly difficult yearly. Mrs. Morse was regarded as fortunate.

Ed had a good year, increased her allowance and gave her a sealskin coat. But she had to be careful of her moods with him. He insisted upon gaiety. He would not listen to admissions of aches or weariness.

"Hey, listen," he would say, "I got worries of my own, and plenty. Nobody wants to hear other people's troubles, sweetie. What you got to do, you got to be a sport and forget it. See? Well, slip us a little smile, then. That's my girl."

She never had enough interest to quarrel with him as she had with Herbie, but she wanted the privilege of occasional admitted sadness. It was strange. The other women she saw did not have to fight their moods. There was Mrs. Florence Miller who got regular crying jags, and the men sought only to cheer and comfort her. The others spent whole evenings in grieved recitals of worries and ills; their escorts paid them deep sympathy. But she was instantly undesirable when she was low in spirits. Once, at Jimmy's, when she could not make herself lively, Ed had walked out and left her.

"Why the hell don't you stay home and not go spoiling everybody's evening?" he had roared.

Even her slightest acquaintances seemed irritated if she were not conspicuously light-hearted.

"What's the matter with you, anyway?" they would say. "Be your age, why don't you? Have a little drink and snap out of it."

When her relationship with Ed had continued nearly three years, he moved to Florida to live. He hated leaving her; he gave her a large check and some shares of a sound stock, and his pale eyes were wet when he said good-by. She did not miss him. He came to New York infrequently, perhaps two or three times a year, and hurried directly from the train to see her. She was always pleased to have him come and never sorry to see him go.

Charley, an acquaintance of Ed's that she had met at Jimmy's, had long admired her. He had always made opportunities of touching her and leaning close to talk to her. He asked repeatedly of all their friends if they had ever heard such a fine laugh as she had. After Ed left, Charley became the main figure in her life. She classified him and spoke of him as "not so bad." There was nearly a year of Charley; then she divided her time between him and Sydney, another frequenter of Jimmy's; then Charley slipped away altogether.

Sydney was a little, brightly dressed, clever Jew. She was perhaps nearest contentment with him. He amused her always; her laughter was not forced.

He admired her completely. Her softness and size delighted him. And he thought she was great, he often told her, because she kept gay and lively when she was drunk.

"Once I had a gal," he said, "used to try and throw herself out of the window every time she got a can on. Jee-*zuss*," he added, feelingly.

Then Sydney married a rich and watchful bride, and then there was Billy. No—after Sydney came Fred, then Billy. In her haze, she never recalled how men entered her life and left it. There were no surprises. She had no thrill at their advent, nor woe at their departure. She seemed to be always able to attract men. There was never another as rich as Ed, but they were all generous to her, in their means.

Once she had news of Herbie. She met Mrs. Martin dining at Jimmy's, and the old friendship was vigorously renewed. The still admiring Joe, while on a business trip, had seen Herbie. He had settled in Chicago, he looked fine, he was living with some woman—seemed to be crazy about her. Mrs. Morse had been drinking vastly that day. She took the news with mild interest, as one hearing of the sex peccadilloes of somebody whose name is, after a moment's groping, familiar.

"Must be damn near seven years since I saw him," she commented. "Gee. Seven years."

More and more, her days lost their individuality. She never

knew dates, nor was sure of the day of the week.

"My God, was that a year ago!" she would exclaim, when an event was recalled in conversation.

She was tired so much of the time. Tired and blue. Almost everything could give her the blues. Those old horses she saw on Sixth Avenue—struggling and slipping along the car-tracks, or standing at the curb, their heads dropped level with their worn knees. The tightly stored tears would squeeze from her eyes as she teetered past on her aching feet in the stubby, champagne-colored slippers.

The thought of death came and stayed with her and lent her a sort of drowsy cheer. It would be nice, nice and restful, to be dead.

There was no settled, shocked moment when she first thought of killing herself; it seemed to her as if the idea had always been with her. She pounced upon all the accounts of suicides in the newspapers. There was an epidemic of self-killings—or maybe it was just that she searched for the stories of them so eagerly that she found many. To read of them roused reassurance in her; she felt a cozy solidarity with the big company of the voluntary dead.

She slept, aided by whisky, till deep into the afternoons, then lay abed, a bottle and glass at her hand, until it was time to dress and go out for dinner. She was beginning to feel toward alcohol a little puzzled distrust, as toward an old friend who has refused a simple favor. Whisky could still soothe her for most of the time, but there were sudden, inexplicable moments when the cloud fell treacherously away from her, and she was sawed by the sorrow and bewilderment and nuisance of all living. She played voluptuously with the thought of cool, sleepy retreat. She had never been troubled by religious belief and no vision of an after-life intimidated her. She dreamed by day of never again putting on tight shoes, of never having to laugh and listen and admire, of never more being a good sport. Never.

But how would you do it? It made her sick to think of jumping from heights. She could not stand a gun. At the theater, if one of the actors drew a revolver, she crammed her fingers into her ears and could not even look at the stage until after the shot had been fired. There was no gas in her flat. She looked long at the bright blue veins in her slim wrists—a cut with a razor blade, and there you'd be. But it would hurt, hurt like hell, and there would be blood to see. Poison—something tasteless and quick and painless—was the thing. But they wouldn't sell it to you in drugstores, because of the law.

She had few other thoughts.

There was a new man now—Art. He was short and fat and exacting and hard on her patience when he was drunk. But there had been only occasionals for some time before him, and she was glad of a little stability. Too, Art must be away for weeks at a stretch, selling silks, and that was restful. She was convincingly gay with him, though the effort shook her.

"The best sport in the world," he would murmur, deep in her neck. "The best sport in the world."

One night, when he had taken her to Jimmy's, she went into the dressing-room with Mrs. Florence Miller. There, while designing curly mouths on their faces with lip-rouge, they compared experiences of insomnia.

"Honestly," Mrs. Morse said, "I wouldn't close an eye if I didn't go to bed full of Scotch. I lie there and toss and turn and toss and turn. Blue! Does a person get blue lying awake that way!"

"Say, listen, Hazel," Mrs. Miller said, impressively, "I'm telling you I'd be awake for a year if I didn't take veronal. That stuff makes you sleep like a fool."

"Isn't it poison, or something?" Mrs. Morse asked.

"Oh, you take too much and you're out for the count," said Mrs. Miller. "I just take five grains—they come in tablets. I'd be scared to fool around with it. But five grains, and you cork off pretty."

"Can you get it anywhere?" Mrs. Morse felt superbly Machiavellian.

"Get all you want in Jersey," said Mrs. Miller. "They won't give it to you here without you have a doctor's prescription. Finished? We'd better go back and see what the boys are doing."

That night, Art left Mrs. Morse at the door of her apartment; his mother was in town. Mrs. Morse was still sober, and it happened that there was no whisky left in her cupboard. She lay in bed, looking up at the black ceiling.

She rose early, for her, and went to New Jersey. She had never taken the tube, and did not understand it. So she went to the Pennsylvania Station and bought a railroad ticket to Newark. She thought of nothing in particular on the trip out. She looked at the uninspired hats of the women about her and gazed through the smeared window at the flat, gritty scene.

In Newark, in the first drug-store she came to, she asked for a tin of talcum powder, a nailbrush, and a box of veronal tablets. The powder and the brush were to make the hypnotic seem also a casual need. The clerk was entirely unconcerned. "We only keep them in bottles," he said, and wrapped up for her a little glass vial containing ten white tablets, stacked one on another.

She went to another drug-store and bought a face-cloth, an orange-wood stick, and a bottle of veronal tablets. The clerk was also uninterested.

"Well, I guess I got enough to kill an ox," she thought, and went back to the station.

At home, she put the little vials in the drawer of her dressing-table and stood looking at them with a dreamy tenderness.

"There they are, God bless them," she said, and she kissed her finger-tip and touched each bottle.

The colored maid was busy in the living-room.

"Hey, Nettie," Mrs. Morse called. "Be an angel, will you? Run around to Jimmy's and get me a quart of Scotch."

She hummed while she awaited the girl's return.

During the next few days, whisky ministered to her as tenderly as it had done when she first turned to its aid. Alone, she was soothed and vague, at Jimmy's she was the gayest of the groups. Art was delighted with her.

Then, one night, she had an appointment to meet Art at Jimmy's for an early dinner. He was to leave afterward on a business excursion, to be away for a week. Mrs. Morse had been drinking all the afternoon; while she dressed to go out, she felt herself rising pleasurably from drowsiness to high spirits. But as she came out into the street the effects of the whisky deserted her completely, and she was filled with a slow, grinding wretchedness so horrible that she stood swaying on the pavement, unable for a moment to move forward. It was a gray night with spurts of mean, thin snow, and the streets shone with dark ice. As she slowly crossed Sixth Avenue, consciously dragging one foot past the other, a big, scarred horse pulling a rickety express-wagon crashed to his knees before her. The driver swore and screamed and lashed the beast insanely, bringing the whip back over his shoulder for every blow, while the horse struggled to get a footing on the slippery asphalt. A group gathered and watched with interest.

Art was waiting, when Mrs. Morse reached Jimmy's.

"What's the matter with you, for God's sake?" was his greeting to her.

"I saw a horse," she said. "Gee, I—a person feels sorry for horses. I—it isn't just horses. Everything's kind of terrible, isn't it? I can't help getting sunk."

"Ah, sunk, me eye," he said. "What's the idea of all the bellyaching? What have you got to be sunk about?"

"I can't help it," she said.

"Ah, help it, me eye," he said. "Pull yourself together, will you? Come on and sit down, and take that face off you."

She drank industriously and she tried hard, but she could not overcome her melancholy. Others joined them and commented on her gloom, and she could do no more for them than smile weakly. She made little dabs at her eyes with her handkerchief, trying to time her movements so they would be unnoticed, but several times Art caught her and scowled and shifted impatiently in his chair.

When it was time for him to go to his train, she said she would leave, too, and go home.

"And not a bad idea, either," he said. "See if you can't sleep yourself out of it. I'll see you Thursday. For God's sake, try and cheer up by then, will you?"

"Yeah," she said. "I will."

In her bedroom, she undressed with a tense speed wholly

unlike her usual slow uncertainty. She put on her nightgown, took off her hair-net and passed the comb quickly through her dry, vari-colored hair. Then she took the two little vials from the drawer and carried them into the bathroom. The splintering misery had gone from her, and she felt the quick excitement of one who is about to receive an anticipated gift.

She uncorked the vials, filled a glass with water and stood before the mirror, a tablet between her fingers. Suddenly she bowed graciously to her reflection, and raised the glass to it.

"Well, here's mud in your eye," she said.

The tablets were unpleasant to take, dry and powdery and sticking obstinately half-way down her throat. It took her a long time to swallow all twenty of them. She stood watching her reflection with deep, impersonal interest, studying the movements of the gulping throat. Once more she spoke aloud.

"For God's sake, try and cheer up by Thursday, will you?" she said. "Well, you know what he can do. He and the whole lot of them."

She had no idea how quickly to expect effect from the veronal. When she had taken the last tablet, she stood uncertainly, wondering, still with a courteous, vicarious interest, if death would strike her down then and there. She felt in no way strange, save for a slight stirring of sickness from the effort of swallowing the tablets, nor did her reflected face look at all different. It would not be immediate, then; it might even take an hour or so.

She stretched her arms high and gave a vast yawn.

"Guess I'll go to bed," she said. "Gee, I'm nearly dead."

That struck her as comic, and she turned out the bathroom light and went in and laid herself down in her bed, chuckling softly all the time.

"Gee, I'm nearly dead," she quoted. "That's a hot one!"

III

Nettie, the colored maid, came in late the next afternoon to clean the apartment, and found Mrs. Morse in her bed. But then, that was not unusual. Usually, though, the sounds of cleaning waked her, and she did not like to wake up. Nettie, an agreeable girl, had learned to move softly about her work.

But when she had done the living-room and stolen in to tidy the little square bedroom, she could not avoid a tiny clatter as she arranged the objects on the dressing-table. Instinctively, she glanced over her shoulder at the sleeper, and without warning a sickly uneasiness crept over her. She came to the bed and stared down at the woman lying there.

Mrs. Morse lay on her back, one flabby, white arm flung up, the wrist against her forehead. Her stiff hair hung untenderly along her face. The bed covers were pushed down, exposing a deep square of soft neck and a pink nightgown, its fabric worn uneven by many launderings; her great breasts, freed from their tight confiner, sagged beneath her arm-pits. Now and then she made knotted, snoring sounds, and from the corner of her opened mouth to the blurred turn of her jaw ran a lane of crusted spittle.

"Mis' Morse," Nettie called. "Oh, Mis' Morse! It's terrible late."

Mrs. Morse made no move.

"Mis' Morse," said Nettie. "Look, Mis' Morse. How'm I goin' get this bed made?"

Panic sprang upon the girl. She shook the woman's hot shoulder.

"Ah, wake up, will yuh?" she whined. "Ah, please wake up."

Suddenly the girl turned and ran out in the hall to the elevator door, keeping her thumb firm on the black, shiny button until the elderly car and its Negro attendant stood before her. She poured a jumble of words over the boy, and led him back to the apartment. He tiptoed creakingly in to the bedside; first gingerly, then so lustily that he left marks in the soft flesh, he prodded the unconscious woman.

"Hey, there!" he cried, and listened intently, as for an echo.

"Jeez. Out like a light," he commented.

At his interest in the spectacle, Nettie's panic left her. Importance was big in both of them. They talked in quick, unfinished whispers, and it was the boy's suggestion that he fetch the young doctor who lived on the ground floor. Nettie hurried along with him. They looked forward to the limelit moment of breaking their news of something untoward, something pleasurably unpleasant. Mrs. Morse had become the medium of drama. With no ill wish to her, they hoped that her state was serious, that she would not let them down by being awake and normal on their return. A little fear of this determined them to make the most, to the doctor, of her present condition. "Matter of life and death," returned to Nettie from her thin store of reading. She considered startling the doctor with the phrase.

The doctor was in and none too pleased at interruption. He wore a yellow and blue striped dressing-gown, and he was lying on his sofa, laughing with a dark girl, her face scaly with inexpensive powder, who perched on the arm. Half-emptied highball glasses stood beside them, and her coat and hat were neatly hung up with the comfortable implication of a long stay. Always something, the doctor grumbled. Couldn't let anybody alone after a hard day. But he put some bottles and instruments into a case, changed his dressing-gown for his coat and started out with the Negroes.

"Snap it up there, big boy," the girl called after him. "Don't be all night."

The doctor strode loudly into Mrs. Morse's flat and on to the bedroom, Nettie and the boy right behind him. Mrs. Morse had not moved; her sleep was as deep, but soundless, now. The doctor looked sharply at her, then plunged his thumbs into the lidded pits above her eyeballs and threw his weight upon them. A high, sickened cry broke from Nettie.

"Look like he tryin' to push her right on th'ough the bed," said the boy. He chuckled.

Mrs. Morse gave no sign under the pressure. Abruptly the doctor abandoned it, and with one quick movement swept the covers down to the foot of the bed. With another he flung her nightgown back and lifted the thick, white legs, cross-hatched with blocks of tiny, iris-colored veins. He pinched them repeatedly, with long, cruel nips, back of the knees. She did not awaken.

"What's she been drinking?" he asked Nettie, over his shoulder.

With the certain celerity of one who knows just where to lay hands on a thing, Nettie went into the bathroom, bound for the cupboard where Mrs. Morse kept her whisky. But she stopped at the sight of the two vials, with their red and white labels, lying before the mirror. She brought them to the doctor.

"Oh, for the Lord Almighty's sweet sake!" he said. He dropped Mrs. Morse's legs, and pushed them impatiently across the bed. "What did she want to go taking that tripe for? Rotten yellow trick, that's what a thing like that is. Now we'll have to pump her out, and all that stuff. Nuisance, a thing like that is; that's what it amounts to. Here, George, take me down in the elevator. You wait here, maid. She won't do anything."

"She won't die on me, will she?" cried Nettie.

"No," said the doctor. "God, no. You couldn't kill her with an ax."

IV

After two days, Mrs. Morse came back to consciousness, dazed at first, then with a comprehension that brought with it the slow, saturating wretchedness.

"Oh, Lord, oh, Lord," she moaned, and tears for herself and for life striped her cheeks.

Nettie came in at the sound. For two days she had done the ugly, incessant tasks in the nursing of the unconscious, for two nights she had caught broken bits of sleep on the living-room couch. She looked coldly at the big, blown woman in the bed.

"What you been tryin' to do, Mis' Morse?" she said. "What kine o' work is that, takin' all that stuff?"

"Oh, Lord," moaned Mrs. Morse, again, and she tried to cover her eyes with her arms. But the joints felt stiff and brittle, and she cried out at their ache.

"Tha's no way to ack, takin' them pills," said Nettie. "You can thank you' stars you heah at all. How you feel now?"

"Oh, I feel great," said Mrs. Morse. "Swell, I feel."

Her hot, painful tears fell as if they would never stop.

"Tha's no way to take on, cryin' like that," Nettie said. "After what you done. The doctor, he says he could have you arrested, doin' a thing like that. He was fit to be tied, here."

"Why couldn't he let me alone?" wailed Mrs. Morse. "Why the hell couldn't he have?"

"Tha's terr'ble, Mis' Morse, swearin' an' talkin' like that," said Nettie, "after what people done for you. Here I ain' had no sleep at all for two nights, an' had to give up goin' out to my other ladies!"

"Oh, I'm sorry, Nettie," she said. "You're a peach. I'm sorry I've given you so much trouble. I couldn't help it. I just got sunk. Didn't you ever feel like doing it? When everything looks just lousy to you?"

"I wouldn' think o' no such thing," declared Nettie. "You got to cheer up. Tha's what you got to do. Everybody's got their troubles."

"Yeah," said Mrs. Morse. "I know."

"Come a pretty picture card for you," Nettie said. "Maybe that will cheer you up."

She handed Mrs. Morse a post-card. Mrs. Morse had to cover one eye with her hand, in order to read the message; her eyes were not yet focusing correctly.

It was from Art. On the back of a view of the Detroit Athletic Club he had written: "Greeting and salutations. Hope you have lost that gloom. Cheer up and don't take any rubber nickels. See you on Thursday."

She dropped the card to the floor. Misery crushed her as if she were between great smooth stones. There passed before her a slow, slow pageant of days spent lying in her flat, of evenings at Jimmy's being a good sport, making herself laugh and coo at Art and other Arts; she saw a long parade of weary horses and shivering beggars and all beaten, driven, stumbling things. Her feet throbbed as if she had crammed them into the stubby champagne-colored slippers. Her heart seemed to swell and harden.

"Nettie," she cried, "for heaven's sake pour me a drink, will you?"

The maid looked doubtful.

"Now you know, Mis' Morse," she said, "you been near daid. I don' know if the doctor he let you drink nothin' yet."

"Oh, never mind him," she said. "You get me one, and bring in the bottle. Take one yourself."

"Well," said Nettie.

She poured them each a drink, deferentially leaving hers in the bathroom to be taken in solitude, and brought Mrs. Morse's glass in to her.

Mrs. Morse looked into the liquor and shuddered back from its odor. Maybe it would help. Maybe, when you had been knocked cold for a few days, your very first drink would give you a lift. Maybe whisky would be her friend again. She prayed without addressing a God, without knowing a God. Oh, please, please, let her be able to get drunk, please keep her always drunk.

She lifted the glass.

"Thanks, Nettie," she said. "Here's mud in your eye."

The maid giggled. "That's the way, Mis' Morse," she said. "You cheer up, now."

"Yeah," said Mrs. Morse. "Sure."

Sunset Gun

Godmother

The day that I was christened—
　　It's a hundred years, and more!—
A hag came and listened
　　At the white church door,
A-hearing her that bore me
　　And all my kith and kin
Considerately, for me,
　　Renouncing sin.
While some gave me corals,
　　And some gave me gold,
And porringers, with morals
　　Agreeably scrolled,
The hag stood, buckled
　　In a dim gray cloak;
Stood there and chuckled,
　　Spat, and spoke:
"There's few enough in life'll
　　Be needing my help,
But I've got a trifle
　　For your fine young whelp.
I give her sadness,
　　And the gift of pain,
The new-moon madness,
　　And the love of rain."
And little good to lave me
　　In their holy silver bowl
After what she gave me—
　　Rest her soul!

The Red Dress

I always saw, I always said
    If I were grown and free,
I'd have a gown of reddest red
    As fine as you could see,

To wear out walking, sleek and slow,
    Upon a Summer day,
And there'd be one to see me so
    And flip the world away.

And he would be a gallant one,
    With stars behind his eyes,
And hair like metal in the sun,
    And lips too warm for lies.

I always saw us, gay and good,
    High honored in the town.
Now I am grown to womanhood. . . .
    I have the silly gown.

Victoria

Dear dead Victoria
    Rotted cosily;
In excelsis gloria,
    And R. I. P.

And her shroud was buttoned neat,
    And her bones were clean and round,
And her soul was at her feet
    Like a bishop's marble hound.

Albert lay a-drying,
    Lavishly arrayed,
With his soul out flying
    Where his heart had stayed.

And there's some could tell you what land
   His spirit walks serene
(But I've heard them say in Scotland
   It's never been seen).

To Newcastle

I met a man the other day—
   A kindly man, and serious—
Who viewed me in a thoughtful way,
   And spoke me so, and spoke me thus:

"Oh, dallying's a sad mistake;
   'Tis craven to survey the morrow!
Go give your heart, and if it break—
   A wise companion is Sorrow.

"Oh, live, my child, nor keep your soul
   To crowd your coffin when you're dead...."
I asked his work; he dealt in coal,
   And shipped it up the Tyne, he said.

Parable for
a Certain Virgin

Oh, ponder, friend, the porcupine;
   Refresh your recollection,
And sit a moment, to define
   His means of self-protection.

How truly fortified is he!
   Where is the beast his double
In forethought of emergency
   And readiness for trouble?

Recall his figure, and his shade—
   How deftly planned and clearly
For slithering through the dappled glade
   Unseen, or pretty nearly.

Yet should an alien eye discern
   His presence in the woodland,
How little has he left to learn
   Of self-defense! My good land!

For he can run, as swift as sound,
   To where his goose may hang high;
Or thrust his head against the ground
   And tunnel half to Shanghai;

Or he can climb the dizziest bough—
   Unhesitant, mechanic—
And, resting, dash from off his brow
   The bitter beads of panic;

Or should pursuers press him hot,
   One scarcely needs to mention
His quick and cruel barbs, that got
   Shakespearean attention;

Or driven to his final ditch,
   To his extremest thicket,
He'll fight with claws and molars (which
   Is not considered cricket).

How amply armored, he, to fend
   The fear of chase that haunts him!
How well prepared our little friend!—
   And who the devil wants him?

Bric-à-Brac

Little things that no one needs—
    Little things to joke about—
Little landscapes, done in beads.
    Little morals, woven out,
Little wreaths of gilded grass,
    Little brigs of whittled oak
Bottled painfully in glass;
    These are made by lonely folk.

Lonely folk have lines of days
    Long and faltering and thin;
Therefore—little wax bouquets,
    Prayers cut upon a pin,
Little maps of pinkish lands,
    Little charts of curly seas,
Little plats of linen strands,
    Little verses, such as these.

Interior

Her mind lives in a quiet room,
    A narrow room, and tall,
With pretty lamps to quench the gloom
    And mottoes on the wall.

There all the things are waxen neat
    And set in decorous lines;
And there are posies, round and sweet,
    And little, straightened vines.

Her mind lives tidily, apart
    From cold and noise and pain,
And bolts the door against her heart,
    Out wailing in the rain.

Reuben's Children

Accursed from their birth they be
Who seek to find monogamy,
Pursuing it from bed to bed—
I think they would be better dead.

On Cheating the
Fiddler

"Then we will have tonight!" we said.
"Tomorrow—may we not be dead?"
The morrow touched our eyes, and found
Us walking firm above the ground,
Our pulses quick, our blood alight.
Tomorrow's gone—we'll have tonight!

There Was One

There was one a-riding grand
  On a tall brown mare,
And a fine gold band
  He brought me there.

A little, gold band
  He held to me
That would shine on a hand
  For the world to see.

There was one a-walking swift
  To a little, new song,
And a rose was the gift
  He carried along,

First of all the posies,
　Dewy and red.
They that have roses
　Never need bread.

There was one with a swagger
　And a soft, slow tongue,
And a bright, cold dagger
　Where his left hand swung—

Craven and gilt,
　Old and bad—
And his stroking of the hilt
　Set a girl mad.

There was one a-riding grand
　As he rode from me.
And he raised his golden band
　And he threw it in the sea.

There was one a-walking slow
　To a sad, long sigh.
And his rose drooped low,
　And he flung it down to die.

There was one with a swagger
　And a little, sharp pride,
And a bright, cold dagger
　Ever at his side.

At his side it stayed
　When he ran to part.
What is this blade
　Struck through my heart?

Incurable

And if my heart be scarred and burned,
The safer, I, for all I learned;
The calmer, I, to see it true
That ways of love are never new—
The love that sets you daft and dazed
Is every love that ever blazed;
The happier, I, to fathom this:
A kiss is every other kiss.
The reckless vow, the lovely name,
When Helen walked, were spoke the same;
The weighted breast, the grinding woe,
When Phaon fled, were ever so.
Oh, it is sure as it is sad
That any lad is every lad,
And what's a girl, to dare implore
Her dear be hers forevermore?
Though he be tried and he be bold,
And swearing death should he be cold,
He'll run the path the others went....
But you, my sweet, are different.

The Second Oldest Story

Go I must along my ways
    Though my heart be ragged,
Dripping bitter through the days,
    Festering, and jagged.
Smile I must at every twinge,
    Kiss, to time its throbbing;
He that tears a heart to fringe
    Hates the noise of sobbing.

`·  ·  ·  ·  ·  ·  ·`

Weep, my love, till Heaven hears;
   Curse and moan and languish.
While I wash your wound with tears,
   Ease aloud your anguish.
Bellow of the pit in Hell
   Where you're made to linger.
There and there and well and well—
   Did he prick his finger!

Partial Comfort

Whose love is given over-well
Shall look on Helen's face in hell,
Whilst they whose love is thin and wise
May view John Knox in paradise.

Fable

Oh, there once was a lady, and so I've been told,
Whose lover grew weary, whose lover grew cold.
"My child," he remarked, "though our episode ends,
In the manner of men, I suggest we be friends."
And the truest of friends ever after they were—
Oh, they lied in their teeth when they told me of her!

A Pig's-Eye View of Literature

The Lives and Times of John Keats,
Percy Bysshe Shelley, and
George Gordon Noel, Lord Byron

Byron and Shelley and Keats
Were a trio of lyrical treats.

The forehead of Shelley was cluttered with curls,
And Keats never was a descendant of earls,
And Byron walked out with a number of girls,
   But it didn't impair the poetical feats
      Of Byron and Shelley,
      Of Byron and Shelley,
   Of Byron and Shelley and Keats.

Oscar Wilde

If, with the literate, I am
Impelled to try an epigram,
I never seek to take the credit;
We all assume that Oscar said it.

Harriet Beecher Stowe

The pure and worthy Mrs. Stowe
Is one we all are proud to know
As mother, wife, and authoress—
Thank God, I am content with less!

D. G. Rossetti

Dante Gabriel Rossetti
Buried all of his *libretti*,
Thought the matter over—then
Went and dug them up again.

Thomas Carlyle

Carlyle combined the lit'ry life
With throwing teacups at his wife,
Remarking, rather testily,
"Oh, stop your dodging, Mrs. C.!"

Charles Dickens

Who call him spurious and shoddy
Shall do it o'er my lifeless body.
I heartily invite such birds
To come outside and say those words!

Alexandre Dumas and His Son

Although I work, and seldom cease,
At Dumas *père* and Dumas *fils*,
Alas, I cannot make me care
For Dumas *fils* and Dumas *père*.

Alfred, Lord Tennyson

Should Heaven send me any son,
I hope he's not like Tennyson.
I'd rather have him play a fiddle
Than rise and bow and speak an idyll.

George Gissing

When I admit neglect of Gissing,
They say I don't know what I'm missing.
Until their arguments are subtler,
I think I'll stick to Samuel Butler.

Walter Savage Landor

Upon the work of Walter Landor
I am unfit to write with candor.
If you can read it, well and good;
But as for me, I never could.

George Sand

What time the gifted lady took
Away from paper, pen, and book,
She spent in amorous dalliance
(They do those things so well in France).

Mortal Enemy

Let another cross his way—
    She's the one will do the weeping!
Little need I fear he'll stray
    Since I have his heart in keeping.

Let another hail him dear—
    Little chance that he'll forget me!
Only need I curse and fear
    Her he loved before he met me.

Penelope

In the pathway of the sun,
    In the footsteps of the breeze,
Where the world and sky are one,
    He shall ride the silver seas,
        He shall cut the glittering wave.
I shall sit at home, and rock;
Rise, to heed a neighbor's knock;
Brew my tea, and snip my thread;
Bleach the linen for my bed.
        They will call him brave.

Bohemia

Authors and actors and artists and such
Never know nothing, and never know much.
Sculptors and singers and those of their kidney
Tell their affairs from Seattle to Sydney.
Playwrights and poets and such horses' necks
Start off from anywhere, end up at sex.
Diarists, critics, and similar roe
Never say nothing, and never say no.
People Who Do Things exceed my endurance;
God, for a man that solicits insurance!

The Searched Soul

When I consider, pro and con,
What things my love is built upon—
A curly mouth; a sinewed wrist;
A questioning brow; a pretty twist
Of words as old and tried as sin;
A pointed ear; a cloven chin;
Long, tapered limbs; and slanted eyes
Not cold nor kind nor darkly wise—
When so I ponder, here apart,
What shallow boons suffice my heart,
What dust-bound trivia capture me,
I marvel at my normalcy.

The Trusting Heart

Oh, I'd been better dying,
  Oh, I was slow and sad;
A fool I was, a-crying
  About a cruel lad!

But there was one that found me,
    That wept to see me weep,
And had his arm around me,
    And gave me words to keep.

And I'd be better dying,
    And I am slow and sad;
A fool I am, a-crying
    About a tender lad!

The Gentlest Lady

They say He was a serious child,
    And quiet in His ways;
They say the gentlest lady smiled
    To hear the neighbors' praise.

The coffers of her heart would close
    Upon their smallest word.
Yet did they say, "How tall He grows!"
    They thought she had not heard.

They say upon His birthday eve
    She'd rock Him to His rest
As if she could not have Him leave
    The shelter of her breast.

The poor must go in bitter thrift,
    The poor must give in pain,
But ever did she get a gift
    To greet His day again.

They say she'd kiss the Boy awake,
    And hail Him gay and clear,
But oh, her heart was like to break
    To count another year.

The Maid-Servant
at the Inn

"It's queer," she said; "I see the light
  As plain as I beheld it then,
All silver-like and calm and bright—
  We've not had stars like that again!

"And she was such a gentle thing
  To birth a baby in the cold.
The barn was dark and frightening—
  This new one's better than the old.

"I mind my eyes were full of tears,
  For I was young, and quick distressed,
But she was less than me in years
  That held a son against her breast.

"I never saw a sweeter child—
  The little one, the darling one!—
I mind I told her, when he smiled
  You'd know he was his mother's son.

"It's queer that I should see them so—
  The time they came to Bethlehem
Was more than thirty years ago;
  I've prayed that all is well with them."

Fulfillment

For this my mother wrapped me warm,
And called me home against the storm,
And coaxed my infant nights to quiet,
And gave me roughage in my diet,
And tucked me in my bed at eight,
And clipped my hair, and marked my weight,

And watched me as I sat and stood:
That I might grow to womanhood
To hear a whistle and drop my wits
And break my heart to clattering bits.

Daylight Saving

My answers are inadequate
To those demanding day and date
And ever set a tiny shock
Through strangers asking what's o'clock;
Whose days are spent in whittling rhyme—
What's time to her, or she to Time?

Thought for a
Sunshiny Morning

It costs me never a stab nor squirm
To tread by chance upon a worm.
"Aha, my little dear," I say,
"Your clan will pay me back one day."

Surprise

My heart went fluttering with fear
Lest you should go, and leave me here
To beat my breast and rock my head
And stretch me sleepless on my bed.
Ah, clear they see and true they say
That one shall weep, and one shall stray
For such is Love's unvarying law....
I never thought, I never saw
That I should be the first to go;
How pleasant that it happened so!

On Being a Woman

Why is it, when I am in Rome,
I'd give an eye to be at home,
But when on native earth I be,
My soul is sick for Italy?

And why with you, my love, my lord,
Am I spectacularly bored,
Yet do you up and leave me—then
I scream to have you back again?

Afternoon

When I am old, and comforted,
    And done with this desire,
With Memory to share my bed
    And Peace to share my fire,

I'll comb my hair in scalloped bands
    Beneath my laundered cap,
And watch my cool and fragile hands
    Lie light upon my lap.

And I will have a sprigged gown
    With lace to kiss my throat;
I'll draw my curtain to the town,
    And hum a purring note.

And I'll forget the way of tears,
    And rock, and stir my tea.
But oh, I wish those blessed years
    Were further than they be!

A Dream Lies Dead

A dream lies dead here. May you softly go
Before this place, and turn away your eyes,
Nor seek to know the look of that which dies
Importuning Life for life. Walk not in woe,
But, for a little, let your step be slow.
And, of your mercy, be not sweetly wise
With words of hope and Spring and tenderer skies.
A dream lies dead; and this all mourners know:

Whenever one drifted petal leaves the tree—
Though white of bloom as it had been before
And proudly waitful of fecundity—
One little loveliness can be no more;
And so must Beauty bow her imperfect head
Because a dream has joined the wistful dead!

The Homebody

There still are kindly things for me to know,
Who am afraid to dream, afraid to feel—
This little chair of scrubbed and sturdy deal,
This easy book, this fire, sedate and slow.
And I shall stay with them, nor cry the woe
Of wounds across my breast that do not heal;
Nor wish that Beauty drew a duller steel,
Since I am sworn to meet her as a foe.

It may be, when the devil's own time is done,
That I shall hear the dropping of the rain
At midnight, and lie quiet in my bed;
Or stretch and straighten to the yellow sun;
Or face the turning tree, and have no pain;
So shall I learn at last my heart is dead.

Second Love

"So surely is she mine," you say, and turn
Your quick and steady mind to harder things—
To bills and bonds and talk of what men earn—
And whistle up the stair, of evenings.
And do you see a dream behind my eyes,
Or ask a simple question twice of me—
"Thus women are," you say; for men are wise
And tolerant, in their security.

How shall I count the midnights I have known
When calm you turn to me, nor feel me start,
To find my easy lips upon your own
And know my breast beneath your rhythmic heart.
Your god defer the day I tell you this:
My lad, my lad, it is not you I kiss!

Fair Weather

This level reach of blue is not my sea;
Here are sweet waters, pretty in the sun,
Whose quiet ripples meet obediently
A marked and measured line, one after one.
This is no sea of mine, that humbly laves
Untroubled sands, spread glittering and warm.
I have a need of wilder, crueler waves;
They sicken of the calm, who knew the storm.

So let a love beat over me again,
Loosing its million desperate breakers wide;
Sudden and terrible to rise and wane;
Roaring the heavens apart; a reckless tide
That casts upon the heart, as it recedes,
Splinters and spars and dripping, salty weeds.

The Whistling Girl

Back of my back, they talk of me,
  Gabble and honk and hiss;
Let them batten, and let them be—
  Me, I can sing them this:

"Better to shiver beneath the stars,
  Head on a faithless breast,
Than peer at the night through rusted bars,
  And share an irksome rest.

"Better to see the dawn come up,
  Along of a trifling one,
Than set a steady man's cloth and cup
  And pray the day be done.

"Better be left by twenty dears
  Than lie in a loveless bed;
Better a loaf that's wet with tears
  Than cold, unsalted bread."

Back of my back, they wag their chins,
  Whinny and bleat and sigh;
But better a heart a-bloom with sins
  Than hearts gone yellow and dry!

Story

"And if he's gone away," said she,
"Good riddance, if you're asking me.
I'm not a one to lie awake
And weep for anybody's sake.
There's better lads than him about!
I'll wear my buckled slippers out
A-dancing till the break of day.

I'm better off with him away!
And if he never come," said she,
"Now what on earth is that to me?
I wouldn't have him back!"
   I hope
Her mother washed her mouth with soap.

Frustration

If I had a shiny gun,
I could have a world of fun
Speeding bullets through the brains
Of the folk who give me pains;

Or had I some poison gas,
I could make the moments pass
Bumping off a number of
People whom I do not love.

But I have no lethal weapon—
Thus does Fate our pleasure step on!
So they still are quick and well
Who should be, by rights, in hell.

Healed

Oh, when I flung my heart away,
   The year was at its fall.
I saw my dear, the other day,
   Beside a flowering wall;
And this was all I had to say:
   "I thought that he was tall!"

Post-Graduate

Hope it was that tutored me,
    And Love that taught me more;
And now I learn at Sorrow's knee
    The self-same lore.

Landscape

Now this must be the sweetest place
    From here to heaven's end;
The field is white and flowering lace,
    The birches leap and bend,

The hills, beneath the roving sun,
    From green to purple pass,
And little, trifling breezes run
    Their fingers through the grass.

So good it is, so gay it is,
    So calm it is, and pure,
A one whose eyes may look on this
    Must be the happier, sure.

But me—I see it flat and gray
    And blurred with misery,
Because a lad a mile away
    Has little need of me.

For a Favorite Granddaughter

Never love a simple lad,
    Guard against a wise,
Shun a timid youth and sad,
    Hide from haunted eyes.

Never hold your heart in pain
  For an evil-doer;
Never flip it down the lane
  To a gifted wooer.

Never love a loving son,
  Nor a sheep astray;
Gather up your skirts and run
  From a tender way.

Never give away a tear,
  Never toss a pine;
Should you heed my words, my dear,
  You're no blood of mine!

Liebestod

When I was bold, when I was bold—
  And that's a hundred years!—
Oh, never I thought my breast could hold
  The terrible weight of tears.

I said: "Now some be dolorous;
  I hear them wail and sigh,
And if it be Love that play them thus,
  · Then never a love will I."

I said: "I see them rack and rue,
  I see them wring and ache,
And little I'll crack my heart in two
  With little the heart can break."

When I was gay, when I was gay—
  It's ninety years and nine!—
Oh, never I thought that Death could lay
  His terrible hand in mine.

I said: "He plies his trade among
    The musty and infirm;
A body so hard and bright and young
    Could never be meat for worm."

"I see him dull their eyes," I said,
    "And still their rattling breath.
And how under God could I be dead
    That never was meant for Death?"

But Love came by, to quench my sleep,
    And here's my sundered heart;
And bitter's my woe, and black, and deep,
    And little I guessed a part.

Yet this there is to cool my breast,
    And this to ease my spell;
Now if I were Love's, like all the rest,
    Then can I be Death's, as well.

And he shall have me, sworn and bound,
    And I'll be done with Love.
And better I'll be below the ground
    Than ever I'll be above.

Dilemma

If I were mild, and I were sweet,
And laid my heart before your feet,
And took my dearest thoughts to you,
And hailed your easy lies as true;
Were I to murmur "Yes," and then
"How true, my dear," and "Yes," again,
And wear my eyes discreetly down,
And tremble whitely at your frown,
And keep my words unquestioning—
My love, you'd run like anything!

Should I be frail, and I be mad,
And share my heart with every lad,
But beat my head against the floor
What times you wandered past my door;
Were I to doubt, and I to sneer,
And shriek "Farewell!" and still be here,
And break your joy, and quench your trust—
I should not see you for the dust!

Theory

Into love and out again,
    Thus I went, and thus I go.
Spare your voice, and hold your pen—
    Well and bitterly I know
All the songs were ever sung,
    All the words were ever said;
Could it be, when I was young,
    Some one dropped me on my head?

Superfluous Advice

Should they whisper false of you,
    Never trouble to deny;
Should the words they say be true,
    Weep and storm and swear they lie.

A Fairly Sad Tale

I think that I shall never know
Why I am thus, and I am so.
Around me, other girls inspire
In men the rush and roar of fire,
The sweet transparency of glass,
The tenderness of April grass,

The durability of granite;
But me—I don't know how to plan it.
The lads I've met in Cupid's deadlock
Were—shall we say?—born out of wedlock.
They broke my heart, they stilled my song,
And said they had to run along,
Explaining, so to sop my tears,
First came their parents or careers.
But ever does experience
Deny me wisdom, calm, and sense!
Though she's a fool who seeks to capture
The twenty-first fine, careless rapture,
I must go on, till ends my rope,
Who from my birth was cursed with hope.
A heart in half is chaste, archaic;
But mine resembles a mosaic—
The thing's become ridiculous!
Why am I so? Why am I thus?

The Last Question

New love, new love, where are you to lead me?
  All along a narrow way that marks a crooked line.
How are you to slake me, and how are you to feed me?
  With bitter yellow berries, and a sharp new wine.

New love, new love, shall I be forsaken?
  One shall go a-wandering, and one of us must sigh.
Sweet it is to slumber, but how shall we awaken—
  Whose will be the broken heart, when dawn comes
    by?

But Not Forgotten

I think, no matter where you stray,
That I shall go with you a way.

Though you may wander sweeter lands,
You will not soon forget my hands,
Nor yet the way I held my head,
Nor all the tremulous things I said.
You still will see me, small and white
And smiling, in the secret night,
And feel my arms about you when
The day comes fluttering back again.
I think, no matter where you be,
You'll hold me in your memory
And keep my image, there without me,
By telling later loves about me.

Pour Prendre Congé

I'm sick of embarking in dories
    Upon an emotional sea.
I'm wearied of playing Dolores
    (A role never written for me).

I'll never again like a cub lick
    My wounds while I squeal at the hurt.
No more I'll go walking in public,
    My heart hanging out of my shirt.

I'm tired of entwining me garlands
    Of weather-worn hemlock and bay.
I'm over my longing for far lands—
    I wouldn't give that for Cathay.

I'm through with performing the ballet
    Of love unrequited and told.
Euterpe, I tender you *vale;*
    Good-by, and take care of that cold.

I'm done with this burning and giving
    And reeling the rhymes of my woes.
And how I'll be making my living,
    The Lord in His mystery knows.

For a Lady
Who Must Write Verse

Unto seventy years and seven,
    Hide your double birthright well—
You, that are the brat of Heaven
    And the pampered heir to Hell.

Let your rhymes be tinsel treasures,
    Strung and seen and thrown aside.
Drill your apt and docile measures
    Sternly as you drill your pride.

Show your quick, alarming skill in
    Tidy mockeries of art;
Never, never dip your quill in
    Ink that rushes from your heart.

When your pain must come to paper,
    See it dust, before the day;
Let your night-light curl and caper,
    Let it lick the words away.

Never print, poor child, a lay on
    Love and tears and anguishing,
Lest a cooled, benignant Phaon
    Murmur, "Silly little thing!"

Two-Volume Novel

The sun's gone dim, and
    The moon's turned black;
For I loved him, and
    He didn't love back.

Rhyme Against Living

If wild my breast and sore my pride,
I bask in dreams of suicide;
If cool my heart and high my head,
I think, "How lucky are the dead!"

Wisdom

This I say, and this I know:
  Love has seen the last of me.
Love's a trodden lane to woe,
  Love's a path to misery.

This I know, and knew before,
  This I tell you, of my years:
Hide your heart, and lock your door.
  Hell's afloat in lovers' tears.

Give your heart, and toss and moan;
  What a pretty fool you look!
I am sage, who sit alone;
  Here's my wool, and here's my book.

Look! A lad's a-waiting there,
  Tall he is and bold, and gay.
What the devil do I care
  What I know, and what I say?

Coda

There's little in taking or giving,
  There's little in water or wine;
This living, this living, this living
  Was never a project of mine.
Oh, hard is the struggle, and sparse is
  The gain of the one at the top,
For art is a form of catharsis,
  And love is a permanent flop,
And work is the province of cattle,
  And rest's for a clam in a shell,
So I'm thinking of throwing the battle—
  Would you kindly direct me to hell?

Just a Little One

I like this place, Fred. This is a nice place. How did you ever find it? I think you're perfectly marvelous, discovering a speakeasy in the year 1928. And they let you right in, without asking you a single question. I bet you could get into the subway without using anybody's name. Couldn't you, Fred?

Oh, I like this place better and better, now that my eyes are getting accustomed to it. You mustn't let them tell you this lighting system is original with them, Fred; they got the idea from the Mammoth Cave. This is you sitting next to me, isn't it? Oh, you can't fool me. I'd know that knee anywhere.

You know what I like about this place? It's got atmosphere. That's what it's got. If you would ask the waiter to bring a fairly sharp knife, I could cut off a nice little block of the atmosphere, to take home with me. It would be interesting to have for my memory book. I'm going to start keeping a memory book tomorrow. Don't let me forget.

Why, I don't know, Fred—what are you going to have? Then I guess I'll have a highball, too; please, just a little one. Is it really real Scotch? Well, that will be a new experience for me. You ought to see the Scotch I've got home in my cupboard; at least it was in the cupboard this morning—it's probably eaten its way out by now. I got it for my birthday. Well, it was something. The birthday before, all I got was a year older.

This is a nice highball, isn't it? Well, well, well, to think of me having real Scotch; I'm out of the bush leagues at last. Are you going to have another one? Well, I shouldn't like to see you drinking all by yourself, Fred. Solitary drinking is what causes half the crime in the country. That's what's responsible for the failure of prohibition. But please, Fred, tell him to make mine just a little one. Make it awfully weak; just cambric Scotch.

It will be nice to see the effect of veritable whisky upon one who has been accustomed only to the simpler forms of entertainment. You'll like that, Fred. You'll stay by me if anything happens, won't you? I don't think there will be anything spectacular, but I want to ask you one thing, just in case. Don't let me take any horses home with me. It doesn't matter so much about stray dogs and kittens, but elevator boys get awfully stuffy when you try to bring in a horse. You might just as well know that about me now, Fred. You can always tell that the crash is coming when I start getting tender about Our Dumb Friends. Three highballs, and I think I'm St. Francis of Assisi.

But I don't believe anything is going to happen to me on these. That's because they're made of real stuff. That's what the difference is. This just makes you feel fine. Oh, I feel swell, Fred. You do too, don't you? I knew you did, because you look better. I love that tie you have on. Oh, did Edith give it to you? Ah, wasn't that nice of her? You know, Fred, most people are really awfully nice. There are darn few that aren't pretty fine at heart. You've got a beautiful heart, Fred. You'd be the first person I'd go to if I were in trouble. I guess you are just about the best friend I've got in the world. But I worry about you, Fred. I do so, too. I don't think you take enough care of yourself. You ought to take care of yourself for your friends' sake. You oughtn't to drink all this terrible stuff that's around; you owe it to your friends to be careful. You don't mind my talking to you like this, do you? You see, dear, it's because I'm your friend that I hate to see you not taking care of yourself. It hurts me to see you batting around the way you've been doing. You ought to stick to this place, where they have real Scotch that can't do you any harm. Oh, darling, do you really think I ought to? Well, you tell him just a little bit of a one. Tell him, sweet.

Do you come here often, Fred? I shouldn't worry about you so much if I knew you were in a safe place like this. Oh, is this where you were Thursday night? I see. Why, no, it didn't make a bit of difference, only you told me to call you up, and like a fool I broke a date I had, just because I thought I was going to see you. I just sort of naturally thought so, when you said to call you up. Oh, good Lord, don't make all that fuss about it. It really didn't make the slightest difference. It just didn't seem a very friendly way to behave, that's all. I don't know—I'd been believing we were such good friends. I'm an awful idiot about people, Fred. There aren't many who are really your friend at heart. Practically anybody would play you dirt for a nickel. Oh, yes, they would.

Was Edith here with you, Thursday night? This place must be very becoming to her. Next to being in a coal mine, I can't think of anywhere she could go that the light would be more flattering to that pan of hers. Do you really know a lot of people that say she's good-looking? You must have a wide acquaintance among the astigmatic, haven't you, Freddie, dear? Why, I'm not being any way at all—it's simply one of those things, either you can see it or you can't. Now to me, Edith looks like something that would eat her young. Dresses well? *Edith* dresses well? Are you trying to kid me, Fred, at my age? You mean you mean it? Oh, my God. You mean those clothes of hers are *intentional?* My heavens, I always thought she was on her way out of a burning building.

Well, we live and learn. Edith dresses well! Edith's got good taste! Yes, she's got sweet taste in neckties. I don't suppose I ought to say it about such a dear friend of yours, Fred, but she is the lousiest necktie-picker-out I ever saw. I never saw anything could touch that thing you have around your neck. All right, suppose I did say I liked it. I just said that because I felt sorry for you. I'd feel sorry for anybody with a thing like that on. I just wanted to try to make you feel good, because I thought you were my friend. My friend! I haven't got a friend in the world. Do you know that, Fred? Not one single friend in this world.

All right, what do you care if I'm crying? I can cry if I want to, can't I? I guess you'd cry, too, if you didn't have a friend in the world. Is my face very bad? I suppose that damned mascara has run all over it. I've got to give up using mascara, Fred; life's too sad. Isn't life terrible? Oh, my God, isn't life awful? Ah, don't cry, Fred. Please don't. Don't you care, baby. Life's terrible, but don't you care. You've got friends. I'm the one that hasn't got any friends. I am so. No, it's me. I'm the one.

l don't think another drink would make me feel any better. I don't know whether I want to feel any better. What's the sense of feeling good, when life's so terrible? Oh, all right, then. But please tell him just a little one, if it isn't too much trouble. I don't want to stay here much longer. I don't like this place. It's all dark and stuffy. It's the kind of place Edith would be crazy about—that's all I can say about this place. I know I oughtn't to talk about your best friend, Fred, but that's a terrible woman. That woman is the louse of this world. It makes me feel just awful that you trust that woman, Fred. I hate to see anybody play you dirt. I'd hate to see you get hurt. That's what makes me feel so terrible. That's why I'm getting mascara all over my face. No, please don't, Fred. You mustn't hold my hand. It wouldn't be fair to Edith. We've got to play fair with the big louse. After all, she's your best friend, isn't she?

Honestly? Do you honestly mean it, Fred? Yes, but how could I help thinking so, when you're with her all the time— when you bring her here every night in the week? Really, only Thursday? Oh, I know—I know how those things are. You simply can't help it, when you get stuck with a person that way. Lord, I'm glad you realize what an awful thing that woman is. I was worried about it, Fred. It's because I'm your friend. Why, of course I am, darling. You know I am. Oh, that's just silly, Freddie. You've got heaps of friends. Only you'll never find a better friend than I am. No, I know that. I know I'll never find a better friend than you are to me. Just give me back my hand a second, till I get this damned mascara out of my eye.

Yes, I think we ought to, honey. I think we ought to have a little drink, on account of our being friends. Just a little one, because it's real Scotch, and we're real friends. After all, friends are the greatest things in the world, aren't they, Fred? Gee, it makes you feel good to know you have a friend. I feel great, don't you, dear? And you look great, too. I'm proud to have you for a friend. Do you realize, Fred, what a rare thing a friend is, when you think of all the terrible people there are in this world? Animals are much better than people. God, I love animals. That's what I like about you, Fred. You're so fond of animals.

Look, I'll tell you what let's do, after we've had just a little highball. Let's go out and pick up a lot of stray dogs. I never had enough dogs in my life, did you? We ought to have more dogs. And maybe there'd be some cats around, if we looked. And a horse, I've never had one single horse, Fred. Isn't that rotten? Not one single horse. Ah, I'd like a nice old cab-horse, Fred. Wouldn't you? I'd like to take care of it and comb its hair and everything. Ah, don't be stuffy about it, Fred, please don't. I need a horse, honestly I do. Wouldn't you like one? It would be so sweet and kind. Let's have a drink and then let's you and I go out and get a horsie, Freddie—just a little one, darling, just a little one.

Well, Mona! Well, you poor sick thing, you! Ah, you look so little and white and *little,* you do, lying there in that great big bed. That's what you do—go and look so childlike and pitiful nobody'd have the heart to scold you. And I ought to scold you, Mona. Oh, yes, I should so, too. Never letting me know you were ill. Never a word to your oldest friend. Darling, you might have known I'd understand, no matter what you did. What do I mean? Well, what do you *mean* what do I mean, Mona? Of course, if you'd rather not talk about—Not even to your oldest friend. All I wanted to say was you might have known that I'm always for you, no matter what happens. I do admit, sometimes it's a little hard for me to understand how on earth you ever got into such—well. Goodness knows I don't want to nag you now, when you're so sick.

All right, Mona, then you're *not* sick. If that's what you want to say, even to me, why, all right, my dear. People who aren't sick have to stay in bed for nearly two weeks, I suppose; I suppose people who aren't sick look the way you do. Just your nerves? You were simply all tired out? I see. It's just your nerves. You were simply tired. Yes. Oh, Mona, Mona, why don't you feel you can trust me?

Well—if that's the way you want to be to me, that's the way you want to be. I won't say anything more about it. Only I do think you might have let me know that you had—well, that you were so *tired,* if that's what you want me to say. Why, I'd never have known a word about it if I hadn't run bang into Alice Patterson and she told me she'd called you up and that maid of yours said you had been sick in bed for ten days. Of course, I'd thought it rather funny I hadn't heard from you, but you know how you are—you simply let people go, and weeks can go by like, well, like *weeks,* and never a sign from you. Why, I could have been dead over and over again, for all you'd know. Twenty times over. Now, I'm not going to scold you when you're sick, but frankly and honestly, Mona, I said to myself this time, "Well, she'll have a good wait before I call her up. I've given in often enough, goodness knows. Now she can just call me first." Frankly and honestly, that's what I said!

And then I saw Alice, and I did feel mean, I really did. And

now to see you lying there—well, I feel like a complete *dog*.
That's what you do to people even when you're in the wrong the
way you always are, you wicked little thing, you! Ah, the poor
dear! Feels just so awful, doesn't it?

Oh, don't keep trying to be brave, child. Not with me. Just
give in—it helps so much. Just tell me all about it. You know
I'll never say a word. Or at least you ought to know. When
Alice told me that maid of yours said you were all tired out and
your nerves had gone bad, I naturally never said anything, but
I thought to myself, "Well, maybe that's the only thing Mona
could say was the matter. That's probably about the best
excuse she could think of." And of course I'll never deny it—
but perhaps it might have been better to have said you had
influenza or ptomaine poisoning. After all, people don't stay in
bed for ten whole days just because they're nervous. All right,
Mona, then they *do*. Then they do. Yes, dear.

Ah, to think of you going through all this and crawling off
here all alone like a little wounded animal or something. And
with only that colored Edie to take care of you. Darling,
oughtn't you have a trained nurse, I mean really oughtn't you?
There must be so many things that have to be done for you.
Why, Mona! Mona, please! Dear, you don't have to get so
excited. Very well, my dear, it's just as you say—there isn't a
single thing to be done. I was mistaken, that's all. I simply
thought that after— Oh, now, you don't have to do that. You
never have to say you're sorry, to *me*. I understand. As a matter
of fact, I was glad to hear you lose your temper. It's a good sign
when sick people are cross. It means they're on the way to
getting better. Oh, I know! You go right ahead and be cross all
you want to.

Look, where shall I sit? I want to sit some place where you
won't have to turn around, so you can talk to me. You stay
right the way you're lying, and I'll—Because you shouldn't
move around, I'm sure. It must be terribly bad for you. All
right, dear, you can move around all you want to. All right, I
must be crazy. I'm crazy, then. We'll leave it like that. Only
please, please don't excite yourself that way.

I'll just get this chair and put it over—oops, I'm sorry I

joggled the bed—put it over here, where you can see me. There. But first I want to fix your pillows before I get settled. Well, they certainly are *not* all right, Mona. After the way you've been twisting them and pulling them, these last few minutes. Now look, honey, I'll help you raise yourself ve-ry, ve-ry slo-o-ow-ly. Oh. Of course you can sit up by yourself, dear. Of course you can. Nobody ever said you couldn't. Nobody ever thought of such a thing. There now, your pillows are all smooth and lovely, and you lie right down again, before you hurt yourself. Now, isn't that better? Well, I should think it was!

Just a minute, till I get my sewing. Oh, yes, I brought it along, so we'd be all cozy. Do you honestly, frankly and honestly, think it's pretty? I'm so glad. It's nothing but a tray-cloth, you know. But you simply can't have too many. They're a lot of fun to make, too, doing this edge—it goes so quickly. Oh, Mona dear, so often I think if you just had a home of your own, and could be all busy, making pretty little things like this for it, it would do so *much* for you. I worry so about you, living in a little furnished apartment, with nothing that belongs to you, no roots, no nothing. It's not right for a woman. It's all wrong for a woman like you. Oh, I wish you'd get over that Garry Mc-Vicker! If you could just meet some nice, sweet, considerate man, and get married to him, and have your own lovely place— and with your *taste*, Mona!—and maybe have a couple of children. You're so simply adorable with children. Why, Mona Morrison, are you crying? Oh, you've got a cold? You've got a cold, *too?* I thought you were crying, there for a second. Don't you want my handkerchief, lamb? Oh, you have yours. Wouldn't you have a pink chiffon handkerchief, you nut! Why on earth don't you use cleansing tissues, just lying there in bed with no one to see you? You little idiot, you! Extravagant little fool!

No, but really, I'm serious. I've said to Fred so often, "Oh, if we could just get Mona married!" Honestly, you don't know the feeling it gives you, just to be all secure and safe with your own sweet home and your own blessed children, and your own nice husband coming back to you every night. That's a woman's *life*. Mona. What you've been doing is really horrible.

Just drifting along, that's all. What's going to happen to you, dear, whatever is going to become of you? But no—you don't even think of it. You go, and go falling in love with that Garry. Well, my dear, you've got to give me credit—I said from the very first, "He'll never marry her." You know that. What? There was never any thought of marriage, with you and Garry? Oh, Mona, now listen! Every woman on earth thinks of marriage as soon as she's in love with a man. Every woman, I don't care who she is.

Oh, if you were only married! It would be all the difference in the world. I think a child would do everything for you, Mona. Goodness knows, I just can't speak *decently* to that Garry, after the way he's treated you—well, you know perfectly well, *none* of your friends can—but I can frankly and honestly say, if he married you, I'd absolutely let bygones be bygones, and I'd be just as happy as happy, for you. If he's what you want. And I will say, what with your lovely looks and what with good-looking as he is, you ought to have simply *gorgeous* children. Mona, baby, you really have got a rotten cold, haven't you? Don't you want me to get you another handkerchief? Really?

I'm simply sick that I didn't bring you any flowers. But I thought the place would be full of them. Well, I'll stop on the way home and send you some. It looks too dreary here, without a flower in the room. Didn't Garry send you any? Oh, he didn't know you were sick. Well, doesn't he send you flowers anyway? Listen, hasn't he called up, all this time, and found out whether you were sick or not? Not in ten days? Well, then, haven't you called him and told him? Ah, now, Mona, there *is* such a thing as being too much of a heroine. Let him worry a little, dear. It would be a very good thing for him. Maybe that's the trouble—you've always taken all the worry for both of you. Hasn't sent any flowers! Hasn't even telephoned! Well, I'd just like to talk to that young man for a few minutes. After all, this is all *his* responsibility.

He's away? He's *what?* Oh, he went to Chicago two weeks ago. Well, it seems to me I'd always heard that there were telephone wires running between here and Chicago, but of course— And you'd think since he's been back, the least he could do would be to do something. He's not back yet? He's not *back* yet? Mona, what are you trying to tell me? Why, just night before last— Said he'd let you know the minute he got home? Of all the rotten, low things I ever heard in my life, this is really the— Mona, dear, please lie down. Please. Why, I didn't mean anything. I don't know what I was going to say, honestly I don't, it couldn't have been anything. For goodness' sake, let's talk about something else.

Let's see. Oh, you really ought to see Julia Post's living-room, the way she's done it now. She has brown walls—not beige, you know, or tan or anything, but brown—and these cream-colored taffeta curtains and—Mona, I tell you I absolutely don't know what I was going to say, before. It's gone completely out of my head. So you see how unimportant it must have been. Dear, please just lie quiet and try to relax. Please forget about that man for a few minutes, anyway. No man's worth getting that worked up about. Catch me doing it! You know you can't expect to get well quickly, if you get yourself so excited. You know that.

What doctor did you have, darling? Or don't you want to say? Your own? Your own Doctor Britton? You don't mean it! Well, I certainly never thought he'd do a thing like— Yes, dear, of course he's a nerve specialist. Yes, dear. Yes, dear. Yes, dear, of course you have perfect confidence in him. I only wish you would in me, once in a while; after we went to school together and everything. You might know I absolutely sympathize with you. I don't see how you could possibly have done anything else. I know you've always talked about how you'd give anything to have a baby, but it would have been so terribly unfair to the child to bring it into the world without being married. You'd have had to go live abroad and never see anybody and— And even then, somebody would have been sure to have told it sometime. They always do. You did the only possible thing, *I* think. Mona, for heaven's sake! Don't scream like that. I'm not deaf, you know. All right, dear, all right, all right, all right. All right, of course I believe you. Naturally I take your word for anything. Anything you say. Only please do try to be quiet. Just lie back and rest, and have a nice talk.

Ah, now don't keep harping on that. I've told you a hundred times, if I've told you once, I wasn't going to say anything at all. I tell you I don't remember *what* I was going to say. "Night before last"? When did I mention "night before last"? I never said any such— Well. Maybe it's better this way, Mona. The more I think of it, the more I think it's much better for you to hear it from me. Because somebody's bound to tell you. These things always come out. And I know you'd rather hear it from your oldest friend, wouldn't you? And the good Lord knows, anything I could do to make you see what that man really is! Only do relax, darling. Just for me. Dear, Garry isn't in Chicago. Fred and I saw him night before last at the Comet Club, dancing. And Alice saw him Tuesday night at El Rhumba. And I don't know how many people have said they've seen him around at the theater and night clubs and things. Why, he couldn't have stayed in Chicago more than a day or so—if he went at all.

Well, he was with *her* when we saw him, honey. Apparently he's with her all the time; nobody ever sees him with anyone else. You really must make up your mind to it, dear; it's the only thing to do. I hear all over that he's just simply *pleading* with her to marry him, but I don't know how true that is. I'm sure I can't see why he'd want to, but then you never can tell what a man like that will do. It would be just good enough *for* him if he got her, that's what *I* say. Then he'd see. She'd never stand for any of his nonsense. She'd make him toe the mark. She's a smart woman.

But, oh, so *ordinary*. I thought, when we saw them the other night, "Well, she just looks cheap, that's all she looks." That must be what he likes, I suppose. I must admit he looked very well. I never saw him look better. Of course you know what I think of him, but I always had to say he's one of the handsomest men I ever saw in my life. I can understand how any woman would be attracted to him—at first. Until they found out what he's really like. Oh, if you could have seen him with that awful, common creature, never once taking his eyes off her, and hanging on every word she said, as if it was pearls! It made me just——

Mona, angel, are you *crying?* Now, darling, that's just plain silly. That man's not worth another thought. You've thought about him entirely too much, that's the trouble. Three years! Three of the best years of your life you've given him, and all the time he's been deceiving you with that woman. Just think back over what you've been through—all the times and times and times he promised you he'd give her up; and you, you poor little idiot, you'd believe him, and then he'd go right back to her again. And *everybody* knew about it. Think of that, and then try telling me that man's worth crying over! Really, Mona! I'd have more pride.

You know, I'm just glad this thing happened. I'm just glad you found out. This is a little too much, this time. In Chicago, indeed! Let you know the minute he came home! The kindest thing a person could possibly have done was to tell you, and bring you to your senses at last. I'm not sorry I did it, for a second. When I think of him out having the time of his life and you lying here deathly sick all on account of him, I could just— Yes, it is on account of him. Even if you didn't have an—well, even if I was mistaken about what I naturally thought was the matter with you when you made such a secret of your illness, he's driven you into a nervous breakdown, and that's plenty bad enough. All for that man! The skunk! You just put him right out of your head.

Why, of course you can, Mona. All you need to do is to pull yourself together, child. Simply say to yourself, "Well, I've wasted three years of my life, and that's that." Never worry about *him* any more. The Lord knows, darling, he's not worrying about you.

It's just because you're weak and sick that you're worked up like this, dear. I know. But you're going to be all right. You can make something of your life. You've got to, Mona, you know. Because after all—well, of course, you never looked sweeter, I don't mean that; but you're—well, you're not getting any younger. And here you've been throwing away your time, never seeing your friends, never going out, never meeting anybody new, just sitting here waiting for Garry to telephone, or Garry to come in—if he didn't have anything better to do. For three years, you've never had a thought in your head but that man. Now you just forget him.

Ah, baby, it isn't good for you to cry like that. Please don't. He's not even worth talking about. Look at the woman he's in love with, and you'll see what kind he is. You were much too good for him. You were much too sweet to him. You gave in too easily. The minute he had you, he didn't want you any more. That's what he's like. Why, he no more loved you than——

Mona, don't! Mona, stop it! Please, Mona! You mustn't talk like that, you mustn't say such things. You've got to stop crying, you'll be terribly sick. Stop, oh, stop it, oh, please stop! Oh, what am I going to do with her? Mona, dear—Mona! Oh, where in heaven's name is that fool maid?

Edie. Oh, Edie! Edie, I think you'd better get Dr. Britton on the telephone, and tell him to come down and give Miss Morrison something to quiet her. I'm afraid she's got herself a little bit upset.

The Little Hours

Now what's this? What's the object of all this darkness all over me? They haven't gone and buried me alive while my back was turned, have they? Ah, now would you think they'd do a thing like that! Oh, no, I know what it is. I'm awake. That's it. I've waked up in the middle of the night. Well, isn't that nice. Isn't that simply ideal. Twenty minutes past four, sharp, and here's Baby wide-eyed as a marigold. Look at this, will you? At the time when all decent people are just going to bed, I must wake up. There's no way things can ever come out even, under this system. This is as rank as injustice is ever likely to get. This is what brings about hatred and bloodshed, that's what *this* does.

Yes, and you want to know what got me into this mess? Going to bed at ten o'clock, that's what. That spells ruin. T-e-n-space-o-apostrophe-c-l-o-c-k: ruin. Early to bed, and you'll wish you were dead. Bed before eleven, nuts before seven. Bed before morning, sailors give warning. Ten o'clock, after a quiet evening of reading. Reading—there's an institution for you. Why, I'd turn on the light and read, right this minute, if reading weren't what contributed toward driving me here. I'll show it. God, the bitter misery that reading works in this world! Everybody knows that—everybody who *is* everybody. All the best minds have been off reading for years. Look at the swing La Rochefoucauld took at it. He said that if nobody had ever learned to read, very few people would be in love. There was a man for you, and that's what *he* thought of it. Good for you, La Rochefoucauld; nice going, boy. I wish I'd never learned to read. I wish I'd never learned to take off my clothes. Then I wouldn't have been caught in this jam at half-past four in the morning. If nobody had ever learned to undress, very few people would be in love. No, his is better. Oh, well, it's a man's world.

La Rochefoucauld, indeed, lying quiet as a mouse, and me tossing and turning here! This is no time to be getting all

254

steamed up about La Rochefoucauld. It's only a question of minutes before I'm going to be pretty darned good and sick of La Rochefoucauld, once and for all. La Rochefoucauld this and La Rochefoucauld that. Yes, well, let me tell you that if nobody had ever learned to quote, very few people would be in love with La Rochefoucauld. I bet you I don't know ten souls who read him without a middleman. People pick up those scholarly little essays that start off "Was it not that lovable old cynic, La Rochefoucauld, who said . . ." and then they go around claiming to know the master backwards. Pack of illiterates, that's all they are. All right, let them keep their La Rochefoucauld, and see if I care. I'll stick to La Fontaine. Only I'd be better company if I could quit thinking that La Fontaine married Alfred Lunt.

I don't know what I'm doing mucking about with a lot of French authors at this hour, anyway. First thing you know, I'll be reciting *Fleurs du Mal* to myself, and then I'll be little more good to anybody. And I'll stay off Verlaine too; he was always chasing Rimbauds. A person would be better off with La Rochefoucauld, even. Oh, damn La Rochefoucauld. The big Frog. I'll thank him to keep out of my head. What's he doing there, anyhow? What's La Rochefoucauld to me, or he to Hecuba? Why, I don't even know the man's first name, that's how close I ever was to *him*. What am I supposed to be, a hostess to La Rochefoucauld? That's what *he* thinks. Sez he. Well, he's only wasting his time, hanging around here. I can't help him. The only other thing I can remember his saying is that there is always something a little pleasing to us in the misfortunes of even our dearest friends. That cleans me all up with Monsieur La Rochefoucauld. *Maintenant c'est fini, ça.*

Dearest friends. A sweet lot of dearest friends *I've* got. All of them lying in swinish stupors, while I'm practically up and about. All of them stretched sodden through these, the fairest hours of the day, when man should be at his most productive. Produce, produce, produce, for I tell you the night is coming. Carlyle said that. Yes, and a fine one *he* was, to go shooting off his face on production. *Oh,* Thomas Carli-*yill,* what *I* know about *you*-oo! No, that will be enough of that. I'm not going to start fretting about Carlyle, at this stage of the game. What did he ever do that was so great, besides founding a college for Indians? (That one ought to make him spin.) Let him keep his face out of this, if he knows what's good for him. I've got enough trouble with that lovable old cynic, La Rochefoucauld—him and the misfortunes of his dearest friends!

The first thing I've got to do is to get out and whip me up a complete new set of dearest friends; that's the first thing. Everything else can wait. And will somebody please kindly be so good as to inform me how I am ever going to meet up with any new people when my entire scheme of living is out of joint—when I'm the only living being awake while the rest of the world lies sleeping? I've got to get this thing adjusted. I must try to get back to sleep right now. I've got to conform to the rotten little standards of this sluggard civilization. People needn't feel that they have to change their ruinous habits and come my way. Oh, no, no; no, indeed. Not at all. I'll go theirs. If that isn't the woman of it for you! Always having to do what somebody else wants, like it or not. Never able to murmur a suggestion of her own.

And what suggestion has anyone to murmur as to how I am going to drift lightly back to slumber? Here I am, awake as high noon what with all this milling and pitching around with La Rochefoucauld. I really can't be expected to drop everything and start counting sheep, at my age. I hate sheep. Untender it may be in me, but all my life I've hated sheep. It amounts to a phobia, the way I hate them. I can tell the minute there's one in the room. They needn't think that I am going to lie here in the dark and count their unpleasant little faces for them; I wouldn't do it if I didn't fall asleep again until· the middle of next August. Suppose they never get counted— what's the worst that can happen? If the number of imaginary sheep in this world remains a matter of guesswork, who is richer or poorer for it? No, sir; *I'm* not their scorekeeper. Let them count themselves, if they're so crazy mad after mathematics. Let them do their own dirty work. Coming around here, at this time of day, and asking me to count them!

And not even *real* sheep, at that. Why, it's the most preposterous thing I ever heard in my life.

But there must be *something* I could count. Let's see. No, I already know by heart how many fingers I have. I could count my bills, I suppose. I could count the things I didn't do yesterday that I should have done. I could count the things I should do today that I'm not going to do. I'm never going to accomplish anything; that's perfectly clear to me. I'm never going to be famous. My name will never be writ large on the roster of Those Who Do Things. I don't do anything. Not one single thing. I used to bite my nails, but I don't even do that any more. I don't amount to the powder to blow me to hell. I've turned out to be nothing but a bit of flotsam. Flotsam and leave'em—that's me from now on. Oh, it's all terrible.

Well. This way lies galloping melancholia. Maybe it's because this is the zero hour. This is the time the swooning soul hangs pendant and vertiginous between the new day and the old, nor dares confront the one or summon back the other. This is the time when all things, known and hidden, are iron to weight the spirit; when all ways, traveled or virgin, fall away from the stumbling feet, when all before the straining eyes is black. Blackness now, everywhere is blackness. This is the time of abomination, the dreadful hour of the victorious dark. For it is always darkest—Was it not that lovable old cynic, La Rouchefoucauld, who said it is always darkest before the deluge?

There. Now you see, don't you? Here we are again, practically back where we started. La Rochefoucauld, we are here. Ah, come on, son—how about your going your way and letting me go mine? I've got my work cut out for me right here; I've got all this sleeping to do. Think how I am going to look by daylight if this keeps up. I'll be a seamy sight for all those rested, clear-eyed, fresh-faced dearest friends of mine—the rats! My *dear*, whatever have you been doing; I thought you were so good lately. Oh, I was helling around with La Rochefoucauld till all hours; we couldn't stop laughing about your misfortunes. No, this is getting too thick, really. It isn't right to have this happen to a person, just because she went to bed at ten o'clock once in her life. Honest, I won't ever do it again. I'll go straight, after this. I'll never go to bed again, if I can only sleep now. If I can tear my mind away from a certain French cynic, *circa* 1650, and slip into lovely oblivion. 1650. I bet ⅃ look as if I'd been awake since then.

How do people go to sleep? I'm afraid I've lost the knack. I might try busting myself smartly over the temple with the night-light. I might repeat to myself, slowly and soothingly, a list of quotations beautiful from minds profound; if I can remember any of the damn things. That might do it. And it ought effectually to bar that visiting foreigner that's been hanging around ever since twenty minutes past four. Yes, that's what I'll do. Only wait till I turn the pillow; it feels as if La Rochefoucauld had crawled inside the slip.

Now let's see—where shall we start? Why—er—let's see. Oh, yes, I know one. This above all, to thine own self be true and it must follow, as the night the day, thou canst not then be false to any man. Now they're off. And once they get started, they ought to come like hot cakes. Let's see. Ah, what avail the sceptered race and what the form divine, when every virtue, every grace, Rose Aylmer, all were thine. Let's see. They also serve who only stand and wait. If Winter comes, can Spring be far behind? Lilies that fester smell far worse than weeds. Silent upon a peak in Darien. Mrs. Porter and her daughter wash their feet in soda-water. And Agatha's Arth is a hug-the-hearth, but my true love is false. Why did you die when lambs were cropping, you should have died when apples were dropping. Shall be together, breathe and ride, so one day more am I deified, who knows but the world will end tonight. And he shall hear the stroke of eight and not the stroke of nine. They are not long, the weeping and the laughter; love and desire and hate I think will have no portion in us after we pass the gate. But none, I think, do there embrace. I think that I shall never see a poem lovely as a tree. I think I will not hang myself today. Ay tank Ay go home now.

Let's see. Solitude is the safeguard of mediocrity and the stern companion of genius. Consistency is the hob-goblin of little minds. Something is emotion remembered in tranquillity.

A cynic is one who knows the price of everything and the value of nothing. That lovable old cynic is one who—oops, there's King Charles's head again. I've got to watch myself. Let's see. Circumstantial evidence is a trout in the milk. Any stigma will do to beat a dogma. If you would learn what God thinks about money, you have only to look at those to whom He has given it. If nobody had ever learned to read, very few people—

All right. That fixes it. I throw in the towel right now. I know when I'm licked. There'll be no more of this nonsense; I'm going to turn on the light and read my head off. Till the next ten o'clock, if I feel like it. And what does La Rochefoucauld want to make of that? Oh, he *will*, eh? Yes, he will! He and who else? La Rochefoucauld and *what* very few people?

Horsie

When young Mrs. Gerald Cruger came home from the hospital, Miss Wilmarth came along with her and the baby. Miss Wilmarth was an admirable trained nurse, sure and calm and tireless, with a real taste for the arranging of flowers in bowls and vases. She had never known a patient to receive so many flowers, or such uncommon ones; yellow violets and strange lilies and little white orchids poised like a bevy of delicate moths along green branches. Care and thought must have been put into their selection that they, like all the other fragile and costly things she kept about her, should be so right for young Mrs. Cruger. No one who knew her could have caught up the telephone and lightly bidden the florist to deliver to her one of his five-dollar assortments of tulips, stock, and daffodils. Camilla Cruger was no complement to garden blooms.

Sometimes, when Miss Wilmarth opened the shiny boxes and carefully grouped the cards, there would come a curious expression upon her face. Playing over shorter features, it might almost have been one of wistfulness. Upon Miss Wilmarth, it served to perfect the strange resemblance that she bore through her years; her face was truly complete with that look of friendly melancholy peculiar to the gentle horse. It was not, of course, Miss Wilmarth's fault that she looked like a horse. Indeed, there was nowhere to attach any blame. But the resemblance remained.

She was tall, pronounced of bone, and erect of carriage; it was somehow impossible to speculate upon her appearance undressed. Her long face was innocent, indeed ignorant, of cosmetics, and its color stayed steady. Confusion, heat, or haste caused her neck to flush crimson. Her mild hair was pinned with loops of nicked black wire into a narrow knot, practical to support her little high cap, like a charlotte russe from a bakeshop. She had big, trustworthy hands, scrubbed and dry, with nails cut short and so deeply cleaned with some small sharp instrument that the ends stood away from the spatulate finger-tips. Gerald Cruger, who nightly sat opposite her at his own dinner table, tried not to see her hands. It irritated him to be reminded by their sight that they must feel like straw matting and smell of white soap. For him, women who were not softly lovely were simply not women.

He tried, too, so far as it was possible to his beautiful manners, to keep his eyes from her face. Not that it was un-pleasant—a kind face, certainly. But, as he told Camilla, once he looked he stayed fascinated, awaiting the toss and the whinny.

"I love horses, myself," he said to Camilla, who lay all white and languid on her apricot satin chaise-longue. "I'm a fool for a horse. Ah, what a noble animal, darling! All I say is, nobody has any business to go around looking like a horse and behaving as if it were all right. You don't catch horses going around looking like people, do you?"

He did not dislike Miss Wilmarth; he only resented her. He had no bad wish in the world for her, but he waited with longing the day she would leave. She was so skilled and rhyth-mic in her work that she disrupted the household but little. Nevertheless, her presence was an onus. There was that thing of dining with her every evening. It was a chore for him, cer-tainly, and one that did not ease with repetition, but there was no choice. Everyone had always heard of trained nurses' bristling insistence that they be not treated as servants; Miss Wilmarth could not be asked to dine with the maids. He would not have dinner out; be away from *Camilla?* It was too much to expect the maids to institute a second dinner service or to carry trays, other than Camilla's, up and down the stairs. There were only three servants and they had work enough.

"Those children," Camilla's mother was wont to say, chuckling. "Those two kids. The independence of them! Struggling along on cheese and kisses. Why, they hardly let me pay for the trained nurse. And it was all we could do, last Christmas, to make Camilla take the Packard and the chauffeur."

So Gerald dined each night with Miss Wilmarth. The small dread of his hour with her struck suddenly at him in the afternoon. He would forget it for stretches of minutes, only to be smitten sharper as the time drew near. On his way home from his office, he found grim entertainment in rehearsing his table talk, and plotting desperate innovations to it.

Cruger's Compulsory Conversations: Lesson I, a Dinner with a Miss Wilmarth, a Trained Nurse. Good evening, Miss Wilmarth. Well! And how were the patients all day? That's good, that's fine. Well! The baby gained two ounces, did she? That's fine. Yes, that's right, she will be before we know it. That's right. Well! Mrs. Cruger seems to be getting stronger every day, doesn't she? That's good, that's fine. That's right, up and about before we know it. Yes, she certainly will. Well! Any visitors today? That's good. Didn't stay too long, did they? That's fine. Well! No, no, no, Miss Wilmarth—*you* go ahead. I wasn't going to say anything at all, really. No, really. Well! Well! I see where they found those two aviators after all. Yes, they certainly do run risks. That's right. Yes. Well! I see where they've been having a regular old-fashioned blizzard out West. Yes, we certainly have had a mild winter. That's right. Well! I see where they held up that jeweler's shop right in broad daylight on Fifth Avenue. Yes, I certainly don't know what we're coming to. That's right. Well! I see the cat. Do you see the cat? The cat is on the mat. It certainly is. Well! Pardon me, Miss Wilmarth, but must you look so much like a horse? Do you like to look like a horse, Miss Wilmarth? That's good, Miss Wilmarth, that's fine. You certainly do, Miss Wilmarth. That's right. Well! Will you for God's sake finish your oats, Miss Wilmarth, and let me get out of this?

Every evening he reached the dining-room before Miss Wilmarth and stared gloomily at silver and candle-flame until she was upon him. No sound of footfall heralded her coming, for her ample canvas oxfords were soled with rubber; there would be a protest of parquet, a trembling of ornaments, a creak, a rustle, and the authoritative smell of stiff linen; and there she would be, set for her ritual of evening cheer.

"Well, Mary," she would cry to the waitress, "you know

what they say—better late than never!"

But no smile would mellow Mary's lips, no light her eyes. Mary, in converse with the cook, habitually referred to Miss Wilmarth as "that one." She wished no truck with Miss Wilmarth or any of the others of her guild; always in and out of a person's pantry.

Once or twice Gerald saw a strange expression upon Miss Wilmarth's face as she witnessed the failure of her adage with the maid. He could not quite classify it. Though he did not know, it was the look she sometimes had when she opened the shiny white boxes and lifted the exquisite, scentless blossoms that were sent to Camilla. Anyway, whatever it was, it increased her equine resemblance to such a point that he thought of proffering her an apple.

But she always had her big smile turned toward him when she sat down. Then she would look at the thick watch strapped to her wrist and give a little squeal that brought the edges of his teeth together.

"Mercy!" she would say. "My good mercy! Why, I had no more idea it was so late. Well, you mustn't blame me, Mr. Cruger. Don't you scold *me*. You'll just have to blame that daughter of yours. She's the one that keeps us all busy."

"She certainly is," he would say. "That's right."

He would think, and with small pleasure, of the infant Diane, pink and undistinguished and angry, among the ruffles and *choux* of her bassinet. It was her doing that Camilla had stayed so long away from him in the odorous limbo of the hospital, her doing that Camilla lay all day upon her apricot satin chaise-longue. "We must take our time," the doctor said, "just ta-a-ake our ti-yem." Yes; well, that would all be because of young Diane. It was because of her, indeed, that night upon night he must face Miss Wilmarth and comb up conversation. All right, young Diane, there you are and nothing to do about it. But you'll be an only child, young woman, that's what you'll be.

Always Miss Wilmarth followed her opening pleasantry about the baby with a companion piece. Gerald had come to know it so well he could have said it in duet with her.

"You wait," she would say. "Just you wait. You're the one that's going to be kept busy when the beaux start coming around. You'll see. That young lady's going to be a heart-breaker if ever I saw one."

"I guess that's right," Gerald would say, and he would essay a small laugh and fail at it. It made him uncomfortable, somehow embarrassed him to hear Miss Wilmarth banter of swains and conquest. It was unseemly, as rouge would have been unseemly on her long mouth and perfume on her flat bosom.

He would hurry her over to her own ground. "Well!" he would say. "Well! And how were the patients all day?"

But that, even with the baby's weight and the list of the day's visitors, seldom lasted past the soup.

"Doesn't that woman ever go out?" he asked Camilla. "Doesn't our Horsie ever rate a night off?"

"Where would she want to go?" Camilla said. Her low, lazy words had always the trick of seeming a little weary of their subject.

"Well," Gerald said, "she might take herself a moonlight canter around the park."

"Oh, she doubtless gets a thrill out of dining with you," Camilla said. "You're a man, they tell me, and she can't have seen many. Poor old horse. She's not a bad soul."

"Yes," he said. "And what a round of pleasure it is, having dinner every night with Not a Bad Soul."

"What makes you think," Camilla said, "that I am caught up in any whirl of gaiety, lying here?"

"Oh, darling," he said. "Oh, my poor darling. I didn't mean it, honestly I didn't. Oh, *lord*, I didn't mean it. How could I complain, after all you've been through, and I haven't done a thing? Please, sweet, please. Ah, Camilla, say you know I didn't mean it."

"After all," Camilla said, "you just have her at dinner. I have her around all day."

"Sweetheart, please," he said. "Oh, poor angel."

He dropped to his knees by the chaise-longue and crushed her limp, fragrant hand against his mouth. Then he remembered about being very, very gentle. He ran little apologetic kisses up and down her fingers and murmured of gardenias and lilies and thus exhausted his knowledge of white flowers.

Her visitors said that Camilla looked lovelier than ever, but they were mistaken. She was only as lovely as she had always been. They spoke in hushed voices of the new look in her eyes since her motherhood; but it was the same far brightness that had always lain there. They said how white she was and how lifted above other people; they forgot that she had always been pale as moonlight and had always worn a delicate disdain, as light as the lace that covered her breast. Her doctor cautioned tenderly against hurry, besought her to take recovery slowly— Camilla, who had never done anything quickly in her life. Her friends gathered, adoring, about the apricot satin chaise-longue where Camilla lay and moved her hands as if they hung heavy from her wrists; they had been wont before to gather and adore at the white satin sofa in the drawing-room where Camilla reclined, her hands like heavy lilies in a languid breeze. Every night, when Gerald crossed the threshold of her fragrant room, his heart leaped and his words caught in his throat; but those things had always befallen him at the sight of her. Motherhood had not brought perfection to Camilla's loveliness. She had had that before.

Gerald came home early enough, each evening, to have a while with her before dinner. He made his cocktails in her room, and watched her as she slowly drank one. Miss Wilmarth was in and out, touching flowers, patting pillows. Sometimes she brought Diane in on display, and those would be minutes of real discomfort for Gerald. He could not bear to watch her with the baby in her arms, so acute was his vicarious embarrassment at her behavior. She would bring her long head down close to Diane's tiny, stern face and toss it back again high on her rangy neck, all the while that strange words, in a strange high voice, came from her.

"Well, her wuzza booful dirl. Ess, her wuzza. Her wuzza, wuzza, wuzza. Ess, her *wuzz*." She would bring the baby over to him. "See, Daddy. Isn't us a gate, bid dirl? Isn't us booful?

Say 'nigh-nigh,' Daddy. Us doe teepy-bye, now. Say 'nigh-nigh.' "

Oh, God.

Then she would bring the baby to Camilla. "Say 'nigh-nigh,' " she would cry. " 'Nigh-nigh,' Mummy."

"If that brat ever calls you 'Mummy,' " he told Camilla once, fiercely, "I'll turn her out in the snow."

Camilla would look at the baby, amusement in her slow glance. "Good night, useless," she would say. She would hold out a finger, for Diane's pink hand to curl around. And Gerald's heart would quicken, and his eyes sting and shine.

Once he tore his gaze from Camilla to look at Miss Wilmarth, surprised by the sudden cessation of her falsetto. She was no longer lowering her head and tossing it back. She was standing quite still, looking at him over the baby; she looked away quickly, but not before he had seen that curious expression on her face again. It puzzled him, made him vaguely uneasy. That night, she made no further exhortations to Diane's parents to utter the phrase "nigh-nigh." In silence she carried the baby out of the room and back to the nursery.

One evening, Gerald brought two men home with him; lean, easily dressed young men, good at golf and squash rackets, his companions through his college and in his clubs. They had cocktails in Camilla's room, grouped about the chaise-longue. Miss Wilmarth, standing in the nursery adjoining, testing the temperature of the baby's milk against her wrist, could hear them all talking lightly and swiftly, tossing their sentences into the air to hang there unfinished. Now and again she could distinguish Camilla's lazy voice; the others stopped immediately when she spoke, and when she was done there were long peals of laughter. Miss Wilmarth pictured her lying there, in golden chiffon and deep lace, her light figure turned always a little away from those about her, so that she must move her head and speak her slow words over her shoulder to them. The trained nurse's face was astoundingly equine as she looked at the wall that separated them.

They stayed in Camilla's room a long time, and there was always more laughter. The door from the nursery into the hall was open, and presently she heard the door of Camilla's room being opened, too. She had been able to hear only voices before, but now she could distinguish Gerald's words as he called back from the threshold; they had no meaning to her.

"Only wait, fellers," he said. "Wait till you see Seabiscuit."

He came to the nursery door. He held a cocktail shaker in one hand and filled glass in the other.

"Oh, Miss Wilmarth," he said. "Oh, good evening, Miss Wilmarth. Why, I didn't know this door was open—I mean, I hope we haven't been disturbing you."

"Oh, not the least little bit," she said. "Goodness."

"Well!" he said. "I—we were wondering if you wouldn't have a little cocktail. Won't you please?" He held out the glass to her.

"Mercy," she said, taking it. "Why, thank you ever so much. Thank you, Mr. Cruger."

"And, oh, Miss Wilmarth," he said, "would you tell Mary there'll be two more to dinner? And ask her not to have it before half an hour or so, will you? Would you mind?"

"Not the least little bit," she said. "Of course I will."

"Thank you," he said. "Well! Thank you, Miss Wilmarth. Well! See you at dinner."

"Thank *you*," she said. "I'm the one that ought to thank *you*. For the lovely little cockytail."

"Oh," he said, and failed at an easy laugh. He went back into Camilla's room and closed the door behind him.

Miss Wilmarth set her cocktail upon a table, and went down to inform Mary of the impending guests. She felt light and quick, and she told Mary gaily, awaiting a flash of gaiety in response. But Mary received the news impassively, made a grunt but no words, and slammed out through the swinging doors into the kitchen. Miss Wilmarth stood looking after her. Somehow servants never seemed to—She should have become used to it.

Even though the dinner hour was delayed, Miss Wilmarth was a little late. The three young men were standing in the dining-room, talking all at once and laughing all together. They stopped their noise when Miss Wilmarth entered, and

Gerald moved forward to perform introductions. He looked at her, and then looked away. Prickling embarrassment tormented him. He introduced the young men, with his eyes away from her.

Miss Wilmarth had dressed for dinner. She had discarded her linen uniform and put on a frock of dark blue taffeta, cut down to a point at the neck and given sleeves that left bare the angles of her elbows. Small, stiff ruffles occurred about the hips, and the skirt was short for its year. It revealed that Miss Wilmarth had clothed her ankles in roughened gray silk and her feet in black, casket-shaped slippers, upon which little bows quivered as if in lonely terror at the expanse before them. She had been busy with her hair; it was crimped and loosened, and ends that had escaped the tongs were already sliding from their pins. All the length of her nose and chin was heavily powdered; not with a perfumed dust, tinted to praise her skin, but with coarse, bright white talcum.

Gerald presented his guests; Miss Wilmarth, Mr. Minot; Miss Wilmarth, Mr. Forster. One of the young men, it turned out, was Freddy, and one, Tommy. Miss Wilmarth said she was pleased to meet each of them. Each of them asked her how she did.

She sat down at the candle-lit table with the three beautiful young men. Her usual evening vivacity was gone from her. In silence she unfolded her napkin and took up her soup spoon. Her neck glowed crimson, and her face, even with its powder, looked more than ever as if it should have been resting over the top rail of a paddock fence.

"Well!" Gerald said.

"Well!" Mr. Minot said.

"Getting much warmer out, isn't it?" Mr. Forster said. "Notice it?"

"It is, at that," Gerald said. "Well. We're about due for warm weather."

"Yes, we ought to expect it now," Mr. Minot said. "Any day now."

"Oh, it'll be here," Mr. Forster said. "It'll come."

"I love spring," said Miss Wilmarth. "I just love it."

Gerald looked deep into his soup plate. The two young men looked at her.

"Darn good time of year," Mr. Minot said. "Certainly is."

"And how it is!" Mr. Forster said.

They ate their soup.

There was champagne all through dinner. Miss Wilmarth watched Mary fill her glass, none too full. The wine looked gay and pretty. She looked about the table before she took her first sip. She remembered Camilla's voice and the men's laughter.

"Well," she cried. "Here's a health, everybody!"

The guests looked at her. Gerald reached for his glass and gazed at it as intently as if he beheld a champagne goblet for the first time. They all murmured and drank.

"Well!" Mr. Minot said. "Your patients seem to be getting along pretty well, Miss Witmark. Don't they?"

"I should say they do," she said. "And they're pretty nice patients, too. Aren't they, Mr. Cruger?"

"They certainly are," Gerald said. "That's right."

"They certainly are," Mr. Minot said. "That's what they are. Well. You must meet all sorts of people in your work, I suppose. Must be pretty interesting."

"Oh, sometimes it is," Miss Wilmarth said. "It depends on the people." Her words fell from her lips clear and separate, sterile as if each had been freshly swabbed with boracic acid solution. In her ears rang Camilla's light, insolent drawl.

"That's right," Mr. Forster said. "Everything depends on the people, doesn't it? Always does, wherever you go. No matter what you do. Still, it must be wonderfully interesting work. Wonderfully."

"Wonderful the way this country's come right up in medicine," Mr. Minot said. "They tell me we have the greatest doctors in the world, right here. As good as any in Europe. Or Harley Street."

"I see,'" Gerald said, "where they think they've found a new cure for spinal meningitis."

"*Have* they really?" Mr. Minot said.

"Yes, I saw that, too," Mr. Forster said. "Wonderful thing. Wonderfully interesting."

"Oh, say, Gerald," Mr. Minot said, and he went from there into an account, hole by hole, of his most recent performance at golf. Gerald and Mr. Forster listened and questioned him.

The three young men left the topic of golf and came back to it again, and left it and came back. In the intervals, they related to Miss Wilmarth various brief items that had caught their eyes in the newspapers. Miss Wilmarth answered in exclamations, and turned her big smile readily to each of them. There was no laughter during dinner.

It was a short meal, as courses went. After it, Miss Wilmarth bade the guests good night and received their bows and their "*Good* night, Miss Witmark." She said she was awfully glad to have met them. They murmured.

"Well, good night, then, Mr. Cruger," she said "See you tomorrow!"

"Good night, Miss Wilmarth," Gerald said.

The three young men went and sat with Camilla. Miss Wilmarth could hear their voices and their laughter as she hung up her dark blue taffeta dress.

Miss Wilmarth stayed with the Crugers for five weeks. Camilla was pronounced well—so well that she could have dined downstairs on the last few nights of Miss Wilmarth's stay, had she been able to support the fardel of dinner at the table with the trained nurse.

"I really couldn't dine opposite that face," she told Gerald. "You go amuse Horsie at dinner, stupid. You must be good at it, by now."

"All right, I will, darling," he said. "But God keep me, when she asks for another lump of sugar, from holding it out to her on my palm."

"Only two more nights," Camilla said, "and then Thursday Nana'll be here, and she'll be gone forever."

" 'Forever,' sweet, is my favorite word in the language," Gerald said.

Nana was the round and competent Scottish woman who had nursed Camilla through her childhood and was scheduled to engineer the unknowing Diane through hers. She was a comfortable woman, easy to have in the house; a servant, and knew it.

Only two more nights. Gerald went down to dinner whistling a good old tune.

"The old gray mare, she ain't what she used to be,
Ain't what she used to be, ain't what she used to
be—"

The final dinners with Miss Wilmarth were like all the others. He arrived first, and stared at the candles until she came.

"Well, Mary," she cried on her entrance, "you know what they say—better late than never."

Mary, to the last, remained unamused.

Gerald was elated all the day of Miss Wilmarth's departure. He had a holiday feeling, a last-day-of-school jubilation with none of its faint regret. He left his office early, stopped at a florist's shop, and went home to Camilla.

Nana was installed in the nursery, but Miss Wilmarth had not yet left. She was in Camilla's room, and he saw her for the second time out of uniform. She wore a long brown coat and a brown rubbed velvet hat of no definite shape. Obviously, she was in the middle of the embarrassments of farewell. The melancholy of her face made it so like a horse's that the hat above it was preposterous.

"Why, there's Mr. Cruger!" she cried.

"Oh, good evening, Miss Wilmarth," he said. "Well! Ah, hello, darling. How are you, sweet? Like these?"

He laid a florist's box in Camilla's lap. In it were strange little yellow roses, with stems and leaves and tiny, soft thorns all of blood red. Miss Wilmarth gave a little squeal at the sight of them.

"Oh, the darlings!" she cried. "Oh, the boo-fuls!"

"And these are for you, Miss Wilmarth," he said. He made himself face her and hold out to her a square, smaller box.

"Why, Mr. Cruger," she said. "For me, really? Why, really, Mr. Cruger."

She opened the box and found four gardenias, with green foil and pale green ribbon holding them together.

"Oh, now, really, Mr. Cruger," she said. "Why, I never in all my life—Oh, now, you shouldn't have done it. Really, you shouldn't. My good mercy! Well, I never saw anything so lovely in all my life. Did you, Mrs. Cruger? They're *lovely*. Well, I just don't know how to *begin* to thank you. Why, I just—well, I just adore them."

Gerald made sounds designed to convey the intelligence that he was glad she liked them, that it was nothing, that she was welcome. Her squeaks of thanks made red rise back in his ears.

"They're nice ones," Camilla said. "Put them on, Miss Wilmarth. And these are awfully cunning, Jerry. Sometimes you have your points."

"Oh, I didn't think I'd *wear* them," Miss Wilmarth said. "I thought I'd just take them in the box like this, so they'd keep better. And it's such a nice box—I'd like to have it. I—I'd like to keep it."

She looked down at the flowers. Gerald was in sudden horror that she might bring her head down close to them and toss it back high, crying "wuzza, wuzza, wuzza" at them the while.

"Honestly," she said, "I just can't take my eyes *off* them."

"The woman is mad," Camilla said. "It's the effect of living with us, I suppose. I hope we haven't ruined you for life, Miss Wilmarth."

"Why, Mrs. Cruger," Miss Wilmarth cried. "Now, really! I was just telling Mrs. Cruger, Mr. Cruger, that I've never been on a pleasanter case. I've just had the time of my life, all the time I was here. I don't know when I—honestly, I can't stop looking at my posies, they're so lovely. Well, I just can't thank you for all you've done."

"Well, we ought to thank you, Miss Wilmarth," Gerald said. "We certainly ought."

"I really hate to say 'good-by,' " Miss Wilmarth said. "I just hate it."

"Oh, don't say it," Camilla said. "I never dream of saying it. And remember, you must come in and see the baby, any time you can."

"Yes, you certainly must," Gerald said. "That's right."

"Oh, I will," Miss Wilmarth said. "Mercy, I just don't dare go take another look at her, or I wouldn't be able to leave, ever. Well, what am I thinking of! Why, the car's been waiting all this time. Mrs. Cruger simply insists on sending me home in the car, Mr. Cruger. Isn't she terrible?"

"Why, not at all," he said. "Why, of course."

"Well, it's only five blocks down and over to Lexington," she said, "or I really couldn't think of troubling you."

"Why, not at all," Gerald said. "Well! Is that where you live, Miss Wilmarth?"

She lived in some place of her own sometimes? She wasn't always disarranging somebody else's household?

"Yes," Miss Wilmarth said. "I have Mother there."

Oh. Now Gerald had never thought of her having a mother. Then there must have been a father, too, some time. And Miss Wilmarth existed because two people once had loved and known. It was not a thought to dwell upon.

"My aunt's with us, too," Miss Wilmarth said. "It makes it nice for Mother—you see, Mother doesn't get around very well any more. It's a little bit crowded for the three of us—I sleep on the davenport when I'm home, between cases. But it's so nice for Mother, having my aunt there."

Even in her leisure, then, Miss Wilmarth was a disruption and a crowd. Never dwelling in a room that had been planned only for her occupancy; no bed, no corner of her own; dressing before other people's mirrors, touching other people's silver, never looking out one window that was hers. Well. Doubtless she had known nothing else for so long that she did not mind or even ponder.

"Oh, yes," Gerald said "Yes, it certainly must be fine for your mother. Well! Well! May I close your bags for you, Miss Wilmarth?"

"Oh, that's all done," she said. "The suitcase is downstairs. I'll just go get my hat-box. Well, good-by, then, Mrs. Cruger, and take care of yourself. And thank you a thousand times."

"Good luck, Miss Wilmarth," Camilla said. "Come see the baby."

Miss Wilmarth looked at Camilla and at Gerald standing beside her, touching one long white hand. She left the room to fetch her hat-box.

"I'll take it down for you, Miss Wilmarth," Gerald called after her.

He bent and kissed Camilla gently, very, very gently.

"Well, it's nearly over, darling," he said. "Sometimes I am practically convinced that there is a God."

"It was darn decent of you to bring her gardenias," Camilla said. "What made you think of it?"

"I was so crazed at the idea that she was really going," he said, "that I must have lost my head. No one was more surprised than I, buying gardenias for Horsie. Thank the Lord she didn't put them on. I couldn't have stood that sight."

"She's not really at her best in her street clothes," Camilla said. "She seems to lack a certain *chic.*" She stretched her arms slowly above her head and let them sink slowly back. "That was a fascinating glimpse of her home life she gave us. Great fun."

"Oh, I don't suppose she minds," he said. "I'll go down now and back her into the car, and that'll finish it."

He bent again over Camilla.

"Oh, you look so lovely, sweet," he said. "So *lovely.*"

Miss Wilmarth was coming down the hall, when Gerald left the room, managing a pasteboard hat-box, the florist's box, and a big leather purse that had known service. He took the boxes from her, against her protests, and followed her down the stairs and out to the motor at the curb. The chauffeur stood at the open door. Gerald was glad of that presence.

"Well, good luck, Miss Wilmarth," he said. "And thank you so much."

"Thank *you*, Mr. Cruger," she said. "I—I can't tell you how I've enjoyed it all the time I was here. I never had a pleasanter— And the flowers, and everything. I just don't know what to say. I'm the one that ought to thank *you.*"

She held out her hand, in a brown cotton glove. Anyway, worn cotton was easier to the touch than dry, corded flesh. It was the last moment of her. He scarcely minded looking at the long face on the red, red neck.

"Well!" he said. "Well! Got everything? Well, good luck, again, Miss Wilmarth, and don't forget us."

"Oh, I won't," she said. "I—oh, I won't do that."

She turned from him and got quickly into the car, to sit upright against the pale gray cushions. The chauffeur placed her hat-box at her feet and the florist's box on the seat beside her, closed the door smartly, and returned to his wheel. Gerald waved cheerily as the car slid away. Miss Wilmarth did not wave to him.

When she looked back, through the little rear window, he had already disappeared in the house. He must have run across the sidewalk—run, to get back to the fragrant room and the little yellow roses and Camilla. Their little pink baby would lie sleeping in its bed. They would be alone together; they would dine alone together by candlelight; they would be alone together in the night. Every morning and every evening Gerald would drop to his knees beside her to kiss her perfumed hand and call her sweet. Always she would be perfect, in scented chiffon and deep lace. There would be lean, easy young men, to listen to her drawl and give her their laughter. Every day there would be shiny white boxes for her, filled with curious blooms. It was perhaps fortunate that no one looked in the limousine. A beholder must have been startled to learn that a human face could look as much like that of a weary mare as did Miss Wilmarth's.

Presently the car swerved, in a turn of the traffic. The florist's box slipped against Miss Wilmarth's knee. She looked down at it. Then she took it on her lap, raised the lid a little and peeped at the waxy white bouquet. It would have been all fair then for a chance spectator; Miss Wilmarth's strange resemblance was not apparent, as she looked at her flowers. They were her flowers. A man had given them to her. She had been given flowers. They might not fade maybe for days. And she could keep the box.

Glory in the Daytime

Mr. Murdock was one who carried no enthusiasm whatever for plays and their players, and that was too bad, for they meant so much to little Mrs. Murdock. Always she had been in a state of devout excitement over the luminous, free, passionate elect who serve the theater. And always she had done her wistful worshiping, along with the multitudes, at the great public altars. It is true that once, when she was a particularly little girl, love had impelled her to write Miss Maude Adams a letter beginning "Dearest Peter," and she had received from Miss Adams a miniature thimble inscribed "A kiss from Peter Pan." (That was a day!) And once, when her mother had taken her holiday shopping, a limousine door was held open and there had passed her, as close as *that*, a wonder of sable and violets and round red curls that seemed to tinkle on the air; so, forever after, she was as good as certain that she had been not a foot away from Miss Billie Burke. But until some three years after her marriage, these had remained her only personal experiences with the people of the lights and the glory.

Then it turned out that Miss Noyes, new come to little Mrs. Murdock's own bridge club, knew an actress. She actually knew an actress; the way you and I know collectors of recipes and members of garden clubs and amateurs of needlepoint.

The name of the actress was Lily Wynton, and it was famous. She was tall and slow and silvery; often she appeared in the role of a duchess, or of a Lady Pam or an Honorable Moira. Critics recurrently referred to her as "that great lady of our stage." Mrs. Murdock had attended, over years, matinee performances of the Wynton successes. And she had no more thought that she would one day have opportunity to meet Lily Wynton face to face than she had thought—well, than she had thought of flying!

Yet it was not astounding that Miss Noyes should walk at ease among the glamorous. Miss Noyes was full of depths and mystery, and she could talk with a cigarette still between her lips. She was always doing something difficult, like designing her own pajamas, or reading Proust, or modeling torsos in plasticine. She played excellent bridge. She liked little Mrs. Murdock. "Tiny one," she called her.

"How's for coming to tea tomorrow, tiny one? Lily Wynton's going to drop up," she said, at a therefore memorable meeting of the bridge club. "You might like to meet her."

The words fell so easily that she could not have realized their weight. Lily Wynton was coming to tea. Mrs. Murdock might like to meet her. Little Mrs. Murdock walked home through the early dark, and stars sang in the sky above her.

Mr. Murdock was already at home when she arrived. It required but a glance to tell that for him there had been no singing stars that evening in the heavens. He sat with his newspaper opened at the financial page, and bitterness had its way with his soul. It was not the time to cry happily to him of the impending hospitalities of Miss Noyes; not the time, that is, if one anticipated exclamatory sympathy. Mr. Murdock did not like Miss Noyes. When pressed for a reason, he replied that he just plain didn't like her. Occasionally he added, with a sweep that might have commanded a certain admiration, that all those women made him sick. Usually, when she told him of the temperate activities of the bridge club meetings, Mrs. Murdock kept any mention of Miss Noyes's name from the accounts. She had found that this omission made for a more agreeable evening. But now she was caught in such a sparkling swirl of excitement that she had scarcely kissed him before she was off on her story.

"Oh, Jim," she cried. "Oh, what do you think! Hallie Noyes asked me to tea tomorrow to meet Lily Wynton!"

"Who's Lily Wynton?" he said.

"Ah, Jim," she said. "Ah, really, Jim. Who's Lily Wynton! Who's Greta Garbo, I suppose!"

"She some actress or something?" he said.

Mrs. Murdock's shoulders sagged. "Yes, Jim," she said. "Yes. Lily Wynton's an actress."

She picked up her purse and started slowly toward the door.

But before she had taken three steps, she was again caught up in her sparkling swirl. She turned to him, and her eyes were shining.

"Honestly," she said, "it was the funniest thing you ever heard in your life. We'd just finished the last rubber—oh, I forgot to tell you, I won three dollars, isn't that pretty good for me?—and Hallie Noyes said to me, 'Come on in to tea tomorrow. Lily Wynton's going to drop up,' she said. Just like that, she said it. Just as if it was anybody."

"Drop up?" he said. "How can you drop *up?*"

"Honestly, I don't know what I said when she asked me," Mrs. Murdock said. "I suppose I said I'd love to—I guess I must have. But I was so simply— Well, you know how I've always felt about Lily Wynton. Why, when I was a little girl, I used to collect her pictures. And I've seen her in, oh, everything she's ever been in, I should think, and I've read every word about her, and interviews and all. Really and truly, when I think of *meeting* her— Oh, I'll simply die. What on earth shall I say to her?"

"You might ask her how she'd like to try dropping down, for a change," Mr. Murdock said.

"All right, Jim," Mrs. Murdock said. "If that's the way you want to be."

Wearily she went toward the door, and this time she reached it before she turned to him. There were no lights in her eyes.

"It—it isn't so awfully nice," she said, "to spoil somebody's pleasure in something. I was so thrilled about this. You don't see what it is to me, to meet Lily Wynton. To meet somebody like that, and see what they're like, and hear what they say, and maybe get to know them. People like that mean—well, they mean something different to me. They're not like this. They're not like me. Who do I ever see? What do I ever hear? All my whole life, I've wanted to know—I've almost prayed that some day I could meet—Well. All right, Jim."

She went out, and on to her bedroom.

Mr. Murdock was left with only his newspaper and his bitterness for company. But he spoke aloud.

" 'Drop up!' " he said. " 'Drop up,' for God's sake!"

The Murdocks dined, not in silence, but in pronounced quiet. There was something straitened about Mr. Murdock's stillness; but little Mrs. Murdock's was the sweet, far quiet of one given over to dreams. She had forgotten her weary words to her husband, she had passed through her excitement and her disappointment. Luxuriously she floated on innocent visions of days after the morrow. She heard her own voice in future conversations. . . .

I saw Lily Wynton at Hallie's the other day, and she was telling me all about her new play—no, I'm terribly sorry, but it's a secret, I promised her I wouldn't tell anyone the name of it. . . . Lily Wynton dropped up to tea yesterday, and we just got to talking, and she told me the most interesting things about her life; she said she'd never dreamed of telling them to anyone else. . . . Why, I'd love to come, but I promised to have lunch with Lily Wynton. . . . I had a long, long letter from Lily Wynton. . . . Lily Wynton called me up this morning. . . . Whenever I feel blue, I just go and have a talk with Lily Wynton, and then I'm all right again. . . . Lily Wynton told me . . . Lily Wynton and I . . . "Lily," I said to her . . .

The next morning, Mr. Murdock had left for his office before Mrs. Murdock rose. This had happened several times before, but not often. Mrs. Murdock felt a little queer about it. Then she told herself that it was probably just as well. Then she forgot all about it, and gave her mind to the selection of a costume suitable to the afternoon's event. Deeply she felt that her small wardrobe included no dress adequate to the occasion; for, of course, such an occasion had never before arisen. She finally decided upon a frock of dark blue serge with fluted white muslin about the neck and wrists. It was her style, that was the most she could say for it. And that was all she could say for herself. Blue serge and little white ruffles—that was she.

The very becomingness of the dress lowered her spirits. A nobody's frock, worn by a nobody. She blushed and went hot when she recalled the dreams she had woven the night before, the mad visions of intimacy, of equality with Lily Wynton. Timidity turned her heart liquid, and she thought of telephoning Miss Noyes and saying she had a bad cold and could not come. She steadied, when she planned a course of conduct to pursue at teatime. She would not try to say anything; if she stayed silent, she could not sound foolish. She would listen and watch and worship and then come home, stronger, braver, better for an hour she would remember proudly all her life.

Miss Noyes's living-room was done in the early modern period. There were a great many oblique lines and acute angles, zigzags of aluminum and horizontal stretches of mirror. The color scheme was sawdust and steel. No seat was more than twelve inches above the floor, no table was made of wood. It was, as has been said of larger places, all right for a visit.

Little Mrs. Murdock was the first arrival. She was glad of that: no, maybe it would have been better to have come after Lily Wynton; no, maybe this was right. The maid motioned her toward the living-room, and Miss Noyes greeted her in the cool voice and the warm words that were her special combination. She wore black velvet trousers, a red cummerbund, and a white silk shirt, opened at the throat. A cigarette clung to her lower lip, and her eyes, as was her habit, were held narrow against its near smoke.

"Come in, come in, tiny one," she said. "Bless its little heart. Take off its little coat. Good Lord, you look easily eleven years old in that dress. Sit ye doon, here beside of me. There'll be a spot of tea in a jiff."

Mrs. Murdock sat down on the vast, perilously low divan, and, because she was never good at reclining among cushions, held her back straight. There was room for six like her, between herself and her hostess. Miss Noyes lay back with one ankle flung upon the other knee, and looked at her.

"I'm a wreck," Miss Noyes announced. "I was modeling like a mad thing, all night long. It's taken everything out of me. I was like a thing bewitched."

"Oh, what were you making?" cried Mrs. Murdock.

"Oh, Eve," Miss Noyes said. "I always do Eve. What else is

there to do? You must come pose for me some time, tiny one.
You'd be nice to do. Ye-es, you'd be very nice to do. My tiny
one."

"Why, I—" Mrs. Murdock said, and stopped. "Thank you
very much, though," she said.

"I wonder where Lily is," Miss Noyes said. "She said she'd
be here early—well, she always says that. You'll adore her, tiny
one. She's really rare. She's a real person. And she's been
through perfect hell. God, what a time she's had!"

"Ah, what's been the matter?" said Mrs. Murdock.

"Men," Miss Noyes said. "Men. She never had a man that
wasn't a louse." Gloomily she stared at the toe of her flat-
heeled patent leather pump. "A pack of lice, always. All of
them. Leave her for the first little floozie that comes along."

"But—" Mrs. Murdock began. No, she couldn't have heard
right. How could it be right? Lily Wynton was a great actress.
A great actress meant romance. Romance meant Grand Dukes
and Crown Princes and diplomats touched with gray at the
temples and lean, bronzed, reckless Younger Sons. It meant
pearls and emeralds and chinchilla and rubies red as the blood
that was shed for them. It meant a grim-faced boy sitting in the
fearful Indian midnight, beneath the dreary whirring of the
punkahs, writing a letter to the lady he had seen but once;
writing his poor heart out, before he turned to the service
revolver that lay beside him on the table. It meant a golden-
locked poet, floating face downward in the sea, and in his
pocket his last great sonnet to the lady of ivory. It meant brave,
beautiful men, living and dying for the lady who was the pale
bride of art, whose eyes and heart were soft with only compassion for them.

A pack of lice. Crawling after little floozies; whom Mrs.
Murdock swiftly and hazily pictured as rather like ants.

"But—" said little Mrs. Murdock.

"She gave them all her money," Miss Noyes said. "She
always did. Or if she didn't, they took it anyway. Took every
cent she had, and then spat in her face. Well, maybe I'm
teaching her a little bit of sense now. Oh, there's the bell—

that'll be Lily. No, sit ye doon, tiny one. You belong there."

Miss Noyes rose and made for the archway that separated the living-room from the hall. As she passed Mrs. Murdock, she stooped suddenly, cupped her guest's round chin, and quickly, lightly kissed her mouth.

"Don't tell Lily," she murmured, very low.

Mrs. Murdock puzzled. Don't tell Lily what? Could Hallie Noyes think that she might babble to the Lily Wynton of these strange confidences about the actress's life? Or did she mean— But she had no more time for puzzling. Lily Wynton stood in the archway. There she stood, one hand resting on the wooden molding and her body swayed toward it, exactly as she stood for her third-act entrance of her latest play, and for a like half-minute.

You would have known her anywhere, Mrs. Murdock thought. Oh, yes, anywhere. Or at least you would have exclaimed, "That woman looks something like Lily Wynton." For she was somehow different in the daylight. Her figure looked heavier, thicker, and her face—there was so much of her face that the surplus sagged from the strong, fine bones. And her eyes, those famous dark, liquid eyes. They were dark, yes, and certainly liquid, but they were set in little hammocks of folded flesh, and seemed to be set but loosely, so readily did they roll. Their whites, that were visible all around the irises, were threaded with tiny scarlet veins.

"I suppose footlights are an awful strain on their eyes," thought little Mrs. Murdock.

Lily Wynton wore, just as she should have, black satin and sables, and long white gloves were wrinkled luxuriously about her wrists. But there were delicate streaks of grime in the folds of her gloves, and down the shining length of her gown there were small, irregularly shaped dull patches; bits of food or drops of drink, or perhaps both, sometime must have slipped their carriers and found brief sanctuary there. Her hat—oh, her hat. It was romance, it was mystery, it was strange, sweet sorrow; it was Lily Wynton's hat, of all the world, and no other could dare it. Black it was, and tilted, and a great, soft plume drooped from it to follow her cheek and curl across her throat.

Beneath it, her hair had the various hues of neglected brass. But, oh, her hat.

"Darling!" cried Miss Noyes.

"Angel," said Lily Wynton. "My sweet."

It was that voice. It was that deep, soft, glowing voice. "Like purple velvet," someone had written. Mrs. Murdock's heart beat visibly.

Lily Wynton cast herself upon the steep bosom of her hostess, and murmured there. Across Miss Noyes's shoulder she caught sight of little Mrs. Murdock.

"And who is this?" she said. She disengaged herself.

"That's my tiny one," Miss Noyes said. "Mrs. Murdock."

"What a clever little face," said Lily Wynton. "Clever, clever little face. What does she do, sweet Hallie? I'm sure she writes, doesn't she? Yes, I can feel it. She writes beautiful, beautiful words. Don't you, child?"

"Oh, no, really I—" Mrs. Murdock said.

"And you must write me a play," said Lily Wynton. "A beautiful, beautiful play. And I will play in it, over and over the world, until I am a very, very old lady. And then I will die. But I will never be forgotten, because of the years I played in your beautiful, beautiful play."

She moved across the room. There was a slight hesitancy, a seeming insecurity, in her step, and when she would have sunk into a chair, she began to sink two inches, perhaps, to its right. But she swayed just in time in her descent, and was safe.

"To write," she said, smiling sadly at Mrs. Murdock, "to write. And such a little thing, for such a big gift. Oh, the privilege of it. But the anguish of it, too. The agony."

"But, you see, I—" said little Mrs. Murdock.

"Tiny one doesn't write, Lily," Miss Noyes said. She threw herself back upon the divan. "She's a museum piece. She's a devoted wife."

"A wife!" Lily Wynton said. "A wife. Your first marriage, child?"

"Oh, yes," said Mrs. Murdock.

"How sweet," Lily Wynton said. "How sweet, sweet, sweet. Tell me, child, do you love him very, very much?"

"Why, I—" said little Mrs. Murdock, and blushed. "I've been married for ages," she said.

"You love him," Lily Wynton said. "You love him. And is it sweet to go to bed with him?"

"Oh—" said Mrs. Murdock, and blushed till it hurt.

"The first marriage," Lily Wynton said. "Youth, youth. Yes, when I was your age I used to marry, too. Oh, treasure your love, child, guard it, live in it. Laugh and dance in the love of your man. Until you find out what he's really like."

There came a sudden visitation upon her. Her shoulders jerked upward, her cheeks puffed, her eyes sought to start from their hammocks. For a moment she sat thus, then slowly all subsided into place. She lay back in her chair, tenderly patting her chest. She shook her head sadly, and there was grieved wonder in the look with which she held Mrs. Murdock.

"Gas," said Lily Wynton, in the famous voice. "Gas. Nobody knows what I suffer from it."

"Oh, I'm so sorry," Mrs. Murdock said. "Is there anything——"

"Nothing," Lily Wynton said. "There is nothing. There is nothing that can be done for it. I've been everywhere."

"How's for a spot of tea, perhaps?" Miss Noyes said. "It might help." She turned her face toward the archway and lifted up her voice. "Mary! Where the hell's the tea?"

"You don't know," Lily Wynton said, with her grieved eyes fixed on Mrs. Murdock, "you don't know what stomach distress is. You can never, never know, unless you're a stomach sufferer yourself. I've been one for years. Years and years and years."

"I'm terribly sorry," Mrs. Murdock said.

"Nobody knows the anguish," Lily Wynton said. "The agony."

The maid appeared, bearing a triangular tray upon which was set an heroic-sized tea service of bright white china, each piece a hectagon. She set it down on a table within the long reach of Miss Noyes and retired, as she had come, bashfully.

"Sweet Hallie," Lily Wynton said, "my sweet. Tea—I adore it. I worship it. But my distress turns it to gall and wormwood in me. Gall and wormwood. For hours, I should have no peace. Let me have a little, tiny bit of your beautiful, beautiful brandy, instead."

"You really think you should, darling?" Miss Noyes said. "You know——"

"My angel," said Lily Wynton, "it's the only thing for acidity."

"Well," Miss Noyes said. "But do remember you've got a performance tonight." Again she hurled her voice at the archway. "Mary! Bring the brandy and a lot of soda and ice and things."

"Oh, no, my saint," Lily Wynton said. "No, no, sweet Hallie. Soda and ice are rank poison to me. Do you want to freeze my poor, weak stomach? Do you want to kill poor, poor Lily?"

"Mary!" roared Miss Noyes. "Just bring the brandy and a glass." She turned to little Mrs. Murdock. "How's for your tea, tiny one? Cream? Lemon?"

"Cream, if I may, please," Mrs. Murdock said. "And two lumps of sugar, please, if I may."

"Oh, youth, youth," Lily Wynton said. "Youth and love."

The maid returned with an octagonal tray supporting a decanter of brandy and a wide, squat, heavy glass. Her head twisted on her neck in a spasm of diffidence.

"Just pour it for me, will you, my dear?" said Lily Wynton. "Thank you. And leave the pretty, pretty decanter here, on this enchanting little table. Thank you. You're so good to me."

The maid vanished, fluttering. Lily Wynton lay back in her chair, holding in her gloved hand the wide, squat glass, colored brown to the brim. Little Mrs. Murdock lowered her eyes to her teacup, carefully carried it to her lips, sipped, and replaced it on its saucer. When she raised her eyes, Lily Wynton lay back in her chair, holding in her gloved hand the wide, squat, colorless glass.

"My life," Lily Wynton said, slowly, "is a mess. A stinking mess. It always has been, and it always will be. Until I am a very, very old lady. Ah, little Clever-Face, you writers don't know what struggle is."

"But really I'm not—" said Mrs. Murdock.

"To write," Lily Wynton said. "To write. To set one word beautifully beside another word. The privilege of it. The blessed, blessed peace of it. Oh, for quiet, for rest. But do you think those cheap bastards would close that play while it's doing a nickel's worth of business? Oh, no. Tired as I am, sick as I am, I must drag along. Oh, child, child, guard your precious gift. Give thanks for it. It is the greatest thing of all. It is the only thing. To write."

"Darling, I told you tiny one doesn't write," said Miss Noyes. "How's for making more sense? She's a wife."

"Ah, yes, she told me. She told me she had perfect, passionate love," Lily Wynton said. "Young love. It is the greatest thing. It is the only thing." She grasped the decanter; and again the squat glass was brown to the brim.

"What time did you start today, darling?" said Miss Noyes.

"Oh, don't scold me, sweet love," Lily Wynton said. "Lily hasn't been naughty. Her wuzzunt naughty dirl 't all. I didn't get up until late, late, late. And though I parched, though I burned, I didn't have a drink until after my breakfast. 'It is for Hallie,' I said." She raised the glass to her mouth, tilted it, and brought it away, colorless.

"Good Lord, Lily," Miss Noyes said. "Watch yourself. You've got to walk on that stage tonight, my girl."

"All the world's a stage," said Lily Wynton. "And all the men and women merely players. They have their entrance and their exitses, and each man in his time plays many parts, his act being seven ages. At first, the infant, mewling and puking——"

"How's the play doing?" Miss Noyes said.

"Oh, lousily," Lily Wynton said. "Lousily, lousily, lousily. But what isn't? What isn't, in this terrible, terrible world? Answer me that." She reached for the decanter.

"Lily, listen," said Miss Noyes. "Stop that. Do you hear?"

"Please, sweet Hallie," Lily Wynton said. "Pretty please. Poor, poor Lily."

"Do you want me to do what I had to do last time?" Miss Noyes said. "Do you want me to strike you, in front of tiny one, here?"

Lily Wynton drew herself high. "You do not realize," she said, icily, "what acidity is." She filled the glass and held it, regarding it as though through a lorgnon. Suddenly her manner changed, and she looked up and smiled at little Mrs. Murdock.

"You must let me read it," she said. "You mustn't be so modest."

"Read—?" said little Mrs. Murdock.

"Your play," Lily Wynton said. "Your beautiful, beautiful play. Don't think I am too busy. I always have time. I have time for everything. Oh, my God, I have to go to the dentist tomorrow. Oh, the suffering I have gone through with my teeth. Look!" She set down her glass, inserted a gloved forefinger in the corner of her mouth, and dragged it to the side. "Oogh!" she insisted. "Oogh!"

Mrs. Murdock craned her neck shyly, and caught a glimpse of shining gold.

"Oh, I'm so sorry," she said.

"As wah ee id a me ass ime," Lily Wynton said. She took away her forefinger and let her mouth resume its shape. "That's what he did to me last time," she repeated. "The anguish of it. The agony. Do you suffer with your teeth, little Clever-Face?"

"Why, I'm afraid I've been awfully lucky," Mrs. Murdock said. "I——"

"You don't know," Lily Wynton said. "Nobody knows what it is. You writers—you don't know." She took up her glass, sighed over it, and drained it.

"Well," Miss Noyes said. "Go ahead and pass out, then, darling. You'll have time for a sleep before the theater."

"To sleep," Lily Wynton said. "To sleep, perchance to dream. The privilege of it. Oh, Hallie, sweet, sweet Hallie, poor Lily feels so terrible. Rub my head for me, angel. Help me."

"I'll go get the Eau de Cologne," Miss Noyes said. She left the room lightly patting Mrs. Murdock's knee as she passed her. Lily Wynton lay in her chair and closed her famous eyes.

"To sleep," she said. "To sleep, perchance to dream."

"I'm afraid," little Mrs. Murdock began. "I'm afraid," she

said, "I really must be going home. I'm afraid I didn't realize how awfully late it was."

"Yes, go, child," Lily Wynton said. She did not open her eyes. "Go to him. Go to him, live in him, love him. Stay with him always. But when he starts bringing them into the house—get out."

"I'm afraid—I'm afraid I didn't quite understand," Mrs. Murdock said.

"When he starts bringing his fancy women into the house," Lily Wynton said. "You must have pride, then. You must go. I always did. But it was always too late then. They'd got all my money. That's all they want, marry them or not. They say it's love, but it isn't. Love is the only thing. Treasure your love, child. Go back to him. Go to bed with him. It's the only thing. And your beautiful, beautiful play."

"Oh, dear," said little Mrs. Murdock. "I—I'm afraid it's really terribly late."

There was only the sound of rhythmic breathing from the chair where Lily Wynton lay. The purple voice rolled along the air no longer.

Little Mrs. Murdock stole to the chair upon which she had left her coat. Carefully she smoothed her white muslin frills, so that they would be fresh beneath the jacket. She felt a tenderness for her frock; she wanted to protect it. Blue serge and little ruffles—they were her own.

When she reached the outer door of Miss Noyes's apartment, she stopped a moment and her manners conquered her. Bravely she called in the direction of Miss Noyes's bedroom.

"Good-by, Miss Noyes," she said. "I've simply got to run. I didn't realize it was so late. I had a lovely time—thank you ever so much."

"Oh, good-by, tiny one," Miss Noyes called. "Sorry Lily went by-by. Don't mind her—she's really a real person. I'll call you up, tiny one. I want to see you. Now where's that damned Cologne?"

"Thank you ever so much," Mrs. Murdock said. She let herself out of the apartment.

Little Mrs. Murdock walked homeward, through the

clustering dark. Her mind was busy, but not with memories of
Lily Wynton. She thought of Jim; Jim, who had left for his
office before she had arisen that morning, Jim, whom she had
not kissed good-by. Darling Jim. There were no others born
like him. Funny Jim, stiff and cross and silent; but only
because he knew so much. Only because he knew the silliness
of seeking afar for the glamour and beauty and romance of
living. When they were right at home all the time, she thought.
Like the Blue Bird, thought little Mrs. Murdock.

Darling Jim. Mrs. Murdock turned in her course, and entered an enormous shop where the most delicate and esoteric of
foods were sold for heavy sums. Jim liked red caviar. Mrs.
Murdock bought a jar of the shiny, glutinous eggs. They would
have cocktails that night, though they had no guests, and the
red caviar would be served with them for a surprise, and it
would be a little, secret party to celebrate her return to contentment with her Jim, a party to mark her happy renunciation
of all the glory of the world. She bought, too, a large, foreign
cheese. It would give a needed touch to dinner. Mrs. Murdock
had not given much attention to ordering dinner, that morning. "Oh, anything you want, Signe," she had said to the maid.
She did not want to think of that. She went on home with her
packages.

Mr. Murdock was already there when she arrived. He was
sitting with his newspaper opened to the financial page. Little
Mrs. Murdock ran in to him with her eyes a-light. It is too bad
that the light in a person's eyes is only the light in a person's
eyes, and you cannot tell at a look what causes it. You do not
know if it is excitement about you, or about something else.
The evening before, Mrs. Murdock had run in to Mr. Murdock
with her eyes a-light.

"Oh, hello," he said to her. He looked back at his paper, and
kept his eyes there. "What did you do? Did you drop up to
Hank Noyes's?"

Little Mrs. Murdock stopped right where she was.

"You know perfectly well, Jim," she said, "that Hallie
Noyes's first name is Hallie."

"It's Hank to me," he said. "Hank or Bill. Did what's-her-name show up? I mean drop up. Pardon me."

"To whom are you referring?" said Mrs. Murdock, perfectly.

"What's-her-name," Mr. Murdock said. "The movie star."

"If you mean Lily Wynton," Mrs. Murdock said, "she is not a movie star. She is an actress. She is a great actress."

"Well, did she drop up?" he said.

Mrs. Murdock's shoulders sagged. "Yes," she said. "Yes, she was there, Jim."

"I suppose you're going on the stage now," he said.

"Ah, Jim," Mrs. Murdock said. "Ah, Jim, please. I'm not sorry at all I went to Hallie Noyes's today. It was—it was a real experience to meet Lily Wynton. Something I'll remember all my life."

"What did she do?" Mr. Murdock said. "Hang by her feet?"

"She did no such thing!" Mrs. Murdock said. "She recited Shakespeare, if you want to know."

"Oh, my God," Mr. Murdock said. "That must have been great."

"All right, Jim," Mrs. Murdock said. "If that's the way you want to be."

Wearily she left the room and went down the hall. She stopped at the pantry door, pushed it open, and spoke to the pleasant little maid.

"Oh, Signe," she said. "Oh, good evening, Signe. Put these things somewhere, will you? I got them on the way home. I thought we might have them some time."

Wearily little Mrs. Murdock went on down the hall to her bedroom.

New York to Detroit

"All ready with Detroit," said the telephone operator.

"Hello," said the girl in New York.

"Hello?" said the young man in Detroit.

"Oh, Jack!" she said. "Oh, darling, it's so wonderful to hear you. You don't know how much I——"

"Hello?" he said.

"Ah, can't you hear me?" she said. "Why, I can hear you just as if you were right beside me. Is this any better, dear? Can you hear me now?"

"Who did you want to speak to?" he said.

"You, Jack!" she said. "You, you. This is Jean, darling. Oh, please try to hear me. This is Jean."

"Who?" he said.

"Jean," she said. "Ah, don't you know my voice? It's Jean, dear. Jean."

"Oh, hello there," he said. "Well. Well, for heaven's sake. How are you?"

"I'm all right," she said. "Oh, I'm not, either, darling. I—oh, it's just terrible. I can't stand it any more. Aren't you coming back? Please, when are you coming back? You don't know how awful it is, without you. It's been such a long time, dear—you said it would be just four or five days, and it's nearly three weeks. It's like years and years. Oh, it's been so awful, sweetheart—it's just——"

"Hey, I'm terribly sorry," he said, "but I can't hear one damn thing you're saying. Can't you talk louder, or something?"

"I'll try, I'll try," she said. "Is this better? Now can you hear?"

"Yeah, now I can, a little," he said. "Don't talk so fast, will you? What did you say, before?"

"I said it's just awful without you," she said. "It's such a long time, dear. And I haven't had a word from you. I—oh, I've

291

just been nearly crazy, Jack. Never even a post-card, dearest, or a——"

"Honestly, I haven't had a second," he said. "I've been working like a fool. God, I've been rushed."

"Ah, have you?" she said. "I'm sorry, dear. I've been silly. But it was just—oh, it was just hell, never hearing a word. I thought maybe you'd telephone to say goodnight, sometimes,—you know, the way you used to, when you were away."

"Why, I was going to, a lot of times," he said,' "but I thought you'd probably be out, or something."

"I haven't been out," she said. "I've been staying here, all by myself. It's—it's sort of better, that way. I don't want to see people. Everybody says, 'When's Jack coming back?' and 'What do you hear from Jack?' and I'm afraid I'll cry in front of them. Darling, it hurts so terribly when they ask me about you, and I have to say I don't——"

"This is the damnedest, lousiest connection I ever saw in my life," he said. "What hurts? What's the matter?"

"I said, it hurts so terribly when people ask me about you," she said, "and I have to say—Oh, never mind. Never mind. How are you, dear? Tell me how you are."

"Oh, pretty good," he said. "Tired as the devil. You all right?"

"Jack, I—that's what I wanted to tell you," she said. "I'm terribly worried. I'm nearly out of my mind. Oh, what will I do, dear, what are we going to do? Oh, Jack, Jack, darling!"

"Hey, how can I hear you when you mumble like that?" he said. "Can't you talk louder? Talk right into the what-you-call-it."

"I can't scream it over the telephone!" she said. "Haven't you any sense? Don't you know what I'm telling you? Don't you know? Don't you know?"

"I give up," he said. "First you mumble, and then you yell. Look, this doesn't make sense. I can't hear anything, with this rotten connection. Why don't you write me a letter, in the morning? Do that, why don't you? And I'll write you one. See?"

Jack, listen, listen!" she said. "You listen to me! I've got to talk to you. I tell you I'm nearly crazy. Please, dearest, hear what I'm saying. Jack, I——"

"Just a minute," he said. "Someone's knocking at the door. *Come in. Well, for cryin' out loud! Come on in, bums. Hang your coats up on the floor, and sit down. The Scotch is in the closet, and there's ice in that pitcher. Make yourselves at home—act like you were in a regular bar. Be with you right away.* Hey, listen, there's a lot of crazy Indians just come in here, and I can't hear myself think. You go ahead and write me a letter tomorrow. Will you?"

"Write you a letter!" she said. "Oh, God, don't you think I'd have written you before, if I'd known where to reach you? I didn't even know that, till they told me at your office today. I got so——"

"Oh, yeah, did they?" he said. "I thought I—*Ah, pipe down, will you? Give a guy a chance. This is an expensive talk going on here.* Say, look, this must be costing you a million dollars. You oughtn't to do this."

"What do you think I care about that?" she said. "I'll die if I don't talk to you. I tell you I'll die, Jack. Sweetheart, what is it? Don't you want to talk to me? Tell me what makes you this way. Is it—don't you really like me any more? Is that it? Don't you, Jack?"

"Hell, I can't hear," he said. "Don't what?"

"Please," she said. "Please, please. Please, Jack, listen. When are you coming back, darling? I need you so. I need you so terribly. When are you coming back?"

"Why, that's the thing," he said. "That's what I was going to write you about tomorrow. *Come on, now, how about shutting up just for a minute? A joke's a joke.* Hello. Hear me all right? Why, you see, the way things came out today, it looks a little bit like I'd have to go on to Chicago for a while. Looks like a pretty big thing, and it won't mean a very long time, I don't believe. Looks as if I'd be going out there next week, I guess."

"Jack, no!" she said. "Oh, don't do that! You can't do that. You can't leave me alone like this. I've got to see you, dearest. I've got to. You've got to come back, or I've got to come there to you. I can't go through this. Jack, I can't, I——"

"Look, we better say good-night now," he said. "No use trying to make out what you say, when you talk all over yourself like that. And there's so much racket here—*Hey, can the harmony, will you? God, it's terrible. Want me to be thrown out of here?* You go get a good night's sleep, and I'll write you all about it tomorrow."

"Listen!" she said. "Jack, don't go 'way! Help me, darling. Say something to help me through tonight. Say you love me, for God's sake say you still love me. Say it. Say it."

"Ah, I can't talk," he said. "This is fierce. I'll write you first thing in the morning. 'By. Thanks for calling up."

"Jack!" she said. "Jack, don't go. Jack, wait a minute. I've got to talk to you. I'll talk quietly. I won't cry. I'll talk so you can hear me. Please, dear, please——"

"All through with Detroit?" said the operator.

"No!" she said. "No, no, no! Get him, get him back again right away! Get him back. No, never mind. Never mind it now. Never——"

Death and Taxes

Prayer for a Prayer

Dearest one, when I am dead
  Never seek to follow me.
    Never mount the quiet hill
    Where the copper leaves are still,
  As my heart is, on the tree
Standing at my narrow bed.

Only, of your tenderness,
  Pray a little prayer at night.
    Say: "I have forgiven now—
    I, so weak and sad; O Thou,
  Wreathed in thunder, robed in light,
Surely Thou wilt do no less."

After Spanish Proverb

Oh, mercifullest one of all,
  Oh, generous as dear,
None lived so lowly, none so small,
  Thou couldst withhold thy tear:

How swift, in pure compassion,
  How meek in charity,
To offer friendship to the one
  Who begged but love of thee!

Oh, gentle word, and sweetest said!
Oh, tender hand, and first
To hold the warm, delicious bread
To lips burned black of thirst.

The Danger of Writing
Defiant Verse

And now I have another lad!
No longer need you tell
How all my nights are slow and sad
For loving you too well.

His ways are not your wicked ways,
He's not the like of you.
He treads his path of reckoned days,
A sober man, and true.

They'll never see him in the town,
Another on his knee.
He'd cut his laden orchards down,
If that would pleasure me.

He'd give his blood to paint my lips
If I should wish them red.
He prays to touch my finger-tips
Or stroke my prideful head.

He never weaves a glinting lie,
Or brags the hearts he'll keep.
I have forgotten how to sigh—
Remembered how to sleep.

He's none to kiss away my mind—
A slower way is his.
Oh, Lord! On reading this, I find
A silly lot he is.

Distance

Were you to cross the world, my dear,
　　To work or love or fight,
I could be calm and wistful here,
　　And close my eyes at night.

It were a sweet and gallant pain
　　To be a sea apart;
But, oh, to have you down the lane
　　Is bitter to my heart.

Sanctuary

My land is bare of chattering folk;
　　The clouds are low along the ridges,
And sweet's the air with curly smoke
　　From all my burning bridges.

The Evening Primrose

You know the bloom, unearthly white,
That none has seen by morning light—
The tender moon, alone, may bare
Its beauty to the secret air.
Who'd venture past its dark retreat
Must kneel, for holy things and sweet,
That blossom, mystically blown,
No man may gather for his own
Nor touch it, lest it droop and fall. . . .
Oh, I am not like that at all!

The Flaw in Paganism

Drink and dance and laugh and lie,
   Love, the reeling midnight through,
For tomorrow we shall die!
   (But, alas, we never do.)

Salome's Dancing-Lesson

She that begs a little boon
   (*Heel and toe! Heel and toe!*)
Little gets—and nothing, soon.
   (*No, no, no! No, no, no!*)
She that calls for costly things
Priceless finds her offerings—
What's impossible to kings?
   (*Heel and toe! Heel and toe!*)

Kings are shaped as other men.
   (*Step and turn! Step and turn!*)
Ask what none may ask again.
   (*Will you learn? Will you learn?*)
Lovers whine, and kisses pall,
Jewels tarnish, kingdoms fall—
Death's the rarest prize of all!
   (*Step and turn! Step and turn!*)

Veils are woven to be dropped.
   (*One, two, three! One, two, three!*)
Aging eyes are slowest stopped.
   (*Quietly! Quietly!*)
She whose body's young and cool
Has no need of dancing-school—
Scratch a king and find a fool!
   (*One, two, three! One, two, three!*)

Cherry White

I never see that prettiest thing—
A cherry bough gone white with Spring—
But what I think, "How gay 'twould be
To hang me from a flowering tree."

My Own

Then let them point my every tear,
    And let them mock and moan;
Another week, another year,
    And I'll be with my own

Who slumber now by night and day
    In fields of level brown;
Whose hearts within their breasts were clay
    Before they laid them down.

Solace

There was a rose that faded young;
I saw its shattered beauty hung
    Upon a broken stem.
I heard them say, "What need to care
With roses budding everywhere?"
    I did not answer them.

There was a bird, brought down to die;
They said, "A hundred fill the sky—
    What reason to be sad?"
There was a girl, whose lover fled;
I did not wait, the while they said,
    "There's many another lad."

Little Words

When you are gone, there is nor bloom nor leaf,
   Nor singing sea at night, nor silver birds;
And I can only stare, and shape my grief
   In little words.

I cannot conjure loveliness, to drown
   The bitter woe that racks my cords apart.
The weary pen that sets my sorrow down
   Feeds at my heart.

There is no mercy in the shifting year,
   No beauty wraps me tenderly about.
I turn to little words—so you, my dear,
   Can spell them out.

Tombstones
in the Starlight

I. The Minor Poet

His little trills and chirpings were his best.
   No music like the nightingale's was born
Within his throat; but he, too, laid his breast
   Upon a thorn.

II. The Pretty Lady

She hated bleak and wintry things alone.
   All that was warm and quick, she loved too well—
A light, a flame, a heart against her own;
   It is forever bitter cold, in Hell.

III.   The Very Rich Man

He'd have the best, and that was none too good;
   No barrier could hold, before his terms.
He lies below, correct in cypress wood,
   And entertains the most exclusive worms.

IV.   The Fisherwoman

The man she had was kind and clean
   And well enough for every day,
But, oh, dear friends, you should have seen
   The one that got away!

V.   The Crusader

Arrived in Heaven, when his sands were run,
   He seized a quill, and sat him down to tell
The local press that something should be done
   About that noisy nuisance, Gabriel.

VI.   The Actress

Her name, cut clear upon this marble cross,
   Shines, as it shone when she was still on earth;
While tenderly the mild, agreeable moss
   Obscures the figures of her date of birth.

Garden-Spot

God's acre was her garden-spot, she said;
   She sat there often, of the Summer days,
Little and slim and sweet, among the dead,
   Her hair a fable in the leveled rays.

She turned the fading wreath, the rusted cross,
　And knelt to coax about the wiry stem.
I see her gentle fingers on the moss
　Now it is anguish to remember them.

And once I saw her weeping, when she rose
　And walked a way and turned to look around—
The quick and envious tears of one that knows
　She shall not lie in consecrated ground.

Ornithology for Beginners

The bird that feeds from off my palm
Is sleek, affectionate, and calm,
But double, to me, is worth the thrush
A-flickering in the elder-bush.

Vers Démodé

For one, the amaryllis and the rose;
　The poppy, sweet as never lilies are;
The ripen'd vine, that beckons as it blows;
　The dancing star.

For one, the trodden rosemary and rue;
　The bowl, dipt ever in the purple stream
And, for the other one, a fairer due—
　Sleep, and no dream.

The Little Old Lady
in Lavender Silk

I was seventy-seven, come August,
  I shall shortly be losing my bloom;
I've experienced zephyr and raw gust
  And (symbolical) flood and simoom.

When you come to this time of abatement,
  To this passing from Summer to Fall,
It is manners to issue a statement
  As to what you got out of it all.

So I'll say, though reflection unnerves me
  And pronouncements I dodge as I can,
That I think (if my memory serves me)
  There was nothing more fun than a man!

In my youth, when the crescent was too wan
  To embarrass with beams from above,
By the aid of some local Don Juan
  I fell into the habit of love.

And I learned how to kiss and be merry—an
  Education left better unsung.
My neglect of the waters Pierian
  Was a scandal, when Grandma was young.

Though the shabby unbalanced the splendid,
  And the bitter outmeasured the sweet,
I should certainly do as I then did,
  Were I given the chance to repeat.

For contrition is hollow and wraithful,
  And regret is no part of my plan,
And I think (if my memory's faithful)
  There was nothing more fun than a man!

Sonnet for the End
of a Sequence

So take my vows and scatter them to sea;
Who swears the sweetest is no more than human.
And say no kinder words than these of me:
"Ever she longed for peace, but was a woman!
And thus they are, whose silly female dust
Needs little enough to clutter it and bind it,
Who meet a slanted gaze, and ever must
Go build themselves a soul to dwell behind it."

For now I am my own again, my friend!
This scar but points the whiteness of my breast;
This frenzy, like its betters, spins an end,
And now I am my own. And that is best.
Therefore, I am immeasurably grateful
To you, for proving shallow, false, and hateful.

The Apple Tree

When first we saw the apple tree
   The boughs were dark and straight,
But never grief to give had we,
   Though Spring delayed so late.

When last I came away from there
   The boughs were heavy hung,
But little grief had I to spare
   For Summer, perished young.

Iseult of Brittany

So delicate my hands, and long,
   They might have been my pride.
And there were those to make them song
   Who for their touch had died.

Too frail to cup a heart within,
   Too soft to hold the free—
How long these lovely hands have been
   A bitterness to me!

"Star Light,
Star Bright—"

Star, that gives a gracious dole,
   What am I to choose?
Oh, will it be a shriven soul,
   Or little buckled shoes?

Shall I wish a wedding-ring,
   Bright and thin and round,
Or plead you send me covering—
   A newly spaded mound?

Gentle beam, shall I implore
   Gold, or sailing-ships,
Or beg I hate forevermore
   A pair of lying lips?

Swing you low or high away,
   Burn you hot or dim;
My only wish I dare not say—
   Lest you should grant me him.

The Sea

Who lay against the sea, and fled,
   Who lightly loved the wave,
Shall never know, when he is dead,
   A cool and murmurous grave.

But in a shallow pit shall rest
   For all eternity,
And bear the earth upon the breası
   That once had worn the sea.

Guinevere
at Her Fireside

A nobler king had never breath—
   I say it now, and said it then.
Who weds with such is wed till death
   And wedded stays in Heaven. Amen.

(And oh, the shirts of linen-lawn,
   And all the armor, tagged and tied,
And church on Sundays, dusk and dawn.
   And bed a thing to kneel beside!)

The bravest one stood tall above
   The rest, and watched me as a light.
I heard and heard them talk of love;
   I'd naught to do but think, at night.

The bravest man has littlest brains;
   That chalky fool from Astolat
With all her dying and her pains!—
   Thank God, I helped him over that.

I found him not unfair to see—
   I like a man with peppered hair!
And thus it came about. Ah, me,
   Tristram was busied otherwhere. . . .

A nobler king had never breath—
   I say it now, and said it then.
Who weds with such is wed till death
   And wedded stays in Heaven. Amen.

Transition

Too long and quickly have I lived to vow
  The woe that stretches me shall never wane,
  Too often seen the end of endless pain
To swear that peace no more shall cool my brow.
I know, I know—again the shriveled bough
  Will burgeon sweetly in the gentle rain,
  And these hard lands be quivering with grain—
I tell you only: it is Winter now.

What if I know, before the Summer goes
Where dwelt this bitter frenzy shall be rest?
What is it now, that June shall surely bring
New promise, with the swallow and the rose?
My heart is water, that I first must breast
The terrible, slow loveliness of Spring.

Lines on Reading
Too Many Poets

Roses, rooted warm in earth,
  Bud in rhyme, another age;
Lilies know a ghostly birth
  Strewn along a patterned page;
Golden lad and chimbley sweep
Die; and so their song shall keep.

Wind that in Arcadia starts
  In and out a couplet plays;
And the drums of bitter hearts
  Beat the measure of a phrase.
Sweets and woes but come to print
Quae cum ita sint.

From a Letter
from Lesbia

. . . So, praise the gods, Catullus is away!
    And let me tend you this advice, my dear:
Take any lover that you will, or may,
    Except a poet. All of them are queer.

It's just the same—a quarrel or a kiss
    Is but a tune to play upon his pipe.
He's always hymning that or wailing this;
    Myself, I much prefer the business type.

That thing he wrote, the time the sparrow died—
    (Oh, most unpleasant—gloomy, tedious words!)
I called it sweet, and made believe I cried;
    The stupid fool! I've always hated birds. . . .

Purposely Ungrammatical Love Song

There's many and many, and not so far,
    Is willing to dry my tears away;
There's many to tell me what you are,
    And never a lie to all they say.

It's little the good to hide my head,
    It's never the use to bar my door;
There's many as counts the tears I shed,
    There's mourning hearts for my heart is sore.

There's honester eyes than your blue eyes,
    There's better a mile than such as you.
But when did I say that I was wise,
    And when did I hope that you were true?

Ballade of Unfortunate Mammals

Love is sharper than stones or sticks;
  Lone as the sea, and deeper blue;
Loud in the night as a clock that ticks;
  Longer lived than the Wandering Jew.
Show me a love was done and through,
  Tell me a kiss escaped its debt!
Son, to your death you'll pay your due—
  Women and elephants never forget.

Ever a man, alas, would mix,
  Ever a man, heigh-ho, must woo;
So he's left in the world-old fix,
  Thus is furthered the sale of rue.
Son, your chances are thin and few—
  Won't you ponder, before you're set?
Shoot if you must, but hold in view
  Women and elephants never forget.

Down from Caesar past Joynson-Hicks
  Echoes the warning, ever new:
Though they're trained to amusing tricks,
  Gentler, they, than the pigeon's coo,
Careful, son, of the cursèd two—
  Either one is a dangerous pet;
Natural history proves it true—
  Women and elephants never forget.

L'ENVOI

Prince, a precept I'd leave for you,
  Coined in Eden, existing yet:
Skirt the parlor, and shun the zoo—
  Women and elephants never forget.

Sweet Violets

You are brief and frail and blue—
Little sisters, I am, too.
You are Heaven's masterpieces—
Little loves, the likeness ceases.

Prayer
for a New Mother

The things she knew, let her forget again—
 The voices in the sky, the fear, the cold,
The gaping shepherds, and the queer old men
 Piling their clumsy gifts of foreign gold.

Let her have laughter with her little one;
 Teach her the endless, tuneless songs to sing,
Grant her her right to whisper to her son
 The foolish names one dare not call a king.

Keep from her dreams the rumble of a crowd,
 The smell of rough-cut wood, the trail of red,
The thick and chilly whiteness of the shroud
 That wraps the strange new body of the dead.

Ah, let her go, kind Lord, where mothers go
 And boast his pretty words and ways, and plan
The proud and happy years that they shall know
 Together, when her son is grown a man.

Midnight

The stars are soft as flowers, and as near;
  The hills are webs of shadow, slowly spun;
No separate leaf or single blade is here—
  All blend to one.

No moonbeam cuts the air; a sapphire light
  Rolls lazily, and slips again to rest.
There is no edgèd thing in all this night,
  Save in my breast.

Ninon de Lenclos, on Her Last Birthday

So let me have the rouge again,
  And comb my hair the curly way.
The poor young men, the dear young men
  They'll all be here by noon today.

And I shall wear the blue, I think—
  They beg to touch its rippled lace;
Or do they love me best in pink,
  So sweetly flattering the face?

And are you sure my eyes are bright,
  And is it true my cheek is clear?
Young what's-his-name stayed half the night;
  He vows to cut his 'throat, poor dear!

So bring my scarlet slippers, then,
  And fetch the powder-puff to me.
The dear young men, the poor young men—
  They think I'm only seventy!

Ultimatum

I'm wearied of wearying love, my friend,
　Of worry and strain and doubt;
Before we begin, let us view the end,
　And maybe I'll do without.
There's never the pang that was worth the tear,
　And toss in the night I won't—
So either you do or you don't, my dear,
　Either you do or you don't!

The table is ready, so lay your cards
　And if they should augur pain,
I'll tender you ever my kind regards
　And run for the fastest train.
I haven't the will to be spent and sad;
　My heart's to be gay and true—
Then either you don't or you do, my lad,
　Either you don't or you do!

The Willow

On sweet young earth where the myrtle presses,
　Long we lay, when the May was new;
The willow was winding the moon in her tresses,
　The bud of the rose was told with dew.

And now on the brittle ground I'm lying,
　Screaming to die with the dead year's dead;
The stem of the rose is black and drying,
　The willow is tossing the wind from her head.

Summary

Every love's the love before
  In a duller dress.
That's the measure of my lore—
  Here's my bitterness:
Would I knew a little more,
  Or very much less!

Of a Woman, Dead Young

(J. H., 1905-1930)

If she had been beautiful, even,
Or wiser than women about her,
Or had moved with a certain defiance;
If she had had sons at her sides,
And she with her hands on their shoulders,
Sons, to make troubled the Gods—
But where was there wonder in her?
What had she, better or eviler,
Whose days were a pattering of peas
From the pod to the bowl in her lap?

That the pine tree is blasted by lightning,
And the bowlder split raw from the mountain,
And the river dried short in its rushing—
That I can know, and be humble.
But that They who have trodden the stars
Should turn from Their echoing highway
To trample a daisy, unnoticed
In a meadow of small, open flowers—
Where is Their triumph in that?
Where is Their pride, and Their vengeance?

Sonnet on
an Alpine Night

My hand, a little raised, might press a star;
Where I may look, the frosted peaks are spun,
So shaped before Olympus was begun,
Spanned each to each, now, by a silver bar.
Thus to face Beauty have I traveled far,
But now, as if around my heart were run
Hard, lacing fingers, so I stand undone.
Of all my tears, the bitterest these are.

Who humbly followed Beauty all her ways,
Begging the brambles that her robe had passed,
Crying her name in corridors of stone,
That day shall know his weariedest of days—
When Beauty, still and suppliant at last,
Does not suffice him, once they are alone.

Requiescat

Tonight my love is sleeping cold
    Where none may see and none shall pass.
The daisies quicken in the mold,
    And richer fares the meadow grass.

The warding cypress pleads the skies,
    The mound goes level in the rain.
My love all cold and silent lies—
    Pray God it will not rise again!

Ballade of
a Talked-off Ear

Daily I listen to wonder and woe,
Nightly I hearken to knave or to ace,
Telling me stories of lava and snow,
Delicate fables of ribbon and lace,
Tales of the quarry, the kill, the chase,
Longer than heaven and duller than hell—
Never you blame me, who cry my case:
"Poets alone should kiss and tell!"

Dumbly I hear what I never should know,
Gently I counsel of pride and of grace;
Into minutiae gayly they go,
Telling the name and the time and the place.
Cede them your silence and grant them space—
Who tenders an inch shall be raped of an ell!
Sympathy's ever the boaster's brace;
Poets alone should kiss and tell.

Why am I tithed what I never did owe?
Choked with vicarious saffron and mace?
Weary my lids, and my fingers are slow—
Gentlemen, damn you, you've halted my pace.
Only the lads of the cursed race,
Only the knights of the desolate spell,
May point me the lines the blood-drops trace—
Poets alone should kiss and tell.

L'ENVOI

Prince or commoner, tenor or bass,
Painter or plumber or never-do-well,
Do me a favor and shut your face—
Poets alone should kiss and tell.

Prologue to a Saga

Maidens, gather not the yew,
    Leave the glossy myrtle sleeping;
Any lad was born untrue,
    Never a one is fit your weeping.

Pretty dears, your tumult cease;
    Love's a fardel, burthening double.
Clear your hearts, and have you peace—
    Gangway, girls: I'll show you trouble.

Sight

Unseemly are the open eyes
    That watch the midnight sheep,
That look upon the secret skies
    Nor close, abashed, in sleep;

That see the dawn drag in, unbidden,
    To birth another day—
Oh, better far their gaze were hidden
    Below the decent clay.

Prisoner

Long I fought the driving lists,
    Plume a-stream and armor clanging;
Link on link, between my wrists,
    Now my heavy freedom's hanging.

The Lady's Reward

Lady, lady, never start
Conversation toward your heart;
Keep your pretty words serene;
Never murmur what you mean.
Show yourself, by word and look,
Swift and shallow as a brook.
Be as cool and quick to go
As a drop of April snow;
Be as delicate and gay
As a cherry flower in May.
Lady, lady, never speak
Of the tears that burn your cheek—
She will never win him, whose
Words had shown she feared to lose.
Be you wise and never sad,
You will get your lovely lad.
Never serious be, nor true,
And your wish will come to you—
And if that makes you happy, kid,
You'll be the first it ever did.

Temps Perdu

I never may turn the loop of a road
  Where sudden, ahead, the sea is lying,
But my heart drags down with an ancient load—
  My heart, that a second before was flying.

I never behold the quivering rain—
  And sweeter the rain than a lover to me—
But my heart is wild in my breast with pain;
  My heart, that was tapping contentedly.

There's never a rose spreads new at my door
   Nor a strange bird crosses the moon at night
But I know I have known its beauty before,
   And a terrible sorrow along with the sight.

The look of a laurel tree birthed for May
   Or a sycamore bared for a new November
Is as old and as sad as my furtherest day—
   What is it, what is it, I almost remember?

Autumn Valentine

In May my heart was breaking—
   Oh, wide the wound, and deep!
And bitter it beat at waking,
   And sore it split in sleep.

And when it came November,
   I sought my heart, and sighed,
"Poor thing, do you remember?"
   "What heart was that?" it cried.

The Custard Heart

No living eye, of human being or caged wild beast or dear, domestic animal, had beheld Mrs. Lanier when she was not being wistful. She was dedicated to wistfulness, as lesser artists to words and paint and marble. Mrs. Lanier was not of the lesser; she was of the true. Surely the eternal example of the true artist is Dickens's actor who blacked himself all over to play Othello. It is safe to assume that Mrs. Lanier was wistful in her bathroom, and slumbered soft in wistfulness through the dark and secret night.

If nothing should happen to the portrait of her by Sir James Weir, there she will stand, wistful for the ages. He has shown her at her full length, all in yellows, the delicately heaped curls, the slender, arched feet like elegant bananas, the shining stretch of the evening gown; Mrs. Lanier habitually wore white in the evening, but white is the devil's own hue to paint, and could a man be expected to spend his entire six weeks in the States on the execution of a single commission? Wistfulness rests, immortal, in the eyes dark with sad hope, in the pleading mouth, the droop of the little head on the sweet long neck, bowed as if in submission to the three ropes of Lanier pearls. It is true that, when the portrait was exhibited, one critic expressed in print his puzzlement as to what a woman who owned such pearls had to be wistful about; but that was doubtless because he had sold his saffron-colored soul for a few pennies to the proprietor of a rival gallery. Certainly, no man could touch Sir James on pearls. Each one is as distinct, as individual as is each little soldier's face in a Meissonier battle scene.

For a time, with the sitter's obligation to resemble the portrait, Mrs. Lanier wore yellow of evenings. She had gowns of velvet like poured country cream and satin with the lacquer of buttercups and chiffon that spiraled about her like golden smoke. She wore them, and listened in shy surprise to the

319

resulting comparisons to daffodils, and butterflies in the sunshine, and such; but she knew.

"It just isn't me," she sighed at last, and returned to her lily draperies. Picasso had his blue period, and Mrs. Lanier her yellow one. They both knew when to stop.

In the afternoons, Mrs. Lanier wore black, thin and fragrant, with the great pearls weeping on her breast. What her attire was by morning, only Gwennie, the maid who brought her breakfast tray, could know; but it must, of course, have been exquisite. Mr. Lanier—certainly there was a Mr. Lanier; he had even been seen—stole past her door on his way out to his office, and the servants glided and murmured, so that Mrs. Lanier might be spared as long as possible from the bright new cruelty of the day. Only when the littler, kinder hours had succeeded noon could she bring herself to come forth and face the recurrent sorrows of living.

There was duty to be done, almost daily, and Mrs. Lanier made herself brave for it. She must go in her town car to select new clothes and to have fitted to her perfection those she had ordered before. Such garments as hers did not just occur; like great poetry, they required labor. But she shrank from leaving the shelter of her house, for everywhere without were the unlovely and the sad, to assail her eyes and her heart. Often she stood shrinking for several minutes by the baroque mirror in her hall before she could manage to hold her head high and brave, and go on.

There is no safety for the tender, no matter how straight their route, how innocent their destination. Sometimes, even in front of Mrs. Lanier's dressmaker's or her furrier's or her lingère's or her milliner's, there would be a file of thin girls and small, shabby men, who held placards in their cold hands and paced up and down and up and down with slow, measured steps. Their faces would be blue and rough from the wind, and blank with the monotony of their treadmill. They looked so little and poor and strained that Mrs. Lanier's hands would fly to her heart in pity. Her eyes would be luminous with sympathy and her sweet lips would part as if on a whisper of cheer, as she passed through the draggled line into the shop.

Often there would be pencil-sellers in her path, a half of a creature set upon a sort of roller-skate thrusting himself along the pavement by his hands, or a blind man shuffling after his wavering cane. Mrs. Lanier must stop and sway, her eyes closed, one hand about her throat to support her lovely, stricken head. Then you could actually see her force herself, could see the effort ripple her body, as she opened her eyes and gave these miserable ones, the blind and the seeing alike, a smile of such tenderness, such sorrowful understanding, that it was like the exquisite sad odor of hyacinths on the air. Sometimes, if the man was not too horrible, she could even reach in her purse for a coin and, holding it as lightly as if she had plucked it from a silvery stem, extend her slim arm and drop it in his cup. If he was young and new at his life, he would offer her pencils for the worth of her money; but Mrs. Lanier wanted no returns. In gentlest delicacy she would slip away, leaving him with mean wares intact, not a worker for his livelihood like a million others, but signal and set apart, rare in the fragrance of charity.

So it was, when Mrs. Lanier went out. Everywhere she saw them, the ragged, the wretched, the desperate, and to each she gave her look that spoke with no words.

"Courage," it said. "And you—oh, wish me courage, too!"

Frequently, by the time she returned to her house, Mrs. Lanier would be limp as a freesia. Her maid Gwennie would have to beseech her to lie down, to gain the strength to change her gown for a filmier one and descend to her drawing-room, her eyes darkly mournful, but her exquisite breasts pointed high.

In her drawing-room, there was sanctuary. Here her heart might heal from the blows of the world, and be whole for its own sorrow. It was a room suspended above life, a place of tender fabrics and pale flowers, with never a paper or a book to report the harrowing or describe it. Below the great sheet of its window swung the river, and the stately scows went by laden with strange stuff in rich tapestry colors; there was no necessity to belong to the sort who must explain that it was garbage. An island with a happy name lay opposite, and on it stood a row of prim, tight buildings, naive as a painting by Rousseau. Sometimes there could be seen on the island the brisk figures of nurses and internes, sporting in the lanes. Possibly there were figures considerably less brisk beyond the barred windows of the buildings, but that was not to be wondered about in the presence of Mrs. Lanier. All those who came to her drawing-room came in one cause: to shield her heart from hurt.

Here in her drawing-room, in the lovely blue of the late day, Mrs. Lanier sat upon opalescent taffeta and was wistful. And here to her drawing-room, the young men came and tried to help her bear her life.

There was a pattern to the visits of the young men. They would come in groups of three or four or six, for a while; and then there would be one of them who would stay a little after the rest had gone, who presently would come a little earlier than the others. Then there would be days when Mrs. Lanier would cease to be at home to the other young men, and that one young man would be alone with her in the lovely blue. And then Mrs. Lanier would no longer be at home to that one young man, and Gwennie would have to tell him and tell him, over the telephone, that Mrs. Lanier was out, that Mrs. Lanier was ill, that Mrs. Lanier could not be disturbed. The groups of young men would come again; that one young man would not be with them. But there would be, among them, a new young man, who presently would stay a little later and come a little earlier, who eventually would plead with Gwennie over the telephone.

Gwennie—her widowed mother had named her Gwendola, and then, as if realizing that no other dream would ever come true, had died—was little and compact and unnoticeable. She had been raised on an upstate farm by an uncle and aunt hard as the soil they fought for their lives. After their deaths, she had no relatives anywhere. She came to New York, because she had heard stories of jobs; her arrival was at the time when Mrs. Lanier's cook needed a kitchen-maid. So in her own house, Mrs. Lanier had found her treasure.

Gwennie's hard little farm-girl's fingers could set invisible stitches, could employ a flatiron as if it were a wand, could be as summer breezes in the robing of Mrs. Lanier and the tend-ing of her hair. She was as busy as the day was long; and her days frequently extended from daybreak to daybreak. She was never tired, she had no grievance, she was cheerful without being expressive about it. There was nothing in her presence or the sight of her to touch the heart and thus cause discomfort.

Mrs. Lanier would often say that she didn't know what she would do without her little Gwennie; if her little Gwennie should ever leave her, she said, she just couldn't go on. She looked so lorn and fragile as she said it that one scowled upon Gwennie for the potentialities of death or marriage that the girl carried within her. Yet there was no pressing cause for worry, for Gwennie was strong as a pony and had no beau. She had made no friends at all, and seemed not to observe the omission. Her life was for Mrs. Lanier; like all others who were permitted close, Gwennie sought to do what she could to save Mrs. Lanier from pain.

They could all assist in shutting out reminders of the sadness abroad in the world, but Mrs. Lanier's private sorrow was a more difficult matter. There dwelt a yearning so deep, so secret in her heart that it would often be days before she could speak of it, in the twilight, to a new young man.

"If I only had a little baby," she would sigh, "a little, little baby, I think I could be almost happy." And she would fold her delicate arms, and lightly, slowly rock them, as if they cradled that little, little one of her dear dreams. Then, the denied madonna, she was at her most wistful, and the young man would have lived or died for her, as she bade him.

Mrs. Lanier never mentioned why her wish was unfulfilled; the young man would know her to be too sweet to place blame, too proud to tell. But, so close to her in the pale light, he would understand, and his blood would swirl with fury that such clods as Mr. Lanier remained unkilled. He would beseech Mrs. Lanier, first in halting murmurs, then in rushes of hot words, to let him take her away from the hell of her life and try to make her almost happy. It would be after this that Mrs. Lanier would be out to the young man, would be ill, would be incapable of being disturbed.

Gwennie did not enter the drawing-room when there was

only one young man there; but when the groups returned she served unobtrusively, drawing a curtain or fetching a fresh glass. All the Lanier servants were unobtrusive, light of step and correctly indistinct of feature. When there must be changes made in the staff, Gwennie and the housekeeper arranged the replacements and did not speak of the matter to Mrs. Lanier, lest she should be stricken by desertions or saddened by tales of woe. Always the new servants resembled the old, alike in that they were unnoticeable. That is, until Kane, the new chauffeur, came.

The old chauffeur had been replaced because he had been the old chauffeur too long. It weighs cruelly heavy on the tender heart when a familiar face grows lined and dry, when familiar shoulders seem daily to droop lower, a familiar nape is hollow between cords. The old chauffeur saw and heard and functioned with no difference; but it was too much for Mrs. Lanier to see what was befalling him. With pain in her voice, she had told Gwennie that she could stand the sight of him no longer. So the old chauffeur had gone, and Kane had come.

Kane was young, and there was nothing depressing about his straight shoulders and his firm, full neck to one sitting behind them in the town car. He stood, a fine triangle in his fitted uniform, holding the door of the car open for Mrs. Lanier and bowed his head as she passed. But when he was not at work, his head was held high and slightly cocked, and there was a little cocked smile on his red mouth.

Often, in the cold weather when Kane waited for her in the car, Mrs. Lanier would humanely bid Gwennie to tell him to come in and wait in the servants' sitting-room. Gwennie brought him coffee and looked at him. Twice she did not hear Mrs. Lanier's enameled electric bell.

Gwennie began to observe her evenings off; before, she had disregarded them and stayed to minister to Mrs. Lanier. There was one night when Mrs. Lanier had floated late to her room, after a theater and a long conversation, done in murmurs, in the drawing-room. And Gwennie had not been waiting, to take off the white gown, and put away the pearls, and brush the bright hair that curled like the petals of forsythia. Gwennie had not yet returned to the house from her holiday. Mrs. Lanier had had to arouse a parlor-maid and obtain unsatisfactory aid from her.

Gwennie had wept, next morning, at the pathos of Mrs. Lanier's eyes; but tears were too distressing for Mrs. Lanier to see, and the girl stopped them. Mrs. Lanier delicately patted her arm, and there had been nothing more of the matter, save that Mrs. Lanier's eyes were darker and wider for this new hurt.

Kane became a positive comfort to Mrs. Lanier. After the sorry sights of the streets, it was good to see Kane standing by the car, solid and straight and young, with nothing in the world the trouble with him. Mrs. Lanier came to smile upon him almost gratefully, yet wistfully, too, as if she would seek of him the secret of not being sad.

And then, one day, Kane did not appear at his appointed time. The car, which should have been waiting to convey Mrs. Lanier to her dressmaker's, was still in the garage, and Kane had not appeared there all day. Mrs. Lanier told Gwennie immediately to telephone the place where he roomed and find out what this meant. The girl had cried out at her, cried out that she had called and called and called, and he was not there and no one there knew where he was. The crying out must have been due to Gwennie's loss of head in her distress at this disruption of Mrs. Lanier's day; or perhaps it was the effect on her voice of an appalling cold she seemed to have contracted, for her eyes were heavy and red and her face pale and swollen.

There was no more of Kane. He had had his wages paid him on the day before he disappeared, and that was the last of him. There was never a word and not another sight of him. At first, Mrs. Lanier could scarcely bring herself to believe that such betrayal could exist. Her heart, soft and sweet as a perfectly made crème renversée, quivered in her breast, and in her eyes lay the far light of suffering.

"Oh, how could he do this to me?" she asked piteously of Gwennie. "How could he do this to poor me?"

There was no discussion of the defection of Kane; it was too painful a subject. If a caller heedlessly asked whatever had become of that nice-looking chauffeur, Mrs. Lanier would lay her hand over her closed lids and slowly wince. The caller would be suicidal that he had thus unconsciously added to her sorrows, and would strive his consecrated best to comfort her.

Gwennie's cold lasted for an extraordinarily long time. The weeks went by, and still, every morning, her eyes were red and her face white and puffed. Mrs. Lanier often had to look away from her when she brought the breakfast tray.

She tended Mrs. Lanier as carefully as ever; she gave no attention to her holidays, but stayed to do further service. She had always been quiet, and she became all but silent, and that was additionally soothing. She worked without stopping and seemed to thrive, for, save for the effects of the curious cold, she looked round and healthy.

"See," Mrs. Lanier said in tender raillery, as the girl attended the group in the drawing-room, "see how fat my little Gwennie's getting! Isn't that cute?"

The weeks went on, and the pattern of the young men shifted again. There came the day when Mrs. Lanier was not at home to a group; when a new young man was to come and be alone with her, for his first time, in the drawing-room. Mrs. Lanier sat before her mirror and lightly touched her throat with perfume, while Gwennie heaped the golden curls.

The exquisite face Mrs. Lanier saw in the mirror drew her closer attention, and she put down the perfume and leaned toward it. She drooped her head a little to the side and watched it closely; she saw the wistful eyes grow yet more wistful, the lips curve to a pleading smile. She folded her arms close to her sweet breast and slowly rocked them, as if they cradled a dream-child. She watched the mirrored arms sway gently, caused them to sway a little slower.

"If I only had a little baby," she sighed. She shook her head. Delicately she cleared her throat, and sighed again on a slightly lower note. "If I only had a little, little baby, I think I could be almost happy."

There was a clatter from behind her, and she turned,

amazed. Gwennie had dropped the hair-brush to the floor and stood swaying, with her face in her hands.

"Gwennie!" said Mrs. Lanier. "Gwennie!"

The girl took her hands from her face, and it was as if she stood under a green light.

"I'm sorry," she panted. "Sorry. Please excuse me. I'm—oh, I'm going to be sick!"

She ran from the room so violently that the floor shook.

Mrs. Lanier sat looking after Gwennie, her hands at her wounded heart. Slowly she turned back to her mirror, and what she saw there arrested her; the artist knows the masterpiece. Here was the perfection of her career, the sublimation of wistfulness; it was that look of grieved bewilderment that did it. Carefully she kept it upon her face as she rose from the mirror and, with her lovely hands still shielding her heart, went down to the new young man.

From the Diary
of a New York Lady

During Days of Horror, Despair, and World Change

Monday. Breakfast tray about eleven; didn't want it. The champagne at the Amorys' last night was *too* revolting, but what *can* you do? You can't stay until five o'clock on just *nothing*. They had those *divine* Hungarian musicians in the green coats, and Stewie Hunter took off one of his shoes and led them with it, and it *couldn't* have been funnier. He is *the* wittiest number in the *entire* world; he *couldn't* be more perfect. Ollie Martin brought me home and we both fell asleep in the car—*too* screaming. Miss Rose came about noon to do my nails, simply *covered* with *the* most divine gossip. The Morrises are going to separate *any minute*, and Freddie Warren *definitely* has ulcers, and Gertie Leonard simply *won't* let Bill Crawford out of her sight even with Jack Leonard *right there in the room*, and it's all *true* about Sheila Phillips and Babs Deering. It *couldn't* have been more thrilling. Miss Rose is *too* marvelous; I really think that a lot of times people like that are a lot more intelligent than a lot of people. Didn't notice until after she had gone that the damn fool had put that *revolting* tangerine-colored polish on my nails; *couldn't* have been more furious. Started to read a book, but too nervous. Called up and found I could get two tickets for the opening of "Run like a Rabbit" tonight for forty-eight dollars. Told them they had *the* nerve of the world, but what *can* you do? Think Joe said he was dining out, so telephoned some *divine* numbers to get someone to go to the theater with me, but they were all tied up. Finally got Ollie Martin. He *couldn't* have more poise, and what do *I* care if he *is* one? *Can't* decide whether to wear the green crepe or the red wool. Every time I look at my finger nails, I could *spit*. *Damn* Miss Rose.

Tuesday. Joe came barging in my room this morning at *practically nine o'clock. Couldn't* have been more furious. Started to fight, but *too* dead. Know he said he wouldn't be home to dinner. Absolutely *cold* all day; couldn't *move*. Last night *couldn't* have been more perfect. Ollie and I dined at Thirty-Eight East, absolutely *poisonous* food, and not one *living* soul that you'd be seen *dead* with, and "Run like a Rabbit" was *the* world's worst. Took Ollie up to the Barlows' party and it *couldn't* have been more attractive—*couldn't* have been more people absolutely *stinking*. They had those Hungarians in the green coats, and Stewie Hunter was leading them with a fork—everybody simply *died*. He had *yards* of green toilet paper hung around his neck like a lei; he *couldn't* have been in better form. Met a *really new number*, very tall, *too* marvelous, and one of those people that you can *really* talk to them. I told him sometimes I get so *nauseated* I could *yip*, and I felt I absolutely *had* to do something like write or paint. He said why didn't I write or paint. Came home alone; Ollie passed out *stiff*. Called up the new number three times today to get him to come to dinner and go with me to the opening of "Never Say Good Morning," but first he was out and then he was all tied up with his mother. Finally got Ollie Martin. Tried to read a book, but couldn't sit still. *Can't* decide whether to wear the red lace or the pink with the feathers. Feel *too* exhausted, but what *can* you do?

Wednesday. The most terrible thing happened *just this minute*. Broke one of my finger nails *right off short*. Absolutely *the* most horrible thing I ever had happen to me in my life. Called up Miss Rose to come over and shape it for me, but she was out for the day. I do have *the* worst luck in the *entire* world. Now I'll have to go around like this all day and all night, but what *can* you do? *Damn* Miss Rose. Last night *too* hectic. "Never Say Good Morning" *too* foul, *never* saw more poisonous clothes on the stage. Took Ollie up to the Ballards' party; *couldn't* have been better. They had those Hungarians in the green coats and Stewie Hunter was leading them with a freesia—*too* perfect. He had on Peggy Cooper's ermine coat and Phyllis Minton's silver turban; *simply* unbelievable. Asked simply *sheaves* of *divine* people to come here Friday night; got the address of those Hungarians in the green coats from Betty Ballard. She says just engage them until four, and then whoever gives them another three hundred dollars, they'll stay till five. *Couldn't* be cheaper. Started home with Ollie, but had to drop him at his house; he *couldn't* have been sicker. Called up the new number today to get him to come to dinner and go to the opening of "Everybody Up" with me tonight, but he was tied up. Joe's going to be out; he didn't *condescend* to say *where, of course.* Started to read the papers, but nothing in them except that Mona Wheatley is in Reno charging *intolerable cruelty.* Called up Jim Wheatley to see if he had anything to do tonight, but he was tied up. Finally got Ollie Martin. *Can't* decide wether to wear the white satin or the black chiffon or the yellow pebble crepe. Simply *wrecked* to the *core* about my finger nail. Can't *bear* it. *Never* knew *anybody* to have such *unbelievable* things happen to them.

Thursday. Simply *collapsing* on my *feet*. Last night *too* marvelous. "Everybody Up" *too* divine, *couldn't* be filthier, and the new number was there, *too* celestial, only he didn't see me. He was with Florence Keeler in that *loathsome* gold Schiaparelli model of hers that every *shopgirl* has had since *God* knows. He must be out of his *mind;* she wouldn't *look* at a man. Took Ollie to the Watsons' party; *couldn't* have been more thrilling. Everybody simply *blind*. They had those Hungarians in the green coats and Stewie Hunter was leading them with a lamp, and, after the lamp got broken, he and Tommy Thomas did adagio dances—*too* wonderful. Somebody told me Tommy's doctor told him he had to absolutely get *right out of town,* he has *the* world's worst stomach, but you'd *never* know it. Came home alone, couldn't find Ollie *anywhere.* Miss Rose came at noon to shape my nail, *couldn't* have been more fascinating. Sylvia Eaton can't go *out the door* unless she's had a hypodermic, and Doris Mason *knows every single word* about Douggie Mason and that girl up in Harlem, and Evelyn North won't be *induced* to keep away from those three acrobats, and they don't *dare* tell Stuyvie Raymond *what* he's got the matter with him. *Never* knew anyone that had a more simply *fascinating* life than Miss Rose. Made her take that *vile* tangerine polish off my nails and put on dark red. Didn't notice until after she had gone that it's practically *black* in electric light; *couldn't* be in a worse state. *Damn* Miss Rose. Joe left a note saying he was going to dine out, so telephoned the new number to get him to come to dinner and go with me to that new movie tonight, but he didn't answer. Sent him three telegrams to *absolutely surely* come tomorrow night. Finally got Ollie Martin for tonight. Looked at the papers, but nothing in them except that the Harry Motts are throwing a tea with Hungarian music on Sunday. Think will ask the new number to go to it with me; they must have meant to invite me. Began to read a book, but too exhausted. *Can't* decide whether to wear the new blue with the white jacket or save it till tomorrow night and wear the ivory moire. Simply *heartsick* every time I think of my nails. *Couldn't* be wilder. Could *kill* Miss Rose, but what *can* you do?

Friday. Absolutely *sunk; couldn't* be worse. Last night *too* divine, movie *simply* deadly. Took Ollie to the Kingslands' party, *too* unbelievable, everybody absolutely *rolling.* They had those Hungarians in the green coats, but Stewie Hunter wasn't there. He's got a *complete* nervous breakdown. Worried *sick* for fear he won't be well by tonight; will absolutely *never* forgive him if he doesn't come. Started home with Ollie, but dropped him at his house because he *couldn't* stop crying. Joe left word with the butler he's going to the country this afternoon for the week-end; *of course* he wouldn't *stoop* to say *what* country. Called up *streams* of marvelous numbers to get someone to come dine and go with me to the opening of "White Man's Folly," and then go somewhere after to dance for a while; can't *bear* to be the first one there at your own party. Everybody was tied up. Finally got Ollie Martin. *Couldn't* feel *more* depressed; never should have gone *anywhere near* champagne and Scotch together. Started to read a book, but too restless. Called up Anne Lyman to ask about the new baby and *couldn't* remember if it was a boy or girl—*must* get a secretary *next week*. Anne *couldn't* have been more of a help; she said she didn't know whether to name it Patricia or Gloria, so then of course I knew it was a girl *right away*. Suggested calling it Barbara; forgot she already had one. Absolutely *walking the floor* like a *panther* all day. Could *spit* about Stewie Hunter. Can't *face* deciding whether to wear the blue with the white jacket or the purple with the beige roses. Every time I look at those *revolting* black nails, I want to absolutely *yip*. I really have *the* most horrible things happen to me of anybody in the *entire* world. *Damn* Miss Rose.

Cousin Larry

The young woman in the crepe de Chine dress printed all over
with little pagodas set amid giant cornflowers flung one knee
atop the other and surveyed, with an enviable contentment, the
tip of her scrolled green sandal. Then, in a like happy calm, she
inspected her finger nails of so thick and glistening a red that it
seemed as if she but recently had completed tearing an ox
apart with her naked hands. Then she dropped her chin
abruptly to her chest and busied herself among the man-made
curls, sharp and dry as shavings, along the back of her neck;
and again she appeared to be wrapped in cozy satisfaction.
Then she lighted a fresh cigarette and seemed to find it, like all
about her, good. Then she went right on with all she had been
saying before.

"No, but really," she said. "Honestly. I get so darn sick of all
this talk about Lila—'Oh, poor Lila' this, and 'Oh, the poor
thing' that. If they want to be sorry for her—well, it's a free
country, I suppose, but all I can say is I think they're crazy. I
think they're absolutely cock-eyed wild. If they want to be sorry
for anybody, go be sorry for Cousin Larry, why don't they?
Then they'd be making some sense, for a change. Listen,
nobody has to be sorry for Lila. She has a marvelous time; she
never does one solitary thing she doesn't want to do. She has
the best time of anybody I know. And anyway, it's all her own
fault, anyway. It's just the way she is; it's her rotten, vile
disposition. Well, you can't be expected to feel sorry for
anybody when it's their own fault, can you? Does that make
any sense? Now I ask you!

"Listen. I know Lila. I've known her for years. I've seen her
practically day in, day out. Well, you know how often I've
visited them, down in the country. You know how well you
know a person after you've visited them; well, that's the way I
know Lila. And I like her. Honestly I do. I like Lila all right

when she's decent. It's only when she starts feeling sorry for herself and begins whining and asking questions and spoiling everybody's fun that she makes me throw up. A lot of the time she's perfectly all right. Only she's selfish, that's all. She's just a rotten, selfish woman. And then the way people talk about Larry for staying in town and going around places without her! Listen to me, she stays home because she wants to. She'd *rather* go to bed early. I've seen her do it night after night, when I've been down there visiting. I know her like a book. Catch *that* one doing anything she doesn't feel like doing!

"Honestly. It just makes me boil to hear anyone say anything against Larry. Just let them try criticizing him to me, that's all. Why, that man's a living saint, that's what he is. How on earth he's got anything at all left, after ten years with that woman, I *don't* see. She can't let him alone a second; always wants to be in on everything, always wants to know what's the joke and what's he laughing about, and oh, tell her, tell her, so she can laugh too. And she's one of those damn serious old fools that can't see anything funny, and can't kid or anything, and then she tries to get cute and play, too, and—well, you just can't *look*, that's all. And poor Larry, who couldn't be funnier or have more of a sense of humor and all. I should think she'd have driven him cock-eyed wild, years ago.

"And then when she sees the poor soul having a little bit of fun with anybody for a few minutes, she gets—well, she doesn't get jealous, she's too self-centered ever to have a jealous moment—she's so rotten suspicious, she's got such a vile, dirty mind, she just gets mean. And to me, of all people. Now I ask you! Me, that's known Larry practically all my life, practically. Why, I've called him Cousin Larry for years—that shows you how I've always felt about him. And the very first time I went down there to stay with them, she started in about why did I call him Cousin Larry, and I said, oh, I'd known him so well, I felt sort of related, and then she got kittenish, the old fool, and said, well, I'd have to take her into the family, too, and I said, yes, that would be great, or something. And I *did* try to call her Aunt Lila, but I just simply couldn't seem to *feel* that way. And it didn't seem to make her any happier, anyway. Well, she's just one of those kind she's never happy unless she's miserable. She *enjoys* being miserable. That's why she does it. Catch her doing anything she doesn't want to do!

"Honestly. Poor Cousin Larry. Imagine that dirty old thing trying to work up something, because I call him Cousin Larry. Well, I certainly didn't let her stop me; I guess my friendship with Larry is worth a little more than *that*. And he calls me Little Sweetheart, too, just the way he always did. He's always called me his little sweetheart. Wouldn't you think she could see, if there was anything in it, he wouldn't call me that right in front of her face all the time?

"Really. It isn't that she means anything in my young life, it's just that I feel so terribly sorry for Larry. I wouldn't set foot in the house again if it wasn't for him. But he says—of course, he's never said one single word against her, he's the kind would always be just like a clam about any woman that happened to be his wife—he says nobody has any idea of what it's like to be there alone with Lila. So that's why I went down in the first place. And I saw what he meant. Why, the first night I was in the house, she went up to bed at ten o'clock. Cousin Larry and I were playing some old phonograph records—well, we had to do *something*, she wouldn't laugh or kid or do anything we were doing, just sat there like an old stick—and it just happened I happened to find a lot of old songs Larry and I used to sing and go dancing to, and everything. Well, you know how it is when you know a man awfully well, you always have things that remind you of things, and we were laughing and playing these records and sort of saying, 'Do you remember the time?' and 'What does that remind you of?' and all, the way everybody does; and the first thing you know, Lila got up and said she was sure we wouldn't mind if she went to bed—she felt so awfully tired. And Larry told me then, that's what she always does when anybody around is having a good time. If there's a guest in the house when she feels so awfully tired, that's just too bad, that's all. A little thing like that doesn't put *that* one out. When she wants to go to bed, she *goes*.

"So that's why I've gone down there so much. You don't know what a real godsend it is for Larry to have someone he can sit up with, after dear Lila goes to bed at ten o'clock. And then I'm somebody the poor soul can play golf with in the daytime, too; Lila can't play—oh, she's got something wrong with her insides, *wouldn't* she have? I wouldn't go near the place if it wasn't such a help to Larry. You know how crazy he is about having a good time. And Lila's *old*—she's an *owe-wuld* woman! Honestly. Larry—well, of course it doesn't make any difference how old a man is, anyway—years, I mean; it's the way he feels that counts. And Larry's just like a kid. I keep telling Lila, trying to clean up her nasty, evil mind, that Cousin Larry and I are nothing but a couple of crazy kids together. Now I ask you, wouldn't you think she'd have sense enough to see she's all through and the only thing for her to do is to sit back and let people have a good time that *can? She* had a good time; going to bed early, that's what she likes. Nobody interferes with her—wouldn't you think she'd mind her own business and stop asking questions and wanting to know what everything's about?

"Well, now look. Once I was down there, and I happened to be wearing orchids. And so Lila said oh, weren't they lovely and all, and who sent them to me. Honestly. She *deliberately* asked me who sent them to me. So I thought, well, it will just do you good, and I told her Cousin Larry did. I told her it was a sort of a little anniversary of ours—you know how it is, when you know a man a long time, you always have sort of little anniversaries, like the first time he ever took you to lunch, or the first time he sent you flowers or something. So anyway, this was one of those, and I told Lila what a wonderful friend Cousin Larry was to me, and how he always remembered things like that, and how much fun it was for him to do them, he seemed to get such pleasure out of doing sweet things. Now I ask you. Wouldn't you think anybody in the *world* would see how innocent it was if you told them that? And do you know what she said? Honestly. She said, 'I like orchids, too.' So I just thought, well, maybe if you were fifteen years younger you might get some man to send you some, baby, but I didn't say a thing. I just said, 'Oh, wear these, Lila; won't you?' Just like that; and Lord knows, I didn't *have* to say it, did I? But oh, no, she wouldn't.

No, she thought she'd just go and lie down a while, if I didn't mind. She was feeling so awfully tired.

"And then—oh, my dear, I nearly forgot to tell you. You'll simply die over this, you'll absolutely collapse. Well, the last time I was there, Cousin Larry had sent me some little chiffon drawers; they couldn't have been cuter. You know, it was just a joke, these little pink chiffon things with '*Mais l'amour viendra*' embroidered on them in black. It means 'Love will come.' You know. He saw them in some window and he just sent them to me, just for this joke. He's always doing things like—hey, for goodness' sake, don't tell anyone, will you? Because, Lord knows if it *meant* anything, I wouldn't be telling you, you *know* that, but you know how people are. And there's been enough talk, just because I go out with him sometimes, to keep the poor soul company while Lila's in bed.

"Well, so anyway, he sent me these things, and so when I came down to dinner—there were just the three of us; that's another thing she does, she doesn't have anybody in unless he absolutely insists—I said to Larry, 'I've got them on, Cousin Larry.' So of course Lila had to hear and she said, 'What have you got on?' and she kept asking and asking, and naturally I wasn't going to tell *her*, and it just struck me so funny I nearly died trying not to laugh and every time I caught Larry's eye we'd both bust right out. And Lila kept saying oh, what was the joke, and oh, tell her, tell her. And so finally, when she saw we wouldn't tell, she had to go to bed, no matter how it made *us* feel. My God, can't people have jokes? This is a free country, isn't it?

"Honestly. And she's getting worse and worse all the time. I'm simply *sick* about Larry. I can't see what he's ever going to do. You know a woman like that wouldn't give a man a divorce in a million years, even if he was the one that had the money. Larry never says a word, but I bet there are times when he just wishes she'd *die*. And everybody saying 'Oh, poor Lila,' 'Oh, poor, dear Lila, isn't it a shame?' That's because she gets them off in corners, and starts sobbing about not having any children. Oh, how she wishes she had a baby. Oh, if she and Larry only had a baby, blah, blah, blah, blah, blah. And then the eyes filling with tears—you know, you've seen her do it. Eyes filling with tears! A lot she's got to cry about, always doing what she wants all the time. I bet that's just a line, about not having a baby. That's just to get sympathy. She's just so rotten selfish she wouldn't have ever given up her own convenience to have one, that's what's the matter with her. She might have had to stay up after ten o'clock.

"Poor Lila! Honestly, I could lose my lunch. Why don't they say poor Larry, for a change? He's the one to feel sorry for. Well. All *I* know is, I'll always do anything I can for Cousin Larry. That's all *I* know."

The young woman in the printed crepe de Chine dress removed her dead cigarette from its pasteboard holder and seemed, as she did so, to find increased enjoyment in the familiar sight of her rich-hued finger nails. Then she took from her lap a case of gold or some substance near it, and in a minute mirror scanned her face as carefully as if it were verse. She knit her brows, she drew her upper eyelids nearly to those below them, she turned her head as one expressing regretful negation, she moved her mouth laterally in the manner of a semi-tropical fish; and when all this was done, she seemed even cooler in confidence of wellbeing. Then she lighted a fresh cigarette and appeared to find that, too, impeccable. Then she went right on over all she had been saying before.

Little Curtis

Mrs. Matson paused in the vestibule of G. Fosdick's Sons' Department Store. She transferred a small parcel from her right hand to the crook of her left arm, gripped her shopping-bag firmly by its German-silver frame, opened it with a capable click, and drew from its orderly interior a little black-bound book and a neatly sharpened pencil.

Shoppers passing in and out jostled her as she stood there, but they neither shared in Mrs. Matson's attention nor hurried her movements. She made no answer to the "Oh, I *beg* your pardons" that bubbled from the lips of the more tender-hearted among them. Calm, sure, gloriously aloof, Mrs. Matson stood, opened her book, poised her pencil, and wrote in delicate, prettily slanting characters: "4 crepe-paper candy-baskets, $.28."

The dollar-sign was gratifyingly decorative, the decimal point clear and deep, the 2 daintily curled, the 8 admirably balanced. Mrs. Matson looked approvingly at her handiwork. Still unhurried, she closed the book, replaced it and the pencil in the bag, tested the snap to see that it was indisputably shut, and took the parcel once more in her right hand. Then, with a comfortable air of duty well done, she passed impressively, and with a strong push, from G. Fosdick's Sons' Department Store by means of a portal which bore a placard with the request, "Please Use Other Door."

Slowly Mrs. Matson made her way down Maple Street. The morning sunshine that flooded the town's main thoroughfare caused her neither to squint nor to lower her face. She held her head high, looking about her as one who says, "Our good people, we are pleased with you."

She stopped occasionally by a shop-window, to inspect thoroughly the premature autumn costumes there displayed. But her heart was unfluttered by the envy which attacked the lesser women around her. Though her long black coat, of that vintage when coats were puffed of sleeve and cut sharply in at the waist, was stained and shiny, and her hat had the general air of indecision and lack of spirit that comes with age, and her elderly black gloves were worn in patches of rough gray, Mrs. Matson had no yearnings for the fresh, trim costumes set temptingly before her. Snug in her was the thought of the rows of recent garments, each one in its flowered cretonne casing, occupying the varnished hangers along the poles of her bedroom closet.

She had her unalterable ideas about such people as gave or threw away garments that might still be worn, for warmth and modesty, if not for style. She found it distinctly lower-class to wear one's new clothes "for every day"; there was an unpleasant suggestion of extravagance and riotous living in the practice. The working classes, who, as Mrs. Matson often explained to her friends, went and bought themselves electric ice-boxes and radios the minute they got a little money, did such things.

No morbid thought of her possible sudden demise before the clothes in her closet could be worn or enjoyed irked her. Life's uncertainty was not for those of her position. Mrs. Matsons pass away between seventy and eighty; sometimes later, never before.

A blind colored woman, a tray of pencils hung about her neck, with a cane tapping the pavements before her, came down the street. Mrs. Matson swerved sharply to the curb to avoid her, wasting a withering glance upon her. It was Mrs. Matson's immediate opinion that the woman could see as well as *she* could. She never bought of the poor on the streets, and was angry if she saw others do so. She frequently remarked that these beggars all had big bank-accounts.

She crossed to the car-tracks to await the trolley that would bear her home, her calm upset by her sight of the woman. "Probably owns an apartment-house," she told herself, and shot an angry glance after the blind woman.

However, her poise was restored by the act of tendering her fare to the courteous conductor. Mrs. Matson rather enjoyed small and legitimate disbursements to those who were appropriately grateful. She gave him her nickel with the manner of one presenting a park to a city, and swept into the car to a desirable seat.

Settled, with the parcel securely wedged between her hip and the window, against loss or robbery, Mrs. Matson again produced the book and pencil. "Car-fare, $.05," she wrote. Again the exquisite handwriting, the neat figures, gave her a flow of satisfaction.

Mrs. Matson, regally without acknowledgment, accepted the conductor's aid in alighting from the car at her corner. She trod the sun-splashed pavement, bowing now and again to neighbors knitting on their porches or bending solicitously over their iris-beds. Slow, stately bows she gave, unaccompanied by smile or word of greeting. After all, she was Mrs. Albert Matson; she had been Miss Laura Whitmore, of the Drop Forge and Tool Works Whitmores. One does not lose sight of such things.

She always enjoyed the first view of her house as she walked toward it. It amplified in her her sense of security and permanence. There it stood, in its tidy, treeless lawns, square and solid and serviceable. You thought of steel-engravings and rows of Scott's novels behind glass, and Sunday dinner in the middle of the day, when you looked at it. You knew immediately that within it no one ever banged a door, no one clattered up- and down-stairs, no one spilled crumbs or dropped ashes or left the light burning in the bathroom.

Expectancy pervaded Mrs. Matson as she approached her home. She spoke of it always as her home. "You must come to see me in my home some time," she graciously commanded new acquaintances. There was a large, institutional sound to it that you didn't get in the word "house."

She liked to think of its cool, high-ceilinged rooms, of its busy maids, of little Curtis waiting to deliver her his respectful kiss. She had adopted him almost a year ago, when he was four. She had, she told her friends, never once regretted it.

In her absence her friends had been wont to comment sadly upon what a shame it was that the Albert Matsons had no child—and with all the Matson and Whitmore money, too.

Neither of them, the friends pointed out, could live forever; it would all have to go to the Henry Matsons' children. And they were but quoting Mrs. Albert Matson's own words when they observed that those children would be just the kind that would run right through it.

Mr. and Mrs. Matson held a joint view of the devastation that would result if their nephews and nieces were ever turned loose among the Matson and Whitmore money. As is frequent in such instances, their worry led them to pay the other Matson family the compliment of the credit for schemes and desires that had never edged into their thoughts.

The Albert Matsons saw their relatives as waiting, with a sort of stalking patience, for the prayed-for moment of their death. For years they conjured up ever more lurid pictures of the Matson children going through their money like Sherman to the sea; for years they carried about with them the notion that their demise was being eagerly awaited, was being made, indeed, the starting-point of bacchanalian plans.

The Albert Matsons were as one in everything, as in this. Their thoughts, their manners, their opinions, their very locutions were phenomena of similarity. People even pointed out that Mr. and Mrs. Matson looked alike. It was regarded as the world's misfortune that so obviously Heaven-made a match was without offspring. And of course—you always had to come back to it, it bulked so before you—there was all that Matson and Whitmore money.

No one, though, ever directly condoled with Mrs. Matson upon her childlessness. In her presence one didn't speak of things like having children. She accepted the fact of babies when they were shown to her; she fastidiously disregarded their mode of arrival.

She had told none of her friends of her decision to adopt a little boy. No one knew about it until the papers were signed and he was established in the Matson house. Mrs. Matson had got him, she explained, "at the best place in New York." No one was surprised at that. Mrs. Matson always went to the best places when she shopped in New York. You thought of her selecting a child as she selected all her other belongings: a good one, one that would last.

She stopped abruptly now, as she came to her gate, a sudden frown creasing her brow. Two little boys, too absorbed to hear her steps, were playing in the hot sun by the hedge—two little boys much alike in age, size, and attire, compact, pink-and-white, good little boys, their cheeks flushed with interest, the backs of their necks warm and damp. They played an interminable, mysterious game with pebbles and twigs and a small tin trolley-car.

Mrs. Matson entered the yard.

"Curtis!" she said.

Both little boys looked up, startled. One of them rose and hung his head before her frown.

"And who," said Mrs. Matson deeply, "who told Georgie he could come here?"

No answer. Georgie, still squatting on his heels, looked inquiringly from her to Curtis. He was interested and unalarmed.

"Was it you, Curtis?" asked Mrs. Matson.

Curtis nodded. You could scarcely tell that he did, his head hung so low.

"Yes, Mother dear!" said Mrs. Matson.

"Yes, Mother dear," whispered Curtis.

"And how many times," Mrs. Matson inquired, "have I told you that you were not to play with Georgie? How many times, Curtis?"

Curtis murmured vaguely. He wished that Georgie would please go.

"You don't know?" said Mrs. Matson incredulously. "You don't know? After all Mother does for you, you don't know how many times she has told you not to play with Georgie? Don't you remember what Mother told you she'd have to do if you ever played with Georgie again?"

A pause. Then the nod.

"Yes, Mother dear!" said Mrs. Matson.

"Yes, Mother dear," said Curtis.

"Well!" Mrs. Matson said. She turned to the enthralled Georgie. "You'll have to go home now, Georgie—go right straight home. And you're not to come here any more, do you understand me? Curtis is not allowed to play with you—not ever."

Georgie rose.

" 'By," he said philosophically, and walked away, his farewell unanswered.

Mrs. Matson gazed upon Curtis. Grief disarranged her features.

"Playing!" she said, her voice broken with emotion. "Playing with a furnaceman's child! After all Mother does for you!"

She took him by a limp arm and led him, unresisting, along the walk to the house; led him past the maid that opened the door, up the stairs to his little blue bedroom. She put him in it and closed the door.

Then she went to her own room, placed her package carefully on the table, removed her gloves, and laid them, with her bag, in an orderly drawer. She entered her closet, hung up her coat, then stooped for one of the felt slippers that were set scrupulously, in the first dancing position, on the floor beneath her nightgown. It was a lavender slipper, with scallops and a staid rosette; it had a light, flexible leather sole, across which was stamped its name, "Kumfy-Toes."

Mrs. Matson grasped it firmly by the heel and flicked it back and forth. Carrying it, she went to the little boy's room. She began to speak as she turned the doorknob.

"And before Mother had time to take her hat off, too," she said. The door closed behind her.

She came out again presently. A scale of shrieks followed her.

"That will do!" she announced, looking back from the door. The shrieks faded obediently to sobs. "That's quite enough of that, thank you. Mother's had just about plenty for one morning. And today, too, with the ladies coming this afternoon, and all Mother has to attend to! Oh, I'd be ashamed, Curtis, if I were you—that's what I'd be."

She closed the door, and retired, to remove her hat.

The ladies came in mid-afternoon. There were three of them. Mrs. Kerley, gray and brittle and painstaking, always thoughtful about sending birthday-cards and carrying glass jars of soup to the sick. Mrs. Swan, her visiting sister-in-law, younger, and given to daisied hats and crocheted lace collars, with her transient's air of bright, determined interest in her hostess's acquaintances and activities. And Mrs. Cook. Only she did not count very much. She was extremely deaf, and so pretty well out of things.

She had visited innumerable specialists, spent uncounted money, endured agonizing treatments, in her endeavors to be able to hear what went on about her and to have a part in it. They had finally fitted her out with a long, coiling, corrugated speaking-tube, rather like a larger intestine. One end of this she placed in her better ear, and the other she extended to those who would hold speech with her. But the shining black mouthpiece seemed to embarrass people and intimidate them; they could think of nothing better to call into it than "Getting colder out," or "You keeping pretty well?" To hear such remarks as these she had gone through years of suffering.

Mrs. Matson, in her last spring's blue taffeta, assigned her guests to seats about the living-room. It was an afternoon set apart for fancy-work and conversation. Later there would be tea, and two triangular sandwiches apiece made from the chopped remnants of last night's chicken, and a cake which was a high favorite with Mrs. Matson, for its formula required but one egg. She had gone, in person, to the kitchen to supervise its making. She was not entirely convinced that her cook was wasteful of materials, but she felt that the woman would bear watching.

The crepe-paper baskets, fairly well filled with disks of peppermint creams, were to enliven the corners of the tea-table. Mrs. Matson trusted her guests not to regard them as favors and take them home.

The conversation dealt, and favorably, with the weather. Mrs. Kerley and Mrs. Swan vied with each other in paying compliments to the day.

"So clear," said Mrs. Kerley.

"Not a cloud in the sky," augmented Mrs. Swan. "Not a one."

"The air was just lovely this morning," reported Mrs. Kerley. "I said to myself, 'Well, this is a beautiful day if there ever *was* one.' "

"There's something so balmy about it," said Mrs. Swan.

Mrs. Cook spoke suddenly and overloudly, in the untrustworthy voice of the deaf.

"Phew, this is a scorcher!" she said. "Something terrible out."

The conversation went immediately to literature. It developed that Mrs. Kerley had been reading a lovely book. Its name and that of its author escaped her at the moment, but her enjoyment of it was so keen that she had lingered over it till 'way past ten o'clock the night before. Particularly did she commend its descriptions of some of those Italian places; they were, she affirmed, just like a picture. The book had been drawn to her attention by the young woman at the Little Booke Nooke. It was, on her authority, one of the new ones.

Mrs. Matson frowned at her embroidery. Words flowed readily from her lips. She seemed to have spoken on the subject before.

"I haven't any use for all these new books," she said. "I wouldn't give them house-room. I don't see why a person wants to sit down and write any such stuff. I often think, I don't believe they know what they're writing about themselves half the time. I don't know who they think wants to read those kind of things. I'm sure *I* don't."

She paused to let her statements sink deep.

"Mr. Matson," she continued—she always spoke of her husband thus; it conveyed an aristocratic sense of aloofness, did away with any suggestion of carnal intimacy between them—"Mr. Matson isn't any hand for these new books, either. He always says, if he could find another book like *David Harum*, he'd read it in a minute. I wish," she added longingly, "I had a dollar for every time I've heard him say that."

Mrs. Kerley smiled. Mrs. Swan threw a rippling little laugh into the pause.

"Well, it's true, you know, it really is true," Mrs. Kerley told Mrs. Swan.

"Oh, it is," Mrs. Swan hastened to reassure her.

"I don't know what we're coming to, *I'm* sure," announced Mrs. Matson.

She sewed, her thread twanging through the tight-stretched circle of linen in her embroidery-hoop.

The stoppage of conversation weighed upon Mrs. Swan. She lifted her head and looked out the window.

"My, what a lovely lawn you have!" she said. "I couldn't help noticing it, first thing. We've been living in New York, you know."

"I often say I don't see what people want to shut themselves up in a place like that for," Mrs. Matson said. "You know, you exist, in New York—we live, out here."

Mrs. Swan laughed a bit nervously. Mrs. Kerley nodded. "That's right," she said. "That's pretty good."

Mrs. Matson herself thought it worthy of repetition. She picked up Mrs. Cook's speaking-tube.

"I was just saying to Mrs. Swan," she cried, and called her epigram into the mouthpiece.

"Live where?" asked Mrs. Cook.

Mrs. Matson smiled at her patiently. "New York. You know, that's where I got my little adopted boy."

"Oh, yes," said Mrs. Swan. "Carrie told me. Now, wasn't that lovely of you!"

Mrs. Matson shrugged. "Yes," she said, "I went right to the best place for him. Miss Codman's nursery—it's absolutely reliable. You can get awfully nice children there. There's quite a long waiting-list, they tell me."

"Goodness, just think how it must seem to him to be up here," said Mrs. Swan, "with this big house, and that lovely, smooth lawn, and everything."

Mrs. Matson laughed slightly. "Oh—well," she said.

"I hope he appreciates it," remarked Mrs. Swan.

"I think he will," Mrs. Matson said capably. "Of course," she conceded, "he's pretty young right now."

"So lovely," murmured Mrs. Swan. "So sweet to get them young like this and have them grow up."

"Yes, I think that's the nicest way," agreed Mrs. Matson. "And, you know, I really enjoy training him. Naturally, now that we have him here with us, we want him to act like a little gentleman."

"Just think of it," cried Mrs. Swan, "a child like that having all this! And will you have him go to school later on?"

"Oh, yes," Mrs. Matson replied. "Yes, we want him to be educated. You take a child going to some nice little school near here, say, where he'll meet only the best children, and he'll make friends that it will be a pretty good thing for him to know some day."

Mrs. Swan waxed arch. "I suppose you've got it all settled what he's going to be when he grows up," she said.

"Why, certainly," said Mrs. Matson. "He's to go right straight into Mr. Matson's business. My husband," she informed Mrs. Swan, "is the Matson Adding Machines."

"Oh-h-h," said Mrs. Swan on a descending scale.

"I think Curtis will do very well in school," prophesied Mrs. Matson. "He's not at all stupid—picks up everything. Mr. Matson is anxious to have him brought up to be a good, sensible business man—he says that's what this country needs, you know. So I've been trying to teach him the value of money. I've bought him a little bank. I don't think you can begin too early. Because probably some day Curtis is going to have— well——"

Mrs. Matson drifted into light, anecdotal mood.

"Oh, it's funny the way children are," she remarked. "The other day Mrs. Newman brought her little Amy down to play with Curtis, and when I went up to look at them, there he was, trying to give her his brand-new flannel rabbit. So I just took him into my room, and I sat him down, and I said to him, 'Now, Curtis,' I said, 'you must realize that Mother had to pay almost two dollars for that rabbit—nearly two hundred pennies,' I said. 'It's very nice to be generous, but you must learn that it isn't a good idea to give things away to people. Now you go in to Amy,' I said, 'and you tell her you're sorry, but she'll have to give that rabbit right back to you.' "

"And did he do it?" asked Mrs. Swan.

"Why, I told him to," Mrs. Matson said.

"Isn't it splendid?" Mrs. Swan asked of the company at large. "Really, when you think of it. A child like that, just suddenly having everything all at once. And probably coming of poor people, too. Are his parents—living?"

"Oh, no, no," Mrs. Matson said briskly. "I couldn't be bothered with anything like that. Of course, I found out all about them. They were really quite nice, clean people—the father was a college man. Curtis really comes of a very nice family, for an orphan."

"Do you think you'll ever tell him that you aren't—that he isn't—tell him about it?" inquired Mrs. Kerley.

"Dear me, yes, just as soon as he's a little older," Mrs. Matson answered. "I think it's so much nicer for him to know. He'll appreciate everything so much more."

"Does the little thing remember his father and mother at all?" Mrs. Swan asked.

"I really don't know if he does or not," said Mrs. Matson.

"Tea," announced the maid, appearing abruptly at the door.

"Tea is served, Mrs. Matson," said Mrs. Matson, her voice lifted.

"Tea is served, Mrs. Matson," echoed the maid.

"*I* don't know what I'm going to do with her," Mrs. Matson told her guests when the girl had disappeared. "Here last night she had company in the kitchen till nearly eleven o'clock at night. The trouble with me is I'm too good to servants. The only way to do is to treat them like cattle."

"They don't appreciate anything else," said Mrs. Kerley.

Mrs. Matson placed her embroidery in her sweet-grass work-basket, and rose.

"Well, shall we go have a cup of tea?" she said.

"Why, how lovely!" cried Mrs. Swan.

Mrs. Cook, who had been knitting doggedly, was informed, via the speaking-tube, of the readiness of tea. She dropped her work instantly, and led the way to the dining-room.

The talk, at the tea-table, was of stitches and patterns. Praise, benignly accepted by Mrs. Matson, was spread by Mrs. Swan and Mrs. Kerley upon the sandwiches, the cake, the baskets, the table-linen, the china, and the design of the silver.

A watch was glanced at, and there arose cries of surprise at the afternoon's flight. There was an assembling of workbags, a fluttering exodus to the hall to put on hats. Mrs. Matson watched her guests.

"Well, it's been just too lovely," Mrs. Swan declared, clasping her hand. "I can't *tell* you how much I've enjoyed it, hearing about the dear little boy, and all. I *hope* you're going to let me see him some time."

"Why, you can see him now, if you'd like," said Mrs. Matson. She went to the foot of the stairs and sang, *"Cur*-tis, *Cur*-tis."

Curtis appeared in the hall above, clean in the gray percale sailor-suit that had been selected in the thrifty expectation of his "growing into it." He looked down at them, caught sight of Mrs. Cook's speaking-tube, and watched it intently, his eyes wide open.

"Come down and see the ladies, Curtis," commanded Mrs. Matson.

Curtis came down, his warm hand squeaking along the banister. He placed his right foot upon a step, brought his left foot carefully down to it, then started his right one off again. Eventually he reached them.

"Can't you say how-do-you-do to the ladies?" asked Mrs. Matson.

He gave each guest, in turn, a small, flaccid hand.

Mrs. Swan squatted suddenly before him, so that her face was level with his.

"My, what a nice boy!" she cried. "I just love little boys like you, do you know it? Ooh, I could just eat you up! I could!"

She squeezed his arms. Curtis, in alarm, drew his head back from her face.

"And what's *your* name?" she asked him. "Let's see if you can tell me what your name is. I just *bet* you can't!"

He looked at her.

"Can't you tell the lady your name, Curtis?" demanded Mrs. Matson.

"Curtis," he told the lady.

"Why, what a *pretty* name!" she cried. She looked up at Mrs. Matson. "Was that his real name?" she asked.

"No," Mrs. Matson said, "they had him called something else. But I named him as soon as I got him. My mother was a Curtis."

Thus might one say, "My name was Guelph before I married."

Mrs. Cook spoke sharply. "Lucky!" she said. "Pretty lucky, that young one!"

"Well, I should say so," echoed Mrs. Swan. "Aren't you a pretty lucky little boy? Aren't you, aren't you, aren't you?" she rubbed her nose against his.

"Yes, Mrs. Swan," Mrs. Matson pronounced and frowned at Curtis.

He murmured something.

"Ooh—*you!*" said Mrs. Swan. She rose from her squatting posture. "I'd like to *steal* you, in your little sailor-suit, and all!"

"Mother bought that suit for you, didn't she?" asked Mrs. Matson of Curtis. "Mother bought him all his nice things."

"Oh, he calls you mother? Now, isn't that sweet!" cried Mrs. Swan.

"Yes, I think it's nice," said Mrs. Matson.

There was a brisk, sure step on the porch; a key turned in the lock. Mr. Matson was among them.

"Well," said Mrs. Matson upon seeing her mate. It was her invariable evening greeting to him.

"Ah," said Mr. Matson. It was his to her.

Mrs. Kerley cooed. Mrs. Swan blinked vivaciously. Mrs. Cook applied her speaking-tube to her ear in the anticipation of hearing something good.

"I don't think you've met Mrs. Swan, Albert," remarked Mrs. Matson. He bowed.

"Oh, I've heard so much about Mr. Matson," cried Mrs. Swan.

Again he bowed.

"We've been making friends with your dear little boy," Mrs. Swan said. She pinched Curtis's cheek. "You sweetie, you!"

"Well, Curtis," said Mr. Matson, "haven't you got a good-evening for me?"

Curtis gave his hand to his present father with a weak smile of politeness. He looked modestly down.

"That's more like it," summarized Mr. Matson. His parental duties accomplished, he turned to fulfill his social obligations. Boldly he caught up Mrs. Cook's speaking-tube. Curtis watched.

"Getting cooler out," roared Mr. Matson. "I thought it would."

Mrs. Cook nodded. "That's good!" she shouted.

Mr. Matson pressed forward to open the door for her. He was of generous proportions, and the hall was narrow. One of the buttons-of-leisure on his coat-sleeve caught in Mrs. Cook's speaking-tube. It fell, with a startling crash, to the floor, and writhed about.

Curtis's control went. Peal upon peal of high, helpless laughter came from him. He laughed on, against Mrs. Matson's cry of "Curtis!" against Mr. Matson's frown. He doubled over with his hands on his little brown knees, and laughed mad laughter.

"Curtis!" bellowed Mr. Matson. The laughter died. Curtis straightened himself, and one last little moan of enjoyment escaped him.

Mr. Matson pointed with a magnificent gesture. "Upstairs!" he boomed.

Curtis turned and climbed the stairs. He looked small beside the banister.

"Well, of all the—" said Mrs. Matson. "I never knew him to do a thing like that since he's been here. I never heard him do such a thing!"

"That young man," pronounced Mr. Matson, "needs a good talking to."

"He needs more than that," his spouse said.

Mr. Matson stooped with a faint creaking, retrieved the speaking-tube, and presented it to Mrs. Cook. "Not at all," he said in anticipation of the thanks which she left unspoken. He bowed.

"Pardon me," he ordered, and mounted the stairs.

Mrs. Matson moved to the door in the wake of her guests. She was bewildered and, it seemed, grieved.

"I never," she affirmed, "never knew that child to go on that way."

"Oh, children," Mrs. Kerley assured her, "they're funny sometimes—especially a little boy like that. You can't expect so much. My goodness, you'll fix all that! I always say I don't know any child that's getting any better bringing up than that young one—just as if he was your own."

Peace returned to the breast of Mrs. Matson. "Oh—goodness!" she said. There was almost a coyness in her smile as she closed the door on the departing.

Sentiment

Oh, anywhere, *driver, anywhere—it doesn't matter. Just keep driving.*

It's better here in this taxi than it was walking. It's no good my trying to walk. There is always a glimpse through the crowd of someone who looks like him—someone with his swing of the shoulders, his slant of the hat. And I think it's he, I think he's come back. And my heart goes to scalding water and the buildings sway and bend above me. No, it's better to be here. But I wish the driver would go fast, so fast that people walking by would be a long gray blur, and I could see no swinging shoulders, no slanted hat. It's bad stopping still in the traffic like this. People pass too slowly, too clearly, and always the next one might be—No, of course it couldn't be. I know that. Of course I know it. But it might be, it might.

And people can look in and see me, here. They can see if I cry. Oh, let them—it doesn't matter. Let them look and be damned to them.

Yes, you look at me. Look and look and look, you poor, queer tired woman. It's a pretty hat, isn't it? It's meant to be looked at. That's why it's so big and red and new, that's why it has these great soft poppies on it. Your poor hat is all weary and done with. It looks like a dead cat, a cat that was run over and pushed out of the way against the curbstone. Don't you wish you were I and could have a new hat whenever you pleased? You could walk fast, couldn't you, and hold your head high and raise your feet from the pavement if you were on your way to a new hat, a beautiful hat, a hat that cost more than ever you had? Only I hope you wouldn't choose one like mine. For red is mourning, you know. Scarlet red for a love that's dead. Didn't you know that?

She's gone now. The taxi is moving and she's left behind forever. I wonder what she thought when our eyes and our lives met. I wonder did she envy me, so sleek and safe and young. Or did she realize how quick I'd be to fling away all I have if I could bear in my breast the still, dead heart that she carries in hers. She doesn't feel. She doesn't even wish. She is done with hoping and burning, if ever she burned and she hoped. Oh, that's quite nice, it has a real lilt. She is done with hoping and burning, if ever she— Yes, it's pretty. Well—I wonder if she's gone her slow way a little happier, or, perhaps, a little sadder for knowing that there is one worse off than herself.

This is the sort of thing he hated so in me. I know what he would say. "Oh, for heaven's sake!" he would say. "Can't you stop that fool sentimentalizing? Why do you have to do it? Why do you *want* to do it? Just because you see an old char-woman on the street, there's no need to get sobbing about her. She's all right. She's fine. 'When your eyes and your lives met'—oh, come on now. Why, she never even saw you. And her 'still, dead heart,' nothing! She's probably on her way to get a bottle of bad gin and have a roaring time. You don't have to dramatize *everything*. You don't have to insist that *everybody's* sad. Why are you always so sentimental? Don't *do* it, Rosalie." That's what he would say. I know.

But he won't say that or anything else to me, any more. Never anything else, sweet or bitter. He's gone away and he isn't coming back. "Oh, of course I'm coming back!" he said. "No, I don't know just when—I told you that. Ah, Rosalie, don't go making a national tragedy of it. It'll be a few months, maybe—and if ever two people needed a holiday from each other! It's nothing to cry about. I'll be back. I'm not going to stay away from New York forever."

But I knew. I knew. I knew because he had been far away from me long before he went. He's gone away and he won't come back. He's gone away and he won't come back, he's gone away and he'll never come back. Listen to the wheels saying it, on and on and on. That's sentimental, I suppose. Wheels don't say anything. Wheels can't speak. But I *hear* them.

I wonder why it's wrong to be sentimental. People are so contemptuous of feeling. "You wouldn't catch *me* sitting alone and mooning," they say. "Moon" is what they say when they mean remember, and they are so proud of not remembering.

It's strange, how they pride themselves upon their lacks. "I never take anything seriously," they say. "I simply couldn't imagine," they say, "letting myself care so much that I could be hurt." They say, "No one person could be that important to *me*." And why, why do they think they're right?

Oh, who's right and who's wrong and who decides? Perhaps it was I who was right about that charwoman. Perhaps she *was* weary and still-hearted, and perhaps, for just that moment, she knew all about me. She needn't have been all right and fine and on her way for gin, just because he said so. Oh. Oh, I forgot. He didn't say so. He wasn't here; he isn't here. It was I, imagining what he would say. And I thought I heard him. He's always with me, he and all his beauty and his cruelty. But he mustn't be any more. I mustn't think of him. That's it, don't think of him. Yes. Don't breathe, either. Don't hear. Don't see. Stop the blood in your veins.

I can't go on like this. I can't, I can't. I cannot stand this frantic misery. If I knew it would be over in a day or a year or two months, I could endure it. Even if it grew duller sometimes and wilder sometimes, it could be borne. But it is always the same and there is no end.

> *"Sorrow like a ceaseless rain*
> *Beats upon my heart.*
> *People twist and scream in pain—*
> *Dawn will find them still again;*
> *This has neither wax nor wane,*
> *Neither stop nor start."*

Oh, let's see—how does the next verse go? Something, something, something, something, something to rhyme with "wear." Anyway, it ends:

> *"All my thoughts are slow and brown:*
> *Standing up or sitting down*
> *Little matters, or what gown*
> *Or what shoes I wear."*

Yes, that's the way it goes. And it's right, it's so right. What is it to me what I wear? Go and buy yourself a big red hat with poppies on it—that ought to cheer you up. Yes—go buy it and loathe it. How am I to go on, sitting and staring and buying big red hats and hating them, and then sitting and staring again—day upon day upon day upon day? Tomorrow and tomorrow and tomorrow. How am I to drag through them like this?

But what else is there for me? "Go out and see your friends and have a good time," they say. "Don't sit alone and dramatize yourself." Dramatize yourself! If it be drama to feel a steady—no, a *ceaseless* rain beating upon my heart, then I do dramatize myself. The shallow people, the little people, how can they know what suffering is, how could their thick hearts be torn? Don't they know, the empty fools, that I could not see again the friends we saw together, could not go back to the places where he and I have been? For he's gone, and it's ended. It's ended, it's ended. And when it ends, only those places where you have known sorrow are kindly to you. If you revisit the scenes of your happiness, your heart must burst of its agony.

And that's sentimental, I suppose. It's sentimental to know that you cannot bear to see the places where once all was well with you, that you cannot bear reminders of a dead loveliness. Sorrow is tranquillity remembered in emotion. It—oh, I think that's quite good. "Remembered in emotion"—that's a really nice reversal. I wish I could say it to him. But I won't say anything to him, ever again, ever, ever again. He's gone, and it's over, and I dare not think of the dead days. All my thoughts must be slow and brown, and I must——

Oh, no, no, no! Oh, the driver shouldn't go through this street! This was our street, this is the place of our love and our laughter. I can't do this, I can't, I can't. I will crouch down here, and hold my hands tight, tight over my eyes, so that I cannot look. I must keep my poor heart still, and I must be like the little, mean, dry-souled people who are proud not to remember.

But, oh, I see it, I see it, even though my eyes are blinded. Though I had no eyes, my heart would tell me this street, out of all streets. I know it as I know my hands, as I know his face. Oh, why can't I be let to die as we pass through?

We must be at the florist's shop on the corner now. That's where he used to stop to buy me primroses, little yellow primroses massed tight together with a circle of their silver-backed leaves about them, clean and cool and gentle. He always said that orchids and camellias were none of my affair. So when there were no spring and no primroses, he would give me lilies-of-the-valley and little, gay rosebuds and mignonette and bright blue cornflowers. He said he couldn't stand the thought of me without flowers—it would be all wrong; I cannot bear flowers near me, now. And the little gray florist was so interested and so glad—and there was the day he called me "madam"! Ah, I can't, I can't.

And now we must be at the big apartment house with the big gold doorman. And the evening the doorman was holding the darling puppy on a big, long leash, and we stopped to talk to it, and he took it up in his arms and cuddled it, and that was the only time we ever saw the doorman smile! And next is the house with the baby, and he always would take off his hat and bow very solemnly to her, and sometimes she would give him her little starfish of a hand. And then is the tree with the rusty iron bars around it, where he would stop to turn and wave to me, as I leaned out the window to watch him. And people would look at him, because people always had to look at him, but he never noticed. It was our tree, he said; it wouldn't dream of belonging to anybody else. And very few city people had their own personal tree, he said. Did I realize that, he said.

And then there's the doctor's house, and the three thin gray houses and then—oh, God, we must be at our house now! Our house, though we had only the top floor. And I loved the long, dark stairs, because he climbed them every evening. And our little prim pink curtains at the windows, and the boxes of pink geraniums that always grew for me. And the little stiff entry and the funny mail-box, and his ring at the bell. And I waiting for him in the dusk, thinking he would never come; and yet the waiting was lovely, too. And then when I opened the door to him— Oh, no, no, no! Oh, no one could bear this. No one, no one.

Ah, why, why, why must I be driven through here? What

torture could there be so terrible as this? It will be better if I uncover my eyes and look. I will see our tree and our house again, and then my heart will burst and I will be dead. I will look, I will look.

But where's the tree? Can they have cut down our tree—*our* tree? And where's the apartment house? And where's the florist's shop? And where—oh, where's our house, where's ——

Driver, what street is this? Sixty-Fifth? Oh. No, nothing, thank you. I—I thought it was Sixty-Third. . . .

Clothe the Naked

Big Lannie went out by the day to the houses of secure and leisured ladies, to wash their silks and their linens. She did her work perfectly; some of the ladies even told her so. She was a great, slow mass of a woman, colored a sound brown-black save for her palms and the flat of her fingers that were like guttapercha from steam and hot suds. She was slow because of her size, and because the big veins in her legs hurt her, and her back ached much of the time. She neither cursed her ills nor sought remedies for them. They had happened to her; there they were.

Many things had happened to her. She had had children, and the children had died. So had her husband, who was a kind man, cheerful with the little luck he found. None of their children had died at birth. They had lived to be four or seven or ten, so that they had had their ways and their traits and their means of causing love; and Big Lannie's heart was always wide for love. One child had been killed in a street accident and two others had died of illnesses that might have been no more than tedious, had there been fresh food and clear spaces and clean air behind them. Only Arlene, the youngest, lived to grow up.

Arlene was a tall girl, not so dark as her mother but with the same firm flatness of color. She was so thin that her bones seemed to march in advance of her body. Her little pipes of legs and her broad feet with jutting heels were like things a child draws with crayons. She carried her head low, her shoulders scooped around her chest, and her stomach slanted forward. From the time that she was tiny, there were men after her.

Arlene was a bad girl always; that was one of the things that had happened to Big Lannie. There it was, and Big Lannie could only keep bringing her presents, surprises, so that the girl would love her mother and would want to stay at home. She brought little bottles of sharp perfume, and pale stockings of tinny silk, and rings set with bits of green and red glass; she tried to choose what Arlene would like. But each time Arlene came home she had bigger rings and softer stockings and stronger perfume than her mother could buy for her. Sometimes she would stay with her mother over a night, and sometimes more than a week; and then Big Lannie would come back from work one evening, and the girl would be gone, and no word of her. Big Lannie would go on bringing surprises, and setting them out along Arlene's bed to wait a return.

Big Lannie did not know it, when Arlene was going to have a baby. Arlene had not been home in nearly half a year; Big Lannie told the time in days. There was no news at all of the girl until the people at the hospital sent for Big Lannie to come to her daughter and grandson. She was there to hear Arlene say the baby must be named Raymond, and to see the girl die. For whom Raymond was called, or if for anyone, Big Lannie never knew.

He was a long, light-colored baby, with big, milky eyes that looked right back at his grandmother. It was several days before the people at the hospital told her he was blind.

Big Lannie went to each of the ladies who employed her and explained that she could not work for some while; she must take care of her grandson. The ladies were sharply discommoded, after her steady years, but they dressed their outrage in shrugs and cool tones. Each arrived, separately, at the conclusion that she had been too good to Big Lannie, and had been imposed upon, therefore. "Honestly, those niggers!" each said to her friends. "They're all alike."

Big Lannie sold most of the things she lived with, and took one room with a stove in it. There, as soon as the people at the hospital would let her, she brought Raymond and tended him. He was all her children to her.

She had always been a saving woman, with few needs and no cravings, and she had been long alone. Even after Arlene's burial, there was enough left for Raymond and Big Lannie to go on for a time. Big Lannie was slow to be afraid of what must come; fear did not visit her at all, at first, and then it slid in only when she waked, when the night hung motionless before another day.

Raymond was a good baby, a quiet, patient baby, lying in his wooden box and stretching out his delicate hands to the sounds that were light and color to him. It seemed but a little while, so short to Big Lannie, before he was walking about the room, his hands held out, his feet quick and sure. Those of Big Lannie's friends who saw him for the first time had to be told that he could not see.

Then, and it seemed again such a little while, he could dress himself, and open the door for his granny, and unlace the shoes from her tired feet, and talk to her in his soft voice. She had occasional employment—now and then a neighbor would hear of a day's scrubbing she could do, or sometimes she might work in the stead of a friend who was sick—infrequent, and not to be planned on. She went to the ladies for whom she had worked, to ask if they might not want her back again; but there was little hope in her, after she had visited the first one. Well, now, really, said the ladies; well, really, now.

The neighbors across the hall watched over Raymond while Big Lannie looked for work. He was no trouble to them, nor to himself. He sat and crooned at his chosen task. He had been given a wooden spool around the top of which were driven little brads, and over these with a straightened hairpin he looped bright worsted, working faster than sight until a long tube of woven wool fell through the hole in the spool. The neighbors threaded big, blunt needles for him, and he coiled the woolen tubes and sewed them into mats. Big Lannie called them beautiful, and it made Raymond proud to have her tell him how readily she sold them. It was hard for her, when he was asleep at night, to unravel the mats and wash the worsted and stretch it so straight that even Raymond's shrewd fingers could not tell, when he worked with it next day, that it was not new.

Fear stormed in Big Lannie and took her days and nights. She might not go to any organization dispensing relief, for dread that Raymond would be taken from her and put in—she would not say that word to herself, and she and her neighbors lowered their voices when they said it to one another—an institution. The neighbors wove lingering tales of what happened inside certain neat, square buildings on the cindery skirts of the town, and, if they must go near them, hurried as if passing graveyards, and came home heroes. When they got you in one of those places, whispered the neighbors, they laid your spine open with whips, and then when you dropped, they kicked your head in. Had anyone come into Big Lannie's room to take Raymond away to an asylum for the blind, the neighbors would have fought for him with stones and rails and boiling water.

Raymond did not know about anything but good. When he grew big enough to go alone down the stairs and into the street, he was certain of delight each day. He held his head high, as he came out into the little yard in front of the flimsy wooden house, and slowly turned his face from side to side, as if the air were soft liquid on which he bathed it. Trucks and wagons did not visit the street, which ended in a dump for rusted bedsprings and broken boilers and staved-in kettles; children played over its cobbles, and men and women sat talking in open windows and called across to one another in gay, rich voices. There was always laughter for Raymond to hear, and he would laugh back, and hold out his hands to it.

At first, the children stopped their play when he came out, and gathered quietly about him, and watched him, fascinated. They had been told of his affliction, and they had a sort of sickened pity for him. Some of them spoke to him, in soft, careful tones. Raymond would laugh with pleasure, and stretch his hands, the curious smooth, flat hands of the blind, to their voices. They would draw sharply back, afraid that his strange hands might touch them. Then, somehow ashamed because they had shrunk from him and he could not see that they had done so, they said gentle good-bys to him, and backed away into the street again, watching him steadily.

When they were gone, Raymond would start on his walk to the end of the street. He guided himself by lightly touching the broken fences along the dirt sidewalk, and as he walked he crooned little songs with no words to them. Some of the men and women at the windows would call hello to him, and he would call back and wave and smile. When the children, forgetting him, laughed again at their games, he stopped and turned to the sound as if it were the sun.

In the evening, he would tell Big Lannie about his walk, slapping his knee and chuckling at the memory of the laughter he had heard. When the weather was too hard for him to go out in the street, he would sit at his worsted work, and talk all day of going out the next day.

The neighbors did what they could for Raymond and Big Lannie. They gave Raymond clothes their own children had not yet worn out, and they brought food, when they had enough to spare and other times. Big Lannie would get through a week, and would pray to get through the next one; and so the months went. Then the days on which she could find work fell farther and farther apart, and she could not pray about the time to come because she did not dare to think of it.

It was Mrs. Ewing who saved Raymond's and Big Lannie's lives, and let them continue together. Big Lannie said that then and ever after; daily she blessed Mrs. Ewing, and nightly she would have prayed for her, had she not known, in some dimmed way, that any intercession for Mrs. Delabarre Ewing must be impudence.

Mrs. Ewing was a personage in the town. When she went to Richmond for a visit, or when she returned from viewing the azalea gardens in Charleston, the newspaper always printed the fact. She was a woman rigorously conscious of her noble obligation; she was prominent on the Community Chest committee, and it was she who planned and engineered the annual Bridge Drive to raise funds for planting salvia around the cannon in front of the D.A.R. headquarters. These and many others were her public activities, and she was no less exacting of herself in her private life. She kept a model, though childless, house for her husband and herself, relegating the supervision of details to no domestic lieutenant, no matter how seemingly trustworthy.

Back before Raymond was born, Big Lannie had worked as laundress for Mrs. Ewing. Since those days, the Ewing wash tubs had witnessed many changes, none for the better. Mrs.

Ewing took Big Lannie back into her employment. She apologized for this step to her friends by the always winning method of self-deprecation. She knew she was a fool, she said, after all that time, and after the way that Big Lannie had treated her. But still, she said—and she laughed a little at her own ways—anyone she felt kind of sorry for could always get around her, she said. She knew it was awful foolish, but that, she said, was the way she was. Mr. Ewing, she said behind her husband's hearing, always called her just a regular little old easy mark.

Big Lannie had no words in which to thank Mrs. Ewing, nor to tell her what two days' assured employment every week could mean. At least, it was fairly assured. Big Lannie, as Mrs. Ewing pointed out to her, had got no younger, and she had always been slow. Mrs. Ewing kept her in a state of stimulating insecurity by referring, with perfect truth, to the numbers of stronger, quicker women who were also in need of work.

Two days' work in the week meant money for rent and stovewood and almost enough food for Raymond and Big Lannie. She must depend, for anything further, on whatever odd jobs she could find, and she must not stop seeking them. Pressed on by fear and gratitude, she worked so well for Mrs. Ewing that there was sometimes expressed satisfaction at the condition of the lady's household linen and her own and her husband's clothing. Big Lannie had a glimpse of Mr. Ewing occasionally, leaving the house as she came, or entering it as she was leaving. He was a bit of a man, not much bigger than Raymond.

Raymond grew so fast that he seemed to be taller each morning. Every day he had his walk in the street to look forward to and experience, and tell Big Lannie about at night. He had ceased to be a sight of the street; the children were so used to him that they did not even look at him, and the men and women at the windows no longer noticed him enough to hail him. He did not know. He would wave to any gay cry he heard, and go on his way, singing his little songs and turning toward the sound of laughter.

Then his lovely list of days ended as sharply as if ripped from some bright calendar. A winter came, so sudden and savage as to find no comparison in the town's memories, and Raymond had no clothes to wear out in the street. Big Lannie mended his outgrown garments as long as she could, but the stuff had so rotted with wear that it split in new places when she tried to sew together the ragged edges of rents.

The neighbors could give no longer; all they had they must keep for their own. A demented colored man in a near-by town had killed the woman who employed him, and terror had spread like brush fire. There was a sort of panic of reprisal; colored employees were dismissed from their positions, and there was no new work for them. But Mrs. Ewing, admittedly soft-hearted certainly to a fault and possibly to a peril, kept her black laundress on. More than ever Big Lannie had reason to call her blessed.

All winter, Raymond stayed indoors. He sat at his spool and worsted, with Big Lannie's old sweater about his shoulders and, when his tattered knickerbockers would no longer hold together, a calico skirt of hers lapped around his waist. He lived, at his age, in the past; in the days when he had walked, proud and glad, in the street, with laughter in his ears. Always, when he talked of it, he must laugh back at that laughter.

Since he could remember, he had not been allowed to go out when Big Lannie thought the weather unfit. This he had accepted without question, and so he accepted his incarceration through the mean weeks of the winter. But then one day it was spring, so surely that he could tell it even in the smoky, stinking rooms of the house, and he cried out with joy because now he might walk in the street again. Big Lannie had to explain to him that his rags were too thin to shield him, and that there were no odd jobs for her, and so no clothes and shoes for him.

Raymond did not talk about the street any more, and his fingers were slow at his spool.

Big Lannie did something she had never done before; she begged of her employer. She asked Mrs. Ewing to give her some of Mr. Ewing's old clothes for Raymond. She looked at the floor and mumbled so that Mrs. Ewing requested her to talk *up*. When Mrs. Ewing understood, she was, she said, surprised. She had, she said, a great, great many demands on her charity, and she would have supposed that Big Lannie, of all people, might have known that she did everything she could, and, in fact, a good deal more. She spoke of inches and ells. She said that if she found she could spare anything, Big Lannie was kindly to remember it was to be just for this once.

When Big Lannie was leaving at the end of her day's work, Mrs. Ewing brought her a package with her own hands. There, she said, was a suit and a pair of shoes; beautiful, grand things that people would think she was just a crazy to go giving away like that. She simply didn't know, she said, what Mr. Ewing would say to her for being such a crazy. She explained that that was the way she was when anyone got around her, all the while Big Lannie was trying to thank her.

Big Lannie had never before seen Raymond behave as he did when she brought him home the package. He jumped and danced and clapped his hands, he tried to speak and squealed instead, he tore off the paper himself, and ran his fingers over the close-woven cloth and held it to his face and kissed it. He put on the shoes and clattered about in them, digging with his toes and heels to keep them on; he made Big Lannie pin the trousers around his waist and roll them up over his shins. He babbled of the morrow when he would walk in the street, and could not say his words for laughing.

Big Lannie must work for Mrs. Ewing the next day, and she had thought to bid Raymond wait until she could stay at home and dress him herself in his new garments. But she heard him laugh again; she could not tell him he must wait. He might go out at noon next day, she said, when the sun was so warm that he would not take cold at his first outing; one of the neighbors across the hall would help him with the clothes. Raymond chuckled and sang his little songs until he went to sleep.

After Big Lannie left in the morning, the neighbor came in to Raymond, bringing a pan of cold pork and corn bread for his lunch. She had a call for a half-day's work, and she could not stay to see him start out for his walk. She helped him put on the trousers and pinned and rolled them for him, and she laced the shoes as snug as they would go on his feet. Then she told him not to go out till the noon whistles blew, and kissed him, and left.

Raymond was too happy to be impatient. He sat and thought of the street and smiled and sang. Not until he heard the whistles did he go to the drawer where Big Lannie had laid the coat, and take it out and put it on. He felt it soft on his bare back, he twisted his shoulders to let it fall warm and loose from them. As he folded the sleeves back over his thin arms, his heart beat so that the cloth above it fluttered.

The stairs were difficult for him to manage, in the big shoes, but the very slowness of the descent was delicious to him. His anticipation was like honey in his mouth.

Then he came out into the yard, and turned his face in the gentle air. It was all good again; it was all given back again. As quickly as he could, he gained the walk and set forth, guiding himself by the fence. He could not wait; he called out, so that he would hear gay calls in return, he laughed so that laughter would answer him.

He heard it. He was so glad that he took his hand from the fence and turned and stretched out his arms and held up his smiling face to welcome it. He stood there, and his smile died on his face, and his welcoming arms stiffened and shook.

It was not the laughter he had known; it was not the laughter he had lived on. It was like great flails beating him flat, great prongs tearing his flesh from his bones. It was coming at him, to kill him. It drew slyly back, and then it smashed against him. It swirled around and over him, and he could not breathe. He screamed and tried to run out through it, and fell, and it licked over him, howling higher. His clothes unrolled, and his shoes flapped on his feet. Each time he could rise, he fell again. It was as if the street were perpendicular before him, and the laughter leaping at his back. He could not find the fence, he did not know which way he was turned. He lay screaming, in blood and dust and darkness.

When Big Lannie came home, she found him on the floor in a corner of the room, moaning and whimpering. He still wore his new clothes, cut and torn and dusty, and there was dried blood on his mouth and his palms. Her heart had leapt in alarm when he had not opened the door at her footstep, and she cried out so frantically to ask what had happened that she frightened him into wild weeping. She could not understand what he said; it was something about the street, and laughing at him, and make them go away, and don't let him go in the street no more, never in the street no more. She did not try to make him explain. She took him in her arms and rocked him, and told him, over and over, never mind, don't care, everything's all right. Neither he nor she believed her words.

But her voice was soft and her arms warm. Raymond's sobs softened, and trembled away. She held him, rocking silently and rhythmically, a long time. Then gently she set him on his feet, and took from his shoulders Mr. Ewing's old full-dress coat.

War Song

Soldier, in a curious land
  All across a swaying sea,
Take her smile and lift her hand—
  Have no guilt of me.

Soldier, when were soldiers true?
  If she's kind and sweet and gay,
Use the wish I send to you—
  Lie not lone till day!

Only, for the nights that were,
  Soldier, and the dawns that came,
When in sleep you turn to her
  Call her by my name.

1944

PART TWO

Later Stories
Reviews and Articles

Later Stories

I Live on Your Visits

The boy came into the hotel room and immediately it seemed even smaller.

"Hey, it's cool in here," he said. This was not meant as a comment on the temperature. "Cool," for reasons possibly known in some department of Heaven, was a term then in use among many of those of his age to express approbation.

It was indeed cool in the room, after the hard gray rain in the streets. It was warm, and it was so bright. The many-watted electric bulbs his mother insisted upon were undimmed by the thin frilled shades she had set on the hotel lamps, and there were shiny things everywhere: sheets of mirror along the walls; a square of mirror backing the mirror-plated knob on the door that led to the bedroom; cigarette boxes made of tiny bits of mirror and matchboxes slipped into little mirror jackets placed all about; and, on consoles and desk and table, photographs of himself at two and a half and five and seven and nine framed in broad mirror bands. Whenever his mother settled in a new domicile, and she removed often, those photographs were the first things out of the luggage. The boy hated them. He had had to pass his fifteenth birthday before his body had caught up with his head; there was that head, in those presentments of his former selves, that pale, enormous blob. Once he had asked his mother to put the pictures somewhere else—preferably some small, dark place that could be locked. But he had had the bad fortune to make his request on one of the occasions when she was given to weeping suddenly and long. So the photographs stood out on parade, with their frames twinkling away.

There were twinklings, too, from the silver top of the fat crystal cocktail shaker, but the liquid low within the crystal was pale and dull. There was no shine, either, to the glass his mother held. It was cloudy from the clutch of her hand, and on the inside there were oily dribbles of what it had contained.

His mother shut the door by which she had admitted him,

and followed him into the room. She looked at him with her head tilted to the side.

"Well, aren't you going to kiss me?" she said in a charming, wheedling voice, the voice of a little, little girl. "Aren't you, you beautiful big ox, you?"

"Sure," he said. He bent down toward her, but she stepped suddenly away. A sharp change came over her. She drew herself tall, with her shoulders back and her head flung high. Her upper lip lifted over her teeth, and her gaze came cold beneath lowered lids. So does one who has refused the white handkerchief regard the firing squad.

"Of course," she said in a deep, iced voice that gave each word its full due, "if you do not wish to kiss me, let it be recognized that there is no need for you to do so. I had not meant to overstep. I apologize. *Je vous demande pardon.* I had no desire to force you. I have never forced you. There is none to say I have."

"Ah, Mom," he said. He went to her, bent again, and this time kissed her cheek.

There was no change in her, save in the slow, somehow offended lifting of her eyelids. The brows arched as if they drew the lids up with them. "Thank you," she said. "That was gracious of you. I value graciousness. I rank it high. *Mille grazie.*"

"Ah, Mom," he said.

For the past week, up at his school, he had hoped—and coming down in the train he had hoped so hard that it became prayer—that his mother would not be what he thought of only as "like that." His prayer had gone unanswered. He knew by the two voices, by the head first tilted then held high, by the eyelids lowered in disdain then raised in outrage, by the little lisped words and then the elegant enunciation and the lofty diction. He knew.

He stood there and said, "Ah, Mom."

"Perhaps," she said, "you will award yourself the privilege of meeting a friend of mine. She is a true friend. I am proud that I may say it."

There was someone else in the room. It was preposterous

that he had not seen her, for she was so big. Perhaps his eyes
had been dazzled, after the dim-lit hotel corridor; perhaps his
attention had been all for his mother. At any rate, there she sat,
the true friend, on the sofa covered with embossed cotton
fabric of the sickened green that is peculiar to hotel
upholsteries. There she sat, at one end of the sofa, and it
seemed as if the other end must fly up into the air.

"I can give you but little," his mother said, "yet life is still
kind enough to let me give you something you will always
remember. Through me, you will meet a human being."

Yes, oh, yes. The voices, the stances, the eyelids—those were
the signs. But when his mother divided the race into people and
human beings—that was the certainty.

He followed her the little way across the room, trying not to
tread on the train of her velvet tea gown that slid along the floor
after her and slapped at the heels of her gilt slippers. Fog
seemed to rise from his raincoat and his shoes cheeped. He
turned out to avoid the coffee table in front of the sofa, came in
again too sharply and bumped it.

"Mme. Marah," his mother said, "may I present my son?"

"Christ, he's a big bastard, isn't he?" the true friend said.

She was a fine one to talk about anybody's being big. Had
she risen, she would have stood shoulder against shoulder with
him, and she must have outweighed him by sixty pounds. She
was dressed in quantities of tweedlike stuff ornamented,
surprisingly, with black sequins set on in patterns of little
bunches of grapes. On her massive wrists were bands and
chains of dull silver, from some of which hung amulets of
discolored ivory, like rotted fangs. Over her head and neck was
a sort of caul of crisscrossed mauve veiling, splattered with
fuzzy black balls. The caul caused her no inconvenience. Puffs
of smoke issued sporadically from behind it, and, though the
veiling was crisp elsewhere, around the mouth it was of a
marshy texture, where drink had passed through it.

His mother became the little girl again. "Isn't he wonderful?" she said. "This is my baby. This is Crissy-wiss."

"*What* is his name?" the true friend said.

"Why, Christopher, of course," his mother said.

Christopher, of course. Had he been born earlier, it would have been Peter; earlier again, Michael; he had been not much too late for Jonathan. In the lower forms of his school, there were various Nicholases, several Robins, and here and there a Jeremy coming up. But the members of his own class were in the main Christophers.

"Christopher," the true friend said. "Well, that's not too bad. Of course, that downward stroke of the 'p' is bound to give him trouble, and I'm never really happy about an 'r' and an 'i' together. But it's not too bad. Not too. When's your birthday?" she asked the boy.

"The fifteenth of August," he said.

His mother was no longer the little girl. "The heat," she said, "the cruel August heat. And the stitches. Oh, God, the stitches!"

"So he's a Leo," the true friend said. "Awfully big for a Leo. You want to be pretty careful, young man, from October 22nd to November 13th. Keep away from anything electrical."

"I will," the boy said. "Thank you," he added.

"Let me see your hand," the true friend said.

The boy gave her his hand.

"Mm," she said, scanning the palm. "M-hmm, m-hmm, m-hmm. Oh. Well—*that* can't be helped. Well, you'll have pretty good health, if you just watch that chest of yours. There's a long sickness in your twenties and a bad accident some time around forty-five, but that's about all. There's going to be an unhappy love affair, but you'll get over it. You'll marry and— I can't see if there's two or three children. Probably two and one born dead, or something like that. I don't see much money, any time. Well, you watch your chest." She gave him back his hand.

"Thank you," he said.

The little girl came back to his mother. "Isn't he going to be famous?" she said.

The true friend shrugged. "It's not in his hand," she said.

"I always thought he'd write," his mother said. "When he was so small you could hardly see him, he used to write little verses. Crissy, what was the one about the bumpety bunny?"

"Oh, Mother!" he said. "I don't remember!"

"Oh, you do so, too!" she said. "You're just being modest. It was all about how the bunny went bumpety, bumpety all day long. Of course you remember. Well, you don't seem to write verses any more—at least none you show to *me*. And your letters—they're like telegrams. When you write at all, that is. Oh, Marah, why do they have to grow up? And now he's going to be married and have all those children."

"Two, anyway," the true friend said. "I'm not too happy about that third one."

"I suppose I'll never see him then," his mother said. "A lonely old woman, sick and trembling, and no one to take care of me."

She picked up the true friend's empty glass from the coffee table, filled it and her own from the cocktail shaker, and returned the friend's. She sat down near the sofa.

"Well, sit down, Crissy," she said. "And why don't you take off your coat?"

"Why, I don't think I'd better, Mom," he said. "You see—"

"He wants to keep his wet coat on," the true friend said. "He likes to smell like low tide."

"Well, you see," the boy said, "I can stay just a minute. You see, the train was late and everything, and I told Dad I'd be sure to be there early."

"Oh?" his mother said. The little girl ran off abruptly. The eyelids came into play.

"It's because the train was late," he said. "If it had been on time, I could have stayed awhile. But it had to go and be late, and they're having dinner awfully early tonight."

"I see," his mother said. "I see. I had thought that you would have dinner with me. With your mother. Her only son. But no, that is not to be. I have only an egg, but I would have shared it with you so gladly. So happily. But you are wise, of course. You must think first of your own comfort. Go and fill your stomach with your father. Go eat stalled ox with him."

"Mother, don't you see?" he said. "We have to have dinner

early because we have to go to bed early. We've got to get up at daybreak because we're driving to the country. You know. I wrote you."

"Driving?" she said. "Your father has a new car, I presume."

"It's the same old heap," he said. "Nearly eight years old."

"Really?" she said. "Naturally, the buses in which I am obliged to ride are all this year's models."

"Ah, Mom," he said.

"Is your father well?" she said.

"He's fine," he said.

"Why not?" she said. "What is there could pierce that heart? And how is Mrs. Tennant? As I suppose she calls herself."

"Let's not do this again, will you, Mom?" he said. "She's Mrs. Tennant. You know that. She and Dad have been married for six years."

"To me," she said, "there is only one woman who may rightfully wear a man's name; the one whose son he has sired. But that is only my humble opinion. Who is to listen to it?"

"You get along all right with your stepmother?" the true friend said.

As always, it took him a moment before he could connect the term. It seemed to have nothing to do with Whitey, with her gay little monkey's face and her flying straw-colored hair.

A laugh fell from his mother's lips, hard, like a pellet of ice. "Such women are sly," she said. "They have ways."

"Well, born on a cusp," the true friend said. "You've got to keep considering that."

His mother turned to the boy. "I am going to do something that you will agree, in any honesty, that I have never done before," she said. "I am going to ask a favor of you. I am going to ask you to take off your coat and sit down, so that for just a few poor minutes it will seem as if you were not going to leave me. Will you let me have that illusion? Do not do it out of affection or gratitude or consideration. Just in simple pity."

"Yes, sit down, for God's sake," the true friend said. "You make people nervous."

"All right, sure," the boy said. He took off his raincoat, hung it over his arm, and sat on a small, straight chair.

"He's the biggest damn thing I ever saw," the true friend said.

"Thank you," his mother said. "If you think I ask too much, I plead guilty. *Mea culpa.* Well, now that we are cozy, let us talk, shall we? I see so little of you—I know so little about you. Tell me some things. Tell me what there is about this Mrs. Tennant that causes you to rank her so high above me. Is she more beautiful than I am?"

"Mom, please," he said. "You know Whitey isn't beautiful. She's just sort of funny-looking. Nice funny."

"Nice funny," she said. "Oh, I'm afraid I could never compete with that. Well, looks aren't everything, I suppose. Tell me, do you consider her a human being?"

"Mother, I don't know," he said. "I can't do that kind of talk."

"Let it pass," she said. "Let it be forgotten. Is your father's country place attractive at this time of year?"

"It isn't a place," he said. "You know—it's just a big sort of shack. There isn't even any heat. Just fireplaces."

"Ironic," she said. "Bitterly, cruelly ironic. I, who so love an open fire; I, who could sit all day looking into its leaping golds and purples and dreaming happy dreams. And I haven't even a gas log. Well. And who is going to this shack, to share the lovely, glowing fires?"

"Just Dad and Whitey and me," he said. "Oh, and the other Whitey, of course."

His mother looked at the true friend. "Is it growing dark in here?" she said. "Or is it just that I think I am going to faint?" She looked again at the boy. "The *other* Whitey?"

"It's a little dog," he said. "Not any particular kind. It's a nice little dog. Whitey saw it out in the street, when it was snowing, and it followed her home, and so they kept it. And whenever Dad—whenever anybody called Whitey, the dog would come, too. So Dad said well, if he thought that was his name, then that was going to *be* his name. So that was why."

"I am afraid," his mother said, "that your father is not aging with dignity. To me, whimsey after forty-five is a matter of nausea."

"It's an awfully nice little dog," he said.

"The management does not allow dogs here," she said. "I suppose that will be held against me. Marah—this drink. It is as weak as the beating of my heart."

"Why doesn't he make us some fresh ones?" the true friend said.

"I'm sorry," the boy said. "I don't know how to make cocktails."

"What do they teach you, anyway, in that fancy school of yours?" the true friend said.

His mother tilted her head at the boy. "Crissy," she said, "want to be a big, brave man? Take the bowl and get some nice, cold ice out of the kitchen."

He took the ice bowl, went into the minuscule kitchen, and took a tray of ice cubes from the tiny refrigerator. When he replaced the tray, he could hardly close the refrigerator door, the shelves were so crowded. There were a cardboard box of eggs, a packet of butter, a cluster of glossy French rolls, three artichokes, two avocados, a plate of tomatoes, a bowl of shelled peas, a grapefruit, a tin of vegetable juices, a glass of red caviar, a cream cheese, an assortment of sliced Italian sausages, and a plump little roasted Cornish Rock hen.

When he returned, his mother was busied with bottles and shaker. He set the bowl of cubes beside them.

"Look, Mom," he said, "honestly I've got to—"

His mother looked at him and her lip trembled. "Just two more minutes," she whispered. "Please, oh, please."

He went and sat again.

She made the drinks, gave one to the true friend, and kept one. She sank into her chair; her head drooped and her body looked as boneless as a skein of yarn.

"Don't you want a drink?" the true friend said.

"No, thanks," the boy said.

"Might do you good," the true friend said. "Might stunt

your growth. How long are you going to stay up in this country where you're going?"

"Oh, just over tomorrow night," he said. "I have to be back at school Sunday evening."

His mother stiffened and straightened. Her former coldnesses were as tropical heat to that which took her now.

"Do I understand you to say that you will not be coming in to see me again?" she said. "Do I understand you aright?"

"I can't, Mom," he said. "I won't have a chance. We've got to drive back, and then I have to get the train."

"I quite comprehend," she said. "I had thought, in my tenderness, I would see you again before your return to your school. I had thought, of course, that if you must rush away like a mad thing today, then I would see you again, to make up for it. Disappointments—I thought I had had them all, I thought life could bring forth no new ones. But this—this. That you will not take a little bit of your time from your relatives, who have so much of it, to give to me, your mother. How it must please them that you do not want to see me. How they must laugh together. What a triumph. How they must howl in merriment."

"Mother, don't say things like that," he said. "You shouldn't, even when you're—"

"Please!" she said. "The subject is closed. I will say no more about your father, poor, weak man, and that woman with the dog's name. But you—you. Have you no heart, no bowels, no natural instincts? No. You have not. I must face the fact. Here, in the presence of my friend, I must say what I had thought never, never to say. My son is not a human being!"

The true friend shook her caul and sighed. The boy sat still.

"Your father," his mother said. "Does he still see his old friends? *Our* old friends?"

"Why, I don't know, Mom," he said. "Yes, they see a lot of people, I guess. There's almost always somebody there. But they're alone a lot of the time. They like it that way."

"How fortunate," she said. "They like being alone. Smug, content, no need— Yes. And the old friends. They do not see me. They are all in twos, they have lives, they know what they're going to be doing six months from now. Why should they see me? Why should they have memories, kindnesses?"

"Probably most of them Pisces," the true friend said.

"Well, you must go," the boy's mother said. "It is late. Late—when is it ever late for me, when my son is with me? But you have told me. I know. I understand, and so I bow my head. Go, Christopher. Go."

"I'm terribly sorry, Mom," the boy said. "But I told you how it is." He rose and put on his coat.

"Christ, he gets bigger and bigger," the true friend said.

This time, the eyelids of the boy's mother were lowered at her friend. "I have always admired tall men," she said. She turned again to the boy. "You must go," she said. "It is so written. But take happiness with you. Take sweet memories of our little time together. See—I shall show you that I bear no vengefulness. I shall show you that I wish only well to those who have wrought but evil to me. I shall give you a present to take one of them."

She rose, moved about the room, touched boxes and tables fruitlessly. Then she went to the desk, moved papers and inkstands, and brought forth a small, square box, on top of which was a little plaster poodle, sitting on its hind legs, its front paws curved endearingly, begging.

"This is a souvenir of happier times," she said. "But I need no reminders. Take this dear, happy thing to one you love. See! See what it is!"

She touched a spring at the back of the box and the "Marseillaise" tinkled forth, hesitantly.

"My little music box," she said. "That moonlit night, the ship so brilliant, the ocean so still and beckoning."

"Hey, that's cool, Mom," he said. "Thanks ever so much. Whitey'll love it. She loves things like that."

"Things like that?" she said. "There are no other things like that, when one gives from one's heart." She stopped and seemed to ponder. "*Whitey* will love it?" she said. "Are you telling me that you propose giving it to that so-called Mrs.

Tennant?" She touched the box; the tinkling ceased.

"I thought you said—" the boy said.

She shook her head at him, slowly. "Curious," she said. "Extraordinary. That my son should have so little perception. This gift, from my poor little store, is not for her. It is for the little dog. The little dog that I may not have."

"Why, thanks, Mom," he said. "Thanks."

"So go," she said. "I would not hold you. Take with you my wishes for your joy, among your loved ones. And when you can, when they will release you for a little while—come to me again. I wait for you. I light a lamp for you. My son, my only child, there are but desert sands for me between your comings. I live on your visits—Chris, I live on your visits."

Lolita

Mrs. Ewing was a short woman who accepted the obligation borne by so many short women to make up in vivacity what they lack in number of inches from the ground. She was a creature of little pats and prods, little crinklings of the eyes and wrinklings of the nose, little runs and ripples of speech and movement, little spirals of laughter. Whenever Mrs. Ewing entered a place, all stillness left it.

Her age was a matter of guesswork, save for those who had been at school with her. For herself, she declared that she paid no attention to her birthdays—didn't give a hoot about them; and it is true that when you have amassed several dozen of the same sort of thing, it loses that rarity which is the excitement of collectors. In the summertime, she wore little cotton play suits, though her only game was bridge, and short socks, revealing the veins along the backs of her legs. For winter, she chose frocks of audible taffeta, frilled and frilled again, and jackets made of the skins of the less-sought-after lower animals. Often, of an evening, she tied a pale ribbon in her hair. Through shimmering heat or stabbing wind Mrs. Ewing trudged to her hairdresser's; her locks had been so frequently and so drastically brightened and curled that to caress them, one felt, would be rather like running one's fingers through julienne potatoes. She decorated her small, square face in a manner not unusual among ladies of the South and the Southwest, powdering the nose and chin sharp white and applying circles of rouge to the cheeks. Seen from an end of a long, softly lighted room, Mrs. Ewing was a pretty woman.

She had long been a widowed lady. Even before her widowhood, she and Mr. Ewing had lived separately, while the sympathy of the town dwelt with her. She had dallied with the notion of divorce, for it is well known that the thought, much less the presence, of a merry divorcee sets gentlemen to pawing the ground and snorting. But before her plans took form, Mr. Ewing, always a devout believer in the doctrine of one more for the road, was killed in an automobile accident. Still, a widow, too, a soft little widow, has repute the world over for causing the hearts of gentlemen to beat warm and fast. Mrs. Ewing and her friends felt sure that she would marry again. Time slid on, and this did not happen.

Mrs. Ewing never vaunted her lorn condition, never shut herself within the shaded chambers of bereavement. She went right along, skipping and tinkling through all the social events of the town, and no week went by without her presiding in her own house over cheerful little dinners or evenings of passionate bridge. She was always the same, and always the same to everyone, although she reached her heights when there were men present. She coquetted with the solid husbands of her friends, and with the two or three bachelors of the town, tremulous antiques pouring pills into their palms at the dinner table, she was sprightly to the verge of naughtiness. To a stranger observing her might have come the thought that Mrs. Ewing was not a woman who easily abandoned hope.

Mrs. Ewing had a daughter: Lolita. It is, of course, the right of parents to name their offspring what they please, yet it would sometimes be easier if they could glimpse the future and see what the little one was going to look like later on. Lolita was of no color at all; she was thin, with insistent knobs at the ends of her bones, and her hair, so fine that it seemed sparse, grew straight. There was a time when Mrs. Ewing, probably hostess to fantasies about a curly-headed tot, took to wetting the child's hair severely and rolling it up on strips of rags when she went to bed. But when the strips were untied in the morning, down fell the hair again, straight as ever. All that came of the project was a series of white nights for Lolita, trying to rest her head on the hard knots of the rags. So the whole thing was given up, and her hair hung as it must thereafter. In her early days at school, the little boys would chase her around the schoolyard at recess, snatching at the limp strands and crying, "Oh, Lolita, give us a curl, willya? Ah, Lolita, give us one of your pretty curls!" The little girls, her little friends, would gather in a group to watch and say "Oo, aren't they terrible?" and press their hands against their mouths to control their giggles.

Mrs. Ewing was always her own sparkling self with her daughter, but her friends, mothers of born belles, tried to imagine themselves in her place and their hearts ached for her. Gallant in their own way, they found cases to relate to her, cases of girls who went through periods of being plain and then turned suddenly into dazzling beauties; some of the more scholarly brought up references to the story of the ugly duckling. But Lolita passed through young girlhood and came of age and the only difference in her was that she was taller.

The friends did not dislike Lolita. They spoke sweetly to her and when she was not present always inquired of her mother about her, although knowing there would be no news. Their exasperation was not with her but with the Fates, who had foisted upon Mrs. Ewing that pale gawk—one, moreover, with no spirit, with never a word to say for herself. For Lolita was quiet, so quiet that often you would not realize she was in the room, until the light shone on her glasses. There was nothing to do about it; there were no hopeful anecdotes to cover the condition. The friends, thinking of their own winging, twittering young, sighed again for Mrs. Ewing.

There were no beaux draped along the railing of the Ewing porch in the evening; no young male voices asked for Lolita over the telephone. At first seldom, then not at all, did the other girls ask her to their parties. This was no mark of dislike; it was only that it was difficult to bear her in mind, since school was done with for all of them and they no longer saw her daily. Mrs. Ewing always had her present at her own little soirees, though the Lord knew she added nothing to them, and, dauntless, took her along to the public events attended by both old and young, festivals for the benefit of church or charity or civic embellishment. Even when brought into such festivities, Lolita would find a corner and stay there in her quiet. Her mother would call to her across the big public room, carolling high and clear above the social clatter: "Well, come on there, little old Miss Stick-in-the-Mud! Get up on your feet and start mixing around with people!" Lolita would only smile and stay where she was, quiet as she was. There was nothing morose about her stillness. Her face, if you remembered to see it, had a look of shy welcoming, and her smile might have been set high in the tiny list of her attractions. But such attributes are valuable only when they can be quickly recognized; who has time to go searching?

It often happens in the instance of an unsought maiden daughter and a gay little mother that the girl takes over the running of the house, lifting the burden from the mother's plump shoulders. But not Lolita. She had no domestic talents. Sewing was a dark mystery to her, and if she ventured into the kitchen to attempt some simple dish, the results would be, at best, ludicrous. Nor could she set a room in pretty order. Lamps shivered, ornaments shattered, water slopped out of flower vases before her touch. Mrs. Ewing never chided the girl for her clumsiness; she made jokes about it. Lolita's hands shook under railleries, and there would be only more spilled water and more splintered shepherdesses.

She could not even do the marketing successfully, although armed with a resume of the needs of the day in her mother's curly handwriting. She would arrive at the market at the proper hour, the time it was filled with women, and then seem to be unable to push her way through them. She stood aside until later arrivals had been served before she could go to the counter and murmur her wants; and so Mrs. Ewing's lunch would be late. The household would have tottered if it had not been for the maid Mrs. Ewing had had for years—Mardy, the super-cook, the demon cleaner. The other ladies lived uneasily with their servants, ridden with fears that they might either leave or become spoiled, but Mrs. Ewing was cozy with Mardy. She was as vigorously winsome with the maid as with the better-born. They enjoyed laughing together, and right at hand was the subject of Lolita's incompetences.

Experiments palled, and finally Lolita was relieved of

domestic offices. She stayed still and silent; and time went on and Mrs. Ewing went on and on, bright as a bubble in the air.

Then there bloomed a certain spring, not gradually but all in a day, a season long to be referred to as the time John Marble came. The town had not before seen the like of John Marble. He looked as if he had just alighted from the chariot of the sun. He was tall and fair, and he could make no awkward move or utter no stumbling phrase. The girls lost all consciousness of the local young men, for they were nowhere as against John Marble. He was older than they—he had crossed thirty—and he must have been rich, for he had the best room at the Wade Hampton Inn and he drove a low, narrow car with a foreign name, a thing of grace and power. More, there was about him the magic of the transitory. There were the local young men, day after day, year in, year out. But John Marble had come on some real-estate dealings for his firm, some matters of properties outside the town limits, and when his business was done, he would go back to the great, glittering city where he lived. Time pressed; excitement heightened.

Through his business John Marble met important men of the town, the fathers of daughters, and there was eager entertaining for the brilliant stranger. The girls put on the fluffiest white, and tucked bunches of pink roses in their pale-blue sashes; their curls shone and swung like bells. In the twilight they sang little songs for John Marble, and one of them had a guitar. The local young men, whose evenings hung like wet seaweed around their necks, could only go in glum groups to the bowling alley or the moving-picture theater. Though the parties in John Marble's honor slackened, for he explained that because of the demands of his business he must regret invitations, still the girls impatiently refused appointments to the local young men, and stayed at home alone on the chance of a telephone call from John Marble. They beguiled the time of waiting by sketching his profile on the telephone pad. Sometimes they threw away their training and telephoned him, even as late as ten o'clock at night. When he answered, he was softly courteous, charmingly distressed that his work kept him from being with them. Then, more and more frequently, there was no answer to their calls. The switchboard operator at the inn merely reported that Mr. Marble was out.

Somehow, the difficulties in the way of coming nearer to John Marble seemed to stimulate the girls. They tossed their fragrant curls and let their laughter soar, and when they passed the Wade Hampton Inn, they less walked than sashayed. Their elders said that never in their memories had the young girls been so pretty and so spirited as they were that spring.

And with the whole townful of bright blossoms bended for his plucking, John Marble chose Lolita Ewing.

It was a courtship curiously without detail. John Marble would appear at the Ewing house in the evening, with no preliminary telephoning, and he and Lolita would sit on the porch while Mrs. Ewing went out among her friends. When she returned, she shut the gate behind her with a clang, and as she started up the brick path she uttered a loud, arch *"A-hem,"* as if to warn the young people of her coming, so that they might wrench themselves one from the other. But there was never a squeal of the porch swing, never a creak of a floor board—those noises that tell tales of scurryings to new positions. The only sound was of John Marble's voice, flowing easily along; and when Mrs. Ewing came up on the porch, John Marble would be lying in the swing and Lolita would be sitting in a wicker chair some five feet away from him, with her hands in her lap, and, of course, not a peep out of her. Mrs. Ewing's conscience would smite her at the knowledge of John Marble's one-sided evening, and so she would sit down and toss the ball of conversation in the air and keep it there with reports of the plot of the moving picture she had seen or the hands of the bridge game in which she had taken part. When she, even she, came to a pause, John Marble would rise and explain that the next day was to be a hard one for him and so he must go. Mrs. Ewing would stand at the porch steps and as he went down the path would call after him roguish instructions that he was not to do anything that she would not do.

When she and Lolita came in from the dark porch to the

lighted hall, Mrs. Ewing would look at her daughter in an entirely new way. Her eyes narrowed, her lips pressed together, and her mouth turned down at the corners. In silence she surveyed the girl, and still in silence not broken by even a good night, she would mount to her bedroom, and the sound of her closing door would fill the house.

The pattern of the evenings changed. John Marble no longer came to sit on the porch. He arrived in his beautiful car and took Lolita driving through the gentle dark. Mrs. Ewing's thoughts followed them. They would drive out in the country, they would turn off the road to a smooth dell with thick trees to keep it secret from passersby, and there the car would stop. And what would happen then? Did they—Would they— But Mrs. Ewing's thoughts could go no farther. There would come before her a picture of Lolita, and so the thoughts would be finished by her laughter.

All the days, now, she contined to regard the girl under lowered lids, and the downturn of her mouth became a habit with her, though not among her prettier ones. She seldom spoke to Lolita directly, but she still made jokes. When a wider audience was wanting, she called upon Mardy. "Hi, Mardy!" she would cry. "Come on in here, will you? Come in and look at her, sitting there like a queen. Little Miss High-and-Mighty, now she thinks she's caught her a beau!"

There was no announcement of engagement. It was not necessary, for the town sizzled with the news of John Marble and Lolita Ewing. There were two schools of thought as to the match: one blessed Heaven that Lolita had gained a man and the other mourned the callousness of a girl who could go away and leave her mother alone. But miracles were scarce in the annals of the town, and the first school had the more adherents. There was no time for engagement rites. John Marble's business was concluded, and he must go back. There were scarcely hours enough to make ready for the wedding.

It was a big wedding. John Marble first suggested, then stated, that his own plan would be for Lolita and him to go off alone, be married, and then start at once for New York; but

Mrs. Ewing paid him no heed. "No, *sir*," she said. "Nobody's going to do *me* out of a great big lovely wedding!" And so nobody did.

Lolita in her bridal attire answered her mother's description of looking like nothing at all. The shiny white fabric of her gown was hostile to her colorless skin, and there was no way to pin the veil becomingly on her hair. But Mrs. Ewing more than made up for her. All in pink ruffles caught up with clusters of false forget-me-nots, Mrs. Ewing was at once bold sunlight and new moonlight, she was budding boughs and opening petals and little, willful breezes. She tripped through the throngs in the smilax-garlanded house, and everywhere was heard her laughter. She patted the bridegroom on arm and cheek, and cried out, to guest after guest, that for two cents she would marry him herself. When the time came to throw rice after the departing couple, she was positively devil-may-care. Indeed, so extravagant was her pitching that one hard-packed handful of the sharp little grains hit the bride squarely in the face.

But when the car was driven off, she stood still looking after it, and there came from her downturned mouth a laugh not at all like her usual trill. "Well," she said, "we'll see." Then she was Mrs. Ewing again, running and chirping and urging more punch on her guests.

Lolita wrote to her mother every week without fail, telling of her apartment and the buying and placing of furniture and the always new adventure of shopping; each letter concluded with the information that John hoped Mrs. Ewing was well and sent her his love. The friends eagerly inquired about the bride, wanting to know above all if she was happy. Mrs. Ewing replied that well, yes, she said she was. "That's what I tell her every time I write to her," she said. "I say, 'That's right, honey, you go ahead and be happy just as long as you can.' "

It cannot be said in full truth that Lolita was missed in the town; but there was something lacking in the Ewing house, something lacking in Mrs. Ewing herself. Her friends could not actually define what it was, for she went on as always, flirting the skirts of her little dresses and trying on her little hair ribbons, and there was no slowing of her movements. Still, the glister was not quite so golden. The dinners and the bridge games continued, but somehow they were not as they had been.

Yet the friends must realize she had taken a stunning blow, for Mardy left her; left her, if you please, for the preposterous project of getting married; Mardy, after all the years and all Mrs. Ewing's goodness to her. The friends shook their heads, but Mrs. Ewing, after the first shock, could be gay about it. "I declare," she said, and her laugh spiralled out, "everybody around me goes off and gets married. I'm just a regular little old Mrs. Cupid." In the long line of new maids there were no Mardys; the once cheerful little dinners were gloomy with grease.

Mrs. Ewing made several journeys to see her daughter and son-in-law, bearing gifts of black-eyed peas and tins of herring roe, for New Yorkers do not know how to live and such delicacies are not easily obtained up North. Her visits were widely spaced; there was a stretch of nearly a year between two of them, while Lolita and John Marble travelled in Europe and then went to Mexico. ("Like hens on hot griddles," Mrs. Ewing said. "People ought to stay put.")

Each time she came back from New York, her friends gathered about her, clamoring for reports. Naturally, they quivered for news of oncoming babies. There was none to tell them. There was never any issue of those golden loins and that plank of a body. "Oh, it's just as well," Mrs. Ewing said comfortably, and left the subject there.

John Marble and Lolita were just the same, the friends were told.

John Marble was as devastating as he had been when he first came to the town, and Lolita still had not a word to say for herself. Though her tenth wedding anniversary was coming close, she could not yet give shape to her dresses. She had closets of expensive clothes—when Mrs. Ewing quoted the prices of some of the garments, the friends sucked in their breath sharply—but when she put on a new dress it might as well have been the old one. They had friends, and they entertained quite nicely, and they sometimes went out. Well, yes, they did seem so; they really did seem happy.

"It's just like I tell Lolita," Mrs. Ewing said. "Just like I always say to her when I write: 'You go ahead and be happy as long as you can.' Because—Well, you know. A man like John Marble married to a girl like Lolita! But she knows she can always come here. This house is her home. She can always come back to her mother."

For Mrs. Ewing was not a woman who easily abandoned hope.

The Bolt behind the Blue

Miss Mary Nicholl was poor and plain, which afflictions compelled her, when she was in the presence of a more blessed lady, to vacillate between squirming humility and spitting envy. The more blessed lady, her friend Mrs. Hazelton, enjoyed Miss Nicholl's visits occasionally; humility is a seemly tribute to a favorite of fate, and to be the cause of envy is cozy to the ego. The visits had to be kept only occasional, though. With the years, Miss Nicholl grew no less flat in the purse and no more delightful to the eye, and it is a boresome business to go on and on feeling tenderness for one whose luck never changes.

Miss Nicholl worked as secretary to a stern and sterling woman. For seven hours a day she sat in a small room lined with filing cabinets where at half-past twelve precisely was put upon her desk, next to her typewriter, a tray set forth with the produce of the stern and sterling one's favorite health-food shop. The job was permanent and the lunches insured Miss Nicholl against constipation, yet it is to be admitted that her daily round lacked color and height. Those were fine occasions for her when, her work done, she might cover her typewriter and go to call on Mrs. Hazelton, to tread the gleaming halls, to sit in the long blue drawing room, to stroke the delicate cocktail glass and warm her spirit in its icy contents.

And her enjoyment did not die with her leave-taking; indeed, it took on strong new life. She would go home to the house where she roomed, summon Miss Christie who lived across the hall, and tell about her excursion into elegance. Miss Nicholl had a keen eye and a magnetic memory; she described every curve of furniture, every stretch of fabric, every ornament, every arrangement of flowers. She went long and full into the details of Mrs. Hazelton's costume, and all but called each pearl by name. Miss Christie was employed in a combined lending library and gift shop, all a-twist with potted philodendron; in her life there was none such as Mrs. Hazelton. She hung on every word of the recital. So did Miss Nicholl.

Fortune had upended her cornucopia to hurtle gifts upon Alicia Hazelton. She was beautiful, modeled after the design of an earlier day, when there were not just good-looking women, there were great beauties. She would have been perfectly placed in a victoria, holding a tiny jointed parasol, or tooling down the avenue on the box of a coach, seated next the gentleman in the grey topper who managed the reins. She was large and soft and white and golden. Though she was quite complacent about her massive shoulders and bosom, her real pride lay in her exquisite feet and ankles. Mrs. Hazelton knew too much about her style to essay short skirts, and she never would have slung one knee over the other, but each time she sat she tweaked up her draperies and left on view those ankles, lightly crossed. And she was rich. She was not wealthy or well-to-do or comfortably off; in the popular phrase, Mrs. Hazelton was loaded. And she had had three husbands and three divorces. To Miss Nicholl, whose experiences had not encompassed so much as a furtive pressure of the hand, there seemed to be always present behind Mrs. Hazelton's chair an invisible trio of the adoring and discarded.

If Mrs. Hazelton had been asked, she would have answered that she had known Miss Nicholl for, oh, Lord, ages and ages—so long she couldn't remember how the acquaintanceship had begun. Miss Nicholl could have reminded her. Once, the stern and sterling one had sent Miss Nicholl to Mrs. Hazelton with tickets for a charity benefit, under orders to see the lady in person and get the money for them right then. Mrs. Hazelton, warmed with the altruistic exercise of writing a check, had invited Miss Nicholl to sit down, had given her a cocktail, and, as she left, had bidden her to drop in any time.

Miss Christie had not had these circumstances explained to her. Exact words were never spoken, but Miss Christie had come to live in the belief that Miss Nicholl and Mrs. Hazelton had grown up together, would in fact have made a joint debut had it not been for the death of Miss Nicholl's father, too innocent a soul to mistrust the dastard who managed his financial affairs; so Miss Nicholl had had to go to work and, naturally, her path had split wide from Mrs. Hazelton's. But they always kept in touch with each other. Miss Christie thought that was simply lovely.

As fervently as she cherished Mrs. Hazelton's invitation given at their first meeting, Miss Nicholl did not presume on it. She never did drop in. She always telephoned to inquire if she might come in for a little while the next day or the day after it, on her way from work. If she was told that Mrs. Hazelton would be out or occupied or ill, she let weeks go by before she tried again. Frequently there were long dry reaches between her visits.

It was after such a lapse that Miss Nicholl telephoned one day and heard Mrs. Hazelton answer the call herself and warmly tell her to come that very afternoon. When Miss Nicholl had replaced the receiver, she went through three different sorts of glow. The first was of pure pleasure, the next of exasperation that the blouse she had on was well into its second day, and the third of stormy frustration that Miss Christie had been summoned to New Jersey to attend the sickbed of someone spoken of as Auntie Dee-dee, and would be away at least overnight.

Still, Miss Nicholl could depend on her memory never to slack; as soon as Miss Christie returned, after Auntie Dee-dee had either recovered or done whatever it was she was going to do, Miss Nicholl would be quite ready with the account of the appointment with Mrs. Hazelton. So the glow of pleasure came back and stayed. It was high in her when she arrived at Mrs. Hazelton's and caroled to the maid who opened the door, "Well, Dellie, it's been a long time since we've seen each other, hasn't it?"

It is heartening to speak easily with the servants. It shows how solidly you are accepted in the house.

Miss Nicholl had made her telephone call at a most fortunate time for herself. For four days, Mrs. Hazelton had not stirred beyond her own walls. For four days, she had heard no voices save those of the maids and that of her little daughter, who was kept at home by a cold. Worse, she had heard scarcely a word of her own. The servants were too adept to require spoken orders, and there are limits to the number of times you can ask a child if she has any fever. Miss Nicholl's proposed visit took on something in the nature of a godsend. The Nicholl admiration was thick and sweet, and Mrs. Hazelton craved honey. Besides, Miss Nicholl was older than Mrs. Hazelton by a year or so and looked it by a decade. A thing like that can be a comfort on a dismal day.

Yet, as she awaited her guest, Mrs. Hazelton's anticipation was not without alloy. The thought of Miss Nicholl always brought with it a nasty little guilt. She supposed she really ought to do more for the poor thing. But what more could she do? It was unthinkable that you could tuck a folded twenty-dollar bill into her dry palm; such people were so impossibly sensitive about being objects of charity. You could have her come to see you, feed her a drink, let her look at your pretty flowers, maybe give her some little thing you were through with—such a donation, unlike cash, wounded no feelings. Perhaps she might let her come oftener, and she must remember to keep Mary Nicholl's name on the Christmas list. Such plans were soothing to a degree, but still the guilt sneaked back, and with it came, of course, the irritation toward the one that caused it. Mrs. Hazelton, sitting waiting for Miss Nicholl, tapped her foot.

But when Miss Nicholl came into the drawing room, she was welcomed charmingly. The two ladies exchanged embraces—Mrs. Hazelton smelled like a summer afternoon in Heaven—and sat down opposite each other, smiling. It was no trouble to smile when looking at Mrs. Hazelton. With the folds of her chiffon tea gown flowing along her figure and her little Yorkshire terrier lying curled at her feet beside the high-heeled tapering slippers that were made for her in Rome, she was like an admirably composed canvas. The dog, Bonne Bouche—she had been christened before Mrs. Hazelton bought her—wore on her head, in the manner of the fashionables among her tribe, a bow of satin ribbon holding back her silvery bangs. Bonne Bouche was all that Mrs. Hazelton could ask of a pet. She was tiny, she was noiseless, and she had a real talent for sleeping. Mrs. Hazelton loved her truly.

Mrs. Hazelton's view from across the room was less agreeable. Before her eyes was Miss Nicholl, sitting there, as was her way, with no part of her touching the back of the chair.

"Dreadful the way we never see each other," Mrs. Hazelton said. "Oh, this city, this city! So rushed you don't have a chance to lay eyes on an old friend. It's been so long, I honestly thought you might have changed—I swear I did. But nothing like that. You never do change, you lucky thing, you."

With the exception of the last four, Mrs. Hazelton could not have uttered truer words. Miss Nicholl had not altered in appearance since back beyond her school days; it is possible, indeed, that those who had gazed on her infant face had found her a seamy baby. Her features were less chiseled than hewn, and long lines ran beside her mouth and across her grainy brow. She was of a ruthless trimness. Her belt was cinched so tight that, looking at it, you could hardly draw your own breath, the stiff waves of her hair were netted to her skull, her skirt snapped sharply at her legs. She wore, to pin the collar of her blouse all shipshape, a pansy of lavender enamel with a minute diamond forming an unconvincing dewdrop on one petal. Mrs. Hazelton had never seen her without this ornament. Nor had anybody else.

"Oh, I'm the same tacky old me," Miss Nicholl said. "But you—well, you're lovelier than ever."

"You really think I don't look too awful?" Mrs. Hazelton said.

"I never heard such talk," Miss Nicholl said. "You're just plain gorgeous, that's all you are."

"Oh, now really!" Mrs. Hazelton said.

The maid entered, carrying a tray on which were cocktail glasses and a crystal shaker. She set the tray on a table, filled two glasses, gave one to Miss Nicholl—who cried out, "Why,

Dellie, how *nice!*"—and the other to the hostess. The ladies sipped. Dellie, as quietly as she had come, left them alone together again.

"Oooo—yummy!" Miss Nicholl said. "What a treat! I haven't had a cocktail since—why it must be since the last time I was here. Sometimes I simply long for one—times when it's just beginning to get dark. Well, one thing about being poor— I'll never fill a drunkard's grave. When you can't afford cocktails, you have to get along without, that's all. Oh, I'm not complaining. I'd be a fine one to complain, now wouldn't I, when I can sit here with you. There you are, just the way I always think about you. No, wait a minute! Isn't there something different? I can't quite decide what it is. Now, don't you go tell me. Oh, I know! Didn't you used to wear two long strings of pearls?"

Mrs. Hazelton had done so; now she wore only one long rope, while around her neck were three tight strands. Some time before, she had chanced to look in her mirror when there was a mean light falling on it. She saw signs, and chilled as she saw them, of certain swags under her chin, if not yet reality, then certainly warning. So she had taken one length of pearls to her jeweler's where it was cut into the triple neckband, to clasp her throat and keep its secret.

"I had the other long one made into these," she said. "They're smarter. So many women are wearing them like this."

"Naturally, after you started the style," Miss Nicholl said. "Yes, they do look smart, I suppose. But if I must be brutally frank, I'd have to say I think I like them better the way they were."

"Oh, you do?" Mrs. Hazelton said.

"I always feel that pearls show up better in a long string," Miss Nicholl said. "You know—like flowing. I suppose it's because I love them so much—well, you know me and pearls. Really, there are times I've thought to myself, if I ever decide to go wrong, I'd do it for pearls."

"Fortunately, I've never had to do quite that," Mrs. Hazelton said. Miss Nicholl laughed. Mrs. Hazelton joined her, courteously, after a moment.

"Just to look at you," Miss Nicholl said, "a person would know you'd always had them."

"Of course, such things are a matter of luck," Mrs. Hazelton said.

"Some people seem to have all of it," Miss Nicholl said. She took rather more than a sip of her cocktail. "Well, tell me about everything. How's our little girl?"

"She's fine," Mrs. Hazelton said. "Oh, no, she isn't, either. She's got a cold."

"Poor little trick!" Miss Nicholl said. "She must be pretty big now, isn't she? It's so long since I've seen her." Miss Nicholl's pause let it be known that the time lag was no fault of hers.

"Yes, she's enormous," Mrs. Hazelton said. "Well, after all, she's eleven."

"Such a fascinating age!" Miss Nicholl said. "You and she must have high old times together."

"Yes, Ewie's great fun," Mrs. Hazelton said.

"You still call her Ewie?" Miss Nicholl asked.

"Everyone does," Mrs. Hazelton said.

"Well, it's kind of cute, of course," Miss Nicholl said. "Still, it does seem a shame. Stephanie is such an adorable name."

"Not," Mrs. Hazelton said, "when you remember that her father's name was Stephen."

"Do you ever talk to her about her father?" Miss Nicholl asked.

"My dear, the child is only eleven years old," Mrs. Hazelton said.

"Now tell me what you've been up to, while my back was turned," Miss Nicholl said. "For all I knew, you might have gone and got yourself married again."

"No, thank you," Mrs. Hazelton said. "No more marrying for me, thank you very much. You know the old saying: once bit, twice shy." She sat back mysteriously confident that the adage applied to her case.

"Oh, you're wise!" Miss Nicholl said. "Wise *and* beautiful— you've got everything. What do you need a husband for? Now me, I don't for a moment regret I never tried marriage. People say, 'But don't you ever get lonely?' I wouldn't pay them the compliment of listening to them. All I do, I just simply say to them, 'If a woman can't think of something to do to keep herself from being lonely, it's her own fault.' "

"That's what *I* think, certainly," Mrs. Hazelton said.

But she did not. She did not know what she thought about such things lately. She had been back from her last visit to Nevada for a long while during which she had done nothing startling to keep herself vivid before her friends—God, how people do get used to you! On her previous returns from her quests for freedom, invitations had whirled about her like blown snow; now they trickled in, slow and thin. Oh, of course there were various bids for her presence, but there was no excitement to them. And actually, once or twice, the plea that she come to dine had concluded with those words that are like the thud of clods on a coffin-lid: "Just us, you know—you don't mind if we don't get a man for you, do you, darling?" Lord in Heaven, was she, Alicia Hazelton, becoming an extra woman?

"You'll never have to worry about being alone," Miss Nicholl said. "You—with the whole town clamoring after you."

"Oh—that," Mrs. Hazelton said. Suddenly she looked closely at Miss Nicholl. "Mary," she said, "tell me. What do you do evenings?"

"Why, I don't know," Miss Nicholl said. "Different things—" She broke off in a high, wild cry; Mrs. Hazelton's daughter had come into the room. "There she is!" shrieked Miss Nicholl. "There her was! There's her mother's ewe lamb!"

Ewie was a pretty thing, tall and slender, with skin white as cherry bloom, waving red-gold hair cut close to her fine head, and long, straight red-gold eyelashes.

"You remember Miss Nicholl, Ewie," Mrs. Hazelton said. "Go say how-do-you-do to her."

Ewie went to Miss Nicholl, let her hand touch Miss Nicholl's hand, and kicked a little curtsy, the very awkwardness of which would have been irresistible in a smaller child.

"She's simply beautiful—the picture of her mother!" Miss

Nicholl said. "Well, aren't I going to get a kiss, Ewie? Just for old times' sake?"

"I've got a head cold," Ewie said. She left Miss Nicholl and rushed to the dog. She picked her up and pressed kisses on her infinitesimal nose.

"Ah, de Bouchie-wouchie," she said. "Ah, de baby angel."

"Ewie!" Mrs. Hazelton said. "Stop kissing the dog. With your cold."

Ewie replaced Bonne Bouche, who immediately returned to slumber. Then she sat down on a sofa and began humming a private, tuneless selection.

"Don't slump like that," Mrs. Hazelton said. "Look at Miss Nicholl. See how nice and straight she sits."

Ewie looked at Miss Nicholl and looked away again.

"I'm so sorry you have a cold," Miss Nicholl said. "It's a shame."

"Oh, it's much better," Mrs. Hazelton said.

"It'll be worse to-night," Ewie said. "Dellie says that's the dangerous thing about head colds, they always get worse at night. They go up into your sinuses or something. She says sometimes they get so bad you have to have a terrible operation."

"Well, you won't have to have anything like that," Mrs. Hazelton said.

"I might," Ewie said. She hummed again.

"Oh, this beautiful room!" Miss Nicholl said. "Those flowers! You always have white flowers, don't you, lady fair?"

"Yes, always," Mrs. Hazelton said. She always did, ever since she had read of a leader of society who permitted none but white blossoms in her home.

"They're just like you," Miss Nicholl said. She looked at an array of stock like a great white fountain, started to count the sprays, felt vertigo coming on, and gave it up.

"These are on their last legs," Mrs. Hazelton said. "The florist will be here tomorrow. He changes them every three days."

"Three days, you extravagant pussy-cat!" Miss Nicholl

cried. "Oh, why can't I take care of your flowers? I've got a green thumb."

Ewie's eyelashes sprang apart. She looked eagerly at Miss Nicholl.

"You have?" she breathed. "Is it on the hand you shook hands with me with? Ah, I didn't see it. Show it to me."

"Oh, no, dear," Miss Nicholl said. "It isn't a real one. It's just a way of saying that flowers will do anything for you."

"Oh, shoot!" Ewie said. She went back to her musical abstraction.

"Ewe lamb, if you could manage to stop that clinging, somehow," Mrs. Hazelton said. "Pour some fresh in Miss Nicholl's glass."

Ewie rose, gave Miss Nicholl a drink ("Why, *thank* you, you sweet thing!"), and watched her sip.

"Do you like that stuff?" she said. "I think it tastes like medicine."

"Well, it is a kind of medicine, you know," Miss Nicholl said. "A lovely kind. It does so much good for poor sick people."

Ewie drew closer. "Are you sick?" she asked. "What've you got the matter with you?"

"I'm not sick, precious," Miss Nicholl said. "I only said that. It was just a sort of figure of speech. Have you had figures of speech in school?"

"That's next year," Ewie said. "With Miss Fosdeck; I hate her. What kind of sick people is it good for?"

"Oh, Ewie, for heaven's sake!" Mrs. Hazelton said.

"I didn't mean really sick," Miss Nicholl said. "I meant people who are, well—people who are blue."

"You know what?" Ewie said. "Dellie knew this baby and it got born too soon, and it was blue. Dark blue. All over."

"But I'm sure Dellie said it's all right now, didn't she?" Miss Nicholl said.

"It died," Ewie said. "Dellie says all those cases are doomed. Doomed from the womb." The remembered phrase caught her fancy, and she chuckled.

"Oh, Dellie says, Dellie says!" Mrs. Hazelton said. "You'll turn into a Dellie-says one of these fine days if you don't watch out. Why don't you go and sit down and be sweet?"

Ewie went and sat down and was sweet, save that she resumed her song, this time adding as a lyric "doomed from the womb, oh-h, doomed from the womb," until her mother's voice drowned her out.

"Ewie, *stop that!*" Mrs. Hazelton screamed.

"You still haven't told me what you've been doing," Miss Nicholl said quickly to Mrs. Hazelton. "But I can guess—I know you, lady fair. Nothing but parties, parties, parties, every day and every night. Aren't I right?"

"No, my dear," Mrs. Hazelton said. "I've taken a vow to let up. Daytime things, lunch and fashion openings and cocktails and all that, yes, but oh, those late nights, every blessed night!"

"Oh, you haven't been out at night for ages," Ewie said.

"Naturally," Mrs. Hazelton said. "When my only child is sick, I'm not going to leave her here alone."

"Dellie was here," Ewie said. "Anyway, you haven't gone out at night since before I got my head cold."

"If I choose to stay at home for an evening of quiet now and then, I can do it without any comment from you," Mrs. Hazelton said.

Ewie took up her aria again, but with no words. She also occupied herself with forming tiny pleats in the skirt of her frock, pressing them sharp with a thumbnail.

"I bet you've been doing a lot of entertaining, yourself," Miss Nicholl said.

"Oh, it's so hard to get up the energy," Mrs. Hazelton said. "And this season's crop of extra men! They're about the right age for Ewie. They make me feel a hundred years old."

"You! Old!" Miss Nicholl said.

"I can't stand them hanging around the house, messing on my carpets," Mrs. Hazelton said. "I know lots of women invite them, but—well, let them. It's their funeral."

Ewie ceased her activities. "You know what?" she said. "I was in a funeral once."

"You were no such thing!" Mrs. Hazelton said.

"Oh, I was so, too!" Ewie said. "There was this big long funeral going down Fifth Avenue, and it was so long some of the last cars had to wait for a light, and so, why, I started to walk across to go to the park, and so there I was, right in the middle of it. Only Dellie yelled and yanked me back. She says it's terrible luck to go through a funeral. Once she had a cousin that did, and in two weeks, right smack to the day, her cousin died."

"I'm not sure that I like all this about Dellie yelling and yanking on Fifth Avenue," Mrs. Hazelton said. "That's the way they get when they've been with you so long—think they can do anything. Still, I can't imagine how I'd have ever got along without her. She practically brought Ewie up, you know."

"Yes, I can see the marks," Miss Nicholl said. "Oh, only fooling, lady fair, just my little joke. I've always said Dellie's a real treasure. Well, you always have perfect servants."

"There I was, bang in the middle of a funeral," Ewie said.

"I don't know what makes Ewie this way," Mrs. Hazelton said.

"Oh, all children are like that," Miss Nicholl said.

"I never was," Mrs. Hazelton said.

"Come to think of it, I don't believe I was either," Miss Nicholl said. "And you couldn't have been anything but perfect. Ever."

They considered Ewie, now both pleating and humming.

"So active," Miss Nicholl said. "Always busy."

"She never got that from her father," Mrs. Hazelton said. "That or anything else."

Ewie hummed higher.

"Ewe lamb, you don't think you've got any fever, do you?" Mrs. Hazelton said.

Ewie felt the back of her neck. "Not yet," she said.

"You're just about all well," Mrs. Hazelton said. "If it's a decent day tomorrow, you and Dellie can go to the park."

"Oh, what fun!" Miss Nicholl cried.

"It's Dellie's day off tomorrow," Ewie said. "She's going

over to see her sister. Her sister's husband's terribly sick."

"Hasn't Dellie got any healthy friends, honey-bunny?" Miss Nicholl said.

"Oh, she's got zillions of them," Ewie said. "There was seventeen, right in her family, only twelve of them died. Some of them were born dead, and the others had a liver condition. Dellie said it was nothing but bile, bile, bile—"

"Ewie, please," Mrs. Hazelton said. "No details, if you don't mind."

"Dellie says all the alive ones feel fine," Ewie said. "It's just this husband of her sister's. He can't work or anything, but Dellie says you wouldn't want to meet a lovelier man. He's good and sick. Dellie says her sister says she wouldn't be surprised if he started spitting blood, any day."

"Kindly stop that disgusting talk," Mrs. Hazelton said. "While we're trying to drink our cocktails."

"Well, I was only answering *her*," Ewie said, jerking her head in the direction of Miss Nicholl. "She asked me if Dellie had any healthy friends, and I told her all except that husband of her sister's and he—"

"That will do," Mrs. Hazelton said. "Now why don't you run along and ask Dellie to take your temperature? And then you can stay in the kitchen and talk to her and Ernestine."

"Can I take Bonne Bouche with me?" Ewie asked.

"I suppose so," Mrs. Hazelton said. She picked up the little dog. "But don't let Ernestine give her anything to eat besides her supper. She's beginning to lose her figure." She kissed Bonne Bouche on her hair ribbon. "Aren't you, darling?"

Ewie joyously received the dog into her arms. "Can we stay in the kitchen to have our supper?" she asked.

"Oh, all right, all right!" Mrs. Hazelton said.

"Oo brother!" Ewie said. She started for the door.

"Ewie, what's the matter with you, anyway?" Mrs. Hazelton said. "I tell you, I'm thinking seriously of changing that school of yours, next year. You have no more manners than a moose. Say good-by to Miss Nicholl, for heaven's sake."

Ewie turned toward Miss Nicholl and smiled at her—her smile, that had the rarity of all truly precious things. "Good-by, Miss Nicker," she said. "Please do come again very soon, won't you?"

"Oh, I will, you angel-pie," Miss Nicholl said.

Ewie, cooing to Bonne Bouche, left them.

"She's simply adorable!" Miss Nicholl said. "Oh, lady fair, why do you have to have everything in the world? Well, you deserve it, that's all I can say. That's what keeps me from murdering you, right this minute."

"Oh, you mustn't do that," Mrs. Hazelton said.

"If I could only have a sweet, happy little girl like Ewie, that's all I would ask," Miss Nicholl said. "You don't know how I've always wanted to have a child all my own. Without having any old man mixed up in it."

"I'm afraid that would be rather hard to accomplish," Mrs. Hazelton said. "I guess you'd just have to take the bitter along with the sweet, like the rest of us. Well. What were we talking about before Ewie barged in? Oh, yes—what *do* you do in the evenings?"

"Why, after I'm through work," Miss Nicholl said, "I really feel I've earned a little enjoyment. So when I get home, after I've cleaned up, Idabel and I—"

"Who?" Mrs. Hazelton said.

"Idabel Christie," Miss Nicholl said. "That has the room across the hall from me. You know—I've told you about her."

"Oh, yes, of course," Mrs. Hazelton said. "I forgot for a moment her name was Idabel. I don't know how I came to."

"It's an odd name," Miss Nicholl said. "But I think it's rather sweet, don't you?"

"Yes, charming," Mrs. Hazelton said.

"Anyway, we do all sorts of things," Miss Nicholl said. "When we're feeling rich, we go to dinner at the Candlewick Tea Room—terribly nice, and just around the corner from us. It's so pretty—candles, and yellow tablecloths and a little bunch of different-colored immortelles, dyed I guess they are, on every table. It's those little touches that make the place. And the food! Idabel and I always say to each other when we go in, 'All diet abandon, ye who enter here.' "

"*You* don't have to diet," Mrs. Hazelton said. "You're one of those fortunate people."

"Me fortunate! Well, that's a new picture of yours truly," Miss Nicholl said. "One thing, though, I don't want to flesh up, if I can help it. But oh, those yummy sticky rolls, served in little baskets, and that prune spin with maraschino cherries in it! Idabel Christie likes the fudge cup-custard, but I can't resist the prune spin."

Only a tiny ripple along her chiffons told that Mrs. Hazelton shuddered.

"Well, of course the Candlewick couldn't be farther away from this," Miss Nicholl said. "You'd probably laugh at it."

"Why, I wouldn't at all," Mrs. Hazelton said.

"Yes, you would," Miss Nicholl said. "You don't know about how, when you can have so few things, you have to like the thing you *can* have. We can't go to the Candlewick very often. It's not at all cheap, I mean for us. You can hardly get out of there much under two dollars apiece with the tip. Listen to me! I bet you never heard of as little as two dollars."

"Now stop it," Mrs. Hazelton said.

"There's another thing about the Candie—we call it the Candie to ourselves," Miss Nicholl said. "You have to get there pretty fairly early. It's so small and it's grown so popular you haven't a chance of a table after six o'clock."

"But when you're through dinner doesn't that make an awfully long evening for you?" Mrs. Hazelton asked.

"That's what we like," Miss Nicholl said. "We have to get up in the morning—we're woiking goils, you know. Usually, when we go to the Candie, we make a real binge of it and go to a movie afterward. And sometimes, when we feel just wild, we go to the theater. But that's pretty seldom. The price of tickets, these days!"

"You do?" Mrs. Hazelton asked. "You go to the theater alone together? Oh, I wouldn't dare do that!"

"I don't think anybody would try to hold us up," Miss Nicholl said. "And if they did, there's two of us."

"I didn't mean holdups," Mrs. Hazelton said. "It's only I've always been told nothing ages a woman so much as being seen at the theater in the evening with just another woman."

"Oh, really?" Miss Nicholl said.

"Oh, it certainly doesn't work with *you*," Mrs. Hazelton said. "Probably some silly old wives' tale, anyway. Well, but look. Suppose you don't go to the movies or the theater. Then what do you do?"

"We just stay home and do our nails and put up our hair and talk," Miss Nicholl said.

"That must be a comfort," Mrs. Hazelton said. "To have somebody to talk to whenever you feel like it right there in the house. A great comfort."

"Well, yes, it is, you know," Miss Nicholl cried.

"It's the only thing that could possibly make me give a thought to having another husband," Mrs. Hazelton said, slowly. "Somebody here, somebody to talk to you."

"Why, you've got Ewie!" Miss Nicholl cried.

"You've heard Ewie," Mrs. Hazelton said.

"Then some evenings," Miss Nicholl said, "when we don't feel like going out or talking or anything, we just go to our own rooms and read. Idabel Christie, oh, she's a wicked one! She works in a library, the way I've told you, and when she sees a book she knows I'd like, she hides it away for me, even if there's a long waiting list. I suppose I'm as bad as she is, for taking it."

"I simply must order some books," Mrs. Hazelton said. "There's not a new book in this house."

"Think of buying books, instead of borrowing them from a library!" Miss Nicholl said. "Think of being the first one to read them! Think of never having to touch another plastic jacket! Well, there's not much use dreaming about buying books, when you haven't got a decent rag to your back, is there? Oh, what a curse it is to be poor!"

"Mary Nicholl, no one would ever think about your being poor if you didn't talk about it so much," Mrs. Hazelton said.

"I don't care if they know," Miss Nicholl said. "I never heard that poverty was any disgrace. I'm not ashamed of it. However little money I may have, I earn every cent of it. There are some people who can't say that much for themselves."

"I'm sure you ought to be very proud," Mrs. Hazelton said.

"Well, I am, " Miss Nicholl said. "But I'd like to have just *some* clothes. The coat I've got to wear with this suit doesn't belong to the skirt. The skirt it belongs to—moths ate the whole seat right out of it. That makes you feel chic, going around with your—with the whole seat out of your skirt."

"I thought what you have on looks awfully nice," Mrs. Hazelton said.

"Well, let's talk about something prettier than my old rags," Miss Nicholl said. "I bet you've been getting yourself heaps and heaps of lovely new clothes, haven't you?"

"Oh, I've picked up a few little things," Mrs. Hazelton said. "Nothing very interesting. Would you like to see them?"

"*Would* I!" Miss Nicholl said.

"Well, come along," Mrs. Hazelton said. She rose, beautifully.

"Could I—" Miss Nicholl said. "I mean would I be awfully greedy if I just took what's left in the shaker of the lovely little cocktails?"

"Oh, of course," Mrs. Hazelton said. "I hope it's still cold."

Bearing her glass, which the remnant in the shaker could fill only partway, Miss Nicholl followed her hostess to a room dedicated to great deep closets. She stood close as Mrs. Hazelton slid along poles hangers bearing dress after dress, the cost of the least of which would have been two years' rent to Miss Nicholl.

"But, they're all new!" she cried. "All of them! Oh, what did you do with the old ones—the ones that weren't even old, I mean. What did you *do* with them?"

"Oh, I don't know," Mrs. Hazelton said. "Told Dellie to get rid of them somehow, I suppose. I was sick of the sight of them." It was apparent that the question had not interested her.

Miss Nicholl went to work, and put her shoulders into it. She piled up praises until she seemed to be building them into dizzy towers. Mrs. Hazelton did not speak, but there was encouragement in the way she looked distractedly about, as if searching her stores for something to give.

Higher and higher Miss Nicholl raised her towers; admiration glugged from her lips like syrup from a pitcher, and Mrs. Hazelton seemed again to be searching. Her quest stopped when she opened a drawer and took from it an evening purse covered with iridescent sequins. She insisted upon Miss Nicholl's accepting it.

Mrs. Hazelton was not an ungenerous lady, but she was not subject to imagination. Her most recent Christmas gift to Miss Nicholl had been a big jar of bath salts and a tall flagon of after-shaving lotion. The four women who lived on Miss Nicholl's floor shared its one bathroom. They all rose at the same hour in the morning; they retired at the same hour at night. To have commandeered the bathroom for the time required for lolling and anointing would have been considered, in their mildest phrase, piggish. So Miss Nicholl had set the unopened jar and flagon on her bureau, where they looked rich indeed and were much admired by Miss Christie. And now a sequinned purse, perfect to be carried with a ball gown.

Still, a present is a present, and Miss Nicholl positively writhed with gratitude.

She took the purse back to the drawing room when they returned from reviewing the wardrobe, and put it in her big black oilcloth handbag which, half a block away, could hardly be told from patent leather. Dellie had been in, removed the cocktail tray, and left no replacement. Miss Nicholl gave a little yelp as she saw darkness beyond the windows, and said she really ought to go. Mrs. Hazelton's protest was neither voiced nor worded stiffly enough to cause her to change her mind. Mrs. Hazelton seemed, in fact, somewhat languid, almost, if it was conceivable that anyone like her could have had anything to make her tired, a trifle weary.

"Mustn't take a chance on wearing out my welcome," Miss Nicholl said. "I always come dangerously near it, when I'm here—I can't tear myself away." She looked around the room.

"I just want to take the picture of this room away with me. Oh, I simply revel in all this wonderful space!"

"Yes, space is the greatest luxury to me," Mrs. Hazelton said.

Miss Nicholl made a small laugh. "It would be to me, too," she said, "but it's the costliest, isn't it? Or wouldn't you know, lady fair? Well, fare thee well. Lovely, lovely time."

"Be sure to come again," Mrs. Hazelton said. "Don't forget."

"I couldn't do that, ever," Miss Nicholl said. "I'm that regular old bad penny. I'll be turning up again before you know it."

"Well, I've got myself rather tangled up, all next week," Mrs. Hazelton said. "The week after, perhaps. Call up anyway."

"Oh, I will, never fear," Miss Nicholl said. "And thanks again, a zillion, for the wonderful evening purse. I'll think of you every time I use it."

Miss Nicholl was going home by bus; before she reached the bus stop, a vicious rain and an ugly wind attacked her. Such demonstrations worked evilly upon her spirit. As she fought through the elements, she talked to herself furiously, though her lips never moved.

"Well, that was a fine visit, I must say. A half-a-shaker of cocktails, and not even a cheese cracker. You'd think a person could do better than that, with all her money. And pushing me out in the pouring rain—never even suggesting staying to dinner. I suppose she's got a lot of her rich society friends coming, and I'm not good enough to associate with them. Not that I would have stayed, if she'd got down on her knees and begged me. I don't want anything to do with those people, thank you very much. I'd just be bored sick.

"And those faded flowers. And that awful Dellie, with never a smile out of her, no matter how democratic you try to be to her. The first thing I'd have, if I was rich, would be nice-mannered servants. You can always tell a lady by her servants' manners. And that little dog—acts to me as if it was drugged

"And all those clothes, on all those hangers. Why, it would take a girl twenty years old the rest of her life to wear half of them. Yes, and that's just who they're appropriate for, too—someone twenty years old. If there's anything I hate to see, it's a woman trying to keep young by dressing like a girl. Simply makes a laughing-stock of herself. And giving me that sequinned purse. What does she think I'm going to do with it, except stick it away in my bottom drawer? Because that's where it's going to go, with not even tissue paper around it—no, not even newspaper. Well, maybe I'll show it to Idabel first. It must have cost a mint; Idabel will enjoy seeing it. Oh, my God, Idabel won't be home. My whole afternoon, just wasted.

"Yes, and the gorgeous Mrs. Hazelton is putting on weight, too. She must be five pounds heavier than she was last time. My, it will just kill her to get fat. Just absolutely finish her. Well, she'll put on many a pound before I telephone her again. She can call me when she wants to see me. And I'm not so sure I'll come, either.

"And that child. That child doesn't look right to me. So pale, and all. And all that talk about sickness and funerals. There's no good behind that. It's like some sort of sign. It will be a big surprise to me if that child ever makes old bones.

"Not that it's the poor thing's fault. Her mother doesn't do a thing about her. Nothing but 'Stop that, Ewie,' and, 'Don't do that, Ewie.' Ewie, indeed—what a name! Sheer affectation. It's no wonder the poor thing likes that Dellie better than her mother. Oh, what a frightful thing it must be to have your own child turn from you! I don't see how she can sleep nights.

"What kind of life is that, sitting around in a teagown, counting her pearls? Pearls that size are nothing but vulgar, anyway. Why should she have all those things? She's never done anything—couldn't even keep a husband. It's awful to think of that empty existence; nothing to do but have breakfast in bed and spend money on herself. No, *sir*, she can have her pearls and her hangers and her money and her twice-a-week florist, and welcome to them. I swear, I wouldn't change places with Alicia Hazelton for anything on earth!"

It is a strange thing, but it is a fact. Though it had every justification, a bolt did not swoop from the sky and strike Miss Nicholl down, then and there.

Mrs. Hazelton, when Miss Nicholl was gone, sank into her chair, crossed her incomparable ankles, and smoothed her chiffon folds. She breathed the soft long sigh that comes after duty well done, though with effort. That was the trouble with such as Miss Nicholl—once they came, God, how they stayed. Well. The poor thing was so delighted with that purse; how little it took! Those binges with Miss What's-her-name from across the hall, in that tearoom with the little touches, the prune spin with cherries in it!

Ewie came in. "You know what?" she said. "Dellie's sister's husband is lots worse. Dellie's sister telephoned, and Dellie says it sounds to her as if her sister's husband is as good as a goner from what her sister says."

"I'm not interested," Mrs. Hazelton said. "It's quite enough to listen to what Dellie says, all day long, without having to hear what her sister says too."

Ewie sat down, mainly on her shoulders and the back of her neck. "Miss Nicker isn't very pretty, is she?" she said.

"Beauty isn't everything," Mrs. Hazelton said.

"I think she's the most terrible-looking person I ever saw," Ewie said. "And her clothes are something awful."

"They're not awful at all," Mrs. Hazelton said. "She dresses herself very sensibly, for her type. You're not to say a word against her, do you hear, Ewie? She's a wonderful woman."

"Why is she?" Ewie asked.

"Well, she works very hard," Mrs. Hazelton said, "and she doesn't do anybody any harm, and people like to do things for her because it gives her so much pleasure."

"I sort of feel sorry for her," Ewie said.

"You needn't," Mrs. Hazelton said. "She has more than a good many people. Much more."

She looked around the big, beautiful room, sweet with shimmering blossoms. She touched the pearls about her throat, twined her fingers in the long rope, and glanced down at the delicate slippers that were made for her in Rome.

"What's she got that's so much more?" Ewie asked.

"Why," Mrs. Hazelton said, "she hasn't any responsibilities, and she has a job that gives her something to do every day, and a nice room, and a lot of books to read, and she and her friend do all sorts of things in the evenings. Oh, let me tell you, I'd be more than glad to change places with Mary Nicholl!"

And again that bolt, though surely sufficiently provoked, stayed where it was, up in back of the blue.

PLAY REVIEWS

From *Vanity Fair*
1918 - 1920

Henrik Ibsen: *Hedda Gabler*

June 1918

In my present state of almost impenetrable gloom brought on by night after night of *April, Nancy Lee,* and *Once Upon a Time,* you don't know how it helps to have one good evening to look back on. You don't know what it means to me to be able to say a few kind words about something. I am almost overcome with happiness to be able to announce with heartfelt appreciation, that *Hedda Gabler* is something else again. Mr. Arthur Hopkins, who produced it, has my undying gratitude. He will never know all that he did for me.

I know all those things that the critics said about Nazimova's performance of *Hedda Gabler,* but I can't help it—I thought she was great. I know she was weird, and morbid, and exaggerated, and neurasthenic, and full of poses, and all those other things they called her, but that is my notion of the way she should have been. Somehow, I never could seem to picture Hedda Tesman as belonging to the Susanna Cocroft type. I thought Nazimova was consistently wonderful, from the moment of her first, bored entrance to the shot that marked her spectacular final exit. Shots almost always do mark the final exit of Mr. Ibsen's heroines.

I do wish that he had occasionally let the ladies take

bichloride of mercury, or turn on the gas, or do something quiet and neat around the house. I invariably miss most of the lines in the last act of an Ibsen play; I always have my fingers in my ears, waiting for the loud report that means that the heroine has just Passed On.

Lionel Atwill, as George Tesman, gave what seemed to me a flawless performance—and George Tesman is one of those parts that can be overdone almost without an effort; just one "Fancy that!" too many and you're gone. His make-up was perfect; I have never seen such a convincingly realistic goatee. That and his gold-rimmed spectacles changed him utterly. I never should have recognized him if he hadn't used the same green and red handkerchief that he did in *The Wild Duck.* Charles Bryant, as Judge Brack, seemed rather out of the picture. Everybody knew that the Judge didn't mean right by Hedda; I did wish he could have managed to look mean occasionally, instead of beaming paternally upon her all the time.

After *Hedda Gabler,* the season was over for me. There just wasn't one other thing that I could get all heated up about. My life was a long succession of thin evenings.

Oscar Wilde: *An Ideal Husband*

November 1918

Over at the Comedy, which has been all done over in honor of the event, John Williams is producing Oscar Wilde's *An Ideal Husband*—invariably spoken of as *The Ideal Husband* by the same group of intellectuals who always refer to *The Doll's House.* The company is one of exceptional brilliance (see advertisements) with Constance Collier, Beatrice Beckley, Norman Trevor, Julian L'Estrange, and Cyril Harcourt among those present. Constance Collier, many critics said, was hopelessly miscast as Mrs. Chevely, but she played the lady just as I have always pictured her, so I was perfectly happy. Beatrice Beckley has the thankless job of playing Lady Chiltern, one of those frightfully virtuous women of Wilde's who can't utter the simplest observation without dragging in such Sabbatical expressions as "we needs must." Norman Trevor, as Sir Robert Chiltern, seems to have adopted a new technique; the idea is to see how quickly he can get through his speeches. He broke all previously existing world's records in the second-act tirade about women's love. I thought that Julian L'Estrange reached the highest point of the whole production. He played Lord Goring apparently without an effort, taking the whole thing quite calmly, uttering his epigrams as if he had just happened to think them up that moment.

Somehow, no matter how well done an Oscar Wilde play may be, I always am far more absorbed in the audience than in the drama. There is something about them that never fails to enthrall me. They have a conscious exquisiteness, a deep appreciation of their own culture. They exude an atmosphere of the *New Republic*—a sort of Crolier-than-thou air. "Look at us," they seem to say. "We are the cognoscenti. We have come because we can appreciate this thing—we are not as you, poor bonehead, who are here because you couldn't get tickets for the Winter Garden." They walk slowly down the aisle and sink gracefully into their seats, trusting that all may note their presence, for the very fact of their being there is a proof of their erudition. From the moment of the curtain's rise they keep up a hum of approbation, a reassuring signal of their patronage and comprehension. "Oh, the lines, the lines!" they sigh, one to another, quite as if they were the first to discover that this Oscar Wilde is really a very promising young writer; and they use the word "scintillating" as frequently and as proudly as if they had just coined it. Yet there is about their enjoyment a slightly strained quality, almost as if they were striving to do what should be expected of those of their intellect. It isn't the sort of enjoyment that just sits back and listens; it is almost as if they felt they must be continually expressing their appreciation, to show that no epigrams get over their heads, to convince those about them of their cleverness and their impeccable taste in drama.

Leo Tolstoi: *Redemption*

December 1918

There is always this to be said for the epidemic of Spanish influenza—it gave the managers something to blame things on. Whenever a manager saw that all was practically over with a play, he hid his aching heart under the guise of a noble solicitude for the public welfare, and with an air of "It is a far, far better thing I do than I have ever done before," announced that the play would be removed, owing to the epidemic. If you are one of those who must ever go about the world finding good in everything, hold the thought that the Spanish influenza has helped many a play to make a graceful getaway.

It was a thin month for the drama, one way or another. There was one dark Saturday night when seven plays slunk out into the Great Unknown, among them *Someone in the House*—and I liked it so much, too—and *I.O.U.*, a dainty trifle in which, as a climax, Jose Ruben branded Mary Nash on the shoulder with a red-hot iron. Though that Saturday marked the crisis, the lean days are not yet over for the plays. Several of them are tossing fitfully, and two or three seem barely able to stagger through the week. It looks as if the managers would have to call in the aid of influenza again, to get them decently off to the warehouse.

There are still a few rays of light, however, even in the gathering gloom of the season. There is Tolstoi's *Redemption*, for instance—although "ray of light" isn't exactly a happy term for it. It isn't what you might call sunny. I went into the Plymouth Theatre a comparatively young woman, and I staggered out of it, three hours later, twenty years older, haggard and broken with suffering. It won't fill you all full of glad thoughts, and it isn't just the sort of thing to take the kiddies to, but won't you please see it, even if you have to mortgage the Dodge, sublet the apartment, and sell everything but your Liberty Bonds, to get tickets? Go and see it, so that you may come out and proclaim to the world that at last you have beheld a perfectly done play.

A more extraordinary production I have never seen. It is

difficult to speak of "atmosphere" and "feeling" without sounding as if one wore sandals and lived below Fourteenth Street, but you just can't mention Robert Jones' scenery without using the words. I never realized that so much atmosphere could be worked into one production. And it is gained with such seeming ease, too—gained by suggestion rather than by painstaking detail. The final curtain rises on "A corridor outside the courtroom"; Mr. Jones' scene consists of a bare, flat wall with two doors—that is all, yet it gives one a sense of mystery, of hopelessness, of unescapable tragedy. There is an unforgettable picture of the gypsies' house, with the gypsies grouped about a fire, and another of a drinking den in the slums—this last gruesomely dark save for the feeble table lights that shine on the ghastly faces of the drinkers. I humbly remove my hat—the bill for which I received for the third time, only this morning—to Mr. Jones. He is indubitably There.

Of John Barrymore's performance of the chief role, I can only say that, to me, it was flawless. I have heard people say that it was all too much in the same key, and I have heard other people observe that it was perhaps a little overdramatic; but then, I thought it should have been both those things. Fedya's life was all in the same key, and he was just the sort of person who would have done things dramatically. I thought Mr. Barrymore consistently fine; his death scene, where he leaps in agony like a mortally wounded animal, was simply remarkable.

There's only one thing I could wish about the whole play—I do wish they would do something about those Russian names. Owing to the local Russian custom of calling each person sometimes by all of his names, sometimes by only his first three or four, and sometimes by a nickname which has nothing to do with any of the other names, it is difficult for one with my congenital lowness of brow to gather exactly whom they are talking about. I do wish that as long as they are translating the thing, they would go right ahead, while they're at it, and translate Fedor Vasilyevich Protosov and Sergei Dmitrievich Abreskov and Ivan Petrovich Alexandrov into Joe and Harry and Fred.

Edward Knoblock: *Tiger! Tiger!*

January 1919

Often, in those long quiet hours when I am caught in a subway block, or sitting in the dentist's antechamber, or waiting for a Broadway car, I ponder sadly on the good old times that have passed beyond recall. Those were the happy days—the days when people rushed gladly to the theater, enjoyed every minute of it, applauded enthusiastically, wished there were more, and came out wreathed in smiles to spread abroad the glad tidings that "The show was great!" Why, some of them even, of their own free will, went back to see the same play over and over again. Yes, those were undoubtedly the days.

Think how hideously different things are now. We go heroically to the theater, hoping always, with piteous faith, that maybe it won't be so bad, after all—yet ever dreading, with the bitter fear born of cruel experience, that probably it will be worse. We sit patiently until we can decently leave, and then we come out with an air of, "Well, thank the Lord that's over." No more does anyone rush up to you on the street, crying hysterically, "You *must* see that show at the Knickerbocker. Best thing that's ever been put on! I've been to see it every night this week, and I'm on my way now to get seats for the matinee tomorrow!"

Do you ever hear anything like that any more? Echo unhesitatingly answers, "Certainly not!" Ask anyone what he thought of the show he went to see last night—just go ahead and ask him. The usual answer—provided he can recall the play at all—is a deep groan, followed by the mournful words, "The worst I ever sat through." The most enthusiastic reply you will get is a cold look and an unflattering, "Well—maybe *you* might like it."

Just what seems to be the trouble, anyway? Is it that the dizzy whirl of modern life has made us cold and blasé? Or is it, perhaps, that the plays themselves are just naturally poisonous?

Personally, I am a trifle inclined towards the latter theory—and the new plays are certainly backing me up in my opinion.

There is *Tiger! Tiger!*, Edward Knoblock's drama at the Belasco, for instance. Somehow, I cannot feel that the dizzy whirl of modern life had anything to do with my intense suffering during the performance—I hold the play itself directly responsible. The plot concerns the affair of a Member of Parliament with a cook—an affair which goes on for nearly three years. When, at the end of that time she decides to leave him, he makes a frightful scene, nearly bursting a blood vessel in his rage and disappointment. It seemed most unreasonable of him to behave that way; how could he expect a cook to stay in the same situation for more than three years? And he needn't have been so worked up, going around saying that he had nothing to live for, and all that. I know it's the natural way to feel when the cook leaves—but then, there are always the want ads.

The M. P. finally goes to war—where he should have gone early in the play—and gets himself killed. And as far as I was concerned, he was unlamented. Even Lionel Atwill's remarkably skillful acting couldn't make him seem anything but a cad to me. I have never beheld anyone who was so ready and willing to stay home from the war as that M. P. was. Goodness knows that I appreciate thoughtfulness and attention in a man; but when a large, strong, able-bodied Britisher won't go to war because a perfectly self-supporting woman says that she would miss him if he went—well, it seems to me to be a trifle over-obliging of him.

The whole play was absolutely unconvincing to me—possibly because Frances Starr never for one moment made me feel that she really was a cook. Then, too, the sentimental passages seemed to leave me cold. Because a young woman says "H'aint" and "you was," and admits that she "don't know nothin' about art," doesn't seem to me to be any particular reason for a man to clasp her passionately in his arms and tell her that she is a wild, sweet, fairy thing—a creature of the spring woods. Miss Starr's ringing recitals of the pathos of a cook's lot also failed to move me. The cooks I have known have never been in any way pathetic; they have always been the self-made, not to say aggressive type, who manage to get along very

well indeed without any outside assistance, and they'll thank
you to keep your sympathy to yourself.

J. M. Barrie: *Dear Brutus*

February 1919

There really isn't much to say for the life of a critic. In the first
place, it is entirely too spotty. There are long, quiet stretches
when he hasn't a thing to do with his evenings, and then there
are sudden outbursts of such violent activity that he nearly
succumbs to apoplexy. If only the managers could be induced
to spread things out a trifle thinner, much unnecessary
suffering would be averted. But no—managers aren't that way.
The congested condition of the new plays is worse than ever.
Before Christmas, for instance, there were two long weeks with
not a single opening anywhere about them; the managers
might just as well have carried out the idea and pasted
decorative placards saying, "Not to be opened till Christmas,"
on the doors of their theaters. But just as soon as the joyous
Yuletide hit town, the managers suddenly unleashed a whole
drove of new plays and set them on the public. It cut in horribly
on the critics' holidays. On Christmas Eve, when everyone else
was safe at home trying to make the children's new mechanical
toys work, there were the critics out in the bitter night, striving
to see seven openings at once. Oh, it's a rough life, a critic's is.

But then, it does have its compensations. For example, there
is *Dear Brutus*, the new Barrie play at the Empire. Seeing that
really does make up for practically everything. So far as I am
concerned, it is one of the big things in life. Of course, the
minute you start to say anything about a Barrie play, you
immediately bore everyone around you to the verge of tears.
There is simply no use in trying to tell about it—the only thing
to do is to go see it as soon as possible, which will probably be
some time in Easter week, from the way the house is selling out.
It is practically impossible to talk about the play without
bringing in "whimsical charm," and that spoils everything.
People are so everlastingly fed up with the poor old term that

they say, "Oh, yes, it must be another of those things—let's go to the movies." But there you are; the play is simply packed with whimsical charm, and what can you do about it? And, after all, it does seem pretty good to call something charming for a change; it is certainly delightfully restful to see a play wherein nobody swears at anybody, or shoots anybody, or seduces anybody, or goes to war about anything. The outstanding feature of the Great Dramas of this season is their thorough and exhaustive lack of charm. You can count the exceptions on the fingers of one hand—and have a thumb and two or three fingers left over.

Well, anyway, *Dear Brutus* is to me the event of the season. Besides the well-known charm, it holds you interested and entertained every second, and there are few other plays of the season that keep you right along with them all the way through. I don't know whether you feel that way about it, but I think it is a far better play than *A Kiss for Cinderella* was. I will admit that I got a bit sunk in the whimsicalities of *A Kiss for Cinderella*, but *Dear Brutus* never cloys for a moment.

It isn't just the play itself—there is the excellence of its acting, too. Those whimsical things can be so completely ruined by an oversweet performance. I shudder to think how sticky the whole thing would have been with a less able performance than that of William Gillette. The ladies' cup goes to Helen Hayes, who does an exquisite bit of acting. Hers is one of those roles that could be overdone without a struggle, yet she never once skips over into the kittenish, never once grows too exuberantly sweet—and when you think how easily she could have ruined the whole thing, her work seems little short of marvelous. I could sit down right now and fill reams of paper with a single-spaced list of the names of actresses who could have completely spoiled the part. The cast of *Dear Brutus* also includes Louis Calvert, Sam Sothern, Hilda Spong, and Violet Kemble Cooper—you can see for yourself it's a big evening.

Altogether, *Dear Brutus* meant practically everything to me. It made me weep—and I can't possibly enjoy a play more than that.

Sem Benelli: *The Jest*

June 1919

Without wishing to infringe in any way on the Pollyanna copyright, there are times when one must say a few kind words for the general scheme of things. After all, the plan really has been worked out rather cleverly. When everything has gone completely bad and suicide seems the one way out, then something good happens, and life is again worth the cost of living. When things have sunk to their lowest depths, some really desirable event occurs, and business goes on again as usual. When clouds are thickest, the sun is due to come out strong in a little while. In fact, the darkest hour is just before the dawn. (No originality is claimed for that last one; it is just brought in for the heart interest and popular appeal.)

The Pollyanna system has recently been worked out with particularly brilliant effect, in the theater. When the latest attractions at the local playhouses were so consistently poisonous that one had just about decided to give up the whole thing and stay at home in the evenings to see if there was anything in family life—then along came Mr. Arthur Hopkins and produced *The Jest*. And, once again, all's well with the world.

It is difficult to write of *The Jest*, for enough has been written about the thing to fill the Public Library comfortably, by this time. Everyone knows that it was written ten years ago by Sem Benelli—then in his late twenties—who was known in these parts heretofore only for his libretto of *L'Amore dei Tre Rei;* that in Italy, where its name is *La Cena Delle Beffe*, it is practically a national institution; that Bernhardt played John Barrymore's part in French and another woman, Mimi Aguglia, played it in Italian; and that the present production at the Plymouth Theatre is the first English version of the play.

The name of the translator is no longer withheld; everyone knows that Edward Sheldon did the deed. Whether or not he has translated it into verse is still the subject of hot debates among the cultured. The ayes seem to have it, so far. If the English version is in what, in our youth, we used to speak of affectionately as dear old iambic pentameter, the actors mercifully abstain from reciting it that way; they speak their lines as good, hardy prose.

The Sunday supplements have printed long excerpts from the text, illustrated with scenes from the play and with weirdly blurred portraits of the author—portraits which look strangely like composite photographs of Harry Houdini and Josef Hofmann. The name Benelli has rapidly become a household word; little children in Greenwich Village chant it at their play, mothers hum it about the house, fathers whisper it through the smoke of their cigars. It is a good name for household pronunciation, too; you can't get into any arguments about it, the way you did about Ibáñez.

It is even more difficult to write about the production and the acting of *The Jest*—superlatives are tiresome reading. The highest praise is the attitude of the audience, every evening. They say—they've been saying it for years—that it is impossible to hold an audience after eleven o'clock. The final curtain falls on *The Jest* at a quarter to twelve; until that time not a coat is struggled into, not a hat is groped for, not a suburbanite wedges himself out of his mid-row seat and rushes out into the night, to catch the 11:26. One wonders, by the way, how the commuters manage; they must just bring along a tube of toothpaste and a clean collar, and make a night of it. Anyway, there is not so much as a rustle before the curtain drops. Every member of the audience is still in his seat, clamoring for more at the end of the last act.

There can be no greater tribute.

Once again the Barrymore brothers have shown what they can do when they try. They have easily outclassed all comers in this season's histrionic marathon—they have even broken their own records in *Redemption* and *The Copperhead*. Their roles—John plays Giannetto, the sensitive young artist, and Lionel, Neri, the great, swashbuckling mercenary—afford a brilliantly effective study in contrasts. The part of Giannetto, exquisitely portrayed no less by gesture and pose than by voice, is, in its morbid ecstasies, its impotent strivings, its subtle shadings, undoubtedly far more difficult than the blustering role of Neri. Yet the physical strain of Lionel Barrymore's performance must in itself be enormous. How his voice can bear up all evening under Neri's hoarse roars of rage and reverberating bellows of geniality is one of the great wonders of the age. Not an extraordinarily big man in reality, he seems tremendous as he swaggers about the stage; in his fight scene, he goes through a mass formation of supernumeraries much as Elmer Oliphant used to go through the Navy line. And in some strange way, he manages to make the character almost likable.

Again, one must present it to the Barrymores; they are, indubitably, *quelque* family.

It is a bit rough on the other actors in *The Jest*, for the Barrymores' acting makes one forget all about the other people concerned. It is all the more credit to Gilda Varesi that she can make her brief characterization stand out so vigorously. Maude Hanaford and E. J. Ballantine also contribute effective performances. But the Big Four of the occasion are unquestionably the Barrymore brothers, Arthur Hopkins, and Robert Edmond Jones.

Scenically, the production of *The Jest* reaches the high-water mark of the season—which isn't putting it nearly strongly enough, unfortunately. Mr. Jones has devised a series of settings which are the most remarkable of his career; the year holds no more impressive picture than that of Giannetto's entrance, as he stands, cloaked in gleaming white, against a deep blue background, the dark figure of his hunchback servitor crouching at his side. The whole production is a succession of unforgettable pictures.

That, indeed, is just the quarrel that some people have with it. Those who have seen *La Cena Delle Beffe* on its home field say that the American production is a bit overspectacular—that the production cuts in on the drama. The attention of the audience, they say, is diverted from the action by the amazing picturesqueness of the scenes. Well, their view is high over the heads of the untraveled. To one who has seen only this production, any better seems impossible. The simple, homely advice of one who has never been outside of these broadly advertised United States is only this: park the children somewhère, catch the first city-bound train, and go to the Plymouth Theatre, if you have to trade in the baby's Thrïft Stamps to buy the tickets. The play will undoubtedly run from now on. You ought to be able to get nice, comfortable standing-rooms, any time after Labor Day.

Actor's Strike Benefits

October 1919

By closing up *Those Who Walk in Darkness* and *Oh, What a Girl!* the Equity Association undoubtedly did a big thing towards ameliorating conditions among theater-goers; but the great achievement of the actors' strike is the series of benefit performances which it has brought about. The striking actors chartered the Lexington Opera House, gave their services to the cause, and showed what they could do in the way of giving a performance without managerial aid. And from the way the public has flocked to the opera house, it looks to even the most casual observer as if only their own relatives can be backing up the managers.

Aside from the excellence of the bill, there is such a nice, homey atmosphere about these benefit performances. You can stand out in the lobby and be jostled by actors and actresses just as if you were one of them. You can buy a program—-and get your change back—from one of a large flock of eminent ingenues. It is, undoubtedly, an evening to send night letters to the dear ones about. Marie Dressler, Eddie Cantor, W. C. Fields, Ivy Sawyer and Joseph Santley, Van and Schenck, John Charles Thomas—you can see for yourself that it is considerable entertainment. Frank Tinney was funnier than ever in a little scene with Pearl White, who proves to be an excellent feeder for him, and a newcomer, Jim Barton, simply drove everybody wild with his comedy dances. The big event of the bill was, of course, the second act of *The Lady of the Camellias,* done by Ethel and Lionel Barrymore, with Conway Tearle and Doris Rankin in the supporting company. The Barrymores can never fail to be the big event of any bill on which they appear.

Unfortunately, the bill closes with what was classed as an oration, entitled "Equity," passionately delivered by Brandon Tynan, and written by Hassard Short and Perceval Knight, who based it on Mark Antony's speech in *Julius Caesar*. A little of it might have been a good idea, but it seems to last for three or four hours. Far more effective propaganda for the actors' cause was the brief speech which, in response to the insistent audience, Lionel Barrymore made on behalf of himself and his sister: "We're proud to be here. We'll be here forever, if necessary."

Pierre Louÿs: *Aphrodite*

January 1920

At last it has happened. The long-awaited great event of our generation has occurred—*Aphrodite* has had its New York production at the Century Theatre. Now we can all go quietly about our trifling little pursuits again. Outwardly, we are practically unchanged; to look at us, you would never suspect that we are far, far different from the simple souls we were before that night of the first of December when Morris Gest hospitably threw wide the doors of the mammoth theater and, at the purely nominal cost of eleven dollars a ticket, permitted the gaping multitudes to view the première of the sensational spectacle of the age. But we—especially those of us who paid for our first-night tickets—we know. We have lived and we have learned, albeit the lesson was a costly one in both time and money. And as we look ahead, down the vista of the future years, we can plainly see that it is going to be an appreciable time before we ever fall that heavily again.

It all comes of reading the papers—that is what was responsible for the block-long queue that patiently stood all day long, waiting a chance to reach the Century box office. Of course, what you think of the results achieved by the Hylan administration is entirely your own affair, but you must admit that our esteemed Mayor got in some great press work for *Aphrodite*. For months beforehand, the professional publicity writers had enthused almost to the point of hysteria over the magnificence of the production; but Honest John did more for the box-office receipts in a single day than the combined efforts of the most talented and experienced press agents could have accomplished in a year. The Mayor had but to say that he had heard a rumor that there were scandalous goings-on at the Century, and if they weren't careful he would send his Committee of Welcome up to investigate, and the house sold out for eight weeks in advance. The press agents racked their brains for such adjectives as "stupendous," "superb," "sensational," and "overwhelming;" but our own Mayor, with the simple word "indecent," did the trick.

Unfortunately, Mayor Hylan was sadly misinformed. The only indecent thing about the production is the price that the ticket agencies demand for its seats. If you have a normal, wholesome interest in that sort of thing you can save yourself about $4.75 and have a far more absorbing evening by the simple process of investing seventy-five cents in a thoroughly reliable French-English dictionary and borrowing the original *Aphrodite* from the bookshelves of the friend who brought it back from Paris.

Mr. George Hazelton's dramatization of Pierre Louÿs' novel has carefully eliminated anything that might hurt anybody's feelings. Barring one undeniably beautiful ballet, directed by Michel Fokine, with unexpressed apologies to Krafft-Ebing, the production is about as decadent as the Hippodrome. It is but an endless series of scenes, held together by an extraordinarily dull story. Many of the scenes are extremely effective; mass hundreds of gaudily clad people together on a huge stage, turn a spotlight upon them, and you can't help having a gorgeous spectacle. But in dignity and impressiveness, save for those scenes played by Dorothy Dalton and McKay Morris, the production is pitifully lacking.

Possibly this is due, in great part, to the fact that most of the feminine members of the cast were recruited from the Century Roof, where they were trained for emotional roles in ancient Egyptian dramas by a course of dancing around between tables, singing "Smiles." Another factor is the casting of Etienne Girardot as physician to the Queen of Egypt, in which role he wears much the same make-up that he used to in *Charley's Aunt.*

The management has spared no expense in its endeavors to purchase atmosphere. There is even a brand new drop-curtain, for the occasion, painted with the mystic letters ΑΦΡΟΔΙΤΗ, which most of the audience take to be the Greek word for "asbestos." Perhaps it is because one is so impressed by the obvious expenditure that one loses sight of the atmosphere in marveling at its cost. The imposing list of names, printed in the program, of all those to whom the producers owe a lifelong debt for invaluable aid in making the production possible, do no small work in shattering any illusion one may have had. Thus, when one beholds the gleaming white arms of Aphrodite bearing on high the sacred necklace of seventy-seven pearls, one can only remember that the seventy-seven pearls were supplied by Jos. H. Meyer Bros.; when a gorgeous pageant troops across the stage, one promptly recalls that the horses and camels were furnished by Dr. Martin J. Potter; when the moon shines on the Grove of Aphrodite—which looks startlingly like Bryant Park—one knows it is not the moon of ancient Alexandria, but the electrical effects of Messrs. Paul Bismarck and Henry Kliegl; when Demetrios, the sculptor, murders the high priestess and steals her sacred comb to gratify the whim of Chrysis, the courtesan, all one can think of is that the sacred comb was made especially for the production by Samstag and Hilder Bros. (Colonial Brand). In fact, the only unacknowledged contribution to the performance is Aphrodite's costume which was evidently furnished by the Atlas Paint Company.

At one place in the performance, the producers have injected a typical Winter Garden song—which gains more applause than anything else in the entertainment. The plaudits which greet this jazz number suggest a great idea—why not put in more of such songs, build a runway down through the orchestra, cast Johnny Dooley as Demetrios, Fanny Brice as

Chrysis, and Kay Laurell as Aphrodite, and, leaving the rest of the *dramatis personae* unchanged, call the production a revue? Why, it would run for a decade.

John Drinkwater: *Abraham Lincoln*

February 1920

For a little while the theatrical traffic has been neatly regulated. The overcrowded conditions that marked the first part of the season have been greatly bettered; the rush hour, so to speak, is over. Each production has had a whole evening to itself, and there have been effective pauses between the premières. Some plays, with an exquisite thoughtfulness, even withdrew, after a brief showing, and resigned their theatres to the incoming entertainments. The outgoing dramas included one curious divertissement called *The Phantom Legion*, which treated of death and the author's astoundingly unattractive conception of an after-life. This play holds the season's record, thus far, with a run of four evening performances and one matinee. By an odd coincidence, it ran just five performances too many.

It was a leisurely period for the theater, but by no means an uneventful one, for it included the long-awaited American production of John Drinkwater's *Abraham Lincoln*. After its amazing success in London, at an inconvenient, uncomfortable playhouse, after months of enthusiastic heralding over here, after the book had sold out, after the author had been welcomed and interviewed and quoted and photographed laying a wreath on Lincoln's tomb, it finally came to the Cort Theatre. And the extraordinary part of the whole thing is that it fully realizes all we have been keyed up to expect of it.

It takes one some little while to comprehend the fact that one is not witnessing a play at all—it isn't until the performers are well into the second act, in fact, that consciousness begins slowly to dawn. There is no attempt at the development of a plot, there are no twists, no surprises, no "big moments"; there is just a succession of quietly played, simply written scenes—

largely unrelated—from the life of Abraham Lincoln. And even those most prolific of advice can offer no suggestion to Mr. Drinkwater as to a more effective way of showing a great character.

Mr. Drinkwater has come to his subject in all reverence; the Lincoln he draws is the idealist, the leader of men, the man of sorrows. Of the shrewd backwoodsman, there is but little trace, and of the crude humorist, the father of the unquestionably questionable story, none whatever; this is a Lincoln that would stalk freezingly from the room if any one said so much as "It seems there was this traveling man."

The author has seldom sought to improve on history. He has introduced a fictitious character into the cabinet, and he has caused Lincoln, from the box at Ford's Theatre, to deliver a speech compounded of the best-known lines of the Gettysburg and the second inaugural addresses—but how could he have thought of a better speech?

The play is so simply written that there is never a suggestion of the theater about it; even such a tried trick as the soft singing of an off-stage army marching off to war somehow loses all theatricalism and becomes grippingly real, so naturally and quietly is it brought in. The management has introduced the same unseen soldiers in another selection, during a scene in Grant's headquarters at Appomattox, and, though it would seem as if, according to the managerial idea, the Union Army was composed of two tenors and a couple of basses, the effect is none the less telling.

Frank McGlynn, hitherto unknown to New York, is the Lincoln of the production, and from the opening night, his unknown days were over. His is an extraordinarily real characterization; though the lasting impression is of the heroic figure, the maker of history, he has somehow managed to suggest the shrewd humor that the playwright so sedulously avoided.

From *The New Yorker*

1931

(*As Substitute for Robert Benchley*)

Kindly Accept Substitutes

February 21, 1931

It is no light task, and I here present to you the world of one who has been at it for the past dozen years, to follow after the regular conductor of this department, even in an amateur way. But to heel him in print spells ruin. Not I nor anyone else—for it might be as well, right in the very first paragraph, to waft humility to hell—can do what he does to the drama. I must say only, in extenuation, that during his current brief stay in Hollywood where he is engaged in scratching the surface of the movie magnates, new plays have swept down Broadway with a menacing rush and roar, and some heroic thumb must be held in the dyke till help arrives.

So it would be my thumb, poor readers, and I can but say, along with you, that I would it were more worthy. Still, as even the best apology, which I certainly never said this was, is a bore, let's get right out of here, like shot through a goose, and barge on into play-reviewing.

If you want to, you can pick me out of any crowd, these days. I am the little one in the corner who did not think that *The Barretts of Wimpole Street* was a great play, nor even a good play. It is true that I paid it the tribute of tears, but that says nothing, for I am one who weeps at Victorian costumes. (I am also, for your files, one who cries at violoncello renditions of "Mighty Lak a Rose," so you see.) It is again true that when the stage maid flung open the door of "Elizabeth Barrett's bed-sitting-room" and announced, "Mr. Robert Browning," I felt it right in the old spine. But the sight of Mr. Jo Mielziner's exquisite setting and costumes, and the sound of a mighty name are not, after all, the stuff of great play-writing. And I found myself, heaven help me, bored by the over-stressings of *The Barretts of Wimpole Street,* when I was not irritated by its pretense nor embarrassed by its comedy.

Mr. Rudolf Besier, whose play has been so highly praised here and so lengthily successful in London, has written of that strange, scared household at 50 Wimpole Street, where numerous souls slunk through their years under the terrible tyranny of a monstrous puritan. I am told that, when the play was first produced in England, the present Moulton-Barretts took it heavily to heart; exclaimed, in effect, "Ooh, you big storyteller! Grandpa never did any such thing!"; and saw to it that certain bits were removed from the text. Here, I believe, the piece is displayed in its entirety, and I find myself lined right up along with the family. That Edward Moulton-Barrett was a monster and a maniac, a self-appointed czar, and, to bring matters to a climax, an old crab, we have all been told. But those scenes in which he seeks to be a little more than kin and less than kind to his daughter Elizabeth—surely those are apocryphal. Everything else we have all heard of him, but isn't it late in the day to drag up incest? He was bad enough just plain, without making him fancy.

There is, I find, a group who claim to see in *The Barretts of Wimpole Street* a stirring melodrama—possibly out of disappointment, possibly from loyalty to Miss Cornell, or, even, possibly because they really thought so. Indeed, so long ago as the first night, there was a distinct tendency to hiss the villainous father. But I could not, myself, seek solace in the notion that here was just a good old ten-twenty-thirty rouser. In the first place, it seems to me that a melodrama must, and most of all, have a hero, and the young Browning, though played by Mr. Brian Aherne, an actor of fire and beauty, was so secure and cocky a character that it was difficult to wring up any worry about him. Besides, he was made, by the playwright, to be absent always when trouble sprang up—and what's a hero who is off-stage during the fights? And in the second place, there should always, shouldn't there?, be just a bit of suspense as to the outcome.

Miss Katharine Cornell is a completely lovely Elizabeth Barrett—far more lovely than the original, I fear. It is little wonder that Miss Cornell is so worshipped; she has that thing we need, and we so seldom have, in our actresses; she has romance, or, if you like better the word of the daily-paper critics, she has glamour. It is, I think, due to her and not to her present playwright that she presents, for the first time, to my knowledge, on any stage, the portrait of a poet who could really have written poetry. Victorian costumes were seemingly designed for her, and it is no misfortune to her that she reclines, as the sick Miss Barrett, against her red couch, and displays the beautiful, clean angle from the tip of her chin to the hollow of her throat to the audience. Her voice is more thrilling than ever, so it is perhaps cavilling to say that, thrilling though the music may be, it would be nice, now and then, to distinguish some of the words. Perhaps cavilling it is, but here I am saying it.

The Barretts of Wimpole Street is Miss Cornell's first venture as an actress-manageress—there should be some defter term for that. For her production, surely there can be nothing but praise; I cannot remember seeing better direction that night. Also, as I think I was saying only a few minutes ago, Mr. Mielziner's set and costumes are enchanting. I do not believe that there is half enough screaming about Mr. Mielziner. Show me, that's all I ask you, anybody better in our theater. Mr. Charles Waldron, in the unholy role of Elizabeth Barrett's father, seemed to me fine, and Miss Joyce Carey did the feat, before this deemed impossible, of performing a superb fit of hysterics in what was, unfortunately, a wholly unnecessary final scene. A word, also, should, and will be here, said for a delightful, though, I am afraid, too-sentimental-for-his-own-good spaniel named Flush, who, on the first night, got sick of the whole thing and tried to walk off the stage, causing Elizabeth Barrett, ill as she was, to leap off her couch and recapture him.

In fact, now that you've got me right down to it, the only thing I didn't like about *The Barretts of Wimpole Street* was the play.

Personal: Robert Benchley, please come home. Nothing is forgiven.

Just Around Pooh Corner

March 14, 1931

In a shifting, sliding world, it is something to know that Mr. A. A. ("Whimsy-the-Pooh") Milne stands steady. He may, tease that he is, delude us into thinking for a while that he has changed; that we are all grown up now, and so he may be delicately bitter and even a little pleasurably weary, in front of us; and then, suddenly as the roguish sun darting from the cloud, or the little crocus popping into bloom, or the ton of coal clattering down the chute, he is our own Christopher Robin again, and everything is hippity-hoppity as of old.

I lay no claim to any gift of clairvoyance, but when I saw by the anticipatory press that the title of Mr. Milne's new play had been changed from *Success* to *Give Me Yesterday,* I knew all. My dearest dread is the world "yesterday" in the name of a play; for I know that sometime during the evening I am going to be transported, albeit kicking and screaming, back to the scenes and the costumes of a tenderer time. And I know, who show these scars to you, what the writing and the acting of those episodes of tenderer times are going to be like. I was not wrong, heaven help me, in my prevision of the Milne work. Its hero is caused, by a novel device, to fall asleep and a-dream; and thus he is given yesterday. Me, I should have given him twenty years to life.

Give Me Yesterday (To Remember You By) opens in the sunlit drawing room of the Cavendish Square house of one of those cabinet ministers. The cabinet minister is, like

Mélisande, not happy; his wife is proud, cold, and ambitious; his daughter is a Bright Young Thing; his son has gone Socialist; and, to crown all, it is rumored that Mowbrey is to be appointed to the coveted position of Chancellor of the Exchequer. "Ah," I said to myself, for I love a responsive audience, "so it's one of those plays. All right, it's one of those plays. At least we shall have no Christopher Robins cocking their heads on the lawn." For a moment, you see, I had forgotten the title, and hope tormented me.

Well. At the end of the first act, the cabinet minister is leaning back in a chintz-covered wing chair, conning the speech he is to deliver in Yorkshire, and murmuring drowsily, "The place of my boyhood. Ah, happy days, happy, happy days." *Then* I knew we were all gone.

In the second act, the cabinet minister has made that speech, and is, for the night, back in the little bedroom in Yorkshire, where, as a boy, he had spent the nights of his holidays. It appears that his boyhood sweetheart, Sally—called, by Mr. Louis Calhern, who has gone British or something, "Selly," just as he says, and as yearningly, "heppy"—had used to occupy the adjoining room, and he had had a nasty habit of tapping on the wall between, to communicate with her. The code was not essentially difficult. There was one tap for "a," two for "b," and so on. I ask you, kind reader, but to bear this in mind for rougher times.

The cabinet minister stretches himself out on his old bed, and slips picturesquely to slumber. Darkness spreads softly over the stage, save for a gentle blue beam on Mr. Calhern. Music quivers; then come lights. Then there appear two—not one, but two— Christopher Robins, each about eleven years of age, both forced, poor kids, to go quaintsy-waintsy in doings about knights and squires and beauteous maidens. (I should have known when the program listed their roles as "Nite" and "Squier" that the Charles Hopkins Theatre was no place for me, nor ever would be.) These are part of the cabinet minister's dream, and into it comes a Buteus (sic) Maiden in the person of a lady of, say, ten years, with all the poise of the Sphinx though but little of her mystery. For a few minutes, everything is so cute that the mind reels. Then the cabinet minister himself gets into the dream—I do not pretend to follow the argument—and meets up with his boyhood sweetheart, who wears, and becomingly, the dress of her day. And then, believe it or not, things get worse.

The cabinet minister talks softly and embarrassingly to Sally—"Ah, Selly, Selly, Selly"—but that is not enough. He must tap out to her, on the garden wall, his message, though she is right beside him. First he taps, and at the length it would take, the letter "I." Then he goes on into "l," and, though surely everyone in the audience has caught the idea, he carries through to "o." "Oh, he's not going on into 'v,' " I told myself. "Even Milne wouldn't do that to you." But he did. He tapped on through "v," and then did an "e." "If he does 'y,'" I thought, "I'm through." And he did. So I shot myself.

It was, unhappily, a nothing—oh, a mere scratch—and I was able to sit up and watch that dream go on through all the expected stages. All the Cavendish Square characters of the first act march in, headed by the cabinet minister's wife in court dress (Miss Gladys Hanson really must brush up on that curtsy). They force the minister to don a chancellor's robe, and line themselves up between him and his little new-found love. Sadly she vanishes, leaving him wildly shrieking her name, or his apppoximation of it. It is all as subtle as a grocer's calendar.

In the next scene, our hero appears with his coat on—to get it over to the audience, one presumes, that he is no longer in bed and asleep—and meets, after all the years, the Selly of his youth, sitting on the steps of the garden wall, just as she used to sit. She is married, for she had had to make something of her life when ambition called him away from her; but she is not, it seems, heppy, either. They will fly together, but the cabinet minister, leashed by caution, must first take time to settle his affairs. He will come back for her, he tells her, in a week. (And I think that there could not be a lovelier performance than that of Miss Sylvia Field, the Selly, as she listens to him, with her aura of remembered anguish, and her silent intimation of her knowledge that all is not to be well.)

The final act takes us all back, two days later, to Cavendish Square. The minister, transformed by love and hope into a new and somewhat stressfully tender man, has started cleaning up his affairs by sending his resignation to the Prime Minister. All seems set for his return to the Real Things of Life. Then comes word that Mowbrey is not, after all, to be Chancellor of the Exchequer; and right after that, little to my surprise, arrives the letter from the Prime Minister asking our hero if he won't please come on over and be Chancellor. It is the job he has always wanted (P.S. He got it) and it comes to him, oh, irony, irony, just at the time he was about to get away from it all. For several minutes, Mr. Calhern must, with no other aid than that of his face and his clenching right hand, show us a man torn, a man in the agonies of indecision. But he has been too long bound by the thongs of success. ("Success," people keep remarking, and always portentously, throughout the play, "closes in.") The daring has been squeezed out of him. The play ends with him sitting at his desk, one hand tapping out "Good-bye, dear"—what a man; he must have had wood-pecker blood in him!—while the other grasps the pen with which he is to write his acceptance of his Chancellorship.

Now I have gone into this opus at such dreary length not only out of masochism, but from bewilderment. On the morning after its unveiling, the critics of the daily papers went into a species of snake-dance over its magnificence. "A deeply moving drama on a human topic," they said. "The recent theatrical depression is over," they caroled. "Mr. Milne had something to say and he said it," they pronounced. (Is my memory going completely, or haven't several people before Milne had something to say on the subject of the stultifying powers of success, and haven't they said it?) "The gallant Mr. A. A. Milne," they chanted, "came galloping to the rescue of our beleaguered drama." . . . Ladies and gentlemen, I have told you the tale of the play they saw. My case rests. If *Give Me Yesterday* is a fine play, I am Richard Brinsley Sheridan.

And there was yet another reason for my dwelling so much more than lingeringly upon the Milne work. Frankly—ah, let's

not have any secrets, what do you say?—there wasn't anything
else to write about. You can't make straws without bricks, after
all.

*Personal: Robert Benchley, please come home. Whimso is
back again.*

No More Fun

March 21, 1931

Misfortune, and recited misfortune in especial, may be
prolonged to that point where it ceases to excite pity and
arouses only irritation. One more week's crabbing out of me,
and I fear that you will take to throwing eggs. Yet I am forced
again to tell a tale of woe, for I have no other. And I can't, you
will admit, just stand up here in front of you and make faces, to
earn my princely salary.

In justice to me, though, I must explain to you that I am not
the only one who is in this state of jitters anent the current
exhibitions of drama. I have lately crouched in awed silence
listening to the various deans of the dramatic critics, as they sat
around on their cracker barrels, spitting at the stove and
whittling. And they have agreed, to a man, that never in their
hardened memories has there been any such flock of little
turkeys as has been presented in the theaters during the past
few weeks. It seems that the season of 1930-31 started in much
as any other; it got, towards its middle, rather better—there
were good plays and deservedly successful, and there was an
appropriate amount of cheering and an adequate number of
hats in the air. Things, I am told, were seldom happier, and
there were countless cases of restored faith in the drama. And
then, dating promptly from the night that Little Horseshoes,
the Mascot of the Troop, took up going to the theater for a
living, everything went to hell, and there it has stayed ever
since.

It is surely indicative that we have been confronted, during
the past week, with the revival of an old play, done by an all-
star cast—or at least, a pretty-nearly-all-star cast. All-star casts

do not, in normal times, come out of the woodwork until the early Summer. That we have displayed to us in the first part of March an elderly comedy of dubious value, engaging the services of many of our most expensive Thespians, amounts, I think, to a virtual throwing-in of the towel. The producers are licked; they can't get a good new play, and so they must present a dull old one rather than do nothing at all. For I must have been misinformed when I was told that that law had been repealed which made it a felony for a manager not to produce anything whatever for a little while.

Mr. George Tyler has given *The Admirable Crichton* of Sir James Matthew Barrie every possible break. He set it bountifully, he permitted himself to go approximately wild on Victorian costumes, he purchased the endeavors of proven actors, and, above all, he presented it in the New Amsterdam Theatre, to enter which splendid place is ever true excitement. Me, I had not before seen *The Admirable Crichton* on the stage, nor had I read the play. I could not even cry, along with the lady who sat back of me, "Hey, I saw this thing in the movies!" I knew only that Crichton had passed into the language, and I thought that a play whose main character had become a symbol must be indeed a fine play. I think that I have seldom gone to a theater with higher hopes. And I think that I have seldom had a duller evening.

It may be that the years have gone so swiftly that *The Admirable Crichton* is piteously dated; or it may be—and this would be Baby's view—that *The Admirable Crichton* was slow and stressed and tedious even in its heyday. It may be, too, that the all-star cast, as is the manner of all-star casts, held hams' holiday, and did every line, every bit of business, for all it was worth and just that little touch more. They all knew—oh, you can't fool an actor!—that their other-day costumes and manners were pretty darned comic, and they smirked the audience into the secret. I have, happily for me, never before seen upon one stage so many discourteous, patronizing, and exaggerated performances. Miss Fay Bainter strutted humorously about in her Victorian flounces, and, clad in the pants of her costume for the deserted island, took to walking cutely pigeon-toed, thus sharply recalling that it was she who first gave us Ming Toy, in *East Is West*. Mr. Ernest Glendinning—and I'll shoot the next man who calls him "Glendenning"!—grasped the comicalities of his part as the precious young lord; grasped them so hard, indeed, that he strangled them. Miss Estelle Winwood, as Tweeny, gave a performance such as would cause your fourteen-year-old sister to be blackballed for the high-school dramatic club, did she attempt to emulate it. And Mr. Walter Hampden, after his years of playing Manson in *The Servant in the House*, kept it right up and did Bill Crichton so that one found oneself looking for the stigmata.

I am told, by the gentler, that it was not the actors' fault—that the antiquities of *The Admirable Crichton* rendered their jobs impossible. I concede that my advisers have reason (I think in French), yet it still seems to me that a good actor, given an impossible task, is there to see that the audience shall not realize its impossibilities. Or do I, like my milliner, ask too much?

I suppose that the fair thing to do is to let the blame for the dullness and the embarrassment of *The Admirable Crichton* rest equally upon the cast and upon Sir J. M. ("Never-Grow-Up") Barrie. It doesn't, I feel, matter. Conciseness is not my gift. All my envy goes to the inspired Mr. Walter Winchell, who walked wanly out into the foyer after the third act—there are four and they are long, long acts—and summed up the whole thing in the phrase, "Well, for Crichton out loud!"

Personal: Robert Benchley, please come home. A joke's a joke.

A Few Minutes of Your Time

April 4, 1931

You won't have to stay indoors very long this bright Spring day. There is but one play about which to tell you, and that will be scarcely the work of five minutes. Then, leaving me here alone in the dingy classroom, out with you into the sweet April sunshine, romping and shouting and skipping! And I hope you all tumble down and break your pretty little faces.

For it is all very well for you. You don't have to labor and ache and strain to bring twigs and feathers and bits of moss to fill up this page. (Somehow those metaphors got mixed while my back was turned; but you know yourself, that is likely to happen to anybody, and there's little use worrying about it at this day and date. I have enough troubles without getting my forehead all over lines with dithering over the English language.) All you have to do is to slant a cursory glance at what and how the play was, and then you're through for the day. Perhaps it might be as well to quicken things up and tell you that the drama of the week was *The Silent Witness;* that it is not at all a bad play, though hardly a good play; and give you your chance to get out of this here and now and leave me to practise turning cartwheels for the remainder of my allotted time.

The Silent Witness, which is the work of the Messrs. Jack De Leon and Jack Celestin, gentlemen hitherto strangers to me, is a tidy, workmanlike, respectable mystery play, brought here from London, where, I feel sure, it left the Thames sopping wet. It is in no way an incendiary contrivance, but it is careful and steady and, if you are of not too impatient a nature, an easy entertainment for an evening. And I, for one, am really piteously grateful for a mystery play without shrieks and shots and clutching hands. From the days of my youth—which occurred during the time that practically nobody was safe from Indians—I have hated being pounced upon from dark closets, I have loathed prankish acquaintances who dressed up in sheets and made moan, I have had a torturing phobia about sudden, sharp, loud noises. So it was as a day in the country to me to witness something that, though it was announced in the papers as a mystery play, was a quietly played drama of self-sacrifice, involving a murder, it is true, but bringing you competently and fairly ingeniously to a happy solution. And it was all played in the light—perhaps you cannot realize what that alone means to one the smash of whose heart and whose career may be directly traced to a dread of the lonely dark.

I cannot, in honor, tell you all about *The Silent Witness*, for if you have seen, as you doubtless have, those shows that were established successes three months ago, there is nothing in town to warrant your attendance but this drama, and you will naturally want to make your own guesses at its ending. But I may announce to you, and I trust, for the sake of the nice play, provocatively, that *The Silent Witness* concerns a certain Sir Austin Howard—to me, who have the soul of a chambermaid, anything about people named Sir Austin Howard is all right— his lovely wife, and his weakling son, who is, shall we say, retaining a woman of once-and-a-half his age and twenty times his experience. The woman is strangled, Sir Austin's pigskin wallet, which he had given to his son, is found in her flat, and hell accordingly rips loose. Sir Austin is arrested for murder, there is a courtroom scene, pretty fairly dull as they generally are, and, towards eleven, the discovery of the real killer. Do you know, I really think you'd like it.

The play is related in a series of flashbacks, and Mr. Harry Wagstaff Gribble, who directed it, is the audience's creditor for speeding up what would have been otherwise slower than January in molasses, and doing a lot of clever work with a revolving stage. But possibly it is Mr. Gribble who has inserted lines that I cannot feel occurred in the British script—notably the one awarded Miss Kay Strozzi, who, in the role of the lady who has lost her amateur standing, must not only consign her husband to the eternal fires of hell, but must bring up the matter of his canine ancestry on the distaff side. It is, to me, a matter of grave doubt that her invective adds anything whatever to the entertainment.

Miss Strozzi, by the way, is featured on the program—why, I cannot fathom, save that she had the temerity to wear as truly horrible a gown as ever I have seen on the American stage. There was a flowing skirt of pale chiffon—you men don't have to listen—and a bodice of rose-colored taffeta, the sleeves of which ended shortly below her shoulders. Then there was an expanse of naked arms, and then, around the wrists, taffeta frills such as are fastened about the unfortunate necks of beaten white poodle-dogs in animal acts. Had she not luckily been strangled by a member of the cast while disporting this garment, I should have fought my way to the stage and done her in, myself.

Mr. Lionel Atwill returns, after a long absence, to play Sir Austin in *The Silent Witness*. Mr. Atwill's performance is far calmer and steadier than those he was wont to give us of old. He plays the father of a grown son with dignity, taste, and perhaps just a dash too much of humor. In the scene where he must stand in the dock at Old Bailey, he does, it is true, let himself go in the old way; but, at that, it is good to know, in these bitter days of unemployment, that Mr. Atwill's face keeps right on working. Mr. Anthony Kemble-Cooper, whose surname would be easier changed to Legion, does the arduous and thankless role of the son gracefully and piteously. The entire cast, indeed, is suave, careful, and skilled. They, and Mr. Gribble, make of *The Silent Witness* a play that it is no hardship whatever to witness.

So I think, my dears, in discoursing to you upon this, the one play of the week, that I am more than delighted to say that— Why, you've all walked out on me! Oh, you snakes!

Personal: Robert Benchley, please come home. What do you think I am, anyway?

Valedictory

April 11, 1931

Even as these short-lived words arrange themselves laboriously along the paper, the regular conductor of this department is speeding over the rails, head-on for home. If all goes well and swiftly with him, he will arrive just in time to take up attending as beguiling a succession of dramatic entertainments as has ever been promised us; for memory is baffled at matching a list of plays so brilliant, fascinating, and provocative as they sound that are scheduled for display from next week steadily on until summertime—plays that were only waiting, it appears, for his return. It is, as has probably been said somewhere, a man's world.

Meanwhile, this past week has proved a fitting climax to what may be called the Reign of Terror in the theater. There is consolation only in the thought that at last it is over; and such solace is but thin liniment for an aching memory. It is a matter of grave doubt that I shall ever be the same again, after night upon night of *A Woman Denied* and *Paging Danger,* of *Gray Shadow* and *Greater Love* and *Heat Wave* and *The Great Barrington,* of *Privilege Car* and *The Admirable Crichton, The House Beautiful, The Gang's All Here,* and *Give Me Yesterday.* Some strange, sickly morbidity, brought out in me only by enforced dramatic criticism, makes me live my recent past over and over. The three plays of the week, which so doggedly upheld the traditions of the weeks preceding them, must be deferred for a bit while I linger among my *souvenirs.* (The fact that there is nothing whatever to report of the new exhibits, save anguish and boredom, may, it is true, have a little something to do with that.) For this is a fairly solemn moment. Here I am, taking my formal leave of the New York theater, before I go, free, white, and eighty-one, out to battle with the larger and, I can but hope, the kindlier world. I have been awaiting this day, I know; but, just as there is in any lover's parting, no matter how tragic, a tiny flicker of relief, so is there in any termination, gaily anticipated though it be, a sweet and twilit melancholy of retrospection. Poor little plays, maybe they did all that they could. Certainly they did what was in their power to turn gray the hair and make weary the eyelids of this, your correspondent.

And I have my acknowledgements to make. To those old, tried friends, tried just this side of endurance, who accompanied me on my excursions into the drama, I can offer only gratitude and apology. To the dear, unknown new ones, who wrote to buoy me by agreeing with me, I can tender only my heart and my life. And to that mostly anonymous and largely feminine legion of Milne-lovers and Pollock-fanciers who took paper by the ream to inform me that they were every bit as good critics as I was—in which they're damn tootin'!—and invariably ended their epistles by exhorting me to go jump in an undesignated lake, I can but toss what may sound like a kiss.

But we're men or we're mice, and so I must shove sentiment behind me and get to the week's work. The initial offering was that of the Theatre Guild, which presented Bernard Shaw's plush horse, *Getting Married*. I regret to say that during the first act of this, I, for what I hope will be my only time in the theater, fell so soundly asleep that the gentleman who brought me piled up a barricade of overcoat, hat, stick, and gloves between us to establish a separation in the eyes of the world, and went into an impersonation of A Young Man Who Has Come to the Theater Unaccompanied. But before I slipped to gracious oblivion, I did some thinking, and thus ran my thoughts: Everyone at seventeen years of age has worked out such humorous and devastating criticisms of marriage, but when he wrote *Getting Married* in 1908—wasn't it?—Shaw was something more than seventeen. . . . If the Guild has seen fit to present this dull and lumbering work of a mighty man, it might at least do him, his actors, and his audience the courtesy to excuse it by costuming its characters in the dress of its day, and not display it as something hot off the pen. . . . Miss Dorothy Gish ought to do something about the pronunciation of such words as "world" and "girl"; Miss Dorothy Gish ought not to be so awful, awful cute. . . . Reginald Mason is always good, no matter what. . . . Nowhere in the world may be seen so much batik, such coils of hammered jewellery, and so many *pince-nez* as at a Guild first night. . . . Oh, my God, Helen Westley's going to come on in the next act, and she has a fifteen-minute speech. . . . I wish I'd never been born. . . . I wish I were home in bed. . . . I wish. . . . I wish. . . .

In the interval after the first act, I was awakened by the cessation of conversation, and went for a cigarette to the street. And somehow, once out in the open, I did not return for the second act of *Getting Married*. (Hell, I've got nothing to lose now. This is my last assignment—I might just as well tell you I was not faithful to it.) But I brought away from the beautiful Guild Theatre a rankling resentment that, with all Shaw to choose from, these ladies and gentlemen had chosen to do this dullest of his plays—although I shall certainly listen to anybody who puts up an argument for *The Apple Cart* for first place—; a strengthened conviction that a batiked audience at a Shaw play, with its extraneous gurgles of appreciation and its coos of "Oh, delicious!"; is one of the less attractive manifestations of modern civilization; and a sense of glowing gratitude for the boon of a long, refreshing slumber. I wonder, really, if it wouldn't be only decent of me to write the Guild a bread-and-butter letter. Or I wonder, on the other hand, if it wouldn't have been only decent of them to have offered me a nightgown and toothbrush.

Of the second play of the week, *Lady Beyond the Moon*, it is difficult to write, and, certainly, redundant. Redundant because the regular critics did all that was necessary to it, and difficult because of the behavior of its first audience. It was a dull, silly, dirty play of some sort of house-party on Lake Como, and there is little to be said of such attempts. But only once before, in my experience, in a New York theater—and that was during the first-night performance of *Greater Love*—has an audience indulged itself in so many comments, titters, and lip noises, and, though God knows the beholders in both cases have been sore tried, it is always free to them to get up and go, and quietly. Such demonstrations have the boomerang effect of turning one's sympathy to the actors; and bad though the acting was on the stage, during *Lady Beyond the Moon*, that of the audience was worse.

But the audience at what must surely have been the world première of *Right of Happiness*—for if it had ever been tried before spectators at any earlier date, it is scarcely conceivable that it would have reached town—conducted itself like a group of little lambs. And could there be an excuse for displayed impatience, it was right there before them. *Right of Happiness* fittingly concluded the horrible little pre-Easter season, and there are no harsher words to say of it. It was a crude, bad, strangely furious play about, as much as I could discern of its theme, the bitter resentment of a cripple for the pity and patronage that must be his portion. There could certainly be a fine play, and a rending one, on that premise, but *Right of Happiness* was so truly abominably written and devised that it would have been ridiculous had it not been so stultifying a bore· that one had no spirit left for laughter. There is little need, and there would be less mercy, to talk about those who acted it. But one does wonder what on earth Anne Sutherland was doing in that company, and one would like to proffer condolence to Mr. Herbert Rawlinson for his having to play the role of the great surgeon—for it has apparently become traditional that great surgeons must be so presented on the stage that nobody in his right mind would trust them with the treatment of a hangnail.

And with that play, ladies and gentlemen, my labors end. Good-byes are best said briefest. So I thank you all so very much, and, though I certainly had a rotten time, I hate to leave you.

BOOK REVIEWS

From Constant Reader:

From *The New Yorker* 1927 - 1933

The Private Papers
of the Dead

October 8, 1927

I think that the *Journal of Katherine Mansfield** is the saddest book I have ever read. Here, set down in exquisite fragments, is the record of six lonely and tormented years, the life's-end of a desperately ill woman. So private is it that one feels forever guilty of prying for having read it.

Her journal was her dear companion. "Come, my unseen, my unknown, let us talk together," she says to it. Only in its pages could she show her tragically sensitive mind, her lovely, quivering soul. She was not of the little breed of the discontented; she was of the high few fated to be ever unsatisfied. Writing was the precious thing in life to her, but she was never truly pleased with anything she had written. With a sort of fierce austerity, she strove for the crystal clearness, the hard, bright purity from which streams perfect truth. She never felt that she had attained them.

This is the book of a writer. Not, I mean, that there

* *Katherine Mansfield* (1888-1923), the short-story writer, was the wife of John Middleton Murry, the English critic. When he published her private journals after her death, some felt that he was exploiting her. [*Footnotes for* Constant Reader *supplied by the publishers.*]

are chummy bits of "literary gossip" or John-Farrar-like*
anecdotes of the bookmen of her acquaintance. But Katherine
Mansfield could look on at herself, so to say, and see even in
her physical sufferings material for her pen. "I must remember
it," she says, after a racking agony of lumbago, "when I write
about an old man." "Let me remember," she prays of a smoky
rain, a violin note, a shiny, blue day. There are plans for
stories—so many that she did not live to carry out—and
sketches of characters. These are not set down in the dreadful
manner of the two-story-a-week writers who carry obnoxious
notebooks about, snapping at "copy." She wrote them in her
journal, this journal that was for her alone, because here was
her life, because the writer and the woman were not and could
never be two separate beings.

The photographs of her that illustrate the journal are of deep
interest. The first was taken in 1913; the last shortly before her
death ten years later. She grew always more beautiful for her
suffering.

Journal of Katherine Mansfield is a beautiful book and an
invaluable one, but it is her own book, and only her dark, sad
eyes should have read its words. I closed it with a little murmur
to her portrait on the cover. "Please forgive me," I said.

An American Du Barry

October 15, 1927

Nan Britton, the author of the American classic, *The
President's Daughter*, affirms that she wrote her book solely as
a plea for more civilized laws affecting the standing of the
children of unmarried mothers. And maybe she did. And
maybe the writer of "Only a Boy" set down that tale just for the
purpose of arousing interest in bigger and better crêches.

The President's Daughter is the most amazing work that has
yet found its way into these jittering hands. It is the story of the
affair between Nan Britton and Warren Gamaliel Harding;

* *John Farrar* (1896-), publisher and patron of young writers, was
editor of *The Bookman*, a literary monthly of the time.

and Miss Britton takes you through their romance in a glass-bottomed boat, as it were. The book bears the subtitle *Revealing the Love-Secret of President Harding*, which is but a mild statement. For when Miss Britton gets around to revealing, Lord, how she does reveal. She is one who kisses, among other things, and tells.

An attempt was made to suppress the book. The author states, in one of her prefaces, that "six burly policemen" (on the day that that man bites that dog, another front-page item is going to concern a policeman who is not burly) "and John S. Sumner, agent for the Society for the Suppression of Vice, armed with a 'Warrant of Search and Seizure,' entered the printing plant where the making of the book was in process. They seized and carried off the plates and printed sheets." "Lady," you want to say to the author, "those weren't policemen; they were critics of literature dressed up." I admit I drank down the whole book; but one swallow would make a Sumner. (That should have been better. I wish I had more time. Something might have been made of that.)

However, "in a magistrate's court the case was dismissed. The seized plates and printed sheets were returned to the publishers—the Elizabeth Ann Guild, Inc." So now the whole literate world may have the privilege of reading, at five dollars a crack, of the indoor life of the mighty.

Of the authenticity of Miss Britton's story I am absolutely convinced. I wish I were not. I wish I could feel that she had made it all up out of her head, for then I could give myself over to high ecstasies at the discovery of the great American satire, the shrewd and savage critique of Middle-Western love. But I am afraid that *The President's Daughter* is only a true story.

Throughout her book, Miss Britton protests, perhaps a shade too much, of the great love that she and Mr. Harding bore each other, a love which she insists, in a phrase that I am fairly sure I have seen before some place, could not have been greater had they been joined together by fifty ministers; yet they seem to have been, at best, but a road-company Paolo and Francesca. Theirs is the tale of as buckeye a romance as you will find. It is, and a hundred per cent, an American comedy.

The one faint glimpse of glamour that Miss Britton allows us is that of her early days, when she had a little-girl's crush on the Marion editor, more than thirty years her senior, who was just stepping off into politics. Then she sees him as a truly romantic figure, in all he does and says, as, for instance, on that memorable day when her mother "allowed me to go up and shake hands with him and tell him how much I enjoyed his speech, for which hesitating utterance I received one of his loveliest smiles and a courtly 'Thank you kindly, thank you kindly!' "

But when she has grown up into his extramural affections, she seems to view him as someone a little less than glamorous. "Between kisses," she says, "we found time to discuss my immediate need for a position." She tells you of the time when, in alighting from a taxi in front of the Manhattan Hotel, "Mr. Harding caught his foot and tripped, falling in a very awkward position. . . . Mr. Harding's blush of confusion after his fall remained a good many minutes and was explained by him, 'You see, dearie, I'm so crazy about you that I don't know where I'm stepping!' " She speaks of his tucking thirty dollars in her brand new silk stocking. She relates of his hiding in the cupboard when there was an unexpected knock upon the door of her apartment. She tells you about that afternoon when the house detective put them firmly though gently out of an hotel room, despite his plea that they weren't disturbing any of the other guests. " 'Gee, Nan,' was Our President's comment upon that occasion, 'I thought I wouldn't get out of that under a thousand dollars!' "

Mr. Harding, one gathers, was scarcely of the drunken-sailor temperament. He paid five dollars a pair for his shoes and announced that "That is all any fellow should pay for shoes." When his bill for a dinner was over fifteen dollars, "Mr. Harding tipped the waiter $1.50. I watched his face as he counted out the money. . . . He looked across at me and shrugged his shoulders. 'You know Nan, I am not penurious, but a bill like that is really ridiculous.' " He took Miss Britton to the theater, and chivalrously begged her to guess what he paid for the tickets; the correct answer turned out to be $5.50

apiece. "Wartime graft" he termed this. One can but feel, after several of these anecdotes, that Miss Britton was doing admirably to get that thirty dollars tucked into her stocking.

Nor was he precisely a poetic lover. "Dearie" was his most flowery term, and sometimes "to show me he was really just human like myself, he would deliberately use words like 'ain't' " or call his lady "you purty thing!" The shy Miss Britton, because of the difference in their ages, could not quite bring herself to call him Warren; she compromised on "sweetheart."

Surely this story of so bare and shabby a love, of these meetings held in hotels recommended by taxi drivers, and, some time after the man had been made President of the United States, of that tryst in a clothes closet, should be a pathetic thing. But so smug is Miss Britton's style, so sure of himself does she make Harding appear, that one can look on this affair only as a comic, and a slightly horrid, matter. There was no wistfulness in either the practical young lady or her pompous lover.

For the unfortunate little Elizabeth Ann, the child of Nan Britton and Warren Gamaliel Harding, one can only wish that no one will show her this book that so unbeautifully exploits her. Undoubtedly, it will make money, and, one trusts, for her. It is lofty on the list of best sellers, despite the fact that it is allowed no advertising. Probably it will become a greater popular favorite than *We*. This is, you remember, America.

Re-enter Margot Asquith—A Masterpiece from the French

October 22, 1927

"Daddy, what's an optimist?" said Pat to Mike while they were walking down the street together one day.

"One who thought that Margot Asquith* wasn't going to

* *Margot (Tennant) Asquith* (1864-1945), wife of the British Prime Minister of 1908-1916, was known as a wit in London literary and social circles.

write any more," replied the absent-minded professor, as he wound up the cat and put the clock out.

That gifted entertainer, the Countess of Oxford and Asquith, author of *The Autobiography of Margot Asquith* (four volumes, neatly boxed, suitable for throwing purposes), reverts to tripe in a new book deftly entitled *Lay Sermons*. It is a little dandy if I have ever seen one, and I certainly have.

I think it must be pleasanter to be Margot Asquith than to be any other living human being; and this is no matter of snap judgment on my part, for I have given long and envious thought to the desirability of being Charles A. Levine.* But the lady seems to have even more self-assurance than has the argumentative birdman. Her perfect confidence in herself is a thing to which monuments should be erected; hers is a poise that ought to be on display in the British Museum. The affair between Margot Asquith and Margot Asquith will live as one of the prettiest love stories in all literature.

In this book of essays, which has all the depth and glitter of a worn dime, the Countess walks right up to such subjects as Health, Human Nature, Fame, Character, Marriage, Politics, and Opportunities. A rather large order, you might say, but it leaves the lady with unturned hair. Successively, she knocks down and drags out each topic. And there is something vastly stirring in the way in which, no matter where she takes off from, she brings the discourse back to Margot Asquith. Such singleness of purpose is met but infrequently.

When she does get around to less personal matters, it turns out that her conclusions are soothingly far from startling. A compilation of her sentiments, suitably engraved upon a nice, big calendar, would make an ideal Christmas gift for your pastor, your dentist, or Junior's music teacher. Here, for instance, are a few ingots lifted from her golden treasury: "The artistic temperament has been known to land people in every kind of dilemma." . . . "Pleasure will always make a stronger appeal than Wisdom." . . . "It is only the fine natures that

* *Charles A. Levine* made headlines in 1927 by following a few days after Lindbergh in a nonstop transatlantic flight, with Clarence D. Chamberlain, which overshot Berlin.

profit by Experience." . . . "It is better to be a pioneer than a passenger, and best of all to try and create." . . . "It is not only what you See but what you Feel that kindles appreciation and gives life to Beauty." . . . "Quite apart from the question of sex, some of the greatest rascals have been loved." . . . "I think it is a duty women owe not only to themselves, but to everyone else, to dress well."

The Thames, I hear, remains as damp as ever in the face of these observations.

Through the pages of *Lay Sermons* walk the great. I don't say that Margot Asquith actually permits us to rub elbows with them ourselves, but she willingly shows us her own elbow, which has been, so to say, honed on the mighty. "I remember President Wilson saying to me"; "John Addington Symonds once said to me"; "The Master of Balliol told me"—thus does she introduce her anecdotes. And you know those anecdotes that begin that way; me, I find them more efficacious than sheep-counting, rain on a tin roof, or alanol tablets. Just begin a story with such a phrase as "I remember Disraeli—poor old Dizzy!—once saying to me, in answer to my poke in the eye," and you will find me and Morpheus off in a corner, necking.

Margot Asquith's is, I am sure, a naive and an annoying (those two adjectives must ever be synonyms to me) and an unimportant book, yet somehow, grudge it though I do, there is a disarming quality to it and to its author. (There I go, getting tender about things, again; it's no wonder men forget me.) Perhaps it is because the lady's cocksureness implies a certain sort of desperate gallantry; perhaps it is because there is a little—oh, entirely unconscious, please, Your Grace—wistfulness in the recurrent references to the dear dead days of "The Souls," in the tales of the hunting-field when the high gentry were wont to exclaim, "You ride with such audacity, Miss Tennant!" I suppose that wistfulness is a fighting word to the countess, but there it stands. She is, from her book, no master mind, God wot; but she is, also from her book, a game woman, gamer, I think, than she knows. I always have to cry a little bit about courage.

However (and how good it feels to get back to the nice, firm ground again), *Lay Sermons* is a naive and an annoying and an unimportant book. The author says, "I am not sure that my ultimate choice for the name of this modest work is altogether happy." Happier I think it would have been if, instead of the word "Sermons," she had selected the word "Off."

*The Counterfeiters** is too tremendous a thing for praises. To say of it "Here is a magnificent novel" is rather like gazing into the Grand Canyon and remarking, "Well, well, well; quite a slice."

Doubtless you have heard that this book is not pleasant. Neither, for that matter, is the Atlantic Ocean.

A Book of Great Short Stories

October 29, 1927

Ernest Hemingway wrote a novel called *The Sun Also Rises.* Promptly upon its publication, Ernest Hemingway was discovered, the Stars and Stripes were reverentially raised over him, eight hundred and forty-seven book reviewers formed themselves into the word "welcome," and the band played "Hail to the Chief" in three concurrent keys. All of which, I should think, might have made Ernest Hemingway pretty reasonably sick.

For, a year or so before *The Sun Also Rises,* he had published *In Our Time,* a collection of short pieces. The book caused about as much stir in literary circles as an incompleted dogfight on upper Riverside Drive. True, there were a few that went about quick and stirred with admiration for this clean, exciting prose, but most of the reviewers dismissed the volume with a tolerant smile and the word "stark." It was Mr. Mencken who slapped it down with "sketches in the bold, bad manner of the Café du Dôme," and the smaller boys, in their manner, took similar pokes at it. Well, you see, Ernest

---

* *The Counterfeiters* was so much talked about on publication that Constant Reader did not need to mention the name of the author: *André Gide* (1869-1951), French writer and intellectual, who later won the Nobel Prize.

Hemingway was a young American living on the left bank of the Seine in Paris, France; he had been seen at the Dôme and the Rotonde and the Select and the Closerie des Lilas. He knew Pound, Joyce, and Gertrude Stein. There is something a little— well, a little *you*-know—in all of those things. You wouldn't catch Bruce Barton* or Mary Roberts Rinehart** doing them. No, sir.

And besides, *In Our Time* was a book of short stories. That's no way to start off. People don't like that; they feel cheated. Any bookseller will be glad to tell you, in his interesting *argot*, that "short stories don't go." People take up a book of short stories and say, "Oh, what's this? Just a lot of those short things?" and put it right down again. Only yesterday afternoon, at four o'clock sharp, I saw and heard a woman do that to Ernest Hemingway's new book, *Men Without Women*. She had been one of those most excited about his novel.

Literature, it appears, is here measured by a yard-stick. As soon as *The Sun Also Rises* came out, Ernest Hemingway was the white-haired boy. He was praised, adored, analyzed, best-sold, argued about, and banned in Boston; all the trimmings were accorded him. People got into feuds about whether or not his story was worth the telling. (You see this silver scar left by a bullet, right up here under my hair? I got that the night I said that any well-told story was worth the telling. An eighth of an inch nearer the temple, and I wouldn't be sitting here doing this sort of tripe.) They affirmed, and passionately, that the dissolute expatriates in this novel of "a lost generation" were not worth bothering about; and then they devoted most of their time to discussing them. There was a time, and it went on for weeks, when you could go nowhere without hearing of *The Sun Also Rises*. Some thought it without excuse; and some, they of the cool, tall foreheads, called it the greatest American novel, tossing *Huckleberry Finn* and *The Scarlet Letter* lightly out the

* *Bruce Barton* (1886-1967), of the famous Madison Avenue advertising establishment, wrote a life of Jesus called *The Man Nobody Knows*.

** *Mary Roberts Rinehart* (1876-1958) was known for her mystery stories and as a popular society novelist.

window. They hated it or they revered it. I may say, with due respect to Mr. Hemingway, that I was never so sick of a book in my life.

Now *The Sun Also Rises* was as "starkly" written as Mr. Hemingway's short stories; it dealt with subjects as "unpleasant." Why it should have been taken to the slightly damp bosom of the public while the (as it seems to me) superb *In Our Time* should have been disregarded will always be a puzzle to me. As I see it—I knew this conversation would get back to me sooner or later, preferably sooner—Mr. Hemingway's style, this prose stripped to its firm young bones, is far more effective, far more moving, in the short story than in the novel. He is, to me, the greatest living writer of short stories; he is, also to me, not the greatest living novelist.

After all the high screaming about *The Sun Also Rises,* I feared for Mr. Hemingway's next book. You know how it is—as soon as they all start acclaiming a writer, that writer is just about to slip downward. The littler critics circle like literary buzzards above only the sick lions.

So it is a warm gratification to find the new Hemingway book, *Men Without Women,* a truly magnificent work. It is composed of thirteen short stories, most of which have been published before. They are sad and terrible stories; the author's enormous appetite for life seems to have been somehow appeased. You find here little of that peaceful ecstasy that marked the camping trip in *The Sun Also Rises* and the lone fisherman's days in "Big Two-Hearted River" in *In Our Time.* The stories include "The Killers," which seems to me one of the four great American short stories. (All you have to do is drop the nearest hat, and I'll tell you what I think the others are. They are Wilbur Daniel Steele's "Blue Murder," Sherwood Anderson's "I'm a Fool," and Ring Lardner's "Some Like Them Cold," that story which seems to me as shrewd a picture of every woman at some time as is Chekhov's "The Darling." Now what do *you* like best?) The book also includes "Fifty Grand," "In Another Country," and the delicate and tragic "Hills like White Elephants." I do not know where a greater collection of stories can be found.

Ford Madox Ford has said of this author, "Hemingway writes like an angel." I take issue (there is nothing better for that morning headache than taking a little issue.) Hemingway writes like a human being. I think it is impossible for him to write of any event at which he has not been present; his is, then, a reportorial talent, just as Sinclair Lewis's is. But, or so I think, Lewis remains a reporter and Hemingway stands a genius because Hemingway has an unerring sense of selection. He discards details with a magnificent lavishness; he keeps his words to their short path. His is, as any reader knows, a dangerous influence. The simple thing he does looks so easy to do. But look at the boys who try to do it.

The Professor
Goes In for
Sweetness and Light

November 5, 1927

Professor William Lyon Phelps,* presumably for God, for Country and for Yale, has composed a work on happiness. He calls it, in a word, *Happiness,* and he covers the subject in a volume about six inches tall, perhaps four inches across, and something less than half an inch thick. There is something rather magnificent in disposing, in an opus the size of a Christmas card, of this thing that men since time started have been seeking, pondering, struggling for, and guessing at. It reminds me, though the sequence may seem a bit hazy, of a time that I was lunching at the Cap d'Antibes (oh, I get around). I remarked, for I have never set up any claim to being a snappy luncheon companion, that somewhere ahead of us in the Mediterranean lay the island where the Man in the Iron Mask had been imprisoned.

"And who," asked my neighbor at the table, "was the Man in the Iron Mask?"

* *William Lyon Phelps* (1865-1943), in addition to teaching at Yale, lectured widely on books to women's-club audiences and was regarded by many in the twenties and thirties as the arbiter of popular reading taste.

My only answer was a prettily crossed right to the jaw. How expect one who had had a nasty time of it getting through grammar school to explain to him, while he finished the rest of his filet, an identity that the big boys had never succeeded in satisfactorily working out, though they gave their years to the puzzle?

Somewhere, there, is an analogy, in a small way, if you have the patience for it. But I guess it isn't a very good anecdote. I'm better at animal stories.

Anyway, there is this to be said for a volume such as Professor Phelps's *Happiness*. It is second only to a rubber duck as the ideal bathtub companion. It may be held in the hand without causing muscular fatigue or nerve strain, it may be neatly balanced back of the faucets, and it may be read through before the water has cooled. And if it slips down the drain pipe, all right, it slips down the drain pipe.

The professor starts right off with "No matter what may be one's nationality, sex, age, philosophy, or religion, everyone wishes either to become or to remain happy." Well, there's no arguing that one. The author has us there. There is the place for getting out the pencil, underscoring the lines, and setting "how true," followed by several carefully executed exclamation points, in the margin. It is regrettable that the book did not come out during the season when white violets were in bloom, for there is the very spot to press one.

"Hence," goes on the professor, "definitions of happiness are interesting." I suppose the best thing to do with that is to let it pass. Me, I never saw a definition of happiness that could detain me after train-time, but that may be a matter of lack of opportunity, of inattention, or of congenital rough luck. If definitions of happiness can keep Professor Phelps on his toes, that is little short of dandy. We might just as well get on along to the next statement, which goes like this: "One of the best" (we are still on definitions of happiness) "was given in my Senior year at college by Professor Timothy Dwight: 'The happiest person is the person who thinks the most interesting thoughts.' " Promptly one starts recalling such Happiness Boys as Nietzsche, Socrates, de Maupassant, Jean-Jacques

Rousseau, William Blake, and Poe. One wonders, with hungry curiosity, what were some of the other definitions that Professor Phelps chucked aside in order to give preference to this one.

Here is a book happily free from iconoclasm. There is not a sentence that you couldn't read to your most conservative relatives and still be reasonably sure of that legacy. If you like—and please do—there might be here set down a few of the professor's conclusions. "Money is not the chief factor in happiness." ... "Leave out the things that injure, cultivate the things that strengthen, and good results follow." ... "I am certain that with the correct philosophy it is possible to have within one's possession sources of happiness that cannot permanently be destroyed." ... "We are in a certain sense forced to lead a lonely life, because we have all the days of our existence to live with ourselves." ... "Many go to destruction by the alcoholic route because they cannot endure themselves." ... "Happiness is not altogether a matter of luck. It is dependent on certain conditions." These are but a few. But I give you my word, in the entire book there is nothing that cannot be said aloud in mixed company. And there is, also, nothing that makes you a bit the wiser. I wonder—oh, what will you think of me—if those two statements do not verge upon the synonymous.

Happiness concludes with a pretty tribute to what the professor calls the American cow. The cow, he points out, does not have to brush her teeth, bob her hair, select garments, light her fire and cook her food. She is not passionate about the income tax or the League of Nations; she has none of the thoughts that inflict distress and torture. "I have observed many cows," says the professor, in an interesting glimpse of autobiography, "and there is in their beautiful eyes no perplexity; they are never even bored." He paints a picture of so sweet, so placid, so carefree an existence, that you could curse your parents for not being Holsteins. And then what does he do? Breaks up the whole lovely thing by saying, "Very few human beings would be willing to change into cows. ... Life, with all its sorrows, perplexities, and heartbreaks, is more interesting than bovine placidity, hence more desirable. The more interesting it is, the happier it is." (Oh, professor, I should like to contest that.) "And the happiest person is the person who thinks the most interesting thoughts."

These are the views, this is the dogma, of Professor William Lyon Phelps, the pride of New Haven. And, of course, at Harvard there is now—and it looks as if there might be always—President Lowell,* of the Fuller Committee. I trust that my son will elect to attend one of the smaller institutions of higher education.

Madame Glyn
Lectures on "It,"
with Illustrations

November 26, 1927

And this, ladies and gentlemen, is the finest day that has yet broken over the bloody and bowed head of your girl-friend. On this day there first fell into these trembling hands The Book, the Ultimate Book. There is grave doubt that I shall ever be able to talk of anything else. Certainly, I have read my last word. Print can hold for me now nothing but anticlimaxes. *It*, the chef d'oeuvre of Madame Elinor Glyn,** has come into my life. And Sherman's coming into Atlanta is but a sneaking, tiptoe performance in comparison.

* *Abbott Lawrence Lowell* (1856-1943), President of Harvard, served on the Commission appointed by Governor Fuller of Massachusetts, after the public clamor against the murder conviction of radicals Sacco and Vanzetti in 1921, to investigate the fairness of the trial. The Commission's finding in favor of the court was widely unpopular with liberals. Dorothy Parker joined the protest demonstrations in Boston and was arrested and fined five dollars. Sacco and Vanzetti were executed on October 22, 1927—a few days before this issue of *The New Yorker* went to press.

** *Elinor Glyn* (1864-1943), English author of sultry romances, is characterized by a popular jingle of the time: "Would you like to sin/With Elinor Glyn/On a tiger skin/Or would you prefer/To err with her/On some other fur?"

I didn't know. Truly, I didn't know. Mine is a life sheltered to the point of stuffiness. I attend no movies, for any motion-picture theater is as an enlarged and a magnificently decorated lethal chamber to me. I have read but little of Madame Glyn. I did not know that things like *It* were going on. I have misspent my days. When I think of all those hours I flung away in reading William James and Santayana, when I might have been reading of life, throbbing, beating, perfumed life, I practically break down. Where, I ask you, have I been, that no true word of Madame Glyn's literary feats has come to me?

But even those far, far better informed than I must work a bit over the opening sentence of Madame Glyn's foreword to her novel. "This is *not*," she says, drawing her emeralds warmly about her, "the story of the moving picture entitled, *It*, but a full character study of the story *It*, which the people in the picture read and discuss." I could go mad, in a nice way, straining to figure that out. But I shall let it stay a mystery. I shall take what comes to me, glad and grateful and unquestioning. After all, what more could one ask than a character study of a story?

Also in her foreword, Madame Glyn goes into the real meaning of "It." "To have 'It,' " she says—and is she the girl that knows?—"the fortunate possessor must have that strange magnetism which attracts both sexes." (Pul-ease, Madame Glyn, pul-ease!) "He or she must be entirely unself-conscious and full of self-confidence, indifferent to the effect he or she is producing, and uninfluenced by others." (Why, it's Levine, that's who it is, it's Levine.) "There must be physical attraction, but beauty is unnecessary. Conceit or self-consciousness destroys 'It' immediately. In the animal world, 'It' demonstrates" (*sic. Sic* as a dog.) "in tigers and cats—both animals being fascinating and mysterious and quite unbiddable."

So there you have it, in a coconut-shell. Now we can go on with the story.

Well, it seems there was this man named John Gaunt. By the time we meet him, there is iron-gray in his hair and he has twenty million dollars to go with it, but things were not always thus with him. At the age of ten, he was selling papers on the Bowery; yet he pulled himself up so sturdily that at forty he "was a person of great cultivation." Also, "he had that nameless charm, with a strong magnetism that can only be called 'It,' and cats, as well as women, always knew when he came into a room." Also, "from his fifteenth year, when the saloonkeeper's wife at the corner of his street groveled before his six feet of magnificent stripling strength, to his fortieth birthday, females of all types and classes manifested ardent passion for him." That, my friends, is living.

Then there was this girl, Ava Cleveland, and her brother Larry. Larry had It something terrible, and he also had a little way of taking opium. (Oh, please wait a minute. I think I'm going to be able to use "opium" in a sentence. I opium mother is feeling better. No, I guess I'm not, either.) Ava was young and slender and proud. And she had It. It, hell; she had Those.

But Ava was worried. There was that big bill at the dressmaker's. And she had been unlucky at baccarat, lately. And she and Larry were but hangers-on of the rich. You see, as one of Madame Glyn's characters explains, "Their father never brought them up to do anything, and then died." Died happy, you gather from this succinct biography, in the knowledge of a task accomplished, and nothing more to do.

So Ava was worried. Indeed, at the end of the very first chapter, we get a sharp flash of her terrible state of mind. " 'What the H—— are we to do?' she said to herself in not very polite English." Madame Glyn, as you see, does not flinch from plain talk. When she presents a street-Arab to us she has him cry, "Well, I'll be d——d!" It looks to me as if, out in Hollywood, she must have been on the adjoining lot to that on which *What Price Glory?* was being filmed.

Well, anyway, Ava was worried. Oh, of course there were things she could have done. But she was one who could not Give All unless she loved. Call it her hard luck, if you will, but that's how she was. She was unapproachable, pure, sacred. She could have made any All-American team in a moment, just on her dexterity at intercepting passes. Take her, for example, when the husband of her friend pleads with her—when he says:

" 'Then my moment will come—you can't do me down forever, child—I love your white skin.'

"A fierce gleam now came into Ava's eyes.

" 'You make me sick—you married men—it is nothing but skin—skin!' "

She did have a rich suitor, and of honorable intent, but he had a mother fixation that belonged by rights in the Smithsonian Institution. Thus did she put him in his place:

" 'I think a man is no man unless the woman he loves—the prospective mother of his children, who will carry on his name—stands above everything in his life—everything except his duty to his country and his own soil!' "

But strong as is the temptation to quote and quote and quote, we must get on with the story. We must respect Madame Glyn's duty to her own soil. Well, it turns out that Ava and John meet, and he begins promptly to "vibrate with passion." But she is too proud to be mastered by one not of her class; indeed, to herself she refers to him as "this parvenue," with a convincingly aristocratic disregard for gender. And John Gaunt is one of those boys that must master his woman. Madame Glyn, in fact, has interestingly entangled his It with sadism all through the book, and maybe there is much to be said on her side. John must humble this disdainful creature; he must draw the net close.

So he gives Larry, the poppy-fancier, a job in his San Francisco office, and who would like to bet, then and there, that Larry isn't going to misappropriate funds? Then, when Ava's worries bring her to it, she seeks a position in his New York office, where he may keep his burning green eyes on her— I give you my word, she can feel them blazing through the massive oak door. She is offered a hundred dollars a week for cutting clippings out of newspapers. P.S. She got the job.

It goes on for nearly three hundred pages, with both of them vibrating away like steam launches. And then Larry comes through and steals two thousand dollars. Ava must have the money to keep Larry out of jail, where he couldn't get his hop. She goes to John's palatial residence. She will do it. She will Go Through. She will Sell Herself.

And then what do you think? She finds out it isn't the money; it isn't the principle of the thing, either. It is because she Loves. And what else do you think? He was going to marry her all the time.

Do you wonder that I am never going to read anything else?

The Socialist Looks at Literature

December 10, 1927

Upton Sinclair* is his own King Charles' head. He cannot keep himself out of his writings, try though he may; or, by this time, try though he doesn't. Let him start off upon an essay on a subject miles away from his own concerns, and in half a minute there he'll be, popping up between the sentences with a tale of some old but still throbbing grievance, or of some recent wrong that has been worked upon him. His *Money Writes!* is far less the collected accusations against American authors that, according to rumor, he intended it to be than it is a running record of personal woes. As such, it is an interesting document, but one a little less than convincing. As the book goes on, you have your choice of two impressions of its author, as he is today: either he is the prey of delusions of persecution—and the man, God knows, has been beset so sorely and so thoroughly that fantasies of a vast conspiracy against him were almost inevitable; or else he has become a confirmed belly-acher. Many Socialists, and I say it though my heart and soul are with the cause of Socialism, get to be that way.

To me, Upton Sinclair is one of the American great. I have no words worthy of being laid before his courage, his passion, his integrity. Also I think, and I choose my phrase with precision, that he is a hell of a good writer. In Russia and the Scandinavian countries, I am told—me, I could number my

* Although *Upton Sinclair* (1878-1968) was already famous for his social-protest novels such as *The Jungle*, about the Chicago meat-packing industry, and *Oil!*, which was banned in Boston, his eleven popular Lanny Budd novels were more than a decade in the future.

Russian and Scandinavian acquaintances on the thumbs of my two hands—he is rated first among American authors, and those boys in the cold lands are no fools about literature. It seems to me that he has good reason to be hurt at the scant critical appreciation he receives in the United States; although I do not believe, as he does, that this indifference is due to the machinations of Wall Street. I think he is a fine novelist. And I think as a literary critic he is simply god-awful.

Of *Money Writes!*—I hate that exclamation point—he says in his foreword, "it is not a polite book, but it is an honest book, and it is needed." "Needed by whom?" one can only murmur, on finishing it. "This book," he says, further, "is a study of American literature from an economic point of view. It takes our living writers, and turns their pockets inside out, asking 'Where did you get it?' and 'What did you do for it?' "

Fired by Mr. Sinclair's example, I tried turning inside out the pockets of a living writer of my acquaintance, a writer considered successful in his work, and one who appears often in the wealthier magazines. The gross receipts were one nail file; one rubberized tobacco pouch; one fountain pen without a top; one Western Union envelope (empty); one folded bit of paper upon which was written "Endicott 6281—about eleven o'clock"; one card bearing the names Tony, Gus, and Joe, and a West Forty-eighth Street address; one small rubber band (broken); one office clip (bent S-shaped); one half-dollar, one dime, and four pennies; one twenty-five centimes piece; and several unpleasantly mouselike formations of gray fluff. I had no heart to ask, "Where did you get it?" much less, "What did you do for it?"

But Mr. Sinclair was luckier. He asked his questions and then supplied his own answers to them. And he did not confine himself, despite his promise in the preface, to turning inside out the pockets of the living. The book contains a piece on Amy Lowell in which he asserts that she was regarded as a poet only because she was of the Boston Lowells (oh, yes, yes, yes, of course he refers to her as a Brahmin) and had a house in Brookline where she entertained those editors whose pages she wished to use. "She had a huge mansion to live in," he says, "full of all the old books, and her mill-slaves enabled her to buy the new ones. . . . Her success is one more demonstration of the fact that if you have money and social prestige you can get away with murder in America." All right, Mr. Sinclair. What about young Cornelius Vanderbilt, for instance?

There is also his essay on George Sterling, which as a piece of good taste ranks with that statuette of the Milo Venus with the clock in her stomach. The poet had loved the woman who is now Upton Sinclair's wife; and Upton Sinclair writes of that deep and agonized love with a curious satisfaction, with a swagger, almost a smirk. He cannot limit his references to it to this one essay; he keeps dragging it in, though he must go and fetch it from afar, all through the book. I know that an author must be brave enough to chop away clinging tentacles of good taste for the sake of a great work. But this is no great work, you see.

Despite his persecutions, Mr. Sinclair reveals himself in *Money Writes!* to be an enviable man. Always the thing he desires to believe is the thing he feels he knows to be true. Regarding American literature, he is not hurt, but terribly, terribly angry. Well, many feel that way, but Mr. Sinclair's is a more specialized soreness. He is off American authors because they do not always write of sweat-shops and child-labor, of mill-slaves and strikes and wages. Let them write of anything else, and he says that their purses are fat, their livers white, and their tongues black with boot-polish. And he says it so loud and so hard that it sounds to him like truth.

Surely there is no denying that a great novel of social conditions would be a boon to American letters. But it does seem to be not especially useful to roar and stamp because certain authors choose to speak of jade and satin and the shining surface of old furniture. There is a certain lack of proportion in bringing heavy artillery to bear on Joseph Hergesheimer* for so innocuous a work as *From an Old House*. Mr. Sinclair quotes from that book: "The bed in the curly maple room had a

---

* *Joseph Hergesheimer* (1880-1954), popular novelist of some literary distinction, was best known for his *Java Head*.

canopy like a film, a suspended tracery of frost; and under it many delicate and beautiful women had slept . . . cooled in the white silence of winter." Immediately he resumes his own words: "And against that lovely sentence" (Mr. Sinclair is never at his happiest in irony) "let us set one from an article in the *Survey*, December 15, 1925, by Dr. I. M. Rubinow, director of the Jewish Welfare Society of Philadelphia: 'The workingman's apartment in Philadelphia is not an apartment at all, but only two or three rooms sublet without any necessary adjustment for a separate decent family existence, for it has no private bathing or toilet facilities, and very frequently no separate water supply.' "

If this, ladies and gentlemen, proves anything at all, I am the Seventh Regiment. And if it is literary criticism, I am the National Guard.

As to the American poets, Mr. Sinclair shudders at the thought of those filthy traitors who write of love and death instead of sweat and oil. Yet his own knowledge of poetry seems to be a shade inadequate. I do not mean that only a Keats may write of poetry, but when Mr. Sinclair deems a certain verse of his own worthy of quoting—well, you'll see what I mean in a minute. It is a burlesque of the famous land-of-the-bean-and-the-cod lines, and it goes like this:

> Here's to the city of Boston,
>   The land of the bean and the cod,
> Where the Lowells won't let you buy *oil!*
>   And you send to New York, by God.

The Short Story, through a Couple of the Ages

December 17, 1927

There was a time, when I still had my strength, that I read nearly all the stories in the more popular magazines. I did not have to do it; I did it for fun, for I had yet to discover that there were other and more absorbing diversions that had the advantage of being no strain on the eyes. But even in those days of my vigor, nearly all the stories was the best that I could do. I could never go the full course. From the time I learned to read—which, I am pretty thoroughly convinced, was when I made my first big mistake—I was always unable to do anything whatever with stories that began in any of these following manners:

(1) "Ho, Felipe, my horse, and *pronto!*" cried *El Sol.* He turned to the quivering girl, and his mocking bow was so low that his *sombrero* swept the flags of the *patio.* "*Adiós,* then, *señorita,* until *mañana!*" And with a flash of white teeth across the lean young swarthiness of his face, he bounded to the back of his horse and was off, swift as a homing *paloma.*

(2) Everybody in Our Village loved to go by Granny Wilkins' cottage. Maybe it was the lilacs that twinkled a cheery greeting in the dooryard, or maybe it was the brass knocker that twinkled on the white-painted door, or maybe—and I suspect this was the real reason—it was Granny herself, with her crisp white cap, and her wise brown eyes, twinkling away in her dear little old winter apple of a face.

(3) The train chugged off down the long stretch of track, leaving the little new school-mistress standing alone on the rickety boards that composed the platform of Medicine Bend station. She looked very small indeed, standing there, and really ridiculously young. "I just won't cry!" she said fiercely, swallowing hard. "I won't! Daddy—Daddy would be disappointed in me if I cried. Oh, Daddy—Daddy, I miss you so!"

(4) The country club was a-hum, for the final match of the Fourth of July Golf Tournament was in full swing. Many a curious eye lingered on Janet DeLancey, rocking lazily, surrounded as usual by a circle of white-flanneled adorers, for the porch was a-whisper with the rumor that the winner of the match would also be the winner of the hitherto untouched heart of the blond and devastating Janet.

(5) I dunno ez I ought to be settin' here, talkin', when there's the vittles to git fer the men-folks. But, Laws, 'tain't often a body hez a chanct ter talk, up this-a-way. I wuz tellin' yuh

'bout li'l Mezzie Meigs, ol' Skin-flint Meigs's da'ter. She wuz a right peart 'un, Mezzie wuz, and purty!

(6) "For God's sake, don't do it, Kid!" whispered Annie the Wop, twining her slim arms about the Kid's bull-like neck. "Yer promised me yer'd go straight, after the last time. The bulls'll get yer, Kid; they'll send yer up, sure. Aw, Kid, put away yer gat, and let's beat it away somewhere in God's nice, clean country, where yer can raise chickens, like yer always dreamed of doin'.' "

But, with these half-dozen exceptions, I read all the other short stories that separated the Ivory Soap advertisements from the pages devoted to Campbell's Soups. I read about bored and pampered wives who were right on the verge of eloping with slender-fingered, quizzical-eyed artists, but did not. I read of young suburban couples, caught up in the fast set about them, driven to separation by their false, nervous life, and restored to each other by the opportune illness of their baby. I read tales proving that Polack servant-girls have their feelings, too. I read of young men who collected blue jade, and solved mysterious murders, on the side. I read stories of transplanted Russians, of backstage life, of shop-girls' evening hours, of unwanted grandmothers, of heroic collies, of experiments in child-training, of golden-hearted cow-punchers with slow drawls, of the comicalities of adolescent love, of Cape Cod fisherfolk, of Creole belles and beaux, of Greenwich Village, of Michigan Boulevard, of the hard-drinking and easy-kissing younger generation, of baseball players, sideshow artists, and professional mediums. I read, in short, more damn tripe than you ever saw in your life.

And then I found that I was sluggish upon awakening in the morning, spots appeared before my eyes, and my friends shunned me. I also found that I was reading the same stories over and over, month after month. So I stopped, like that. It is only an old wives' tale that you have to taper off.

Recently, though, I took the thing up again. There were rumors about that the American short story had taken a decided turn for the better. Crazed with hope, I got all the more popular and less expensive magazines that I could carry on my shoulders, and sat down for a regular old read. And a regular old read is just what it turned out to be. There they all were—the golden-hearted cow-punchers, the suburban couples, the baseball players, the Creole belles—even dear old Granny Wilkins was twinkling away, in one of them. There were the same old plots, the same old characters, the same old phrases—dear Heaven, even the same old illustrations. So that is why I shot myself.

It is true that in the magazines with quieter covers, with smaller circulations, and with higher purchasing prices, there are good short stories. Their scholarly editors have extended a courteous welcome to the newer writers. And the newer writers are good; they write with feeling and honesty and courage, and they write well. They do not prostitute their talents for money; they do not add words because they are to be paid by the word; scarcely, indeed, do they violate their amateur standing. But here, just as one did in the old days, does one get the feeling of reading the same stories over and over, month after month. There are no golden-hearted cow-punchers, but there are the inevitable Midwestern farm families; the laughing Creole belles have given place to the raw tragedies of the Bayou; but the formulae are as rigorous. You must write your story as starkly as it was written just before you did it; if you can out-stark the previous author, you are one up. Sedulous agony has become as monotonous as sedulous sunshine. Save for those occasions when you come upon a Hemingway or an Anderson or a Lardner in your reading, the other stories that meet your eye might all have come from the same pen.

I do not see how Mr. Edward O'Brien stands the strain. Season after season, as inescapable as Christmas, he turns out his collection of what he considers to be the best short stories of their year. To do this, and he does it conscientiously, he must read and rate every short story in every American magazine of fiction. Me, I should liefer adopt the career of a blood donor.

The Best Short Stories of 1927 is distinguished by the inclusion in it of Ernest Hemingway's superb "The Killers." This is enough to make any book of stories a notable one. There is also Sherwood Anderson's "Another Wife," which seems to me one of his best. But in the other stories I can find only disappointment. They seem to me wholly conventional, in this recent conventionality of anguish. There is no excitement to them; they have all the dogged quiet of too-careful writing. Separate, each one might possibly—oh, possibly—grip you. Grouped together, they string out as flat as Kansas.

Their compiler shows himself, in this volume, to be more than ever the unsung hero. In the back of the book, where he lists all the short stories of the year, and grades them, unasked, without a star, with one star, with two stars, or with three stars, according to his notion of their merits, you may gain some idea of what the man has been through. I give you some of the titles of the stories that he has wrestled with:

"Vomen is Easily Veak-Minded"; "Ma Bentley's Christmas Dinner"; "Archibald in Arcady" (there is always one of those, every year); "Fred and Circuses"; "Willie Painter Stays on the Level"; "Sylvia Treads among the Goulds"; "Betty Use Your Bean"; "Daddy's Nondetachable Cuffs"; "Ann 'n' Andy"; "Freed 'Em and Weep" (I bet that was a little love); "Jerry Gums the Game"; "Blue Eyes in Trouble"; "Grandflapper" (you can practically write that one for yourself); "She Loops to Conquer"; "Yes, Sir, He's My Maybe"; and "Dot and Will Find Out What It Means to Be Rich," which last sets me wondering into the night just what were the titles that the author threw out as being less adroit.

They say Mr. O'Brien makes ample money, on his sales of these stories written by others, and I hope it is true. But no matter how much it is, he deserves more.

Mrs. Post Enlarges on Etiquette

December 31, 1927

Emily Post's *Etiquette* is out again, this time in a new and an enlarged edition, and so the question of what to do with my evenings has been all fixed up for me. There will be an empty chair at the deal table at Tony's, when the youngsters gather to discuss life, sex, literature, the drama, what is a gentleman, and whether or not to go on to Helen Morgan's Club when the place closes; for I shall be at home among my book. I am going in for a course of study at the knee of Mrs. Post. Maybe, some time in the misty future, I shall be Asked Out, and I shall be ready. You won't catch me being intentionally haughty to subordinates or refusing to be a pallbearer for any reason except serious ill health. I shall live down the old days, and with the help of Mrs. Post and God (always mention a lady's name first) there will come a time when you will be perfectly safe in inviting me to your house, which should never be called a residence except in printing or engraving.

It will not be a grueling study, for the sprightliness of Mrs. Post's style makes the textbook as fascinating as it is instructive. Her characters, introduced for the sake of example, are called by no such unimaginative titles as Mrs. A., or Miss Z., or Mr. X.; they are Mrs. Worldly, Mr. Bachelor, the Gildings, Mrs. Oldname, Mrs. Neighbor, Mrs. Stranger, Mrs. Kindhart, and Mr. and Mrs. Nono Better. This gives the work all the force and the application of a morality play.

It is true that occasionally the author's invention plucks at the coverlet, and she can do no better by her brain-children than to name them Mr. Jones and Mrs. Smith. But it must be said, in fairness, that the Joneses and the Smiths are the horrible examples, the confirmed pullers of social boners. They deserve no more. They go about saying "Shake hands with Mr. Smith" or "I want to make you acquainted with Mrs. Smith" or "Will you permit me to recall myself to you?" or "Pardon *me!*" or "Permit me to assist you" or even "Pleased to meet you!" One pictures them as small people, darting about the outskirts of parties, fetching plates of salad and glasses of punch, applauding a little too enthusiastically at the end of a song, laughing a little too long at the point of an anecdote. If you could allow yourself any sympathy for such white trash, you might find something pathetic in their eagerness to please, their desperate readiness to be friendly. But one must, after all, draw that line somewhere, and Mr. Jones, no matter how expensively he is dressed, always gives the effect of being in his shirt-sleeves, while Mrs. Smith is so unmistakably the daughter of a hundred Elks. Let them be dismissed by somebody's phrase (I wish to heaven it were mine)—"the sort of people who buy their silver."

These people in Mrs. Post's book live and breathe; as Heywood Broun once said of the characters in a play, "they have souls and elbows." Take Mrs. Worldly, for instance, Mrs. Post's heroine. The woman will live in American letters. I know of no character in the literature of the last quarter-century who is such a complete pain in the neck.

See her at that moment when a younger woman seeks to introduce herself. Says the young woman: " 'Aren't you Mrs. Worldly?' Mrs. Worldly, with rather freezing politeness, says 'Yes,' and waits." And the young woman, who is evidently a glutton for punishment, neither lets her wait from then on nor replies, "Well, Mrs. Wordly, and how would you like a good sock in the nose, you old meat-axe?" Instead she flounders along with some cock-and-bull story about being a sister of Millicent Manners, at which Mrs. Worldly says, "I want very much to hear you sing some time," which marks her peak of enthusiasm throughout the entire book.

See Mrs. Worldly, too, in her intimate moments at home. "Mrs. Worldly seemingly pays no attention, but nothing escapes her. She can walk through a room without appearing to look either to the right or left, yet if the slightest detail is amiss, an ornament out of place, or there is one dull button on a footman's livery, her house telephone is rung at once!" Or watch her on that awful night when she attends the dinner where everything goes wrong. "In removing the plates, Delia, the assistant, takes them up by piling one on top of the other, clashing them together as she does so. You can feel Mrs. Worldly looking with almost hypnotized fascination—as her attention might be drawn to a street accident against her will."

There is also the practical-joker side to Mrs. W. Thus does Mrs. Post tell us about that: "For example, Mrs. Worldly writes:

" 'Dear Mrs. Neighbor:

" 'Will you and your husband dine with us very informally on Tuesday, the tenth, etc.'

"Whereupon, the Neighbors arrive, he in a dinner coat, she in her simplest evening dress, and find a dinner of fourteen people and every detail as formal as it is possible to make it. . . . In certain houses—such as the Worldlys' for instance—formality is inevitable, no matter how informal may be her 'will you dine informally' intention."

One of Mrs. Post's minor characters, a certain young Struthers, also stands sharply out of her pages. She has caught him perfectly in that scene which she entitles "Informal Visiting Often Arranged by Telephone" (and a darn good name for it, too). We find him at the moment when he is calling up Millicent Gilding, and saying, " 'Are you going to be in this afternoon?' She says, 'Yes, but not until a quarter of six.' He says, 'Fine, I'll come then.' Or she says, 'I'm sorry, I'm playing bridge with Pauline—but I'll be in tomorrow!' He says, 'All right, I'll come tomorrow.' " Who, ah, who among us does not know a young Struthers?

As one delves deeper and deeper into *Etiquette*, disquieting thoughts come. That old Is-It-Worth-It Blues starts up again, softly, perhaps, but plainly. Those who have mastered etiquette, who are entirely, impeccably right, would seem to arrive at a point of exquisite dullness. The letters and the conversations of the correct, as quoted by Mrs. Post, seem scarcely worth the striving for. The rules for the finding of topics of conversation fall damply on the spirit. "You talk of something you have been doing or thinking about—planting a garden, planning a journey, contemplating a journey, or similar safe topics. Not at all a bad plan is to ask advice: "We want to motor through the South. Do you know about the roads?' Or, 'I'm thinking of buying a radio. Which make do you think is best?' "

I may not dispute Mrs. Post. If she says that is the way you should talk, then, indubitably, that is the way you should talk. But though it be at the cost of that future social success I am counting on, there is no force great enough ever to make me say, "I'm thinking of buying a radio."

It is restful, always, in a book of many rules—and *Etiquette* has six hundred and eighty-four pages of things you must and mustn't do—to find something that can never touch you, some law that will never affect your ways. . . .

And in *Etiquette*, too, I had the sweetly restful moment of chancing on a law which I need not bother to memorize, let come no matter what. It is in that section called "The Retort Courteous to One You Have Forgotten," although it took a deal of dragging to get it in under that head. "If," it runs, "after being introduced to you, Mr. Jones" (of course, it would be Mr. Jones that would do it) "calls you by a wrong name, you let it pass, at first, but if he persists you may say: 'If you please, my name is Stimson.' "

No, Mrs. Post; persistent though Mr. Smith be, I may not say, "If you please, my name is Stimson." The most a lady may do is give him the wrong telephone number.

Poor, Immortal Isadora

January 14, 1928

My Life, the posthumously published autobiography of Isadora Duncan, is to me an enormously interesting and a profoundly moving book. Here was a great woman; a magnificent, generous, gallant, reckless, fated fool of a woman. There was never a place for her in the ranks of the terrible, slow army of the cautious. She ran ahead, where there were no paths.

She was no writer, God knows. Her book is badly written, abominably written. There are passages of almost idiotic naiveté, and there are passages of horrendously flowery verbiage. There are veritable Hampton Court mazes of sentences. There are long, low moans of poetry, painstakingly interpolated. There are plural pronouns, airily relating to singular nouns. She knew all about herself as an author. She says, in her introduction, "It has taken me years of struggle, hard work and research to learn to make one simple gesture, and I know enough about the Art" (that word she always capitalizes) "of writing to realise that it would take me again just so many years of concentrated effort to write one simple, beautiful sentence." But, somehow, the style of the book makes no matter.

Out of this mess of prose come her hope, her passion, her suffering; above all, comes the glamour that was Isadora Duncan's.

"Glamour" and "glamorous" are easy words, these days. The, shall we say, critical writers scoop them up by the handsful and plaster the fences of the town with them. The, shall we also say, intelligentsia fling them about like coppers, for the urchins to dive for. The other day, I heard the term "glamorous" applied three times within minutes. It was bestowed upon (*a*) a pretty little actress correctly performing a suitable little part in a neat little play; (*b*) an expensively dressed, nervous woman in whose drawing-room one may meet over-eager portrait-painters, playwrights of dubious sexes, professional conversationalists, and society ladies not yet quite divorced; and (*c*) a graceful young man ever carefully dropping references to his long, unfinished list of easy conquests. Well, there are always those who cannot distinguish between glitter and glamour, just as there are always those who cannot understand why you should desire real pearls when they can't be told from the imitations. But you can, you see, tell them from the imitations. The neat surfaces of the imitations shine prettily; the real glow from within. And the glamour of Isadora Duncan came from her great, torn, bewildered, foolhardy soul.

This book takes her up only to her departure for Russia to found a school of dancing, in 1921; it does not tell of her fantastically ill-advised marriage, and of her few blurred, dizzy years thereafter. There was to be another volume, but she never started it.

A little while after this one had reached her publishers, she was dead. She died as she should die, dramatically and without warning. It is curious that, almost on the first page of her book, she says, "I was born by the sea, and I have noticed that all the great events of my life have taken place by the sea." She died by the sea, on that shiny avenue of Nice that follows the

Mediterranean. It is curious, too, that she died in an automobile accident, as did her two exquisite children. She never recovered from their deaths. Oh, she tried. You follow, in her ill-written pages, the way she tried to live again. She drank, and she loved, and she danced. But she never again became the Bacchante, the beloved, the high priestess of her Art. From the day they were killed until the day of her own death, she was Niobe.

I do not know how honest her book is. I am convinced that as she set down each event, she believed that she was representing it in absolute truth, for she was of the accursed race of artists, who believe each thing they say while they are saying it; yes, and who would go to the stake for that moment's belief. She speaks with frankness—though frankness, if you will forgive dogma, is no synonym for honesty—of her lovers. She had a knack for selecting the unworthy—perhaps all great women have; one and all, they treated her with an extraordinary shabbiness. She calls only one by name. The others, she refers to by gloriously romantic titles—"Romeo," or the "Archangel" (the Archangel, by the way, threw her flat for one of the little girls in her band of dancers), or "Lohengrin." "Lohengrin," whose true name we all know, was perhaps the most important figure in her life; certainly he was the most frequent. He was generous to her only with money, and he had so much of that that it was a tiny, an imperceptible, form of generosity. But she never writes of them ungallantly. She does not whine, nor seek pity. She was a brave woman. We shall not look upon her like again.

There is another heroine in her book, though I doubt if the author realized it. That heroine is her mother. Dora Duncan, a little, prim, convention-bound music-teacher, divorced her roving husband. But she followed her children as anxiously and as loyally as a hen does a brood of fluffy ducklings. Uncomplaining, she lived with them in bare studios, where the only furniture, the mattresses upon which they slept, was hidden by day under Isadora's famous blue curtains. She went with them to Greece, donned, with them, tunic and chlamys and peplum—one hears her saying, plaintively, "How does this thing go on?"—and watched her son, Raymond, who always was the boy to do the one thing too much, kneeling down and kissing the soil, to the reasonable astonishment of the natives. She saw Isadora come into fame and fortune; beheld the contracts, that would have meant a secure old age for her, awaiting her daughter's signature; and then saw Isadora tear them up because she was interested, at the moment, in some transient young man. Finally, she came back to America, to live the rest of her days—you see, in the book you see only Isadora's version, but you can guess what a magnificent battle it must have been—wanting no more to do with any of her offspring. Isadora says that the elderly crabbedness, and the desertion, of her mother was due to the fact that never, since her husband left, had she taken a lover. But you can't help feeling that this is not quite so. Mrs. Duncan must have been so tired. Oh, so very tired.

Please read Isadora Duncan's *My Life*. You will find you won't care how it is written; you will find you will not be eager to trace to their sources the current rumors that it has been expurgated. There is enough in these pages. Here is the record of a grand person. Undoubtedly she was trying. She could not do anything that was not dramatic. Take, for instance, the occasion of her cutting her hair short. Other women go and have their hair bobbed, and that is all there is to it. But Isadora—she was in Albania with Raymond at the time—writes, "I cut off my hair, and threw it in the sea." She was like that. It comes, again, from belonging to that accursed race that cannot do anything unless they see, before and after, a tableau of themselves in the deed.

Possibly I am unfair about the shabbiness of her lovers. Surely there is much to be said on their side. She must have been trying, with her constant drama, with her intensity, with her pitiful, undying hope that here was the love, the great, beautiful love, that was to endure for all time. But she gave them Excitement. She gave them Glamour. She gave them a glimpse of Beauty.

Fortunate they
Who though once on¹ʸ, and then but far away
Have heard her massive sandal set on stone.

They were lucky men, they were. But she was not a lucky lady.

Re-enter Miss Hurst,
Followed by
Mr. Tarkington

January 28, 1928

It is with a deep, though a purely personal, regret that the conductor of this department announces the visitation upon her of a nasty case of the rams.

The rams, as I hope you need never find out for yourself, are much like the heebie-jeebies, except that they last longer, strike deeper, and are, in general, fancier. The illness was contracted on Thursday night at an informal gathering, and I am convinced it may be directly traced to the fact that I got a stalk of bad celery at dinner. It must have been bad celery; because you can't tell me that two or three sidecars, some champagne at dinner, and a procession of mixed Benedictines-and-brandies, taking seven hours to pass a given point, are going to leave a person in that state where she is afraid to turn around suddenly lest she see again a Little Mean Man about eighteen inches tall, wearing a yellow slicker and roller-skates. Besides the continued presence of the Little Mean Man, there are such minor symptoms as loss of correct knee action, heartbreak, an inability to remain either seated or standing, and a constant sound in the ears as of far-off temple bells. These, together with a readiness to weep at any minute and a racking horror of being left alone, positively identify the disease as the rams. Bad celery will give you the rams quicker than anything else. You want to look out for it. There's a lot of it around.

Additional proof that contaminated food was served to those

attending Thursday night's *fiesta* is offered by a fellow guest—
who, by the way, is also a contributor to this lucky magazine.
Ever since the event, he has had the rams, and had them good.
To the list of familiar lesser symptoms he adds an involuntary
jittering movement of the hands, so pronounced as to render an
ordinary teacup and saucer almost deafening in his clutch. He
has not yet been followed about by any Little Mean Men on
roller-skates; but, from the time of his awakening on Friday
morning—an awakening which was entirely contrary to any
wish of his—he has been attended by a personal beaver. He is
all right so long as he keeps his eyes straight ahead. But if he
forgets, and looks quickly up and to the left, he sees this beaver
run like lightning across the ceiling. It is an unusually large
beaver, he says, with the broadest, flattest tail he ever saw in his
life. He says it looks to him to be a beaver of about four or five
years of age.

He is assured that he owes his new pet to his having been the
recipient, at Thursday night's social function, of a bad string
bean. (The second quickest way to contract the rams is through
bad string beans; you should always have your string beans
analyzed.) So you can see for yourself what sort of food was
provided for us. Criminal penny-pinching, that's what a thing
like that is.

You can always tell if you have the genuine rams by the fact
that you cannot like anything much, even your nearest and
dearest. The milder form of the rams—called the German
rams, or Jacob's Evil—attacks so lightly that it leaves you
vitality enough occasionally to give a whoop about something.
In the real, old-fashioned rams, there are two things that you
desire to do less than all the things in the world. One is to read
new books; and the other is to write about them. This latter
activity is not only distasteful but downright dangerous. In the
first place, it is practically impossible to keep the forehead off
the typewriter keys. And in the second, the sufferer from the
rams is very likely to contract a bad case of Author's Elbow,
due to constant strenuous erasing of the curious designs made
by his frequently hitting, in his weakened condition, several

of the wrong letters and punctuation marks at once.

I give you these grim details only in apology. My tiny, begrudged enthusiasm and slow, reluctant words are not the results of a fit of the sulks, truly they are not. It must have been that bad celery that begot them. For I have read two novels that are selling by the thousands every day, and are, also daily, winning the plaudits of press and public. And for my life, I cannot discern what all the applause is about. That's what the rams do to a person.

A President Is Born—no, it is not a companion piece to the Nan Britton book, and if I never hear any such crack again, it will be too soon—is the latest Fannie Hurst* novel. I have a deep admiration for Miss Hurst's work; possibly in your company I must admit this with a coo of deprecating laughter, as one confesses a fondness for comic strips, motion-picture magazines, chocolate-almond bars, and like too-popular entertainments. There have been times when her sedulously torturous style, her one-word sentences and her curiously compounded adjectives, drive me into an irritation that is only to be relieved by kicking and screaming. But she sees and she feels, and she makes you see and feel; and those are not small powers. She has written nothing that has not, in some degree, moved me—nothing, at least, until she wrote *A President Is Born*.

This is, they say, her Big Novel. (If you were a real book reviewer, you would say, "Miss Hurst has chosen a far larger canvas than is her wont." I wish I could talk like that without getting all hot and red.) It is one of those things supposedly written from some time in the future—a trick which is to me, though I have no notion why, always vaguely annoying—and it relates the early life of one David Schuyler, a legendary and a heroic President of the United States. This early life occurs in the mid-western farmlands, and the boy is the youngest member of one of those mid-western farm families so

* *Fannie Hurst* (1889-1968) was known at this time chiefly for her earlier novels *Humoresque* and *Lummox*.

numerous that you are constantly losing track of their names, dispositions, occupations, and spouses. There is among them one of those big, wise, calm, broad-hipped, level-eyed women who puts the farm on a paying basis by her efforts—why do our lady authors so love to write of those? This one, David's sister, is supposed to contribute the footnotes that, in their turn, are supposed to lend an air of authenticity to the book. Her manner of writing shows that she has been much influenced by Miss Hurst.

I can find in *A President Is Born* no character nor any thought to touch or excite me. (There go those rams again.) I am awfully sorry, but it is to me a pretty dull book.

And I am sorry, too, about my feelings in regard to Booth Tarkington's* new novel, *Claire Ambler.* It is, of course, written with finish and skill and a sense of leisured care. But its characters have extraordinarily few dimensions, even for Tarkington characters. It is the study of a girl, who wants to make men fall in love with her but doesn't want them to tell her about it, from the time she is eighteen until she reaches twenty-five. The first part of the book is perhaps the best, certainly the most amusing, for there Mr. Tarkington is dealing with adolescent love. And he has no equal at setting down in exquisite words the comic manifestations of youthful love-agony, though never does he dare let his pen touch the agony itself. He is, I am afraid, too merciful a man for greatness.

Claire Ambler was a disappointment to me, who have a naive trust in what the critics say. I read it all; but I found that neither during the process nor after did I care very much.

There. Now you see what the rams can do. Please, oh, please, take warning, and be careful about celery and string beans.

* *Booth Tarkington* (1869-1946) twice won the Pulitzer Prize for his novels, and his stories of adolescence, *Penrod* and *Seventeen,* were beloved by a whole generation.

A Good Novel,
and a Great Story

February 4, 1928

You don't want a general houseworker, do you? Or a traveling companion, quiet, refined, speaks fluent French entirely in the present tense? Or an assistant billiard-maker? Or an elevator girl? Or a magician's helper? Or a private librarian? Or a lady car-washer? Because if you do, I should appreciate your giving me a trial at the job. Any minute, now, I am going to become one of the Great Unemployed. I am about to leave literature flat on its face. I don't want to review books any more. It cuts in too much on my reading.

In order that my public—my boy and girl, I call them—may have the inestimable benefit of my report, I am supposed to have read *The Last Post*, by Ford Madox Ford (*né* Hueffer).* I have been faithful to my duty, in my fashion. I have read the book. But I did not behave like a regular little soldier about it. I did not sit me down in a hard, straight chair, and read it sternly through at one stretch. I kept putting it down, and sneaking off to the dear, strange things I truly ached to read and to ponder.

It is not that *The Last Post* is not a good book. It is not that I do not think Ford Madox Ford is a fine novelist. (There was a time, there, when I thought I was never going to get out of those negatives, but the crisis is passed, now, and I am expected to pull through.) It is that there are certain things set down in black on white beside which even distinguished, searching, passionate novels pale to mediocrity.

There is, for example, a brief story lately printed in a morning paper. I cannot take my mind from that story. I read it over and over, and then I crawl off in a corner and think and think and think. If it were only any of my business, I should tell you about that story. It concerns a man who shall here be

* *Ford Madox Ford* (1873-1939) changed his surname from Hueffer during World War I. He later withdrew *The Last Post* from the *Parade's End* tetralogy, preferring to have the first three novels stand alone as a trilogy.

called William Doe, because he has enough trouble already. He was charged with writing what are journalistically called poison-pen letters to various city officials; the charge was dismissed when handwriting experts declared that the letters were written not by him but by a woman. That, I think, is a fairly good start, but wait. If it were any possible affair of mine, I should quote the cool, exact words of that newspaper story. "Look at this, will you?" I should say, and then I should write down these lines:

"Mr. Doe from the first stoutly denied that he had anything to do with the letters or knew anything about them. He was at a loss to explain them and the use of his name in the signatures. Yesterday he said that the only explanation he could think of was the fact that his mother had kept him and his brother in long dresses until they were nine years old and that he had since then frequently been a victim of practical jokes perpetrated by his childhood acquaintances."

The Last Post is a tale of human anguish, but it rings flat and thin compared with this short piece. "The Life of William Doe"—there would be a book. I do not know who could worthily set down this wretched, grinding tragedy, this tale of small, steady tortures, of little obscene agonies dropping, slowly, ceaselessly, upon the heart of a man. Dreiser's pen is too heavy; Hemingway's, too sharp. Lardner, I think, might do it. Sherwood Anderson—no, I guess not. But God send that someone does it, and does it fittingly, for there will be a great book—perhaps the great book.

I wish I could stop thinking about it, for, as you have so crisply remarked, it is none of my damn business. I am here to write about books, not to review newspaper stories. Who do I think I am, anyway—Guy Fawkes?

Well, about this latest novel of Ford Madox Ford's. It is the last of his series of four books—what do you call a series of four books, anyway? I can only count up to "trilogy"—beginning with *Some Do Not . . .* and going on through *No More Parades* and *A Man Could Stand Up*. To me, *The Last Post* ranks fourth not only in sequence. Ford's style has here become so tortuous that he writes almost as if he were parodying himself.

There are grave hardships for the reader in the long interior monologues which make up much of the book. It is a novel to be read with a furrow in the brow. You must constantly turn back pages, to ascertain from inside which character's head the author is writing.

(What do you suppose were some of the other dainty little practical jokes that William Doe's childhood acquaintances played on him?)

Yet *The Last Post* is a novel worth all its difficulties. There is always, for me, a vastly stirring quality in Ford's work. His pages are quick and true. I know of few other novelists who can so surely capture human bewilderment and suffering, for his is a great pity. To me, his best book, and far and away his best, is *The Good Soldier*—the novel separate from the books about Christopher Tietjens. Yet all the books of the Tietjens saga have in them some of the same power, the same depth, the same rackingly moving honesty that makes *The Good Soldier* so high and fine a work. They are sad books, filled with sad and skinless people. There are some who do not like such books. The world, too, is crowded with the sorrowful and the sensitive. There are many who do not like such a world.

(Do you think that William Doe must trace every bitter thing that befalls him back to those first nine terrible years of his life? Do you think he has become obsessed with the thought? And if he has, why under Heaven shouldn't he have?)

In his dedicatory letter, which serves as a preface to *The Last Post*, Ford says that the book is written to satisfy a certain "stern, contemptuous, and almost virulent insistence on knowing 'what became of Tietjens.' " There was a demand for an ending; "if possible a happy ending." But that he was not able to supply. "For in this world of ours," he says, "though lives may end, Affairs do not. Even though Tietjens and Valentine were dead the Affair that they set going would go rolling on down the generations. . . . The rest will go on beneath the nut-boughs or over the seas—or in the best Clubs. It is not your day or mine that shall see the end of them."

So at the end of this last book, Christopher Tietjens, "The Last Tory," is left with Valentine and the child that is to be born to them, to carry on the Tietjens gentleness and courage and bewilderment. It has always been a thorn to me that the man should have so difficult a name as Christopher Tietjens; and as for the woman he loved, fine and brave though Ford has made her, I could never let her near my heart because her name was Valentine Wannop. That is quibbling, I know, and of the silliest sort. But that's the way I am. Take me or leave me; or, as is the usual order of things, both.

(I wonder if William Doe's brother, who was also condemned to those pitiful long dresses, has been a like victim of the hellish jokes of the childhood acquaintants. Or was it only William who was singled out?)

The Last Post is mainly the story of the life's end of Mark Tietjens, Christopher's brother, who neither spoke nor moved from the moment he heard a bugler blow the last post, the call for the dead, on the night of the Armistice that he thought shamed England and betrayed her sons, to the quarter-hour before his own death. Then he speaks one brief phrase of deep and contemptuous pity to Christopher's wife, the glamorous and devilish Sylvia. Sylvia, the villainess of the piece, is the character who stands out sharpest to me from the Tietjens saga. It is she that I am sorriest to see leave forever.

(Who do you suppose that woman was who wrote those atrocious letters and signed William Doe's name to them? She must be overwhelmed with the success of her prank. It was such a long, thorough, far-reaching bit of savagery. He was arrested in October, and knew three months of being out on a thousand dollars' bail.)

Through *The Last Post*, as through all his books, there run the long fibers of Ford's hatreds. That is all very well for a writer; that, in fact, is fine for a writer; but it may get him into messes. And it gets Ford into a nasty jam, when he comes to one of his characters, his Amurrican lady, Mrs. De Bray Pape. I am as ready as the next to take a joke on my native sex and my own country-women, but here is as clumsy a caricature as you can find. I suggest that Mr. Ford go some place and get good and ashamed of himself for smearing this blemish of heavy buffoonery across the honest pages of his book.

(I wonder if William Doe ever has easy moments. Or does he dwell always in the fear of what will happen next? Do you suppose he ever has any fun? And how does he?)

And now that this review is over, do you mind if I talk business for a moment? If you yourself haven't any spare jobs for a retired book-reviewer, maybe some friend of yours might have something. Maybe you wouldn't mind asking around. Salary is no object; I want only enough to keep body and soul apart. The one thing I ask is that I have an occasional bit of time to myself. I want to read the papers.

Literary Rotarians

February 11, 1928

The town, these days, is full of them. You cannot go ten yards, on any thoroughfare, without being passed by some Rotarian of Literature, hurrying to attend a luncheon, banquet, tea, or get-together, where he may rush about from buddy to buddy, slapping shoulders, crying nicknames, and swapping gossip of the writing game. I believed for as long as possible that they were on for their annual convention; and I thought that they must run their little span and disappear, like automobile shows, six-day bicycle races, ice on the pavements, and such recurrent impedimenta of metropolitan life. But it appears that they are to go on and on. Their fraternal activities are their livings—more, their existences. They are here, I fear, to stay. But they will never take the place of the horse.

The members of this benevolent order do not wear any such jolly paraphernalia as fezzes, plumed hats, animals' teeth, or fringed silk badges—or, at least, they have not yet done so. But you can spot any one of them at a glance. They are all bright and brisk and determinedly young. They skitter from place to place with a nervous quickness that suggests the movements of those little leggy things that you see on the surface of ponds, on hot Summer days. The tips of their noses are ever delicately a-quiver for the scent of news, and their shining eyes are puckered a bit, with the strain of constant peering. Their words are quicker than the ear, and spoken always in syncopation, from their habitually frantic haste to get out the news that the Doran people have tied up with the Doubleday, Page outfit, or that *McCall's Magazine* has got a new high-pressure editor. Some of them are women, some of them are men. This would indicate that there will probably always be more of them.

They have, I should judge, the best time of any people in the world. Running from guild to league to club to committee, and round the course again, they meet only those of their kind, only those who speak their language and share their interests. They see no misunderstanding outsiders, need listen to no tedious tales of struggle and terror and injustice. Round and round they go, ever up on their toes, giving and receiving hands and smiles and cozily intimate words. It is all as gay and active and wholesome as a figure in the lancers.

Naturally, people so happy cannot keep all their bliss bottled up inside themselves. It must overflow somewhere; and it does, baby, it does. Pick up a newspaper (it would be just like you to pick up the *Wall Street Journal* and make a fool out of me) and there, snug on an inside page, you will find one of the jolly brotherhood bubbling away about the good times he and his buddies have been having. These accounts are called diaries or day-books or "Letters from a Penman" or "Jottings on a Cuff" or "Helling Around with the Booksy Folk" or—but no; there is one weekly treat actually headed, "Turns with a Bookworm," so you can see how much use it is to try to kid their titles. Anyway, it doesn't matter. All I wanted to point out is that if a compositor, in some moment of dreamy confusion, ran any such column under the head of "Gleanings from Rotary," he would still keep his job.

These reports are all written in the chatty, intimate manner; personality must be injected and liveliness, so that you shall see that the writer, for all his lofty connection with things literary, can be just as good company as an electrician, say, or a certified public accountant. And of what hot doings do they tell! From noon to morning, theirs is one mad whirl of literary gatherings. You read and wonder, enviously, how they ever stand the pace.

I went to a literary gathering once. How I got there is all misty to me. I remember that, on that afternoon, I was given a cup of tea which tasted very strange. Drowsiness came over me, and there was a humming noise in my ears; then everything went black. When I came to my senses, I was in the brilliantly lighted banquet-hall of one of the large hotels, attending a dinner of a literary association. The place was filled with people who looked as if they had been scraped out of drains. The ladies ran to draped plush dresses—for Art; to wreaths of silken flowerets in the hair—for Femininity; and, somewhere between the two adornments, to chain-drive *pince-nez*—for Astigmatism. The gentlemen were small and somewhat in need of dusting. There were guests of honor: a lady with three names, who composed pageants; a haggard gentleman, who had won the prize of $20 offered by *Inertia: a Magazine of Poesy* for the best poem on the occupation of the Ruhr district; and another lady, who had completed a long work on "Southern Californian Bird-Calls" and was ready for play.

There was apparently some idea of seating the guests at various small oval tables, but the plan was not followed. Instead, there was incessant visiting, from table to table. No introductions were needed, for each guest wore a card with his or her name plainly written upon it, and everybody talked to everybody else. And the night hung still, to bear the weight of those words of who was cleaning up how much in the fiction game, or the poetry racket.

By pleading a return of that old black cholera of mine, I got away before the speeches, the songs, and the probable donning of paper caps and marching around the room in lockstep. I looked with deep interest, the next morning, for the bookmen's and bookwomen's accounts of the event. One and all, they declared that never had there been so glamorous and brilliant a function. You inferred that those who had been present would require at least a week to sleep it off. They wrote of it as they write of every other literary gathering—as if it were like one of those parties that used to occur just before Rome fell.

From that day to this, I have never touched another cup of tea.

Never has any member of literary Rotary been known to have a dull time. He meets no writer but to love him, no publisher but to praise. (Or however it goes, please.) He has yet to have a thin evening. He no more knows the meaning of the word "boredom" than he does that of the word "taste."

It is not only the altruism of effervescence that causes these scribes to share their gaieties with the public. There is prestige to be had from these accounts. To have written anything, whether it be a *Ulysses* or whether it be a report of who sat next to whom at the P.E.N. Club dinner, is to be a writer. "And what does *he* do?" "Why, he writes." It is impossible to say it without shading the voice with awe. There is an air to it, a distinction. The literary Rotarians have helped us and themselves along to the stage where it doesn't matter a damn what you write; where all writers are equal. They can put precisely the same amount of high and sincere excitement into the sentences "Ernest Hemingway has completed another novel" and "Anne Parrish* confesses she is having so much fun finishing her new book that she almost cries when she has to leave her desk at bedtime." Perfectly level, always, is the business basis.

There are other ways than luncheons, teas, and banquets for the members of the brotherhood to get their fun, as well as their coffee and cakes. They can organize and run Book Weeks, at popular department stores (to some ways of thinking, if this world were anything near what it should be there would be no more need of a Book Week than there would be of a Society for the Prevention of Cruelty to Children); they can appear in bookshops, to shake hands with the public, or any portion of it; and they can tour the country, to talk to the ladies upon what Ford Madox Ford said about American oysters, and how Fannie Hurst wears her hair. In our smaller towns, the literary lecturer has practically replaced the seamstress-in-by-the-day.

An enviable company, these joiners-up, with good cheer and

* *Anne Parrish* (1888-1957) had a minor reputation as a novelist; her *All Kneeling* was a favorite of Alexander Woollcott.

appreciation for their daily portion. And about them always, like the scent of new violets, is the sweet and reassuring sense of superiority. For, being literary folk, they are licensed to be most awfully snooty about the Babbitts.

Excuse It, Please

February 18, 1928

When you have to apologize it is well, I suppose, to get the thing over quickly, and then go quietly along about your parlor games. So this week's piece of living literature must start off with the gifted author, thumb in mouth and head hanging like an old catalpa pod, publicly suing for pardon. It is not a comfortable thing to do. We are a proud lot, we mad Varicks.

When Ernest Hemingway's *Men Without Women* was published, I went promptly, sincerely, and, I do think, pardonably wild. That would have been all very sweet and pretty if I had kept it in the sanctity of my hotel room, but no; never the half-measure girl, I had to go leaping into print with my excitement. For Mr. Hemingway, I selected these words: "He is, to me, the greatest living writer of short stories." For his book, I worked up this combination: "I do not know where you can find a finer collection of stories." That's what I said. Loud and clear and cocky, I said it.

Lately I have had a letter (I can feel again my surprise and delight at receiving it, for it is ever like a day in the country to me to find in my mail a plain white envelope, without the name of a collection agency printed in the upper left-hand corner), a patient and courteous letter from a gentleman who quoted my words about *Men Without Women*, and suggested for my attention a book of short stories called *Seven Men*—in especial, he said, the tale "A. V. Laider" contained therein. I read the note with a sickening sensation that threatened to become definite action. "Oh, my God," I said—I was brought up in a mining town, and the old phrases come back in moments of emotion—"I forgot about *Seven Men!*"

That was all I had done. I had only forgotten about *Seven Men*. In my excitement over Ernest Hemingway, all I did was forget about Max Beerbohm.

I thank my correspondent, damn him, for reminding me. Even, in my humility, I sit silent while he says that "A. V. Laider" is the best story in Beerbohm's book, although I am an old "Enoch Soames" girl myself. This is me apologizing. I am a fool, a bird-brain, a liar and a horse-thief. I promise to try to be better; never again will I mess about with such phrases as "greatest living writer" and "do not know where you can find a finer collection." (While I am crawling this far, I had better keep right along and say that another little lapse of memory was my overlooking the fact that Mr. Rudyard Kipling, not only alive but feeling fine, has been no slouch at short-story writing.) I am done. I wouldn't touch a superlative again with an umbrella.

But it would be all right, wouldn't it, if I amended my remarks to read: "Ernest Hemingway is, to me, the greatest living American writer of short stories?" Or maybe this would do better: "Ernest Hemingway is, to me, the greatest living American short-story writer who lives in Paris most of the time but goes to Switzerland to ski, served with the Italian Army during the World War, has been a prize-fighter and has fought bulls, is coming to New York in the spring, is in his early thirties, has a black moustache, and is still waiting for that two hundred francs I lost to him at bridge." Or maybe, after all, the only thing to do is to play safe and whisper: "Ernest Hemingway is, to me, a good writer."

And now that that is done, I'll be getting up off my hands and knees, and doing the week's wash.

Our Lady
of the Loudspeaker

February 25, 1928

It was to be expected, I suppose, that Aimee Semple Mc-

Pherson,* that Somewhat Different Entertainer, would write a book. Anybody might have foreseen that that would be. Anybody, that is, except me. I am the one who believes, when things are calm and peaceful, that there is a chance of their staying so. That is the way I have gone about all my life. I really must make a note on my desk calendar to have my head examined one day next week. I am beginning to have more and more piercing doubts that my fontanel ever closed up properly.

Well, Aimee Semple McPherson has written a book, and were you to call it a little peach, you would not be so much as scratching its surface. It is the story of her life, and it is called *In the Service of the King,* which title is perhaps a bit dangerously suggestive of a romantic novel. It may be that this autobiography is set down in sincerity, frankness, and simple effort. It may be, too, that the Statue of Liberty is situated in Lake Ontario.

I have never heard Mrs. McPherson preach—a record which, Heaven helping me, I purpose keeping untarnished—but from her literary style, I get the idea. I give you, for your birthday, a typical bit from her opus:

"Quicksand!

"Pernicious quicksand!

"Cloying, treacherous, relentless quicksand!

"The soul-destroying quicksand"—no, no; not "that hung in the well." "The soul-destroying quicksand of unbelief!"

You see? And she can go on like that for hours. Can, hell—does.

On the occasions that she drifts into longer and broader sentences, she writes as many other three-named authoresses have written before. Her manner takes on the thick bloom of rich red plush. The sun becomes "that round orb of day" (as opposed, I expect, to those square orbs you see about so much lately); maple syrup is "Springtide's liquid love gift from the

* *Aimee Semple McPherson's* story is told in this review, but present-day readers might not know of the newspaper sensation caused by the famous lady evangelist's reported abduction and escape in 1927.

heart of the maple wood"; the forest, by a stroke of inspiration, turns out to be "a cathedral of stately grandeur and never ceasing wonder and awe" (argue, if you will, for "cloying quicksand" as the phrase superb, but me, I'll hold out for "stately grandeur"); the ocean—you'll never guess—is "a broad expanse of sparkling silver"; icy panes are portrayed by the delicate whimsy "Jack Frost had completely painted the windows with his magic brush"; and the gifted author is frequently asking you to "But Hold!" It is difficult to say whether Mrs. McPherson is happier in her crackling ex-clamations or in her bead-curtain-and-chenille-fringe style. Presumably the lady is happy in both manners. That would make her two up on me.

As for the plot of the work—oh, do sit down; I've got so much to tell you. She starts off with a bang in a chapter called "The Escape." It tells about her return over the desert from that mysterious hut where those two mean men and that big, strong woman had held her for ransom—you remember about that. Lost at night in trackless sand and rustling undergrowth, she prays to be brought to safety. It is here, in her first quoted prayer, that you glimpse Mrs. McPherson's relations with her Maker. She is patient, always, with the Almighty, and explicit, and she is a firm believer in jogging His memory. Thus the prayer of forensic desperation that bubbles from her heart:

"O God, Thou who didst lead the Children of Israel across the wilderness and guide them in all their journeys—Thou who didst provide for them insomuch that they were fed from the skies and watered from the rock, and didst even keep their shoes from wearing out—Thou who didst care for the three Hebrew children, and kept them safe, though cast into the fiery furnace, so that not a hair of their head was singed, nor was the smell of burning upon their garments—Thou who hast ever looked down in pity upon Thy children in their trials—heard and answered their prayers—Thou hast never failed me before and Thou wilt not fail me now—hear my prayer and guide my weary footsteps to safety, for I am lost and sore distressed."

And so she got back to Los Angeles, and—as was later

developed at the trial—her shoes were not only kept from wearing out, but were not even scuffed.

But there was trouble awaiting her. Dose ole debbil unbelievers greeted her account of her kidnaping and escape with roars of gay laughter. Reporters and photographers—Mrs. McPherson's bêtes noires—descended upon her and tore her privacy from her; and you know what her privacy means to our little lady. True, the members of her congregation made whoopee in the streets, practically smothered her with roses, and carried her about in a flower-decked chair to celebrate her restoration to them. But it was not enough. "I turned," she says, "toward the window of memory and looked back for respite to the peaceful green meadows of childhood.

"I can see it all now—"

All right, Eddie. Black-out, and into the story of the early life.

She was born in Canada, lived peacefully, went through a couple of pages of doubt, and then decided to go in for saving souls. She married an evangelist named Robert Semple, and went with him to China to convert the natives, a strange, yellow people who put food on the graves of their dead and speak an outlandish language. There Mr. Semple died, and, after her little daughter was born, she returned to the United States, to do mission work. But loneliness took her, and she made a second marriage, to which she devotes one grudging paragraph. "I took up my household duties," she says, "with the understanding that I should go back to the Lord's work if ever the call came." Well, the call came, sharp and clear as if from the whistle of some celestial doorman, and back she went. "My husband," she says, "recognizing the call, went with me and helped me for a time, but decided to go back to his world of business."

And that is the only peep we get at Mr. McPherson. I wish that one day he would write the story of his life; there is a book I should love to read. Meanwhile, I can only hope that he has enjoyed a fraction of the success in "his world of business" that his wife has in hers.

There were years, then, of touring the country holding revival meetings. Early in her career, Mrs. McPherson proved herself adept at advertising. In one small town was a poor, drunken half-wit, the butt of the local jokesters, who earned a tiny living as town crier. Mrs. McPherson conceived the charming idea of sending him through the streets, ringing his bell and crying, "Hear ye! Hear ye! I have given my heart to Christ. Come down to the revival tonight and hear Sister McPherson preach about the Christ who saved even me!"

On another occasion, she arrived in St. Petersburg at carnival time, when the streets were thronged with floats. It looked as if business were going thus to be taken away from her, but she thought up a dear little scheme to call herself to the attention of the romping public. She dressed up her flivver in leaves and boughs, and erected upon it an evangelist's tent of sheets, on which was painted: "Jesus Saves! Repent and be Converted! I'm on the way to the Tent Revival. R. U.?"

The car was entered in the parade of floats, and, Mrs. McPherson blushingly admits, was the wow of the entertainment.

Thus she progressed triumphantly along the bright way that led to the mighty temple in Los Angeles. Hers is a story of virtue victorious. Occasionally she was mildly in need, but never for long; for Heaven—which seems, from Mrs. McPherson's personal testimony, to be a sort of gold-paved mail-order house—promptly shipped her food, clothing, money, houses, and even canary birds, as she required them. But never did she endure the little daily heartaches, the quarrels and partings and ugliness that are the lot of the rest of us. She dwelt ever in the blissful amity that is the due of the virtuous. (Not even does she dignify by mention that pretty little jam she got into with her mother, at the time of the kidnaping episode.) Never, indeed, have I known an autobiographer so lavishly to award herself all the breaks.

In the Service of the King has caused an upset in my long-established valuations. With the publication of this, her book,

Aimee Semple McPherson has replaced Elsie Dinsmore* as my favorite character in fiction.

The Compleat Bungler

March 17, 1928

His publishers say of Mr. George Reith, the author of *The Art of Successful Bidding*, that he, "by virtue of his new position as Chairman of the Card Committee of the Knickerbocker Whist Club, is now the highest authority in the auction bridge world." So you see there is something wrong. Obviously the publishers have never met a certain gentleman who shall be nameless— being already possessed of all the other characteristics of one born out of wedlock—who was my bridge partner last Saturday night. Had they listened to him, they could never have rated Mr. Reith as anything more than second highest authority.

I do not know if my quondam partner was ever chairman of any card committee, and I doubt if he is so much as up for the Knickerbocker Whist Club. There is even some room for argument as to whether or not he was the boy that wrote the game. But it was he who was elected, by an overwhelming vote of one, to expound its principles to all those in darkness. He was Elwell's** representative on earth. I would draw him for a partner; one hundred and ten million people in the country, and I would draw him.

My own bridge is of the experimentalist school; it has been suggested, indeed, that what it really needs are backing from Otto Kahn and stage-settings by John Dos Passos. There is youth to my game, youth and hope and fearlessness and a wild, hungry seeking. People have been known to gather from blocks

---

* The name of *Elsie Dinsmore*, the virtuous and put-upon heroine of a series of twenty-six books for girls by *Martha Finley* (1828-1909), was a byword for all who began to read in the late nineteenth century, and for a generation into this one.

** *Joseph Elwell*, a leading authority on bridge, was found murdered in 1920—a crime still unsolved.

around, to stand back of my chair and puzzle out just what it all meant. High have run the bets as to precisely what I was playing, with the speculations ranging all the way from Authors to Prisoners' Base. You can see that mine is no ordinary, patterned, box-office bridge. It is more a symbol of life, really, than a game of cards. Why, I have ever asked, be a slave to form? Look at Cézanne. Is he a slave? Is he shackled to conventions? Is he afraid of the laughter of the herd? Is he untrue to his gift? Is he mineral? Is he in this room?

Emotionally, I am a bridge-player of the manic-depressive type. If I can get all the way through a rubber without once mistaking a spade for a club, I want to go right up and slap Milton Work on the back. If, on the other hand, my partner gives me a dirty, even a slightly soiled, look, I am broken for the evening, and all my thoughts are of the emptiness of life and the sweet solace of the grave. And my partner at last Saturday night's lynching-bee began bestowing positively insanitary looks upon me, even before I had finished my first deal. (All right, suppose I did spill seven or eight cards on the floor. That doesn't make me any less a fellow creature, with blood and bones and an immortal soul and decent, human feelings, does it?)

He turned out to be one of those icily patient boys; he did a good deal of deep sighing, and of asking me, in an heroically mild voice, such questions as "Would you mind telling me what was your idea in leading me a diamond? Or is it a secret?" I kept back the tears, however, like a little soldier, until that moment in our last rubber—our last rubber on earth, undoubtedly—when he suggested that he and the others stop playing and just sit back and watch me do my card tricks.

It was those words that led me to take steps about leashing my bridge game to the standards of the mob. I was advised to study Mr. Reith's *The Art of Successful Bidding*. They told me that it was sane, simple, instructive, and authoritative. I do not question that it is all those things; it is, I have no moment's doubt, a fine textbook. But it is well over my head. I can't even jump for it. There is no use in my poring over advanced stuff, when what I am seeking is some simple, kindly, one-syllabled formula for the way to remember What's Out.

However, the book has done one great thing to salve my ego. In the blurb on its dust-cover, it is stated: "His book is entirely unusual. Any ordinary bridge-player will find he can study it without a deck of cards and he will improve his game." So now I have found out what I am. I am no ordinary bridge-player— can Whitehead say more? It is comforting, it is heartening to know, on the highest authority, a thing like that about oneself. I am no ordinary bridge-player. Say I'm weary, say I'm sad, say that health and wealth have missed me, say I'm growing old, but add I'm no ordinary bridge-player. And if I ever see that Saturday-night boy again, God forbid, I'll take no more cracks about card tricks out of him.

Well, now that that is settled for all time, there are better things to be done. There is a good book out. It is *Home to Harlem*, the first novel by Claude McKay, who has written no prose, to my knowledge, before this. It is a rough book; a bitter, blunt, cruel, bashing novel. I cannot quite pull myself to the point of agreeing with those who hail it as a wholly fine work. It seems to me that there are parts of it that do not come off; I feel, a little uncomfortably, that Mr. McKay has not yet found himself as a novelist. ("Do not come off" and "found himself," both in one sentence! Tie that for coining phrases, if you can.) There are times when his style is regrettably close to that of Miss Fannie Hurst, and there is, of course, his debt— part of what is rapidly assuming the proportions of a National Debt—to the manner of Ernest Hemingway. But it is a good book, and I have yet to see the reader who can put it down once he has opened it.

We needed, and we needed badly, a book about Harlem Negroes by a Negro. White men can write, and have written, Heaven knows, such tales, but one never loses consciousness, while reading them, of the pallor of the authors' skins. Mr. McKay's novel seems to me a vitally important addition to American letters. And for his easily achieved feat of putting even further into their place the writings of Mr Carl Van Vechten, I shall be grateful to him from now on.

Ethereal Mildness

March 24, 1928

Oh, I feel terrible. Rotten, I feel. I've got Spring Misery. I've got a mean attack of Crocus Urge. I bet you I'm running a temperature right at this moment; running it ragged. I ought to be in bed, that's where I ought to be. Not that it would do any good if I were. I can't sleep. I can't sleep for a damn. I can't sleep for sour apples. I can't sleep for you and who else.

I'm always this way in the Spring. Sunk in Springtime: or Take Away Those Violets. I hate the filthy season. Summer makes me drowsy, Autumn makes me sing, Winter's pretty lousy, but I hate Spring. They know how I feel. They know what Spring makes out of me. Just a Thing That Was Once a Woman, that's all I am in the Springtime. But do they do anything about it? Oh, no. Not they. Every year, back Spring comes, with the nasty little birds yapping their fool heads off, and the ground all mucked up with arbutus. Year after year after year. And me not able to sleep, on account of misery. All right, Spring. Go ahead and laugh your girlish laughter, you big sap. Funny, isn't it? People with melancholic insomnia are screams, aren't they? You just go on and laugh yourself simple. That's the girl!

It isn't as if I hadn't tried practically every way I ever heard of to induce sleep. I've taken long walks around the room in the midnight silence, and I've thought soothing thoughts, and I've recited long passages of poetry; I have even tried counting Van Dorens.* But nothing works, drugs nor anything else. Not poppy nor mandragora. There was a book called *Not Poppy*, and now there's one called *Not Magnolia*, and is it any wonder a person goes crazy? What with Spring and book titles and loss of sleep, acute melancholia is the least I could have. I'm having a bad time. Oh, awful.

There has been but one sweet, misty interlude in my long

---

* Currently famous, among others, were *Carl Van Doren*, historian and author of *Benjamin Franklin*; *Mark Van Doren*, his brother, the poet; *Irita Van Doren* (then Carl's wife), editor of the *New York Herald Tribune* "Books."

stretch of white nights. That was the evening I fell into a dead dreamless slumber brought on by the reading of a book called *Appendicitis*. (Well, picture my surprise when this turned out to be a book review, after all! You could have knocked me over with a girder.) *Appendicitis* is the work of Thew Wright, A.B., M.D., F.A.C.S., who has embellished his pages with fascinatingly anatomical illustrations, and has remarked, in his dedication, that he endeavors through this book to bring an understanding of appendicitis to the laity. And it is really terribly hard to keep from remarking, after studying the pictures, "That was no laity; that's my wife." It is hard, but I'll do it if it kills me.

You might, and with good reasons, take for your favorite picture the "Front View of Abdominal Cavity." It is good, I admit; it has nice nuances, there is rhythm to the composition, and clever management is apparent in the shadows. But my feeling is that it is a bit sentimental, a little pretty-pretty, too obviously done with an eye toward popularity. It may well turn out to be another "Whistler's Mother" or a "Girl with Fan." My own choice is the impression of "Vertical Section of Peritoneum." It has strength, simplicity, delicacy, pity, and irony. Perhaps, I grant you, my judgment is influenced by my sentiment for the subject. For who that has stood, bareheaded, and beheld the Peritoneum by moonlight can gaze unmoved upon its likeness?

The view of the Peritoneum induces waking dreams, but not slumber. For that I had to get into the text of the book. In his preface, Dr. Wright observes that "The chapter on anatomy, while it may appear formidable, will, it is believed, well repay the reader for his effort in reading it." Ever anxious to be well repaid, I turned to the chapter. It did appear formidable; it appeared as formidable as all get-out. And when I saw that it started "Let us divide the abdominal cavity into four parts by means of four imaginary lines," I could only murmur, "Ah, let's don't. Surely we can think up something better to play than that."

From there, I went skipping about through the book, growing ever more blissfully weary. Only once did I sit up sharply, and dash sleep from my lids. That was at the section having to do with the love-life of poisonous bacteria. That, says the author, "is very simple and consists merely of the bacterium dividing into two equal parts." Think of it—no quarrels, no lies, no importunate telegrams, no unanswered letters. Just peace and sunshine and quiet evenings around the lamp. Probably bacteria sleep like logs. Why shouldn't they? What is Spring to them?

And, at the end of twenty-four hours, the happy couple—or the happy halves, if you'd rather—will have 16,772,216 children to comfort them in their old age. Who would not be proud to have 16,772,216 little heads clustered about his knee, who would not be soothed and safe to think of the young people carrying on the business after the old folks have passed on? I wish, I wish I were a poisonous bacterium. Yes, and I know right now where I'd go to bring up my family, too. I've got that all picked out. What a time I'd show *him!*

Barring the passages dealing with the life and times of bacteria, there is nothing in Dr. Wright's work to block repose. It is true that I never did find out whether I really had appendicitis—which is why I ever started the book, anyway—or whether it was just the effects of that new Scotch of mine which, friends tell me, must have been specially made by the Borgias. But *Appendicitis* gave me a few blessed hours of forgetfulness, and for that I am almost cringingly grateful to Thew Wright, A.B., M.D., F.A.C.S., and all-around good fellow.

I didn't have such luck with George Jean Nathan's* *Art of the Night*. In fact, it acted upon me like so much black coffee, and this in spite of the fact that any book with "Art" in its title usually renders me unconscious as soon as I've cracked it.

In several reviews of his book that I have seen, his critics have taken Mr. Nathan to task—and taking Mr. Nathan to

---

* *George Jean Nathan* (1882-1958), the drama critic, was writing in *The New Yorker* at this time, after having been associated with H. L. Mencken in editing the magazines *Smart Set* and *The American Mercury*.

tusk ranks as a productive pastime with beating the head against a granite wall—for repeating himself. I cannot see that this is so grave a charge. Mr. Nathan has written many books on the theater, his convictions are always his convictions, and they are invariably present in his writings. This would not seem to be unintentional, so far as I can fathom. Perhaps he emphasizes the same points that he has long been emphasizing, but he has always something more to say on them, and he always has new points to make.

Art of the Night, it seems to me, is the most valuable of his works on the theater, as well as the most entertaining. The piece called "Advice to a Young Critic," though it be frequently phrased in flippancy, is deeply sound and thoughtful, and the paper on "Writers of Plays" highly important. Mr. Nathan has his enthusiasms, but they do not attack his control, as do the penchants of many of our other dramatic critics besiege theirs, causing them to produce not so much compilations of critical papers as bundles of fragrant love-letters. George Jean Nathan does his selected subject the courtesy of knowing about it. He writes of it brilliantly, bravely, and authoritatively. He can, in short, write. And so he makes almost all of the other dramatic commentators (I can think, in fact, of but three exceptions, and I'm not sure of two of those) look as if they spelled out their reviews with alphabet blocks.

So I couldn't, you see, find even a wink of sleep in *Art of the Night.* And I couldn't, either, in James Stephens' *Etched in Moonlight,* a collection of his strange, sad, beautiful stories. The slow, relentless agony of the story he names "Hunger" will, indeed, probably keep me awake from now until Summer comes. It is a superb story; but it was just the thing to undo any pitiful little trifles of good I had picked up for myself, and throw me right back into galloping Spring Misery. Oh, I'm sunk.

Spring. Yeah. Spring.

Mr. Lewis Lays It On
with a Trowel

April 7, 1928

In the combined names of Social Intercourse, Meeting Interesting People, and Getting Out of a Rut, I have taken, in my time, some terrible beatings. I have listened to poets rendering their own odes. I have had the plots of yet unwritten plays given me in tiniest detail, I have assisted in charades, I have been politely mystified by card tricks, I have even been sent out of the room and been forced, on my return, to ask the assembled company such questions as I hoped might reveal to me what Famous Character in Fiction they represented. I have spent entire evenings knee-deep in derry-down-derries, listening to quaint old English ballads done without accompaniment; I have been backed into cold corners by pianos while composers showed me how that thing they wrote three years before Gershwin did "The Man I Love" went; I know a young man who has an inlaid ukelele. You see these gray hairs? Well, making whoopee with the intelligentsia was the way I earned them.

But, strait though my gate has been and charged with punishment my scroll, there is one licking I have yet to take. I have never heard Mr. Sinclair Lewis recite the monologues which make up his new book, *The Man Who Knew Coolidge*. I know that he performs this feat, for Dr. Henry Seidel Canby says so in his review of the book, and Dr. Canby would be the last one to tease a person. But for me, thus far, Mr. Lewis's monologues exist only on the printed page. And that way lies the silver lining. It is no breach of manners to close a book before its end is reached.

I have, at the moment, a friend who is trying to make a lady out of me, and the first step in the uphill climb has been the gaining of my promise to keep from employing certain words. So I can't tell you that I think *The Man Who Knew Coolidge*, whether regarded as an entertainment, a portrait, a contribution to American letters, or as all three, is rotten. I could say that if I could use the word "rotten," but I can't use the word "rotten." The question of honor is involved. I gave my solemn pledge that I wouldn't say "rotten" any more. "Rotten" is not a nice word for a lady to use. It sounds lousy.

But I can say—and, if you don't mind, I will—that I think Mr. Lewis's latest work is as heavy-handed, clumsy, and dishonest a burlesque as it has been my misfortune to see in years. I say it, I admit, waiting for a bolt of lightning to come and flatten me permanently, for it is dangerous business for the likes of me to go about saying harsh things of Sinclair Lewis. Two of our most literary critics have already gone wild, in a booksy way, over *The Man Who Knew Coolidge*, and, though I have not yet seen any words of Mr. Mencken's on it, he printed the first piece in the book in his *American Mercury*. I am trembling like a what's-this leaf for my presumption, but I stick to my story.

It seems to me that *The Man Who Knew Coolidge* is *Babbitt* broadened by a mile, and *Babbitt*, Lord knows, was never instanced as an exercise in the subtle. Mr. Lewis is no longer the reporter; he has become the parodist. Doubtless it is all very well to sacrifice honesty and accuracy for the sake of comic effect, but when the comic effect doesn't come off, then where are you? Well, of course you are, and a pretty uncomfortable place to be, too.

I have been one who has for years marched under a banner inscribed "Sinclair Lewis for Pope." I think he is of vast importance. To my mind *Main Street* and *Babbitt* are invaluable historical documents. It seems to me that *Arrowsmith* belongs with the few American novels that have real magnificence. And *Elmer Gantry*—well, they say it's great. I never told anybody this in my life before, and please, for Heaven's sake, don't get it around, but I couldn't read *Elmer Gantry*. I simply could not read it. I know that is a shocking confession to make, and I shall undoubtedly fry in hell for my failure, but there you are. Now you know the worst, or maybe it's the second worst, about me.

But I am not a bit ashamed to admit my inability to finish *The Man Who Knew Coolidge*. (All right, lightning; what are you going to do about it? Let's see you knock this typewriter out from under me, if you think you're so good.) It is to me, because of its deliberate untruth, an outrageously irritating book. It is not caricature; it is absolute misrepresentation. I hold not even the briefest brief for the Babbittry, but there was never any one as bad as Mr. Lewis's hundred-percent American, Lowell Schmaltz. The more I think of it, the madder I get. I am in a fair way towards getting on into what is locally known as "one of those spells of hers."

I wish I could say "rotten." You don't know how much I need to say it.

These Much Too Charming People

April 21, 1928

And so the butterfly days are over. For me, there shall be no more lolling in the sweet, pale sunshine, no more laughing and singing and using words in sentences through the dear and fragrant little hours of the night, no more getting up in the steely noons with a hangover that ought to be in the Smithsonian Institution, under glass. I have flung the last of my roses, roses riotously before the throng. I have gone earnest. I have a purpose. I have a Cause. My white plume, please, Meadows, and tell them to have my favorite charger at the door in ten minutes.

My life and my arms are now and hereafter consecrated to the services of the Society for the Abolition of Charm. It would be advisable, perhaps, for the Society to make a drive for new members; for, thus far, I am the president, vice-president, secretary, board of directors, list of members, and greens committee, and there is such a thing as keeping an organization too exclusive. Yet there is little reason to fear that the Society will pine and die for want of new blood, for surely there must be countless numbers of strong and restless souls who are so good and sick of conscious charm that they would willingly drop everything and join in the movement for its stamping-out. There is entirely too much charm around, and something must be done to stop it.

For a time, I was passive about the thing. I came up against all the better-known varieties of charm in succession—the wistful, the hearty, the puckish, the sparkling, the shy, the naive (that's the kind I should like to get after first, if it's all right with you), the mysterious, the dry, the sporadic, the quaint, and the Purely Physical—and took them meekly as part of the fardels to which we all are heir.

But then it began to get a little thick and sticky. Everywhere I looked, I saw people going charming. Charm flowed like water, and appeared to be turned on and off in the manner of the same necessary liquid. I couldn't get away from it; the only place I was safe from charm was in my own bed, and you know yourself you do have to get out of bed once in a while, if only to see what the headlines say. My first idea was to flee the whole works, and escape to some mountain fastness, some wild and thunderous pass—I was holding out, I recall, for a spot called Rising Gorge as appropriate to my condition—where These Over-Charming People would never penetrate. But that would have been the deed of a coward, and though we may ride hard, we mad Marches, and lie and swear and raise cheques, there are two things we cannot do: we never resist an officer (or a private) and we never turn yellow.

The thing to do was to face the evil, and strive to wipe it out. That was how I got into my Cause. Then and there was born the Society for the Abolition of Charm. It has not yet been definitely decided how the Society is to go about its work of banishing charm from the face of the earth, but as soon as there are some more members we might meet out in back of the barn and see what can be done.

An event that speeded up the founding of the Society was the publication of Miss G. B. Stern's* novel, *Debonair*. The book takes its faintly revolting title from its hero's conception of its heroine. Thus does he think of her, and thus, I regret to say, does he address her. So, in like manner, did I ever have a beau he might ponder on me and apostrophize me as "Shiftless."

I yield to nobody that I can think of in my admiration for

* *G. B. Stern* (1890-), the British novelist, was already held in high regard for her *Matriarch* series of novels of a Jewish family.

Miss Stern. She is, I think, a fine and sharp and skillful writer. It has been ever a source of sad amazement to me that there was not international screaming over her *The Dark Gentleman*, which is as delicate and shrewd a satire as I know, and the best dog story I have ever read. (I wish that the last bit of that sentence were higher praise, for, though I am one who turns practically faint with love at the sight of a dog a block away, the usual uplifting tale of the noble beast who gives his life for his master, his master's girl-friend, or his master's enemy, according to the powers of the author, is a thing that I am utterly unable to spell out.) Miss Stern wrote of her dogs without coquetry, sentimentality, or brutality, thus establishing a record. Her dogs were none of your cold, pure, brave, noble beasts, and so their doings were absorbing reading; well, you know—it's the same way with books about people who are not all cold, pure, brave, and noble. It is a thorn to me that nothing much is done about *The Dark Gentleman*. I knew of few who had heard of it; and I know of none to whom I have suggested it who ever wants to read much of anything else.

Oh, I beg your pardon. I was supposed to be talking about *Debonair*, wasn't I? Well, it seems to me that in this latest book of hers, Miss Stern has had that thing happen to her which befalls most fine satirists. By the nature of her gift, she writes superbly of the people she hates; but when she tries to do a character whom she likes and wishes her readers to like, the result is appalling.

The heroine of *Debonair*—her name is Loveday, which, looked at from any angle, is pretty hard to do with—is one of those charming girls. Indeed, she is so full of charm that she is practically panting with it. Now charm is bad enough to meet with in daily life as we were saying not five minutes ago, but God deliver you and me from charm on paper. I have yet to have an author inform me that a character is charming, and then, by that character's deeds and conversation, convince me of the fact.

Loveday—would you mind if I referred to her simply as "L"? I have my health to think of—is one of those cute, cute, cute, reckless, scatter-brained, daring, but golden-hearted young women that always make me want to get out the trusty old gun that Grandpa carried all through the Civil War without firing a shot. Oh, how gaily and irresponsibly she does rattle on, all during the book! "Happy Me!" she calls herself, and she addresses her mother as "Lamb-bird." Then she has a little way of saying "quee" instead of "queer," and there is one occasion when she employs "pew" rather than use the less whimsical "pure." In short, I cannot tell you how not hungry it makes me to follow her conversation. "Debonair" may be her lover's word for her, but "God-awful" will ever be her nickname with me.

There is unfortunately so very much of L. in the book—and it's quee how little of that pew young thing is enough to last you a lifetime—that you close it with her alone in your mind. And that is too bad, for in *Debonair* Miss Stern has done, out of her bright and exquisite bitterness, two fine portraits—those of L.'s mother, and of the mother of the hero. L.'s mother seems to me a little less successful than the other; she is the silver cord lady, portrayed unerringly at first, but, as the book progresses, gone over into exaggeration. But the hero's mother, Petal— "Petal-to-my-Friends"; "Petal—it suits her"—that sweet, fragile, beloved, gentle devil of a woman, is, I think, as true and sure and skilled a portrayal as I have seen in twenty years of hard reading.

I wish, so that a fine novel need not have been betrayed, that *Debonair* could have been done without its title role. But there is a little comfort to be had from the quee young lady. Read about her, and you will immediately send in your application for membership in the Society for the Abolition of Charm. That girl will do much to put the Society on its feet.

Put the white plume back in the cupboard, Meadows, if you please. Miss Stern's Loveday is taking over my work for the Cause.

Duces Wild

September 15, 1928

Signor Benito Mussolini, back in the days when he was wearing white shirts, if any, wrote a book. It has lately been translated into English and stacked high on the local book-counters. It is called *The Cardinal's Mistress*. Just when you think that things are beginning to break a little better, it turns out that Mussolini has been writing books about prelates' girl-friends. That's the way life is. That's how things are managed in this world of yours. Sometimes I think I'll give up trying, and just go completely Russian and sit on a stove and moan all day.

It is rumored that Il Duce is having one of those old-fashioned Latin tantrums over the translation and publication of his literary gem. That would be, for me, the one bit of cheer in the whole performance. Anything that makes Mussolini sore is velvet so far as I am concerned. If only I had a private income, I would drop everything right now, and devote the scant remainder of my days to teasing the Dictator of All Italy. If anybody comes up to you on the street and tells you that he is my favorite character in history, would you mind saying it's all a black lie? I want to scotch any rumor that I am what Mr. Walter Winchell would call "that way" about him. Indeed, my dream-life is largely made up of scenes in which I say to him, "Oh, Il Duce, yourself, you big stiff," and thus leave him crushed to a pulp.

The Cardinal's Mistress was written when Mussolini was a cunning little shaver of twenty-six, at which time he was secretary to the Socialist Chamber of Labor. His salary was twenty-four dollars a month and the use of the parlor, and he eked it out—he has never been a heavy eker—by giving French lessons and pursuing literature. For this book, first published serially, he thought up the title, *Claudia Particella, L'Amante del Cardinale: Grande Romanzo dei Tempi del Cardinale Emanuel Madruzzo*. Well do I know, from reading the newspapers, that those who attempt disagreement with the Dictator trifle with their health; so I shall but remark, in **a** quiet way, that if *The Cardinal's Mistress* is a *grande romanzo*, I am Alexandre Dumas, *père et fils*.

On the memorable day that *The Cardinal's Mistress* arrived in the office of this lucky magazine, I was the girl who pled, "Please teacher, may I have it to take home with me? Honest, I don't want a cent of money for reviewing it. I'll do it free of charge; I'll even pay handsomely for the privilege." Well, of course, they wouldn't hear a word of that—or at least I hope to heaven they didn't—but I got the book. I had all sorts of happy plans about it. I was going to have a lot of fun. I was going to kid what you Americans call the tripe (*les tripes*) out of it. At last, I thought, had come my big chance to show up this guy Mussolini. A regular Roman holiday, that's what it was going to be.

Well, the joke was on me. There will be little kidding out of me on the subject of the Mussolini masterpiece, for I am absolutely unable to read my way through it. I tried—the Lord knows I tried. I worked, to employ the most inept simile in the language, like a dog. I put on my oldest clothes (first carefully hanging my second oldest in the cupboard), denied myself to my bill-collectors, backed the bureau against the door, and set myself to my task. And I got just exactly nowhere with that book. From the time I cracked its covers to that whirling moment, much later, when I threw myself exhausted on my bed, it had me licked. I couldn't make head, tail, nor good red herring of the business.

In fairness to the author—and I would strip a gear any time in an effort to be square toward that boy—it is in my line of duty to admit that with any book on the general lines of *The Cardinal's Mistress*, I start 'way back of scratch. When I am given a costume romance beginning, "From the tiny churches hidden within the newly budding verdure of the valleys, the evensong of the Ave Maria floated gently forth and died upon the lake," my only wish is that I, too, might float gently forth and die, and I'm not particular whether it's upon the lake or on dry land. I go on to read of a lady whose "half-closed eyes understood the sorcery of poisonous passions," and my one longing is to close those eyes all the way for her. And then I get into a mess of characters named the Count di Castelnuovo and Don Benizio and Carl Emanuel Madruzzo, Cardinal and Archbishop of Trent and secular prince of the Trentino, and Filiberta, and Madonna Claudia—and everything goes black before my eyes. I know that I am never going to understand who is who and what side they are on, and I might just as well give up the unequal struggle.

There seem to be a lot of things going on in *The Cardinal's Mistress.* There are political intrigues, and subtle poisons, and broken-hearted novices dying in convents, and mysterious horsemen dashing away in clouds of dust, and appropriate characters in history, and all the rest of that stock company. But such things are not for me. Even when they are fairly good, the Sandman has me, before I have so much as reached the middle of them.

For me, the one good bit of the book is its preface by Hiram Motherwell (he also translated the novel). Mr. Motherwell writes his introduction with an irreproachable seriousness, almost a solemnity, in his bearing toward Il Duce as a literary figure; and yet there is that something about it which makes the thoughtful reader feel that the translator would be just as well off if he kept out of the uncertain Italian climate for a time. It is to be hoped that he decides on some nice, faraway place—such as New York City, say—as the ideal winter resort.

Weak though the ordeal has left me, I shall never be the one to grudge the time and effort I put into my attempts at reading *The Cardinal's Mistress.* The book has considerably enlarged that dream-life I was telling you about a few minutes ago. It has broadened now to admit that scene in which I tell Mussolini, "And what's more, you can't even write a book that anyone could read. You old Duce, you." You can see for yourself how flat that would leave him.

There are, as you are not the only one who has been thinking, better things to talk about than the literary output of Benito

("Little Bennie") Mussolini, the Nathalia Crane* of Italy. One of the very much better things is *All Kneeling*, Miss Anne Parrish's new novel. It is a quick and deft and constantly amusing satire, the portrait of a lady who so sharply suggests almost all other ladies that you get a little bit frightened. Some years ago, Miss Parrish wrote a book called *A Pocketful of Poses*, which was a promise of what she would some day do in the way of a shrewd and merciless exposal of a pretentious, terrible, and victorious woman. *All Kneeling* is the performance. It is true that the book is occasionally over-written, that certain points are hammered rather too heavily. But, as I was saying to the landlord only this morning, you can't have everything.

Far from Well

October 20, 1928

> The more it
> *Snows*-tiddely-pom,
> The more it
> *Goes*-tiddely-pom
> The more it
> *Goes*-tiddely-pom
> On
> Snowing.
>
> And nobody
> *Knows*-tiddely-pom,
> How cold my
> *Toes*-tiddely-pom
> How cold my
> *Toes*-tiddely-pom
> Are
> Growing.

The above lyric is culled from the fifth page of Mr. A. A. Milne's new book, *The House at Pooh Corner*, for, although

Nathalia Crane (1913-) had a meteoric reputation as a prodigy when her poems, written before the age of eleven, were published in 1924.

the work is in prose, there are frequent droppings into more cadenced whimsy. This one is designated as a "Hum," that pops into the head of Winnie-the-Pooh as he is standing outside Piglet's house in the snow, jumping up and down to keep warm. It "seemed to him a Good Hum, such as in Hummed Hopefully to Others." In fact, so Good a Hum did it seem that he and Piglet started right out through the snow to Hum It Hopefully to Eeyore. Oh, darn—there I've gone and given away the plot. Oh, I could bite my tongue out.

As they are trotting along against the flakes, Piglet begins to weaken a bit.

" 'Pooh,' he said at last and a little timidly, because he didn't want Pooh to think he was Giving In, 'I was just wondering. How would it be if we went home now and *practised* your song, and then sang it to Eeyore tomorrow—or—or the next day, when we happen to see him.'

" 'That's a very good idea, Piglet,' said Pooh. 'We'll practise it now as we go along. But it's no good going home to practise it, because it's a special Outdoor Song which Has To Be Sung In The Snow.'

" 'Are you sure?' asked Piglet anxiously.

" 'Well, you'll see, Piglet, when you listen. Because this is how it begins. *The more it snows, tiddely-pom—*'

" 'Tiddely what?' said Piglet." (He took, as you might say, the very words out of your correspondent's mouth.)

" 'Pom,' said Pooh. 'I put that in to make it more hummy.' "

And it is that word "hummy," my darlings, that marks the first place in *The House at Pooh Corner* at which Tonstant Weader Fwowed up.

Wallflower's Lament

November 17, 1928

It has lately been drawn to your correspondent's attention that, at social gatherings, she is not the human magnet she would be. Indeed, it turns out that as a source of entertainment, conviviality, and good fun, she ranks somewhere between a sprig of parsley and a single ice-skate. It would appear, from the actions of the assembled guests, that she is about as hot company as a night nurse.

I don't mean that these facts have been pointed out to her in so many words. Not as yet; although there is a fair chance that a certain young gentleman of her acquaintance, who gets the frankies after the fourth *anis de loso* and goes around telling people what makes them so terrible, will shortly be sitting by her side and beginning, "Look, you know what's the matter with you?" Thus far, she has drawn her deductions from the fact that the invitations have been dying off like flies; so that most of her evenings are given to powdering her friends' backs or straightening their ties, as the case may be, saying, "Now have a good time and be sure to tell me who was there," waving by-by smilingly, and then settling down for a hearty attack of the left-all-alone-again yips. On such occasions as she does make those parties where the hosts apparently assemble the list of guests by drawing names out of a hat, she sits in a corner with her thoughts, smiling brightly the while in order to indicate a pathetic willingness to play; or else she listens to something that used to be in the S.O.S. explain, with the aid of paper and a gold pencil, the course of the war from April 7, 1917, until the late afternoon of Armistice Day. So, being one who can take a hint after the first thirty repetitions, she is now conceding her flop, and retiring constructively from society. Do you know anyone who would want a comparatively young woman—young as compared with the Grand Canyon, for instance—fairly free, and looks white under electric light, to sit up with the children evenings, and let the nurse go out?

It is not that she has not tried to improve her condition before acknowledging its hopelessness. (Oh, come on, let's get the hell out of this, and get into the first person.) I have sought, by study, to better my form and make myself Society's Darling. You see, I had been fed, in my youth, a lot of old wives' tales about the way men would instantly forsake a beautiful woman to flock about a brilliant one. It is but fair to say that, after getting out in the world, I had never seen this happen, but I thought that maybe I might be the girl to start the vogue. I would become brilliant. I would sparkle. I would hold whole dinner tables spellbound. I would have throngs fighting to come within hearing distance of me while the weakest, elbowed mercilessly to the outskirts, would cry, "What did she say?" or "Oh, please ask her to tell it again." That's what I would do. Oh, I could just hear myself.

So I got a book called *Favorite Jokes of Famous People* and settled down to read it, memorize its gems, and repeat them at select gatherings. And from the time of the world premiere of my recital until this very living moment, I haven't had an evening off my hands.

It was doubtless ill-advised for me, a very tyro—or, at least, a pretty tyro—as a raconteuse to start off with the selection given in the book as the favorite of Mr. Bruce Barton,* a selection which, by the way, could scarcely be classified as "The Joke Nobody Knows." Thus does Mr. Barton begin his chosen story:

"In the pre-prohibition days two young men set forth one evening from Detroit in an automobile. Awakening the next morning, after a somewhat tempestuous night, they found themselves parked in front of a large building which they assumed to be a hotel but was in fact a sanitarium. The proprietor of the institution was not only a vegetarian, but a zealous member of a religious order."

That, you will admit, is a rough start for the amateur story-teller. You have to remember practically everything except your stance. Pre-prohibition, Detroit, two young men, automobile, next morning, hotel which wasn't a hotel, proprietor who was not only a vegetarian but a member of a religious order—that's advanced stuff. It is perhaps sufficient to say that I made a fool of the anecdote. I represented the two young men as coming from Fort Wayne.

Since then, I have had no heart for *Favorite Jokes of Famous People*. I can't even do much about reading it in moments of leisure. The book has been compiled by Frank Nicholson, who

* *Bruce Barton*: see note for page 459.

dedicates it to "A famous man whose favorite joke is not included in this collection . . . he did not choose to pun," so you can see that he is just the boy who was cut out to collect the best in humor. Mr. Nicholson adds his own touches in giving brief biographies of each celebrity who is represented—one recalls perhaps most sharply his dainty line in his Gene Tunney* piece: "Gene says if he gets married he'll quit fighting. What an optimist that guy is!"—which is my entrant for the 1928 Pulitzer prize for the *mot* doing most to advance American manners and standards of culture. It is to be guessed, too, that Mr. Nicholson does not confine his authoring to the biographies; here and there it seems as if he must have crashed into the jokes themselves. For example, in Donald Ogden Stewart's** favorite story, the magnificent epic of the horse that sat on eggs, Mr. Nicholson has Mr. Stewart referring to "that blankety blank horse." It has been my privilege to have known Mr. Stewart since he wore sailor-suits—he was in the navy during the war—and never yet have I heard him use any such expression as "blankety blank." Or, at least, certainly not in the presence of any woman.

Out of *Favorite Jokes of Famous People* comes one ray of light, one breath of strange, new fragrance, one cool and silver star. That is the selection given by Mr. Ring Lardner. It is too frail, too exquisite to reproduce here, though I can scarcely tear myself away from quoting it. And it is a source of perpetual amazement that Mr. Frank Ernest Nicholson, author of "What an optimist that guy is!," could have admitted this white violet to his collection. Probably he figured out some meaning to the masterpiece, and will never, never realize that it was Mr. Lardner at his sublime best, in the act of kidding the living tripe out of all such collections of famous things of famous whose-thises.

* *Gene Tunney*, who won the World Heavyweight Boxing Championship from Jack Dempsey in 1926, was also known for his literary interests as a student and disciple of William Lyon Phelps.

** *Donald Ogden Stewart* (1894-), man-about-town, author of humorous books and plays and later of movie scripts, was a member with Dorothy Parker of the Algonquin Round Table group.

Well—to get back to me as quickly as possible—when Our Heroine found that she was the bust of the season as a wit and an elocutionist, she decided to turn to that good old stand-by, sex. "Let others raconteur if they will," I said, "but gangway while I go Garbo!" To that end, I acquired a book called *The Technique of the Love Affair*, by one who signs herself "A Gentlewoman," and set out to learn how to loop the Usual Dancing Men.

I have thought, in times past, that I had been depressed. I have regarded myself as one who had walked hand-in-hand with sadness. But until I read that book, depression, as I knew it, was still in its infancy. I have found out, from its pages, that never once have I been right. Never once. Not even one little time.

You know how you ought to be with men? You should always be aloof, you should never let them know you like them, you must on no account let them feel that they are of any importance to you, you must be wrapped up in your own concerns, you may never let them lose sight of the fact that you are superior, you must be, in short, a regular stuffed chemise. And if you could see what I've been doing!

Despite its abominable style and its frequent sandy stretches, *The Technique of the Love Affair* makes, I am bitterly afraid, considerable sense. If only it had been written and placed in my hands years ago, maybe I could have been successful, instead of just successive.

And Again,
Mr. Sinclair Lewis

March 16, 1929

The industry of Mr. Sinclair Lewis is a thing to marvel at, to ponder of a white night, and, if such is your way, to hoist high as an example. To my own admittedly slanted vision, industry ranks with such sour and spinster virtues as thrift, punctuality, level-headedness, and caution. I think that Aldous Huxley utters the loud truth when he says, in *Point Counter Point*, that industry can never substitute for talent. There exists, especially in the American mind, a sort of proud confusion between the two. A list of our authors who have made themselves most beloved and, therefore, most comfortable financially, shows that it is our national joy to mistake for the first-rate, the fecund rate.

Ah, I thought that that was going to turn out better. Oh, dear . . .

Anyhow, the industry of Mr. Lewis is not short of marvelous. There are times, such as after reading *The Man Who Knew Coolidge* and after accomplishing the long trek through the major part of his latest book, *Dodsworth*, when one feels that it might be put to higher purposes; properly hitched up, say, it might supply heat, light, and power to the whole Middle West. It is an almost terrifying force. Think what the man—the man who had behind him such stupendous feats of labor as *Main Street* and *Arrowsmith* and *Elmer Gantry*—has done in this last year. There was *The Man Who Knew Coolidge*, like it or not, there were countless pieces for the weeklies and for the Sunday magazine sections of the newspapers, there was the aching grind of all that posing for all those rotogravure pictures of the honeymoon trip through rural England in the Caravan, and now there is a new novel of three hundred and seventy-seven closely printed pages. Three hundred and seventy-seven pages. And I, after the creative labors involved in composing a telegram to the effect that I won't be able to come to dinner Thursday on account of a severe cold, have to go and lie down for the rest of the day.

It is difficult for me to pass upon *Dodsworth*. I find myself in the unenviable position of the early crocus. As I toss and turn at my typewriter—I shouldn't have drunk that coffee—no reviews of the novel have yet appeared. And how am I to know, until I have read the Book Supplement of the New York Sunday *Times*, whether or not this is a truly important work? I cannot, with the slightest sureness, tell you if it will sweep the country, like *Main Street*, or bring forth yards of printed praise, as did *Elmer Gantry*. My guess would be that it will not. Other guesses which I have made in the past half-year have been that Al Smith would carry New York state, that St. John Ervine would be a great dramatic critic for an American newspaper, and that I would have more than twenty-six dollars in the bank on March first. So you see my confidence in my judgment is scarcely what it used to be.

The book concerns Samuel Dodsworth, inhabitant of Zenith, maker of the Revelation automobile, and millionaire. But he is not a Babbitt, his author points out in just those words. (Now why is it that one experiences slight squirms of discomfort when Mr. Lewis, as he does several times in *Dodsworth,* uses "Babbitt" as a descriptive term? It is his own word, Heaven knows; he has seen it firmly fastened to the language, has heard it applied, perhaps a bit too easily, a million times. It is undeniable that no one has a better right to use it than has he. And yet, somehow, one's deeper respect must always go to the writer—or the grocer or the friend or the stock-broker or the tragedian—who stops just this side of doing those things that no one has a better right to do.)

Well, at any rate, Dodsworth is fifty or so, to his wife's forty-one; their two children are grown up, and no longer in need of them. So he gives up business, and he and his wife embark on a prolonged holiday abroad, to relax, to broaden, and to absorb. Surely, if Mr. Lewis in outlining his plot to some friend, had only said, "Stop me if you've heard this," more than two hundred pages of *Dodsworth* need never have been written.

The greater part of the book seems to me dull with a long and wide and thick heaviness. Mr. Lewis has been a veritable sailor in his prodigality of words. He has given all his characters far too rich a gift of utterance. For weeks, it seems, they argue the relative merits of the old world and the new; no one ever falters, no one ever searches for a phrase, no one, God help us all, ever stops. When Mr. Lewis's ideas—for you feel, too surely, that they are Mr. Lewis's own, and not those of his characters—are not set down in the form of debates, they are given as long mental monologues of Dodsworth's. Dodsworth's thoughts come with a curious neatness, an admirable round- ness of style; he broods in such apt sentences as "travel consists in perpetually finding new things that you have to do if you're going to be respectable." It is obvious that Mr. Lewis likes his main figure, and expects his reader to sympathize with the man's seekings and bafflements. But it is difficult to give tenderness to one who muses in epigrams.

And then, after all those pages and pages and pages, Dodsworth and those near to him seem to come sharply and suddenly alive. Mr. Lewis spares his words, and spends his emotion. Dodsworth's wife leaves him for a young German nobleman; the husband's dull agony and wild bewilderment, his poor, clumsy tries at finding an anodyne in little lively ladies, make a line of gripping, deep-drawn pictures. At last there is the Other Woman—the one who can give him calm and sweetness and companionship; and then there is the inevitable return of the pretentious she-dog of a wife. He goes back with her to their hopeless quarrelling, but he is a stronger man for having known beauty, and the book ends with his return to the woman who gave it to him—ends on a phrase bitter, and troubling, and cruelly deep in its knowledge.

So there you are, or, rather, there I am, in regard to *Dodsworth*. May Heaven help you, as it assisted me, through the travelogues, the debates, and the grotesquely over-drawn figures that clutter it—Mr. Lewis, who never was one to lay himself open to charges of subtilty, here frequently runs over into the realm of comic valentines. But there is the last part, to make up for the rest. You really can't know, until you have managed the first two-thirds, how high that goes in praise.

Hero Worship

April 27, 1929

Round Up—and if there were ever a cup given for the most unfortunate title of the year, it would be resting at this very moment upon the Ring Lardner mantelpiece—is a collection of the previously published short stores of a great artist. There are two classes of people whom it is my cross to meet in my small daily round: those who think that Ring Lardner is a humorist, and those who have just discovered that Ring Lardner is something more than a humorist—the latter group makes me perhaps a shade sicker than the former. There is hope that the Literary Guild's wide distribution of these stories, written over a period of years, may not only serve to establish Ring Lardner in his place, but to put all the head-patters in theirs. If it doesn't, I shall have to go around shooting people again, and I had more or less retired from that line of work.

Round Up bears on its dust-cover sound and dignified appreciation for the author from Mencken, Edmund Wilson, and Dr. Carl Van Doren. And Sir James Barrie lights there, like Tinker Bell, to add: "Congratulations to Ring Lardner. He is the real thing." It is indeed high time to render "congratulations to Ring Lardner"; time so high as to be positively gamey. For one cannot help recalling that when "Some Like Them Gold" (to my mind, Lardner's masterpiece) was published, Edward J. O'Brien listed it in his *Best Short Stories* for that year without even one of his trick stars to signify distinction; and that the exquisite "Golden Honeymoon" was turned down by the noted editor of a famous weekly—which act should send the gentleman down to posterity along with that little band whose members include the publisher who rejected *Pride and Prejudice*, the maid who lighted the hearth with the manuscript of Carlyle's *French Revolution*, and Mrs. O'Leary's cow.*

It is difficult to review these spare and beautiful stories; it would be difficult to review the Gettysburg address. What more are you going to say of a great thing than that it is great? You could, I suppose, speak of Ring Lardner's unparalled ear and eye, his strange, bitter pity, his utter sureness of characterization, his unceasing investigation, his beautiful economy. Or you could, as has been done, go in for comparing him with Ernest Hemingway and Sherwood Anderson. But it seems to me that Lardner's qualities are not to be listed but to be felt, as you read his work. And it also seems that there is no reason for comparison with Anderson and Hemingway. True, they are all writers of short stories (although, if you will kindly keep off

* *Mrs. O'Leary's cow,* in the legend of the times, kicked over the lamp that started the great Chicago fire of 1871.

those bolts of lightning that are just getting all set to strike me, it is my conviction that only his production of "I'm a Fool" passes Mr. Anderson into such high company), but, in the words of our hero, what of it? It is not clear to me why Ring Lardner need be compared to anybody. And may Heaven help those short-story writers who are compared to him.

Home Is the Sailor

January 24, 1931

Maybe you think I was just out in the ladies' room all this time, but there isn't a word of truth in it. In case the question ever comes up, I was in Switzerland, that's where I was. It seems that there was some novel notion of Getting Away from It All, coupled with a wistful dream of Trying to Forget. And when the day comes that you have to tie a string around your finger to remind yourself of what it was you were forgetting, it is time for you to go back home.

The Swiss are a neat and an industrious people, none of whom is under seventy-five years of age. They make cheeses, milk chocolate, and watches, all of which, when you come right down to it, are pretty fairly unnecessary. It is all true about yodelling and cowbells. It is, however, not true about St. Bernard dogs rescuing those lost in the snow. Once there was something in the story; but, what with the altitude and the long evenings and one thing and another, the present dogs are of such inclinations that it is no longer reasonable to send them out to work, since they took to eating the travelers. Barry, the famous dog hero, credited with the saving of seven lives, is now on view, stuffed; stuffed, possibly, with the travelers he did not bring home. Skiing is extremely difficult, and none of my affair. The most frequent accident, among ski-jumpers, is the tearing off of an ear. The edelweiss is a peculiarly unpleasant-looking flower. During the early summer, the natives fling themselves into the sport of watching one cow fight another cow; the winning lady is hung with blossoms and escorted, by her fans, from café to café, all night long. There is a higher consumption of alcohol, per capita, in Switzerland than in any other country in Europe (although there may be some slight change in those figures, now that your correspondent has returned to Tony's). The country itself is extravagantly beautiful, and practically crawling with lakes and mountains. And, while we are on that subject, how are you fixed for mountains, anyway? Because, after a year in the Alps, I should be glad to give them to you for your birthday, and throw in a mandolin.

End, and none too soon, of travelogue. But I just wanted to show you I really have been in Switzerland.

God keep me from chauvinism, but New York is beautiful. Oh, this is a lovely city you have here! I think that your skyline is astounding, and that your women are the most attractive in the world, but that there is a certain amount of exaggeration in the report that your men think of nothing but business, business, business, all the time. If it is true, then wherever *did* I get these bruises on my neck?

But there is a catch to home-coming. Welcome is surely warmer than brandy to the heart, yet there is something a little sinister in the eagerness of those people up at that bank of mine to catch a sight of, and, even, to lay a hand upon, the returned voyager. It isn't, I feel, the gesture of real friendship; there is something either a little more or a little less than that behind it. It is true that I have been wearing a catcher's mask ever since I sent out those last cheques; but what of that? Must they think of nothing but money? Can they set no value upon imagination? Surely that one cheque—numbered XXX—which I made out for three hundred and eighty-six dollars had more of pure fantasy than ever Barrie knew. But they don't care. Not they. It is not agreeable, when you wake in the night, to reflect that you have been dealing for years with an entirely material trust company. Why, those have been virtually the best years of my life, too. Just for this, just for this one thing, I hope they have a run on their old bank. The minute I finish this piece, I am going out and start a lot of dirty rumors.

Unfortunately, until then there is work to be done. When your bank account is so overdrawn that it is positively photographic, steps must be taken. Here, before I am cold off the boat, before—well, I was going to say "before I am used to American money again," but I never was used to it, really, so the phrase rather loses force—before, at any rate, I have shaken the Tauchnitz novels out of my shoes, I have to go to work. I have to write a book review. A hell of a welcome that is, I must say. A person was a fool ever to have got down off that Alp.

For I haven't, you see, been doing much reading while you had your backs turned. I am not quite ashamed of the fact. Reading, according to Bacon—and if it wasn't Bacon, you will correct me, won't you, you big stiffs?—reading makes a full man; but to achieve the same end, I know a trick worth two of it. It is, nevertheless, somewhat appalling to return to what may be loosely called God's Country and find that my friends, all three of them, are saturated with literature, and are running around like hot cakes, reporting in considerably more words than it takes to tell it on the works they claim to have devoured. I am at just that interesting age where I cannot keep out of things. I, too, must be in the know; I, too, must quote and sigh and nod wisely. You know yourself that I cannot, in a week, do book by book what they have done. But it has been my fortune to have all literature brought to me at one crack.

The crack in question comes in two volumes—two good, thick, close-printed volumes. I can hardly bear to part with the title, for once that is out, there goes the whole review. But I shall steel myself, and give it you. The work is scattered by the *Christian Herald* (Louis Klopsch, publisher, Bible House, New York), and it is called *Forty Thousand Sublime and Beautiful Thoughts*. Yes, sir, *Forty Thousand Sublime and Beautiful Thoughts*. It is compiled by a Mr. Charles Noel Douglas, before this a stranger to me, and he has, out of his generosity, not been content with his title; barging on into the practically drunken-sailor stages of lavishness, he has shot the works on an explanatory note, printed, and appropriately, in the red. It runs: "Gathered from the Roses, Clover Blossoms, Geraniums, Violets, Morning Glories, and Pansies of Literature." It is not given to me, as it has been to Mr. Douglas, to discern who are the roses, clover blossoms, geraniums, violets, and morning glories of literature. But I can say, from what I learn by getting around, that the pansies are splendidly represented. Pansies—that's for remembrance.

I tried, for my first duty is toward you, to check up on Mr. Douglas. I wanted to see if there were really forty thousand sublimes and beautifuls for you. Unhappily, it was like counting those sheep over that fence; before I had listed the first hundred I was safely asleep. But I did come upon one page that gave me a little thought, and a shade of distrust toward Mr. Douglas and even toward Mr. Louis Klopsch, of Bible House. On page four-thirty-two of the first volume, in the division of sublimes and beautifuls ranking under the head of "Death"—for Mr. Douglas has thoughtfully categoried all the thoughts alphabetically—there is Shelley's "How wonderful is Death, Death and his brother Sleep!" Then comes a quotation from Horace, one from Young, one from Marcus Antoninus. Then follows, from Shelley, "How wonderful is Death, Death and his brother Sleep!" I do not know how often such little slip-ups occur in the volumes, but having noted this one, I fear the title must be amended to "Thirty-nine Thousand Nine Hundred and Ninety-nine Sublime and Beautiful Thoughts." And that is probably big.

Mr. Douglas, as I have said, has listed his subjects alphabetically, and then collected his garden flowers to enlarge upon them. Thus, were you ever hard up for sublime thoughts upon Arbor Day or Cornerstone Laying or Heraldry or Grant's Birthday or Fish or Dimples or Agriculture (one of the sublime thoughts under "Agriculture" is: "Methinks I have a great desire to a bottle of hay; good hay, sweet hay, hath no fellow") or Aches or Corporations or Aversion (and under "Aversion" comes, sublimely and beautifully, this: "I do not like thee, Doctor Fell . . ."), all you have to do is turn to Mr. Douglas's index, and then go ahead.

You will possibly notice that the allusions, in this fascinating composition, go no further than the "H"s. There is a second volume, but, conscientious though I be, I am but flesh and blood. Up to the "H"s will hold me, Mr. Douglas and Mr. Klopsch.

Now can I go back and talk some more about Switzerland?

Oh, I see. No, it doesn't matter at all. Of course I don't mind. But there was no harm in asking, was there?

Kiss and Tellegen

February 21, 1931

Mr. Lou Tellegen* has recently seen fit to write his memoirs; and, though it is at least debatable that it would have been more public-spirited of him to have sent the results to the zoo, he has caused them to be bound within costly blue covers, and has entitled them *Women Have Been Kind.* After reading the work, or, indeed, after reading only some of it, it is borne home that the name is the most gentlemanly of understatements. "Kind" is but a feeble word for what the girls have been to Mr. Tellegen. It could have been only his chivalry that held him back from stronger terms; for you will see that he is one who carries chivalry to the point of fanaticism. You do not even have to open the book to find out that—it can be learned from the note on the dust-cover. This runs: "In recalling past love affairs, etc., Mr. Tellegen prefers to use fictitious names in cases where the lady is still alive, although the facts will be accurate." Surely one must applaud that spirit in the gentleman, and none does so more heartily than I. Only, after reading the accounts of the "love affairs, etc.," one is given to pondering how strange it is that there *are* "cases where the lady is still alive." Mr. Tellegen, Mr. Tellegen—I'm afraid there's been soldiering somewhere.

The blurb on the dust-cover announces, with rather more than the usual bang, that "here are the intimate reminiscences of the man who was called 'the perfect lover.'" (It is not stated who gave him this name, but I feel, somehow, that I have guessed. I won't say yes, nor I won't say no, but if you were to whisper to me your conjecture that the phrase-coiner's initials are L. T., I might admit that you were, like the countless

* All that needs to be added to what this tells us about *Lou Tellegen* is that he was a well-known actor in his time, and that *Geraldine Farrar* was one of the first famous American-born sopranos at the Metropolitan Opera. Her female admirers were known as "Gerryflappers."

heroines of *Women Have Been Kind,* getting warm.) "Mr. Tellegen's life," the blurb goes breathlessly on, "has been, in every sense of the word, an adventure." (What, one wonders, are those other senses of the word?) "By turn actor, artist, baker, bullfighter, gambler, model, pugilist, prospector" (How come, again one wonders, that he never took up soccer?), "Mr. Tellegen has lived more romance than others read of, and his memoirs are as exciting as a score of novels." (I shall not dispute that last statement, providing the publishers will let me name the score in question.) "His frankness is thoroughly refreshing, and in these reminiscences he has spared no one." And that, Heaven knows, is no blurb-writer's fantasy; indeed Mr. Tellegen has spared no one, including, or, in fact, beginning with, the reader.

The book proper—and that adjective achieves an almost historical distinction as an example of unhappy selection—is written in a style that has all the elegance of a quirked little finger and all the glitter of a pair of new rubbers. Mr. Tellegen's English is of the fanciest persuasion; it even includes such refinements as the exquisite participle "gotten." It develops, by the way, that the gentleman is no slouch as a linguist. He has French, Flemish, Dutch, and Portuguese right where he wants them. But Russian, alas, threw him. Although he embarked on a nice long jaunt with a lady called Sonia, and she did everything she could, he confesses that "to this day I know only one word of Russian." The word, as one can doubtless go without saying, must have been *"da."*

Mr. Tellegen's childhood was not a happy one. He was brought up by a somewhat unnecessarily strict tutor, who taught him, among other things, "the art of the rapier." (Thank God for that little letter "i"!) But he had such good fun, and so frequently, in after years that he surely cannot grudge the brief gray span of his youth. For at fifteen he started out, and from then on he had no dull moments. It was when he was fifteen that he set out with Sonia. The lady was not, strictly speaking, in the market at the time; she was, in fact, the girl-friend of Mr. Tellegen's father. "My father," he explains, "never forgave me for the outrage." Yet it might seem that the older Tellegen was of a nature that magnified an offense. For Sonia appears to have been a young woman that many a man would have been proud and happy to have had lifted from his life. "She conceived," Lou Tellegen says, "the rather eccentric idea of traveling in man's attire." Surely the thing for any right-thinking man to have done would have been to have presented the abductor of a young lady of any such rather eccentric ideas with a suitably inscribed silver trophy, and kissed him on both cheeks.

After Sonia, Mr. Tellegen went from love to love with a speed that sets the reader's reason to tottering. How on earth he ever found time for his other pursuits cannot be figured, even though he sets them down chronologically. He was a baker, and he was a circus performer, and he was a model for Rodin and lesser, and he was a sculptor himself, and he was a prizefighter, and he was an actor, and he wrote plays, and he spent a half-year in the South American jungle, and he gambled night and day, and he perfected a technique of self-defense by knife-throwing. Yet these things were but incidents. His life has been, first and always, the ladies—those women who have been kind to the point of sappiness. Well, I suppose that's what we all want to hear about. Nobody is much interested in the careers of bakers or playwrights.

It is a strange thing that for a few pages Lou Tellegen's book gives out a glamour. That is when he writes of Isadora Duncan (though, while we're up, I cannot recall, can you, any mention of him in her memoirs?). It seems to be impossible for any writer, no matter how bad—and goodness knows some of the worst in the world have had a crack at it—to speak of that woman without conveying something of greatness. Resent though one does the constant exhuming, and by dirty little hands, of those beautiful bones, there is always grandeur there. . . .

His account of his American tour with Sarah Bernhardt is, in a word, terrible. You get no bit of her quality; the author is too much occupied with his own concerns at the time. They were not, in another word, interesting. Nor is there much to the story of his stretch of time with Geraldine Farrar. (Miss Farrar was not his first wife, nor, so much as I can figure out events, his second or third. There came a time when it was drawn, somehow, to Mr. Tellegen's attention that gentlemen sometimes married ladies, and from then on he became a regular marryin' fool.) He is too careful about being courteous to Miss Farrar to give much realism to the record.

In all his descriptions of the great, it is the great, with that one mighty exception, who suffer. You see them all only in their relation to the escapades of Mr. Tellegen, and Mr. Tellegen's escapades are of a certain sameness. True, toward the middle of the book, there is the sprightly account of a sudden home-coming of a husband, when Mr. Tellegen was, shall we say, visiting a lovely lady in her apartment in Venice; and the distinguished guest was forced first to throw his clothes out of the window and then dive out after them, into the Grand Canal. But even before and after that, things are pretty wet.

Not the least amazing bit of the book is the postscript by Eve Casanova, the present Mrs. Tellegen. She likes him, it seems— and surely any such bad writing as her afterword must be sincere—fine. She says, among stronger things, that "he is the true type all women adore—a lover who pursues!" That has made me a little thoughtful. Maybe we both, Mr. Tellegen and I, have been giving too much credit. Maybe it isn't so kind of women to fall for a type like that. Maybe it is not kindness but gratitude. "A lover who pursues"—oh, think what that sounds like to one whose eyes have so often rested on the ugliest modern gesture: that of a man looking at his wristwatch!

Two Lives
and Some Letters

March 14, 1931

"There was no one further from sadness than Henri Gaudier,*" Ford Madox Ford once wrote, "whether in his

* *Henri Gaudier* (1891-1915), the French Vorticist sculptor, was a hero of Ezra Pound and the Vorticist school of writers; his name was unknown to most readers when *Savage Messiah* was published.

being or his fate. He had youth, he had grace of person and of physique, he had a great sense of the comic. He had friendships, associates in his work, loves, the hardships that help youth. He had genius and he died a hero. Who could ask for more? Who could have better things?"

There was no resisting this setting down of Ford's words, for their beauty. But I think that there is more of music than of truth in them. "He had genius and he died a hero"—that is sure. But could there be written a sentence more compact of tragedy?

And it is evident from the letters of Henri Gaudier-Brzeska that he could have asked for more. He could have asked, and he did ask, for tenderness and for understanding. He had friendships, but they were violent and tortured and they smashed to their endings; it was his curse that calmer relations were impossible for him. Of his associates in his work he had those doubts of the man whose fevered faith is all in himself; there buzzed in his mind strange, sly noises that he took for the whisperings of a world in conspiracy against him. I know of his life only from the fine biography that stands before me, and his loves are not there listed, so I cannot say as to them. Yet it would seem to me that in that very plural lie anguish and defeat. And those "hardships that help youth" were so small and dirty and incessant that there could be no stimulus in them. That there is no sadness in his fate, I feel; for it is not his tragedy, nor anybody's, to die young. But in his being, I think indeed he could have had better things.

His letters form a part of this new book by H. S. Ede, who has held himself back from praises and from evaluations, and has not once indulged in the coquetries of the modern biographical manner. He consulted diaries and collected letters, marshalled his facts, and set down, in the dignity of simple English, the story of a star-crossed artist. I am told that it is largely due to the efforts of Mr. Ede, who is curator of the Tate Gallery in London, that the drawings and sculptures of Gaudier-Brzeska have become widely known; that his enthusiasm stands back of the artist's posthumous fame. But his book is not soiled by propaganda, nor sicklied by hero-worship.

He had a wild, sad story to tell, and so he has told it. He has a
fine book.

But he has, to this reader's unease and bewilderment, entitled it *Savage Messiah.* I can only conclude that the names of
many of the new books are arrived at by a species of parlor
game. You write down, each on a neat slip of paper, all the
nouns you can think of. Then you put them in a hat. On an
equal number of paper slips, you write all the adjectives you
ever knew; these you heap in another hat. Then you get some
innocent party to plunge his left hand into one hat and his right
into the other, and to grasp tightly one slip in each. Then he
must pull out his clenched hands, and be made to relinquish
the papers. These are laid next to each other, and there you
have your title. But of course, my idea of the procedure is the
purest guess-work. Possibly they don't use hats at all; maybe
it's baskets.

Savage Messiah, which is published by Knopf, begins with
the meeting in a Paris library of Henri Gaudier and Sophie
Brzeska. She was reading German, to some indefinite end, and
he was studying anatomy. He was nineteen, and she was thirty-
eight. ("The woman I love is thirty years old," he wrote to a
friend, but it was in chivalry, not in ignorance.) She was badly
battered by life and love, and fairly started along the road to
the madhouse where she was to die. But he found her beautiful,
and so, from her photograph, she was. They were both sick and
starved and lonely. They found each other and they lived
together, though in no closer physical communion than that
imposed by the crowded rooms of the poor, until five years later
when, in 1915, he went out to the War to be killed.

Mr. Ede has concerned himself, save for a quick blocking-in
of the background of each, with the story of the life together of
this woman and this man. It is the record of a strange and
sorrowful relationship. There was no medium to it—there were
nothing but shrieking quarrels and florid reconciliations;
eternally the irresistible temperament met the immovable ego.
"I will be a mother to you," she offered, at their meeting, and
she called him "Little Son," but it was he who was maternal
toward her. He cared for her and worried over her and cheered

her. His beautiful letters to her in her absences—she was often away, searching for health and writing on a lavishly conceived trilogy with which she was to stun the world—have a tenderness that squeezes the throat. It was he who put into their life together any glory and gallantry that it had.

They went to live in London, the Polish woman and the French boy; he added her name to his, and they proclaimed themselves brother and sister. In the quick years there, he did his life work. He sold an occasional drawing—during one stretch of their most horrible poverty, he went from public-house to public-house, making sketches, for pennies—but it was sculpture that he loved. ("You will have noticed," he wrote, "that civilizations begin with sculpture and end with it.") His letter announcing to a friend his dedication to his art—"I have put by the brushes and tubes and have snatched the chisel and the boaster, two simple instruments which so admirably second the most wonderful of modeling tools, the human thumb"—is written in high rapture. All his letters, indeed, have about them a clear, bright excitement. In much too long a time, I have read nothing so stirring.

They met many of the famous in London, but friendships were too difficult for them. Brzeska was hysterical, at best, and always wild with jealousy, and the boy was no easy companion. An acquaintance wrote of him, with "his long front hair hanging in a string down the side of his white brow," as "throwing his future and his past and his passion into any discussion." His need for companionship was so great that when he was asked for an evening's visit he could not bear to leave; he had to be invited, with lessening delicacy as the night waned, please to go home. So he was not asked again, and another friendship was over just as it might have been beginning.

One of the most absorbing chapters of the book is the account of the swift and turbulent acquaintanceship of the two foreigners with Katherine Mansfield and her husband, Middleton Murry,* who were then editing a magazine called

* For *Katherine Mansfield* and *John Middleton Murry*, see note on page 451.

Rhythm. The affair started on the loftiest plane—"with rich hand-shakes, we swore eternal friendship"—but the ladies were difficult, Gaudier-Brzeska started throwing his future and his past and his passion into things again, and poor dear Mr. Murry, one gathers, was bewildered and a trifle scared. Possibly those handshakes were too rich; at any rate, they did not endure, and the eternal friendship ended, with a crash, in a blazingly dramatic letter from the artist to Murry, with whom, he said, he "still sympathized as a poor boy, chased by the Furies."

Recommendations seem to me always impudent; but perhaps I know you well enough to ask a favor of you. Please, will you put down whatever that thing is that you're doing and read *Savage Messiah*? It is no fun, but, if only for the sake of the letters it contains, it is a great book. And you don't get "great" out of me for red apples.

Oh, Look—
A Good Book!

April 25, 1931

It seems to me that there is entirely too little screaming about the work of Dashiell Hammett. My own shrill yaps have been ascending ever since I first found *Red Harvest*, and from that day the man has been, God help him, my hero; but I talked only yesterday, I forget why, with two of our leading booksy folk, and they had not heard of that volume, nor had they got around to reading its better, *The Maltese Falcon*.

It is true that Mr. Hammett displays that touch of rare genius in his selection of undistinguished titles for his mystery stories—*The Maltese Falcon* and *The Glass Key*, his new one, sound like something by Carolyn Wells.* It is true that had the literary lads got past those names and cracked the pages, they would have found the plots to be so many nuisances; confusing

* *Carolyn Wells* (1869-1942), the popular mystery writer, used a detective named Fleming Stone in her somewhat ladylike stories.

to madness, as in *Red Harvest;* fanciful to nausea, as in *The Maltese Falcon;* or, as in the case of the newly published *The Glass Key,* so tired that even this reviewer, who in infancy was let drop by a nurse with the result that she has ever since been mystified by amateur coin tricks, was able to guess the identity of the murderer from the middle of the book. It is true that he has all the mannerisms of Hemingway, with no inch of Hemingway's scope nor flicker of Hemingway's beauty. It is true that when he seeks to set down a swift, assured, well-bred young woman, he devises speeches for her such as are only equalled by the talk Mr. Theodore Dreiser compiled for his society flapper in *An American Tragedy.* It is true that he is so hard-boiled you could roll him on the White House lawn. And it is also true that he is a good, hell-bent, cold-hearted writer, with a clear eye for the ways of hard women and a fine ear for the words of hard men, and his books are exciting and powerful and—if I may filch the word from the booksy ones—pulsing. It is difficult to conclude an outburst like this. All I can say is that anybody who doesn't read him misses much of modern America. And hot that sounds!

Dashiell Hammett is as American as a sawed-off shotgun. He is as immediate as a special extra. Brutal he is, but his brutality, for what he must write, is clean and necessary, and there is in his work none of the smirking and swaggering savageries of a Hecht or a Bodenheim.* He does his readers the infinite courtesy of allowing them to supply descriptions and analyses for themselves. He sets down only what his characters say, and what they do. It is not, I suppose, any too safe a recipe for those who cannot create characters; but Dashiell Hammett can and does and has and, I hope, will. On gentle ladies he is, in a word, rotten; but maybe sometime he will do a novel without a mystery plot, and so no doggy girls need come into it. But it is denied us who read to have everything, and it is little

* *Ben Hecht* (1893-1964), the journalist, novelist, and playwright, collaborated with Charles McArthur on the play *The Front Page.* Two of his novels, *Count Bruga* and *A Jew in Love,* lampooned his fellow novelist *Maxwell Bodenheim* (1893-1954), author of *Naked on Roller Skates,* who had lampooned Hecht in his *Ninth Avenue.*

enough to let him have his ladies and his mysteries, if he will give us such characters as Sam Spade, in *The Maltese Falcon*, and such scenes as the beating-up of Ned Beaumont in *The Glass Key*.

His new book, *The Glass Key*, seems to me nowhere to touch its predecessor. Surely it is that Beaumont, the amateur detective of the later story, a man given perhaps a shade too much to stroking his moustache with a thumbnail, can in no way stack up against the magnificent Spade, with whom, after reading *The Maltese Falcon*, I went mooning about in a daze of love such as I had not known for any character in literature since I encountered Sir Launcelot when I hit the age of nine. (Launcelot and Spade—ah well, they're pretty far apart, yet I played Elaine to both of them, and in that lies a life-story.) The new book, or, indeed, any new book, has no figure to stand near Sam Spade, but maybe all the matter is not there. For I thought that in *The Glass Key* Mr. Hammett seemed a little weary, a little short of spontaneous, a little dogged about his simplicity of style, a little determined to make startling the ordering of his brief sentences, a little concerned with having his conclusion approach the toughness of the superb last scene of *The Maltese Falcon*. But all that is not to say that *The Glass Key* is not a good book and an enthralling one, and the best you have read since *The Maltese Falcon*. And if you didn't read that, this is the swiftest book you've ever read in your life.

Words, Words, Words

May 30, 1931

There are times when images blow to fluff, and comparisons stiffen and shrivel. Such an occasion is surely at hand when one is confronted by Dreiser's latest museum piece, *Dawn*. One can but revise a none-too-hot dialectic of childhood; ask, in rhetorical aggressiveness, "What writes worse than a Theodore Dreiser?"—loudly crow the answer, "*Two* Theodore Dreisers"; and, according to temperament, rejoice at the merciful absurdity of the conception, or shudder away from the thought.

The reading of *Dawn* is a strain upon many parts, but the worst wear and tear fall on the forearms. After holding the massive volume for the half-day necessary to its perusal (well, look at that, would you? "massive volume" and "perusal," one right after the other! You see how contagious Mr. D.'s manner is?), my arms ached with a slow, mean persistence beyond the services of aspirin or of liniment. I must file this distress, I suppose, under the head of "Occupational Diseases"; for I could not honestly chalk up such a result against "Pleasure" or even "Improvement." And I can't truly feel that *Dawn* was worth it. If I must have aches, I had rather gain them in the first tennis of the season, and get my back into it.

This present Dreiser book is the record of its author's first twenty years. It requires five hundred and eighty-nine long, wide, and closely printed pages. Nearly six hundred sheets to the title of *Dawn;* God help us one and all if Mr. Dreiser ever elects to write anything called "June Twenty-first"!

The actual account of the writer's early life, and of the lives of his mother, his father, and his nine brothers and sisters which colored and crossed it, is wholly absorbing; but, if I may say so, without that lightning bolt coming barging in the window, what honest setting-down of anyone's first years would not be? And Mr. Dreiser had, in addition, the purely literary good fortune to be a child of poverty—for when, in print, was the shanty not more glamorous than the salon?

Nor should I cavil at the length, and hence the weight, of the book, were it all given over to memories, since if a man were to write down his remembrances and his impressions up to the age of five, much less of twenty, six hundred pages could not begin to contain them. But I do fret, through *Dawn*, at the great desert patches of Mr. Dreiser's moralizing, I do chafe at such monstrous bad writing as that with which he pads out his tale. I have read reviews of this book, written by those whose days are dedicated to literature. "Of course," each one says airily, "Dreiser writes badly," and thus they dismiss that tiny fact, and go off into their waltz-dream. This book, they cry, ranks well beside the *Confessions* of Rousseau; and I, diverted, as is every layman, by any plump red herring, mutter, "Oh,

Rousseau, my eye," and am preoccupied with that.

But on second thinking, I dare to differ more specifically from the booksie-wooksies. It is of not such small importance to me that Theodore Dreiser writes in so abominable a style. He is regarded, and I wish you could gainsay me, as one of our finest contemporary authors; it is the first job of a writer who demands rating among the great, or even among the good, to write well. If he fails that, as Mr. Dreiser, by any standard, so widely muffs it, he is, I think, unequipped to stand among the big.

For years, you see, I have been crouching in corners hissing small and ladylike anathema of Theodore Dreiser. I dared not yip it out loud, much less offer it up in print. But now, what with a series of events that have made me callous to anything that may later occur, I have become locally known as the What-the-Hell Girl of 1931. In that, my character, I may say that to me Dreiser is a dull, pompous, dated, and darned near ridiculous writer. All right. Go on and bring on your lightning bolts.

Of the earlier Dreiser, the author of *Sister Carrie* and *Jennie Gerhardt*, the portrayer of Muldoon and of Paul Dresser, in *Twelve Men*, you don't think I could be so far gone as to withhold all the reverent praise that is in me, do you? But then I read all those hundreds of thousands of words that made up *An American Tragedy* and, though I hung upon some of them, I later read the newspaper accounts of the Snyder-Gray case, and still later, of the cornering by a hundred or so of New York's finest of the nineteen-year-old "Shorty" Crowley. And I realized, slowly and sadly, that any reporter writes better and more vividly than the man who has been proclaimed the great reporter. It is a quite fair comparison. Mr. Dreiser, with the Chester Gillette case, had a great story; the unnamed men of the daily and the evening papers with the tales of the unhappy Ruth Snyder and the bewildered Judd Gray, and the little Crowley boy who never had a prayer—they had fine stories, too. But they would have lost their jobs, had they written too much.

The booksy ones, with that butterfly touch of theirs, flutter away from Dreiser's bad writing and but brush their wings over the admission that he possesses no humor. Now I know that the term "sense of humor" is dangerous (there's a novel idea!) and that humor is snooted upon, in a dignified manner, by the lofty-minded. Thus Professor Paul Elmer More raises a thin and querulous pipe in his essay on Longfellow—I think it is—to say that there were those who claimed that Longfellow had no humor—of whom I am the first ten. All right, suppose he hadn't, he says, in effect; humor may be all very well for those that like it ("Only fools care to see," said the blind man), but there's no good making a fetish of it. I wouldn't for the world go around making fetishes; yet I am unable to feel that a writer can be complete without humor. And I don't mean by that, and you know it perfectly well, the creation or the appreciation of things comic. I mean that the possession of a sense of humor entails the sense of selection, the civilized fear of going too far. A little humor leavens the lump, surely, but it does more than that. It keeps you, from your respect for the humor of others, from making a dull jackass of yourself. Humor, imagination, and manners are pretty fairly interchangeably interwoven.

Mr. Theodore Dreiser has no humor.

I know that Mr. Dreiser is sincere, or rather I have been told it enough to impress me. So, I am assured, is Mrs. Kathleen Norris* sincere; so, I am informed, is Mr. Zane Grey** sincere; so, I am convinced, was Mr. Horatio Alger***—whose work, to me, that of Mr. Dreiser nearest approximates—sincere. But I will not—oh, come on with your lightning again!—admit that sincerity is the only thing. A good thing, a high thing, an admirable thing; but not the only thing in letters.

The thing that most distressed me in *Dawn* was the philosophizing of its author. His is a sort of pre-war bitterness, a sort of road-company anger at conditions. Once does Mr.

* *Kathleen Norris* (1880-1966) was widely read as a writer of "women's fiction."
** The famous Westerns of *Zane Grey* (1875-1939), including *Riders of the Purple Sage.* are still read.
*** *Horatio Alger* (1832-1899) wrote 120 books for boys.

Dreiser quote a youthful sister: "When men proposed marriage, I found I didn't like them well enough to marry them, but when they told me I was beautiful and wanted to give me things and take me places, it was a different matter. Where I liked a man, it was easy enough to go with him—it was fun—there wasn't really anything wrong with it that I could see. Aside from the social scheme as people seem to want it, I don't even now see that it was."

On this the author comments: "At this point I am sure any self-respecting moralist will close this book once and for all!" But, you know, I must differ. I don't think that's enough to warrant the closing of a book by even the most self-respecting of moralists. I think that Mr. Dreiser believes that the world is backward, hypocritical, and mean, and so, I suppose, it is; but times have changed and Mr. D. is not now the only advanced one. I think the self-respecting moralists are much less apt to close the book "at this point" than are those that get a bit squeamish over the authenticity of a woman who says, "Aside from the social scheme as people seem to want it—"

Early in this little dandy, you saw that I had been affected by the Dreiser style. That, maybe, is responsible for this plethora of words. I could have checked all this torrent, and given you a true idea of Theodore Dreiser's *Dawn*, had I but succumbed to the influence of the present-day Nash and the sweeter-day Bentley,* and had written:

> Theodore Dreiser
> Should ought to write nicer.

* *E. C. Bentley* (1895-1956), the English versifier and mystery writer (*Trent's Last Case*), invented a form of biographical couplets called "Clerihews" after his middle name.

The Grandmother
of the Aunt
of the Gardener

July 25, 1931

Once I went through Spain, like a bat out of hell, with a party that included—nay, grew to center upon—a distinguished American of letters. He spoke French as a Frenchman, rather than like one; his German was flawless; he was persuasive in Italian, and read Magyar for easy amusement; but, at the hour of our start, he did not have a stitch of Spanish to his name. Yet, when the train clacked out of Hendaye, he began trading droll anecdotes with the guard, and by the time we were set in Zaragoza, he was helping the natives along with their subjunctives. It was enough to make me, in a word, sick.

For so lavish a gift of ear and of tongue has, to one forever denied any part of it, something of the repellent quality of black magic. How am I not to be bitter, who have stumbled solo round about Europe, equipped only with *"Non, non et non!"* and *"Où est le lavabo des dames?"* How shall I leash my envy, who have lived so placed that there were weeks at a stretch when I heard or saw no word of English; who was committed entirely and eagerly to French manners, customs, and abbreviations, yet could never get it through the head that the letter "c" on a water-faucet does not stand for "cold"?

It isn't that I have not been given every opportunity; it is simply and dismally that I am incapable of acquiring an extramural language. It is true that I can read French at glacier speed, muffing only the key-word of every sentence. It is true that I can understand it as spoken, provided the speaker is reasonably adept at pantomime. It is also, I am afraid, true that, deep in New York, there are certain spells during certain evenings—cognac is best for a starter—when my English slips from me like the shucked skin of a snake, and I converse only in the elegant French tongue. But what French! O God, O Montreal, what French! It must be faced. Struggle though I have and I do and I will, I am no darned use as a linguist. And to think that there are those, like that man of letters, to whom other languages than their own come as sweetly and as naturally as so many Springtimes is to acquire a pain in the neck for which there is no relief.

But I don't give up; I forget why not. Annually I drag out the conversation books and begin that process called brushing up. It always happens about this time, when the *Wanderlust* is as overpowering as the humidity, and I develop my yearly case of the get-away-from-it-alls. And it seems to me only the part of wisdom to dust off the Continental tongues, because you can't tell—maybe any time now one of the steamship lines will listen to reason and accept teeth instead of money, and I will be on my way back to the Old Country.

And annually I am licked right at the start. It is happening to me even now. I have here before me a small green book called *The Ideal System for Acquiring a Practical Knowledge of French* by Mlle. V. D. Gaudel (who, in case you're going over and you don't know anyone in Paris, lives at 346 Rue Saint-Honoré). Well, everything might have been all right if Mlle. Gaudel—now why do I picture her as fond of dancing and light wines, with a way of flipping up her skirts at the back, to the cry of "Oh-la-la"?—had not subtitled her work *Just the French One Wants to Know*. Somehow, those words antagonized me, by their very blandness, so that I forgot the thirst for knowledge and searched the tome only for concrete examples of just the French one will never need. Oh-la-la, yourself, Mademoiselle, and go on and get the hell back into *La Vie Parisienne*!

Now you know perfectly well that at my time of life it would be just a dissipation of energy for me to learn the French equivalent of "Either now, or this afternoon at five." It is, at best, a matter of dark doubt that I shall ever be in any position in which it will be necessary for me to cry: "Although the captain is far from here, I always think of him." It is possible, of course, but it's a nasty wrench to the arm of coincidence that I shall find occasion for the showing-off of the phrase "Her marriage took place (*eut lieu*) on the 2nd of April, 1905"; or that it will be given me to slide gently into a conversation with

"I admire the large black eyes of this orphan." Better rest I silent forever than that I pronounce: "In this case, it is just that you should not like riding and swimming"; or that I inquire: "Are you pleased that they will bring the cricket set?"; or that I swing into autobiography with the confession: "I do not like to play blindman's buff"; or that I so seriously compromise myself as to suggest: "I propose that you breakfast with me and afterwards look for our friends."

The future is veiled, perhaps mercifully, and so I cannot say that never, while I live, shall I have occasion to announce in French: "It was to punish your foster-brother"; but I know which way I would bet. It may be that some day I shall be in such straits that I shall have to remark: "The friend of my uncle who took the quill feather bought a round black rice-straw hat trimmed with two long ostrich feathers and a jet buckle." Possibly circumstances will so weave themselves that it will be just the moment for me to put in: "Mr. Fouchet would have received some eel." It might occur that I must thunder: "Obey, or I will not show you the beautiful gold chain." But I will be damned if it is ever going to be of any good to me to have at hand Mlle. Gaudel's masterpiece: "I am afraid he will not arrive in time to accompany me on the harp."

Oh, "Just the French One Wants to Know" *mon oeil*, Mademoiselle. And you know what you can do, far better than I could tell you.

There is a little more comfort in a booklet called *The American in Europe*, where neat sentences are listed for use in almost every contingency. Yet, somehow there sneaked in under the curious heading of "The Theatre, the Music" this monologue: "I love you; Don't forget me; The beautiful blue eyes; Let us love one another; I play all my pieces by heart without any music." Doubtless they order those things rather better in France, but I feel that, according to our New York ideas, that last phrase is all wrong. It should run, for its place in the sequence: "Come on down to my apartment—I want to show you some remarkably fine etchings I just bought."

To turn to Spanish proves small good. Here I have a stamp-sized work, sent out by Hugo's Simplified System, entitled *How to Get All You Want While Travelling in Spain* (and a pretty sweeping statement, too, Mr. Hugo, if I may say so). Mr. Hugo has captured the Iberian spirit so cleverly as to enable his pupils phonetically to learn "I don't like this table—this waiter—this wine," and to go on from there into truly idiomatic crabbing.

Mr. Hugo is good, but his book can never touch that manual of Spanish conversation that it was once my fortune to pick up in Madrid; though I curse myself for leaving it there, one scene in it is forever branded on my brain and engraved upon my heart. The premise is that a mother and her engaged daughter visit a furniture shop to select the double bed (*matrimonio*) for the future bride's home. (The work was titled, as I recall it, *Easy Conversations for Everyday Occasions*.) The mother sees a bed that she approves—the daughter, in the Latin manner, never opens her trap. Mom asks the salesman the price of the piece of furniture, and he tells her, with respect, "Thirteen pesetas," To which the dear little grayhaired lady replies, very simply, "Jesu!" . . .

Well. I got a long way from the place I started. All I meant to do was moan over my trouble in working on foreign languages. And it took me all these words to do it. The thing to do, surely, is to give the French and the Spanish books to some deserving family, and get to work on that English.

Not Even Funny

March 18, 1933

When one had put sex carefully away on the highest cupboard-shelf, in a box marked "Winter Hats—1916," it is somewhat melancholy to read a book by Tiffany Thayer*—melancholy,

* *Tiffany Thayer* (1902-1959) attained wide notoriety and sales for his sex novels, daring in their day, including his own version of *The Three Musketeers*.

that is, in that no wistful memories whatever are thus evoked. Mr. Thayer, it is deplorably unnecessary to explain, has achieved great prominence in that school of American authors which may be described as the boys who ought to go regularly to a gym. He is beyond question a writer of power; and his power lies in his ability to make sex so thoroughly, graphically, and aggressively unattractive that one is fairly shaken to ponder how little one has been missing. Bewildered is the fox who lives to find that grapes beyond reach can be *really* sour.

Mr. Thayer's latest work is called, with that simplicity which is the gaudiest flower of pretentiousness, *An American Girl*. I am at a loss to comprehend why this was the selected title, since the book displays any number of American girls, all alike in seeming to be, as Henry James said of George Sand, highly accessible. Perhaps it was felt that the name established an excellent base for a superstructure of sequels—*An American Girl at Yale*, *An American Girl on a Gunboat*, and so forth. Or perhaps Mr. Thayer, too, sometimes nods, and simply couldn't think of another thing to call the blamed book. Only in the friendliest spirit is it suggested that for later editions he might care to change his present rather pastel title to the possibly more provocative *I Am a Fugitive from a Daisy Chain Gang*.*

It is not, alas, the mention of sex but that of dullness which brings up the matter of Mabel Dodge Luhan's** *Background*, the entering volume of a proposed series that will comprise her *Intimate Memories*. Last year, Mrs. Luhan gave us *Lorenzo in Taos*, which seems to me one of the most valuable works of our time. It is extraordinarily well written, swift, sure, and excited; it is of enormous importance as a portrait of D. H. Lawrence; and it is in all literature the most staggering survey of the wrong things a woman will do who sets out to wrest from a man

* *I Am a Fugitive from a Georgia Chain Gang*, an autobiographical book by Robert Elliot Burns, was a best seller in 1932.
** *Mabel Dodge*, born into a socialite family in Buffalo, was known for her salon and her literary friends. In the D. H. Lawrence circle in Taos she met and married an Indian, Tony Luhan.

his romantic devotion. I am convinced that Mrs. Luhan had no idea of all she was revealing, nor even of what she was revealing, for no woman could knowingly so display herself and go on walking the world; and it is, I think, in that preposterous naivete, somehow so terrible, somehow so moving, that lies the eternal value of the book.

In *Lorenzo in Taos*, Mrs. Luhan includes Lawrence's letters to her on the subject of her *Intimate Memories*, which work she had in progress during those last hopeful, heart-breaking months when he was in Italy awaiting the health that did not come. Apparently, she wrote him about her work, and she wrote him about it, and she *wrote* him about it, and finally she sent him the manuscript. Lawrence told her to publish her memoirs in the United States, but to substitute invented names for real; he told her to distribute them by private subscription; he told her to try having them published in Germany; he told her to have them printed in Paris on her own money; he told her to lock them in a safe-deposit vault for fifty years; he told her to give them, sealed, to the French Academy, to be opened after her death; he all but told her, in all but words, to tie them around her neck and go jump in the lake. So the first volume of them is now out, published by Harcourt, Brace and Company at three dollars the throw.

This book takes the author only as far as her presentation to the society of her native city of Buffalo, but it does it with unflagging attention to dusty detail. Mrs. Luhan is a woman of relentless memory, and no littlest scroll in the woodwork of any room she ever entered in her girlhood eludes her recall or her description. It may be in her forthcoming volumes, when she gets into her stride of marrying people, things will liven up a bit. But *Background* is to me as dull, and with that same stuffy, oppressive, plush-thick dullness, as an album of old snapshots of somebody else's family group.

From *Esquire*

1957 - 1962

Best Fiction of 1957

December 1957

In taking that traditional backward look, over the fiction of the year, I am afraid it is impossible to avoid the word "trends"; so there it is, and here are some of them, set down, separately, as they seem to me. Books are handsomer than they have ever been before, of lovely print on lovely paper, held in bindings both brave and dignified. Books are much more expensive than they used to be and, especially in the cases of new writers, much longer; apparently there exists a curious convention that length is what gives you your money's worth. Save for a remarkably few works, from expected pens, 1957 is no banner year for the American novel. The cases of euphoria among book reviewers have reached alarming figures; perhaps my opportunity to see, this once-a-year, what they are daily faced with makes a little more understandable to me the fact that any reasonably grammatical novel brings on such attacks of cheer-leading, hat-tossing, and dancing in the streets as make the critiques of the late Alexander Woollcott seem those of a man of ice and iron. Miserable-child stories are surprisingly absent. English authors, though their books may not quite succeed, write better than almost anybody, and Irish authors, better than anybody. The flags of new novelists are their photographs on the back dust-covers of their books, and you never saw so many lumberjack shirts in your life. Poor dear sex is crammed into spaces where there is scarcely room for it by itself, and its joy must be left outside. The nowadays ruling that no word is unprintable has, I think, done nothing whatever for beautiful letters. The boys have gone hog-wild with liberty, yet the short flat terms used over and over, both in dialogue and narrative, add neither vigor nor clarity; the effect is not of shock but of something far more dangerous—tedium. Obscenity is too valuable a commodity to chuck around all over the place; it should be taken out of the safe on special occasions only. Well. So I am growing old, a process that goes on at a gallop even as I sit here, for I find my heart turns tenderly to that yesterday when there were those two demure dashes between the first and fourth letters of the words used with telling infrequency.

Now about those books we all want to give. For myself, to open the holiday exercises, I should dearly wish to send those I most love and respect William Faulkner's *The Town*. The only drawback to this otherwise smooth-flowing plan is that the beloved and venerated go buy and read every Faulkner book as soon as it comes out—which is among the reasons for my feelings toward them, and *The Town* must long have been on their bed tables. It is presumptuous to offer such small awards as these to the greatest writer we have (oh, all right, all right; to the man I believe to be the greatest writer we have, then), even if there were any room left on Mr. Faulkner on which to hang them. Nor can I say that this is William Faulkner's finest work, for his books are so variegated that comparisons among them are not possible. *The Town* comes after *The Hamlet* in his triptych of the horrible, evil, greedy, irresistible Snopes family, on their way of taking over full power in Yoknapatawpha County. I hope you will permit me to crawl back to those words I once said about this being no banner year for American novels. This is the year in which *The Town* appeared; I was a fool and a liar.

If you want to give James Gould Cozzens' enormous novel, *By Love Possessed*, as you probably do and certainly have been told you should, I am afraid you are going to be in trouble, for all those belonging to the Book-of-the-Month Club will have it, and non-members must have emptied the bookshops of it, if they read its rousing reviews. The work caused one reviewer to compare the author to Tolstoy, another to Thackeray, and still another to place him with George Eliot and Joseph Conrad; all of these, you understand, were writing about the same book. *By Love Possessed* seemed to me cold, distant, and exasperatingly patronizing. It is a vast enterprise encompassing all sorts of love, except, naturally, those branches which extend to Jews, Negroes, and people who have lost track of their great-grandparents; that is the way Mr. Cozzens feels and Lord knows he has a right to his feelings, yet it is somewhat obscure to me why he should take such pride in them; unfortunately, he is not the only one who has them. The scene of the book is a small, correct town paved with tradition, and the characters are comfortably, not vulgarly, rich, with a pride in their breeding that virtually amounts to ancestor worship; most of them are lawyers, which accounts, perhaps, for their being so overly articulate. The hero looks around him at a world snagged by love and tries to do what he can, but he is so icy a creature that it is hard to feel compassion for him that he may accomplish so little. He has a child by his first wife—I imagine he swam over her; that wife dies; he has a most unattractive affair; he marries again, this time to as horrendous an example of the games-mistress type as can be met in literature, though it is obviously assumed that she is to be revered. It seems to me that we might all admire Mr. Cozzens' people and their world more if Mr. Cozzens himself did not admire them so much.

Books I think you would want to give—everyone would—are John Cheever's *The Wapshot Chronicle,* about some highly special citizens of a New England village, shrewdly written and swift to read; *A Legacy,* Sybille Bedford's almost terrifyingly brilliant novel of the Berlin of the old, elegant world; *Pnin,* which its author, Vladimir Nabokov, calls a novel, though it is, and nothing against it either, a series of sketches, touching and funny and perfectly written, all at once; and, to my mind more than all of these, *The Feast of Lupercal,* by Brian Moore, the Irishman now a citizen of Canada, who also wrote the strong and pitying *The Lonely Passion of Judith Hearne.*

The choice widens, and I think you must go into careful consideration, among these entries, of the tastes of the recipients. Nevil Shute's *On the Beach* is no Christmas carol, but it seems to me a remarkably fine novel, one which I read, in the peculiarly repulsive phrase, with my eyes glued to the page. It concerns almost the last people left in a world destroyed by radiation, after a war of little, vague beginnings. Mr. Shute does not select his characters in the usual manner of an author doing up a group faced with doom—a nun, a millionaire, a whore, a beggar, a poet; his are people, just people, who know that they must die within a few months, yet cannot stand the thought and go on buying presents for the next Christmas and planning gardens for the next spring. The book is, I suppose, a tour de force, and there are those who think that is an ugly thing to say of a work. One reviewer went farther and dismissed it as "unnecessary," which dictum helped me through the white nights by causing me to try making a list of necessary books. To date, I have got as far as *The Settlement Cook Book* and *Madame Bovary.*

Let's see. *In the Time of Greenbloom,* by the English doctor who writes under the name of Gabriel Fielding, is dramatic, inventive, and somehow tender, with a strange and stunning character in Greenbloom himself. There is *The Black Obelisk* by Erich Maria Remarque, which might be covered by the word "lusty," for want of anything less fragrant. There is Julian Green's *The Transgressor,* beautifully written, of course, and exquisitely translated from his French by his sister, but over it flickers the delicate green light that springs from decayed things, and around it swirls the sweetish odor of what is rotting. There is *Rage on the Bar,* Geoffrey Wagner's story of British colonialism, the more bloodcurdling for the grace of its writings. If you are one who likes to give something by Evelyn Waugh, I beg of you to hold back, this year, for his *The Ordeal of Gilbert Pinfold* must have been written while he was waiting for the lift to reach his floor. And another disappointment is Samuel Beckett's *Murphy,* to one who was and is a devotee of his play, *Waiting for Godot.* Some of it is outrageously funny, but the style is so convoluted that, as Huckleberry Finn said of *Pilgrim's Progress:* The statements was interesting, but tough.

If you want to give something really enchanting to someone who answers the same description, I should like to suggest *The China Shepherdess* by Felicien Marceau; it is rather coolly sharp, with a combination of worldliness and innocence.

I include in this composition a novel called *Silver Spoon* by Edwin Gilbert, only because it was at the top of the best-seller list, and you might happen to have a friend with a morbid interest in seeing something that for a time beat out *Peyton Place.* It concerns the preposterously rich, and there may be some idea behind it of proving that money isn't everything; but I am not sure. As to its length, you get 509 pages for your $4.95, pages which take in just about everything. It is said that George Moore—I *think* it was George Moore—described a fantasy he had had of Tolstoy, when *War and Peace* had gone to press after his seventh complete rewriting of it, springing up in his bed in the middle of the night, shrieking, "I forgot to put in a yacht race!" Mr. Gilbert's sleep need be troubled by no such sense of omission. In *Silver Spoon*, he threw in a blow-by-blow account of a steeplechase.

Of the novels by new writers, I think most often of one by Myron S. Kaufmann, not for its art or its skill, but for the strange passionate innocence the author brings to his story of the son of an orthodox Jewish family, who finds at Harvard that it would be better for him to join the Episcopalian church; it is impossible not to respect Mr. Kaufmann's fervor, and it is almost impossible, so fairly and strongly does he put down his argument, not to be convinced by both sides. I admire the book, but I was first impressed, as I still am, by its title, *Remember Me to God,* which sounds like a phrase Graham Greene and Evelyn Waugh might exchange as they took leave of each other.

I can think of no book anyone would want to give and to receive more than *The Complete Works of Nathanael West.* "Complete" is a saddening word here, for this one volume contains the four short novels—*Miss Lonelyhearts, The Dream Life of Balso Snell, A Cool Million,* and *The Day of the Locust*—that were the entire output of Nathanael West before his outrageously unnecessary death in a motor accident. Wildly funny, desperately sad, brutal and kind, furious and patient, there was no other like Nathanael West.

If you were to say that you do not want to give books of short stories, I should try to be nice about it, of course, but I should have a bad time believing you, for they are sure of welcome always. First, and there is naturally no other place for it ever, is the book of *The Finest Stories of Sean O'Faolain*, and I can say no more than does its title. Then I find the good new writers I so doggedly sought, in Robie Macauley, whose *The End of Pity*, though a somewhat up-and-down collection, has very high ups in his stories of the C.I.C., in Germany; and in Evan S. Connell, Junior, the author of *The Anatomy Lesson*, a writer of fine style and amazing variety. So shut your little face, Virginia, for yes, there is a Santa Claus.

Well, then. A Merry Christmas to all, and God bless us every one, especially William Faulkner.

Edmund Wilson: *The American Earthquake;*
Jack Kerouac: *The Subterraneans;*
Edna Ferber: *Ice Palace*

May 1958

The late Robert Benchley, rest his soul, could scarcely bear to go into a bookshop. His was not a case of so widely shared an affliction as claustrophobia; his trouble came from a great and grueling compassion. It was no joy to him to see the lines and tiers of shining volumes, for as he looked there would crash over him, like a mighty wave, a vision of every one of the authors of every one of those books saying to himself as he finished his opus, "There—I've done it! I have written *the* book. Now it and I are famous forever." Long after Mr. Benchley had rushed out of the shop, he would be racked with pity for poor human dreams. Eventually, he never went anywhere near a bookshop. If he wanted something to read, he either borrowed it or sent for it by mail.

I cannot, of course, lay claim to any of the deep mercy of

that extraordinary man, but I have lately experienced a small attack of his special melancholy; at least, I have been visited by a sort of depressive puzzlement which is somewhere near it. Like many a better one before me, I have gone down under the force of numbers, under the books and books and books that keep coming out and coming out and coming out, shoals of them, spates of them, flash floods of them, too blame many books, and no sign of an end. And this at the time of what is recognized as the slack season in the publishing industry! The slack season comes after the holiday rush and before the big spring drive. (You see, a monthly magazine does not go to press at the double; it takes many weeks to make it all nice and tidy; so that, though you may pick up this issue to leaf it through before you go out a Maying, here am I carving these deathless words on jade in blackest January.) Slack or no slack, out come books, any kind of books, any kind at all. The publishers take no advantage of their blessed leisure. They go right on publishing, all out of control. It seems to be a compulsive activity, a species, I should suppose, of tic.

And so we have books about the moonlit beauty of East Indian maidens; books about journeys in Spain—for no matter where you are or what you are doing or what time it is, someone has always just done a book about travels in Spain; whimsical accounts of the vagaries of household servants; histories of jazz bands and ballet organizations; books supposedly written by cats, though maybe it isn't only supposedly; historical works whose authors have the gift of knowing the exact words and thoughts of their characters at all moments of their lives; books about people who write about people who write; books about families of murderous hatreds and cozy incests; books about experiments in group therapy—in one of these, curious to the layman, the patients are cured by each member choosing one other member as his or her father or mother, as the case may be, although the cases become somewhat confused when one pretty young sufferer selects the presiding psychiatrist, a mild and amiable gentleman, to be her Mama; books about— Please, shall we stop now?

Yet there is a reward for slogging through all these, for out of the heaps comes one fine and lasting book, Edmund Wilson's *The American Earthquake*. It is a chronicle done in essays—though perhaps reports is a better word—on the country from the middle Twenties to the middle of the New Deal. Mr. Wilson has included only a few of his critical pieces—only a handful of bits from his reviews of the theatre of the Twenties, written at the time. He has put in, suddenly, a wildly funny expressionistic drama, a deadly picture of one of those deadly Greenwich Village cocktail parties that go on and on into the deadly dawn, some glimpses of those who long ago were graduated from college, but still keep shinnying up the silver cord that binds them to Alma Mater; these, however, are just here and there. The main book is a series of startlingly clear accounts of the idiocies and brutalities of times that were neither good nor old. Mr. Wilson, scholar, poet, playwright, critic, and novelist, is also a truly wonderful reporter. I think that there is no one as yet to share his eminence with him. If he is lonely up there, I am afraid there is nothing to be done about it.

Surely there is no longer distance between two points than the way from Edmund Wilson to Jack Kerouac, but here is the new Kerouac novel, and so—

Mr. Kerouac, possibly the inventor and certainly the historian of the Beat Generation, calls his latest work *The Subterraneans*. The Subterraneans "are hip without being slick, they are intelligent without being corny, they are intellectual as hell and know all about Pound without being pretentious or talking too much about it, they are very quiet, they are very Christlike." So those are the Subterraneans. The only point in the summary with which I can agree is that they are hip; or, as Grandma used to say, hep.

Doubtless my absence of excitement over Mr. Kerouac's characters is due to a gaping lack in me, for, and I regret the fact, I do not dig bop. I cannot come afire when I hear it, and I am even less ecstatic in reading about it. I am honestly sorry about this, for who could not do with a spot of ecstasy now and then? I envy the generation its pleasure in its music. And that is all I envy it.

It says, on the dust-cover of *The Subterraneans,* that the Beat Youth believe that how to live seems much more crucial to them than why. (I don't know why they need give themselves such airs about it; if memory serves me, that is the way most generations believed.) But the "how" of the Beat Boys and Girls is of an appalling monotony. Nights and days flow into one. They go swoon to that music, they get themselves stoned on beer (which I believe is a possibility in one's tender years), they fight and forget it, they are forever piling into rickety cars and driving furiously to the far-away house of some unexpecting friend, where they establish themselves for days. These practices, I admit, were not unknown on occasion to members of that Lost Generation you may have heard about, but such was not their entire way of life; there were among the Lost those who made fairly important contributions to their times. The Beat Ones never have to be anywhere, never want to go anywhere except just to some other place. There is little laughter among them, and they speak mainly to tell one another how great they are. Through all the wild whirl of their days and nights, they find time, or so they tell, to perform the act of love as constantly as do Japanese beetles. The hero of *The Subterraneans* repeatedly describes his intimate moments with the beautiful young Negro girl with whom he is in love— "love" is his word. He narrates these episodes play-by-play— what do these new writers do, anyway? Keep score-cards?

I think, as perhaps you have discerned, that if Mr. Kerouac and his followers did not think of themselves as so glorious, as intellectual as all hell and very Christlike, I should not be in such a bad humor.

I must say, though, for *The Subterraneans* that it is brought out by the Grove Press in a most pleasing form—a small book with excellent print and paper, and hard covers, though not of cloth. I hope they will do many.

Well. It was my privilege to have a sort of preview of what is surely to be one of the big events of the springtime—Miss Edna Ferber's massive novel *Ice Palace*. Miss Ferber, who so thoroughly travels her country, came most recently upon Alaska. She was deeply impressed with the dramatic beauty of the place, and so, through her eyes, are you, and she is finely indignant over the stupidity of not admitting the territory to statehood—I wish there were several millions like her. Otherwise, the book, which is going to be a movie, has the plot and characters of a book which is going to be a movie.

The heroine, Christine Storm, has yellow hair and dark slanting eyes, and she is Miss Alaska from the start—the very start, for she was born in a caribou. You heard me, she was born in a caribou.

Well, it seems this young couple was out walking in the wilds, and suddenly there were unmistakable signs that Baby was about to make three. It was perishing cold; so the expectant father shot a caribou who happened to be passing and slit it up the front. He assisted his wife to climb inside, and there, all snug and warm, she gave birth to our heroine. The baby was fine, but, unhappily, the mother died. So, a short time later, did the father, in an altercation won by a bear. I felt real sorrow at these two deaths, for it meant that the girl was brought up by both of her grandfathers; two of the most smashing old bores you'd ever want to meet. There is also a salty outspoken old lady—the Thelma Ritter part, surely—who came to Alaska as a colleen, and stayed to boss the whole territory. One grandfather is in love with Alaska and the other with money and power; through the second, Christine is exposed to the wealth and standards of social family in Seattle. But Christine's heart is as pure Alaskan gold as is her hair, and there in the distance is a fine young part-Eskimo aviator, and. . . .

The United States is, as has somewhere been said before, a big country, and there are still reaches of it that Miss Ferber has not attended to. And in every one, there awaits a gold mine for the lady who is, surely, America's most successful writeress.

And so while the January sleet snaps at my windowpanes here, I wish you a merry, merry May.

George P. Elliott: *Parktilden Village;*
John Barth: *The End of the Road;*
Vance Bourjaily: *The Violated;*
Vladimir Nabokov: *Lolita*

October 1958

After a short but thick study of recently published fiction, you will find yourself fully equipped to empty many a drawing room in the capacity of authoritative lecturer on the topic of Sex: Plain and Fancy. Under the latter adjective, you could start things off by citing the fact that each of five new novels deals, either largely or just as a little extra dividend, with a busied young man who enjoys the concurrent favors of a mother and her daughter. Is this, you might ask such listeners as have been unable to get out the door, a fresh trend in American letters? Or is it, perhaps, merely a glancing blow at the housing shortage?

Of the works with this motif, it seems to me that *Parktilden Village* is the best written, and certainly the most swiftly readable. The author, George P. Elliott, stays with the traditional course of his theme only in obeying the rule that the ladies must each find out about the other's relationship with the young man, and must each be broken by the knowledge. (O, women, women—not a flicker of humor in a carload of you!) For much of the time, Mr. Elliott forsakes the homey triangle and gives his attention to a whole parade of other characters, from professors to hot-rodders, all drawn with notable sharpness. He can curse his bad luck that *Parktilden Village* (it is the name of a housing project, and I wish I could stop confusing the title with *Peyton Place*) came out at the same time as those others of like story design, so that the reader can only greet it with a droop of the shoulders and a low moan of, "Oh, Lord, *that* again!" The book glitters with Mr. Elliott's style, though as a sincere admirer of it and a wisher of all good to him, one must hope that somewhere there is somebody who can warn him to watch his pen; because if he doesn't, one of these fine days he is going to simile himself to death.

As to plain sex, there is a bumper crop of it in new publications—well, maybe "plain" is not quite the word; "explicit" would be nearer. Sex, of course, is as old and as prevalent as weather; they both will go right along, and it's pretty tiresome to talk such a lot about either of them—a bit of advice that I should like to see taken by many of our newer writers. Certainly, nobody wants to complain about sex itself; but I think we all have a legitimate grievance in the fact that, as it is shown in present-day novels, its practitioners are so unmercifully articulate about it. Before the actual consummation, after it, and worst of all, during it, they discuss and analyze and debate and question and compare and prophesy and reminisce; and so any joy is talked right out the window. There is no more cruel destroyer of excitement than painstaking detail. Who reads these play-by-play reports of passion responds with much the same thrill he would experience in looking over the blueprints for some stranger's garage. . . . Can you remember, venerable subscriber, the days when there used to be rows of asterisks? How those little stars twinkled and gleamed, and how warmly they shone upon the imagination!

I believe it will be a long time before you will come again upon three people so hell-bent on going over and over a subject as are the woman, the other man, and the husband—especially the husband—in John Barth's *The End of the Road*. They are strange, somber beings; indeed, the other man, the narrator of the story, is caused by the dark disturbances of his mind to cling to the services of a curiously mystic doctor. The woman admits her act of transgression to her husband—it is less cynical than axiomatic to say that when any such lady in fiction has a good long discussion with her lover as to whether it would not be the square thing to confess, she is practically set to get up and put on her shoes and go home and tell all. The husband, once he knows she has committed adultery, has the strange, somber compulsion to make her go back to her fellow sinner and commit it again. Thus all three need never lack conversation, for they can analyze the events of both occasions. The book ends, inevitably, in deep, wide tragedy; it is, in fact, tragic all its way, and there is nothing admirable in being impatient about the work of so good a writer as John Barth. But I am old and grey and full of sleep, and I wish to heaven that his people would, if only occasionally, strip their souls in silence.

Whatever else there may be about this brief between-season stretch in the publishing world, it has brought forth some extraordinarily fine writers. High among them is Vance Bourjaily, whose name I should like to hail long and loud, if I had any idea how to pronounce it. In his novel, *The Violated*, he has taken upon himself a mighty task, and has accomplished it brilliantly. His book travels in time through the Twenties, the Great Depression, the Second World War, and on until almost this minute. It is mainly the story of three young men, and the sister of one of them; but there must be hundreds, literally, of the people whose lives theirs touch, and Mr. Bourjaily has drawn in his background characters superbly. All during the earlier part of the book, the boyhood and the college years of the three young men, you are reminded of Scott Fitzgerald by the descriptive skill and the honest sadness in these accounts of youth, and to say that a writer recalls Scott Fitzgerald is no bad word to spread about him. It is true that the girls encountered along the way of youth are far, far from the Fitzgerald flapper, who was considered a "speed" because of her willingness to nestle close and her sporadic compulsion to dive off yachts; Mr. Bourjaily deals with more untidy manifestations of girlish playfulness. Yet these, too, seem surely true and somehow touching.

The boys are companions at college and, though not together in the war, have each a part in it. I think I have not read more graphic reports on what that latest war was like than these passages about their several experiences.

After the war, the people of the book are the explanation of its title—"violated," Mr. Bourjaily says, "by their inability to communicate, to love, to comprehend, to create—violated by neurotic commitments to preposterous goals, or, more tragically, to no goals at all." Violated by all they have seen and been through, and all they have missed that they should not have.

But it is the after-war section of the book that seems to me to go off. It is as if the author was unable to stop himself. There is, for instance, an all-but-interminable account of a children's performance of *Hamlet*, with the melancholy one played by a fourteen-year-old girl and the ghost something aged eight, who has, or so it says, a most extraordinarily harrowing voice for the part. The audience, seated on orange crates, for the work is given in a bare, dusty room in a deserted house, weeps and shudders and succumbs extravagantly to emotion, an effect which I cannot remember John Barrymore or John Gielgud as ever having created. I cannot help feeling that Mr. Bourjaily, in quoting line after line of the play, and pointing out how each child rendered it and what was the result on the audience, has perhaps rather lost his head. Then there is a long history of a heartsick young man—oh, not one of the principals, for heaven's sake!—who wings homeward to Fire Island for comfort, only to find it is out of season, and he must sleep in cold sands and eat from battered cans until his boy friend comes to what I suppose might be called his rescue. The pathos, indeed the necessity of this interlude eluded me entirely.

But such bits are, and I hope to be first to say it, crabbed bits of nagging at a fine book. Which is what *The Violated* is.

The last item on this list presents difficulties in the telling about it. It is *Lolita*, by Vladimir Nabokov, and as this is being beaten out on the typewriter, it has not reached its publication in the United States.

Lolita, as you undoubtedly know, has had an enormous share of trouble, and caused a true hell of a row. It was first published in Paris, and was promptly banned throughout France. (As it was written in English, there does seem to have been a certain amount of oversolicitude that the French masses would have had their morals upended by the reading of it.) Then it fell into more trouble in England. There were those who, more power to them though their force was great before, struck out stoutly in its defense as a work of art; and there was also one John Gordon who wrote in the London *Sunday Express:* "Without doubt it is the filthiest book I ever read. Sheer unrestrained pornography." Things reached such a pass that, once the French authorities removed the ban as casually as they remove one of their governments, if someone sneaked a copy into this country and presented it to you, you could sell it, under the counter, at any price you wanted to ask. It so happens that I never met anybody who made money on it in the black market, but that is what was said. Then the house of G. P. Putnam's Sons, in New York, quietly announced that they had acquired the rights to the book and were bringing it out virtually immediately. And may honors and blessings light upon the heads of G. P. Putnam's Sons, however many there may be of them.

I do not think that *Lolita* is a filthy book. I cannot regard it as pornography, either sheer, unrestrained, or any other kind. It is the engrossing, anguished story of a man, a man of taste and culture, who can love only little girls. They must be between the ages of nine and fourteen, and he calls them nymphets. But not every child in the age group is a nymphet, nor is even the prettiest one. She must have that quality for which there is no one word, unless you want to call it "It," which I do not. In twelve-year-old Lolita, he finds his ideal nymphet.

She is a dreadful little creature, selfish, hard, vulgar, and foul-tempered. He knows that; he knows all of what she is. That the knowledge cannot turn away his obsession with her is his agony.

An anguished book, but sometimes wildly funny, as in the saga of his travel across and around the United States with her, in search of some place that might possibly please her; and in the account of that trek are descriptions of the American hinterlands that Sinclair Lewis could never touch. Lolita leaves him, of course, for a creature even worse than she is, but he is so riddled with his need of her that he follows the trail of her and her new lover, losing it and picking it up again, over and over. When he finds her, she is seventeen, haggard in the face and swollen with pregnancy, married to a poor, simple fool. He gives her all the money he has—she has a fondness for money—and starts on another weary quest: to find and kill the man who took her from him.

No. There is no good, I see at this late moment, to try to melt down the story. It is in its writing that Mr. Nabokov has made it the work of art that it is. Mr. Nabokov—the same man, you know, that wrote the delicate stories in *Pnin*—started writing in English long after his first youth. His command of the language is absolute, and his *Lolita* is a fine book, a distinguished book—all right, then—a great book.

And how are *you*, John Gordon, Esq., of the London *Sunday Express*?

Ellery Queen: *The New York Murders*

January 1959

Though you may not have accounts of factual crimes every day, life can still be sweet. For fictional murders valiantly hold their own, from the stunning works of the mighty Dashiell Hammett, on down, down, down. And long before you get into the down, down, downs—tall among the very highest-ups, in fact— are the stories of Ellery Queen, an author somewhat difficult to explain. Ellery Queen is two men. Or perhaps it is better to say that two men are Ellery Queen—no, that doesn't look right, either. Well, anyway, it seems there are two gentlemen named, respectively, Frederic Dannay and Manfred Lee, who banded together to write as one, signing their products as Ellery Queen. Then, possibly to make shorter the way on which lies madness, they named their crack brain-child, the hero of their many tales, Ellery Queen, too. So there, if you can clear your head, you are.

Ellery Queen, the hero, is not a detective so much as a detector; that is he comes in when everything is thoroughly balled up and straightens it out, just for the love of justice. He is, I think, the most attractive of current investigators; though he must watch a nasty little habit of quoting from the classics and dropping into foreign tongues, which is creeping up on him. He is slightly built and a wearer, perpetually, of pince-nez, but quick and lethal with his fists, especially if he feels that something impolite has been said to his father, Inspector Queen of the New York Police Force. Women sigh and swoon for the young man, but he has yet to respond. His heart, so far as I can gather, belongs to Daddy. Not the least interesting passages in the Ellery Queen books are those that show glimpses of the home life of father and son, who live in a brownstone of the Upper West Side—I believe they have separate suites, but this has not been entirely clear—are served by a treasure of a sixteen-year-old houseboy named Djuna, and drink great pitchers of lemonade on hot nights. The reader would like to see more of this menage, perhaps, but, despite its fascination, it would hold up the rush of the story. And the rush of the story is, almost unfailingly, magnificent.

The latest Queen book is, actually, three books bound into one under the title of *The New York Murders.* (Ellery Queen deals entirely in murders; you are not fobbed off, as you are with Mr. Leslie Charteris's *Saint,* with pablum about the rape of the dowager's emeralds, or the theft of the blueprint of the newest submarine.) These three murder novels seem to me the best of the Queen stories, which, on the word of one who has watched closely for years, is serious praise. They have speed, ingenuity, and really brilliant examples of detection, and the ending consists more often of a double surprise than a single one.

The joint authors also toss off prize contests, gather anthologies, and get out a monthly magazine containing their own stories and those of other writers. That it appears only monthly is too seldom for me.

Of course, I should like to read of my beloved subject only as it is treated by the best; but the best is not always or even often available, and so, like all aging lovers, I must settle for what is easiest to get. Therefore, I am become a confirmed user of Whodunits. I make the admission without shame, let shrink from me who will. (Have I ever, by the way, told you about an elegant friend of mine who refers to the school as Whodidits? She is the same lady that speaks of Woolworth's as the five-and-ten-cent shop.)

To me, the raveled sleeve of care is never more painlessly knitted up than in an evening alone in a chair snug yet copious, with a good light and an easily held little volume sloppily printed and bound in inexpensive paper. I do not ask much of it—which is just as well, for that is all I get. It does not matter if I guess the killer, and if I happen to discover, along around page 208, that I have read the work before, I attribute the fact not to the less than arresting powers of the author, but to my own lazy memory. I like best to have one book in my hand, and a stack of others on the floor beside me, so as to know the supply of poppy and mandragora will not run out before the small hours. In all reverence I say Heaven bless the Whodunit, the soothing balm on the wound, the cooling hand on the brow, the opiate of the people.

Truman Capote: *Breakfast at Tiffany's;*
John Updike: *The Poorhouse Fair*

February 1959

Long, only too long, can the human frame bear up under cruel and inhuman punishment; but at last comes the day, as it must, as it is bound to, when endurance ravels out and the human frame gets up on its hind legs. This observation, crackling with originality, arises from the fact that that day, that shining day, has at length come to me. It was a dreary while on the road, but finally it is here. Therefore, I should like to issue a short, stiff statement, to be notarized if considered necessary, that I am through and done with novels containing scenes in which young ladies stand mother-naked before long mirrors, and evaluate, always favorably, their unveiled surfaces. Further, I will have no more of books in which various characters tell their dreams; tell, with prodigious extension of memory and ruthless courtesy to details, dreams which, unlike yours and mine, have to do with the plot of the piece. And finally and forever, I am come to the parting of the ways from works where Nature lore invades the telling of the tale. When the author gives me a scene of wild young passion, then I can no longer slog through the immediate follow-up of a tender description of the bendings of wheat in the breeze, nor yet of a report on the intricate delicacies of fern fronds, nor again of the fact that the wild jonquils are thicker than ever this year. Yes, and I will have no more of accounts of the behavior of the undersides of leaves at the approach of a shower. I realize that all this will cut down my reading drastically, nevertheless— There!

So it is fine to come, safe and sure, to a book by Truman Capote. As an author, Mr. Capote has three speeds, of each of which, I think, he is a master. He is a novelist, a writer of short stories, and a reporter of murderous accuracy—if you know his accounts of the travels in Russia of the *Porgy and Bess* company and those who came along with them for the ride, and his interview with Mr. Marlon Brando in an hour of ease. Mr. Capote kills with no such clumsy aids as the butt of a revolver or a tape-wrapped length of pipe. He does it with a sharp clip of the side of the palm to the base of the skull. It is an admirable method, tidy, bloodless, and quicker than the eye. The only catch to it is that you must be expert at it. Mr. Capote is fully that.

His latest book, *Breakfast at Tiffany's,* is a collection of a short novel or, if you wish, a long short story (I promised my mother I should never use that wretched word "novella") and several stories. The long one, the title story of the book, concerns an extravagantly unconventional young lady, entertaining to read about, certainly, but the reader, though the author and the characters in the tale in which he places her admire her vastly, has always the feeling that to know the young woman would be to find her a truly awful pest. But that, of course, is no sort of criticism; it is doubtful if Hamlet would have been fun to be with day on day.

The lesser stories are not especially memorable—I am afraid Mr. Capote does not always write as well as he can—until the last one in the book, *A Christmas Memory*. That is as tender and as beautifully done as anything you can read this year, or, for that matter, in a number of years. I am sick of those who skate fancily over the work of Mr. Capote, to give their time to the beat boys. They neglect to say one thing which is, to me, the most important; Truman Capote can *write*.

To get into the matter of writing well is to come immediately to John Updike's *The Poorhouse Fair*—I think it is his first novel, I have known before this only his poems and his verses. Perhaps this is a purely personal matter, but I am always drawn to reading a book about a poorhouse—after all, it is only the normal curiosity to find out what it will be like in my future residence. Mr. Updike's book is neither light nor easy reading, but it stays with you on and on. What comes to you most strongly about the souls in the house is their dreadful, riddling, day-after-day boredom—so that a sudden rain, a childish, idiotic revolt against the man who tries to run the place with decency, is Christmas to them. Mr. Updike draws his characters permanently. I think the most memorable is the blind woman, still elegant, still beautiful, who tells of her idea of heaven as a place where there will be no appearances, where everyone will be blind. . . . "Don't be afraid, I know about it and none of you does". . . . The story is concerned with the annual fair held by the poorhouse inmates, where people come from all around "to see the freaks." They are not freaks. This is not a grotesque exhibition nor a funny book. But I think— no, I am sure—it is a fine one.

James Thurber: *The Years With Ross*

September 1959

James Thurber, the while that St. Jude, patron of impossible things, must surely have been interceding for him, set himself the task of making believable, in writing, the facade and the workings of the late Harold Wallace Ross, father and editor of *The New Yorker*. It is not only that Mr. Thurber accomplished this. It's that he did it thoroughly but vitally, did it with deep love but a sort of benign outrage. It's that his *The Years With Ross* is a fine, funny, touching book, and an admirably written one, though that last goes without saying—after all, it was written by James Thurber.

Ross, like Heathcliffe, whom he in no other way resembled, went by just one name. There must, of course, have been those who called him Mr. Ross, though never to his back, and semi-occasionally some abraded contributor to the magazine would howl "Harold!" at him, but in all other instances he was Ross. His improbabilities started with his looks. His long body seemed to be only basted together, his hair was quills upon the fretful porcupine, his teeth were Stone-henge, his clothes looked as if they had been brought up by somebody else. Poker-faced he was not. Expressions, sometimes several at a time, would race across his countenance, and always, especially when he thought no one was looking, not the brow alone but the whole expanse would be corrugated by his worries, his worries over his bitch-mistress, his magazine. But what he did and what he caused to be done with *The New Yorker* left his mark and his memory upon his times.

Over every scrap of material he fussed like a hen. His writers would get the proofs of their pieces with the margins taken up by his cablese questions, in pencil: "What mean?", "Who he?", "Why in hell?". The late Robert Benchley—dear Lord, how many too many of the best are "the late"—would simply cross out the questions, write below them, "You keep out of this, Ross," and send back the proof. Once I used the word "stigmata" in a piece. The proof came to me from Ross with no questions: only the exclamation "No such word," in the margin. When friendship was restored, Ross conceded that maybe "stigmata" had something to do with defective vision.

He took me, once upon a time, to see Nazimova in *The Cherry Orchard.* At first he sat silent. Then he said, and over and over through the evening, in the all-but-voiceless voice of one who comes suddenly upon a trove of shining treasure, "Say, this is quite a play—quite a play!" He had not seen it before. He had not heard of it.

People reeled when they learned that the editor of the not-for-the-old-lady-from-Dubuque weekly was this monolith of unsophistication. (The dictionary says firmly that "sophisticated" means "adulterated," and Ross was probably the least adulterated human that ever walked.) Moreover, his ignorance was a very Empire State Building among ignorances: you had to admire it for its size. He was as void of knowledge of all matters cultural, scientific, and sociological as a child in a parochial orphanage. Yet his ignorance was not, as it so often is in an adult, either exasperating or tiresome. There was an innocence to it—no airs, no pretenses; if he did not know a thing, he asked about it. Usually the answer delighted him, and always it astonished him. I think it was his perpetual astonishment that kept him from ever in his life being bored.

Where they came from to Ross, first the conception of an entirely different sort of magazine, and then the power to get it going—maybe that is known in some department of Heaven. Revolutionary is a large word, but that is what *The New Yorker* was. Think, for instance, of the one-line caption under a comic drawing. There was a time when such captions were in dialogue, most frequently between He and She, though sometimes Senator Sorghum and Miss Cayenne took over the act: the Senator would ask the question, and Miss Cayenne would deliver the punch line. Now all magazines that run comic drawings have one-line jokes below them; originally it was Ross's doing. That is no mean monument to a man.

The writing of *The Years With Ross* was beset with peril; the danger, of course, was that readers might consider the strange creature who is the hero of the work to be a product of Mr. Thurber's invention. It is one of the less sanguinary marvels of this our day that the book proves its protagonist to be a breathing man, who had his existence among us only a short time ago, for it is possible to see that readers might have had a moment or so of doubt at first. After all, only God or James Thurber could have invented Ross.

Katherine Anne Porter: *Ship of Fools*

July 1962

Katherine Anne Porter's novel *Ship of Fools* took twenty years in the writing. There is never a slackening of its pace, never a lazily written passage, never a portrait roughed in. To those of us who, after filling a postcard, are obliged to lie down and have wet cloths applied to our brow, this is not a book. It's the Pyramid.

The first reviewers of the novel wrote of it to a man as allegorical, a word that always causes me to writhe with inferiority for I've had my difficulties in recognizing an allegory unless it, so to say, jumps up into my lap and licks my face. But Miss Porter made it, as she makes everything, beautifully clear in the brief explanation of her title which acts as preface. *Ship of Fools* is from a tale by Sebastian Brant published in 1494. "When I began thinking about my novel," she says, "I took for my own this simple, almost universal image of the ship of this world on its voyage to eternity. It is by no means new—it was very old and durable and dearly familiar when Brant used it; and it suits my purpose exactly. I am a passenger on that ship." She chose for the ship of her book the *Vera* out of Vera Cruz, bound for Bremerhaven. She peopled it as thickly as a battlefield. Indeed, the novel suggests a Meissonier battle scene in the perception with which each individual member of the hordes is rendered. The *Vera* is a German liner. The ship's officers are German, the year is 1931. Already there are hideous spurts of anti-Semitism—a man, impeccably Aryan, is banished from the captain's table because it had leaked out that the wife waiting at home is Jewish.

The passengers are in the thousands. In the steerage there are more than eight hundred Spaniards who had worked in the Cuban cane fields and were deported, when the sugar market collapsed, to whatever part of Spain they had come from, where no livelihood awaited them. Night and day they are jammed together on the deck, each one alone in his hopelessness, each one frantic in his bewilderment. The rest of the list are mostly Germans, and there are only four

Americans—not one of whom should make us proud. There are some Cubans and Mexicans, a lone vehement Swede, and a gaggle of migratory Spanish dancers on the way back from being stranded in Mexico—four young women of many too many evenings and four of their slinky salesmen and, somehow attached to them, a pair of six-year-old twins, brats straight out of hell. The twins, knowing that the ladies and gentlemen of the group plan to steal pearls from an elderly Spanish noblewoman, fix their wagon by getting the pearls first and tossing them overboard. Crazed by the success of this caper they seize a poor old bulldog, a big bumbling creature not overbright and afflicted with seasickness from the moment the gangplank was up, but still the shining light in the life of two gentle souls, his owners. The twins throw the old dog overboard; a young man in the steerage sees, and jumps after him into the water. The dog is saved, but the man himself is drowned to live afterward in the indignant memory of the passengers as a fool.

There are very few glimpses of happy young love so far as I can see—these are of a Mexican honeymoon couple, and there is other young love in the persons of two American painters who, living together without benefit of clergy, express their passions only by quarrels.

There is a fine portrait of a raffish old Spanish noblewoman—the one without her pearls—long resident in Cuba, now sent away into exile. She is attended by perhaps the most decent character in the book—a doctor who would like to help her and she, I suppose, would like to help him, but her help is always amatory. You cannot begin to go into the sadnesses of this pair, for she is going into exile and he is going back home to die of his long illness. There is . . . there is . . . there are . . . for heaven's sake who do I think I am trying to put twenty years of work into half a glossy page.

I never said it was a cheery book. I never said it was like those books that have so often been written about ship's companies—those bubbly bits of gaiety on the high seas. But I do say and I think I shall go on saying: My God, here is a book.

Shirley Jackson:
We Have Always Lived in the Castle

December 1962

There is still sunshine for us. The miracle is wrought by Shirley Jackson, God bless her, as ever unparalleled, more than ever in her latest book, *We Have Always Lived in the Castle,* as leader in the field of beautifully written, quiet, cumulative shudders.

This novel brings back all my faith in terror and death. I can say no higher of it and her.

UNCOLLECTED ARTICLES

Good Souls

Their Characteristics, Habits, and Innumerable Methods of Removing the Joy from Life

June 1919

All about us, living in our very families, it may be, there exists a race of curious creatures. Outwardly, they possess no marked peculiarities; in fact, at a hasty glance, they may be readily mistaken for regular human beings. They are built after the popular design; they have the usual number of features, arranged in the conventional manner; they offer no variations on the general run of things in their habits of dressing, eating, and carrying on their business.

Yet, between them and the rest of the civilized world, there stretches an impassable barrier. Though they live in the very thick of the human race, they are forever isolated from it. They are fated to go through life, congenital pariahs. They live out their little lives, mingling with the world, yet never a part of it.

They are, in short, Good Souls.

And the piteous thing about them is that they are wholly unconscious of their condition. A Good Soul thinks he is just like anyone else. Nothing could convince him otherwise. It is heartrending to see him, going cheerfully about, even whistling or humming as he goes, all unconscious of his terrible plight. The utmost he can receive from the world is an attitude of good-humored patience, a perfunctory word of approbation, a praising with faint damns, so to speak—yet he firmly believes that everything is all right with him.

There is no accounting for Good Souls.

They spring up anywhere. They will suddenly appear in families which, for generations, have had no slightest stigma attached to them. Possibly they are throw-backs. There is scarcely a family without at least one Good Soul somewhere in it at the present moment—maybe in the form of an elderly aunt, an unmarried sister, an unsuccessful brother, an indigent cousin. No household is complete without one.

The Good Soul begins early; he will show signs of his condition in extreme youth. Go now to the nearest window, and look out on the little children playing so happily below. Any group of youngsters that you may happen to see will do perfectly. Do you observe the child whom all the other little dears make "it" in their merry games? Do you follow the child from whom the other little ones snatch the cherished candy, to consume it before his streaming eyes? Can you get a good look at the child whose precious toys are borrowed for indefinite periods by the other playful youngsters, and are returned to him in fragments? Do you see the child upon whom all the other kiddies play their complete repertory of childhood's winsome pranks—throwing bags of water on him, running away and hiding from him, shouting his name in quaint rhymes, chalking coarse legends on his unsuspecting back?

Mark that child well. He is going to be a Good Soul when he grows up.

Thus does the doomed child go through early youth and adolescence. So does he progress towards the fulfillment of his destiny. And then, some day, when he is under discussion, someone will say of him, "Well, he means well, anyway." That settles it. For him, that is the end. Those words have branded him with the indelible mark of his pariahdom. He has come into his majority; he is a full-fledged Good Soul.

The activities of the adult of the species are familiar to us all. When you are ill, who is it that hastens to your bedside bearing molds of blanc-mange, which, from infancy, you have hated with unspeakable loathing? As usual, you are way ahead of me, gentle reader—it is indeed the Good Soul. It is the Good Souls who efficiently smooth out your pillow when you have just worked it into the comfortable shape, who creak about the room on noisy tiptoe, who tenderly lay on your fevered brow damp cloths which drip ceaselessly down your neck. It is they who ask, every other minute, if there isn't something that they can do for you. It is they who, at great personal sacrifice, spend long hours sitting beside your bed, reading aloud the continued stories in the *Woman's Home Companion,* or chatting cozily on the increase in the city's death rate.

In health, as in illness, they are always right there, ready to befriend you. No sooner do you sit down, than they exclaim that they can see you aren't comfortable in that chair, and insist on your changing places with them. It is the Good Souls who just *know* that you don't like your tea that way, and who bear it masterfully away from you to alter it with cream and sugar until it is a complete stranger to you. At the table, it is they who always feel that their grapefruit is better than yours and who have to be restrained almost forcibly from exchanging with you. In a restaurant the waiter invariably makes a mistake and brings them something which they did not order—and which they refuse to have changed, choking it down with a wistful smile. It is they who cause traffic blocks, by standing in subway entrances arguing altruistically as to who is to pay the fare.

At the theater, should they be members of a box-party, it is the Good Souls who insist on occupying the rear chairs; if the seats are in the orchestra, they worry audibly, all through the performance, about their being able to see better than you, until finally in desperation you grant their plea and change seats with them. If, by so doing, they can bring a little discomfort on themselves—sit in a draught, say, or behind a pillar—then their happiness is complete. To feel the genial glow of martyrdom—that is all that they ask of life.

Good Souls are punctilious in their observation of correct little ceremonies. If, for example, they borrow a postage stamp, they immediately offer two pennies in return for it—they insist upon this business transaction. They never fail to remember birthdays—their little gift always brings with it a sharp stab of remembrance that you have blissfully ignored their own natal day. At the last moment, on Christmas Eve, comes a present from some Good Soul whose existence, in the rush of holiday shopping you have completely overlooked. When they go away, be it only for an overnight stay, they never neglect to send postcards bearing views of the principal buildings of the place to all their acquaintances; to their intimates, they always bring back some local souvenir—a tiny dish, featuring the gold-lettered name of the town; a thimble in an appropriate case, both bearing the name of their native city; a tie-rack with the name of its place of residence burned decoratively on its wood; or some such useful novelty.

The lives of Good Souls are crowded with Occasions, each with its own ritual which must be solemnly followed. On Mothers' Day, Good Souls conscientiously wear carnations; on St. Patrick's Day, they faithfully don boutonnieres of shamrocks; on Columbus Day, they carefully pin on miniature Italian flags. Every feast must be celebrated by the sending out of cards—Valentine's Day, Arbor Day, Groundhog Day, and all the other important festivals, each is duly observed. They have a perfect genius for discovering appropriate cards of greeting for the event. It must take hours of research.

If it's too long a time between holidays, then the Good Soul will send little cards or little mementoes, just by way of surprises. He is strong on surprises, anyway. It delights him to drop in unexpectedly on his friends. Who has not known the joy of those evenings when some Good Soul just runs in, as a surprise? It is particularly effective when a chosen company of other guests happens to be present—enough for two tables of bridge, say. This means that the Good Soul must sit wistfully by, patiently watching the progress of the rubber, or else must cut in at intervals, volubly voicing his desolation at causing so much inconvenience, and apologizing constantly during the evening.

His conversation, admirable though it is, never receives its just due of attention and appreciation. He is one of those who believe and frequently quote the exemplary precept that there is good in everybody; hanging in his bedchamber is the whimsically phrased, yet vital, statement, done in burned leather—"There is so much good in the worst of us and so much bad in the best of us that it hardly behooves any of us to talk about the rest of us." This, too, he archly quotes on appropriate occasions. Two or three may be gathered together, intimately discussing some mutual acquaintance. It is just getting really absorbing, when comes the Good Soul, to utter his dutiful, "We mustn't judge harshly—after all, we must always remember that many times our own actions may be misconstrued." Somehow, after several of these little reminders, there seems to be a general waning of interest; the little gathering breaks up, inventing quaint excuses to get away and discuss the thing more fully, adding a few really good details, some place where the Good Soul will not follow. While the Good Soul, pitifully ignorant of their evil purpose, glows with the warmth of conscious virtue, and settles himself to read the Contributors' Club, in the *Atlantic Monthly,* with a sense of duty well done.

Yet it must not be thought that their virtue lifts Good Souls above the enjoyment of popular pastimes. Indeed, it does not; they are enthusiasts on the subject of good, wholesome fun. They lavishly patronize the drama, in its cleaner forms. They flock to the plays of Miss Rachel Crothers, Miss Eleanor Porter, and Mr. Edward Childs Carpenter. They are passionate admirers of the art of Mr. William Hodge. In literature, they worship at the chaste shrines of Harold Bell Wright, Gene Stratton-Porter, Eleanor Hallowell Abbott, Alice Hegan Rice, and the other triple-named apostles of optimism. They have never felt the same towards Arnold Bennett since he sprung "The Pretty Lady" on them; they no longer give "The Human Machine" and "How to Live on Twenty-four Hours a Day" as birthday offerings to their friends. In poetry, though Tennyson, Whittier, and Longfellow stand for the highest, of course, they have marked leaning toward the later works of Mrs. Ella Wheeler Wilcox. They are continually meeting people who know her, encounters of which they proudly relate. Among humorists, they prefer Mr. Ellis Parker Butler.

Good Souls, themselves, are no mean humorists. They have a time-honored formula of fun-making, which must be faithfully followed. Certain words or phrases must be whimsically distorted every time they are used. "Over the river," they dutifully say, whenever they take their leave. "Don't you cast any asparagus on me," they warn, archly; and they never fail to speak of "three times in concussion." According to their ritual, these screaming phrases must be repeated several times, for the most telling effect, and are invariably followed by hearty laughter from the speaker, to whom they seem eternally new.

Perhaps the most congenial role of the Good Soul is that of advice-giver. He loves to take people aside and have serious little personal talks, all for their own good. He thinks it only right to point out faults or bad habits which are, perhaps unconsciously, growing on them. He goes home and laboriously writes long, intricate letters, invariably beginning, "Although you may feel that this is no affair of mine, I think that you really ought to know," and so on, indefinitely. In his desire to help, he reminds one irresistibly of Marcelline, who used to try so pathetically and so fruitlessly to be of some assistance in arranging the circus arena, and who brought such misfortunes on his own innocent person thereby.

The Good Souls will, doubtless, gain their reward in Heaven; on this earth, certainly, theirs is what is technically known as a rough deal. The most hideous outrages are perpetrated on them. "Oh, he won't mind," people say. "He's a Good Soul." And then they proceed to heap the rankest impositions upon him. When Good Souls give a party, people who have accepted weeks in advance call up at the last second and refuse, without the shadow of an excuse save that of a subsequent engagement. Other people are invited to all sorts of entertaining affairs; the Good Soul, unasked, waves them a cheery good-bye and hopes wistfully that they will have a good time. His is the uncomfortable seat in the motor; he is the one to ride backwards in the train; he is the one who is always chosen to solicit subscriptions and make up deficits. People borrow his money, steal his servants, lose his golf balls, use him as a sort of errand boy, leave him flat whenever something more attractive offers—and carry it all off with their cheerful slogan, "Oh, he won't mind— he's a Good Soul."

And that's just it—Good Souls never do mind. After each fresh atrocity they are more cheerful, forgiving and virtuous, if possible, than they were before. There is simply no keeping them down—back they come, with their little gifts, and their little words of advice, and their little endeavors to be of service, always anxious for more.

Yes, there can be no doubt about it—their reward will come to them in the next world.

Would that they were even now enjoying it!

The Artist's Reward

November 30, 1929

Once there was a traveller who journeyed alone to the Grand Canyon. He came to the brink just as the day died, and the slow mists circled upward. There he stood and he looked.

And there came, from behind him, the sound of footsteps— large, firm steps dealt by the accustomed feet of a lady tourist. She gained his side and stopped there, radiating native friendliness and the good cheer provided by Fred Harvey. She, too, looked. And woman's world-old need of speech seized her, and seemed as if it would rack her very tweeds apart.

"Well!" she said. "It certainly *is* attractive."

And I feel, my friends—for I think of every one of you gathered here tonight as my friend, and I want *you* to think of *me* that way, too!—I feel not unlike that good lady of the Canyon when I am asked by this hospitable house-organ to speak a few words about Ernest Hemingway. Well! He cer- tainly *is* attractive.

For it is so heat in my mind that the author of *In Our Time*, *Men Without Women*, and *A Farewell to Arms* is far and away the first American artist, that it is the devil's own task to find anything more complicated or necessary to say about him.

It is no misses' size assignment to dash off a description of Ernest Hemingway, Writer and Human Being. One hesitates, in the first place, to add to the measure of bilge that has already been written; probably of no other living man has so much tripe been penned and spoken. And it is the present vogue to rip off sketches of the famous in a sort of delicate blend of the Anecdotal, or Brightest-Things-Our-Baby-Ever-Said, manner, and the Tender, or Lavender-and-Old-Rubbers, school. As a subject, Mr. Hemingway does not lend himself to the style. He will not—indeed, it is my belief that he can not—pluck you down from his memory any cobwebby pretties about his favorite school-teacher; nor will he help you along with your work by uttering Good Ones that you can set promptly on clean white paper. There are anecdotes about him, and beauties, too; and there are quotations from his conversations that, I think, must pass eventually into folklore. But I may not give them to you here. I am sorry but I really can not feel that we are well enough acquainted for that. Mrs. Parker to you, if you please.

But people want to hear things about Ernest Hemingway. As the boys used to say, before they left the phrase flat and ran off in all directions with "gesture," "good theater," and "the American scene," he intrigues the imagination. People so much wanted him to be a figure out of a saga that they went to the length of providing the saga themselves. And a little peach it is.

I have heard of him, both at various times and all in one great bunch, that he is so hard-boiled he makes a daily practice of busting his widowed mother in the nose; that he dictates his stories because he can't write, and has them read to him because he can't read; that he is expatriate to such a degree that he tears down any American flag he sees flying in France; that no woman within half-a-mile of him is a safe woman; that he not only commands enormous prices for his short stories, but insists, additionally, on taking the right eye out of the editor's face; that he has been a tramp, a safe-cracker, and a stockyard attendant; that he is the Pet of the Left Bank, and may be found at any hour of the day or night sitting at a little table at the Select, rubbing absinthe into his gums; that he really hates all forms of sport, and only skis, hunts, fishes, and fights bulls in order to be cute; that a wound he sustained in the Great War was of a whimsical, inconvenient, and inevitably laughable description; and that he also writes under the name of Morley Callaghan. About all that remains to be said is that he is the Lost Dauphin, that he was shot as a German spy, and that he is actually a woman, masquerading in man's clothes. And those rumors are doubtless being started, even as we sit here.

For it is hard not to tell spectacular things of Ernest Hemingway; people are so eager to hear that you haven't the heart to send them away empty. Young women, in especial, are all of a quiver for information. (Sometimes I think that the wide publication of that smiling photograph, the one with the slanted cap and the shirt flung open above the dark sweater, was perhaps a mistake.)

"Ooh," they say, "do *you* know Ernest Hemingway? Ooh, I'd just *love* to meet him! Ooh, tell me what he's *like!*"

Well, I warned you the task sinks me. Ernest Hemingway is something—not exactly—like this:

He has, I should think, the best and the worst times of anybody living; he experiences several examples of both, every day. He has an uncounted number of interests, and a passionate concentration. Whatever he does, he goes in for hook, line, and good red herring. He has a generosity of energy that is absolute. He has a capacity for enjoyment so vast that he gives away great chunks to those about him, and never even misses them. I can say no more of him than that he can take you to a bicycle-race, and make it raise your hair.

He is in his early thirties, he weighs about two hundred pounds, and he is even better than those photographs. The effect upon women is such that they want to go right out and get him and bring him home, stuffed. Heaven help him, if he ever settles in New York and is displayed to the sabre-toothed ladies of stage, pen, salon, and suburb who throng the local

Bohemian gatherings. He is susceptible to flattery, and then is stuck with the flatterer. He is afflicted with deep-seated illness in the presence of unhappily married women who are interested in the Arts.

His father was a Middle-Western doctor. I can find out nothing about his education—probably he read a lot of things. Anyway, he left home at something below the conventional early age, with the englamoured idea of being a prizefighter. (He was a bad prizefighter, so he is now a good amateur boxer.) Then he became a reporter, somehow, and then he went abroad, and Then Came the War, and there he was, in the Italian army. He suffered seven major wounds, and has a life-sentence to wear an aluminum kneecap. He received medals; it makes him sick if you ask him about them. He does not talk about the War, especially if you lead up to it.

He lives, for a bit of every year, in Paris—which is how the expatriation stories started. He and his wife do this because they like it, and because their rent is not high. (He doesn't make much money—not half as much as you do.) They form no part of the dancing-and-light-drugs life of the French capital. Their apartment has no telephone; and any engagement made by telegram, letter, or word-of-mouth for a time set several days ahead throws Mr. Hemingway into one of those states of his—he hates anything, bad or fair, hanging over him. He writes there, mostly in bed, and he reads books that have a great many things going on in them—novels by the elder Dumas, and books and books and books about the Crusades.

When the Hemingways come to the United States, they dwell in the outlands. Their baby was born in Arkansas, and they spent last Winter in Key West, deep-sea fishing, and killing with harpoon or gun the major items of their menus. He avoids New York, for he has the most valuable asset an artist can possess—the fear of what he knows is bad for him. Somehow, you cannot fit him into the jig-saw puzzle of New York life. Drink he does and did and will again, but he was not designed for night-clubs, and it is virtually an impossibility for him to speak easy. The mind refuses to function over the idea of his presence at a literary tea, or an evening of parlor games. Nor is his ambition beckoned toward the North Shore of Long Island. "Scratch a writer," once I heard him say, "and find a social climber." But nobody, including himself, can be with him, and keep remembering that he is a Writer.

With the possible exception of Ring Lardner, he is less the literary character-part than any author I have ever seen. Nothing is done about the thrill of creating, nor the need for expression, nor even the jolly good fun of spinning a yarn. He works like hell, and through it. Nothing comes easily to him; he struggles, sets down a word, scratches it out, and begins all over. He regards his art as hard and dirty work, with no hope of better conditions. He listens, with something of the expression of the tattered orphan outside the bakeshop window, to the literati's tales of the necessity of still and pleasant surroundings and the employment of expensive devices to ease the gestating mind. Once he heard the odyssey of a highly-valued American writer; an account of ceaseless, fruitless flights to the more *luxe*, yet recondite, nooks of the globe, in quest of what was called "a good place to work."

"———" Ernest Hemingway said, mentioning a certain word by name, "the only good place to work is in your head."

Seventy times he rewrote the concluding pages of *A Farewell to Arms*. He had no idea of ever being completely satisfied with them; he merely hoped that the words would eventually come nearer to his meaning. The pile of scribbled-out sheets made a formidable manuscript. Seventy times . . . "Now I suppose," he remarked, "they'll say that the ending is hurried."

He is outrageously sensitive to criticism—probably because his work has begot some specimens that should really be preserved in alcohol. The *American Mercury* dismissed *In Our Time* as "sketches in the bold, bad manner of the Café du Dôme." A certain young gentleman dedicated to beautiful letters confessed with a sort of laughing pride—in the pages of an organ also dedicated to beautiful letters—that he just wasn't able to "understand some of the stories in *Men Without Women*." There was another young gentleman who once occupied the editorial chair of a now defunct magazine of culture, and sought, from there, to form the taste of the American public; he was shown some of Hemingway's work, then unpublished in the United States, refused it, and pronounced, "I hear he has been a reporter—tell him to go on reporting and not try to write."

As I wrote this, the reviews of *A Farewell to Arms* had not yet reached Ernest Hemingway in Paris. All those by what are called the big critics may be laudatory, serious, and understanding; but it is safe to say that if there be included among them one tiny clipping announcing that Miss Harriet McBlease, who does "Book-Looks" for the Middletown *Observer-Companion*, does not find the new Hemingway book to her taste, that will be the one Our Hero will select to brood over. . . .

He has an immense, ill-advised, and indiscriminate tenderness. It is nice to note, by the dust-cover of a recent novel, that its author is "a Hemingway become compassionate," and one hastens to congratulate the lad on what must be such a pleasant change; but the original model was compassionate to start with. As always happens, the people for whom he is sorry eat greedily into his time. He is far more lavish with his sympathy than with his friendship. That goes in few directions, and is given with a little lingering, as if in the expectation of betrayal. But once you have it, there it is, and neither neglect nor bad usage can touch it.

Well—I told you it would sink me. Ernest Hemingway is something—not exactly—like that.

Questioners, in my experience, never conclude with the "What's he *like?*" number. There is always one more interrogation, put in a delicately lowered, and yet lightly rippling, voice. "Does he," it runs, "does he talk like he writes?"

Yes, he does talk like he writes. In fact, liker. But how do you know what his writing is like, when you can see in it only the rough words? (At least, that's what I always mean to answer, and I may get around to it any day.)

It is a strange thing about Ernest Hemingway. Somebody— the public, the city of Boston, a blurb-writer, a reviewer, somebody—has bandied his name about until it has become a synonym for profanity generously laced with obscenity. They read him, and, with a nudge and a snicker, let him go at that.

The title of this interesting composition is taken, unasked, from a letter from Ernest Hemingway to his friend, Scott Fitzgerald. "I am now," he wrote, "in the state of depression where you've gone over and over until you can't tell whether anything you've written is any good or not; this is called the Artist's Reward."

And Mr. Hemingway has gained an additional, and an equally comforting, prize for his travail. He has lived to see any writer who employs the word "bastard" hailed as "another Hemingway."

There is a thing about him that I have not yet mentioned, for I am a slow worker. He has the most profound bravery that it has ever been my privilege to see; and I am not the one who over-readily discerns examples of courage among my opposite sex. He has had pain, ill-health, and the kind of poverty that you don't believe—the kind of which actual hunger is the attendant; he has had about eight times the normal allotment of responsibilities. And he has never once compromised. He has never turned off on an easier path than the one he staked himself. It takes courage.

That brings me to the point which I have been trying to reach all this time: Ernest Hemingway's definition of courage—his phrase that, it seems to me, makes Barrie's "Courage is immortality" sound like one of the more treble trillings of Tinker Bell. Mr. Hemingway did not use the term "courage." Ever the euphemist, he referred to the quality as "guts," and he was attributing its possession to an absent friend.

"Now just a minute," somebody said, for it was one of those argumentative evenings. "Listen. Look here a minute. Exactly what do you mean by 'guts'?"

"I mean," Ernest Hemingway said, "grace under pressure."

That grace is his. The pressure, I suppose, comes in, *gratis*, under the heading of the Artist's Reward.

The Siege of Madrid

November 23, 1937

I want to say first that I came to Spain without my ax to grind. I didn't bring messages from anybody, nor greetings to anybody. I am not a member of any political party. The only group I have ever been affiliated with is that not especially brave little band that hid its nakedness of heart and mind under the out-of-date garment of a sense of humor. I heard someone say, and so I said it too, that ridicule is the most effective weapon. I don't suppose I ever really believed it, but it was easy and comforting, and so I said it. Well, now I know. I know that there are things that never have been funny, and never will be. And I know that ridicule may be a shield, but it is not a weapon.

I was puzzled, as you may have been, about Spain. I read in our larger newspapers that here was a civil war, with the opposing factions neatly divided into Reds and Whites—rather as if they were chessmen. Even I could figure out that there is something not quite right when Moors are employed to defend Christianity. Since I have been here, I have heard what the people in the streets say. Not many of them call it the "war." They speak of it as the "invasion." Theirs is the better word.

There cannot be, in all the world, any place like the city of Madrid today. It has been under seige for nearly a year. You read about besieged cities in medieval days and you say, how awful things must have been, thank goodness they don't happen now. It has happened in Madrid and it goes on happening. In a city as big and as beautiful and as modern as Washington, D. C.

The dispatches say that there is not much doing on the Madrid front now—there is very little activity. It is what is called a lull. But all day long you hear the guns, the dull boom of the big guns and the irritable cackle of machine guns. And you know that gunners no longer need to shoot just for practice. When there is firing, that means there is blood and blindness and death.

And the streets are crowded, and the shops are open, and the people go about their daily living. It isn't tense and it isn't hysterical. What they have is not morale, which is something created and bolstered and directed. It is the sure, steady spirit of those who know what the fight is about and who know that they must win.

In spite of all the evacuation, there are still nearly a million people here. Some of them—you may be like that yourself—won't leave their homes and their possessions, all the things they have gathered together through the years. They are not at all dramatic about it. It is simply that anything else than the life they have made for themselves is inconceivable to them. Yesterday I saw a woman who lives in the poorest quarter of Madrid. It has been bombed twice by the fascists; her house is one of the few left standing. She has seven children. It has often been suggested to her that she and the children leave Madrid for a safer place. She dismisses such ideas easily and firmly. Every six weeks, she says, her husband has forty-eight hours' leave from the front. Naturally, he wants to come home to see her and the children. She, and each one of the seven, are calm and strong and smiling. It is a typical Madrid family.

There are fifty thousand babies still here. All food is scarce, and dairy products are almost memories. But the republican government has stations all over the city where a mother may get milk and eggs and cereals for her baby, regularly, without delay. If she has any money, she may buy them at cost. If she hasn't any, she is given them. Doctors say that the little children of Madrid are better nourished than they ever were in the old days.

The bigger children play in the streets, just as happily and just as noisily as the children in America. That is, they play after school hours. For during siege and under shell fire, education in republican Spain goes on. I do not know where you can see a finer thing.

Six years ago, when the royal romp, Alfonso, left his racing cars and his racing stables and also left, by popular request, his country, there remained twenty-eight million people. Of them, twelve million people were completely illiterate. It is said that Alfonso himself had been taught to read and write, but he had not troubled to bend his accomplishments to the reading of statistics nor the signing of appropriations for schools.

Six years ago almost half the population of this country was illiterate. The first thing that the republican government did was to recognize this hunger, the starvation of the people for education. Now there are schools even in the tiniest, poorest villages; more schools in a year than ever were in all the years of the reigning kings. And still more are being established every day. I have seen a city bombed by night, and the next morning the people rose and went on with the completion of their schools. Here in Madrid, as well as in Valencia, a workers' institute is open. It is a college, but not a college where rich young men may go to make friends with other rich young men who may be valuable to them in business later. It is a college where workers, forced to start as children in fields and factories, may study to be teachers or doctors or lawyers or scientists, according to their gifts. Their intensive university course takes two years. And while they are studying, the government pays their families the money they would have been earning.

In the schools for young children, there is none of the dread thing you have heard so much about—depersonalization. Each child has, at the government's expense, an education as modern and personal as a privileged American school child has at an accredited progressive school. What the Spanish republican government has done for education would be a magnificent achievement, even in days of peace, when money is easy and supplies are endless. But these people are doing it under fire. . . .

The government takes care, too, of the unfortunates of war. There are a million refugee children in Spain. A million is an easy number to say. But how can you grasp what it means? Three hundred thousand of them are in the homes of families and seven hundred thousand are in children's colonies. When it can, the government wants to have all in colonies. I hope that will happen, because I have seen some of the colonies. There is no dreadful orphan-asylum quality about them. I never saw finer children—free and growing and happy. One colony was in a seaside resort, near Valencia. There were sixty children, from four to fourteen, who had been going to a school in Madrid. And the fascist planes had bombed the school.

It was amazing to see how many of these children could draw and draw well—and it was heartening to see how their talent was encouraged by the teachers. When they first came to the colony, the children drew the things that were nearest and deepest to them—they drew planes and bursting bombs and houses in flames. You could see by the dreadful perfection of detail, how well they knew their subjects. Now they are drawing flowers and apples and sailboats and little houses with smoke coming out of the chimneys. They are well children now.

And in Valencia, a few miles away, the fascist planes come over and the bombs drop, and so there will be more children who will draw planes and flames and fragments‘ of bodies blown in the air. That is if there are any children left.

I can't get any pleasing variety into this talk. I can't tell you amusing anecdotes of the boys in the trenches. I don't think there are any such stories. The men who fight for republican Spain, the men, who in less than a year have come from a mob wearing overalls and carrying sticks to a formidable disciplined army, are no gangling lambs, endearingly bewildered as to what is which front and who is on whose side. These are thinking men, knowing what they do, and what they must go on doing.

They are fighting for more than their lives. They are fighting for the chance to live them, for a chance for their children, for the decency and peace of the future.

Their fight is the biggest thing, certainly, that we shall see in our time, but it is not a good show. This is no gay and handsome war, with brass bands and streaming banners. These men do not need such assurances. They are not mad glamorous adventurers, they are not reckless young people plunged into a chaos. I don't think there will be any lost generation after this war.

But I, as an onlooker, am bewildered. While I was in Valencia the fascists raided it four times. If you are going to be in an air raid at all, it is better for you if it happens at night.

Then it is unreal, it is almost beautiful, it is like a ballet with the scurrying figures and the great white shafts of the searchlights. But when a raid comes in the daytime, then you see the faces of the people, and it isn't unreal any longer. You see the terrible resignation on the faces of old women, and you see little children wild with terror.

In Valencia, last Sunday morning, a pretty, bright Sunday morning, five German planes came over and bombed the quarter down by the port. It is a poor quarter, the place where the men who work on the docks live, and it is, like all poor quarters, congested. After the planes had dropped their bombs, there wasn't much left of the places where so many families had been living. There was an old, old man who went up to everyone he saw and asked, please, had they seen his wife, please, would they tell him where his wife was. There were two little girls who saw their father killed in front of them, and were trying to get past the guards, back to the still crumbling, crashing houses to find their mother. There was a great pile of rubble, and on the top of it a broken doll and a dead kitten. It was a good job to get those. They were ruthless enemies to fascism.

I have seen the farms outside of Valencia—the lovely green quiet farms. There is soil so fertile, since the government has irrigated it, that it yields three harvests a year. So hospitable that oranges and beans and potatoes and corn and pomegranates all grow in one field. I have seen the people in the country and in the cities wanting only to go about their lives, only to secure the future of their children. They ask only as much as you have because they are people like you—they want to get up from their tables and go to their beds, to wake to a quiet morning, and the sending of their children off to school. They don't think of accumulated money. They want to do their own work in self-respect and peace. They want the same thing that you have—they want to live in a democracy. And they will fight for it, and they will win.

But in the meantime it makes you sick to think of it. That these people who pulled themselves up from centuries of oppression and exploitation cannot go on to decent living, to peace and progress and civilization without the murder of their children, and the blocking of their way because two men—two men—want more power. It is incredible, it is fantastic, it is absolutely beyond all belief . . . except that it is true.

The Middle or Blue Period

December 1944

And what was it I had to remember, the minute I woke up? I know there was something, something pretty terrible, too. Not just plain terrible. This was fancy terrible; this was terrible with raisins in it. Ah, yes, I have it. This is my birthday. Here's the anniversary of my nativity, come around again on that cosmic belt. The Lord knows I didn't ask for it. Like a hole in the head I need another birthday. I'm birthday poor as it is.

Well. The best you can do about it is the best you can do about it. Many happy returns, my dear; there, that made you laugh out loud, didn't it? Well, that's better. What place have those salt tears on your cheek, on this, your day of fete? This is fiesta. See, the fountains run wine, and already there is dancing in the square. Come, then, a song, a song! Happy birthday to you, happy birthday to you, happy birthday, poor bastard, happy birthday to-o-o you!

This is it, you know, baby. This is the one that does it. You have said farewell to the thirties for the tenth and last time. Now you face it, baby. Now you take it smack in the teeth, baby. Quote baby unquote.

A fine lot of good that ever did, trying to lie about your age. The most you could plausibly knock off was a couple of years, and what's a couple of sandspits to an archipelago? Perhaps, if you had moved to a strange city and given it out that you had had a terribly tragic life, spent mostly in the tropics, you might have been able to subtract something worthwhile.

No; you couldn't have done it. Though the city were Trebizond, you would have met there someone who used to be in your class in school. They go all over the earth, those schoolmates of yours; there can't be a soul left in Upper

Montclair. Close your eyes and put your finger anywhere on the spinning globe, and whatever spot it touches, land or sea, someone who used to be in your class in school is there. It passes credibility that fourteen dirty little girls could have grown up to be so far-flung.

Even at home, there is no safety from them. Put on your best and walk out your door into the tender light, all set to sign "Faithfully, Katharine Hepburn" in any proffered autograph books; and there, waiting to pounce, will be something that used to sit next to you at the Jackson Whites' Academy for the Digitally Over-Privileged, Native Clay Lunches a Feature, which you seem to have attended in your youth. You can tell your fellow alumnae a block off by their gait, which is that of those assisted by prison guards along the last mile. Other show points are the hair like blown ashes, the mouth like a horseshoe with the luck running out, and the general air, no matter how glorious the weather, of being dressed in the expectation of heavy rains. Oh, Oh, God. Maybe you look like that to them. No; no, of course you don't. Stop it. You don't, you don't, you don't.

You know perfectly well they look like that because that's the way they are and the way they always have been; years have nothing to do with it. Years are only garments, and you either wear them with style all your life, or else you go dowdy to the grave. And these are the prettiest years, the most becoming, these that are about to be given you. Can't you get that through your head, you poor cluck? Oh, the gratitude with which you are going to look back on this day! You're going to think of it as the delicate arch through which you passed into the enchanted garden. Sure you are. You know what's happening today? The birthday of your life is come, as Miss Rossetti has it. If you had any sense, your heart would be like a singing bird whose nest is in the watered shoot. (Dear Christina Rossetti: we are taking up English poets, in school, and I have chosen you for the subject of a composition. Please write me any interesting facts you can remember about yourself, also how you came to make up poetry, and what the hell a watered shoot is.) Very well, then, *don't* go around all day with your heart like a soaking wet bird, if that's the way you feel about it. But you might at least have the decency to show a little enthusiasm. Why, you've got the world by the tail. Everything is going to be fine for you from now on. You will have all that you never had before—tranquillity and grace and usefulness and tribute. You're going to have the true time of your life. Oh, you'll love it. Honestly, you will. Honestly.

Well, all right. Middle Age. You've been hanging around here for ten years. Take your foot out of the door and come on in . . . No—please wait a minute . . . Please, just another minute . . . I can't quite . . .

It's that word "middle." Any phrase it touches becomes the label of the frump; middle of the road, middle class, middle age. If only you could leap these dreary decades and land up in the important numbers. There is chic to seventy, elegance to eighty.

People ought to be one of two things, young or old. No; what's the good of fooling? People ought to be one of two things, young or dead.

Well. Taking it like a little soldier, aren't you? And what is there to take, for heaven's sake? If you hadn't ripped the back pages off the calendar last night, you'd never have known the difference.

You probably don't even look any more than twenty-four hours older than you did yesterday. It's only your personal piece of hard luck that you are what you are today, when, inside, you never felt cuter.

You're just the same, within, as you were fifteen years ago, twenty; does any gentleman want to make it thirty? The only noticeable differences are a tendency to believe that your friends are several years older than they say they are, and a disposition to regard sixty as the age of consent. There are certain outer changes you could make, if you feel up to it. You might, for instance, give away that apple-blossom hat; some poor tot would be glad to have it for Sunday school. And now is the time to throw in the towel and stop ordering your dresses a little too big, so you can grow into them.

Take it easy, that's all you have to do. Don't fight it. You're the only one who is passionately interested in your age; other people have their own troubles. The matter will probably never come up, unless you fetch it up. After all, how often does the McKinley Inaugural normally creep into the conversation?

Pretty behavior. The best years of your life opening before you like a painted fan, and here you are, sulking. Look at the women who were famous long after they became, shall we say, full-blown. Look at Ninon de Lenclos. No; don't go off thinking about all the other poor souls who sought to cheer themselves by looking at Ninon de Lenclos. Just keep your eye on Ninon de Lenclos, and you can't go wrong; what woman has done, woman can do. And keep thinking about what's ahead of you. There will be friends and work and communication and laughter. There might very well be a series of rather stately adventures. It is not even impossible that you will be invited to take part in the dance. For God's sake, there must be somebody, somewhere, who has read Benjamin Franklin's letter to the young man!

Your path stretches so smooth, so gracious. There are no more ways for you to make a fool of yourself; you have assembled the complete set. There are no more mistakes; you have made them all. There are, for you, only ease and fulfillment and tenderness. And you did not work to gain them. They are given to you as gifts for this, your happiest birthday.

Oh, come in, Middle Age, come in, come in! Come close to me, give me your hand, let me look in your face . . . Oh . . . Is that what you are really like? . . . Oh, God help me . . . help me . . .

VARIATIONS ON A THEME
from the original introduction
by W. Somerset Maugham

Once when I was in Hollywood I was invited to dinner by Miss
Fanny Brice. It was by way of being a literary party. Aldous
Huxley was there, his sardonic gusto in the horribleness of
human beings not yet greatly mitigated by non-attachment and
brotherly love. Dorothy Parker was there demure in black silk,
but with a demureness fraught with peril to the unwary. I
forget who the remaining guests were but they were evidently
grand, for at dinner Dorothy Parker and I found ourselves
seated together a good way down the table and well below the
salt. The food was good, the wine choice, and we were waited
on by Russian noblemen or Japanese Samurai. I forget which.
After my neighbor and I had discoursed for some while upon
the weather and the crops, with fleeting references to
Shakespeare and the musical glasses, I said:

"Why don't you write a poem for me?"

"I will if you like," she replied. "Give me a pencil and a
piece of paper."

Now I am not one of those prudent authors who keep a little
book in their pocket so, whatever they are, wherever they may
be (as I hear my radio announcer remark every evening) they
can jot down any happy thought that occurs to them. I too
sometimes have a happy thought, but I always think I will
make a note of it later and then forget what on earth it was. I
had neither pencil nor paper.

"Let's ask for it," I said, and turned to the Russian
nobleman or the Japanese Samurai (whichever the case might
be) and told him what we wanted.

He was gone a long time, evidently having some difficulty in
finding what we asked for in that sumptuous house, but at last
returned with a ragged piece of wrapping paper and a blunt
pencil. Dorothy Parker took it and wrote:

> Higgledy Piggledy, my white hen;
> She lays eggs for gentlemen.

"Yes, I've always liked those lines," I said.

She gave a thin, cool smile and without an instant's hesitation, added:

> You cannot persuade her with gun or lariat
> To come across for the proletariat.

With this brilliant rhyme she gathered Higgledy Piggledy into the august company of Jove's Eagle, Sindbad the Sailor's Roc, the Capitoline Geese, Boccaccio's Falcon, Shelley's Skylark, and Poe's Raven. Chaucer's Chanticleer is her fitting mate.

But enough; I must now speak of Dorothy Parker's published work.

I have an old friend who is by profession a literary critic, and going to see him one day, I found him somewhat discomposed. I asked him what was the matter.

"I've lost a friend," he sighed. "X says he'll never forgive me for the review of his book I wrote last week. I praised it for a column and a half; I only made a few reservations in a few lines at the end. After all, I am a critic and a critic must criticize. To read his letter you'd think I'd panned the damned book."

I was concerned to find that a distinguished critic could be so ingenuous. Fancy not knowing that a writer will accept fulsome praise as only his due, but will grizzle and grieve over a hint of imperfection as though his publisher had gypped him, his wife betrayed him, and his son gone in the movies. You can butter him up till you are exhausted but one word of censure will turn all your butter rancid. Now I am not a critic and it is not my business to criticize. Nor in the present case have I any inclination to do so. In her stories Dorothy Parker has a sense of form which in these days, to my old-fashioned mind, is all too rare. Whether in a sketch or a story she knows exactly where to begin and where to end and when you have done reading it you have no questions to ask (What happened next? Why did he do that?) for she has told you all you need to know. She has a tidy mind and leaves no loose ends. She has a wonderfully delicate ear for human speech and with a few words of dialogue, chosen you might think haphazardly, will give you a character complete in all its improbable plausibility. Her style is easy without being slipshod and cultivated without affectation. It is a perfect instrument for the display of her many-sided humor, her irony, her sarcasm, her tenderness, her pathos. Perhaps what gives her writing its peculiar tang is her gift for seeing something to laugh at in the bitterest tragedies of the human animal. It is a devastating truth that she has discovered, and a salutary one, that there is something irresistibly comic in our most heartfelt woes. Who can but laugh wryly when he reads "A Telephone Call," that heartrending monologue, for which of us has not thus awaited with agonizing suspense a call on the phone, a telegram, a letter or a visit? Only a nitwit—but what a happy nitwit he! I do not want to go through these stories one by one, pointing out the peculiar excellence of each, for here they are for the reader to read and the reader is for himself the only judge that matters. He is silly if he lets anyone else, however well qualified, judge for him. In this volume he will find stories aimed only to make him laugh, and a very good aim too, too seldom attempted and less seldom achieved; he will find stories that are cruel, moving, sardonic, tragic, funny, sometimes separately and sometimes all together. But I should like to single out "The Standard of Living" for its humorous and tender handling of those two little stenographers as they wander up Fifth Avenue looking into the shop windows. They have all the charm, the impertinence, the pathos, and the absurdity of youth.

If you are going to judge an author at all he has the right to demand that you shall judge him by his best. "Big Blonde" has all the earmarks of a masterpiece. It is worthy to take its place with the short stories, and very few they are, that men have retained in their memories for many, many years. It displays to perfection all Dorothy Parker's enviable gifts. There are few things more difficult than to write a short story the events of which take place over a long period of time, and yet maintain that unity of effect which is the essence of the short story. In

"Big Blonde" Dorothy Parker has succeeded with peculiar skill in doing just this so that notwithstanding the passage of years you have the same poignancy as is generally only possible to achieve in the narration of a single incident. I think it is done by a determined concentration on the pathetic, feckless, hopeless, tragic, sloppy wanton who is Hazel Morse. People don't often realize how much luck comes into the writing of a good story. A lot of things have to go right. The heaven-sent idea is waiting at the street corner, but you must chance to pass that way to pick it up; it is only by a fluke that you come across the persons who will suggest the characters you need; you have to be in the right mood; time and place must be auspicious. It is no wonder that few good stories are written; it is only a wonder that as many are. In "Big Blonde" Dorothy Parker had all the luck on her side.

Only a very mediocre writer is always at his best, and Dorothy Parker is not a mediocre writer. Sometimes things don't go so well with one as they might, and in such case one can do nothing about it. A carping critic of these stories might suggest that their author on occasion shows an inclination to imitate Dorothy Parker, but I as an admiring friend would answer stoutly that she could not have a better model.

No such reservation could be made with regard to her verse. Now verse is a matter on which I cannot pretend to speak with any authority whatever. I have never written it; I have never understood the mysteries of prosody, and I have never even seen a rhyming dictionary, which I understand is as invaluable to poets as Roget's *Thesaurus* is to us lesser fry. It is a pity, because I have a notion that Dorothy Parker's verse has a technical perfection and I can only speak of it as a delighted reader. (It is true that great poets have unanimously agreed that poetry is for delight, though you wouldn't think so if you read some critics and, still more, some modern poets.) But this I do know, that Dorothy Parker has a beautiful clarity—you never need to rack your brains to ask yourself, now what the devil does this mean?—and she has that great gift of nature, a faultless ear. The felicity of her rhymes is enchanting. In too many poems you get the feeling that a line is there not because it is necessary to the meaning or adds to the emotion the verse seeks to create, but because a rhyme was wanted. With Dorothy Parker never. Her rhymes are as inevitable as they are often unexpected. I should like to give examples to prove the truth of what I say, but it would be foolish to quote when the pages that follow this disquisition are there for the reader to read. Admirable as are Dorothy Parker's stories, I think it is in her poems that she displays the quintessence of her talent. Like Heine, she has made little songs out of her great sorrows; we, heartless readers, endure them with fortitude, for have they not wrung from her these gay, tragic poems? And how fresh and various they are! Though beautifully polished, they have an air of spontaneity and none can know better than a writer what patient industry is needed to acquire that quality. They reflect her personality in its manifold completeness, and what, I ask you, can an artist give you more or better than himself? I shall never grow tired of asserting that it is the artist's personality, and that alone, which gives the work of art its enduring significance. In a few short perfect lines she presents herself to you, to take or to leave, with her pain, her laughter, her tenderness, her feeling for beauty, her ribaldry and her common sense. Now that I come to consider these affections and proclivities that I have ascribed to her, it occurs to me that we all, except bishops and elder statesmen, possess them; but she possesses them in a heightened, more concentrated form, so that when you read almost any one of her verses you seem to see her as through the wrong end of a perfectly focused telescope. It is a great gift to be able to do so much in such a little space. However lyrical her mood, and when she likes she can be as lyrical as Herrick and Landor at their charming best, her aerial flight is anchored to this pendent world (the phrase is Milton's) by the golden chain of common sense. I think it is her common sense that gives her poems their singular and characteristic savor, and what is it but common sense that makes this uncertain, absurd, harsh, and transitory life not only tolerable, but amusing?

INDEX
of Titles of Stories and Poems,
and First Lines of Poems